The xVA Challenge

The xVA Challenge

Counterparty Credit Risk, Funding,
Collateral and Capital

Third Edition

Jon Gregory

This edition first published 2015
© 2015 John Wiley & Sons, Ltd
First edition published 2009, second edition published 2012 by John Wiley & Sons, Ltd

Registered office
John Wiley & Sons Ltd, The Atrium, Southern Gate, Chichester, West Sussex PO19 8SQ, United Kingdom

For details of our global editorial offices, for customer services and for information about how to apply for permission to reuse the copyright material in this book please see our website at www.wiley.com.

Library of Congress Cataloging-in-Publication Data is available

A catalogue record for this book is available from the British Library.

ISBN 978-1-119-10941-9 (hbk)   ISBN 978-1-119-10943-3 (ebk)
ISBN 978-1-119-10942-6 (ebk)   ISBN 978-1-119-10944-0 (ebk)

Cover design: Wiley
Cover image: © Julia Kopacheva/shutterstock

Set in 10/12pt Times by Sparks – www.sparkspublishing.com
Printed in Great Britain by TJ International Ltd, Padstow, Cornwall, UK

10 9 8 7 6 5 4 3 2

To Sylvia, Mimsie, Stella, Cara, Eliza-Joy, Stevie, Peach, Jim, Ginnie, George and Christy

Contents

List of Spreadsheets

One of the key features of the first and second editions of this book was the accompanying spreadsheets that were prepared to allow the reader to gain some simple insight into some of the quantitative aspects discussed. Many of these examples have been used for training courses and have therefore evolved to be quite intuitive and user-friendly.

The spreadsheets can be downloaded freely from Jon Gregory's website, www. cvacentral.com, under the counterparty risk section. New examples may be added over time.

List of Appendices

The following is a list of Appendices that contain additional mathematical detail. These Appendices can be downloaded freely from www.cvacentral.com.

Acknowledgements

The first edition of this book focused on counterparty credit risk and was written in 2009, during the aftermath of the global financial crisis. Since then, the subject matter has necessarily broadened to give more attention to aspects such as funding, collateral and capital. It has been less than three years since the second edition was finished and again, the subject has changed dramatically. Indeed, as before, this is much more than a new edition because most of the content has been rewritten and expanded with several new chapters. I hope this will be a comprehensive reference for the subject we now generally refer to as xVA.

As with the last edition, I have saved space by putting mathematical appendices together with the accompanying spreadsheets on my personal website at www.cvacentral. com. Since many do not study this material in depth, this has proved to be a reasonable compromise for most readers.

I have also made use of a number of survey results and I am grateful to Solum Financial and Deloitte for allowing me to reproduce these results. I am also grateful to IBM and Markit who have provided calculation examples. These will all be mentioned in the text.

Finally, I would like to thank the following people for feedback on this and earlier editions of the book: Manuel Ballester, Ronnie Barnes, Raymond Cheng, Vladimir Cheremisin, Michael Clayton, Daniel Dickler, Wei-Ming Feng, Julia Fernald, Piero Foscari, Teddy Fredaigues, Dimitrios Giannoulis, Arthur Guerin, Kale Kakhiani, Henry Kwon, David Mengle, Ivan Pomarico, Hans-Werner Pfaff, Erik van Raaij, Guilherme Sanches, Neil Schofield, Florent Serre, Masum Shaikh, Ana Sousa, Richard Stratford, Carlos Sterling, Hidetoshi Tanimura, Todd Tauzer, Nick Vause, Frederic Vrins and Valter Yoshida.

Jon Gregory
May 2015

About the Author

Jon Gregory is an independent expert specialising in counterparty risk and related aspects. He has worked on many aspects of credit risk in his career, being previously with Barclays Capital, BNP Paribas and Citigroup. He is a senior advisor for Solum Financial Derivatives Advisory and is a faculty member for the Certificate of Quantitative Finance (CQR).

Jon has a PhD from Cambridge University.

1
Introduction

In 2007, a so-called credit crisis began. This crisis eventually became more severe and long-lasting than could have ever been anticipated. Along the way, there were major casualties such as the bankruptcy of the investment bank Lehman Brothers. Many banks were seen as being extremely reckless in the run-up to the crisis by taking excessive risks to provide gains for their employees and shareholders, and yet were inadequately capitalised for these risks. Governments around the world had to bail out other financial institutions such as American International Group (AIG) in the US and the Royal Bank of Scotland in the UK, and it became clear that it was essentially the taxpayer that was implicitly providing the capital against the risks being taken. AIG required more than $100 billion of taxpayers' money to cover losses due to the excessive risk-taking. Many taxpayers have since faced poor economic conditions and have experienced the cost of these bailouts via higher taxes and reduced government spending.

One result of the "global financial crisis" (as the events from 2007 onwards shall generally be referred to in this book) was a clear realisation that banks needed to be subject to much stricter regulation and conservative requirements over aspects such as capital. It has become all too clear that there has been a significant "too big to fail" problem in that the biggest banks and financial firms could not be allowed to fail and therefore should be subject to even tighter risk controls and oversight. It was therefore obvious that there would need to be a massive shift in the regulatory oversight of banks and large financial firms. Rules clearly needed to be improved, and new ones introduced, to prevent a repeat of the global financial crisis.

It is not, therefore, surprising that new regulation started to emerge very quickly with the Dodd–Frank Act, for example, being signed into law in July 2010, and totalling almost one thousand pages of rules governing financial institutions. In addition, Basel III guidelines for regulatory capital have been developed and implemented relatively rapidly (compared with, for example, the previous Basel II framework). Much of the regulation is aimed squarely at the over-the-counter (OTC) derivatives market where aspects such as counterparty risk and liquidity risk were shown to be so significant in the global financial crisis.

This pace and range of new regulation has been quite dramatic. Additional capital charges, a central clearing mandate and bilateral rules for posting of collateral have all been aimed at counterparty risk reduction and control. The liquidity coverage ratio and net stable funding ratio have taken aim more at liquidity risks. A leverage ratio has been introduced to restrict a bank's overall leverage. An idea of the proliferation of new regulation in OTC derivatives can be seen by the fact that the central clearing mandate led to new capital requirements for exposure to central counterparties which in turn (partially) required a new bilateral capital methodology (the so-called SA-CCR discussed in Chapter 8) to be developed. Not surprisingly, there are also initiatives aimed at rationalising the complex regulatory landscape such as the fundamental review of the trading book. For a typical bank, even keeping up with regulatory change and the underlying requirements is challenging, let alone actually trying to adapt their business model to continue to be viable under such a new regulatory regime.

At the same time as the regulatory change, banks have undertaken a dramatic reappraisal of the assumptions they make when pricing, valuing and managing OTC derivatives. Whilst counterparty risk has always been a consideration, its importance has grown, which is seen via significant credit value adjustment (CVA) values reported in bank's financial statements. Banks have also realised the significant impact that funding costs, collateral effects and capital charges have on valuation. Under accounting rules, CVA was subject to a very strange marriage to DVA (debt value adjustment). Nonetheless, this marriage has produced many offspring such as FVA (funding value adjustment), ColVA (collateral value adjustment), KVA (capital value adjustment) and MVA (margin value adjustment). OTC derivatives valuation is now critically dependent on those terms, now generally referred to as xVA.

It is important not to focus only on the activities of banks but also to consider the end-users who use OTC derivatives for hedging the economic risks that they face. Whilst such entities did not cause or catalyse the global financial crisis, they have been on the wrong end of increasing charges via xVA, partially driven by the regulation aimed at the banks they transact with. The activities of these entities has also changed as they have aimed to understand and optimise the hedging costs they face.

Hence, there is a need to fully define and discuss the world of xVA, taking into account the nature of the underlying market dynamics and new regulatory environment. This is the aim of this book. In Chapters 2–4 we will discuss the global financial crisis, OTC derivatives market and birth of xVA in more detail. Chapters 5–9 will cover methods for mitigating counterparty risk and underlying regulatory requirements. Chapters 10–12 will discuss the quantification of key components such as exposure, default probability and funding costs. Chapters 13–16 will discuss the different xVA terms and give examples of their impact. Finally, in Chapters 17–20 we will discuss the management of xVA at a holistic level and look at possible future trends.

2

The Global Financial Crisis

Life is like playing a violin solo in public and learning the instrument as one goes on.

Samuel Butler (1835–1902)

2.1 PRE-CRISIS

Counterparty risk first gained prominence in the late 1990s when the Asian crisis (1997) and default of Russia (1998) highlighted some of the potential problems of major defaults in relation to derivatives contracts. However, it was the failure of Long-Term Capital Management (LTCM) (1998) that had the most significant impact. LTCM was a hedge fund founded by colleagues from Salomon Brothers' famous bond arbitrage desk, together with two Nobel Prize winners Robert Merton and Myron Scholes. LTCM made stellar profits for several years and then became insolvent in 1998. LTCM was a very significant counterparty for all the large banks and the fear of a chain reaction driven by counterparty risk led the Federal Reserve Bank of New York to organise a bailout whereby a consortium of 14 banks essentially took over LTCM. This failure was a lesson on the perils of derivatives; LTCM has been running at a very significant leverage, much of which was achieved using OTC derivatives together with aspects such as favourable collateral terms. This in turn exposed banks to counterparty risk and raised the prospect of a knock-on impact, causing a cascade of defaults. It was the possibility of this chain reaction that led to the rescue of LTCM because of a perceived threat to the entire financial system.

One of the responses to the above was the Counterparty Risk Management Policy Group (CRMPG) report in June 1999. CRMPG is a group of 12 major international banks with the objective of promoting strong counterparty credit risk and market risk management. Further major defaults such as Enron (2001), WorldCom (2002) and Parmalat (2003) were not as significant as LTCM, but provided a continued lesson on the dangers of counterparty risk. Many banks (typically the largest) devoted significant time and resources into quantifying and managing this. The CRMPG issued a report in January 2005, stating that:

> Credit risk, and in particular counterparty credit risk, is probably the single most important variable in determining whether and with what speed financial disturbances become financial shocks with potential systemic traits.

Meanwhile, efforts to ensure that banks were properly capitalised were being initiated. The Basel Committee on Banking Supervision (BCBS) was established by the Group of Ten (G10) countries in 1974. The Basel Committee does not possess any formal authority and simply formulates broad supervisory standards. However, supervisory authorities in the relevant countries generally follow the BCBS guidelines when they develop their national regulation rules. In 1988, the BCBS introduced a capital measurement framework now known as Basel I that was more or less adopted universally. A more risk-sensitive framework, Basel II, started in 1999. The Basel II framework, now covering the G20 group of countries, is described in the Basel Committee's document entitled *International Convergence of Capital Measurement and Capital Standards* (BCBS, 2006). It consists of three "pillars":

- *Pillar 1, minimum capital requirements.* Banks compute regulatory capital charges according to a set of specified rules.
- *Pillar 2, supervisory review.* Supervisors evaluate the activities and risk profiles of banks to determine whether they should hold higher levels of capital than the minimum requirements in Pillar 1.
- *Pillar 3, market discipline.* This specifies public disclosures that banks must make. They provide greater insight into the adequacy of banks" capitalisation (including disclosure about methods used to determine capital levels required).

Requirements for counterparty risk capital were introduced in Basel I and were clearly set out under Pillar 1 of Basel II.

Meanwhile, the growth of the derivatives markets and the default of some significant clients, such as Enron and WorldCom, led banks to better quantify and allocate such losses. Banks started to price in counterparty risk into transactions, generally focusing on the more risky trades and counterparties. Traders and salespeople were charged for this risk, which was often then managed centrally. This was the birth of the CVA desk. Initially, most banks would not actively manage counterparty risk but adopted some sort of income deferral, charging a CVA to the profit of a transaction. Calculations were typically based on historic probabilities of default and the CVA amounted to an expected loss that built up a collective reserve to offset against counterparty defaults. A CVA desk generally acted as an insurer of counterparty risk and there was not active management of CVA risk.

The above approach to counterparty risk started to change around 2005 as accounting standards developed the concept of "fair value" through IAS 39 ("Financial Instruments: Recognition and Measurement") and FAS 157 ("Financial Accounting Standard 157: Fair Value Measurement"). This required derivatives to be held at their fair value associated with the concept of "exit price", defined as:

> The price that would be received to sell an asset or paid to transfer a liability in an orderly transaction between market participants at the measurement date.

This implied that CVA was a requirement since the price of a derivative should be adjusted to reflect the value at which another market participant would price in the underlying counterparty risk. FAS 157 accounting standards (applicable to US banks, for example) were more prescriptive, requiring:

> A fair value measurement should include a risk premium reflecting the amount market participants would demand because of the risk (uncertainty) in the cashflows.

This suggests that credit spreads, and not historical default probabilities, should be used when computing CVA. Furthermore, FAS 157 states:

> The reporting entity shall consider the effect of its credit risk (credit standing) on the fair value of the liability in all periods in which the liability is measured at fair value.

This suggests that a party's own credit risk should also be considered as part of the exit price. This is generally known as debt value adjustment (DVA).

None of the aforementioned focus on counterparty risk seen in regulation, market practice or accounting rules prevented what happened in 2007. Banks made dramatic errors in their assessment of counterparty risk (e.g. monoline insurers, discussed below), undertook regulatory arbitrage to limit their regulatory capital requirements, were selective about reporting CVA in financial statements and did not routinely hedge CVA risk. These aspects contributed to a major financial crisis.

2.2 THE CRISIS

Between 2004 and 2006, US interest rates rose significantly, triggering a slowdown in the US housing market. Many homeowners, who had barely been able to afford their mortgage payments when interest rates were low, began to default on their mortgages. Default rates on subprime loans (made to those with poor or no credit history) hit record levels. US households had also become increasingly in debt, with the ratio of debt to disposable personal income rising. Many other countries (although not all) had ended up in a similar situation. Years of poor underwriting standards and cheap debt were about to start a global financial crisis for which derivatives and counterparty risk would be effective catalysts.

Many of the now toxic US subprime loans were held by US retail banks and mortgage providers such as Fannie Mae and Freddie Mac. However, the market had been allowed to spread due to the fact that the underlying mortgages had been packaged up into complex structures (using financial engineering techniques), such as mortgage-backed securities (MBSs), which had been given good credit ratings from the ratings agencies. As a result, the underlying mortgages ending up being held by institutions that did not originate them, such as investment banks and even institutional investors outside the US. In mid-2007, a credit crisis began, caused primarily by the systematic mispricing of US mortgages and MBSs. Whilst this caused excessive volatility in the credit markets, it was not believed to be a severe financial crisis – for example, the stock market did not react particularly badly. The crisis, however, did not go away.

In July 2007, Bear Stearns informed investors that they would get very little of their money back from two hedge funds due to losses in subprime mortgages. In August 2007, BNP Paribas told investors that they would be unable to take money out of two funds because the underlying assets could not be valued due to "a complete evaporation of liquidity in the market." Basically, this meant that the assets could not be sold at any reasonable price. In September 2007, Northern Rock (a British bank) sought emergency funding from the Bank of England as a "lender of last resort." This prompted the first run on a bank[1] for more than a century. Northern Rock, in 2008, would be taken into state ownership to save depositors and borrowers.

By the end of 2007, some insurance companies, known as "monolines", were in serious trouble. Monolines provided insurance to banks on mortgage and other related debt through contracts that were essentially derivatives. The triple-A ratings of monolines had meant that banks were not concerned with a potential monoline default, despite the obvious misnomer that a monoline insurance company appeared to represent. Banks' willingness to ignore the counterparty risk had led them to build up large monoline exposures without the ability to receive collateral, at least as long as monolines maintained strong credit ratings. However, monolines were now reporting large losses and making it clear that any downgrading of their credit ratings may trigger collateral calls that they would not be able to make. Such downgrades began in December 2007 and banks were forced to take losses totalling billions of dollars due to the massive counterparty risk they now faced. This was a particularly bad form of counterparty risk, known as wrong-way risk, where the exposure to a counterparty and their default probability were inextricably linked.

In March 2008, Bear Stearns was purchased by JP Morgan Chase for just $2 a share, assisted by a loan of tens of billions of dollars from the Federal Reserve, who were essentially taking $30 billion of losses from the worst Bear Stearns assets to push through the sale. This represented a bailout via the US taxpayer of sorts. In early September 2008, mortgage lenders Fannie Mae and Freddie Mac, who combined accounted for more than half the outstanding US mortgages, were placed into conservatorship (a sort of short-term nationalisation) by the US Treasury.

In September 2008 the unthinkable happened when Lehman Brothers, a global investment bank and the fourth largest investment bank in the US, with a century-long tradition, filed for Chapter 11 bankruptcy protection (the largest in history). The bankruptcy of Lehman Brothers had not been anticipated with all major ratings agencies (Moody's, Standard & Poor's, and Fitch) all giving at least a single-A rating right up to the point of Lehman's failure and the credit derivative market not indicating an impended default.

Saving Lehman Brothers would have cost the US taxpayer and exasperated moral hazard problems since a bailout would not punish their excessive risk taking. However, a Lehman default was not an especially pleasant prospect either. Firstly, there was estimated to be around $400 billion of credit default swap (CDS) insurance written on Lehman Brothers that would trigger massive pay-outs on the underlying CDS contracts; and yet the opacity of the OTC derivatives market meant that it was not clear who actually transacted most of this. Another counterparty might then have had financial problems due to suffering large losses because of providing CDS protection on Lehman. Secondly, Lehman Brothers had around a million derivatives trades with around 8,000 different counterparties that all needed to be unwound, a process that would take years and lead to many legal proceedings. Most counterparties probably never considered that their counterparty risk to Lehman Brothers was a particular issue; nor did they realise that the failure of counterparty risk mitigation methods such as collateral and special purpose vehicles (SPVs) would lead to legal problems.

---

[1] This occurs when a large number of customers withdraw their deposits because they believe the bank is, or might become, insolvent.

On the same day as Lehman Brothers failed, Bank of America agreed a $50 billion rescue of Merrill Lynch. Soon after the remaining two investment banks, Morgan Stanley and Goldman Sachs, opted to become commercial banks. Whilst this would subject them to more strict regulation, it allowed full access to the Federal Reserve's lending facilities and prevented a worse fate. In case September 2008 was not exciting enough, the US government provided American International Group (AIG) with loans of up to $85 billion in exchange for a four-fifths stake in AIG.[2] Had AIG been allowed to fail, their derivative counterparties (the major banks) would have experienced significant losses. AIG was "too big to fail".

By now, trillions of dollars had simply vanished from the financial markets and therefore the global economy. Whilst this was related to the mispricing of mortgage risk, it was also significantly driven by the recognition of counterparty risk. On October 6, the Dow Jones Industrial Average dropped more than 700 points and fell below 10,000 for the first time in four years. The systemic shockwaves arising from the failure of the US banking giants led to the Troubled Asset Relief Program (TARP) of not too much short of $1 trillion to purchase distressed assets and support failing banks. In November 2008, Citigroup – prior to the crisis the largest bank in the world, but now reeling following a dramatic plunge in its share price – needed TARP assistance via a $20 billion cash injection and government backing for around $300 billion of loans.

The contagion had spread far beyond the US. In early 2009, the Royal Bank of Scotland (RBS) reported a loss of £24.1 billion, the biggest in British corporate history. The majority of this loss was borne by the British government, now the majority owner of RBS, having paid £45 billion[3] to rescue RBS in October 2008 (in June 2015 the UK government announced plans to sell the majority of their RBS stake at a price around around 25% less than they acquired it for). In November 2008 the International Monetary Fund (IMF), together with other European countries, approved a $4.6 billion loan for Iceland after the country's banking system collapsed in October. This was the first IMF loan to a Western European nation since 1976.

From late 2009, fears of a sovereign debt crisis developed in Europe driven by high debt levels and a downgrading of government debt in some European states. In May 2010, Greece received a €110 billion bailout from Eurozone counties and the IMF. Greece was to be bailed out again (and has since defaulted on an IMF loan) and support was also given to other Eurozone sovereign entities, notably Portugal, Ireland and Spain. Banks again were heavily exposed to potential failures of European sovereign countries. Again, the counterparty risk of such entities had been considered low, but was now extremely problematic and made worse by the fact that sovereign entities generally did not post collateral.

By now, it was clear that no counterparty (triple-A entities, global investment banks, retail banks and sovereigns) could ever be regarded as risk-free. Counterparty risk, previously hidden via spurious credit ratings, collateral or legal assumptions, was now present throughout the global financial markets. CVA (credit value adjustment), which defined the price of counterparty risk, had gone from being a rarely used technical term to a buzzword constantly associated with derivatives. The pricing of counterparty risk into trades (via a CVA charge) was now becoming the rule and not the exception. Whilst the

---

[2] AIG would receive further bailouts.
[3] Hundreds of billions of pounds were provided in the form of loans and guarantees.

largest investment banks had built trading desks, complex systems and models around managing CVA, all banks (and some other financial institutions and large derivatives users) were now focused on expanding their capabilities in this respect. Banks were also becoming acutely aware of their increasing costs of funding and capitalising their balance sheets.

2.3 REGULATORY REFORM

Despite the CRMPG initiatives, regulatory capital requirements and accounting rules aimed at counterparty risk, a major financial crisis had occurred with failures or rescues of (amongst others) AIG, Bear Stearns, Lehman Brothers, Fannie Mae, Freddie Mac and the Royal Bank of Scotland. The crisis highlighted many shortcomings of the regulatory regime. For example, Basel II capital requirements were seen to produce insufficient capital levels, excessive leverage, procyclicality and systemic risk.

From 2009, new fast-tracked financial regulation started to be implemented and was very much centered on counterparty risk and OTC derivatives. The US Dodd–Frank Wall Street Reform and Consumer Protection Act 2009 (Dodd–Frank) and European Market Infrastructure Regulation (EMIR) were aimed at increasing the stability of the over-the-counter (OTC) derivative markets. The Basel III rules were introduced to strengthen bank capital bases and introduce new requirements on liquidity and leverage. In particular, the completely new CVA capital charge was aimed directly at significantly increasing counterparty risk capital requirements. Additionally, the G20 agreed a clearing mandate whereby all standardised OTC derivatives be cleared via central counterparties with the view that this would, among other things, reduce counterparty risk. Later, the G20 introduced rules that were to require more collateral to be posted against those OTC derivatives that could not be cleared (bilateral collateral rules). Other regulatory rules such as the leverage ratio and liquidity coverage ratio would also have significant impacts on the derivatives market.

Although not driven as much by the recent crisis, IFRS 13 accounting guidelines were introduced from 2013 to replace IAS 39 and FAS 157. IFRS 13 provided a single framework for the guidance around fair value measurement for financial instruments and started to create convergence in practices around CVA. In particular, IRFS 13 (like the aforementioned FAS 157) uses the concept of exit price, which implies the use of market-implied information as much as possible. This is particularly important in default probability estimation, where market credit spreads must be used instead of historical default probabilities. Exit price also introduces the notion of own credit risk and leads to DVA as the CVA charged by a replacement counterparty when exiting a transaction.

2.4 BACKLASH AND CRITICISMS

The above regulatory changes are not without controversy and criticism. Of course there is the obvious complaint that banks will suffer much higher costs in transacting OTC derivatives. This will make them less profitable and higher costs will ultimately also be passed on to end-users. For example an airline predicted more volatile earnings "not because of unpredictable passenger numbers, interest rates or jet fuel prices," but rather due to the OTC derivatives it used.[4] End-users of derivatives, although not responsible, were now being hit as badly as the orchestrators of the global financial crisis. A negative impact on the economy in general was almost inevitable.

However, more subtle were the potential unintended consequences of increased regulation on counterparty risk. The regulatory focus on CVA seemed to encourage active hedging of counterparty risk so as to obtain capital relief. However, the CDS transactions that were most important for such hedging (single-name and index OTC instruments) introduced their own form of counterparty risk, which was the wrong-way type highlighted by the monoline failures. Indeed, the CDS market is even more concentrated than the overall OTC market and has become less, rather than more, liquid in recent years. Problems could be seen as early as 2010 when, for example, the Bank of England commented that:[5]

> ... given the relative illiquidity of sovereign CDS markets a sharp increase in demand from active investors can bid up the cost of sovereign CDS protection. CVA desks have come to account for a large proportion of trading in the sovereign CDS market and so their hedging activity has reportedly been a factor pushing prices away from levels solely reflecting the underlying probability of sovereign default.

Since it was the new CVA capital charge that was partially driving the buying of CDS protection that in turn was apparently artificially inflating CDS prices, there was a question over the methodology (if not the amount) for the additional capital charges for counterparty risk. This led to the controversial European exemptions for CVA capital, discussed later in Chapter 8.

Questions were also raised about the central clearing of large amounts of OTC derivatives and what would happen if such a CCP failed. Since CCPs were likely to take over from the likes of Lehman, Citigroup and AIG as the hubs of the complex financial network, such a question was clearly key, and yet not particularly extensively discussed. Furthermore, the increased collateral requirements from CCPs and the bilateral collateral rules were questioned as potentially creating significant funding costs and liquidity risks. In particular, the fact that initial margin (overcollateralisation) was to become much more common was a concern.

Perhaps the most vociferous criticism was for the DVA component under IFRS 13 accounting standards. DVA required banks to account for their own default in the value of transactions and therefore acted to counteract CVA losses. However, many commentators believed this to be nothing more than an accounting trick as banks reported profits from DVA simply due to the fact that their own credit spread implied they were more likely to default in the future. Some banks aimed to monetise their DVA by selling protection on their peers, a sure way to increase, not reduce, systemic risk. Basel III capital rules moved to remove DVA benefits to avoid effects such as "an increase in a bank's capital when its own creditworthiness deteriorates." Banks then had to reconcile a world where their accounting standards said DVA was real but their regulatory capital rules said it was not.

---

[4] "Corporates fear CVA charge will make hedging too expensive", *Risk*, October 2011.
[5] See www.bankofengland.co.uk/publications/Documents/quarterlybulletin/qb1002.pdf.

2.5   A NEW WORLD

Other changes in derivative markets were also taking place. A fundamental assumption in the pricing of derivative securities had always been that the discounting rate could be appropriately proxied by LIBOR. However, practitioners realised that the OIS (overnight indexed spread) was actually a more appropriate discounting rate and was also a closer representation of the "risk-free rate". The LIBOR–OIS spread had historically hovered around ten basis points, showing a close linkage. However, this close relationship had broken down, even spiking to around 350 basis points around the time of the Lehman Brothers bankruptcy. This showed that even the simplest types of derivative, which had been priced in the same way for decades, needed to be valued differently, in a more sophisticated manner. Another almost inevitable dynamic was that the spreads of banks (i.e. where they could borrow unsecured cash on a longer term than in a typical LIBOR transaction) had increased. Historically, this borrowing cost of a bank was in the region of a few basis points but had now entered the realms of hundreds of basis points in most cases.

It was clear that these now substantial funding costs should be quantified alongside CVA. The cost of funding was named FVA (funding value adjustment) which had the useful effect of consuming the strange DVA accounting requirements (from a bank's point of view at least). Not surprisingly, the increase in funding costs also naturally led banks to tighten up collateral requirements. However, this created a knock-on effect for typical end-users of derivatives that historically have not been able or willing to enter into collateral agreement for liquidity and operational reasons. Some sovereign entities considered posting collateral, not only to avoid the otherwise large counterparty risk and funding costs levied upon them, but also to avoid the issue that banks hedging their counterparty risk may buy CDS protection on them, driving their credit spread wider and potentially causing borrowing problems. Some such entities posted their own bonds as collateral, solving the funding problems if not the counterparty risk ones. It also became clear that there was hidden value in collateral agreements that should be considered using collateral value adjustment (ColVA). Finally, the dramatic increase in capital requirements led to the consideration of capital value adjustment (KVA) and impending requirements to post initial margin to margin value adjustment (MVA).

Regulation aimed at reducing counterparty risk and therefore CVA was becoming better understood and managed. However, this in turn was driving the increased importance of other components such as DVA, FVA, ColVA, KVA and MVA. CVA, once an only child, had been joined by a twin (DVA) and numerous other relatives. The xVA family was growing and, bizarrely, regulation aimed at making OTC derivatives simpler and safer was driving this growth.

3

The OTC Derivatives Market

3.1 THE DERIVATIVES MARKET

3.1.1 Derivatives

Derivatives contracts represent agreements either to make payments or to buy or sell an underlying security at a time or times in the future. The times may range from a few weeks or months (for example, futures contracts) to many years (such as long-dated swaps). The value of a derivative will change with the level of one of more underlying rates, assets or indices, and possibly decisions made by the parties to the contract. In many cases, the initial value of a traded derivative will be contractually configured to be zero for both parties at inception.

Derivatives are not a particularly new financial innovation; for example, in medieval times, forward contracts were popular in Europe. However, derivatives products and markets have become particularly large and complex in the last three decades.

One of the advantages of derivatives is that they can provide very efficient hedging tools. For example, consider the following risks that an institution, such as a corporate, may experience:

- *IR risk*. They need to manage liabilities such as transforming floating- into fixed-rate debt via an interest rate swap.
- *FX risk*. Due to being paid in various currencies, there is a need to hedge cash inflow or outflow in these currencies via FX forwards.
- *Commodity*. The need to lock in commodity prices either due to consumption (e.g. airline fuel costs) or production (e.g. a mining company) via commodity futures or swaps.

There are many different users of derivatives, such as sovereigns, central banks, regional/local authorities, hedge funds, asset managers, pension funds, insurance companies and corporates. All use derivatives as part of their investment strategy or to hedge the risks they face from their business activities.

---

[1] Quote from 2002.

In many ways, derivatives are no different from the underlying cash instruments. They simply allow one to take a very similar position in a synthetic way. For example, an airline wanting to reduce their exposure to a potential rise in aviation fuel price can buy oil futures, which are cash-settled and therefore represent a very simple way to go "long oil" (with no storage or transport costs). An institution wanting to reduce their exposure to a certain asset can do so via a derivative contract, which means they do not have to sell the asset directly in the market.

The credit risk of derivatives contracts is usually called counterparty risk. As the derivatives market has grown, so has the importance of counterparty risk. Furthermore, the lessons from events such as the failure of Long-Term Capital Management and Lehman Brothers (as discussed in the last chapter) have highlighted the problems when a major player in the derivatives market defaults. This in turn has led to an increased focus on counterparty risk and related aspects.

3.1.2   Exchange traded and OTC derivatives

Within the derivatives markets, many of the simplest products are traded through exchanges. A derivatives exchange is a financial centre where parties can trade standardised contracts such as futures and options at a specified price. An exchange promotes market efficiency and enhances liquidity by centralising trading in a single place, thereby making it easy to enter and exit positions. The process by which a financial contract becomes exchange-traded can be thought of as a long journey where a reasonable trading volume, standardisation and liquidity must first develop. Whilst an exchange provides efficient price discovery,[2] it also typically provides a means of mitigating counterparty risk. Modern-day exchanges have a central counterparty clearing function to guarantee performance and therefore reduce counterparty risk. Since the mid-1980s, all exchanges have had such central clearing facilities.

Compared to exchange-traded derivatives, OTC derivatives tend to be less standard structures and are typically traded bilaterally, i.e., between two parties. They are private contracts, traditionally not reported or part of any customer asset protection programme. Hence, each party takes counterparty risk with respect to the other party. Many players in the OTC derivatives market do not have strong credit quality, nor are they able to post collateral to reduce counterparty risk. This counterparty risk is therefore an unavoidable consequence of the OTC derivatives market. A relatively small number of banks are fairly dominant in OTC derivatives: generally these are large and highly interconnected, and are generally viewed as being "too big to fail".

3.1.3   Market size

In 1986, the total notional of OTC derivatives was slightly less than that of exchange traded derivatives at $500 billion.[3] Arguably, even at this point OTC markets were more significant due to the fact that they are longer-dated (for example, a ten-year OTC interest rate swap is many times more risky than a three-month interest rate futures contract).

---

[2] This is the process of determining the price of an asset in a marketplace through the interactions of buyers and sellers.

[3] Source: ISDA survey, 1986, covering only swaps.

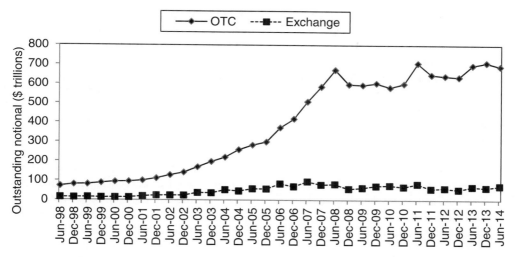

Figure 3.1   Total outstanding notional of OTC and exchange-traded derivatives transactions. The figures cover interest rate, foreign exchange, equity, commodity and credit derivative contracts. Note that notional amounts outstanding are not directly comparable to those for exchange-traded derivatives, which refer to open interest or net positions, whereas the amounts outstanding for OTC markets refer to gross positions, i.e., without netting.
Source: BIS.

Nevertheless, in the following two decades, the OTC derivatives market grew exponentially in size (Figure 3.1). This was due to the use of OTC derivatives as customised hedging instruments and also investment vehicles. The OTC market has also seen the development of completely new products (for example, the credit default swap market increased by a factor of ten between the end of 2003 and the end of 2008). The relative popularity of OTC products arises from the ability to tailor contracts more precisely to client needs, for example, by offering a particular maturity date. Exchange-traded products, by their very nature, do not offer customisation.

The total notional amount of all derivatives outstanding was $601 trillion at 2010 year-end. The curtailed growth towards the end of the history can be clearly attributed to the global financial crisis, where banks have reduced balance sheets and reallocated capital, and clients have been less interested in derivatives, particularly as investments. However, the reduction in recent years is also partially due to compression exercises that seek to reduce counterparty risk via removing offsetting and redundant positions (discussed in more detail in Section 5.3).

A significant amount of OTC derivatives are collateralised: parties pledge cash and securities against the mark-to-market (MTM) of their derivative portfolio with the aim of neutralising the net exposure between the counterparties. Collateral can reduce counterparty risk but introduces additional legal and operational risks. Furthermore, posting collateral introduces funding costs, as it is necessary to source the cash or securities to deliver. It also leads to liquidity risks in case the required amount and type of collateral cannot be sourced in the required timeframe.

Since the late 1990s, there has also been a growing trend to centrally clear some OTC derivatives, primarily aimed at reducing counterparty risk. Centrally cleared derivatives retain some OTC features (such as being transacted bilaterally) but use the central clearing function developed for exchange-traded derivatives. This is discussed in more detail in Chapter 9. It is possible to centrally clear an OTC derivative that is not liquid enough to trade on an exchange. However, central clearing does still require an OTC derivative to have a certain level of standardisation and liquidity, and to not be too complex. This means that many types of OTC derivatives may never be suitable for central clearing.

Broadly speaking, derivatives can be classified into several different groups by the way in which they are transacted and collateralised. These groups, in increasing complexity and risk are:

- *Exchange traded.* These are the most simple, liquid and short-dated derivatives that are traded on an exchange. All derivatives exchanges now have central clearing functions whereby collateral must be posted and the performance of all exchange members is guaranteed. Due to the lack of complexity, the short maturities and central clearing function, this is probably therefore the safest part of the derivatives market.
- *OTC centrally cleared.* These are OTC derivatives that are not suitable for exchange-trading due to being relatively complex, illiquid and non-standard, but are centrally cleared. Indeed, incoming regulation is requiring central clearing of standardised OTC derivatives (Section 9.3.1).
- *OTC collateralised.* These are bilateral OTC derivatives that are not centrally cleared but where parties post collateral to one another in order to mitigate the counterparty risk.
- *OTC uncollateralised.* These are bilateral OTC derivatives where parties do not post collateral (or post less and/or lower quality collateral). This is typically because one of the parties involved in the contract (typically an end-user such as a corporate) cannot commit to collateralisation. Since they have nothing to mitigate their counterparty risk, these derivatives generally receive the most attention in terms of their underlying risks and costs.

The question, of course, is how significant each of the above categories is. Figure 3.2 gives a breakdown in terms of the total notional. Only about a tenth of the market is exchange-traded with the majority being OTC. However, more than half of the OTC market is already centrally cleared. Of the remainder, four-fifths is collateralised, with only 20% remaining under-collateralised. For this reason it is this last category that is the most dangerous and the source of many of the problems in relation to counterparty risk, funding and capital.

The majority of this book is about the seemingly small 7% (20% of the 40% of the 91% in Figure 3.2) of the market that is not well collateralised bilaterally or via a central clearing function. However, it is important to emphasise that this still represents tens of trillions of dollars of notional and is therefore extremely important from a counterparty risk perspective. Furthermore, it is also important to look beyond just counterparty risk and consider funding, capital and collateral. This in turn makes all groups of derivatives in Figure 3.2 important.

3.1.4 Market participants

The range of institutions that take significant counterparty risk has changed dramatically over recent years – or, more to the point, institutions now fully appreciate the extent

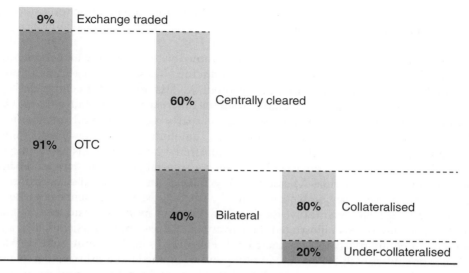

Figure 3.2   Breakdown of different types of derivatives by total notional.
Source: Eurex (2014).

of counterparty risk they may face. It is useful to characterise the different players in the OTC derivatives market. Broadly, the market can be divided into three groups:

- *Large players.* This will be a large global bank, often known as a dealer. They will have a vast number of OTC derivatives trades on their books and have many clients and other counterparties. They will usually trade across all asset classes (interest rate, foreign exchange, equity, commodities, credit derivatives) and will post collateral against positions (as long as the counterparty will make the same commitment and sometimes even if they do not).
- *Medium-sized player.* This will typically be a smaller bank or other financial institution that has significant OTC derivatives activities, including making markets in certain products. They will cover several asset classes although may not be active in all of them (they may, for example, not trade credit derivatives or commodities, and will probably not deal with the more exotic derivatives). Even within an asset class, their coverage may also be restricted to certain market (for example, a regional bank transacting in certain local currencies). They will have a smaller number of clients and counterparties but will also generally post collateral against their positions.
- *End-user.* Typically this will be a large corporate, sovereign or smaller financial institution with derivatives requirements (for example, for hedging needs or investment). They will have a relatively smaller number of OTC derivatives transactions on their books and will trade with only a few different counterparties. They may only deal in a single asset class: for example, some corporates trade only foreign exchange products; a mining company may trade only commodity forwards; or a pension fund may only be active in interest rate and inflation products. Due to their needs, their overall position will be very directional (i.e. they will not execute offsetting transactions). Often,

they may be unable or unwilling to commit to posting collateral or will post illiquid collateral and/or post more infrequently.

The OTC derivatives market is highly concentrated with the largest 14 dealers holding around four-fifths of the total notional outstanding.[4] These dealers collectively provide the bulk of the market liquidity in most products. Historically, these large derivatives players have had stronger credit quality than the other participants and were not viewed by the rest of the market as giving rise to counterparty risk. (The credit spreads of large, highly rated, financial institutions prior to 2007 amounted to just a few basis points per annum.[5]) The default of Lehman Brothers illustrated how wrong this assumption had been. Furthermore, some smaller players, such as sovereigns and insurance companies, have had very strong (triple-A) credit quality. Indeed, for this reason such entities have often obtained very favourable terms such as one-way collateral agreements as they were viewed as being practically risk-free. The failure of monoline insurance companies and near-failure of AIG illustrated the naivety of this assumption. Historically, a large amount of counterparty risk has therefore been ignored simply because large derivatives players or entities with the best credit ratings were assumed to be risk-free. Market practice, regulation and accounting standards have changed dramatically over recent years in reaction to these aspects.

Finally, there are many third parties in the OTC derivative market. These may offer, for example, collateral management, software, trade compression and clearing services. They allow market participants to reduce counterparty risk, the risks associated with counterparty risk (such as legal) and improve overall operational efficiency with respect to these aspects.

3.1.5   Credit derivatives

The credit derivatives market grew swiftly in the decade before the global financial crisis due to the need to transfer credit risk efficiently. The core credit derivative instrument, the credit default swap (CDS), is simple and has transformed the trading of credit risk. However, CDSs themselves can prove highly toxic: whilst they can be used to hedge counterparty risk in other products, there is counterparty risk embedded within the CDS itself. The market has recently become all too aware of the dangers of CDSs and their usage has partly declined in line with this realisation. Credit derivatives can, on the one hand, be very efficient at transferring credit risk but, if not used correctly, can be counterproductive and highly toxic. The growth of the credit derivatives market has stalled in recent years since the crisis.

One of the main drivers of the move towards central clearing of standard OTC derivatives is the wrong-way counterparty risk represented by the CDS market. Furthermore, as hedges for counterparty risk, CDSs seem to require the default remoteness that central clearing apparently gives them. However, the ability of central counterparties to deal with the CDS product, which is much more complex, illiquid and risky than other cleared products, is crucial and not yet tested.

---

[4] Source: ISDA market survey, 2010.
[5] Meaning that the market priced their debt as being of very high quality and practically risk-free.

3.1.6   The dangers of derivatives

Derivatives can be extremely powerful and useful. They have facilitated the growth of global financial markets and have aided economic growth. Of course, not all derivatives transactions can be classified as "socially useful". Some involve arbitraging regulatory capital amounts, tax requirements or accounting rules. As almost every average person now knows, derivatives can be highly toxic and cause massive losses and financial catastrophes if misused.

A key feature of derivatives instruments is leverage. Since most derivatives are executed with only a small (with respect to the notional value of the contract) or no upfront payment made, they provide significant leverage. If an institution has the view that US interest rates will be going down, they may buy US treasury bonds. There is a natural limitation to the size of this trade, which is the cash that the institution can raise in order to invest in bonds. However, entering into a receiver interest rate swap in US dollars will provide approximately the same exposure to interest rates but with no initial investment.[6] Hence, the size of the trade, and the effective leverage, must be limited by the institution themselves, the counterparty in the transaction or a regulator. Inevitably, it will be significantly bigger than that in the previous case of buying bonds outright. Derivatives have been repeatedly shown to be capable of creating or catalysing major market disturbances with their inherent leverage being the general cause.

As mentioned above, the OTC derivatives market is concentrated in the hands of a relatively small number of dealers who trade extensively with one another. These dealers act as common counterparties to large numbers of end-users of derivatives and actively trade with each other to manage their positions. Perversely, this used to be perceived by some as actually adding stability – after all, surely none of these big counterparties would ever fail? Now it is thought of as creating significant systemic risk: where the potential failure in financial terms of one institution creates a domino effect and threatens the stability of the entire financial markets. Systemic risk may not only be triggered by actual losses; just a heightened perception of losses can be problematic.

3.1.7   The Lehman experience

The bankruptcy of Lehman Brothers in 2008 provides a good example of the difficulty created by derivatives. Lehman had more than 200 registered subsidiaries in 21 countries and around a million derivatives transactions. The insolvency laws of more than 80 jurisdictions were relevant. In order to fully settle with a derivative counterparty, the following steps need to be taken:

- reconciliation of the universe of transactions;
- valuation of each underlying transaction; and
- agreement of a net settlement amount.

As shown in Figure 3.3, carrying out the above steps across many different counterparties and transactions has been a very time-consuming process. The Lehman settlement of OTC derivatives has been a long and complex process lasting many years.

---

[6] Aside from initial margin requirements and capital requirements.

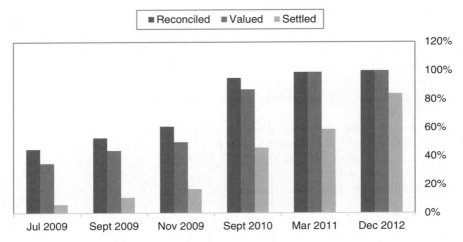

Figure 3.3   Management of derivative transactions by the Lehman Brothers estate.
Source: Fleming and Sarkar (2014).

3.2   DERIVATIVE RISKS

An important concept is that financial risk is generally not reduced per se but is instead converted into different forms; for example, collateral can reduce counterparty risk but creates market, operational and legal risks. Often these forms are more benign, but this is not guaranteed. Furthermore, some financial risks can be seen as a combination of two or more underlying risks (for example, counterparty risk is primarily a combination of market and credit risk). Whilst this book is primarily about counterparty risk and related aspects such as funding, it is important to understand this in the context of other financial risks.

3.2.1   Market risk

Market risk arises from the (short-term) movement of market variables. It can be a linear risk, arising from an exposure to the movement of underlying quantities such as stock prices, interest rates, foreign exchange (FX) rates, commodity prices or credit spreads. Alternatively, it may be a non-linear risk arising from the exposure to market volatility or basis risk, as might arise in a hedged position. Market risk has been the most studied financial risk over the past two decades, with quantitative risk management techniques widely applied in its measurement and management. This was catalysed by some serious market risk-related losses in the 1990s (e.g. Barings Bank in 1995) and the subsequent amendments to the Basel I capital accord in 1995 that allowed financial institutions to use proprietary mathematical models to compute their capital requirements for market risk. Indeed, market risk has mainly driven the development of the value-at-risk (Section 3.3.1) approach to risk quantification.

Market risk can be eliminated by entering into an offsetting contract. However, unless this is done with the same counterparty[7] as the original position(s), then counterparty risk will be generated. If the counterparties to offsetting contracts differ, and either counterparty fails, then the position is no longer neutral. Market risk therefore forms a component of counterparty risk. Additionally, the imbalance of collateral agreements and central clearing arrangements across the market creates a funding imbalance and leads to funding costs.

3.2.2 Credit risk

Credit risk is the risk that a debtor may be unable or unwilling to make a payment or fulfil contractual obligations. This is often known generically as default, although this term has slightly different meanings and impact depending on the jurisdiction involved. The default probability must be characterised fully throughout the lifetime of the exposure (e.g. swap maturity) and so too must the recovery value (or equivalently the loss given default). Less severe than default, it may also be relevant to consider deterioration in credit quality, which will lead to a mark-to-market loss (due to the increase in future default probability). In terms of counterparty risk, characterising the term structure of the counterparty's default probability is a key aspect.

The credit risk of debt instruments depends primarily on default probability and the associated recovery value since the exposure is deterministic (e.g. the par value of a bond). However, for derivatives the exposure is uncertain and driven by the underlying market risk of the transactions. Counterparty risk is therefore seen as a combination of credit and market risk.

3.2.3 Operational and legal risk

Operational risk arises from people, systems and internal and external events. It includes human error (such as trade entry mistakes), failed processes (such as settlement of trades or posting collateral), model risk (inaccurate or inappropriately calibrated models), fraud (such as rogue traders), and legal risk (such as the inability to enforce legal agreements, for example those covering netting or collateral terms). Whilst some operational risk losses may be moderate and common (incorrectly booked trades, for example), the most significant losses are likely to be a result of highly improbable scenarios or even a "perfect storm" combination of events. Operational risk is therefore extremely hard to quantify, although quantitative techniques are increasingly being applied. Counterparty risk mitigation methods, such as collateralisation, inevitably give rise to operational risks.

Legal risk (defined as a particular form of operational risk by Basel II) is the risk of losses due to the assumed legal treatment not being upheld. This can be due to aspects such as incorrect documentation, counterparty fraud, mismanagement of contractual rights, or unanticipated decisions by courts. Mitigating financial risk generally gives rise to legal risk due to the mitigants being challenged in some way at a point where they come into force. Defaults are particularly problematic from this point of view, because they are relatively rare and very sensitive to the jurisdiction in question.

---

[7] Or via a central counterparty, or later reduced via trade compression.

3.2.4   Liquidity risk

Liquidity risk is normally characterised in two forms. Asset liquidity risk represents the risk that a transaction cannot be executed at market prices, perhaps due to the size of the position and/or relative illiquidity of the underlying market. Funding liquidity risk refers to the inability to fund contractual payments or collateral requirements, potentially forcing an early liquidation of assets and crystallisation of losses. Since such losses may lead to further funding issues, funding liquidity risk can manifest itself via a "death spiral" caused by the negative feedback between losses and cash requirements. Reducing counterparty risk often comes at the potential cost of increased funding liquidity risk via mechanisms such as collateralisation or central clearing.

3.2.5   Integration of risk types

A particular weakness of financial risk management over the years has been the lack of focus on the integration of different risk types. It has been well known for many years that crises tend to involve a combination of different financial risks. Given the difficulty in quantifying and managing financial risks in isolation, it is not surprising that limited effort is given to integrating their treatment. As noted above, counterparty risk itself is already a combination of two different risk types, market and credit. Furthermore, the mitigation of counterparty risk can create other types of risk, such as liquidity and operational. It is important not to lose sight of counterparty risk as an intersection of many types of financial risk, and that mitigating counterparty risk creates even more financial risks. This is one of the reasons that this book, since the first and second editions, has evolved to cover more material in relation to collateral, funding and capital.

3.2.6   Counterparty risk

Counterparty risk is traditionally thought of as credit risk between OTC derivatives counterparties. Since the global financial crisis, the importance of OTC derivatives counterparty risk has been a key focus of regulation. Historically, many financial institutions limited their counterparty risk by trading only with the most sound counterparties. The size and scale of counterparty risk has always been important, but for many years has been obscured by the myth of the creditworthiness of the "too big to fail" institutions. However, the financial crisis showed that these are often the entities that represent the most counterparty risk. The need to consider counterparty risk in all OTC derivative relationships and the decline in credit quality generally has caused a meteoric rise in interest in and around the subject. Regulatory pressure has continued to fuel this interest. Whereas in the past, only a few large dealers invested heavily in assessed counterparty risk, it has rapidly become the problem of all financial institutions, big or small. At the same time, the assessment of the impact of collateral, funding and capital has become a key topic.

3.3   RISK MANAGEMENT OF DERIVATIVES

3.3.1   Value-at-risk

Financial risk management of derivatives has changed over the last two decades. One significant aspect has been the implementation of more quantitative approaches, the

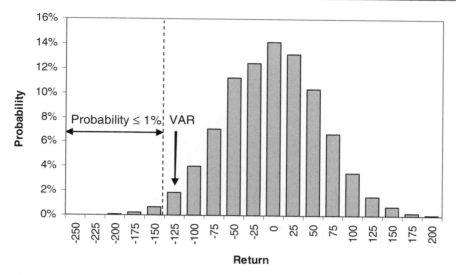

Figure 3.4 Illustration of the value-at-risk (VAR) concept at the 99% confidence level. The VAR is 125, since the chance of a loss greater than this amount is no more than 1%.

most significant probably being value-at-risk (VAR). Initially designed as a metric for market risk, VAR has subsequently been used across many financial areas as a means for efficiently summarising risk via a single quantity. For example, the concept of PFE (potential future exposure), when used to assess counterparty risk, is strongly related to the definition of VAR.

A VAR number has a simple and intuitive explanation as the worst loss over a target horizon to a certain specified confidence level. The VAR at the α% confidence level gives a value that will be exceeded with *no more* than a $(1 - \alpha)$% probability. An example of the computation of VAR is shown in Figure 3.4. The VAR at the 99% confidence level is -125 (i.e. a loss) since the probability that this will be exceeded is no more than 1%. (It is actually 0.92% due to the discrete[8] nature of the distribution.) To find the VAR, one finds the *minimum* value that will be exceeded with the specified probability.

VAR is a very useful way in which to summarise the risk of an entire distribution in a single number that can be easily understood. It also makes no assumption as to the nature of distribution itself, such as that it is a Gaussian.[9] It is, however, open to problems of misinterpretation since VAR says nothing at all about what lies beyond the defined (1% in the above example) threshold. To illustrate this, Figure 3.5 shows a slightly different distribution with the same VAR. In this case, the probability of losing 250 is 1% and hence the 99% VAR is indeed 125 (since there is zero probability of other losses in-between). We can see that changing the loss of 250 does not change the VAR since it is only the *probability* of this loss that is relevant. Hence, VAR does not give an

---

[8] For a continuous distribution, VAR is simply a quantile. (A quantile gives a value on a probability distribution where a given fraction of the probability falls below that level.)

[9] Certain implementations of a VAR model (notably the so-called variance-covariance approach) may make normal (Gaussian) distribution assumptions, but these are done for reasons of simplification and the VAR idea itself does not require them.

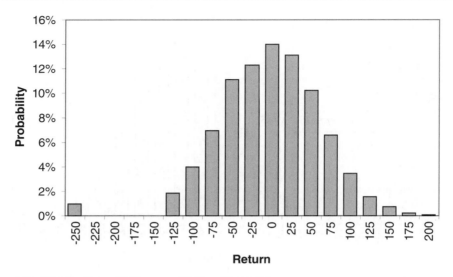

Figure 3.5   Distribution with the same VAR as Figure 3.4.

indication of the possible loss outside the confidence level chosen. Over-reliance upon VAR numbers can be counterproductive as it may lead to false confidence.

Another problem with VAR is that it is not a *coherent* risk measure (Artzner et al., 1999), which basically means that in certain (possibly rare) situations it can exhibit non-intuitive properties. The most obvious of these is that VAR may not behave in a sub-additive fashion. Sub-additivity requires a combination of two portfolios to have no more risk than the sum of their individual risks (due to diversification).

A slight modification of the VAR metric is commonly known as expected shortfall (ES). Its definition is the average loss equal to or above the level defined by VAR. Equivalently, it is the average loss knowing that the loss is at least equal to the VAR. ES does not have quite as intuitive an explanation as VAR, but has more desirable properties such as not completely ignoring the impact of large losses (the ES in Figure 3.5 is indeed greater than that in Figure 3.4) due to being a coherent risk measure. For these reasons, *The Fundamental Review of the Trading Book* (BCBS, 2013) has suggested that banks use ES rather than VAR for measuring their market risk (this may eventually also apply to the calculation of CVA capital, as discussed in Section 8.7).

The most common implementation of VAR and ES approaches is using historical simulation. This takes a period (usually several years) of historical data containing risk factor behaviour across the entire portfolio in question. It then resimulates over many periods how the current portfolio would behave when subjected to the same historical evolution. For example, if four years of data were used, then it would be possible to compute around 1,000 different scenarios of daily movements for the portfolio. If a longer time horizon is of interest, then quite commonly the one-day result is simply extended using the "square root of time rule". For example, in market risk VAR models used by banks, regulators allow the ten-day VAR to be defined as $\sqrt{10}$=3.14 multiplied by the one-day VAR. VAR models can also be "backtested" to check their predictive performance empirically. Backtesting involves performing an *ex-post* comparison of actual outcomes with those predicted by the model. VAR lends itself well to backtesting since a 99% number should be exceeded once every hundred observations.

It is important to note that the use of historical simulation and backtesting are relatively straightforward to apply for VAR and ES due to the short time horizon (ten days) involved. For counterparty risk assessment (and xVA in general), much longer time horizons are involved and quantification is therefore much more of a challenge.

3.3.2   Models

The use of metrics such as VAR relies on quantitative models in order to derive the distribution of returns from which such metrics can be calculated. The use of such models facilitates combining many complex market characteristics such as volatility and dependence into one or more simple numbers that can represent risk. Models can compare different trades and quantify which is better, at least according to certain predefined metrics. All of these things can be done in minutes or even seconds to allow institutions to make fast decisions in rapidly moving financial markets.

However, the financial markets have something of a love/hate relationship with mathematical models. In good times, models tend to be regarded as invaluable, facilitating the growth in complex derivatives products and dynamic approaches to risk management adopted by many large financial institutions. The danger is that models tend to be viewed either as "good" or "bad" depending on the underlying market conditions. Whereas, in reality, models can be good or bad depending on how they are used. An excellent description of the intricate relationship between models and financial markets can be found in MacKenzie (2006).

The modelling of counterparty risk is an inevitable requirement for financial institutions and regulators. This can be extremely useful and measures such as PFE, the counterparty risk analogue of VAR, are important components of counterparty risk management. However, like VAR, the quantitative modelling of counterparty risk is complex and prone to misinterpretation and misuse. Furthermore, unlike VAR, counterparty risk involves looking years into the future rather than just a few days, which creates further complexity not to be underestimated. Not surprisingly, regulatory requirements over backtesting of counterparty risk models[10] have been introduced to assess performance. In addition, a greater emphasis has been placed on stress testing of counterparty risk, to highlight risks in excess of those defined by models. Methods to calculate xVA are, in general, under increasing scrutiny.

3.3.3   Correlation and dependency

Probably the most difficult aspect in understanding and quantifying financial risk is that of co-dependency between different financial variables. It is well known that historically estimated correlations may not be a good representation of future behaviour. This is especially true in a more volatile market environment, or crisis, where correlations have a tendency to become very large. Furthermore, the very notion of correlation (as used in financial markets) may be heavily restrictive in terms of its specification of co-dependency.

---

[10] Under the Basel III regulations.

Counterparty risk takes difficulties with correlation to another level, for example compared to traditional VAR models. Firstly, correlations are inherently unstable and can change significantly over time. This is important for counterparty risk assessment, which must be made over many years, compared with market risk VAR, which is measured over just a single day. Secondly, correlation (as it is generally defined in financial applications) is not the only way to represent dependency, and other statistical measures are possible. Particularly in the case of wrong-way risk (Chapter 19), the treatment of co-dependencies via measures other than correlation is important. In general, xVA calculations require a careful assessment of the co-dependencies between credit risk, market risk, funding and collateral aspects.

4

Counterparty Risk

4.1 BACKGROUND

Counterparty credit risk (often known just as counterparty risk) is the risk that the entity with whom one has entered into a financial contract (the counterparty to the contract) will fail to fulfil their side of the contractual agreement (for example, if they default). Counterparty risk is typically defined as arising from two broad classes of financial products: OTC derivatives (e.g. interest rate swaps) and securities financial transactions (e.g. repos). The former category is the more significant due to the size and diversity of the OTC derivatives market (see Figure 3.1 in the last chapter) and the fact that a significant amount of risk is not collateralised. As has been shown in the market events of the last few years, counterparty risk is complex, with systemic traits and the potential to cause, catalyse or magnify serious disturbances in the financial markets.

4.1.1 Counterparty risk versus lending risk

Traditionally, credit risk can generally be thought of as lending risk. One party owes an amount to another party and may fail to pay some or all of this due to insolvency. This can apply to loans, bonds, mortgages, credit cards and so on. Lending risk is characterised by two key aspects:

- The notional amount at risk at any time during the lending period is usually known with a degree of certainty. Market variables such as interest rates will typically create only moderate uncertainty over the amount owed. For example, in buying a bond, the notional amount at risk for the life of the bond is close to par. A repayment mortgage will amortise over time (the notional drops due to the repayments) but one can predict with good accuracy the outstanding balance at some future date. A loan or credit card may have a certain maximum usage facility, which may reasonably be assumed fully drawn[1] for the purpose of credit risk.
- Only one party takes lending risk. A bondholder takes considerable credit risk, but an issuer of a bond does not face a loss if the buyer of the bond defaults.[2]

---

[1] On the basis that an individual unable to pay is likely to be close to any limit.

[2] This is not precisely true in the case of bilateral counterparty risk (DVA), discussed in Chapter 14, although conventions regarding close-out amounts can correct for this.

With counterparty risk, as with all credit risk, the cause of a loss is the obligor being unable or unwilling to meet contractual obligations. However, two aspects differentiate contracts with counterparty risk from traditional credit risk:

- The value of the contract in the future is uncertain – in most cases significantly so. The MTM value of a derivative at a potential default date will be the net value of all future cashflows required under that contract. This future value can be positive or negative, and is typically highly uncertain (as seen from today).
- Since the value of the contract can be positive or negative, counterparty risk is typically *bilateral*. In other words, each counterparty in a derivatives transaction has risk to the other.

4.1.2   Settlement and pre-settlement risk

A derivatives portfolio contains a number of settlements equal to multiples of the total number of transactions; for example, a swap contract will have a number of settlement dates as cashflows are exchanged periodically. Counterparty risk is mainly associated with pre-settlement risk, which is the risk of default of the counterparty prior to expiration (settlement) of the contract. However, we should also consider settlement risk, which is the risk of counterparty default *during* the settlement process.

- *Pre-settlement risk.* This is the risk that a counterparty will default prior to the final settlement of the transaction (at expiration). This is what "counterparty risk" usually refers to.
- *Settlement risk.* This arises at settlement times due to timing differences between when each party performs on its obligations under the contract.

The difference between pre-settlement and settlement risk is illustrated in Figure 4.1.

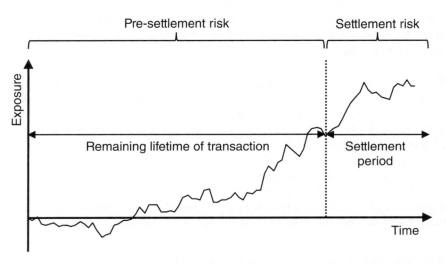

Figure 4.1   Illustration of pre-settlement and settlement risk. Note that the settlement period is normally short (e.g., hours) but can be much longer in some cases.

Example

Suppose an institution enters into a forward FX contract to exchange €1m for $1.1m at a specified date in the future. The settlement risk exposes the institution to a substantial loss of $1.1m, which could arise if €1m was paid but the $1.1m was not received. However, this only occurs for a single day on expiry of the FX forward. This type of cross-currency settlement risk is sometimes called Herstatt risk (see box below). Pre-settlement risk (counterparty risk) exposes the institution to just the difference in market value between the dollar and Euro payments. If the foreign exchange rate moved from 1.1 to 1.15, this would translate into a loss of $50,000, but this could occur at any time during the life of the contract.

Unlike counterparty risk, settlement risk is characterised by a very large exposure – potentially, 100% of the notional of the transaction. Whilst settlement risk gives rise to much larger exposures, default prior to expiration of the contract is substantially more likely than default at the settlement date. However, settlement risk can be more complex when there is a substantial delivery period (for example, as in a commodity contract where one may be required to settle in cash against receiving a physical commodity over a specified time period).

Whilst all derivatives technically have both settlement and pre-settlement risk, the balance between the two will be different depending on the contract. Spot contracts have mainly settlement risk whilst long-dated swaps have mainly pre-settlement (counterparty) risk. Furthermore, various types of netting (see Chapter 5) provide mitigation against settlement and pre-settlement risks.

Case study: Bankhaus Herstatt

A well-known example of settlement risk is the failure of a small German bank, Bankhaus Herstatt. On 26th June 1974, the firm defaulted but only after the close of the German interbank payments system (3:30pm local time). Some of Herstatt Bank's counterparties had paid Deutschemarks to the bank during the day, believing they would receive US dollars later the same day in New York. However, it was only 10:30am in New York when Herstatt's banking business was terminated, and consequently all outgoing US dollar payments from Herstatt's account were suspended, leaving counterparties fully exposed.

Settlement risk is a major consideration in FX markets, where the settlement of a contract involves a payment of one currency against receiving the other. Most FX now goes through CLS[3] and most securities settle DVP,[4] but there are exceptions, such as cross-currency swaps, and settlement risk should be recognised in such cases.

---

[3] A multi-currency cash settlement system – see www.cls-group.com.

[4] Delivery versus payment, where payment is made at the moment of delivery, aiming to minimise settlement risk in securities transactions.

Settlement risk typically occurs for only a small amount of time (often just days, or even hours). To measure the period of risk to a high degree of accuracy would mean taking into account the contractual payment dates, the time zones involved and the time it takes for the bank to perform its reconciliations across accounts in different currencies. Any failed trades should also continue to count against settlement exposure until the trade actually settles. Institutions typically set separate settlement risk limits and measure exposure against this limit rather than including settlement risk in the assessment of counterparty risk. It may be possible to mitigate settlement risk, for example by insisting on receiving cash before transferring securities.

Recent developments in collateral posting have the potential to increase currency settlement risk. The standard CSA (Section 6.4.6), the regulatory collateral requirements (Section 6.7) and central clearing mandate (Section 9.3.1) incentivise or require cash collateral posting in the currency of a transaction. These potentially create more settlement risk, and associated liquidity problems, as parties have to post and receive large cash payment in silos across multi-currency portfolios.

4.1.3 Mitigating counterparty risk

There are a number of ways of mitigating counterparty risk. Some are relatively simple contractual risk mitigants, whilst other methods are more complex and costly to implement. Obviously, no risk mitigant is perfect, and there will always be some residual counterparty risk, however small. Furthermore, quantifying this residual risk may be more complex and subjective. In addition to the residual counterparty risk, it is important to keep in mind that risk mitigants do not remove counterparty risk *per se*, but instead convert it into other forms of financial risk, some obvious examples being:

- *Netting*. Bilateral netting agreements (Section 5.2.4) allow cashflows to be offset and, in the event of default, for MTM values to be combined into a single net amount. However, this also creates **legal risk** in cases where a netting agreement cannot be legally enforced in a particular jurisdiction and also exposes other creditors to more significant losses.
- *Collateral*. Collateral agreements (Section 6.2) specify the contractual posting of cash or securities against MTM losses. Taking collateral to minimise counterparty risk creates **operational risk** due to the necessary logistics involved and **market risk**, since exposure exists in the time taken to receive the relevant collateral amount. Collateralisation of counterparty risk also leads to **liquidity risk**, since the posting of collateral needs to be funded and collateral itself may have price and FX volatility. Aspects such as rehypothecation (reuse) and segregation of collateral are important considerations here (Section 6.4.2 and 6.4.3). Like netting, collateral also increases the losses of other creditors in a default scenario (Section 6.6.1).
- *Other contractual clauses*. Other features, such as resets or additional termination events (Section 5.5.2), aim to periodically reset MTM values or terminate transactions early. Like collateral, these can create **operational** and **liquidity** risks.
- *Hedging*. Hedging counterparty risk with instruments such as credit default swaps (CDSs) aims to protect against potential default events and adverse credit spread movements. Hedging creates **operational** risk and additional **market risk** through the mark-to-market (MTM) volatility of the hedging instruments. Taking certain types of

collateral can create **wrong-way risk** (Chapter 17). Hedging may lead to **systemic risk** through feedback effects (see the statement from the Bank of England in Section 2.4).

- *Central counterparties*. Central counterparties (CCPs) guarantee the performance of transactions cleared through them and aim to be financially safe themselves through the collateral and other financial resources that they require from their members. CCPs act as intermediaries to centralise counterparty risk between market participants. Whilst offering advantages such as risk reduction and operational efficiencies, they require the centralisation of counterparty risk, significant collateralisation and mutualisation of losses. They can therefore potentially create **operational** and **liquidity** risks, and also **systemic risk**, since the failure of a central counterparty could amount to a significant systemic disturbance. This is discussed in more detail in Chapter 9.

Mitigation of counterparty risk is a double-edged sword. On the one hand, it may reduce existing counterparty risks and contribute to improving financial market stability. On the other hand, it may lead to a reduction in constraints such as capital requirements and credit limits, and therefore lead to a growth in volumes. Indeed, without risk mitigants such as netting and collateral, the OTC derivatives market would never have developed to the size it is today. Furthermore, risk mitigation should really be thought of as risk transfer, since new risks and underlying costs are generated.

Another way to see some of the risk conversion described above is in xVA terms. CVA may be reduced but another xVA component created. Indeed, later chapters of this book will discuss this conversion between xVA terms in detail. For now, some obvious examples are:

- *Collateral*. Creates FVA (due to the need to fund collateral posting) and ColVA (due to the optionality inherent in the collateral agreement).
- *Termination clauses*. Aspects such as early termination events (possibly linked to downgrade triggers) create MVA that has been exasperated due to regulatory requirements regarding liquidity buffers (Section 16.2.1).
- *Central clearing and bilateral collateral rules*. The requirement to post additional collateral in the form of initial margin creates MVA.
- *Hedging*. Hedging CVA for accounting purposes may create additional capital requirements and therefore increase KVA. On the other hand, reducing KVA may lead to greater CVA volatility (Section 18.3.8).

The above explains why it is critical to manage xVA centrally and make consistent decisions regarding pricing, valuation and risk mitigation so as to optimise aspects such as capital utilisation and achieve the maximum *overall* economic benefit.

4.1.4 Exposure and product type

The split of OTC derivatives by product type is shown in Figure 4.2. Interest rate products contribute the majority of the outstanding notional but this gives a somewhat misleading view of the importance of other asset classes, especially foreign exchange and credit default swaps. Whilst most foreign exchange products are short-dated, the long-dated nature and exchange of notional in cross-currency swaps means they have considerable

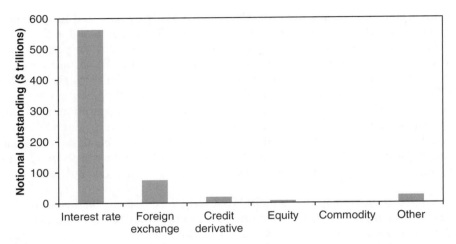

Figure 4.2   Split of OTC gross outstanding notional by product type as of June 2014.
Source: BIS.

counterparty risk. Credit default swaps not only have a large volatility component but also constitute significant "wrong-way risk" (discussed in detail in Chapter 17).

The above can be seen when looking at the averaged response from banks on their CVA breakdown by asset class in Figure 4.3. Although interest rate products make up a significant proportion of the counterparty risk in the market (and indeed are most commonly used in practical examples), one must not underestimate the important (and sometimes more subtle) contributions from other products. It is also important to note that, while large global banks have exposure to all asset classes, smaller banks may have a more limited exposure (for example, mainly interest rate and FX products). End-users

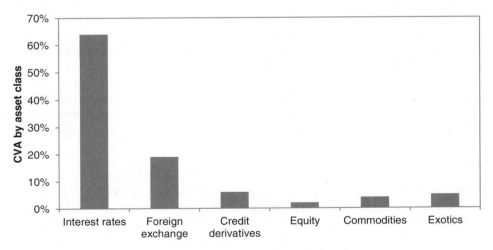

Figure 4.3   Split of CVA by asset class (average over all respondents).
Source: Deloitte/Solum CVA survey, 2013.

Table 4.1 Comparison of the total notional outstanding and the market value of derivatives ($ trillions) for different asset classes as of December 2014.

	Gross notional outstanding	Gross market value*	Ratio
Interest rate	505.5	15.6	3.1%
Foreign exchange	75.9	2.9	3.9%
Credit default swaps	16.4	0.6	3.6%
Equity	7.9	0.6	7.8%
Commodity	1.9	0.3	17.0%

* This is calculated as the sum of the absolute value of gross positive and gross negative market values, corrected for double counting.
Source: BIS.

may also have limited exposure: for example, a corporate may use only interest rate and cross-currency swaps.

A key aspect of derivatives products is that their exposure is substantially smaller than that of an equivalent loan or bond. Consider an interest rate swap as an example; this contract involves the exchange of floating against fixed coupons, and has no principal risk because only cashflows are exchanged. Furthermore, even the coupons are not fully at risk because, at coupon dates, only the difference in fixed and floating coupons or net payment will be exchanged. Comparing the actual total market of derivatives against the total notional amount outstanding therefore shows a significant reduction, as illustrated in Table 4.1. For example, the total market value of interest rate contracts is only 3.1% of the total notional outstanding. It is the market value that is more relevant, since this is representative of the loss that is suffered in a default scenario and is the amount that has to be funded or collateralised.

4.1.5 Setups

Broadly speaking, there are two situations in which counterparty risk and related aspects such as funding, collateral and capital arise. The most obvious (Figure 4.4) would apply to an end-user using OTC derivatives for hedging purposes. Their overall portfolio will be typically directional (but not completely so, as mentioned below), since the general aim will be to offset economic exposures elsewhere. The result of this will be that MTM volatility will be significant and any associated collateral flows may vary substantially. Indeed, the fact that substantial collateral may be required over a short time horizon is one reason why many end-users do not enter into collateral agreements. Another implication of directional portfolios is that there may be less netting benefit available.

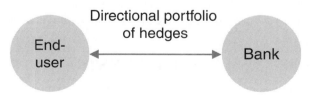

Figure 4.4 Illustration of the classic end-user counterparty risk setup.

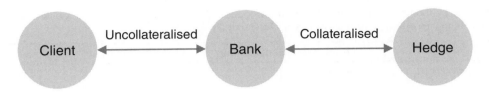

Figure 4.5   Illustration of the classic bank setup.

In practice, an end-user will trade with a reasonable number of bank counterparties depending on the volume of their business and risk appetite.

Another important feature is that end-users may hedge risks on a one-for-one basis; for example, the terms of a swap may be linked directly to those of bonds issued rather than the interest rate exposure being hedged more generically on a macro basis. End-users may find it problematic when unwinding transactions, since the original counterparty will not necessarily quote favourable terms. Furthermore, if they do execute offsetting transactions – for example, a supranational may execute receiver swaps to hedge their lending whilst also having payer swaps to hedge borrowing – the terms received will be less favourable than if they macro-hedged the overall risk. This is a consequence of hedging borrowing and lending on a one-to-one basis. For a similar reason, default situations will be problematic because an end-user may want to replace transactions on a one-for-one basis rather than macro-hedging their exposure to the defaulted counterparty. This will likely be more expensive and time-consuming.

For a bank, the classic counterparty risk situation is rather different (Figure 4.5). Banks will typically aim to run a relatively flat (i.e. hedged) book from a market risk perspective. This means that a transaction with a client will be hedged (either on a macro basis or one-for-one) with another market participant. This is likely to lead to a series of hedges through the interbank market, ending with another opposite exposure to another end-user. In this situation, the bank may have little or no MTM volatility or market risk. However, they do have counterparty risk to both counterparties A and B, because if either were to default it would leave market risk with respect to the other side of the trade.

Another important feature of this situation is that client transactions will often be uncollateralised, whereas the hedges will be collateralised (or centrally cleared). The counterparty risk problem exists mainly on the uncollateralised transactions (although there is still material risk on the hedges). Whilst the overall MTM is neutralised, this introduces an asymmetry in collateral flows that can be problematic. Dealers also suffer from the directional hedging needs of clients. For example, they may transact mainly receiver interest rate swaps with corporate clients. In a falling interest rate environment, the bank's exposure will increase substantially and the hedges of these swaps will require significant collateral posting. Figure 4.5 is very important as a starting point for many different types of analysis and will be referred back to at several later points in this book.

4.2 COMPONENTS

Counterparty risk represents a combination of market risk, which defines the exposure and credit risk that defines the counterparty credit quality. A counterparty with a large default probability and a small exposure may be considered preferable to one with a larger exposure and smaller underlying default probability – but this is not clear. CVA puts a value on counterparty risk and is one way to distinguish numerically between the aforementioned cases. CVA will be discussed in detail later, but we now define the important components that define counterparty risk and related metrics.

4.2.1 Mark-to-market and replacement cost

Mark-to-market (MTM) is the starting point for analysis of counterparty risk and re-lated aspects. Current MTM does not constitute an immediate liability by one party to the other, but rather is the present value of all the payments that a party is expecting to receive, less those it is obliged to make. These payments may be scheduled to occur many years in the future and may have values that are strongly dependent on market variables. MTM will be positive or negative, depending on the magnitude of remaining payments and current market rates.

The MTM with respect to a particular counterparty defines the net value of all posi-tions and is therefore directly related to what could potentially be lost today in the event of a default. However, other aspects are important in this regard, such as the ability to net transactions in default and the possibility to adjust positions with collateral amounts. Both of these aspects are subject to legal agreements and their potential interpretation in a court of law.

Contractual features of transactions, such as close-out netting and termination fea-tures, refer to *replacement costs*. MTM is clearly closely related to replacement cost, which defines the entry point into an equivalent transaction(s) with another counter-party. However, the actual situation is more complicated. To replace a transaction, one must consider costs such as bid–offer spreads, which may be significant especially for particularly illiquid products. Note that even a standard and liquid contract might be non-standard and illiquid at the default time. In such a case, one must then decide whether to replace with an expensive non-standard derivative or with a more standard one that does not match precisely the original one. Large portfolios can be replaced one-for-one or macro-hedged. Broadly speaking, documentation suggests that default costs can effectively be passed on via the replacement cost concept, although this is discussed in more detail later via the definition of close-out amount (Section 5.2.6).

Contractual agreements generally reference replacement costs (and not MTM) in defining a surviving party's position in a default scenario. Although this represents the economic reality in a default, it can cause further problems. By their nature, replacement costs will include CVA (and more generally xVA) components that create a recursive problem, since one cannot define xVA today without knowing the future xVA. Chapter 14 addresses this topic in more detail (Section 14.6.5). For now, we note that quanti-fication will assume, for reasons of simplicity, that MTM is a good proxy for the real replacement cost and this is in general not a bad approximation.

4.2.2 Credit exposure

Credit exposure (hereafter often simply known as exposure) defines the loss in the event of a counterparty defaulting. It is also representative of other costs such as capital and funding that appear in other xVA terms. Exposure is characterised by the fact that a positive value of a portfolio corresponds to a claim on a defaulted counterparty, where-as in the event of negative value, a party is still obliged to honour their contractual payments (at least to the extent that they exceed those of the defaulted counterparty). This means that if a party is owed money and their counterparty defaults then they will incur a loss, while in the reverse situation they cannot gain[5] from the default by being somehow released from their liability.

Exposure is clearly a very time-sensitive measure, since a counterparty can default at any time in the future and one must consider the impact of such an event many years from now. Essentially, characterising exposure involves answering the following two questions:

- What is the current exposure (the maximum loss if the counterparty defaults today)?
- What is the exposure in the future (what could be the loss if the counterparty defaults at some point in the future)?

The second point above is naturally far more complex to answer than the first, except in some simple cases.

All exposure calculations, by convention, will ignore any recovery value in the event of a default. Hence, the exposure is the loss, as defined by the value or replacement cost that would be incurred, assuming no recovery value. Exposure is relevant only if the counterparty defaults and hence the quantification of exposure would be conditional on counterparty default. Having said this, we will often consider exposure independently of any default event and so assume implicitly no "wrong-way risk". Such an assumption is reasonable for most products subject to counterparty risk, although the reader should keep the idea of conditional exposure in mind. We will then address wrong-way risk, which defines the relationship between exposure and counterparty default, in more detail in Chapter 17.

Note that exposure from other points of view (most obviously funding-related) need not be conditional on counterparty default.

4.2.3 Default probability, credit migration and credit spreads

When assessing counterparty risk, one must consider the credit quality of a counter-party over the entire lifetime of the relevant transactions. Such time horizons can be extremely long. Ultimately, there are two aspects to consider:

- What is the probability of the counterparty defaulting[6] over a certain time horizon?
- What is the probability of the counterparty suffering a decline in credit quality over a certain time horizon (for example, a ratings downgrade and/or credit spread widening)?

Credit migrations or discrete changes in credit quality (such as those due to ratings changes) are crucial, since they influence the term structure of default probability. They should also be considered, since they may cause issues even when a counterparty is not yet in default. Suppose the probability of default of a counterparty between the current

---

[5] Except in some special and non-standard cases.

[6] We will generally use the term "default" to refer to any "credit event" that could impact the counterparty.

time and a future date of (say) one year is known. It is also important to consider what the same annual default rate might be in four years – in other words, the probability of default between four and five years in the future. There are three important aspects to consider:

- Future default probability[7] as defined above will have a tendency to decrease due to the chance that the default may occur before the start of the period in question. The probability of a counterparty defaulting between 20 and 21 years in the future may be very small – not because they are very creditworthy (potentially, quite the reverse), but rather because they are unlikely to survive for 20 years!
- A counterparty with an expectation[8] of deterioration in credit quality will have an increasing probability of default over time (although at some point the above phenomenon will reverse this).
- A counterparty with an expectation of improvement in credit quality will have a decreasing probability of default over time, which will be accelerated by the first point above.

Spreadsheet 4.1   Counterparty risk for a forward contract-type exposure.

There is a well-known empirical mean-reversion in credit quality, as evidenced by historical credit ratings changes. This means that good (above-average) credit quality firms tend to deteriorate and vice versa. So a counterparty of good credit quality will tend to have an increasing default probability over time, whereas a poor credit quality counterparty will be more likely to default in the short term and less likely to do so in the longer term. The term structure of default is very important to consider.

Finally, we note that default probability may be defined as real-world or risk-neutral. In the former case, we ask ourselves what the *actual* default probability of the counterparty is, which is often estimated via historical data. In the latter case, we calculate the risk-neutral (or market-implied) probability from market credit spreads. The difference between real-world and risk-neutral default probabilities is discussed in detail in Chapter 12, but it is worth emphasising now that risk-neutral default probabilities have become virtually mandatory for CVA calculations in recent years due to a combination of accounting guidelines, regulatory rules and market practice.

4.2.4 Recovery and loss given default

Recovery rates typically represent the percentage of the outstanding claim recovered when a counterparty defaults. An alternative variable to recovery is loss given default (LGD), which in percentage terms is 100% minus the recovery rate. Default claims can vary significantly, so LGD is therefore highly uncertain. Credit exposure is traditionally measured independently, but LGD is relevant in the quantification of CVA.

---

[7] Here we refer to default probabilities in a specified period, such as annual.

[8] This can refer to a real expectation (historical) or one implied from market spreads (risk-neutral) as discussed below.

In the event of a bankruptcy, the holders of OTC derivatives contracts with the counterparty in default would generally be pari passu[9] with the senior bondholders. OTC derivatives, bonds and CDSs generally reference senior unsecured credit risk and may appear to relate to the same LGD. However, there are timing issues: when a bond issuer defaults, LGD is realised immediately, since the bond can be sold in the market. CDS contracts are also settled within days of the defined "credit event" via the CDS auction that likewise defines the LGD. However, OTC derivatives cannot be freely traded or sold, especially when the counterparty to the derivative is in default. This essentially leads to a potentially different LGD for derivatives. These aspects, which were very important in the Lehman Brothers bankruptcy of 2008 (see Figure 3.3 in the previous chapter), are discussed in more detail in Section 12.2.5.

4.3   CONTROL AND QUANTIFICATION

To control and quantify counterparty risk, one must first recognise that it varies substantially depending on aspects such as the transaction and counterparty in question. In addition, it is important to give the correct benefit arising from the many risk mitigants (such as netting and collateral) that may be relevant. Control of counterparty risk has traditionally been the purpose of credit limits, used by most banks for well over a decade.

However, *credit limits* only cap counterparty risk. While this is clearly the first line of defence, there is also a need to correctly quantify and ensure a party is being correctly compensated for the counterparty risk that they take. This is achieved via CVA, which has been used increasingly in recent years as a means of assigning an economic value on the counterparty risk and/or complying with accounting requirements. In some cases, this CVA is actively managed (for example, through hedging).

Below we analyse credit limits and CVA, and how they complement one another.

4.3.1   Credit limits

Let us consider the first and most basic use of exposure, which is as a means to control the amount of risk to a given counterparty over time. Counterparty risk can be diversified by limiting exposure to any given counterparty, broadly in line with the perceived default probability of that counterparty. This is the basic principle of credit limits (or credit lines). By trading with a greater number of counterparties, a party is not so exposed to the failure of any one of them. Diversification across counterparties is not always practical due to the relationship benefits from trading with certain key clients. In such cases, exposures can become excessively large and should be, if possible, mitigated by other means.

Credit limits are generally specified at the counterparty level, as illustrated in Figure 4.6. The idea is to characterise the potential future exposure (PFE) to a counterparty over time and ensure that this does not exceed a certain value (the credit limit). The PFE represents a worst-case scenario and is similar to the well-known VAR measure described in Section 3.3.1. The credit limit will be set subjectively according to the risk appetite of the party in question. It may be time-dependent, reflecting the fact that exposures

---

[9] This means they have the same seniority and therefore should expect to receive the same recovery value.

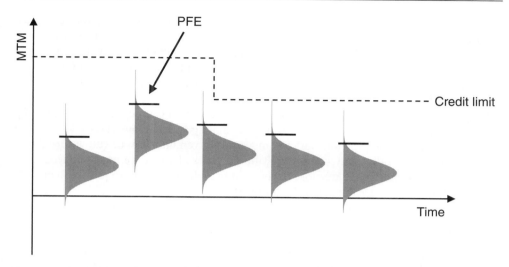

Figure 4.6   Illustration of the use of PFE and credit limits in the control of counterparty risk.

at different times in the future may be considered differently. PFE will be described in more detail in Section 7.2.2 but, broadly, the follow aspects must be accounted for in its quantification:

- the transaction in question;
- the current relevant market variables (e.g. interest rates and volatilities);
- netting of the new transaction with existing transactions with the same counterparty;
- collateral terms with the counterparty (if any); and
- hedging aspects.

Credit limits will often be reduced over time, effectively favouring short-term exposures over long-term ones. This is due to the chance that a counterparty's credit quality may deteriorate over a long time horizon. Indeed, empirical and market-implied default probabilities for good quality (investment grade) institutions tend to increase over time, which suggests the reduction of a credit limit. The credit limit of a counterparty with poor credit quality (sub-investment grade) should arguably increase over time, because if the counterparty does not default then its credit quality will be expected to improve eventually. Note that credit limits should be conditional on non-default before the point in question, because the possibility of an earlier default is captured via a limit at a previous time.

Credit limits are typically used to assess trading activity on a dynamic basis. Any transaction that would breach a credit limit at any point in the future is likely to be refused unless specific approval is given. Limits could be breached for two reasons: either due to new transactions or market movements. The former case is easily dealt with by refusing transactions that would cause a limit breach. The latter is more problematic, and banks sometimes have concepts of hard and soft limits: the latter may be breached through market movements rather than new transactions, whereas a breach of the former would require remedial action (e.g. transactions must be unwound or restructured, or hedges must be sourced). For example, a credit limit of $10m ("soft limit") might restrict trades that cause an increase in PFE above this value, and may allow the PFE to move up to $15m ("hard limit") as a result of changes in market conditions. When close to a limit, only risk-reducing transactions would be approved. Due to the directional nature of end-users activity in OTC derivatives, this is a challenge.[10]

Credit limits allow a consolidated view of exposure with each counterparty and represent a first step in portfolio counterparty risk management. However, they are rather binary in nature, which is problematic. Sometimes a given limit can be fully utilised, preventing transactions that may be more profitable. Banks have sometimes built measures to penalise transactions that are close to (but not breaching) a limit, requiring them to be more profitable, but these are generally quite ad hoc.

4.3.2 Credit value adjustment

Traditional counterparty risk management, as described above, works in a binary fashion. The problem with this is that the risk of a new transaction is the only consideration, whereas the return (profit) should surely be a factor also. By pricing counterparty risk through CVA, the question becomes whether it is profitable once the counterparty risk component has been "priced in". The calculation of CVA (and DVA) will be discussed in more detail in Chapter 14, but in addition to the components required for PFE quantification mentioned above, the following are also important:

- the default probability and expected LGD of the counterparty; and
- the parties' own default probability (in the case of bilateral pricing and DVA).

An important aspect of CVA is that it is a counterparty level calculation.[11] CVA should be calculated incrementally by considering the increase (or decrease) in exposure, taking into account netting effects due to any existing trades with the counterparty. This means that CVA will be additive across different counterparties and does not distinguish between counterparty portfolios that are highly concentrated. Such concentration could arise from a very large exposure with a single counterparty or exposure across two or more highly correlated counterparties (e.g. in the same region or sector).

4.3.3 CVA and credit limits

Traditional credit limits and CVA have their own weaknesses. Broadly speaking, there should be three levels to assess the counterparty risk of a transaction:

- *Trade level.* Incorporating all characteristics of the trade and associated risk factors. This defines the counterparty risk of a trade at a "stand-alone" level.

---

[10] For example, see "Consumers exceeding bank credit lines slows oil hedging", *Risk*, 2nd April 2015.

[11] Strictly speaking, it is a netting set level calculation, as there can possibly be more than one netting agreement with a given counterparty.

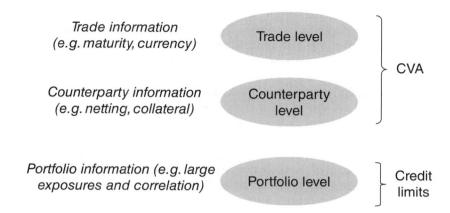

Figure 4.7   High-level illustration of the complimentary use of CVA and credit limits to manage counterparty risk.

- *Counterparty level.* Incorporating the impact of risk mitigants such as netting and collateral for each counterparty (or netting set) individually. This defines the incremental impact that a trade has with respect to existing transactions.
- *Portfolio level.* Consideration of the risk to all counterparties, knowing that only a small fraction may default in a given time period. This defines the impact a trade has on the total counterparty risk faced by an institution.

CVA focuses on evaluating counterparty risk at the trade level (incorporating all specific features of the trade) and counterparty level (incorporating risk mitigants). In contrast, credit limits essentially act at the portfolio level by limiting exposures to avoid concentrations. When viewed like this, we see that CVA and credit limits act in a complementary fashion, as illustrated in Figure 4.7. Indeed, CVA encourages minimising the number of trading counterparties, since this maximises the benefits of netting, whilst credit limits encourage maximising this number to encourage smaller exposures and diversification. Hence, CVA and credit limits are typically used together as complementary ways to quantify and manage counterparty risk. In practice, this means that the credit risk department in a bank will approve a trade (or not) and then, if approved, the xVA desk will price in the CVA component to determine the actual price before transacting.

4.3.4   What does CVA represent?

The price of a financial product can generally be defined in one of two ways:

- The price represents an expected value of future cashflows, incorporating some adjustment for the risk being taken (the risk premium). We will call this the *actuarial price*.
- The price is the cost of an associated hedging strategy. This is the *risk-neutral* (or market-implied) price.

The latter is a well-known concept for banks in pricing derivatives, whereas the former is more common in other areas, most obviously insurance. The biggest difference between the two definitions above is default probability: typically, historical default probabilities in the actuarial approach and credit spread implied default probabilities in the risk-neutral one. This will be discussed more in Section 12.2.

It is hard to objectively define how CVA should be defined with respect to the two very different definitions above. On the one hand, CVA is associated with derivatives for which risk-neutral pricing is standard and there are ways in which CVA can be hedged (e.g. CDS). On the other hand, the credit risk defining CVA is often illiquid and unhedgeable, so CVA may therefore more naturally fit into an actuarial assessment. Historically, the practices of banks have reflected this dichotomy: in the past, it was common to see the actuarial approach being followed where CVA was interpreted as a statistical estimate of the expected future losses from counterparty risk and held as a reserve (analogous to a loan loss reserve in a bank). More recently, CVA is typically defined in a risk-neutral fashion, interpreted as a MTM of the counterparty risk and closely associated with hedging strategies. The more sophisticated and larger banks were much quicker to adopt this risk-neutral approach.

There is no need to debate the above definition problem, since in recent years the risk-neutral approach to CVA has become dominant. The drivers for this have been:

- *Market practice.* Larger banks, in particular those in the US, were early adopters of the risk-neutral CVA approach. This would then be seen by other banks via aspects such as prices for novations. In practical terms, this could mean that a bank stepping into another bank's shoes on a given client portfolio would price the CVA differently, which in turn would lead the original bank to question whether their CVA calculation was market standard.
- *Accounting.* The FAS 157 and IFRS 13 accounting standards (Section 2.1) clearly reference an exit price concept and imply the use of risk-neutral default probabilities, and this has increasingly been the interpretation of auditors. Note that US and Canadian banks reporting under FAS 157 were early adopters of risk-neutral CVA at a time when many European banks (then under IAS 39 accounting standards) still used actuarial CVA. The introduction of IFRS 13 from 2013 has tended to create convergence here. However, the exit price concept also generally requires one's own credit spread to be recognised via debt value adjustment (DVA), which is a problematic component since monetising such a benefit is clearly unlikely to be practical (see Chapter 14 for further discussion).
- *Basel III.* Basel III capital rules (Chapter 8) clearly define CVA with respect to credit spreads and therefore advocate the risk-neutral approach. However, these do not permit DVA, which creates a conflict with accounting standards.
- *Regulators' opinions.* Local regulators have also commented on the need to use credit spreads when calculating CVA. Typical statements[12] are "it is not acceptable to have CCR models based on expected loss or historical calculations ignoring risk premia" and "market implied credit risk premia can be observed from active market like CDS and bonds".

---

[12] Translated from FMA (2012).

The result of the above is that it is now increasingly uncommon to see historical default probabilities used in the calculation of CVA (although other historical parameters are still more commonly used, especially for unobservable parameters such as correlations). For example, in a 2012 survey, Ernst and Young[13] commented:

> Two banks use a blended approach, combining market and historical data, and four banks use primarily historical data, which is generally consistent with their Basel II reporting. Given the requirements of IFRS 13, these six banks are preparing for a potential move to a more market-driven methodology for CVA, recording a DVA on derivative liabilities, and amending their hedging policies in the near future.

This does raise the question of how to define risk-neutral default probabilities when no traded credit spread is observed. This is discussed in Chapter 12.

4.3.5 Hedging counterparty risk

The growth of the credit derivatives market has facilitated hedging of counterparty credit risk. One obvious use of hedging (Figure 4.8) could be to purchase CDS protection on the counterparty in question so as to increase the credit limit.[14] More tailored credit derivative products such as contingent CDS (CCDS) have been designed to hedge counterparty risk even more directly. CCDSs are essentially CDSs but with the notional of protection indexed to the exposure on a contractually specified derivative (or even

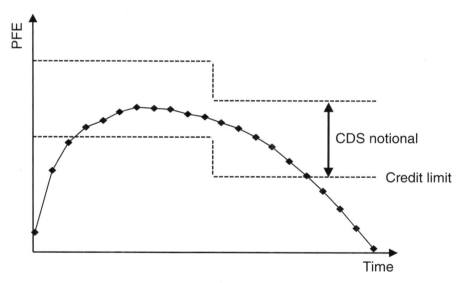

Figure 4.8   Illustration of CDS hedging in order to increase a credit limit (this assumes the maturity of the CDS contract is longer than the maximum time shown)..

---

[13] See www.ey.com.

[14] There are some technical factors that should be considered here such as the possibility of wrong-way risk (Chapter 17).

portfolio of derivatives). They allow the synthetic transfer of counterparty risk linked to a specific trade and counterparty to a third party. However, the CCDS market has never developed any significant liquidity.

More practically, hedging of CVA is done on a dynamic basis with reference to credit spreads (often via CDS indices) and other dynamic market variables (interest rates, FX rates, etc.). This will be discussed in more detail in Chapter 18.

4.3.6   The CVA desk

The concept of a CVA desk (or xVA desk) in a large bank has been around for many years. However, in recent years, smaller banks, other financial institutions and even end-users have had some internal CVA team. This development has been driven by some of the points mentioned in Section 4.3.4, with accounting requirements having a particularly significant impact. The development of the credit derivatives market has facilitated hedging of counterparty credit risk and also allowed CVA desks to treat CVA on a more dynamic basis, although CDSs have not significantly increased in liquidity in recent years.

The general role of a CVA desk in a bank is depicted in Figure 4.9 with reference to the previous discussion in Section 4.1.5. Although the precise setup varies and will be discussed in Chapter 18, in general the aim is for the counterparty risk of the originating trading or sales desk to be priced and managed by the CVA desk. Obviously certain transactions will be more significant from a CVA point of view – more obviously long-dated with more risky and/or uncollateralised counterparties – so a CVA desk may price only certain transactions, although coverage tends to increase as they develop. As discussed below, CVA desks have also needed to broaden their coverage to consider other aspects such as collateral, funding and capital. Indeed, the more general term "xVA desk" will be used from now on.

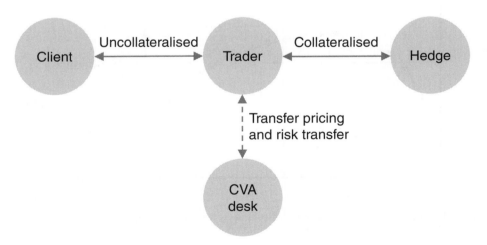

Figure 4.9   Illustration of the role of a CVA desk (xVA desk) in a bank.

4.4   BEYOND CVA

4.4.1   Overview

If the aftermath of the global financial crisis, CVA attracted huge interest due to the problems associated with counterparty risk, the reaction of regulators with the Basel III CVA capital charge (Section 8.7) and accounting changes with IFRS 13. However, related to these changes, other aspects started to gain considerable interest, all of which are connected to CVA. In order to understand these aspects, it is useful to refer to the classic situation represented in Figure 4.5, where an uncollateralised derivative is hedged with a collateralised one. Consider what happens when the market moves, and, for the sake of argument, assume that the uncollateralised transaction has a positive MTM and the collateralised hedge therefore has a negative one. In additional to the obvious counterparty risk problems, the following economic aspects are also relevant:

- *Funding.* It will be necessary to post collateral on the hedge and this amount will need to be funded. (Note that it is probably more realistic to see funding as being driven by the positive MTM of the uncollateralised transaction, as discussed in more detail in Chapter 16.) Furthermore, any initial margin posted will also need to be funded.
- *Collateral.* There will be a choice of the currency of cash and type of securities that can be used to collateralise the negative MTM.
- *Capital.* There will be capital requirements and these will change – which is important, because capital is a cost. The capital for the uncollateralised transaction will increase as it becomes in-the-money. The capital for the hedge will not offset this due to being collateralised – and even if it was uncollateralised, there would likely be a convexity impact (the capital for one transaction would increase by more than the capital reduction on the other).

4.4.2   Economic costs of an OTC derivative

The xVA concept really arises from extending the above analysis to fully assess the lifetime cost of an OTC derivative, including all economically relevant terms as illustrated in Figure 4.10. The explanation of the different aspects is as follows:

- *Positive MTM.* When the transaction is in-the-money (above the centre line), then the uncollateralised component gives rise to counterparty risk and funding costs. If some or all of the MTM is collateralised, then the counterparty can choose what type of collateral to post (with the range specified contractually).
- *Negative MTM.* When the transaction is out-of-the-money, then there is counterparty risk from the party's own default and a funding benefit to the extent they are not required to post collateral. If collateral is posted, then the party can choose the type to post.
- *Overall.* Whether or not the transaction has a positive or negative MTM, there are costs from funding the capital that must be held against the transaction and any initial margin that needs to be posted.

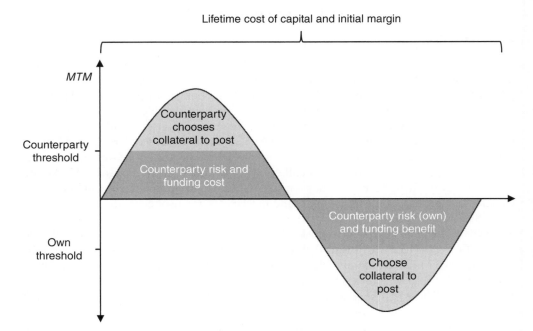

Figure 4.10   Illustration of the lifetime cost of an OTC derivative. Note that this representation is general; in reality, thresholds are often zero or infinity.

The above is a general explanation of the economic costs of a derivative throughout its lifetime. The relevant economics around collateral, funding and capital will be discussed in later chapters.

4.4.3   xVA terms

The general concept of any xVA term is illustrated in Figure 4.11. This quantifies the value of a component such as counterparty risk, collateral, funding or capital. Generally the terms are associated with a cost (positive y-axis) but note that in some cases they can be benefits (in which case they would be negative). In order to compute xVA we have to integrate the profile shown against the relevant cost or benefit such as a credit spread, collateral, funding or cost of capital metric.

When valuing derivatives, we typically start from a basic idealised valuation that may be relevant in certain specific cases. This will be discussed in Chapter 13. After this, there are a variety of xVA terms defined as follows:

- *CVA and DVA*. Defines the bilateral valuation of counterparty risk. DVA (debt value adjustment) represents counterparty risk from the point of view of a party's own default. These components will be discussed in Chapter 14.
- *FVA*. Defines the cost and benefit arising from the funding of the transaction. This will be discussed in Chapter 15.

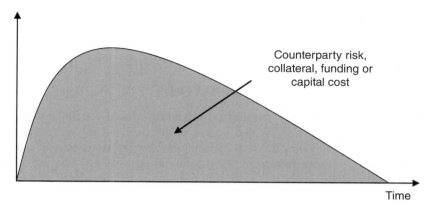

Figure 4.11   Generic illustration of an xVA term. Note that the some xVA terms represent benefits and not costs and would appear on the negative y-axis.

- *ColVA*. Defines the costs and benefits from embedded optionality in the collateral agreement (such as being able to choose the currency or type of collateral to post), and any other non-standard collateral terms (compared to the idealised starting point). This will be discussed in Chapter 13.
- *KVA*. Defines the cost of holding capital (typically regulatory) over the lifetime of the transaction. This will be discussed in Chapter 16.
- *MVA*. Defines the cost of posting initial margin over the lifetime of the transaction. This will also be discussed in Chapter 16.

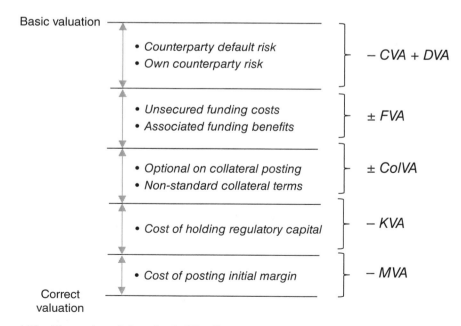

Figure 4.12   Illustration of the role of xVA adjustments.

It is also important to note that there are potential overlaps between the above terms – such as those between DVA and FVA, where own default risk is widely seen as a funding benefit. These overlaps are important and will be discussed in Chapters 18 and 19.

4.5   SUMMARY

In this chapter, we have defined counterparty risk, introduced the key components of credit exposure, default probability and recovery, and outlined the risk mitigation approaches of netting and collateralisation. We have discussed various ways of quantifying and managing counterparty risk, from the traditional approach of credit limits to the more sophisticated approaches of pricing via CVA and the consideration of portfolio and hedging aspects. We have also explained the emergence of other xVA terms to represent the economic impact of collateral, funding and capital.

Netting, Close-out and Related Aspects

5.1 INTRODUCTION

5.1.1 Overview

This chapter describes the role of netting and close-out in OTC derivatives markets. Netting is a traditional way to mitigate counterparty risk where there may be a large number of transactions of both positive and negative value with a given counterparty. Close-out refers to the process of terminating and settling contracts with a defaulted counterparty. We will describe the contractual and legal basis for netting and close-out and their impact in terms of risk reduction and effect on xVA. We will also discuss some other related forms of risk mitigation such as trade compression and break clauses.

5.1.2 The need for netting and close-out

OTC derivatives markets are fast-moving, with some participants (e.g. banks and hedge funds) regularly changing their positions. Furthermore, derivative portfolios may contain a large numbers of transactions, which may partially offset (hedge) one another. These transactions may themselves require contractual exchange of cashflows and/or assets through time. These would ideally be simplified into a single payment where possible (netting). Furthermore, in such a situation, the default of a counterparty (especially a major one) is a potentially very difficult event. A given party may have hundreds or even thousands of separate derivatives transactions with that counterparty. They need a mechanism to terminate their transactions rapidly and replace (rehedge) their overall position. Furthermore, it is desirable for a party to be able to offset what it owes to the defaulted counterparty against what they themselves are owed.

In order to understand netting and close-out in more detail, consider the situation illustrated in Figure 5.1. Suppose parties A and B trade bilaterally and have two transactions with one another, each with its own set of cashflows. This situation is potentially over-complex for two reasons:

- *Cashflows.* Parties A and B are exchanging cashflows or assets on a periodic basis in relation to transaction 1 and transaction 2. However, where equivalent cashflows occur on the same day, this requires exchange of gross amounts, giving rise to settlement

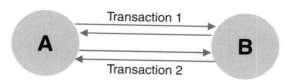

Figure 5.1   Illustration of the need for netting in bilateral markets.

risk. It would be preferable to amalgamate payments and exchange only a net amount (see the discussion on settlement risk in Section 4.1.2).

- *Close-out*. In the event that either party A or B defaults, the surviving party may suffer from being responsible for one transaction that has moved against them but not be paid for the other transaction that may be in their favour. This can lead to uncertainty over cashflow payments or the ability to replace the transactions with another counterparty.

Recent years have highlighted the need for risk mitigants for OTC derivatives. For example, the Lehman Brothers bankruptcy led to extensive litigation in relation to the ability to offset different obligations and the valuation of OTC derivative assets or liabilities (for example, refer to Figure 3.3). This illustrates the importance of documentation in defining the processes that will occur in the event of a counterparty default.

5.1.3   Payment and close-out netting

Bilateral OTC derivatives markets have historically developed netting methods whereby parties can offset what they owe to one another. The following two mechanisms facilitate this in relation to the two points raised in Section 5.1.2:

- *Payment netting*. This gives a party the ability to net cashflows occurring on the same day sometimes even if they are in different currencies. This typically relates to settlement risk.
- *Close-out netting*. This allows the termination of all contracts between an insolvent and a solvent counterparty, together with the offsetting of all transaction values (both in a party's favour and against it). This typically relates to counterparty risk.

Netting legislation covering derivatives has been adopted in most countries with major financial markets. The International Swaps and Derivatives Association (ISDA) has obtained legal opinions supporting the close-out and netting provisions in their Master Agreements in most relevant jurisdictions. (At the time of writing, they currently have such opinion covering 54 jurisdictions.) Thirty-seven countries have legislation that provides explicitly for the enforceability of netting. However, jurisdictions remain where netting is not clearly enforceable in a default scenario.[1]

---

[1] For example, see "Malaysia close to becoming a clean netting jurisdiction", *Risk*, 16th February 2015.

5.2   DEFAULT, NETTING AND CLOSE-OUT

5.2.1   The ISDA Master Agreement

The rapid development of the OTC derivative market could not have occurred without the development of standard documentation to increase efficiency and reduce aspects such as counterparty risk. ISDA is a trade organisation for OTC derivatives practitioners. The market standard for OTC derivative documentation is the ISDA Master Agreement, which was first introduced in 1985 and is now used by the majority of market participants to document their OTC derivative transactions.

The ISDA Master Agreement is a bilateral framework that contains terms and conditions to govern OTC derivative transactions. Multiple transactions will be covered under a general Master Agreement to form a single legal contract of an indefinite term, covering many or all of the transactions. The Master Agreement comprises a common core section and a schedule containing adjustable terms to be agreed by both parties. This specifies the contractual terms with respect to aspects such as netting, collateral, termination events, definition of default and the close-out process. By doing this, it aims to remove legal uncertainties and to provide mechanisms for mitigating counterparty risk. The commercial terms of individual transactions are documented in a trade confirmation, which references the Master Agreement for the more general terms. Negotiation of the agreement can take considerable time but once it has been completed, trading tends to occur without the need to update or change any general aspects. Typically, English or New York law is applied, although other jurisdictions are sometimes used.

From a counterparty risk perspective, the ISDA Master Agreement has the following risk mitigating features:

- the contractual terms regarding the posting of collateral (covered in detail in the next chapter);
- events of default and termination;
- all transactions referenced are combined into a single net obligation; and
- the mechanics around the close-out process are defined.

5.2.2   Events of default

In relation to counterparty risk, default events lead to the termination of transactions before their original maturity date and the initiation of a close-out process. Events of default covered in the ISDA Master Agreement are:

- failure to pay or deliver;
- breach of agreement;
- credit support default;
- misrepresentation;
- default under specified transaction;
- cross default;
- bankruptcy; and
- merger without assumption.

The most common of the above are failure to pay (subject to some defined threshold amount) and bankruptcy.

5.2.3 Payment netting

Payment netting involves the netting of payments between two counterparties in the same currency and in respect of the same transaction, for example netting the fixed and floating interest rate swap payments due on a particular day. For example, if on a particular day an IRS has a fixed payment of 60 by party A to party B and a floating payment of 100 by party B to party A, then payment netting means party B pays party A 40 (Figure 5.2). Parties may also elect to net payments across multiple transaction payments on the same day and in the same currency. This further reduces settlement risk and operational workload.

Settlement risk is also a major consideration in FX markets where the settlement of a contract involves a payment of one currency against receiving the other. In such situations, it is often inconvenient or impossible to settle the currencies on a net basis. To mitigate FX settlement risk, banks established Continuous Linked Settlement (CLS)[2] in 2002. For example, Bank A may deliver €100 million to CLS and Bank B delivers $125 million to CLS. When both deliveries arrive, CLS then make the payments to A and B. This is called payment versus payment (PVP). Parties still make the intended cashflows, but CLS ensures that one cannot occur without the other (which is a risk if one counterparty defaults). The settlement obligations are also reduced through multilateral netting between members.

Payment netting would appear to be a simple process that gives the maximum reduction of any risk arising from payments made on the same day. However, it does leave operational risk, which was illustrated in a high-profile case during the financial crisis (see box below).

Case study: The case of KfW Bankengruppe ("Germany's dumbest bank")

As the problems surrounding Lehman Brothers developed, most counterparties stopped doing business with the bank. However, government-owned German bank KfW Bankengruppe made what they described as an "automated transfer" of €300m to Lehman Brothers literally hours before the latter's bankruptcy. This provoked an outcry, with one German newspaper calling KfW "Germany's dumbest bank".[3] Two of the bank's management board members (one of whom has since successfully sued the bank for his subsequent dismissal) and the head of the risk-control department were suspended in the aftermath of the "mistake".

The KfW Bankengruppe transaction, giving rise to the problem outlined below, was a regular cross-currency swap with euros being paid to Lehman and dollars paid back to KfW. On the day Lehman Brothers declared bankruptcy, KfW made an automated

---

[2] See www.cls-group.com.

[3] For example, see "German bank is dubbed 'dumbest' for transfer to bankrupt Lehman Brothers", *New York Times*, 18th September 2008.

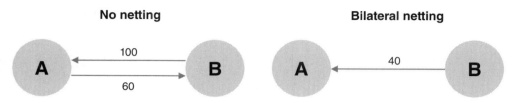

Figure 5.2   Illustration of the impact of payment netting.

transfer of €300m despite the fact that the stricken Lehman Brothers would not be making the opposite dollar payment; nowadays this type of cross-currency swap could be safely settled via CLS. It should be noted that if KfW had withheld the payment, this may have been challenged by the administrator of the Lehman Brothers estate.

5.2.4   Close-out netting

As mentioned above, it is not uncommon to have many different OTC derivative transactions with an individual counterparty. Such transactions may be simple or complex, and may cover a small or wider range of products across different asset classes. Furthermore, transactions may fall into one of the following three categories (especially from the point of view of banks):

- They may constitute hedges (or partial hedges) so that their values should naturally move in opposite directions.
- They may reflect unwinds in that, rather than cancelling a transaction, the reverse transaction may have been executed. Hence two transaction with a counterparty may have equal and opposite values, to reflect the fact that the original transaction has been cancelled.
- They may be largely independent, e.g. from different asset classes or on different underlyings.

Bankruptcy proceedings are, by their nature, long and unpredictable processes. During such processes, likely counterparty risk losses are compounded by the uncertainty regarding the termination of the proceedings. A creditor who holds an insolvent firm's debt has a known exposure, and while the eventual recovery is uncertain, it can be estimated and capped. However, this is not the case for derivatives, where constant rebalancing is typically required to maintain hedged positions. Furthermore, once a counterparty is in default, cashflows will cease and a surviving party will be likely to want or need to execute new replacement contracts.

Whilst payment netting reduces settlement risk, close-out netting is relevant to counterparty risk since it reduces pre-settlement risk. Netting agreements are crucial in order to recognise the benefit of offsetting transactions with the same counterparty. Close-out netting comes into force in the event that a counterparty defaults and aims to allow a timely termination and settlement of the net value of all transactions with that counterparty. Essentially, this consists of two components:

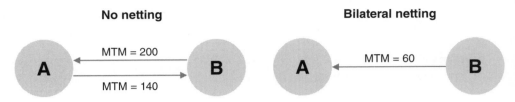

Figure 5.3   Illustration of the impact of close-out netting. In the event of the default of party A, without netting, party B would need to pay 200 to party A and would not receive the full amount of 140 owed. With netting, party B would simply pay 60 to party A and suffer no loss.

- *Close-out*. The right to terminate transactions with the defaulted counterparty and cease any contractual payments.
- *Netting*. The right to offset the value[4] across transactions and determine a *net balance*, which is the sum of positive and negative values, for the final close-out amount.

Close-out netting permits the immediate termination of all contracts with a defaulted counterparty and the settlement of a net amount reflecting the total value of the portfolio (Figure 5.3). In essence, with close-out netting, all covered transactions (of any maturity, whether in- or out-of-the-money) collapse to a single net value. If the surviving party owes money then it makes this payment; if it is owed money then it makes a bankruptcy claim for that amount. Close-out netting allows the surviving institution to immediately realise gains on transactions against losses on other transactions and effectively jump the bankruptcy queue for all but its net exposure, as illustrated in Figure 5.3. Note that close-out netting is general since it only depends on mark-to-market (MTM) values at the time of default and not matching cashflows.

Netting is not just important to reduce exposure but also to reduce the complexity involved in the close-out of transactions in the event that a counterparty defaults. In OTC derivatives markets, surviving parties will usually attempt to replace defaulted transactions. Without netting, the total number of transactions and their notional value that surviving parties would attempt to replace may be larger – and hence may be more likely to cause market disturbances.

5.2.5   Product coverage and set-off rights

Some institutions trade many financial products such as loans and repos as well as interest rate, foreign exchange, commodity, equity and credit products. The ability to apply netting to most or all of these products is desirable in order to reduce exposure. However, legal issues regarding the enforceability of netting arise due to transactions being booked with various different legal entities across different regions. The legal and other operational risks introduced by netting should not be ignored.

Bilateral netting is generally recognised for OTC derivatives, repo-style transactions and on-balance-sheet loans and deposits. Cross-product netting is typically possible

---

[4] The calculations made by the surviving party may be disputed later in litigation. However, the prospect of a valuation dispute and an uncertain recovery value does not affect the ability of the surviving party to immediately terminate and replace the contracts with a different counterparty.

within one of these categories (for example, between interest rate and foreign exchange transactions). However, netting across these product categories (for example, OTC derivatives and repos) is not straightforward as they are documented differently.

However, there is a concept of "set-off" that is similar to close-out netting and involves obligations between two parties being offset to create an obligation that represents the difference. Typically, set-off relates to actual obligations, whilst close-out netting refers only to a calculated amount. Set-off can be treated differently in different jurisdictions but is sometimes used interchangeably with the term "close-out netting". Set-off may therefore potentially be applied to offsetting amounts from other agreements against an ISDA close-out amount representing OTC derivatives. One obviously relevant example for banks is when both a loan and a derivative are executed with the same counterparty. This is most often the case where, for example, a bank lends money to a counterparty under a loan agreement and then hedges the interest rate risk associated with the loan via an interest rate swap (with terms linked to those of the loan) to effectively create a fixed rate loan.

Under the 2002 ISDA Master Agreement, a standard set-off provision is included that would allow for offset of any termination payment due against amounts owing to that party under other agreements (for example a loan master agreement, if the relevant loan documentation permits this). It is therefore possible from a legal perspective to set-off derivatives against other products such as loans. However, this will depend on the precise wording of the different sets of documentation, legal entities involved and legal interpretation in the relevant jurisdiction. Some banks have investigated set-off between contracts such as loans and derivatives in order to reduce exposure and CVA (and potentially CVA capital), but this is not standard market practice.

5.2.6   Close-out amount

The close-out amount represents the amount that is owed by one party to another in a default scenario. If this amount is positive from the point of view of the non-defaulting party, then they will have a claim on the estate of the defaulting party. If it is negative, then they will be obliged to pay this amount to the defaulting party. Although the defaulting party will be unable to pay any claim in full, establishing the size of the claim is important. The determination of the appropriate close-out amount is complex because parties will inevitably disagree. The non-defaulting party will likely consider their value of executing replacement transactions ("replacement cost") as the economically correct close-out amount. The defaulting party is unlikely to agree with this assessment, since it will reflect charges such as bid-offer costs that it does not experience.

The concept of replacement cost led to the development of "market quotation" as a means to define the close-out amount, as in the 1992 ISDA Master Agreement with an alternative known as the "loss method". these are characterised as follows:

- *Market quotation.* The determining (non-defaulting) party obtains a minimum of three quotes from market-makers and uses the average of these quotations in order to determine the close-out amount. This obviously requires a reasonable amount of liquidity in the market for the particular transactions in question. Such liquidity is not always present especially in the aftermath of a major default (e.g. Lehman Brothers) and in more exotic or non-standard products. It has therefore sometimes been problematic to find market-makers willing to price complex transactions realistically following a major default.

- *Loss method.* This is the fallback mechanism in the event that it is difficult for the determining party to achieve the minimum three quotes required by market quotation for all relevant transactions. In such a case, the determining party is required to calculate its loss in good faith and using reasonable assumptions. This gives a large amount of discretion to the determining party and introduces major subjectivity into the process.

Market quotation generally works well for non-complex transactions in relatively stable market conditions. However, since 1992 there have been an increasing number of more complex and structured OTC derivative transactions. This led to a number of significant disputes in the determination of the market quotation amount (e.g. see Figure 3.3). Furthermore, the loss method was viewed as too subjective and as giving too much discretion to the determining party. This was further complicated by contradictory decisions made by the English and US courts.

Because of the above problems and market developments (such as the availability of more external pricing sources), the 2002 ISDA Master Agreement replaced the concepts of market quotation and loss method with a single definition of "close-out amount". This was intended to offer greater flexibility to the determining party and to address some of the practical problems in achieving market quotations for complex products during periods of market stress. Close-out amounts are essentially a diluted form of market quotation as they do not require actual tradable quotes but can instead rely on indicative quotations, public sources of prices and market data, and internal models to arrive at a commercially reasonable price. In addition, the determining party's own creditworthiness may be taken into consideration and costs of funding and hedging may be included.

In summary, market quotation is an objective approach that uses actual firm quotes from external parties. The loss method is more flexible, with the determining party choosing any reasonable approach to determine its loss or gain. The close-out amount method is somewhere in between, giving the determining party flexibility to choose its approach but aiming to ensure that such an approach is commercially reasonable. Following the publication of the 2002 ISDA Master Agreement, some parties continued to use market quotation via the 1992 ISDA Master Agreement on the basis that it produced a more objective result. However, during the global financial crisis, the problems associated with this payment method (especially in relation to the Lehman Brothers bankruptcy) were again highlighted. As a result, there has been a growing trend towards using the 2002 close-out amount definition. In 2009, ISDA published a close-out amount protocol to provide parties with an efficient way to amend older Master Agreements to close-out amount with only one signed document rather than changing bilateral documentation on a counterparty-by-counterparty basis.

Note that the contractual definition regarding close-out is crucial in defining the economics of a counterparty default and as such is a key element in defining credit exposure (Chapter 7) and related aspects such as CVA (Chapter 14).

5.2.7 The impact of netting

Close-out netting is the single biggest risk mitigant for counterparty risk and has been critical for the growth of the OTC derivatives market. Without netting, the current size and liquidity of the OTC derivatives market would be unlikely to exist. Netting means that the overall credit exposure in the market grows at a lower rate than the notional growth of the market itself. Netting has also been recognised (at least partially) in regulatory capital rules, which was also an important aspect in allowing banks to grow their OTC derivative businesses. The expansion and greater concentration of derivatives markets has increased the extent of netting steadily over the last decade such that netting currently reduces exposure by close to 90% (Figure 5.4). However, note that netted positions are inherently more volatile than their underlying gross positions, which can create systemic risk.

Netting has some subtle effects on the dynamics of OTC derivative markets. Suppose an institution wants to trade out of a position. Executing an offsetting position with another market participant, whilst removing the market risk as required, will leave counterparty risk with respect to the original and new counterparties. A counterparty knowing that an institution is heavily incentivised to trade out of the position with them may offer unfavourable terms to extract the maximum financial gain. The institution can either accept these unfavourable terms or transact with another counterparty and accept the resulting counterparty risk.

The above point extends to establishing multiple positions with different risk exposures. Suppose an institution requires both interest rate and foreign exchange hedges. Since these transactions are imperfectly correlated then by executing the hedges with the same counterparty, the overall counterparty risk is reduced, and the institution may

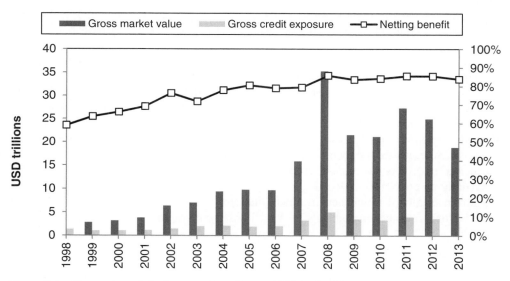

Figure 5.4 Illustration of the impact of netting on OTC derivatives exposure. The netting benefit (right hand y-axis) is defined by dividing the gross credit exposure by the gross market value and subtracting this ratio from 100%.
Source: BIS.

obtain more favourable terms. However, this creates an incentive to transact repeatedly with the same counterparty, leading to potential concentration risk.

An additional implication of netting is that it can change the way market participants react to perceptions of increasing risk of a particular counterparty. If credit exposures were driven by gross positions, then all those trading with the troubled counterparty would have strong incentives to attempt to terminate existing positions and stop any new trading. Such actions would be likely to result in even more financial distress for the troubled counterparty. With netting, an institution will be far less worried if there is no current exposure (MTM is negative). Whilst they will be concerned about potential future exposure and may require collateral, netting reduces the concern when a counterparty is in distress, which may in turn reduce systemic risk.

Interestingly, the benefits from netting are under threat from the drive towards mandatory clearing of OTC derivatives since clearable transactions will be removed from the portfolio (and cleared at one or more central counterparties), thereby removing potential netting benefits from the residual bilateral portfolio. This is discussed in more detail in Chapter 9.

5.3   MULTILATERAL NETTING AND TRADE COMPRESSION

5.3.1   Overview

Whilst netting reduces OTC derivative exposure by almost an order of magnitude, there is still a need to find ways of reducing it still further. Typical ISDA netting agreements by their nature operate bilaterally between just two counterparties. Trade compression can go further and achieve multilateral netting benefits via the cooperation of multiple counterparties.

Compression aims to minimise the gross notional of positions in the market. Whilst it does not and cannot change the market risk profile, it does potentially reduce:

- counterparty credit risk via reducing the overall exposure to multiple counterparties;
- operational costs by reducing the number of transactions;
- regulatory capital for banks not using advanced models where capital is partially driven by gross notional (for example, the so-called current exposure method discussed in Section 8.2);
- regulatory capital for banks with advanced model approval where the margin period of risk (Section 6.6.2) may otherwise need to be increased;
- other components such as the leverage ratio (section 8.8.2) since Basel III bases this partially on gross notional; and
- legal uncertainty around netting since offsetting transactions are replaced with a net equivalent transaction.

5.3.2   Multilateral netting

Suppose that party A has an exposure to party B, whilst B has exposure to a third party C that in turn has exposure to the original party A. Even using bilateral netting, all three parties have exposure (A has exposure to B, B to C and C to A). Some sort of trilateral

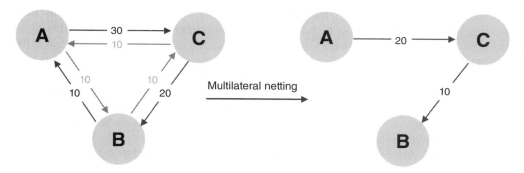

Figure 5.5 Illustration of the potential exposure reduction offered by multilateral netting. The black and grey exposures indicate positions in contractually identical (and therefore fungible) transactions, differing only in notional amount. The exposures in grey are removed completely, whilst those in black are reduced by ten units.

(and by extension multilateral) netting between the three (or more) parties would allow the exposures to be netted further as illustrated in Figure 5.5.

5.3.3   Bilateral compression services

Compression in exchange-traded and centrally cleared markets is a natural extension of the nature of trading and/or clearing through a central entity. However, the implementation of multilateral netting in bilateral OTC markets is not trivial and some sort of third party clearly needs to facilitate the process.

Initiatives such as TriOptima's TriReduce service[5] provides compression services covering major OTC derivatives products such as interest rate swaps (in major currencies), credit default swaps (CDS) on single-name, indices and tranches and energy swaps across around 200 members. This has been instrumental in reducing exposures in OTC derivatives markets, especially in rapidly growing areas such as credit derivatives.[6]

Compression has developed since OTC derivatives portfolios grow significantly through time but contain redundancies due to the nature of trading (e.g. with respect to unwinds). This suggests that the transactions can be reduced in terms of number and gross notional without changing the overall risk profile. This will reduce operational costs and also minimise counterparty risk. It may also reduce systemic risk by lowering the number of contracts that need to be replaced in a counterparty default scenario. Compression is subject to diminishing marginal returns over time as the maximum multilateral netting is achieved. It also relies to some degree on counterparties being readily interchangeable, which implies they need to have comparable credit quality.

A typical compression cycle will start with participants submitting their relevant transactions, which are matched according to the counterparty to the transaction and cross-referenced against a trade-reporting warehouse. An optimal overall solution may involve positions between pairs of counterparties increasing or changing sign. For this

---

[5] See www.trioptima.com.

[6] For example, "CDS dealers compress $30 trillion in trades in 2008", Reuters, 12th January 2009.

and other reasons, participants can specify constraints (such as the total exposure to a given counterparty, which may be related to internal credit limits of a participant). Participants must also specify tolerances since, whilst the aim of compression is to be totally market risk and cash neutral, allowing some small changes in MTM valuations and risk profile can increase the extent of the compression possible. Based on trade population and tolerances, changes are determined based on redundancies in the multilateral trade population. Once the process is finished, all changes are legally binding. Such changes can take effect by unwinding portions of transactions, executing new transactions and novating transactions to other counterparties.

Compression services are also complimentary to central clearing[7] as reducing the total notional and number of contracts cleared will be operationally more efficient and reduce complexity in close-out positions in the event of a clearing member default. However, since trades are generally cleared very quickly after being executed, the trade compression process must be done at the CCP level.

In the future, development of more advanced compression services may be important to optimise the costs of transacting OTC derivatives. In particular, compressing across both bilateral and central cleared products and using metrics such as xVA instead of gross notional may be particularly important.

5.3.4   The need for standardisation

Trade compression by its nature requires standard contracts, which are therefore fungible. OTC derivatives that do not fit the standard product templates cannot be compressed. A good example of producing standardisation of this type is the CDS market. In the aftermath of the global financial crisis, large banks together with ISDA made swift progress in standardising CDS contracts in terms of coupons and maturity dates to aid compression (and indeed facilitate central clearing). CDS contracts now trade with both fixed premiums and upfront payments, and scheduled termination dates of 20th March, 20th June, 20th September or 20th December. This means that positions can be bucketed according to underlying reference entity (single name or index) and maturity, but without any other differences (such as the previous standard where coupons and maturity dates would differ).

Standardisation of contracts to aid compression is not always possible. For example, interest rate swaps typically trade at par via a variable fixed rate. In such cases, compression is less easy and methods such as "coupon blending"[8] are being developed where swaps with the same maturity but different coupon rates can be combined.

5.3.5   Examples

In order to understand trade compression, consider the example "market" represented by Figure 5.6. This shows position sizes[9] between different counterparties in a certain

---

[7] For example, see www.swapclear.com/Images/lchswapcompression.pdf.

[8] For example, see www.cmegroup.com/trading/otc/files/cme-otc-irs-clearing-coupon-blending.pdf.

[9] This will be referred to as notional but could represent exposure or another measure, as it is the relative values that are important.

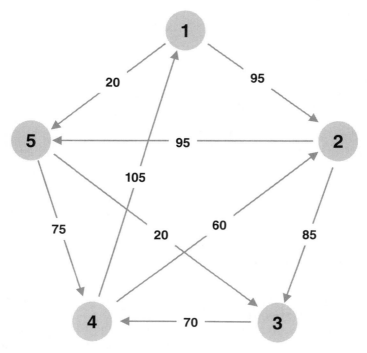

Figure 5.6   Illustration of a simple "market" made up of positions in fungible (interchangeable) contracts.

fungible (interchangeable) products. Note that the total gross notional between counterparties is 1250.

The aim of compression is to reduce the gross notional in Figure 5.6 without changing the net position of any counterparty. However, this is likely to be a subjective process for a number of reasons. Firstly, it is not clear what should be minimised. An obvious choice may be the total notional, although this would not penalise large positions or the total number of non-zero positions. Alternative choices could be to use the squared notional or the total number of positions, which would reduce large exposure and interconnectedness respectively. (O'Kane (2013) discusses this point in more detail.) Secondly, there may need to be constraints applied to the optimisation, such as the size of positions with single counterparties. In the above example, there is no transaction between counterparties 1 and 3. It may be that one or both of them would like to impose this as a constraint. Many different algorithms could be used to optimise the market above and commercial applications have tended to follow relatively simple approaches (for example, see Brouwer, 2012). The example below, albeit for a very small market, will provide some insight on how they work in practice.

One obvious method to reduce the total notional is to look for opportunities for netting within rings in the market. A trilateral possibility occurs between counterparties 2, 3 and 4 (as illustrated in Figure 5.7) where notionals of 60, 70 and 85 occur in a ring and can therefore be reduced by the smallest amount (assuming positions cannot be

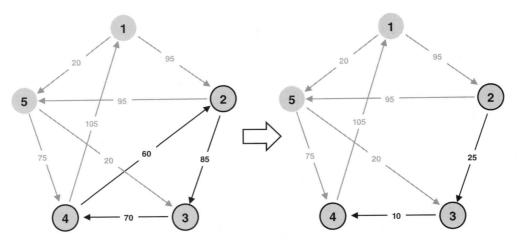

Figure 5.7   Illustration of using trilateral netting between counterparties 2, 3 and 4 to reduce the overall notional of the system shown in Figure 5.6.

reversed) of 60. This leads to the total notional of the compressed system being reduced to 890 (from 1250) on the right-hand side of Figure 5.7.

Continuing a process such as the one above could lead to a number of possible solutions, two of which are shown in Figure 5.8. Note that the solution on the left-hand side has reversed the exposure between counterparties 4 and 5, whilst on the right-hand side there is a transaction between counterparties 1 and 3 where none existed previously. The latter solution has a lower total notional of 110 (compared to 130 for the former), however, this also illustrates that constraints imposed by counterparties (for example, 1 and 3 not wanting exposure to one another) will weaken the impact of compression. Figure 3.1 in Chapter 3 shows the impact of the much greater emphasis on compression in OTC derivatives in the last few years.

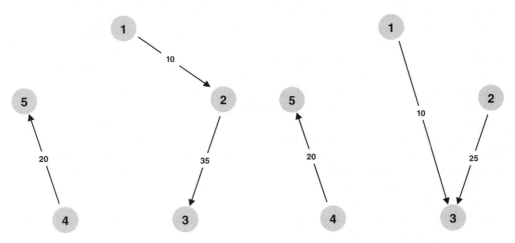

Figure 5.8   Illustration of two possible final results of compressing the original market in Figure 5.6 leading to total notionals of 130 (left-hand side) and 110 (right-hand side).

Table 5.1 Simple illustration of trade compression for single name CDS contracts. A party has three contracts on the same reference credit and with identical maturities but transacted with different counterparties. It is beneficial to "compress" the three into a net contract, which represents the total notional of the long and short positions. This may naturally be with counterparty A as a reduction of the initial transaction. The coupon of the new contract is the weighted average of the three original ones.

Reference	Notional	Long/short	Maturity	Coupon	Counterparty
ABC index	40	Long	20/12/2019	200	Counterparty A
ABC index	25	Short	20/12/2019	150	Counterparty B
ABC index	10	Short	20/12/2019	300	Counterparty C
ABC index	5	Long	20/12/2019	250	Counterparty A

A simple example of the potential result of a CDS compression exercise for one market participant is given in Table 5.1. Here, the net long position resulting from transactions with three counterparties is reduced to a single identical long position with one of the counterparties. Note that in this example, the coupons are assumed different and the weighted coupon is maintained.[10] This is not typically the case in the CDS market, as mentioned above[11] but may be a problem for compression of other products such as interest rate swaps, which do not trade with up-front premiums.

5.4 TERMINATION FEATURES AND RESETS

Long-dated derivatives have the problem that, whilst the current exposure might be relatively small and manageable, the exposure years from now could have easily increased to a relatively large, unmanageable level. An obvious way to mitigate this problem is to have a contractual feature in the transaction that permits action to reduce a high exposure. This is the role of termination features such as break clauses and reset agreements.

5.4.1 Walkaway features

Although no longer common, some OTC derivatives were historically documented with "walkaway" or "tear-up" features. Such a clause effectively allows an institution to cancel transactions in the event that their counterparty defaults. They would clearly only choose to do this in case they were in debt to the counterparty. Whilst a feature such as this does not reduce credit exposure, it does allow a surviving party to benefit from ceasing payments and not being obliged to settle amounts owed to a counterparty. These types of agreements, which were common prior to the 1992 ISDA Master Agreement, have been less usual since and are not now part of standardised ISDA documentation. However, they have sometimes been used in transactions since 1992. Whilst walkaway features do not mitigate counterparty risk *per se*, they do result in potential gains that offset the risk of potential losses.

---

[10] $(40 \times 200) - (25 \times 150) - (10 \times 300) = (5 \times 250)$.

[11] Although CDSs trade with at least two different coupons of 100 bps and 500 bps, which are standards for investment and speculative grade credits respectively. A credit or index could potentially have trades outstanding with both coupons used (for example, due to a significantly changing credit quality through time).

Walkaway agreements were seen in the Drexel Burnham Lambert (DBL) bankruptcy of 1990. Interestingly, in this case counterparties of DBL decided not to walk away and chose to settle net amounts owed. This was largely due to relatively small gains compared with the potential legal cost of having to defend the validity of the walkaway agreements or the reputational cost of being seen as taking advantage of the DBL default.

Even without an explicit walkaway agreement, an institution can still attempt to gain in the event of a counterparty default by not closing out contracts that are out-of-the-money to them but ceasing underlying payments. Another interesting case is that between Enron Australia (Enron) and TXU Electricity (TXU), involving a number of electricity swaps that were against TXU when Enron went into liquidation in early 2002. Although the swaps were not transacted with a walkaway feature, ISDA documentation supported TXU avoiding paying the MTM owed to Enron (A\$3.3 million) by not terminating the transaction (close-out) but ceasing payments to their defaulted counterparty. The Enron liquidator went to court to try to force TXU to settle the swaps but the New South Wales Supreme Court found in favour of TXU in that they would not have to pay the owed amount until the individual transactions expired (i.e. the obligation to pay was not cancelled but it was postponed).

Some Lehman Brothers counterparties also chose (like TXU) not to close-out swaps and stop making contractual payments (as their ISDA Master Agreements seemed to support). Since the swaps were very out-of-the-money from the counterparties' point of view (and therefore strongly in-the-money for Lehman), there were potential gains to be made from doing this. Again, Lehman administrators challenged this in the courts. US and English courts came to different conclusions with respect to the enforceability of this "walkaway event", with the US court[12] ruling that the action was improper whilst the English court[13] ruled that the withholding of payments was upheld.

Any type of walkaway feature is arguably rather unpleasant and should be avoided due to the additional costs for the counterparty in default and the creation of moral hazard, since an institution is potentially given the incentive to contribute to their counterparty's default due to the financial gain they can make.

5.4.2   Termination events

Another important aspect of the ISDA Master Agreement is an additional termination event (ATE), which allows a party to terminate OTC derivative transactions in certain situations. The most common ATE is in relation to a rating downgrade of one or both counterparties (for example, below investment grade). For unrated parties such as hedge funds, other metrics such as market capitalisation, net asset value or key man departure may be used. ATEs are obviously designed to mitigate against counterparty risk by allowing a party to terminate transactions or apply other risk-reducing actions when their counterparty's credit quality is deteriorating. This may be considered particularly useful when trading with a relatively good credit quality counterparty and/or long-maturity transactions. Over such a time horizon, there is ample time for both the MTM of the transaction to become significantly positive and for the credit quality of the counterparty to decline. If the ATE is exercised then the party can terminate the transactions at

---

[12] The Bankruptcy Court for the Southern District of New York.
[13] High Court of England and Wales.

their current replacement value. This introduces a complexity in terms of the definition of the replacement cost and whether it, for example, incorporates the credit quality of the replacement counterparty (similar to the discussion in relation to default close-out in Section 5.2.6). ATEs may not always lead to a termination of transactions and alternatively the affected party may be required to post (additional) collateral, or provide third party credit protection.

As an alternative to ATEs that apply to all transactions under a given ISDA Master Agreement, individual transactions may reference similar terms which have often been termed "break clauses" or "mutual puts". It may be considered advantageous to attach such a clause to a long-dated transaction (e.g. ten years or above), which carries significant counterparty risk over its lifetime. For example, a 15-year swap might have a mutual put in year five and every two years thereafter. Such break clauses may be mandatory, optional or trigger-based, and may apply to one or both parties in a transaction.

Recent years have highlighted the potential dangers of ATEs and other break clauses, in particular:

- *Risk-reducing benefit.* Whilst an idiosyncratic rating downgrade of a given counterparty may be a situation that can be mitigated against, a systematic deterioration in credit quality is much harder to nullify. Such systematic deteriorations are more likely for larger financial institutions, as observed in the global financial crisis.
- *Weaknesses in credit ratings.* Breaks clearly need to be exercised early before the counterparty's credit quality declines significantly and/or exposure increases substantially. Exercising them at the "last minute" is unlikely to be useful due to systemic risk problems. Ratings are well-known to be somewhat unreactive as dynamic measures of credit quality. By the time the rating agency has downgraded the counterparty, the financial difficulties will be too acute for the clause to be effective. This was seen clearly in relation to counterparties such as monoline insurers (see Section 2.2) in the global financial crisis. Indeed, under the Basel III rules for capital allocation, no positive benefit for ratings-based triggers is allowed (discussed later in Section 8.6.1).

Furthermore, ratings have in many circumstances been shown to be extremely slow in reacting to negative credit information, leading to the following problems:[14]

- *Cliff-edge effects.* The fact that many counterparties could have similar clauses may cause cliff-edge effects where a relatively small event such as a single-notch rating downgrade may cause a dramatic consequence as multiple counterparties all attempt to terminate transactions or demand other risk mitigating actions. The near-failure of AIG (see later discussion in Section 6.2.2) is a good example of this.
- *Determination of valuation in the event of a termination.* As discussed with respect to the definition of the close-out amount in Section 5.2.6, the market price used for termination is difficult and non-subjective to define.
- *Relationship issues.* Exercising break clauses may harm the relationship with a counterparty irrevocably and would therefore often not be used, even when contractually

---

[14] One obvious extension of this idea is to create triggers based on more continuous quantities such as credit spreads. However, these may be almost as problematic and may lead to further concerns such as the definition of the credit spread.

available. Clients do not generally expect break clauses to be exercised and banks, for relationship reasons, have historically avoided exercising these. Although banks have used break clauses more in recent years, in hindsight many have been no more than gimmicks. This is essentially part of a moral hazard problem, where front-office personnel may use the presence of a break clause to get a transaction executed but then later argue against the exercise of the break to avoid a negative impact on the client relationship. Banks should have clear and consistent policies over the exercise of optional break clauses and the benefit they assign to them from a risk reduction point of view.[15] There is typically a lack of internal clarity around who in a bank is empowered to exercise an ATE or other type of break clause.

- *Modelling difficulty*. Breaks are often very difficult to model since it is hard to determine the dynamics of rating changes in relation to potential later default events and the likelihood that a break would be exercised. Unlike default probability, rating transitions probabilities cannot be implied from market data. This means that historical data must be used, which is, by its nature, scarce and limited to some broad classification. This also means that there is no obvious means to hedge such triggers. One exception is where the break is mandatory (relatively uncommon) where the model may simply assume it will occur with 100% probability.

Although traditionally popular with credit and sales departments in banks, break clauses are seen by xVA desks as adding significant complexity and potentially very limited benefit. They are generally becoming less common, either being modified to permit cures such as posting of additional collateral or removed completely. Using other measures of credit quality such as CDS spreads may resolve some (but not all) of the problems of traditional breaks mentioned above and is not currently practical due to the illiquidity of the CDS market.

Prior to the financial crisis, break clauses were typically required by banks trading with certain (often uncollateralised) counterparties. More recently, it has become common for counterparties such as asset managers and pension funds to require break clauses linked to banks' own credit ratings due to the unprecedented credit quality problems within the banking sector during the global financial crisis. These breaks are also problematic since declines in banks' ratings and credit quality are likely to be linked to significant systemic problems generally. This means that finding a replacement counterparty for a given transaction may not be easy. Additionally, in recent times the liquidity coverage ratio (Section 8.8.4) has had an impact of such clauses as regulation has required banks to hold a liquidity buffer according to a worst-case change in their credit rating.

5.4.3   Reset agreements

A reset agreement is a different type of clause which avoids a transaction becoming strongly in-the-money (to either party) by means of adjusting product-specific parameters that reset the transaction to be more at-the-money. Reset dates may coincide with payment dates or be triggered by the breach of some market value. For example, in a resettable cross-currency swap, the MTM on the swap (which is mainly driven by FX

---

[15] Furthermore, usage of break clauses is becoming common. Parties will exercise break clauses or use their presence as leverage for agreeing other risk-mitigating actions.

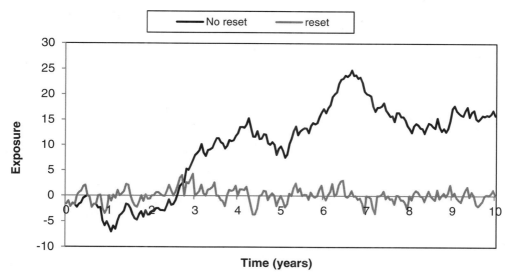

Figure 5.9   Illustration of the impact of reset features on the exposure of a long-dated cross-currency swap. Resets are assumed to occur quarterly.

movements on the final exchange of notional) is exchanged at each reset time in cash. In addition, the FX rate is reset to (typically) the prevailing spot rate. The reset means that the notional on one leg of the swap will change. Such a reset is similar to the impact of closing out the transaction and executing a replacement transaction at market rates, and consequently reduces the exposure. An example of the impact of such a reset is shown in Figure 5.9. It can also be seen as a weaker form of collateralisation which is discussed in the next chapter.

5.5   SUMMARY

In this chapter, we have described the primary ways of mitigating counterparty risk via exposure reduction. Payment netting allows offsetting cashflows to be combined into a single amount and reduces settlement risk. Close-out netting is a crucial way to control exposure by being legally able to offset transactions with positive and negative MTM values in the event a counterparty does default. Compression reduces gross notional and improves efficiency, although the associated net exposure is not materially reduced. ATEs or break clauses allow the termination of a transaction to mitigate an exposure combined with a deterioration of the credit quality of a counterparty, possibly linked to some event such as a credit ratings downgrade. Reset features allow the periodic resetting of an exposure.

In the next chapter, we discuss the use of collateral, which is the other main method for reducing exposure. However, when discussing collateral it is important to consider the associated funding implications.

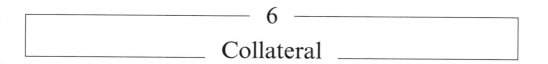

6

Collateral

6.1 INTRODUCTION

This chapter explains the role of collateral (also known as margin[1]) in reducing counter-party risk beyond the benefit achieved with netting and the other methods described in the previous chapter. We also highlight the important link between collateralisation and funding.

6.1.1 Rationale for collateral

Collateral is an asset supporting a risk in a legally enforceable way. The fundamental idea of OTC derivatives collateralisation is that cash or securities are passed (with or without actual ownership changing) from one party to another primarily as a means to reduce counterparty risk. Whilst break clauses and resets (discussed in the last chapter) can provide some risk-mitigating benefit in these situations, collateral is a more dynamic and generic concept. Indeed, the use of collateral is essentially a natural extension of break clauses and resets. A break clause can be seen as a single payment of collateral and cancellation of the transaction. A reset feature is essentially the periodic (typically infrequent) payment of collateral to neutralise an exposure. Standard collateral terms simply take this further to much more frequent collateral posting.

A collateral agreement reduces risk by specifying that collateral must be posted by one counterparty to the other to support such an exposure. The collateral receiver only becomes the permanent economic owner of the collateral (aside from any potential legal challenge) if the collateral giver defaults. In the event of default, the non-defaulting party may seize the collateral and use it to offset any losses relating to the MTM of their portfolio. Like netting agreements, collateral agreements may be two-way, which means that either counterparty is required to post collateral against a negative mark-to-market value (from their point of view). Both counterparties will periodically mark all positions to market and calculate the net value. They will then check the terms of the collateral agreement to calculate if they are owed collateral and vice versa. To keep operational costs under control, posting of collateral will not be continuous and will

---

[1] "Collateral" is the term commonly used for exchange-traded and centrally cleared derivatives. Since this book mainly focuses on bilateral OTC derivatives, the term collateral will be used except when referencing specific terms such as variation margin and initial margin.

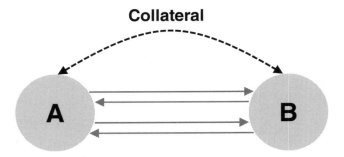

Figure 6.1   Illustration of the basic role of collateral.

occur in blocks according to predefined rules. Collateral agreements may be negotiated prior to any trading activity between counterparties, or may be agreed or updated prior to an increase in trading volume or change in other conditions.

The basic idea of collateralisation is illustrated in Figure 6.1. Parties A and B have one or more OTC derivative transactions between them and therefore agree that one or both of them will exchange collateral in order to offset the exposure that will otherwise exist. The rules regarding the timings, amounts and type of collateral posted should naturally be agreed before the initiation of the underlying transaction(s). In the event of default, the surviving party may be able to keep some or all of the collateral to offset losses that they may otherwise incur.

Note that, since collateral agreements are often bilateral, collateral must be returned or posted in the opposite direction when exposure decreases. Hence, in the case of a positive MTM, a party will call for collateral and in the case of a negative MTM they will be required to post collateral themselves (although they may not need to return if their counterparty does not make a request). Posting collateral and returning previously received collateral are not materially very different. One exception is that when returning, a party may ask for specific securities back.

Collateral posted against OTC derivatives positions is, in most cases, under the control of the counterparty and may be liquidated immediately upon an event of default. This arises due to the laws governing derivatives contracts and the nature of the collateral (cash or liquid securities). Counterparty risk, in theory, can be completely neutralised as long as a sufficient amount of collateral is held against it. However, there are legal obstacles to this and issues such as rehypothecation. Bankruptcies such as Lehman Brothers and MF Global have provided evidence of the risks of rehypothecation (see Section 6.4.3). It is therefore important to note that, whilst collateral can be used to reduce counterparty risk, it gives rise to new risks, such as market, operational and liquidity. These risks will be discussed in detail later in this chapter.

Collateral also has funding implications. Consider either of the classic situations depicted in Section 4.1.5. An end-user posting collateral will have to source this collateral. A bank hedging an uncollateralised transaction with a collateralised one will be exposed to asymmetric collateral posting. These aspects require a consideration of funding that will be discussed in Section 6.6.6. This is also the basis of funding value adjustment (FVA), discussed in Chapter 15.

6.1.2   Analogy with mortgages

Collateral can perhaps be best understood by a simple everyday example of a mortgaged house that also provides an insight into some of the risk arising from collateralising. The mortgage lender has *credit risk*, since the mortgagor may fail to make future mortgage payments. This risk is mitigated by the house playing the role of collateral and being pledged against the value borrowed. It is worth noting that there are a number of residual risks introduced in this arrangement:

- The risk that the value of the property in question falls below the outstanding value of the loan or mortgage. This is often known as "negative equity" and corresponds to *market risk*. Note that this depends on both the value of the property (collateral) and the value of the mortgage (exposure).
- The risk that the mortgage lender is unable, or faces legal obstacles, to take ownership of the property in the event of a borrower default, and faces costs in order to evict the owners and sell the property. This corresponds to *operational* or *legal risk*.
- The risk that the property cannot be sold immediately in the open market and will have a falling value if property prices are in decline. To achieve a sale, the property may then have to be sold at a discount to its fair value if there is a shortage of buyers. This is *liquidity risk*.
- The risk that there is a strong dependence between the value of the property and the default of the mortgagor. For example, in an economic downturn, high unemployment and falling property prices make this rather likely. This is a form of *correlation* (or even *wrong-way*) risk.

Note that in the above example, there is no equivalent of variation margin: for example, the mortgagor does need to post additional collateral if their house price declines or if interest rates increase. However, there is the equivalent of initial margin generally built-in, as the loan-to-value ratio of a mortgage is generally less than 100%.[2] These aspects of collateral are discussed in section 6.1.3.

6.1.3   Variation margin and initial margin

There are two fundamentally different types of collateral that should be explained up-front. In OTC derivatives, collateral would most obviously reflect the MTM of the underlying transactions, which can generally be positive or negative from each party's point of view. This idea forms the basis of variation margin (sometimes called "market-to-market margin"). The MTM is used for variation margin calculations because it is the most obvious and easy way to define a proxy for the actual loss arising from the default of one of the parties. However, in an actual default scenario, the variation margin may be insufficient due to aspects such as delays in receiving collateral and close-out costs (e.g. bid-offer). For these and other reasons, additional collateral is sometimes used in the form of initial margin. Figure 6.2 shows conceptually the roles of variation and initial margins.

---

[2] Except in highly risky mortgages such as the ones that partially led to the global financial crisis.

Figure 6.2 Illustration of the difference between variation and initial margins as forms of collateralisation. Variation margin aims to track the MTM of the relevant portfolio through time whilst initial margin represents an additional amount that may be needed due to delays and close-out costs in the event of a counterparty default.

Historically, the bilateral OTC derivative market has used collateral almost entirely in the form of variation margin, and initial margin has been rare. Initial margin is a much more common concept on derivative exchanges and central counterparties (CCPs). However, future regulation covering collateral posting in bilateral markets will make initial margin much more common (Section 6.7).

6.2   COLLATERAL TERMS

6.2.1   The credit support annex (CSA)

There is no obligation in an OTC derivatives contract for either party to post collateral. However, within an ISDA Master Agreement (see Section 5.2.1), it is possible to append a Credit Support Annex (CSA) that permits the parties to mitigate their counterparty risk further by agreeing to contractual collateral posting. The CSA has become the market standard collateral agreement in bilateral markets.[3] As with netting, ISDA has legal opinions throughout a large number of jurisdictions regarding the enforceability of the provisions within a CSA. The CSA will typically cover the same range of transactions as included in the Master Agreement and it will be the net MTM of these transactions that will form the basis of collateral requirements. However, within the CSA the parties can choose a number of key parameters and terms that will define the collateral posting requirements (known as the "credit support amount") in detail. These cover many different aspects such as:

- method and timings of the underlying valuations;
- the calculation of the amount of collateral that will be posted;
- the mechanics and timing of collateral transfers;
- eligible collateral;
- collateral substitutions;

---

[3] 87% of collateral agreements in use are ISDA agreements. Source: ISDA (2013).

- dispute resolution;
- remuneration of collateral posted;
- haircuts applied to collateral securities;
- possible rehypothecation (reuse) of collateral securities; and
- triggers that may change the collateral conditions (for example, ratings downgrades that may lead to enhanced collateral requirements).

One important point with bilateral CSA documentation is that the underlying terms are agreed upfront on signing the CSA and can only be changed by mutual agreement through an amendment to the documentation. This is clearly a cumbersome process and not sensitive to changes in market conditions. In contrast, a CCP can unilaterally change terms in response to market changes; (for example, some CCPs have increased and/or restricted collateral requirements in illiquid and volatile markets in recent years). This lack of flexibility in a CSA is a factor in funding liquidity risk (Section 6.6.6).

The process by which two counterparties will agree to collateralise their exposures can be summarised as follows:

- Parties negotiate and sign a CSA containing the terms and conditions under which they will operate.
- Transactions subject to collateral are regularly marked-to-market, and the overall valuation including netting is agreed (unless this amount is disputed as discussed later).
- The party with negative MTM delivers collateral (subject to minimum transfer amounts and thresholds, as discussed later). Initial margins are also posted or updated if relevant.
- The collateral position is updated to reflect the transfer of cash or securities.
- Periodic reconciliations may also be performed to reduce the risk of disputes (see Section 6.3.2).

6.2.2 Types of CSA

The parameters of a CSA are a matter of negotiation[4] between the two parties, with the stronger (credit quality) or larger party often able to dictate terms. Due to the very different nature of OTC derivatives counterparties, many different collateral arrangements exist. Some institutions (e.g. corporates) are unable to post collateral: this is generally because they cannot commit to the resulting operational and liquidity requirements. Other institutions (e.g. supranationals) receive collateral but are unwilling to post it, a position partially supported by their exceptional (generally triple-A) credit quality. Non-collateral posting entities generally prefer (or have no choice) to pay charges for the counterparty risk (CVA), funding (FVA), collateral terms (ColVA) and capital requirements (KVA) they impose on a bank[5] rather than agreeing to post collateral to mitigate these charges.

---

[4] Although future regulatory requirements will reduce the need for negotiation (Section 6.7).
[5] Note that FVA and ColVA can be benefits as well as costs, as discussed in the relevant chapters later.

Broadly speaking, three possible collateral agreements exist in practice:

- *No CSA.* In some OTC derivatives trading relationships, CSAs are not used because one or both parties cannot commit to collateral posting. A typical example of this is the relationship between a bank and a corporate where the latter's inability to post collateral means that a CSA is not usually in place (for example, a corporate treasury department may find it very difficult to manage their liquidity needs under a CSA).[6]
- *Two-way CSA.* A two-way CSA is more typical for two financial counterparties, where both parties agree to post collateral. Two-way CSAs with low thresholds are standard in the interbank market and aim to be beneficial (from a counterparty risk point of view at least) to both parties.
- *One-way CSA.* In some situations, a one-way CSA is used where only one party can receive collateral. This actually represents additional risk for the collateral giver and puts them in a worse situation than if they were in a no-CSA relationship. A typical example is a high quality entity such as a triple-A sovereign or supranational trading with a bank. Banks themselves have typically been able to demand one-way CSAs in their favour when transacting with some hedge funds. The consideration of funding and capital costs have made such agreements particularly problematic in recent years (Section 7.5.3).

Note that the above are general classifications and are not identified contractually. For example, a one-way CSA would specify a threshold (Section 6.2.3) of infinity for the non-posting party. Hence, an endless number of different CSA agreements actually exist based on the terms that will be defined in the next sections.

Historically, OTC derivative markets have sometimes also linked collateral requirements to credit quality (most commonly credit ratings[7]). The motivation for doing this is to minimise the operational workload whilst a counterparty is unlikely to default but to have the ability to tighten the collateralisation terms when their credit quality deteriorates. This type of agreement can lead to problems, since a downgrade of a counterparty's credit rating can occur rather late and then cause further credit issues due to the requirement to post collateral (similar to the discussions around ATEs in Section 5.4.2). Prior to the global financial crisis, triple-A entities such as monoline insurers traded through one-way collateral agreements (i.e. they did not post collateral), but with triggers specifying that they must post if their ratings were to decline. Such agreements can lead to rather unpleasant discontinuities, since a downgrade of a counterparty's credit rating can occur rather late with respect to the actual decline in credit quality, which in turn may cause further credit issues due to the requirement to post collateral. This is exactly what happened with AIG (see box) and monoline insurers (Section 2.2) in the global financial crisis, and is therefore a good argument against collateral being linked to ratings or credit quality in general.

---

[6] Some large corporates post collateral but most do not.
[7] Other less common examples are net asset value, market value of equity or traded credit spreads.

Case study: The dangers of credit rating triggers

The case of American International Group (AIG) is probably the best example of the funding liquidity problems that can be induced by collateral posting. In September 2008, AIG was essentially insolvent due to the collateral requirements arising from credit default swap transactions executed by their financial products subsidiary AIGFP. In this example, one of the key aspects was that AIGFP posted collateral as a function of their credit rating. The liquidity problems of AIG stemmed from the requirement to post an additional $20 billion[8] of collateral as a result of its bonds being downgraded. Due to the systemic importance of AIG, the Federal Reserve Bank created a secured credit facility of up to $85 billion to allow AIGFP to post the collateral they owed and avoid the collapse of AIG.

A collateral agreement must explicitly define all the parameters of the collateralisation and account for all possible scenarios. The choice of parameters will often come down to a balance between the workload of calling and returning collateral versus the risk mitigation benefit of doing so. Funding implications, not historically deemed important, should also be considered. We will now analyse the components that make up the collateral process in more detail.

6.2.3 Threshold

The threshold is the amount below which collateral is not required, leading to *undercollateralisation*. If the MTM is below the threshold then no collateral can be called and the underlying portfolio is therefore uncollateralised. If the MTM is above the threshold, only the *incremental* amount of collateral can be called for. (For example, a threshold of 5 and MTM of 8 would lead to collateral of 3 being required.) Although this clearly limits the risk reducing benefit of the collateralisation, it does lessen the operational burden and underlying liquidity costs.

Thresholds typically exist because one or both parties can gain in operational and liquidity costs and the associated weakening of the collateralisation is worth this. Some counterparties may be able to tolerate uncollateralised counterparty risk up to a certain level (for example, banks will be comfortable with this up to the credit limit for the counterparty in question – see Section 4.3.1). A threshold of zero means that collateral would be posted under any circumstance and an infinite threshold is used to specify that a counterparty will not post collateral under any circumstance (as in a one-way CSA, for example).

It is increasingly common to see zero thresholds for both parties since collateral agreements are as much about funding (FVA) and capital (KVA) costs as well as pure counterparty risk issues (CVA). This is also being driven by the move towards central clearing, where zero thresholds and initial margins are ubiquitous, and incoming bilateral collateral rules (Section 6.7). The regulatory capital treatment of CSAs with non-zero thresholds also tends to be rather conservative (Chapter 8).

---

[8] AIG 2008 Form 10-K.

6.2.4   Initial margin

Initial margin defines an amount of extra collateral that must be posted irrespective of the MTM of the underlying portfolio. It is generally independent of the MTM and is usually required upfront at trade inception. The general aim of this is to provide the added safety of *overcollateralisation* to give a cushion against potential risks such as delays in receiving collateral and costs in the close-out process.

Historically, the term "independent amount" has been used in bilateral markets (via CSAs) and "initial margin" is the equivalent term used on exchanges and CCPs (and will be used from now on). Initial margin has been uncommon in bilateral markets, two obvious exceptions being hedge funds posting to banks and banks posting to sovereigns/ supranationals. These are both cases where one party has a significantly inferior/superior credit quality and initial margin has not been common in more balanced relationships (e.g. the interbank market). However, initial margin is now becoming more usual in bi-lateral markets due to incoming bilateral collateral rules (Section 6.7) that are especially relevant for transactions between financial counterparties. Note also that initial margins have historically been relatively static amounts (e.g. percentage of notional) but are in-creasingly being driven by more dynamic methodologies.

Note that thresholds and initial margins essentially work in opposite directions and an initial margin can be thought of (intuitively and mathematically) as a negative thresh-old. For this reason, these terms are not seen together: either undercollateralisation is specified via a threshold (with zero initial margin) or an initial margin defines overcol-lateralisation (with a threshold of zero).

Initial margin acts as a cushion against "gap risk", the risk that the value of a portfolio may gap substantially in a short space of time. Indeed, initial margins are more common (and larger) for products such as credit derivatives where such gap events are more likely and severe. There is no market standard for calculating initial margin, although methods based on VAR models are becoming common. When setting the initial margin, the aim is to ensure that the portfolio will be overcollateralised in most plausible counterparty default scenarios, and it is therefore unlikely that any loss will be suffered. Not surpris-ingly, a risk-sensitive statistical estimation of initial margin may reference confidence levels of 99% or more (see Section 6.7.6).

6.2.5   Minimum transfer amount and rounding

A minimum transfer amount is the smallest amount of collateral that can be transferred. It is used to avoid the workload associated with a frequent transfer of insignificant amounts of (potentially non-cash) collateral. The size of the minimum transfer amount again represents a balance between risk mitigation versus operational workload. The minimum transfer amount and threshold are additive in the sense that the exposure must exceed the sum of the two before any collateral can be called. We note this does not mean that the minimum transfer amount can be incorporated into the threshold – this would be correct in defining the point at which the collateral call can be made but not in terms of the collateral due (more details are given in Section 6.2.8).

A collateral call or return amount may also be rounded to a multiple of a certain size to avoid dealing with awkward quantities. This is especially relevant when posting collat-eral in securities that by their nature cannot be divided infinitely like cash. The rounding may be always up (or down), or might always be in favour of one counterparty (i.e. up when they call for collateral and down when they return collateral). This is typically a relatively small amount and will have a small effect on the impact of collateralisation. However, the impact of rounding can be considered alongside the other factors above and will cause minor but noticeable impacts on the overall exposure (Chapter 11).

Note that minimum transfer amounts and rounding quantities are relevant for non-cash collateral where transfer of small amounts is problematic. In cases where cash-only collateral is used (e.g. variation margin and central counterparties) then these terms are generally zero.

6.2.6   Haircuts

Cash is the most common type of collateral posted (around three-quarters of all collateral is cash). However, a CSA allows each party to specify the assets they are comfortable accepting as collateral and to define a "haircut" that allows for the price variability of each asset. The haircut is a reduction in the value of the asset to account for the fact that its price may fall between the last collateral call and liquidation in the event of the counterparty's default. As such, the haircut is theoretically driven by the volatility of the asset, and its liquidity. In practice, haircut levels are set when a CSA is negotiated and are not adjusted in line with changes in the market. Cash collateral in a major currency may require no haircut[9] but other securities will have pre-specified haircuts depending on their individual characteristics. A haircut of $x\%$ means that for every unit of that security posted as collateral, only $(1-x)\%$ of credit ("valuation percentage") will be given, as illustrated in Figure 6.3. The collateral giver must account for the haircut when posting collateral.

Haircuts are primarily used to account for market risk stemming from the price volatility of the type of collateral posted. Collateral with significant credit or liquidity risk is generally avoided as haircuts cannot practically be large enough to cover the default of the collateral asset or having to liquidate it at a substantially reduced price. Aside from this, volatile assets such as equities or gold are not as problematic as their behaviour

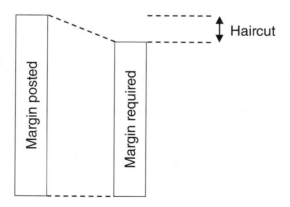

Figure 6.3   Illustration of a haircut applied to collateral.

---

[9] Although this may change with the introduction of the bilateral collateral rules discussed in Section 6.7.

Table 6.1   Example haircuts in a collateral agreement

	Party A	Party B	Valuation percentage	Haircut
Cash in eligible currency	X	X	100%	0%
Debt obligations issued by the governments of the US, UK or Germany with a maturity less than one year	X	X	98%	2%
Debt obligations issued by the governments of the US, UK or Germany with a maturity between one and ten years	X	X	95%	5%
Debt obligations issued by the governments of the US, UK or Germany with a maturity greater than ten years	X		90%	10%

in a default scenario is more predictable and relatively large haircuts can be taken as compensation for their price volatility and potential illiquidity.

Some examples of haircuts, together with eligible collateral types, are shown in Table 6.1. For example, a high-quality long-dated government or corporate bond has significant interest rate volatility due to the long maturity, although default and liquidity risk will probably not be of great concern. Such a security might therefore attract a haircut of around a few percent.

The important points to consider in determining eligible collateral and assigning haircuts are:

- time taken to liquidate the collateral;
- volatility of the underlying market variable(s) defining the value of the collateral;
- default risk of the security;
- maturity of the security;
- liquidity of the security; and
- any relationship between the value of the collateral and either the default of the counterparty or the underlying exposure (wrong-way risk).

The last point above is often the hardest to implement in a prescriptive fashion. For example, high quality (above some credit rating) sovereign bonds are likely to be deemed as eligible collateral. They will likely have good liquidity, low default risk and reasonably low price volatility (depending on their maturity). However, the CSA may not prevent (for example) a bank posting bonds from their own sovereign. CSAs do not typically go into such detailed descriptions, which can sometimes lead to surprises later.

Finally, it is important to consider the potential correlation between the exposure and the valuation of collateral. All these points will be discussed in a more quantitative fashion in Chapter 11.

Example

Consider a security that attracts a haircut of 5% and is being posted to cover a collateral call of $100,000. Only 95% of the value of this security is credited for collateral purposes (valuation percentage) and so the actual amount of collateral posted must be as follows:

Market value of collateral	=	$105,263
Haircut	=	$5,263 (5% of $105,263)
Credit given	=	$100,000 (difference between the above)

It is the collateral giver's responsibility to account for haircuts when posting collateral so that if a collateral call is made as above then (assuming they do not dispute the amount) the counterparty could post $100,000 in cash but $105,263 in terms of the market value of a security attracting a 5% haircut.

6.2.7 Linkage to credit quality

As mentioned above, thresholds, initial margin and minimum transfer amounts may all be linked to credit quality (usually in the form of ratings), an example of which is shown in Table 6.2. The logic of this is clearly that collateral becomes important as the credit quality of a counterparty deteriorates, and being able to take more collateral (lower threshold and possibly an initial margin) more frequently (lower minimum transfer amount) is worthwhile. When facing a lower rated counterparty, greater operational costs of collateral management are worthwhile to achieve greater counterparty risk mitigation. Note that in the case of a two-way CSA, both parties are subject to the impact of thresholds and minimum transfer amounts.

Rating triggers used to be viewed as useful risk mitigants but have been highlighted in the global financial crisis as being ineffective due to the slow reaction of credit ratings and the cliff-edge effects they produce (for example, see the AIG example in Section 6.2.2). On the one hand, if a counterparty's credit quality deteriorates, then such rating triggers may be of limited benefit (if at all). On the other hand, an institution suffering

Table 6.2   Example of rating linked collateral parameters. This could be for a one- or two-way CSA.

Rating	Initial margin	Threshold	Minimum transfer amount
AAA/Aaa	0	$250m	$5m
AA+/Aa1	0	$150m	$2m
AA/Aa2	0	$100m	$2m
AA–/Aa3	0	$50m	$2m
A+/A1	0	0	$1m
A/A2	1%*	0	$1m
A–/A3	1%*	0	$1m
BBB+/Baa1	2%*	0	$1m

*Expressed in terms of the total notional of the portfolio

a downgrade themselves can suffer greatly from the need to post more collateral and the potentially problematic funding issues this may well introduce. Such linkages to credit quality are therefore becoming less common, although, since CSA terms are not changed frequently (they may not be renegotiated for many years), they are still often observed. Incoming regulatory rules in the liquidity coverage ratio (Section 8.8.4) require the consideration of outflows including collateral posting that would arise from a downgrade in a bank's credit rating by up to and including three notches. This means a bank must consider a worst case scenario (with respect to their own rating only) in terms of the reduction of threshold and/or initial margin posting as defined in a schedule such as Table 6.2.

6.2.8   Credit support amount

ISDA CSA documentation defines the "credit support amount" as the amount of collateral that may be requested at a given point in time. The parameters in a typical CSA may not aim for a continuous posting of collateral due to the operational cost and liquidity requirements. The threshold and minimum transfer amount discussed above serve this purpose.

Spreadsheet 6.1   Collateral calculation including thresholds and initial margins

---

If the MTM of the portfolio minus the threshold is positive from either party's view, then they may be able to call collateral subject to the minimum transfer amount. The following steps define the amount of collateral that can be called by either party at a given time:

1 Calculate the hypothetical collateral amount, taking into account the thresholds using the formula

$$\max\,(MTM - threshold_C, 0) - \max(-MTM - threshold_I, 0) - C, \tag{6.1}$$

where MTM represents the current mark-to-market value[10] of the relevant transactions, $threshold_I$ and $threshold_C$ represent the thresholds for the institution and their counterparty respectively, and C represents the amount of collateral held already. If the above calculation results in a positive value then collateral can be called (or requested to be returned), whilst a negative value indicates the requirement to post (or return) collateral (subject to the points below).

2 Determine whether the absolute value of the amount calculated above is above the minimum transfer amount. If not, then no call can be made.

3 If the amount is above the minimum transfer amount then round it to the relevant figure.

4 Compute the value of any initial margins separately as these are usually independent from the variation margin amount above. Note that in the case where both parties

---

[10] In comparison to the discussion in Section 5.2.4, this is typically defined as the actual MTM value and does not have any other components in relation to close-out definitions, for example.

Table 6.3   Example collateral calculation.

	Collateral calculation
Portfolio MTM	1,754,858
MTM of collateral held	–
Required collateral (Equation 6.1)	754,858
Above minimum transfer amount?	Yes
Credit support amount	775,000

Table 6.4   Example collateral calculation with existing collateral.

	Collateral calculation
Portfolio MTM	1,623,920
MTM of collateral held	775,000
Required collateral (Equation 6.1)	−151,080
Above minimum transfer amount?	Yes
Credit support amount	−150,000

would post initial margin (not common historically but required under future regulation as described in Section 6.7) then the initial margins would not be netted and would be paid separately. Whilst, in theory, initial margin could be represented within Equation 6.1, in practice aspects such as segregation (discussed below) mean that they are probably best dealt with independently.

Consider a collateral calculation assuming a two-way CSA with the threshold, minimum transfer amount and rounding equal to $1,000,000, $100,000 and $25,000 respectively. Initially we show an example in Table 6.3 where there is an exposure resulting in $775,000 of collateral being called for. Whilst the mark-to-market of the underlying transactions or "portfolio value" is $1,754,858, the first million dollars of exposure cannot be collateralised due to the threshold. The required collateral is assumed to be rounded up to the final amount of $775,000. Of course, assuming the counterparty agrees with all the calculations they will calculate a value of –$775,000 meaning that they will agree to post this amount.

In Table 6.4, the situation has changed since the collateral has been received and the exposure of the institution has dropped. The result of this is that they are required to post collateral back. Note that, whilst they still have uncollateralised exposure, they are required to do this because of the threshold, i.e. they must return collateral as their net exposure of $848,920[11] has fallen below the threshold.

6.2.9   Impact of collateral on exposure

The impact of collateral on a typical exposure profile is shown in Figure 6.4. There are essentially two reasons why collateral cannot perfectly mitigate exposure. Firstly, the presence of a threshold[12] means that a certain amount of exposure cannot be

---

[11] This is the portfolio MTM of $1,623,920 less the MTM of collateral held of $775,000.

[12] Note that a threshold can be zero, in which case this is not an issue. However, even many interbank CSAs have non-zero thresholds.

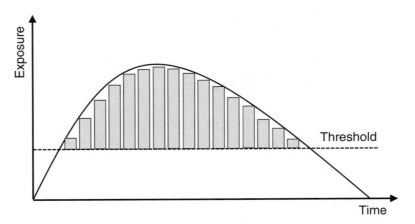

Figure 6.4 Illustration of the impact of collateral on exposure. The collateral amount is depicted by the grey areas.

collateralised. Secondly, the delay in receiving collateral and parameters such as the minimum transfer amount create a discrete effect, as the movement of exposure cannot be tracked perfectly[13] (this is illustrated by the grey blocks in Figure 6.4). Note that an initial margin can be thought of as making the threshold negative and can therefore potentially reduce the exposure to zero, depending on its magnitude.

In order to maximise the benefits of counterparty risk mitigation, ideally there should be no adverse correlation between the collateral and the credit quality of the counterparty, which represents wrong-way risk. A sovereign entity posting their own bonds provides an example of this.[14] Note that adverse correlations can also be present with cash collateral: an example would be receiving euros from European sovereigns or European banks. Funding considerations should also be taken into account when considering the benefit of various types of collateral, as will be discussed in Section 6.4.

6.3   MECHANICS OF COLLATERAL

6.3.1   Collateral call frequency

Collateral call frequency refers to the periodic timescale with which collateral may be called and returned. A longer collateral call frequency may be agreed upon, most probably to reduce operational workload and in order for the relevant valuations to be carried out. Some smaller institutions may struggle with the operational and funding requirements in relation to the daily collateral calls required by larger counterparties. Whilst a collateral call frequency longer than daily might be practical for asset classes

---

[13] The purpose of an initial margin is to mitigate this risk by providing a buffer.

[14] We note that there are benefits in taking collateral in this form. Firstly, more collateral can be called for as the credit quality of the sovereign deteriorates. Secondly, even a sudden jump to default event provides the recovery value of the debt as collateral. After this, the party would have access to a second recovery value as an unsecured creditor.

and markets that are not so volatile, daily calls have become standard in most OTC derivatives markets. Furthermore, intraday collateral calls are common for more vanilla and standard products such as repos and for derivatives cleared via CCPs (Chapter 9).

6.3.2   Valuation agents, disputes and reconciliations

The valuation agent refers to the party making the calculations regarding the credit support amount. Large counterparties trading with smaller counterparties may insist on being valuation agents for all purposes. In such a case, the "smaller" counterparty is not obligated to return or post collateral if they do not receive the expected notification, whilst the valuation agent may be under obligation to make returns where relevant. Alternatively, both counterparties may be the valuation agent and each will call for (return of) collateral when they have an exposure (less negative MTM). In these situations, the potential for collateral disputes is significant.

The role of the valuation agent in a collateral calculation is to calculate:

- current MTM under the impact of netting;
- the market value of collateral previously posted and adjust this by the relevant haircuts;
- the total uncollateralised exposure; and
- the credit support amount (the amount of collateral to be posted by either counterparty).

A dispute over a collateral call is common and can arise due to one or more of a number of factors:

- trade population;
- trade valuation methodology;
- application of CSA rules (e.g. thresholds and eligible collateral);
- market data and market close time;
- valuation of previously posted collateral.

Given the non-transparent and decentralised nature of the OTC market, significant disagreements can occur about collateral requirements. If the difference in valuation or disputed amount is within a certain tolerance specified in the collateral agreement, then the counterparties may "split the difference". Otherwise, it will be necessary to find the cause of the discrepancy. Obviously, such a situation is not ideal and will mean that one party will have a partially uncollateralised exposure, at least until the origin of the disputed amount can be traced, agreed upon and corrected. The following steps are normally followed in the case of a dispute:

- The disputing party is required to notify its counterparty (or the third-party valuation agent) that it wishes to dispute the exposure or collateral calculation, no later than the close of business on the day following the collateral call.

- The disputing party agrees to transfer the undisputed amount and the parties will attempt to resolve the dispute within a certain timeframe (the "resolution time"). The reason for the dispute will be identified (e.g. which transactions have material differences in valuation).
- If the parties fail to resolve the dispute within the resolution time, they will obtain mark-to-market quotations from several market makers (typically four), for the components of the disputed exposure (or value of existing collateral in case this is the component under dispute).

Rather than being *reactive* and focusing on dispute resolution, it is better to be proactive and aim to prevent disputes in the first place. Reconciliations aim to minimise the chance of a dispute by agreeing on valuation figures even though the resulting netted exposure may not lead to any collateral changing hands. They can be performed using dummy trades before two counterparties even transact with one another. It is good practice to perform reconciliations at periodic intervals (for example, weekly or monthly) so as to minimise differences in valuation between counterparties. Such reconciliations can pre-empt later problems that might arise during more sensitive periods. Reconciliations may be rather detailed and therefore highlight differences that otherwise may be within the dispute tolerance or that by chance offset one another. Hence, problems that may otherwise appear only transiently should be captured in a thorough reconciliation. Around 32% of OTC derivatives portfolios are currently reconciled on a daily basis with large trade populations more commonly reconciled less frequently.[15] Third-party valuation agents provide operational efficiencies, and can help prevent disputes that are common in bilateral collateral relationships. In an attempt to improve dispute management, especially in light of collateral requirements for non-cleared derivatives, ISDA has developed the "ISDA 2013 EMIR Portfolio Reconciliation, Dispute Resolution and Disclosure Protocol", which is based around European regulatory requirements.

Note that for centrally cleared transactions, collateral disputes are not problematic since the central counterparty is the valuation agent. However, central counterparties will clearly aim to ensure that their valuation methodologies are market standard, transparent and robust.

The global financial crisis highlighted many problems in the collateral management practices of banks. Regulators have reacted to this in the Basel III proposals for bilateral transactions (Section 8.6.3), which reduce (in some cases) the capital savings that can be achieved via collateralising. Collateral management practices are being continually improved. One example of this is the increase in electronic messaging in order for collateral management to move away from manual processes. ISDA (2014) reports a recent significant increase in electronic messaging.

6.3.3 Title transfer and security interest

In practice, there are two methods of collateral transfer:

- *Security interest*. In this case, the collateral does not change hands but the receiving party acquires an interest in the collateral assets and can use them only under certain

---

[15] Source: ISDA (2014).

contractually defined events (e.g. default). Other than this, the collateral giver general-ly continues to own the securities.

• *Title transfer*. Here, legal possession of collateral changes hands and the underlying collateral assets (or cash) are transferred outright but with potential restrictions on their usage. Aside from any such restrictions, the collateral holder can generally use the assets freely and the enforceability is therefore stronger.

ISDA (2014) reports 47.6% of collateral agreements as being New York law pledge (a type of security interest) and 28.3% being English law title transfer. Title transfer is more beneficial for the collateral receiver since they hold the physical assets and are less exposed to any issues such as legal risk. Security interest is more preferable for the collateral giver since they still hold the collateral assets and are less exposed to problems such as overcollateralisation if the collateral receiver defaults (where under title transfer the additional collateral may form part of the bankruptcy estate and not be returned).

6.3.4   Coupons, dividends and remuneration

As long as the giver of collateral is not in default, then they remain the collateral owner from an economic point of view. Hence, the receiver of collateral must pass on coupon payments, dividends and any other cashflows. One exception to this rule is in the case where an immediate collateral call would be triggered. In this case, the collateral receiver may typically keep the minimum component of the cashflow (e.g. coupon on a bond) in order to remain appropriately collateralised.

The collateral agreement will also stipulate the rate of interest to be paid on cash and when interest is to be transferred between parties irrespective of whether title transfer or security interest is used. Interest will typically be paid on cash collateral at the overnight indexed swap (OIS[16]) rate (for example, EONIA in Europe, Fed Funds in the US). Some counterparties, typically sovereigns or institutional investors, may subtract a spread on cash to discourage receiving cash collateral (and encourage securities), since cash must be invested to earn interest or placed back in the banking system.

The logic behind using the OIS rate is that since collateral may only be held for short periods (due to potentially substantial daily MTM changes), then only a short-term in-terest rate can be paid. However, OIS is not necessarily the most appropriate collateral rate, especially for long-dated OTC derivatives where collateral may need to be posted in substantial amounts for a long period. This may lead to a negative carry problem due to a party funding the collateral posted at a rate significantly higher than the OIS rate they receive. This is one source of FVA (Chapter 15). Occasionally, a collateral receiver may agree to pay a rate higher than OIS to compensate for this funding mismatch or to incentivise the posting of cash. These carry mismatches are generally quantified via ColVA (Chapter 13).

---

[16] Discussed in more detail in Section 13.2.2.

6.4   COLLATERAL AND FUNDING

6.4.1   Overview

In recent years, collateral eligibility and re-use have gained significant interest, as funding costs have been viewed as significant. Therefore, the consideration of the type of collateral that will be posted and received is important, since different forms of collateral have different funding costs and remuneration rates. When posting and receiving collateral, institutions are becoming increasingly aware of the need to optimise this process and maximise funding efficiencies. Collateral management is no longer a back-office operations centre but can be an important asset optimisation tool delivering (and substituting) the most cost-effective collateral. A party should consider the cheapest-to-deliver cash collateral and account for the impact of haircuts and the ability to rehypothecate non-cash collateral. For example, different currencies of cash will pay different OIS rates and non-cash collateral, if rehypothecated, will earn different rates on repo. Chapter 13 provides a more in-depth study of these aspects.

The traditional role of collateral for bilateral OTC derivatives has been as a counterparty risk mitigant. However, there is another role of collateral, which is as provision of funding. Without collateral, a party could be owed money but would not be paid immediately for this asset. Since institutions are often engaged in hedging transactions this can create funding problems (for example, a bank not receiving collateral on a transaction may have to post collateral on the associated hedge trade). As collateral has relevance in funding as well as counterparty risk reduction, one point to bear in mind is that different types of collateral may offer different counterparty risk and funding benefits. An important distinction is that collateral as a counterparty risk mitigant is by definition required only in an actual default scenario. On the other hand, collateral as a means of funding is relevant in all scenarios. For example, an entity posting their own bonds provides a funding benefit but is a poor counterparty risk mitigant. This balance between counterparty risk and funding is seen in aspects such as rehypothecation and segregation (discussed below) and is a key feature in understanding xVA.

6.4.2   Substitution

Sometimes a party may require or want collateral securities returned. This may be for operational reasons (for example, they require the securities for some reason[17]) or more likely it will be for optimisation reasons. In such a case, it is possible to make a substitution request to exchange an alternative amount of eligible collateral (with the relevant haircut applied). If consent is not required for the substitution then such a request cannot be refused[18] (unless the collateral type is not admissible under the agreement), although the requested collateral does not need to be released until the alternative collateral has been received. More commonly, substitution may only be allowed if the holder of the collateral gives consent. Whether or not collateral can be substituted freely is an important consideration in terms of the funding costs and benefits of collateral and valuing

---

[17] Note that the collateral returned needs not be exactly the same but must be equivalent (e.g. the same bond issue).

[18] For example, on grounds that the original collateral has been repoed, posted to another counterparty, sold or is otherwise inaccessible.

the cheapest-to-deliver optionality inherent in collateral agreements. However, in some situations there seems to be a gentleman's agreement with respect to giving consent for substitution requests. This will be discussed in more detail in Chapter 13.

6.4.3 Rehypothecation

Another aspect in relation to funding efficiencies is the reuse of collateral. For collateral to provide benefit against funding costs, it must be usable. Whilst cash collateral and collateral posted under title transfer are intrinsically reusable, other collateral must have the right of rehypothecation, which means it can be used by the collateral holder (for example, in another collateral agreement or a repo transaction). Due to the nature of the OTC derivatives market, where intermediaries such as banks generally hedge transactions, rehypothecation is important, as illustrated in Figure 6.5.

Where rehypothecation is allowed then it is often utilised (as seen in Figure 6.6), which is not surprising as this reduces funding costs and demand for high quality collateral.

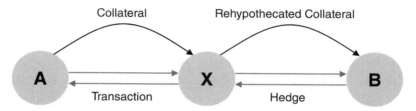

Figure 6.5   Illustration of the importance of rehypothecation of collateral. Party X transacts with counterparty A and hedges this transaction with counterparty B, both under collateral agreements. If counterparty B posts collateral then reuse or rehypothecation means that it is possible to pass this collateral on to counterparty A, as the hedge will have an equal and opposite value.

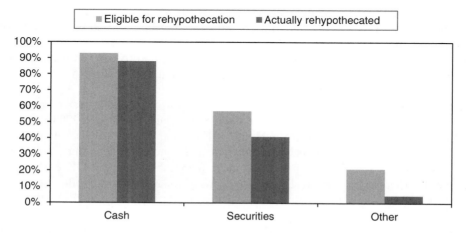

Figure 6.6   Illustration of rehypothecation of collateral (large dealers only).
Source: ISDA (2014).

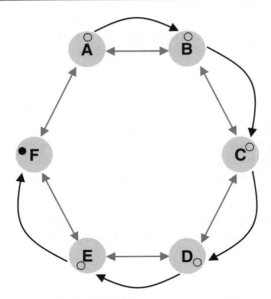

Figure 6.7 Illustration of the potential risks of rehypothecation of collateral (empty circles indicate collateral that has been rehypothecated; the dark circle represents the actual collateral).

Rehypothecation would seem to be obvious in OTC derivatives markets where many parties have multiple hedges and offsetting transactions. In such a situation, rehypothecation can allow a flow of collateral through the system without creating additional liquidity problems. From the point of view of funding, rehypothecation is important. However, from the point of view of counterparty risk, rehypothecation is dangerous since it creates the possibility that rehypothecated collateral will not be received in a default scenario (Figure 6.7). A party faces two possible risks in this respect:

- Collateral pledged in a collateral agreement against a negative MTM to another counterparty may be rehypothecated and consequently not be returned (in the event of a default of the counterparty coupled to an increase in the MTM).
- Collateral received from party A and then rehypothecated to party B may not be retrieved in the event that party B defaults, creating a liability to party A.

Prior to the global financial crisis, the rehypothecation of collateral was common and was viewed as a critical feature (for example, Segoviano and Singh, 2008). However, bankruptcies such as Lehman Brothers and MF Global illustrated the potential problems where rehypothecated assets were not returned. One example is that customers of Lehman Brothers Inc. (US) were treated more favourably than the UK customers of Lehman Brothers International (Europe) in terms of the return of rehypothecated assets (due to differences in customer protection between the UK and the US[19]). Singh and

---

[19] The liquidator of Lehman Brothers (PricewaterhouseCoopers) stated in October 2008, shortly after the bankruptcy, that certain assets provided to Lehman Brothers International (Europe) had been rehypothecated and may not be returned.

Aitken (2009) reported a significant drop in rehypothecation in the aftermath of the crisis. This is safer from the point of view of counterparty risk but creates higher funding costs.

6.4.4 Segregation

Even if collateral is not rehypothecated, there is a risk that it may not be retrieved in a default scenario. Segregation of collateral is designed to reduce counterparty risk and entails collateral posted being legally protected in the event that the receiving counterparty becomes insolvent. In practice, this can be achieved either through legal rules that ensure the return of any collateral not required (in priority over any bankruptcy rules), or alternatively by a third party custodian holding the initial margin. Segregation is therefore contrary and incompatible with the practice of rehypothecation. The basic concept of segregation is illustrated in Figure 6.8.

There are three potential ways in which segregated collateral can be held:

- directly by the collateral receiver;
- by a third party acting on behalf of one party; and
- in tri-party custody where a third party holds the collateral and has a three-way contract with the two parties concerned.

It is important to note that there is the concept of legal segregation (achieved by all three methods above) and operational segregation (achieved by only the latter two). In the MF Global default, parties had legal but not operational segregation and due to fraudulent behaviour lost collateral that they would have expected to have had returned (see Section 6.6.4). Since cash is fungible by its nature, it is difficult to segregate on the balance sheet of the collateral receiver. Hence, a tri-party arrangement where the collateral is held in a designated account, and not rehypothecated or reinvested in any way, may be desirable. On the other hand, this limits investment options and makes it difficult for the collateral giver to earn any return on their cash. Even if collateral is held with a third- or tri-party agent then it is important to consider potential concentration risk with such third parties.

As mentioned in section 6.3.3, there are two methods of posting collateral, namely title transfer and security interest. Segregation and non-rehypothecation of collateral

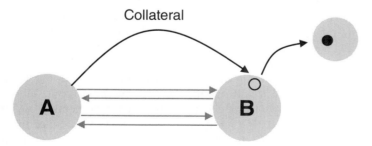

Figure 6.8   Illustration of the concept of segregation. Party A posts collateral to party B, which is segregated.

is relevant and practical in the latter case. Title transfer leaves the collateral giver as an unsecured creditor in the event of default of the collateral receiver, since ownership of the underlying asset passes to the collateral receiver at the time of transfer (and title is passed on in the event of rehypothecation). Around half of the OTC derivatives market is collateralised via title transfer, as it forms the basis of English law CSAs. Collateral requiring segregation should ideally be governed by a security interest type of relationship, or additional legal requirements.

Note that segregation, whilst clearly the optimal method for reducing counterparty risk, causes potential funding issues for replacing collateral that would otherwise simply be rehypothecated. This is at the heart of the cost/benefit balance of counterparty risk and also the funding and regulatory requirements over central clearing and bilateral collateral rules.

6.4.5   Variation and initial margin rehypothecation and segregation

So should rehypothecation be avoided to reduce counterparty risk or encouraged to minimise funding costs? There is no obvious answer to this question but there are more natural answers when considering the two types of collateral: variation and initial margin (Section 6.1.3).

Variation margin is generally the amount of collateral that on a MTM basis, is owed from one party to another. Since this amount is a direct liability, then its rehypothecation is a natural concept although this can create counterparty risk in two ways:

- There is counterparty risk created by collateral that needs to be returned against a positive change in MTM. However, under frequent exchange of collateral (e.g. daily) this should be a relatively small problem.
- Collateral assets subject to haircuts require overcollateralisation, which also creates counterparty risk due to the extra amount posted. Again, with small haircuts for many securities this is a relatively minimal effect.

Hence, rehypothecation of variation margin is not particularly problematic. However, initial margin is not owed and therefore would increase counterparty risk if it were rehypothecated/not segregated, since it may not be returned in a default scenario. Indeed, the problems of excessive rehypothecation mentioned in Section 6.4.3 arise largely from the initial margins which, where received, were often comingled with variation margin and not segregated. In recent years, hedge funds (as significant posters of initial margin) have become increasing unwilling to allow rehypothecation of initial margin.

The answer to the above question is therefore that, generally, variation margin is never segregated and can be commonly rehypothecated or reused. This is because it does not represent overcollateralisation, and should have a close relationship to the amount owed by the giver to the receiver (see Figure 6.2). In the event of default, the variation margin can be retrieved via right of set-off against the underlying positions. Initial margin, on the other hand, is increasingly being given the protective treatments of segregation/non-rehypothecation to avoid creating additional counterparty risk. Since initial margin is not owed by the collateral giver then this protection is relevant as it would be otherwise be lost in a default of the collateral receiver.

In line with the above comments, the regulatory requirements over bilateral collateral posting (discussed later in Section 6.7) generally require segregation of initial but not variation margin.

6.4.6   Standard CSA

A large amount of optionality exists in most bilateral CSAs since there are so many possibilities about the type of collateral that can be delivered (and substituted) across currency, asset class and maturity. A concept known as the "cheapest-to-deliver" collateral has developed: this is the most favourable collateral type to choose to post and with the choice driven primarily by the remuneration received (Section 13.4.3 discusses this in more detail). Knowing the cheapest-to-deliver collateral in the future depends on many aspects such as the future exposure, OIS rates in different currencies, cross-currency basis swap spreads, haircuts and substitution criteria. For these reasons, CSAs are generally being simplified and the concept of a standard CSA has been developed.

The ISDA Standard Credit Support Annex (SCSA) aims to achieve such standardisation and greatly reduce embedded optionality in CSAs whilst promoting the adoption of standard pricing (for example, what is now typically known as OIS discounting discussed in Section 13.2.5). At the same time, the mechanics of a SCSA are focussed on being closely aligned to central clearing collateral practices.

In a typical CSA, a single amount is calculated at each period for a portfolio, which may cover many currencies. Cash collateral may therefore be posted in different currencies and also typically in other securities. In addition, thresholds and minimum transfer amounts are commonly not zero. A SCSA makes the process more robust, requiring:

- cash collateral only (with respect to variation margin, any initial margins will be allowed in other securities);
- only currencies with the most liquid OIS curves (USD, EUR, GBP, CHF and JPY) will be eligible;
- zero thresholds and minimum transfer amounts; and
- one collateral requirement per currency (cross-currency products are put into the USD bucket).

The SCSA will require parties to calculate one collateral requirement per currency per day, with collateral exchanged in each relevant currency independently. This gives rise to settlement risk (Section 4.1.2). To mitigate this, it is possible to convert each currency amount into a single amount in one of seven "transport currencies", with an accompanying interest adjustment overlay (to correct for interest rate differences between the currencies, known as the Implied Swap Adjustment (ISA) Mechanism.

The SCSA has not yet become very popular due to the currency silo issue mentioned above and to a large extent will likely be superseded by future regulatory rules on bilateral collateral posting (Section 6.7) that impose similar requirements to the SCSA.

6.5   COLLATERAL USAGE

This section reviews market practice in the OTC derivative markets, which has been changing significantly in recent years.

6.5.1   Extent of collateralisation

Collateral posting across the market is quite mixed depending on the type of institution (Table 6.5). The main reasons for differences are the liquidity needs and operational workload related to posting cash or high-quality securities under stringent collateral agreements. Other aspects may include internal or external restrictions (for example, monoline insurers were only able to gain triple-A credit ratings by virtue of not posting collateral, as discussed in Section 2.2) and the economic view that uncollateralised trading is cheaper than collateralised trading (when liquidity costs are factored in).

Nevertheless, collateral usage has increased significantly over the last decade, as illustrated in Figure 6.9, which shows the estimated amount of collateral and gross credit exposure. The ratio of these quantities gives an estimate of the fraction of credit exposure that is collateralised. This has grown year on year to a ratio of around 50%, although this is a slightly misleading figure as it is essentially a blend of the following broad, distinct cases:[20]

- uncollateralised (no CSA, 0% collateral);
- collateralised (two-way CSA, around 100% collateral or less depending on the thresholds); and
- overcollateralised (CSA with initial margin, greater than 100% collateral).

Nevertheless, the impact of collateralisation is reported to reduce overall exposure by around four-fifths (Ghosh et al., 2008). Incorporating the fact that credit exposures are first decreased through netting and the remaining net exposures are further mitigated by the pledging of collateral reduces total market exposure by nearly 93% (Bliss and Kaufman, 2005).

Table 6.5   Collateral posting by type of institution.

Institution type	Collateral posting
Dealers	Very high
Hedge funds	Very high
Non-dealer banks	High
Pension funds	High
Corporates	Low
Supranationals	Low
Sovereigns	Very low

Source: ISDA (2010).

---

[20] The case of a one-way CSA would either be uncollateralised or collateralised depending on the direction (sign) of the MTM.

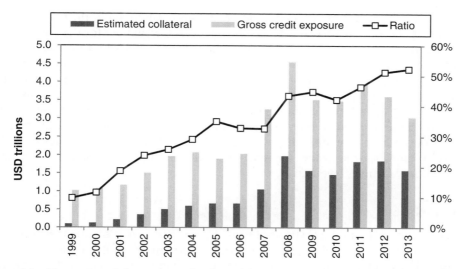

Figure 6.9   Illustration of the amount of collateral for non-cleared OTC derivatives compared to the gross credit exposure and the ratio giving the overall extent of collateralising of OTC derivatives. Note that the collateral numbers are halved to account for double counting as discussed in ISDA (2014).
Sources: BIS (2013) and ISDA (2014).

6.5.2   Coverage of collateralisation

As illustrated in Figure 6.10, a large proportion of all OTC derivatives trade under collateral agreements. The proportion is highest for credit derivatives, which is not surprising due to the high volatility of credit spreads[21] and the concentration of these transactions

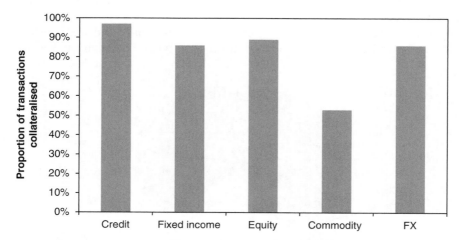

Figure 6.10   Illustration of the proportion of OTC derivatives collateralised shown by product type.
Source: ISDA (2014).

---

[21] In addition, the wrong-way risk embedded in credit derivatives may be driving this aspect.

with financial counterparties (as opposed to end-users). Additionally, the fact that many FX transactions are short-dated explains the relatively low number for this asset class.

Collateral agreements will reference the netted value of some or all transactions with a specific counterparty. From a risk-mitigation point of view, one should include the maximum number of transactions, but this should be balanced against the need to value effectively all such transactions. Product and regional impacts are often considered when excluding certain transactions from collateral agreements. Collateral agreements do require the transfer of the undisputed amount immediately, which means that the majority of products should still be collateralised even when there are disputes regarding a minority. However, the cleaner approach of leaving such products outside a collateral agreement is sometimes favoured.

6.5.3   Collateral type

Non-cash collateral also creates the problems of reuse or rehypothecation (Section 6.4.3) and additional volatility arising from the price uncertainty of collateral posted and its possible adverse correlation to the original exposure. On the contrary, cash is generally more costly to post and, in extreme market conditions, may be in limited supply.

Cash is the major form of collateral taken against OTC derivatives exposures (Figure 6.11). The ability to post other forms of collateral is often highly preferable for liquidity reasons. However, the global financial crisis provided stark evidence of the way in which collateral of apparent strong credit quality and liquidity can quickly become risky and illiquid (for example, Fannie Mae and Freddie Mac securities and triple-A mortgage backed securities). Cash collateral has become increasingly common over recent years, a trend that is unlikely to reverse – especially due to cash variation margin requirements in situations such as central clearing. Government securities comprise a further 14.8% of total collateral, with the remaining 10.3% comprising government agency securities, supranational bonds, US municipal bonds, covered bonds, corporate bonds, letters of credit and equities.

If the credit rating of an underlying security held as collateral declines below that specified in the collateral agreement, then normally it will be necessary to replace this

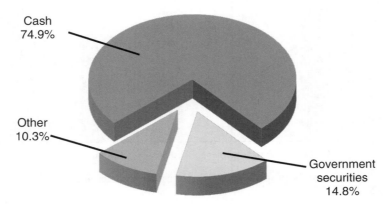

Figure 6.11   Breakdown of the type of collateral received against non-cleared OTC derivatives.
Source: ISDA (2014).

security immediately. When two counterparties do not have the same local currency, one of them will have to take FX risk linked to the collateral posted, even when it is in the form of cash. Securities in various currencies may be specified as admissible collateral but may also attract haircuts due to the additional FX risk. FX risk from posted collateral can be hedged in the spot and forward FX markets, but it must be done dynamically as the value of collateral changes.

6.6   THE RISKS OF COLLATERAL

Whilst collateralisation is a useful mechanism for reducing counterparty risk, it has significant limitations that must be considered. It is also important to emphasise that collateral, like netting, does not reduce risk overall but merely redistributes it. Essentially, collateral converts counterparty risk into other forms of financial risk. The most obvious aspect is the linkage of collateral to increased funding liquidity risk (Section 6.6.6). Collateralisation also gives rise to other risks such as legal risk, if the envisaged terms cannot be upheld within the relevant jurisdiction. Other potential issues such as wrong-way risk (where collateral is adversely correlated to the underlying exposure), credit risk (where the collateral securities may suffer from default or other adverse credit effects) and FX risk (due to collateral being posted in a different currency) are also important.

6.6.1   Collateral impact outside OTC derivatives markets

Risk mitigants such as collateral are often viewed narrow-mindedly only in their impact on reducing exposure to a defaulted counterparty. However, more precisely, what actually happens is a *redistribution* of risk, where OTC derivative creditors are paid more in a default scenario at the expense of other creditors. Figure 6.12 shows the impact of the posting of collateral against an OTC derivative transaction. Assume that in default of party B, party A and the other creditors (OC) of B, have the same seniority of claim

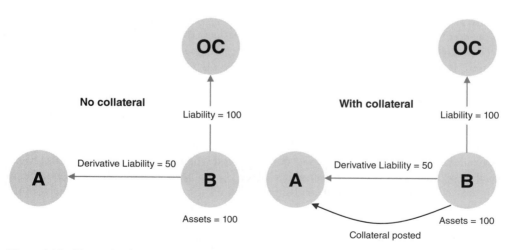

Figure 6.12   Example of the impact of derivatives collateral on other creditors (OC). The collateral posted (variation and possibly also initial margin) will reduce the claims of the other creditors.

(pari passu). Party B owes derivatives creditors 50, and other creditors 100, and has assets of 100.

With respect to the amount of collateral posted in Figure 6.12, it is useful to consider the following three cases:

- *No collateral.* In the no collateral case, the other creditors will have a claim on two-thirds (100 divided by 150) of the assets of B, with the derivative claims of A receiving the remaining third. The derivative creditors and other creditors will both recover 67% of their claims.
- *Variation margin.* If party B posts 50 variation margin to A against their full derivative liability, then this will reduce the value received by the OCs in default. Now the remaining assets of B in default will be only 50, to be paid to the other creditors (recovery 50%). OTC derivatives creditors will receive 100% of their claim (ignoring close-out costs).
- *Initial margin.* Suppose that B pays 50 variation margin and 25 initial margin and that the entire initial margin is used by A in the close-out and replacement costs of their transactions with B. In such a case, the OCs would receive only the remaining 25 (recovery 25%). (Of course, it could be argued that some or all of the initial margin may be returned, but a significant portion may be used in close-out costs).

Collateral does not reduce risk, it merely redistributes it (although possibly in a beneficial way). Other creditors will be more exposed, leading to an increase in risk in this (non-OTC derivative) market. Furthermore, the other creditors will react to their loss of seniority, for example by charging more when lending money.

6.6.2   Market risk and the margin period of risk

Collateral can never completely eradicate counterparty risk and we must consider the residual risk that remains under the collateral agreement. Residual risk can exist due to contractual parameters such as thresholds and minimum transfer amounts that effectively delay the collateral process. This is a market risk as it is defined by market movements since the counterparty last posted collateral.

Thresholds and minimum transfer amount can, of course, be set to small (or zero) values. However, another important aspect is the inherent delay in receiving collateral. Frequent contractual collateral calls obviously maximise the risk reduction benefit but may cause operational and liquidity problems. For variation margin, daily collateral calls have become fairly standard in OTC derivative markets, although longer periods do sometimes exist – initial margins, where they apply, may be adjusted on a less frequent basis. The margin period of risk (MPR) is the term used to refer to the effective time between a counterparty ceasing to post collateral and when all the underlying transactions have been successfully closed-out and replaced (or otherwise hedged), as illustrated in Figure 6.13. Such a period is crucial since it defines the effective length of time without receiving collateral where any increase in exposure (including close-out costs) will remain uncollateralised. Note that the MPR is a counterparty risk specific concept (since it is related to default) and is not relevant when assessing funding costs (discussed in more detail in Chapter 15).

In general, it is useful to define the MPR as the combination of two periods:

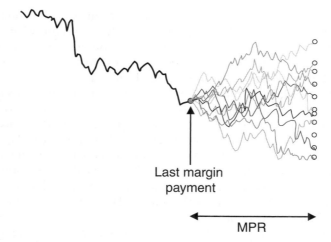

Last margin
payment

MPR

Figure 6.13   Illustration of the role of the margin period of risk (MPR).

- *Pre-default.* This represents the time prior to the counterparty being in default and includes the following components:
  - *Valuation/collateral call.* This represents the time taken to compute current MTM and market value of collateral already held, working out if a valid call can be made and making that call. This should include the time delay due to the contractual period between calls.
  - *Receiving collateral.* The delay between a counterparty receiving a collateral request to the point at which they release collateral. The possibility of a dispute (i.e. the collateral giver does not agree with the amount called for) should be incorporated here.
  - *Settlement.* Collateral will not be received immediately as there is a settlement period depending on the type of collateral. Cash collateral may settle on an intraday basis whereas other securities will take longer. For example, government and corporate bonds may be subject to one-day and three-day settlement periods respectively.
  - *Grace period.* In the event a valid collateral call is not followed by the receipt of the relevant collateral, there may be a relevant grace period before the counterparty would be deemed to be in default. This is sometimes known as the cure period.
- *Post-default.* This represents the process after the counterparty is contractually in default and the close-out process can begin:
  - *Close-out of transactions.* The contractual termination of transactions and representation of the future cashflow as a single MTM value.
  - *Rehedging and replacement.* The replacement or rehedging (including macro hedging) of defaulted transactions.
  - *Liquidation of collateral.* The liquidation (sale) of collateral securities.[22]

Note that the assessment of the MPR will be much longer than the time taken to receive collateral in normal cases and normal market conditions (which may well be small)

---

[22] Note that this aspect should be included in the haircuts assigned to the collateral assets.

because collateral performs no function (at least in terms of mitigating counterparty risk[23]) in these situations. Instead, a party must consider a scenario where their counterparty is in default and market conditions may be far from normal. Reflecting the above problems, Basel II capital requirements specified that banks should use a *minimum*[24] of ten days MPR for OTC derivatives in their modelling. The Basel III regime defines a more conservative 20-day minimum in certain cases. By contrast, CCPs make assumptions regarding the MPR of around five business days. (see Section 9.3.4).

The MPR should also potentially be extended due to the "ISDA Resolution Stay Protocol"[25] that would temporarily restrict certain default rights (by 24 or 48 hours) in the event of a counterparty default. The 18 major global banks have agreed to sign this protocol, which is intended to give regulators time to facilitate an orderly resolution in the event that a large bank becomes financially distressed. Although it is intended primarily to apply to globally systemically important financial institutions (G-Sifis), in time the protocol may apply to other market participants.

The MPR is the primary driver of the need for initial margin. Assuming only variation margin, the *best-case* reduction of counterparty risk can be shown to be approximately half the square root of the ratio of the maturity of the underlying portfolio to the MPR (see more detailed discussion in Section 11.3.3). For a five-year OTC derivatives portfolio, with a MPR of ten business days, this would lead to an approximate reduction of $0.5 \times \sqrt{(5 \times 250/10)} \approx 5.6$ times. In reality, due to aspects such as thresholds and minimum transfer amounts, the improvement would be less than this and to reduce counterparty risk further would require additional initial margin. The choice of initial margin is closely tied to the assumed MPR, as is clearly illustrated in Figure 6.13. This will be discussed more in Section 11.3.3.

For the examples in Chapter 11, we will use a period of ten days (or multiples thereof). The MPR is a rather simple "catch-all" parameter and should not be compared too literally with the actual time it may take to affect a close-out and replacement of transactions. This is discussed in more detail in Section 11.2.

6.6.3   Operational risk

The time-consuming and intensely dynamic nature of collateralisation means that operational risk is a very important aspect. The following are examples of specific operational risks:

- missed collateral calls;
- failed deliveries;
- computer error;
- human error; and
- fraud.

---

[23] For example, in such a situation collateral may provide funding benefit.

[24] Assuming daily collateral calls. If this is not the case, then the additional number of contractual days must be added to the time interval used.

[25] For example, see "ISDA publishes 2014 resolution stay protocol", 12th November 2014, www.isda.org.

Operational risk can be especially significant for the largest banks that may have thousands of relatively non-standardised collateral agreements with clients, requiring posting and receipt of billions of dollars of collateral on a given day. This creates large operational costs in terms of aspects such as manpower and technology. As noted in Section 6.6.2, Basel III recognises operational risk in such situations by requiring a MPR of 20 days for netting sets where the number of transactions exceeds 5,000 or the portfolio contains illiquid collateral or exotic transactions that cannot easily be valued under stressed market conditions (Section 8.6.3). Furthermore, if there have been more than two collateral call disputes with a counterparty over the previous two quarters lasting longer than the MPR, then the MPR for that counterparty must be doubled for the next two quarters.

The following is a list of points to consider in relation to operational risk:

- legal agreements must be accurate and enforceable;
- systems must be capable of automating the many daily tasks and checks that are required;
- the regular process of calls and returns of collateral is complex and can be extremely time-consuming, with a workload that increases in markets that are more volatile;
- timely, accurate valuation of all transactions and collateral securities is paramount;
- information on initial margins, minimum transfer amounts, rounding, collateral types and currencies must be maintained accurately for each counterparty; and
- failure to deliver collateral is a potentially dangerous signal and must be followed up swiftly.

The supervisory review process under Pillar II of Basel III states that the collateral management unit is adequately resourced (staff and systems) to process collateral calls under periods of stress in a timely manner. In addition, the collateral management unit must produce reports for senior management, showing aspects such as the amount and type of collateral posted and received, concentrations of assets, and the occurrence and causes of any disputes.

6.6.4   Legal risk

As already discussed above, rehypothecation and segregation are subject to possible legal risks. Holding collateral gives rise to legal risk in that the non-defaulting party must be confident that the collateral held is free from legal challenge by the administrator of their defaulted counterparty.

In the case of MF Global (see box), segregation was not effective and customers lost money as a result. This raises questions about the enforcement of segregation, especially in times of stress. Note that the extreme actions from senior members of MF Global in using segregated customer collaterals were caused by desperation to avoid bankruptcy. It is perhaps not surprising that in the face of such a possibility, extreme and even illegal actions may be taken. There is obviously the need to have very clear and enforceable rules on collateral segregation.

Case study: MF Global and segregation

The case of MF Global provides a good illustration of the potential risks of segregation. MF Global was a major derivatives broker that filed for bankruptcy in October 2011. The aim of segregation is to prevent rehypothecation and make collateral safe in the event of default of the collateral receiver (this applies mainly to overcollateralisation in the form of initial margin, as discussed in Section 6.4.5). Unfortunately, it became clear that prior to bankruptcy, MF Global had illegally transferred a total of $1.6 billion of segregated customer collateral to third parties to meet overdrafts and collateral calls.

6.6.5   Liquidity risk

Holding collateral creates liquidity risk in the event that collateral has to be liquidated (sold) following the default of a counterparty. In such a case, the non-defaulting party faces transaction costs (e.g. bid-offer) and market volatility over the liquidation period when selling collateral securities for cash needed to rehedge their derivatives transactions. This risk can be minimised by setting appropriate haircuts to provide a buffer against prices falling between the counterparty defaulting and the party being able to sell the securities in the market. There is also the risk that by liquidating an amount of a security that is large compared with the volume traded in that security, the price will be driven down and a potentially larger loss (well beyond the haircut) incurred. If a party chooses to liquidate the position more slowly in small blocks, then there is exposure to market volatility for a longer period.

When agreeing to collateral that may be posted and when receiving securities as collateral, important considerations are:

• What is the total issue size or market capitalisation posted as collateral?
• Is there a link between the collateral value and the credit quality of the counterparty? Such a link may not be obvious and predicted by looking at correlations between variables.[26]
• How is the relative liquidity of the security in question likely to change if the counterparty concerned is in default?

Because of liquidity impacts, a concentration limit of 5–10% may be imposed to prevent severe liquidation risk in the event of a counterparty defaulting. Most OTC derivatives collateral is in cash, government and agency securities (Figure 6.11), ensuring good liquidity even in stressed markets.

6.6.6   Funding liquidity risk

The above liquidity considerations only come into play when a counterparty has actually defaulted. A more significant aspect of liquidity risk stems from the funding needs that

---

[26] In the case of the Long-Term Capital Management (LTCM) default, a very large proprietary position on Russian government bonds made these securities far from ideal as collateral. Even a European bank posting cash in euros gives rise to a potentially problematic linkage, as noted earlier.

arise due to collateral terms, especially when collateral needs to be segregated and/or cannot be rehypothecated. We refer to this as funding liquidity risk.

It is easy to understand how an end-user of OTC derivatives might have significant funding liquidity risk. Most end-users (for example corporates) do not have substantial cash reserves or liquid assets that can be posted as collateral (and if they did, they would rather be able to use them to fund potential projects). Some end-users (such as pension funds) have liquid assets such as government and corporate bonds but hold limited amounts of cash. It is also important to note that end-users, due to their hedging needs, have directional positions (for example, paying the fixed rate in interest rate swaps to hedge floating rate borrowing). This means that a significant move in market variables (interest rates, for example) can create substantial MTM moves in their OTC derivatives portfolio and large associated collateral requirements. This is why many end-users do not have CSAs with their bank counterparties.

Some non-financial clients such as institutional investors, large corporates and sovereigns do trade under CSAs with banks. They may do this to increase the range of counterparties they can deal with and achieve lower transaction costs (due to reduced xVA charges). In volatile market conditions, such CSA terms can cause funding liquidity problems due to significant collateral requirements. Consider a corporate entering into a collateralised five-year cross-currency swap to hedge a bond issue in another currency. The potential MTM move and therefore collateral could be as much as 55% of the notional of the swap.[27] Clients entering into collateral agreements need to include an assessment of the worst-case collateral requirements in their cash management and funding plans, and understand how they would source eligible collateral. This is illustrated in Chapter 11 (Section 11.3.8).

Whilst the previously discussed AIG case (Section 6.2.2) can be blamed on rating triggers, other examples of end-users undertaking hedging activities illustrate the problem of funding liquidity risk (see the Ashanti example below).

Case study: The Ashanti case

Ashanti (now part of AngloGold Ashanti Limited) was a Ghanaian gold producer. When gold prices rose in September 1999, Ashanti experienced very large losses of $450 million on OTC derivatives contracts (gold forward contracts and options) used to hedge (possibly excessively[28]) their exposure to a falling gold price. The negative value of Ashanti's' hedge book meant that its OTC derivatives counterparties were due further variation margin payments totalling around $280 million in cash. Ashanti had a funding liquidity problem: it had the physical gold to satisfy contracts but not the cash or securities to make the collateral payments. To solve its liquidity crisis, Ashanti then struck an agreement making it exempt from posting collateral for just over three years.[29]

---

[27] This assumes a five-year FX move at the 95% confidence level with FX volatility at 15%.

[28] Sam Jonah, the chief executive of Ashanti, commented: "I am prepared to concede that we were reckless. We took a bet on the price of gold. We thought that it would go down and we took a position."

[29] "Ashanti wins three-year gold margin reprieve", GhanaWeb, 2nd November 1999.

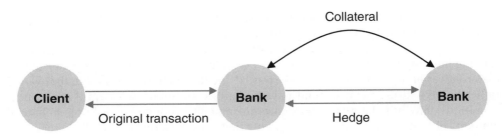

Figure 6.14   Illustration of the funding issues caused when a bank transacts with a non-collateral posting client and hedges the transaction with a collateralised counterparty (usually another bank).

End-users face funding liquidity risks when posting collateral since it may possibly cause them to default in a case where they are solvent but unable to meet the collateral demands in eligible securities within the timescale required. In turn, their bank counterparties may carry some of the risk since they may waive the receipt of collateral to avoid this, with the obvious problem that it will be converted back into uncollateralised counterparty risk and funding requirements for the banks in question. Funding liquidity risk may also mean that a rating agency may have a more negative view on a company's credit quality if they agree to post collateral. (Note that monolines could only achieve triple-A ratings through not posting collateral – see Section 2.2.)

For banks, funding liquidity issues arise due to the nature of trading with clients. Since most banks aim to run mainly flat (hedged) OTC derivatives books, funding costs arise from the nature of hedging: an uncollateralised transaction being hedged via a transaction within a collateral arrangement (Figure 6.14). The bank will need to fund the collateral posted on the hedge when the uncollateralised (client) transaction moves in their favour and will experience a benefit when the reverse happens. Many banks will have directional client portfolios, which can lead to large collateral requirements on the associated hedges. This problem is one way to explain the need for funding value adjustment (FVA) discussed in more detail in Chapter 15. It also explains why banks are keen for more clients to sign collateral agreements to balance the collateral flows in the situation depicted in Figure 6.14.

The problem with collateral is that it converts counterparty risk into funding liquidity risk. This conversion may be beneficial in normal, liquid markets where funding costs are low. However, in abnormal markets where liquidity is poor, funding costs can become significant and may put extreme pressure on a party. As discussed in Section 6.8, this can be seen as a conversion of counterparty risk (CVA) into funding liquidity risk components (FVA and MVA).

6.7   REGULATORY COLLATERAL REQUIREMENTS

6.7.1   Background

In addition to already-formulated rules for mandatory central clearing of standardised OTC derivatives (Section 9.3.1) and higher capital requirements for non-cleared

transactions (Section 8.6), G20 leaders agreed in 2011 to add bilateral collateral requirements for non-clearable OTC derivatives (so-called bilateral margin requirements).
These collateral requirements apply mainly to sophisticated OTC derivatives players
(e.g. banks) and not end-users, who are generally exempt. Note that these incoming rules
mean that some collateral arrangements will be partly defined by regulation and not
simply a bilateral negotiation between the two parties involved.

Bilateral collateral requirements cover both variation and initial margins, with the
latter being more important due to being quite rare in bilateral markets. Such bilateral
initial margins are intended to reduce systemic risk and to bridge the divide between
clearable and non-clearable transactions (which could otherwise encourage regulatory
arbitrage). The rules have attracted criticism[30] for requiring dramatically higher levels of
collateralisation than have been used historically in OTC derivative markets. The overall
thrust of criticisms is two-fold. Firstly, initial margin requirements will be very costly
and cause banks to find new ways of funding, diverting resources from other areas (e.g.
lending businesses), or simply withdrawing from OTC derivatives markets. An estimate
of initial margin requirements is made by ISDA (2012), who state that total initial margin requirements could range from $1.7 trillion to $10.2 trillion (depending on the use of
internal models and standard collateral schedules, and the level of thresholds). They also
suggest that in stressed market conditions, initial margin requirements could increase
dramatically, perhaps by a factor of three. The second criticism is that, as discussed
in Section 6.6.6, higher collateral requirements will create funding liquidity risk, which
could be problematic in distressed market conditions.

The rules can be found in BCBS-IOSCO (2015) and aim to ensure that "appropriate
margining practices should be in place with respect to all derivatives transactions that
are not cleared by CCPs". Below is a summary of the rules, which are discussed in more
detail in Gregory (2014).

6.7.2   Covered entities

Initial and variation margin requirements will apply to financial entities and systemically
important non-financial entities ("covered entities"). The rules do not apply to:

- sovereigns;
- central banks;
- multilateral development banks;
- the Bank for International Settlements; and
- other non-financial institutions that are not systemically important.

The precise definition of covered entities is likely to have slightly different interpretations
in different regions. In addition to the exemption of various entities, certain products are
also exempt, notably FX forwards and swaps, and repos and security lending transactions. A transaction can be exempt either due to the nature of either one of the entities
trading or the transaction type itself.

---

[30] For example, see "WGMR proposals raise procyclicality fears", *Risk*, 5th April 2013.

6.7.3   General requirements

The concepts of variation and initial margin are intended to reflect current and potential future exposure respectively. With respect to each, standards state that covered entities for non-centrally cleared derivatives must exchange:

- Variation margin:
  - must be exchanged bilaterally on a regular basis (e.g. daily);
  - full collateral must be used (i.e. zero threshold);
  - the minimum transfer amount must not exceed €500,000 ($650,000); and
  - must be posted in full for all new transactions after the implementation date (see below).
- Initial margin:
  - to be exchanged by both parties with no netting of amounts;
  - should be bankruptcy protected;
  - should be based on an extreme but plausible move in the underlying portfolio value at a 99% confidence level;
  - a ten-day time horizon should be assumed on top of the daily variation margin exchanged (as discussed in Section 6.6.2, this is consistent with minimum Basel capital requirements for the MPR);
  - can be calculated based on internal (validated) models or regulatory tables; and
  - follows a phased-in implementation and applies only to new transactions after the implementation date and includes a threshold amount (see below).

Since initial margin is required to be segregated, it will be held separately from variation margin. Margin requirements will be phased in by the use of declining thresholds from 1st September 2016 (extended from 1st December 2015), as shown in Table 6.6 (potentially also dependent on local regulator). Rigorous and robust dispute resolution procedures should be in place in case of disagreements over collateral amounts. This is an important point since risk-sensitive initial margin methodologies will be, by their nature, quite complex and likely to lead to disputes. Note that the requirements allow a party to remain exempt if they have a total notional of less than €8 billion of OTC derivatives.

The requirements will therefore create a phasing in effect. Covered counterparties will probably agree new CSAs incorporating the rules to cover future transactions but can keep old transactions under existing CSAs. New or modified CSAs will need to consider the following aspects:

- thresholds and minimum transfer amounts;
- collateral eligibility;
- haircuts;
- calculations, timings and deliveries;
- dispute resolution; and
- initial margin calculations and mechanisms for segregation.

Regarding the quality of initial margin, the collateral should be "highly liquid" and in particular should hold its value in a stressed market (accounting for the haircut).

Table 6.6 Timescales for the implementation of collateral requirements for covered entities and transactions based on aggregate group-wide month-end average notional amount of non-centrally cleared derivatives (including physically settled FX forwards and swaps), newly executed during the immediately preceding June, July and August.

Date	Requirement
Variation margin	
1 September 2016	Exchange variation margin with respect to new non-centrally cleared derivative transactions if average aggregate notionals exceed €3 trillion for both parties
1 March 2017	As above but with no threshold
Initial margin	
1 September 2016 to 31 August 2017	Exchange initial margin if average aggregate notionals exceed €3 trillion
1 September 2017 to 31 August 2018	Exchange initial margin if average aggregate notionals exceed €2.25 trillion
1 September 2018 to 31 August 2019	Exchange initial margin if average aggregate notionals exceed €1.5 trillion
1 September 2019 to 31 August 2020	Exchange initial margin if average aggregate notionals exceed €0.75 trillion
From 1 September 2020	Exchange initial margin if average aggregate notionals exceed €8 billion

Risk-sensitive haircuts should be applied and collateral should not be exposed to excessive credit, market or FX risk. Collateral must not be "wrong-way", meaning correlated to the default of the counterparty (for example, a counterparty posting their own bonds or equity). Examples of satisfactory collateral are given as:

- cash;
- high quality government and central bank securities;
- high-quality corporate/covered bonds;
- equity in major stock indices; and
- gold.

Collateral must be subject to haircuts, as discussed in the next section. Note that US regulatory proposals limit eligible collateral for variation margin to cash only in US dollars or the currency of the underlying payment obligations.

As mentioned above, FX swaps and forwards are exempt from collateral rules, which followed lobbying from the industry. This, like a similar exemption over clearing, is controversial (for example, see Duffie, 2011). On the one hand, such FX products are often short-dated and more prone to settlement risk than counterparty risk. On the other hand, FX rates can be quite volatile and occasionally linked to sovereign risk, and cross-currency swaps are typically long-dated.

To manage the liquidity impact associated with collateral requirements, it is possible to use an initial margin threshold (not to be confused with the threshold defined in a CSA discussed in Section 6.2.3). The introduction of this threshold followed the results of a quantitative impact study (QIS), which indicated that such a measure could reduce the total liquidity costs by 56% (representing more than half a trillion dollars).[31] This would work in much the same way as a threshold in a typical CSA in that initial margin would not need to be posted until this threshold is reached, and above the threshold only the incremental initial margin would be posted.[32] The threshold can be no larger than €50m and must apply to a consolidated group of entities where relevant. This means that if a firm engages in separate derivatives transactions with more than one counterparty, but belonging to the same larger consolidated group (such as a bank holding company), then the threshold must essentially be *shared* in some way between these counterparties.

The threshold rules imply that a firm must have in place a system to identify the exposure to a counterparty across an entire group. It would then be necessary to decide how to identify the benefit created by the threshold. It could be allocated across entities *a priori* or used on a first-come-first-served basis.

Note that, whilst the threshold of €50m would relieve the liquidity strain created via the collateral requirements, it would increase the procyclicality problem as collateral amounts will be even more sensitive to market conditions.

6.7.4 Haircuts

As in the case of initial margin models, approved risk-sensitive internal or third party quantitative models can be used for establishing haircuts so long as the model for doing this meets regulatory approval. BCBS-IOSCO (2015) defines that haircut levels should be risk-sensitive and reflect the underlying market, liquidity and credit risks that affect the value of eligible collateral in both normal and stressed market conditions. As with initial margins, haircuts should be set in order to mitigate procyclicality and to avoid sharp and sudden increases in times of stress. The time horizon and confidence level for computing haircuts is not defined explicitly, but could be argued to be less (say, two to three days) than the horizon for initial margin, since the collateral may be liquidated independently and more quickly than the portfolio would be closed-out and replaced.

Instead of model-based haircuts, an entity is allowed to use standardised haircuts as defined in Table 6.7. The FX add-on of 8% is particularly problematic as it forces significant overcollateralisation when collateral is posted in the "wrong currency". It seems that this may not be required in the European implementation of the rules.[33]

Table 6.7   Standardised haircut schedule as defined by BCBS-IOSCO (2015). Note that the FX add-on corresponds to cases where the currency of the derivative differs from that of the collateral asset.

	0–1 years	1–5 years	5+ years
High-quality government and central bank securities	0.5%	2%	4%
High-quality corporate/covered bonds	1%	4%	8%
Equity/gold	15%		
Cash (in the same currency)	0%		
FX add-on for different currencies	8%		

[31] See www.bis.org/press/p130215a.htm.

[32] For example, for a threshold amount of 50 and a calculated initial margin of 35, no collateral is required. However, if the calculated collateral is 65, then an amount of 15 needs to be posted.

[33] For example, see "EU revisions to uncleared margin rules address industry fears", Risk, 10th June 2015.

6.7.5   Segregation and rehypothecation

As mentioned in Section 6.4.5, variation margin can be rehypothecated and netted whereas initial margin must be exchanged on a gross basis (i.e. amounts posted between two parties cannot cancel), must be segregated and cannot be rehypothecated, re-pledged or reused (except potentially in one case mentioned below). The use of a third party to achieve such segregation is likely. Third-party custodians would most likely offer the most robust protection, although this does raise the issue as to whether such entities (the number of which is currently quite small) would become sources of systemic risk with the amount of collateral they would need to hold. Arrangements for segregation will vary across jurisdictions depending on the local bankruptcy regime and need to be effective under the relevant laws, and supported by periodically updated legal opinions.

Rehypothecation of initial margin is allowed in very limited situations where the transaction is a hedge of a client position, and will be suitably protected once rehypothecated with the client having a priority claim under the relevant insolvency regime. It must be ensured that the initial margin can only be rehypothecated once and the client must be informed and agree to the rehypothecation. This is of limited benefit due the potentially large chain of hedges that is executed across the interbank market in response to a client transaction.[34]

6.7.6   Initial margin calculations

There is then the question of how to define initial margin amounts for portfolios. Rules require that initial margins should calculated separately for different asset classes, with the total requirement being additive across them. It is not therefore possible to benefit from potentially low historic correlations between risk factors in these assets. The relevant asset classes are defined as:

- currency/rates;
- equity;
- credit; and
- commodities.

Separate calculations must also be made for derivatives under different netting agreements. The calculation of initial margins can be done via two methods:

- regulatory defined collateral schedule; and
- entities' own or third party quantitative models (that must be validated by the relevant supervisory body).

There can be no "cherry picking" by mixing these approaches based on which gives the lowest requirement in a given situation, although it is presumably possible to choose

---

[34] For example, see "Industry 'won't bother' with one-time rehypothecation", *Risk*, 12th September 2013.

Table 6.8   Standardised initial margin schedule as defined by BCBS-IOSCO (2015).

	0–2 years	2–5 years	5+ years
Interest rate	1%	2%	4%
Credit	2%	5%	10%
Commodity	15%		
Equity	15%		
Foreign exchange	6%		
Other	15%		

different approaches for different asset classes, as long as there is no switching between these approaches.[35]

Where an entity used their own quantitative model for calculating collateral, this should be calibrated to a (equally weighed) period of not more than five years, which includes a period of financial stress. These requirements, in particular the use of a stress period, are aimed at avoiding procyclicality. Large discrete calls for initial margin (as could presumably arise due to procyclicality of the collateral model) should be avoided, as these tend to produce cliff-edge effects.

For entities not using their own models for collateral calculations, a standardised initial margin schedule can be used (Table 6.8). The quantities shown should be used to calculate gross initial margin requirements by multiplying by the notional amount. To account for portfolio effects when using the standardised margin schedule, the well-known NGR (net gross ratio) formula is used (see Section 8.2.2), which is defined as the net replacement divided by the gross replacement of transactions. The NGR is used to calculate the net standardised initial margin requirement via:

$$Net\ initial\ margin = (0.4 + 0.6 + NGR) \times Gross\ initial\ margin$$

NGR gives a simple representation of the future offset between positions, the logic being that 60% of the current offset can be assumed for future exposures. For example, consider two four-year interest rate products with notional values of 100 and 50 and respective mark-to-market (replacement cost) valuations of 10 and –3. This means that the NGR is 70% (the net exposure of 7 divided by the gross exposure of 10). From Table 6.8, the gross initial margin of the two transactions would be 2% of 150 multiplied by NGR, which would then lead to a net initial margin of 2.1.

6.7.7   Standardised initial margin method (SIMM)

The choice of either internal models or standardised collateral schedules is a difficult one. The latter are very simple and transparent but will yield more conservative require-ments However, the design of internal models is open to substantial interpretation and would inevitably lead to disputes between counterparties and a large effort of regulatory approvals of different models. Together with the major banks, ISDA has been developing

---

[35] The precise wording here from BCBS-IOSCO (2015) is as follows: "Accordingly, the choice between model- and schedule-based initial margin calculations should be made consistently over time for all transactions within the same well defined asset class."

the SIMM[36] in an attempt to avoid a proliferation of collateral models where parties would inevitably dispute the initial margin requirements.

A general model for initial margin needs to have the following characteristics:

- risk-sensitivity and recognising diversification effects;
- relatively easy to implement;
- transparent so that disputes can be managed and predictions made; and
- have general regulatory approval, potentially within all relevant jurisdictions across all parties wanting to use the model.

Note that since the bilateral collateral rules apply to transactions that cannot be centrally cleared, then by definition this will need to capture the more non-standard, complex and illiquid OTC derivatives.

In order to meet the objectives above, the SIMM follows a sensitivity-based approach (SBA) based on the Standardised Capital Calculation in the Basel Committee's Fundamental Review of the Trading Book (Section 8.8.1). Transactions are divided into the four asset classes as required (see previous section). Within each asset class the initial margin requirements are driven by:

- sensitivities to various risk factors (e.g. interest rate delta in a particular currency);
- risk weights (essentially defining the variability of a risk factor); and
- correlations and aggregation (defining the extent of offset between positions in the same asset class).

Inputs such as risk weights will be recalibrated periodically with the aim of avoiding significant moves that may contribute to volatile collateral requirements.

6.8   CONVERTING COUNTERPARTY RISK INTO FUNDING LIQUIDITY RISK

It is important to emphasise the high-level issue around aspects discussed in this chapter, which is that increasing collateralisation may reduce counterparty risk, but it increases funding liquidity risk. Figure 6.15 illustrates the increasing strength of collateral use, starting by moving from uncollateralised to collateralised via a typical CSA. The bilateral collateral rules increase collateral further through requiring initial margin, and central clearing takes this even further by adding default funds and potentially more conservative initial margin requirements.[37]

What is important to appreciate is that, whilst the conversion of counterparty risk to funding liquidity risk is an inevitable result of the completely realistic need to take collateral, it may be pushed too far. A key decision for market participants and regulators alike is the concentration of various trading on the spectrum represented by Figure 6.15

---

[36] See "Dealers plan standard margin model for WGMR regime", *Risk*, 21st June 2013. Updates and more information can be found at www.isda.org.

[37] CCPs are generally more conservative in their initial margin methodologies. This is not surprising as they do not have to post initial margin themselves, although they can be more competitive via lowering such requirements.

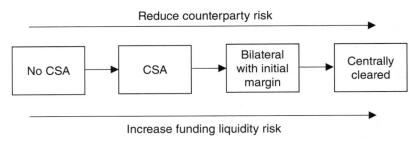

Figure 6.15   Illustration of the increasing impact of collateral on counterparty risk and funding liquidity risk.

and the risks that this presents. Whilst pushing to the right minimises counterparty risk, it also increases more opaque and complex funding liquidity risks. Indeed, the reduction of counterparty risk and CVA and KVA has been a driver for creating other xVA terms such as FVA and MVA, as discussed later in Chapters 15 and 16 respectively.

6.9   SUMMARY

This chapter has discussed the use of collateral in OTC derivatives transactions, which is a crucial method to reduce counterparty risk. We have described the mechanics of collateral management and the variables that determine how much collateral is posted. The use of collateral in OTC derivative markets has been reviewed. The significant risks that arise from collateral use have also been considered, with particular emphasis on collateral usage increasing funding liquidity risks. The incoming rules on collateral posting for non-clearable OTC derivatives have also been described.

7
Credit Exposure and Funding

Exposure is the key determinant in xVA because it represents the core value that may be at risk in default scenarios and that otherwise needs to be funded. Indeed, exposure of some sort is a common component of all xVA adjustments. This chapter will be concerned with defining exposure in more detail and explaining the key characteristics. We start with credit exposure, including the important metrics used for its quantification. Typical credit exposure profiles for various products will be discussed and we will explain the impact of netting and collateral on credit exposure. We also describe the link between credit exposure and funding costs that are driven by similar components but have some different features, especially when aspects such as segregation are involved. This leads us to define funding exposure, which is similar to credit exposure but has some distinct differences.

7.1   CREDIT EXPOSURE

7.1.1   Definition

A defining feature of counterparty risk arises from the asymmetry of potential losses with respect to the value[1] of the underlying transaction(s). In the event that a counterparty has defaulted, a surviving institution may close-out the relevant contract(s) and cease any future contractual payments. Following this, they may determine the net amount owing between them and their counterparty and take into account any collateral that may have been posted or received. Note that collateral may be held to reduce exposure but any posted collateral may have the effect of increasing exposure. Also note that the precise impact of netting and collateral will discussed in Section 7.4.

Once the above steps have been followed, there is a question of whether the net amount is positive or negative. The main defining characteristic of credit exposure (hereafter referred to simply as exposure) is related to whether the effective value of the contracts (including collateral) is positive (in a party's favour) or negative (against them), as illustrated in Figure 7.1:

- *Negative value*. In this case, the party is in debt to its counterparty and is still legally obliged to settle this amount (they cannot "walkaway" from the transaction(s) except in specific cases – see Section 5.4.1). Hence, from a valuation perspective, the position

---

[1] The definition of value will be more clearly defined below.

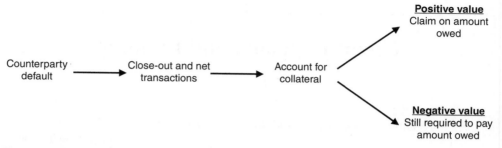

Figure 7.1   Illustration of the impact of a positive or negative value in the event of the default of a counterparty.

appears largely unchanged. A party does not generally gain or lose from their counterparty's default in this case.

- *Positive value*. When a counterparty defaults, they will be unable to undertake future commitments and hence a surviving party will have a claim on the positive value at the time of the default, typically as an unsecured creditor. They will then expect to recover some fraction of their claim, just as bondholders receive some recovery on the face value of a bond. This unknown recovery value is, by convention, not included in the definition of exposure.

The above feature – a party loses if the value is positive and does not gain if it is negative – is a defining characteristic of counterparty risk. We can define exposure simply as:

$$Exposure = \max(value, 0) \tag{7.1}$$

This would mean that defining exposure at a given time is relatively easy. One simply values the relevant contracts, aggregates them according to the relevant netting rules, applies an adjustment corresponding to any collateral held against the positions and finally takes the positive value of this net final amount.

7.1.2   Bilateral exposure

A key feature of counterparty risk is that it is bilateral: both parties to a transaction can default and therefore both can experience losses. For completeness, we may need to consider losses arising from both defaults. From a party's point of view, their own default will cause a loss to any counterparty to whom they owe money. This can be defined in terms of negative exposure, which by symmetry is:

$$Negative\ exposure = \min(value, 0) \tag{7.2}$$

A negative exposure leads to a gain, which is relevant since the counterparty is making a loss.[2]

---

[2] This is a symmetry effect where one party's gain must be another's loss. There may be reasonable concern with defining a gain in the event of a party's own default. This will be discussed in more detail in Chapter 14.

7.1.3   The close-out amount

The amount represented by "value" in the above discussion represents the effective value of the relevant contracts at the default time of the counterparty (or party themselves), including the impact of risk mitigants such as netting and collateral. However, this is the actual value agreed with the counterparty (the administrators of their default) and may not conform to any definite representation that can be defined and modelled. A party will obviously aim for the relevant documentation and legal practices to align the actual value agreed bilaterally after the default to their own unilateral view prior to any default.

As discussed in Section 5.2.6, there is a concept of close-out amount defined by the relevant documentation and its legal interpretation in the appropriate jurisdiction. Whilst efforts have been made to define close-out language in the most appropriate way and to learn from problems relating to historic bankruptcies, there will clearly always be the chance of a dispute over amounts. A party clearly wants their own definition of value in the representation of exposure to correspond to the actual value that is agreed in a default scenario. When quantifying exposure and other xVA terms, Equations 7.1 and 7.2 above are fundamental starting points and will typically rely on definition of mark-to-market (MTM) value that may come from a standard valuation model. Whilst this theoretical definition of value cannot practically include aspects such as the type of documentation used, jurisdiction or market behaviour at the time of default, it will be hoped that issues such as these only constitute small uncertainties.

Quantification of exposure and xVA will therefore rely on relatively clean measures of value driven from the MTM of the transactions in question that can readily drive quantitative calculations. However, it should be remembered that documentation will tend to operate slightly differently. For example, ISDA documentation (Section 5.2.6) specifically references that the "Close-out Amount" may include information related to the creditworthiness of the surviving party. This implies that a party can potentially reduce the amount owed to a defaulting counterparty, or increase their claims in accordance with charges they experience in replacing the transaction(s) at the point where their counterparty defaults. Such charges may themselves arise from the xVA components that depend on exposure in their calculation. The result of this is a recursive problem where the very definition of current exposure depends on potential xVA components in the future. We will discuss this issue in more detail in Chapter 14. Until then, we emphasise that it is general market practice to base exposure quantification on a concept of value that is relatively easy to define and model, and that any errors in doing this are usually relatively small.

A final point to note about the above problems in determining close-out amounts is the time delay. Until an agreement is reached, a party cannot be sure of the precise amount owed or the value of their claim as an unsecured creditor. This will create particular problems for managing counterparty risk. In a default involving many contracts (such as the number of OTC derivatives in the Lehman bankruptcy), the sheer operational volumes can make the time taken to agree on such valuations considerable.

7.1.4   Exposure as a short option position

Counterparty risk creates an asymmetric risk profile, as shown by Equation 7.1. When a counterparty defaults, a party loses if the value is positive but does not gain if it is negative. The profile can be likened to a short[3] option position. Familiarity with basic options-pricing theory would lead to two obvious conclusions about the quantification of exposure:

- Since exposure is similar to an option payoff, a key aspect will be volatility (of the value of the relevant contracts and collateral).
- Options are relatively complex to price (at least compared with the underlying instruments). Hence, to quantify exposure even for a simple instrument may be quite complex.

By symmetry, a party has long optionality from their own default (via DVA, discussed in Chapter 14).

We can extend the option analogy further, for example by saying that a portfolio of transactions with the same counterparty will have an exposure analogous to a basket option and that a collateral agreement will change the *strike* of the underlying options. However, thinking of xVA as one giant exotic options pricing problem is correct but potentially misleading. One reason for this is that, as already noted in the last section, we cannot even write the payoff of the option, namely the exposure, down correctly (since we cannot precisely define the *value* term in Equation 7.1). Furthermore, xVA contains many other subjective components such as credit and funding curves (Chapter 12) and wrong-way risk (Chapter 17). At the core of the exposure calculation there is an option pricing type problem, but this cannot be treated with the accuracy and sophistication normally afforded to this topic due to the sheer complexity of the underlying options and the other components that drive xVA. Treating xVA quantification as a purely theoretical option pricing problem tends to under-emphasise other important but more qualitative aspects.

7.1.5   Future exposure

A *current* valuation of all relevant positions and collateral will lead us to a calculation of current exposure – admittedly with some uncertainty regarding the actual close-out amount, as noted in the last section. However, it is even more important to characterise what the exposure might be at some point in the future. This concept is illustrated in Figure 7.2, which can be considered to represent any situation from a single transaction to a large portfolio with associated netting and collateral terms. Whilst the current (and past) exposure is known with certainty, the future exposure is defined probabilistically by what may happen in the future in terms of market movements and contractual features of transactions, both of which are uncertain. Hence, in understanding future exposure one must define the *level* of the exposure and also its underlying *uncertainty*.

Quantifying exposure is extremely complex due to the long periods involved, the many different market variables that may influence the exposure, and risk mitigants such as netting and collateral. Doing this will be the subject of Chapters 10 and 11, whereas this chapter focuses on the following topics:

---

[3] The short option position arises since exposure constitutes a loss.

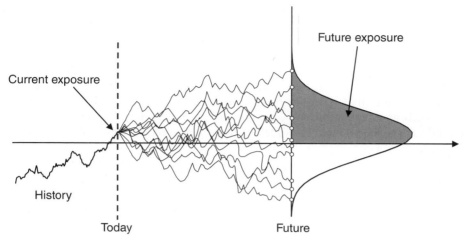

Figure 7.2 Illustration of future exposure with the grey area representing exposure (positive future values). The white area represents negative exposure.

- defining exposure;
- discussing intuitively the impact of aspects such as netting and collateral; and
- introducing the concept of funding exposure.

7.1.6   Comparison to value-at-risk

In financial risk management, value-at-risk (VAR) methods (Section 3.3.1) have, for almost two decades, been a popular methodology to characterise market risk. Any reader familiar with VAR will recognise from Figure 7.2 that the characterisation of exposure shares similarities with the characterisation of VAR. This is indeed true, although we note that in quantifying exposure we are faced with additional complexities, most notably:

- *Time horizon.* Unlike VAR, exposure needs to be defined over multiple time horizons (often far in the future) so as to understand fully the impact of time and specifics of the underlying contracts. There are two important implications of this.
  - Firstly, "ageing" of transactions must be considered. This refers to understanding a transaction in terms of all future contractual payments and changes such as cashflows, termination events, exercise decisions and collateral postings. Such effects may also create path dependency where the exposure at one date depends on an event defined at a previous date. In VAR models, due to the ten-day horizon used,[4] such aspects can be neglected.
  - The second important point here is that, when looking at longer time horizons, the trend (also known as drift) of market variables, in addition to their underlying volatility and co-dependence structure, is relevant (as depicted in Figure 7.2). In VAR the drift can be ignored, again since the relevant time horizon is short.

---

[4] In many cases this is a one-day horizon that is simply scaled to ten days.

- *Risk mitigants*. Exposure is typically reduced by risk mitigants such as netting and collateral, and the impact of these mitigants must be considered in order to properly estimate future exposure. In some cases, such as applying the correct netting rules, this requires knowledge of the relevant contractual agreements and their legal interpretation in the jurisdiction in question. In the case of future collateral amounts, another degree of subjectivity is created since there is no certainty over the type of collateral and precise time that it would be received. Other contractual features of transactions, such as termination agreements (Section 5.4.2), may also create subjectivity and all such elements must be modelled, introducing another layer of complexity and uncertainty.
- *Application*. VAR is a risk management approach. Exposure must be defined for both risk management and pricing (i.e., xVA). This creates additional complexity in quantifying exposure and may lead to two completely different sets of calculations, one to define exposure for risk management purposes and one for pricing purposes. This debate is discussed in Section 10.4.

In other words, exposure is much more complex than VAR and yet is only one component of counterparty risk and the different xVA terms.

7.2   METRICS FOR EXPOSURE

In this section, we define the measures commonly used to quantify exposure. The different metrics introduced will be appropriate for different applications. There is no standard nomenclature used and some terms may be used in other context(s) elsewhere. We follow the original regulator definitions (BCBS, 2005).

We begin by defining exposure metrics for a given time horizon. Note that in discussing exposure below, we are referring to the total number of relevant transactions, netted appropriately and including any relevant collateral amounts. We will refer to this as the "netting set".

7.2.1   Expected future value

This component represents the forward or expected value of the netting set at some point in the future. As mentioned above, due to the relatively long time horizons involved in measuring counterparty risk, the expected value can be an important component, whereas for market risk VAR assessment (involving only a time horizon of ten days), it is not. Expected future value (EFV) represents the expected (average) of the future value calculated with some probability measure in mind (to be discussed later). EFV may vary significantly from current value for a number of reasons:

- *Cashflow differential*. Cashflows in derivatives transactions may be rather asymmetric. For example, early in the lifetime of an interest rate swap, the fixed cashflows will typically exceed the floating ones, assuming the underlying yield curve is upwards-sloping as is most common. Another example is a cross-currency swap where the payments may differ by several per cent annually due to a differential between the associated interest rates. The result of asymmetric cashflows is that a party may expect a transaction in the future to have a value significantly above (below) the current one due to paying out (receiving) net cashflows. Note that this can also apply to transactions maturing due to final payments (e.g. cross-currency swaps).

- *Forward rates*. Forward rates can differ significantly from current spot variables. This difference introduces an implied drift (trend) in the future evolution of the underlying variables in question (assuming one believes this is the correct drift to use, as discussed in more detail in Section 10.4). Drifts in market variables will lead to a higher or lower future value for a given netting set, even before the impact of volatility. Note that this point is related to the point above on cashflow differential, since some or all of this is a result of forward rates being different from spot rates.
- *Asymmetric collateral agreements*. If collateral agreements are asymmetric (such as a one-way collateral posting) then the future value may be expected to be higher or lower reflecting respectively unfavourable or favourable collateral terms. More discussion on the impact of collateral terms is given in Chapter 11.

7.2.2   Potential future exposure

In risk management, it is natural to ask ourselves what would be the worse exposure that we could have at a certain time in the future. PFE will answer this question with reference to a certain confidence level. For example, the PFE at a confidence level of 99% will define an exposure that would be exceeded with a probability of no more than 1% (one hundred percent minus the confidence level). PFE is a similar metric to VAR and is illustrated in Figure 7.3. Note also that, as shown, the centre of the distribution can differ significantly from zero (this represents the EFV of the transactions having a significantly positive or negative expected value).[5]

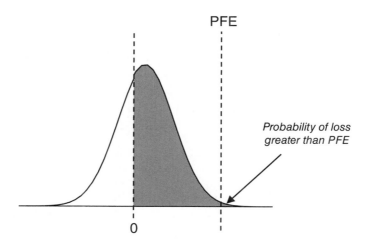

Figure 7.3   Illustration of potential future exposure. The grey area represents (positive) exposures.

---

[5] Note that the normal distribution used to depict the distribution of future values does not need to be assumed and also that PFE is often defined at confidence levels other than 99%.

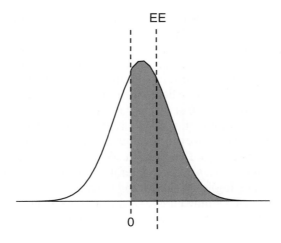

Figure 7.4   Illustration of expected exposure. The grey area represents (positive) exposures.

7.2.3   Expected exposure

In addition to PFE, which is clearly a risk management measure, the pricing of some xVA terms will involve expected exposure (EE), as illustrated in Figure 7.4. This is the average of all exposure values. Note that only positive values (the grey area) give rise to exposures and other values have a zero contribution (although they contribute in terms of their probability). This means that the expected exposure will be above the EFV defined in Section 7.2.1 – this is similar to the concept of an option being more valuable than the underlying forward contract. Note that EE is sometimes called EPE.

7.2.4   EE and PFE for a normal distribution

In Appendix 7A we give simple formulas for the EE and PFE for a normal distribution. These formulas are reasonably simple to compute and are useful examples.

Spreadsheet 7.1   EE and PFE for a normal distribution

Example

Suppose future value is defined by a normal distribution with mean 2.0 and standard deviation 2.0. As given by the formulae in Appendix 7A, the EE and PFE (at the 99% confidence level) are

EE   =   2.17
PFE   =   6.65

If the standard deviation was increased to 4.0, we would obtain

EE   =   2.79
PFE =   11.31

Note that the EE, like the PFE, is sensitive to standard deviation (volatility).

7.2.5   Maximum PFE

Maximum or peak PFE simply represents the highest PFE value over a given time interval, thus representing the worst-case exposure over the entire interval. This is illustrated in Figure 7.5. Maximum PFE is sometimes used as a metric in credit limits management.

7.2.6   Expected positive exposure

Expected positive exposure (EPE) is defined as the average exposure across all time horizons. It can therefore be represented as the weighted average of the EE across time, as illustrated in Figure 7.6. If the EE points are equally spaced (as in this example) then it is simply the average.

Spreadsheet 7.2   EPE and EEPE example

This single EPE number is often called a "loan equivalent", as the average amount effectively lent to the counterparty in question. It is probably obvious that expressing a highly uncertain exposure by a single EPE or loan-equivalent amount can represent a fairly

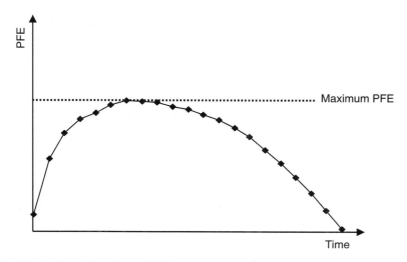

Figure 7.5   Illustration of maximum PFE.

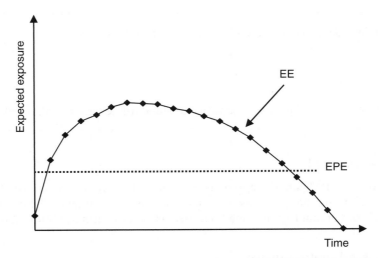

Figure 7.6 Illustration of expected positive exposure, which is the weighted average (the weights being the time intervals) of the EE profile.

crude approximation, as it averages out both the randomness of market variables and the impact of time. However, we shall see later that EPE has a strong theoretical basis for assessing regulatory capital (Chapter 8) and quantifying xVA (Chapter 14).

7.2.7 Negative exposure

Exposure is represented by positive future values. Conversely, we may define negative exposure as being represented by negative future values. This will obviously represent the exposure from a counterparty's point of view. We can therefore define measures such as negative expected exposure (NEE) and expected negative exposure (ENE), which are the precise opposite of EE and EPE. Such measures will be used for computing metrics such as DVA (Chapter 14) and FVA (Chapter 15).

7.2.8 Effective expected positive exposure (EEPE)

A final metric to define here is a term used only in regulatory capital calculations and known as effective expected positive exposure (EEPE). The motivation for EEPE is as a more conservative version of EPE that deals with the following two problems:

- Since EPE represents an average of the exposure, it may neglect very large exposures that are present for only a small time.
- EPE may underestimate exposure for short-dated transactions and not properly capture "rollover risk". This arises from current short-dated transactions that will be rolled over into new transactions at their maturity.

For these reasons, EEPE was introduced for regulatory capital purposes (BCBS, 2005). It is the average of the effective EE (EEE), which is simply a non-decreasing version of

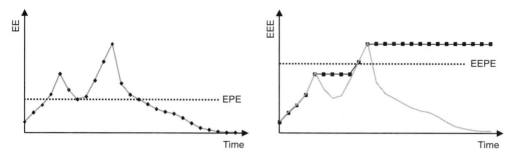

Figure 7.7   Illustration of effective EE (EEE) and effective EPE (EEPE).

the EE profile. These terms are shown in comparison with EE and EPE in Figure 7.7. Loosely speaking, EEPE assumes that any reduction in the EE profile is a result of a maturing transaction that will be replaced.[6] Note that, due to the definition of regulatory capital calculations, only a one-year time horizon is relevant in the EEPE definition. The use and definition of EEPE for regulatory capital calculations is discussed in more detail in Chapter 8.

We emphasise that some of the exposure metrics defined above, whilst common definitions, are not always used. In particular, banks often use EPE to refer to what is defined here as EE. The definitions above were introduced by the BCBS (2005) and are used consistently throughout this book (including earlier editions).

7.3   FACTORS DRIVING EXPOSURE

We now give some examples of the significant factors that drive exposure, illustrating some important effects such as maturity, payment frequencies, option exercise, roll-off and default. Our aim here is to describe some key features that must be captured, whilst Chapter 10 will give actual examples from real transactions. In all the examples below we will depict EE defined as a percentage of the notional of the transaction in question.

7.3.1   Loans and bonds

Although not generally characterised as counterparty risk, the exposures of debt instruments such as loans and bonds can usually be considered almost deterministic and approximately equal to the notional value. Bonds typically pay a fixed rate and therefore will have some additional uncertainty, because if interest rates decline, the exposure may increase and vice versa. In the case of loans, they are typically floating-rate instruments, but the exposure may decline over time due to the possibility of prepayments.

---

[6] They essentially assume that any reduction in exposure is a result of maturing transactions. This is not necessarily the case.

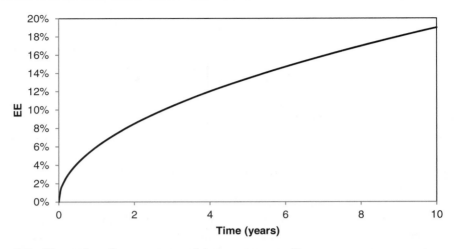

Figure 7.8   Illustration of a square root of time exposure profile.

7.3.2   Future uncertainty

The first and most obvious driving factor in exposure is future uncertainty. Forward contracts such as forward rate agreements (FRAs) and FX forwards are usually characterised by having just the exchange of two cashflows or underlyings (often netted into a single payment) at a single date, which is the maturity of the contract. This means that the exposure is a rather simple increasing function reflecting the fact that, as time passes, there is increasing uncertainty about the value of the final exchange. Based on fairly common assumptions,[7] such a profile will follow a "square root of time" rule, meaning that it will be proportional to the square root of the time (t):

$$Exposure \propto \sqrt{t} \tag{7.3}$$

This is described in more mathematical detail in Appendix 7B and such a profile is illustrated in Figure 7.8. We can see from Equation 7.3 that the maturity of the contract does not influence the exposure (except for the obvious reason that there is zero exposure after this date). For similar reasons, much the same shape is seen for vanilla options with an upfront premium, although more exotic options may have more complex profiles (for example, see Section 7.3.5).

7.3.3   Periodic cashflows

Many OTC derivatives include the periodic payment of cashflows, which has the impact of reversing the effect of future uncertainty. The most obvious and common example here is an interest rate swap, which is characterised by a peaked shape, as shown in Figure 7.9. The shape arises from the balance between future uncertainties over payments,

---

[7] Specifically, that the returns of the underlying market variable (e.g. FX) are independently identically distributed (i.i.d.).

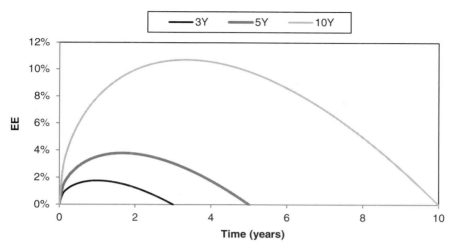

Figure 7.9   Illustration of the EE of swaps of different maturities.

combined with the roll-off of fixed against floating payments over time. This can be represented approximately as:

$$Exposure \propto (T-t)\sqrt{t} \tag{7.4}$$

where T represents the maturity of the transaction in question. This is described in more mathematical detail in Appendix 7B. The above function is initially increasing due to the $\sqrt{t}$ term, but then decreases to zero as a result of the $(T-t)$ component, which is an approximate representation of the remaining maturity of the transaction at a future time t. It can be shown that the maximum of the above function occurs at T/3, i.e. the maximum exposure occurs at one-third of the lifetime.

As seen in Figure 7.9, a swap with a longer maturity has much more risk due to both the increased lifetime and the greater number of payments due to be exchanged. An illustration of the swap cashflows is shown in Figure 7.10.

An exposure profile can be substantially altered due to the more specific nature of the cashflows in a transaction. Transactions such as basis swaps, where the payments are made more frequently than they are received (or vice versa) will then have more (less) risk than the equivalent equal payment swap. This effect is illustrated in Figures 7.11 and 7.12.

Another impact that the cashflows have on exposure is in creating an asymmetry between opposite transactions. In the case of an interest rate swap, this occurs because of the different cashflows being exchanged. In a "payer swap", fixed cashflows are paid periodically at a deterministic amount (the "swap rate") whilst floating cashflows are received. The value of future floating cashflows is not known until the fixing date, although at inception their (risk-neutral) expected value will be equal to that of the fixed cashflows. The value of the projected[8] floating cashflows depends on the shape of the

---

[8] "Projected" here means the risk-neutral expected value of each cashflow.

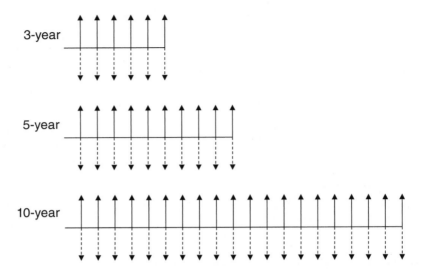

Figure 7.10 Illustration of a cashflows swap transaction of different maturities (semi-annual payment frequencies are assumed).

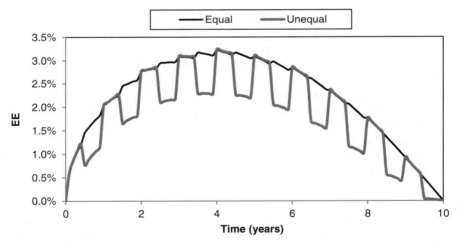

Figure 7.11 Illustration of EE for swaps with equal and unequal payment frequencies. The latter corresponds to a swap where cashflows are received quarterly but paid only semi-annually.

underlying yield curve. In the case of a typical upwards-sloping yield curve, the initial floating cashflows will be expected to be smaller than the fixed rate paid, whilst later in the swap the trend is expected to reverse. This is illustrated schematically in Figure 7.13.

The net result of this effect is that the EE of the payer swap is higher due to the expectation to pay net cashflows (the fixed rate against the lower floating rate) in the first periods of the swap, and receive net cashflows later in the lifetime (Figure 7.14). The NEE is

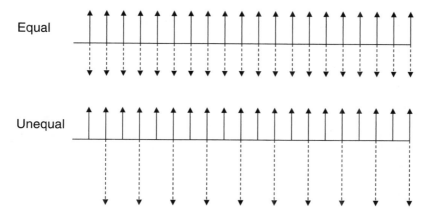

Equal

Unequal

Figure 7.12   Illustration of the cashflows in a swap transaction with different payment frequencies.

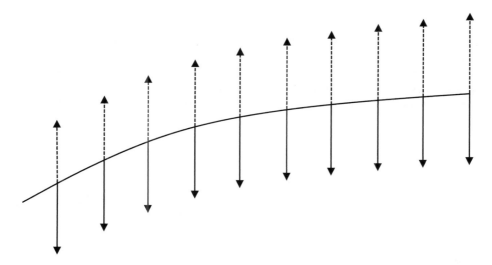

Figure 7.13   Illustration of the floating (dotted lines) against fixed cashflows in a swap where the yield curve is upwards-sloping. Whilst the (risk-neutral) expected value of the floating and fixed cashflows is equal, the projected floating cashflows are expected to be smaller at the beginning and larger at the end of the swap.

correspondingly less negative. Another way to state this is that the EFV (expected future value, defined in Section 7.2.1) of the swap is positive (by an amount defined by the expected net cashflows). For an opposite "receiver" swap, this effect would be reserved with the EE being lower, NEE more negative and the sign of the EFV reversed.

The above effect can be even more dramatic in cross-currency swaps where a high-interest-rate currency is paid against one with lower interest rates (as was the case, for example, with widely traded dollar versus yen swaps for many years before the dramatic US interest rate cuts of 2008/09), as illustrated in Figure 7.15. The overall high interest

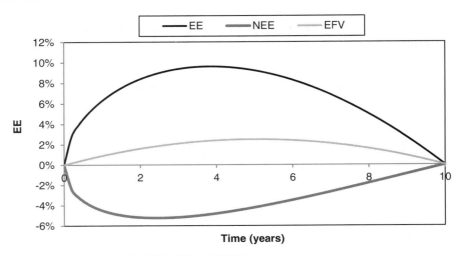

Figure 7.14   Illustration of the EFV, EE and NEE for a payer interest rate swap.

rates paid are expected to be offset by the gain on the notional exchange at the maturity of the contract,[9] and this expected gain on exchange of notional leads to a significant exposure for the payer of the high interest rate. In the reverse swap, it is increasingly likely that there will be a negative MTM on the swap when paying the currency with the lower interest rates. This creates a "negative drift", making the exposure much lower.

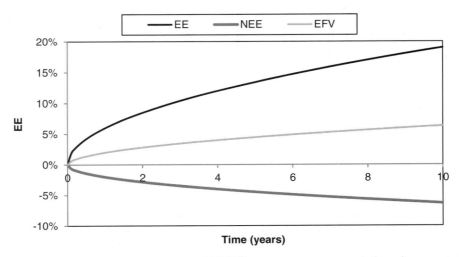

Figure 7.15   Illustration of the EFV, EE and NEE for a cross-currency swap where the pay currency has the higher interest rate.

---

[9] From a risk-neutral point of view.

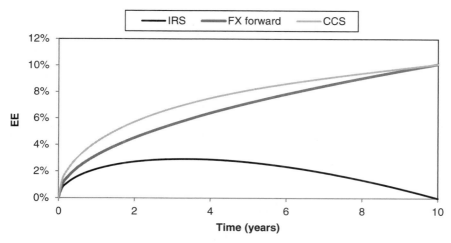

Figure 7.16   Illustration of the EE of a cross-currency swap (CCS) profile as a combination of an interest rate swap (IRS) and FX forward.

7.3.4   Combination of profiles

Some products have an exposure that is driven by a combination of two or more underlying risk factors. An obvious example is a cross-currency swap, which is essentially a combination of an interest rate swap and an FX forward transaction.[10] This would therefore be represented by a combination of the profiles shown in Figures 7.8 and 7.9, and as described in more mathematical detail in Appendix 7C. Figure 7.16 illustrates the combination of two such profiles. Cross-currency swap exposures can be considerable due to the high FX volatility driving the risk, coupled with the long maturities and final exchanges of notional. The contribution of the interest rate swap is typically smaller, as shown. We note also that the correlation between the two interest rates and the FX rate is an important driver of the exposure (Figure 7.16 assumes a relatively low correlation, as often seen in practice, which increases the cross-currency exposure[11]).

Spreadsheet 7.3   Simple example of a cross-currency swap profile

In Figure 7.17 we illustrate the exposure for cross-currency swaps of different maturities. The longer-maturity swaps have slightly more risk due to the greater number of interest rate payments on the swap.

---

[10] Due to the interest rate payments coupled with an exchange of notional in the two currencies at the end of the transaction.

[11] The impact of correlation can be seen in Spreadsheet 7.3.

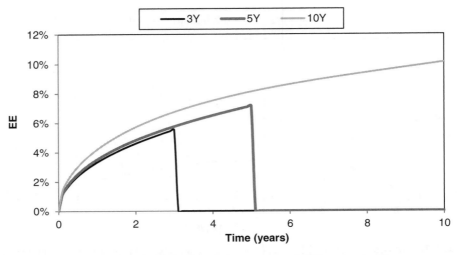

Figure 7.17   Illustration of the EE for cross-currency swaps of different maturities.

7.3.5   Optionality

The impact of exercise decisions creates some complexities in exposure profiles, since after the exercise date(s) the underlying transaction will have a certain probability of being "alive" or not. This is particularly important in the case of physical settlement. Figure 7.18 shows the exposure for a European-style interest rate swaption that

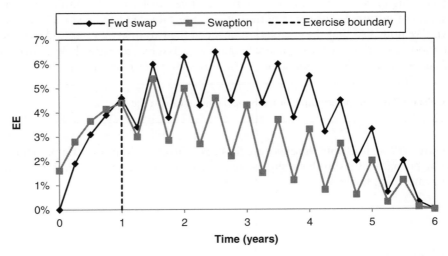

Figure 7.18   EE for a swap-settled (physically settled) interest rate swaption and the equivalent forward swap. The option maturity is one year and the swap maturity is five years.

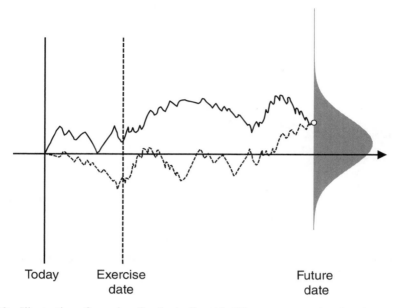

Today   Exercise   Future
              date   date

Figure 7.19   Illustration of exercise of a physically settled European swaption showing two potential scenarios of future value for the underlying swap. The solid line corresponds to a scenario where the swaption would be exercised, giving rise to an exposure at the future date. The dotted line shows a scenario that would give rise to an identical exposure but where the swaption would not have been exercised, and hence the exposure would be zero. The exercise boundary is assumed to be the x-axis.

is swap-settled (physical delivery) rather than cash-settled.[12] The underlying swap has different payment frequencies also. We compare it with the equivalent forward starting swap. Before the exercise point, the swaption must always have a greater exposure than the forward starting swap,[13] but thereafter this trend will reverse, since there will be scenarios where the forward starting swap has positive value but the swaption would not have been exercised. This effect is illustrated in Figure 7.19, which shows a scenario that would give rise to exposure in the forward swap but not the swaption.

We can make a final comment about the swaption example, which is that in exercising one should surely incorporate the views on aspects such as counterparty risk, funding and capital at that time. In other words, the future xVA should be a component in deciding whether to exercise or not. This therefore leads to a recursive problem for the calculation of xVA for products with exercise boundaries.

---

[12] The cash-settled swaption has an identical exposure until the exercise date and then zero exposure thereafter. Physically settled swaptions are standard in some interest rate markets. Depending on the currency, either swap or physical settlement may be most common.

[13] The option to enter into a contract cannot be worth less than the equivalent obligation to enter into the same contract.

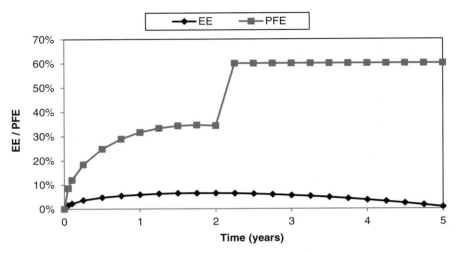

Figure 7.20   EE and PFE for a long protection single-name CDS transaction. A PFE of 60% arises from default with an assumed recovery rate of 40%.

7.3.6   Credit derivatives

Credit derivatives represent a challenge for exposure assessment due to wrong-way risk, which will be discussed in Chapter 17. Even without this as a consideration, exposure profiles of credit derivatives are hard to characterise due to the discrete payoffs of the instruments. Consider the exposure profile of a single-name CDS, as shown in Figure 7.20 (long CDS protection) for which we show the EE and PFE. Whilst the EE shows a typical swap-like profile, the PFE has a jump due to the default of the reference entity. This is a rather unnatural effect[14] (see also Hille et al., 2005), as it means that PFE may or may not represent the actual credit event occurring and is sensitive to the confidence level used. Using a measure such as expected shortfall[15] partially solves this problem. This effect will also not be apparent for CDS indices due to the large number of reference credits where single defaults have a less significant impact.

Spreadsheet 7.4   Simple calculation of the exposure of a CDS

---

[14] We comment that the above impact could be argued to be largely a facet of common modelling assumptions, which assume default as a sudden unanticipated jump event with a known recovery value (40%). Using a more realistic modelling of default and an unknown recovery value gives behaviour that is more continuous.

[15] Expected shortfall is recommended by the Fundamental Review of the Trading Book (Section 8.8.1) and is a measure used in preference to VAR in some cases since it has more mathematically convenient properties and, unlike VAR, is a "coherent risk measure". In this case, it corresponds to the expected exposure conditional on being above the relevant PFE value.

7.4   THE IMPACT OF NETTING AND COLLATERAL ON EXPOSURE

Netting effectively allows the future values of different transactions to offset one another thanks to contractual terms (Section 5.2). This means that the aggregate effect of all transactions in a netting set must be considered. As we shall see, there are several different aspects to contemplate before understanding the full netting impact on overall exposure with respect to a particular netting set and counterparty. We will describe the general points to consider before analysing netting from a more detailed, quantitative view in Chapter 10.

7.4.1   The impact of netting on future exposure

We illustrate the impact of netting on exposure in Figure 7.21 with exactly opposite transactions. When there is no legal agreement to allow netting, then exposures must be considered additive. This means that the positions do not offset one another. With netting permitted (and enforceable), one can add values at the netting set level before calculating the exposure and therefore the profiles shown give a zero exposure at all points in the future. This means that two opposite transactions (as shown in the example) will give a zero exposure with netting.

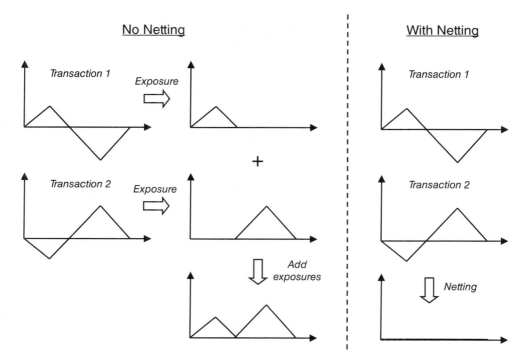

Figure 7.21   Illustration of the impact of netting on exposure.

7.4.2   Netting and the impact of correlation

> **Spreadsheet 7.5**   Simple two-transaction example of netting effects

Netting is essentially a diversification effect. When considering the netting benefit of two or more transactions, the most obvious consideration is the correlation between the future values (and therefore exposures also). A high positive correlation between two transactions means that future values are likely to be of the same sign. This means that the netting benefit will be small or even zero. We illustrate this in Table 7.1, where we can see that the two sets of values create very little netting benefit. Netting will only help in cases where the values of the transactions have opposite signs, which occurs only in scenario 3 in the table. The EE (average of the exposures assuming equally weighted scenarios) is reduced by only a small amount.

Note that the correlation of future values (columns two and three in Table 7.1) is 100% but the correlation of the exposures (only the positive parts of these values) is 96%. The latter number explains the small netting benefit. In practical terms, this corresponds to otherwise identical transactions that have different current MTM values (for example, two interest rate swaps of the same currency and maturity but with different swap rates). In such a case, the relative offset of the MTM values creates a netting effect. This is also discussed in Section 7.4.3 below.

On the other hand, negative correlations are clearly more helpful as future values are much more likely to have opposite signs and hence the netting benefit will be stronger. We illustrate this in Table 7.2 where we see that netting is beneficial in four out of the five scenarios. The EE is almost half the value without netting. In this case the correlation of future values is –100% but the correlation of exposures is –81%. The extreme case of perfect negatively correlated exposures corresponds to opposite transactions and would give the maximum netting benefit and a total exposure of zero.[16]

The majority of netting may occur across transactions of different asset classes that may be considered to have only a small correlation. One should note that this would still create a positive benefit. Indeed, for a simple example in Appendix 7D we show the

Table 7.1   Illustration of the impact of netting when there is positive correlation between MTM values. The expected exposure is shown assuming each scenario has equal weight.

| Scenario | Future value | | Total exposure | | Netting benefit |
	Trade 1	Trade 2	No netting	Netting	
Scenario 1	25	15	40	40	0
Scenario 2	15	5	20	20	0
Scenario 3	5	–5	5	0	5
Scenario 4	–5	–15	0	0	0
Scenario 5	–15	–25	0	0	0
EE			13	12	1

---

[16] For example, subtract 10 from transaction 2 in each scenario in Table 7.3 to see this.

Table 7.2 Illustration of the impact of netting when there is negative correlation between future values. The expected exposure is shown assuming each scenario has equal weight.

Scenario	Future value		Total exposure		Netting benefit
	Trade 1	Trade 2	No netting	Netting	
Scenario 1	25	−15	25	10	15
Scenario 2	15	−5	15	10	5
Scenario 3	5	5	10	10	0
Scenario 4	−5	15	15	10	5
Scenario 5	−15	25	25	10	15
EE			18	10	8

reduction corresponding to the case of normal variables with zero mean and equal variance. We derive the following formula for the "netting factor" with respect to exposure under the assumption that future values follow a multivariate normal distribution:

$$\text{Netting factor} = \frac{\sqrt{n + n(n-1)\bar{\rho}}}{n}, \tag{7.5}$$

where n represents the number of exposures and $\bar{\rho}$ is the average correlation. The netting factor represents the ratio of net to gross exposure and will be +100% if there is no netting benefit ($\bar{\rho} = 100$)% and 0% if the netting benefit is maximum.[17] We illustrate the above expression in Figure 7.22, where we can see that the netting benefit improves (lower netting value) for a large number of exposures and low correlation as one would expect, since these conditions maximise the diversification benefit. We note that this is

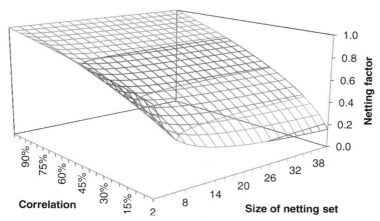

Figure 7.22 Illustration of the netting benefit in a simple example as a function of the size of the netting set (number of transactions) and correlation as derived in Appendix 7D. Only positive correlations are shown.

---

[17] Note that there is a restriction on the correlation level here of $\bar{\rho} = -(n-1)^{-1}$ that ensures the term inside the square root in Equation 7.5 does not become negative. This is explained in Appendix 7D.

a stylised example but it shows the general impact of correlation and the size of the netting set.

With no correlation, the simple formula tells us that the overall netting factor is $1/\sqrt{n}$. This means, for example, that two independent transactions with zero mean and equal volatility have a netted exposure reduced to 71% of their exposure without netting. For five exposures, the netting factor decreases to 45%.

7.4.3   Netting and relative MTM

In Table 7.1, the correlation between future values is 100% but the correlation of exposures is only 96%. We can therefore see that the netting benefit depends not only on the correlation of future values but also on their relative offset.

An illustration of the impact of negative future value of a netting set is shown in Figure 7.23. Negative future value will create netting benefit irrespective of the structural correlation between transactions. This is because an out-of-the-money portfolio is unlikely to have an exposure unless the MTM of the transactions moves significantly.

A positive future value can also be considered to have a beneficial impact with respect to netting. An illustration of the impact of the positive future value of a netting set is shown in Figure 7.24. The negative MTM of a new transaction will have an impact in offsetting the in-the-money portfolio. These effects are important since they show that even directional portfolios can have significant netting effects.

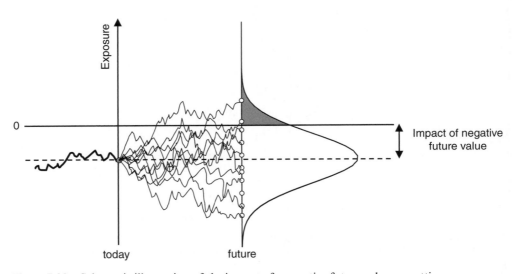

Figure 7.23   Schematic illustration of the impact of a negative future value on netting.

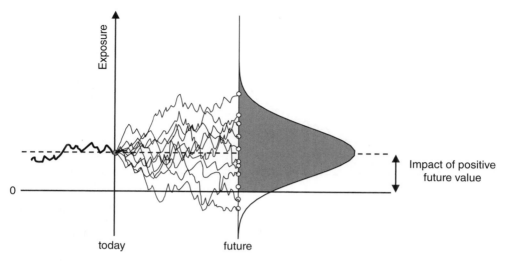

Figure 7.24   Schematic illustration of the impact of a positive future value on netting.

7.4.4   Impact of collateral on exposure

A simple example of the impact of collateral on exposure is given in Table 7.3, assuming a two-way collateral agreement. In scenarios 1–3 the exposure is reduced significantly, since collateral is held. The exposure is not perfectly collateralised, which may be the case in practice due to factors such as a sudden increase in MTM, or contractual aspects such as thresholds and minimum transfer amounts (Section 6.2). In scenario 4, the value of the portfolio is negative and collateral must therefore be posted but this does not increase the exposure (again, in practice due to aspects such as thresholds and minimum transfer amounts). Finally, in scenario 5, the posting of collateral *creates* exposure.[18] In comparison with the benefits shown in the other scenarios, this is not a particularly significant effect, but it is important to note that collateral can increase as well as reduce exposure. These effects will be seen in actual cases in Chapter 11.

Table 7.3   Illustration of the impact of collateral on exposure. The expected exposure is shown assuming each scenario has equal weight.

| | Future value | | Exposure | | |
Scenario	No collateral	With collateral	No collateral	With collateral	Benefit
Scenario 1	25	23	25	2	23
Scenario 2	15	12	15	3	12
Scenario 3	5	3	5	2	3
Scenario 4	−5	−2	0	0	0
Scenario 5	−15	−18	0	3	−3
EE			9	2	7

[18] In practice, this can happen when previously posted collateral has not yet been returned as required.

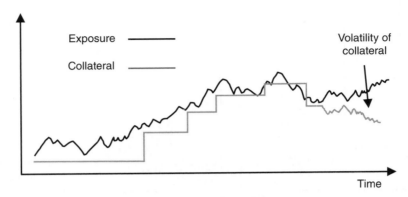

Figure 7.25 Illustration of the impact of collateral on exposure showing the delay in receiving collateral and the granularity receiving and posting collateral amounts discontinuously. Also shown is the impact of the volatility of collateral itself (for ease of illustration this is shown in the last period only).

Collateral typically reduces exposure but there are many (sometimes subtle) points that must be considered in order to assess properly the true extent of any risk reduction. To account properly for the real impact of collateral, parameters such as thresholds and minimum transfer amounts must be properly understood and represented appropriately. Furthermore, the "margin period of risk" (MPR) must be carefully analysed to determine the true risk horizon with respect to collateral transfer. Quantifying the extent of the risk mitigation benefit of collateral is not trivial and requires many, sometimes subjective, assumptions.

To the extent that collateral is not a perfect form of risk mitigation, there are three considerations, which are illustrated in Figure 7.25:

- There is a granularity effect because it is not always possible to ask for all of the collateral required, due to parameters such as thresholds and minimum transfer amounts. This can sometimes lead to a beneficial overcollateralisation (as seen in Figure 7.25) where the collateral amount is for a short period greater than the exposure. Note that this must also consider the impact of collateral that a party must themselves post.
- There is a delay in receiving collateral that involves many aspects such as the operational components of requesting and receiving collateral to the possibility of collateral disputes. These aspects are included in the assessment of the MPR.
- We must consider a potential variation in the value of the collateral itself (if it is not cash in the currency in which the exposure is assessed).

We also emphasise that the treatment of collateral is path-dependent, since the amount of collateral required at a given time depends on the amount of collateral called (or posted) in the past. This is especially important in the case of two-way collateral agreements.

The impact of collateral on exposure is discussed in more detail in Chapter 11. However, Figure 7.26 shows the qualitative impact for three broadly defined cases:

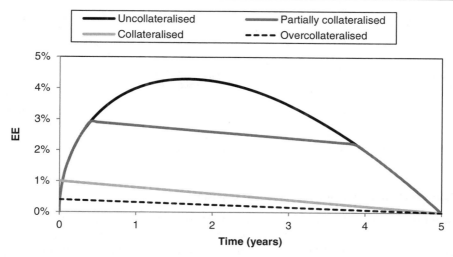

Figure 7.26   Illustration of the EE of an interest rate swap with different levels of collateralisation.

- *Partially collateralised.* Here, the presence of contractual aspects such as thresholds means that the reduction of exposure is imperfect. A threshold can be seen as approximately capping the exposure.
- *Collateralised.* In the collateralised case, we assume aspects such as thresholds are zero and therefore the exposure is reduced significantly. However, the MPR still leads to a reasonably material value.
- *Overcollateralised.* In this case, we assume there is initial margin (Section 6.2.4) and therefore the exposure is reduced further compared to the above case (and potentially to zero if the initial margin is large enough).

7.5   FUNDING, REHYPOTHECATION AND SEGREGATION

7.5.1   Funding costs and benefits

Over recent years, market consensus has emerged that uncollateralised derivatives exposures need to be funded and therefore give rise to costs that are generally recognised via funding value adjustment (FVA). It is therefore appropriate to define the concept of funding exposure. The basic logic is that an exposure (positive MTM) is a funding cost, while a negative exposure (negative MTM) represents a funding benefit (Figure 7.27). The more detailed explanation and arguments around funding costs will be discussed in Chapter 15, but a basic explanation is as follows. A positive MTM represents a derivative asset that cannot be monetised economically (for example, unlike a treasury bond, it is not possible to repo a derivative and receive cash for the positive MTM), and hence it has to be funded like any other asset with an associated cost. In the reverse situation, a negative MTM creates a derivative liability that represents a loss that does not need to be paid immediately and acts rather like a loan, providing a funding benefit.

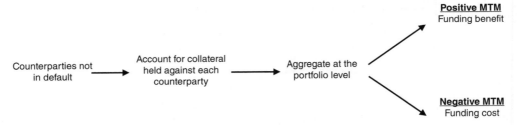

Figure 7.27   Illustration of the impact of a positive or negative MTM on funding.

7.5.2   Differences between funding and credit exposure

The concept of funding costs and benefits can therefore be seen to have clear parallels with the definition of exposure earlier (compare Figure 7.27 with Figure 7.1). A positive value (exposure in Equation 7.1) is at risk when a counterparty defaults, but is also the amount that has to be funded when the counterparty does not. A negative exposure (Section 7.2.7) is associated with a funding benefit. However, whilst exposure defined for credit purposes has clear parallels with funding exposure, there are some distinct differences that must be considered:

- *Close-out.* The consideration of potential close-out adjustments (Section 7.1.3) is relevant only in the definition of credit exposure in a default scenario and does not apply when considering funding aspects that should be based on the MTM (note the difference in the use of the terms value and MTM in Figures 7.1 and 7.27 respectively).
- *Margin period of risk.* The MPR is a concept that is defined assuming the default of the counterparty and is relevant for credit exposure. In assessing the equivalent delay in receiving collateral against a derivatives portfolio, the normal collateral posting frequency (which is likely much shorter) should be assumed. As discussed in Chapter 15, this is one reason why the FVA of a collateralised derivative may be considered to be zero, even though the equivalent CVA is not.
- *Netting.* Close-out netting is a concept that applies in a default scenario and hence credit exposure is defined at the netting set level (which may correspond or be a sub-set of the counterparty level). On the other hand, funding applies at the overall portfolio level since MTM for different transactions is additive and collateral received from one counterparty may be posted to another.
- *Segregation.* As discussed in the next section, segregation has different impacts on credit exposure and funding.

Despite the above differences, credit, debt and funding value adjustments (CVA, DVA and FVA) have many similarities and should most obviously be quantified using shared methodologies.

7.5.3   Impact of segregation and rehypothecation

Collateral in OTC derivative transactions can be seen to serve two purposes: it has a traditional role in mitigating counterparty risk and it also provides a funding position.

Whilst the former role is the traditional use of collateral, the latter has been seen as increasingly important in recent years. Collateral may be complimentary in mitigating both counterparty risk and funding costs. For example, receiving collateral from a counterparty against a positive MTM has a two-fold benefit:

- Counterparty risk reduction. In the event of the counterparty defaulting, it is possible to hold on to (or take ownership of) the collateral to cover close-out losses.
- Funding benefit. The collateral can be used for other purposes[19] such as being posted as collateral against a negative MTM in another transaction. Indeed, it could be posted against the hedge of the transaction (which by definition will have a negative MTM).

However, as Table 7.4 illustrates, the type of collateral must have certain characteristics to provide benefits against both counterparty risk and funding costs. Firstly, in order to maximise the benefits of counterparty risk mitigation, there must be no adverse correlation between the collateral and the credit quality of the counterparty (wrong-way risk). A second important consideration is that, for collateral to be used for funding purposes, it must be reusable. This means that collateral must not be segregated and non-cash collateral must be reusable (transferred by title transfer or rehypothecation allowed) so that the collateral can be reused. In the case of cash collateral this is trivially the case, but for non-cash collateral rehypothecation must be allowed so that the collateral can be reused or pledged via repo.

Let us consider the counterparty risk mitigation and funding benefit from various types of collateral under certain situations:

- *Cash that does not need to be segregated.* As discussed above, this provides both counterparty risk and funding benefits.
- *Securities that can be rehypothecated.* As above, as long as the haircuts are sufficient to mitigate against any adverse price moves and also the corresponding haircuts associated with reusing the securities (e.g. the repo market or the collateral terms for another transaction).
- *Cash/securities that must be segregated/cannot be rehypothecated.* These provide a counterparty mitigation benefit since they may be monetised in a default scenario but do not provide a funding benefit, since they cannot be reused in a non-default scenario.

Table 7.4   Impact of collateral type on counterparty risk and funding.

	Collateral can be used	Segregated or rehypothecation not allowed
No wrong-way risk	Counterparty risk reduction and funding benefit	Counterparty risk reduction only
Wrong-way collateral	Funding benefit and limited counterparty risk reduction	Limited counterparty risk reduction

---

[19] As long as it does not need to be segregated and can be rehypothecated, as discussed below.

- *Counterparty posting own bonds (that can be rehypothecated).* These provide a questionable counterparty risk mitigation benefit since they will obviously be in default when needed.[20] However, as long as they can be rehypothecated (and the haircuts are sufficient for this purpose) then they provide a funding benefit.

One example of the above balance can be seen in the recent behaviour of sovereigns, supranationals and agencies (SSA) counterparties who have traditionally enjoyed one-way CSAs with banks and not posted collateral due to their high credit quality (typically triple-A). SSAs have begun to move to two-way CSA and post collateral, sometimes in the form of their own bonds.[21] This is because the traditional one-way agreement creates a very significant funding obligation for the banks, which is in turn reflected in the cost of the swaps that SSAs use to hedge their borrowing and lending transactions. As banks have become more sensitive to funding costs that in turn have been higher, the move to a two-way CSA means that a counterparty can achieve a significant pricing advantage (see a later example in Section 19.4.2). Posting own bonds may be seen as optimal for a high credit quality counterparty because it minimises the liquidity risk that they face from posting other collateral. Furthermore, thanks to their strong credit quality, the counterparty risk[22] that they impose is less significant than the funding costs, and hence they most obviously need to reduce the latter.

7.5.4   Impact of collateral on credit and funding exposure

When considering the benefit of collateral on exposure, we must therefore carefully define the counterparty risk and funding exposure components with reference to the type of collateral required. In general, collateral should be subtracted (added) to the exposure when received from (posted to) the counterparty. However, segregation and rehypothecation create distinct differences. From the more general Equation 7.1, the credit exposure from the point of counterparty risk is:

$$Exposure_{CCR} = \max(value - CR + CP_{NS}, 0), \tag{7.6}$$

where *value* is as defined in Section 7.1.3, CR is the total collateral received from the counterparty (assuming no wrong-way risk) and CP_{NS} is the collateral posted to the counterparty that is not segregated. Any collateral received, irrespective of segregation and rehypothecation aspects, can be utilised in a default situation. However, if collateral posted is not segregated it will create additional counterparty risk, since it cannot be retrieved in the event that the counterparty defaults.[23]

---

[20] Note that they will provide some counterparty risk reduction benefits. Firstly, if the bonds decline in value, it is possible to request more collateral; and secondly, the bonds will be worth something in default. However, a rapid default of the counterparty, coupled with a low recovery value, will make this form of collateral almost worthless.

[21] For example, see "Bank of England to post collateral in OTC derivatives trades", *Risk*, 22nd June 2014, and "Europe's SSAs embrace two-way collateral", IFR SSA Special Report 2014.

[22] As discussed in Chapter 8, the capital requirements for counterparty risk (KVA) may still be quite significant, even if the counterparty risk charge itself (CVA) is not.

[23] Note that negative exposure is defined differently, since this is relevant in the case the party themselves default (DVA): *Negative exposure_{CCR}* = $\min(value + CP - CR_{NS}, 0)$.

On the other hand, the exposure from the point of view of funding aspects is defined as:

$$Exposure_{Funding} = MTM - CR_{RH} + CP \tag{7.7}$$

where MTM is used instead of *value* as discussed in Section 7.5.2, CR_{RH} represents the collateral received that can be rehypothecated (or more generally reused) and CP represents all collateral posted, irrespective of segregation and rehypothecation aspects.

To make this definition more precise we can distinguish between the two general types of collateral (Section 6.1.3):

- *Initial margin.* As seen from Equation 7.6, this needs to be segregated otherwise posted initial margin will increase credit exposure. Furthermore, if initial margin is posted and received, then the amounts will offset one another – in practice, initial margin received could be simply returned to the counterparty! For this reason, unilateral initial margin ideally should be segregated and bilateral initial margin must be segregated. The latter case indeed applies in the future regulatory collateral rules (Section 6.7).[24]
- *Variation margin.* From Equation 7.7 we can see that variation margin should be rehypothecable (or reusable) so as to provide a funding benefit. Whilst this potentially creates more counterparty risk when posting – since variation margin is typically already owed against a MTM loss – this should not be a major concern. Variation margin is never segregated and can typically be rehypothecated, since it is posted against a MTM loss and does not represent overcollateralisation.

Making the above assumptions regarding initial and variation margins, we can write the above formulas more specifically as:[25]

$$Exposure_{CCR} = \max(value - VM - IM^R, 0), \tag{7.8}$$

$$Exposure_{Funding} = MTM - VM + IM^P \tag{7.9}$$

The exposure for counterparty risk purposes can be offset by variation margin (which may be positive or negative) and initial margin received (IM^R). The exposure for funding is fully adjusted by variation margin and increased by the initial margin posted (IM^P). Note finally that in the absence of initial margin, the formulas above become identical except for the first three points in Section 7.5.2. This is one reason why we will separate the funding of IM into MVA so that the remaining exposure for CVA and FVA purposes will be more closely aligned.

Note that there are also some other points that may need to be considered above. For example, initial margin received may be considered to have a funding cost due to the need to segregate it with a third party custodian. The above expressions will be relevant

---

[24] Except for the one-time rehypothecation of initial margin mentioned in Section 6.7.5.

[25] As before, note that the concept of negative exposure for counterparty risk purposes is defined as *Negative exposure*$_{CCR}$ = $\min(value + VM - IM^P, 0)$ with posted variation margin being negative. The funding exposure can be positive or negative, and is defined directly by Equation 7.9.

later in the definition of CVA and DVA (Chapter 14), FVA (Chapter 15), and MVA (Chapter 16).

7.5.5 Examples

To understand the concepts introduced above, we give several examples below illustrating exposure from counterparty risk and funding points of view.

Example 1

Suppose the current MTM of a portfolio is 20 and 15 of variation margin is held, together with 6 of (unilateral) segregated initial margin. Ignore close-out costs and so $value \equiv MTM$. We have:

$$Exposure_{CCR} = \max(20-15-6,0) = 0$$

$$Exposure_{Funding} = 20-15 = 5$$

The current counterparty risk exposure is zero, whereas the amount that has to be funded is 5 since the initial margin held does not provide a funding benefit.

Example 2

Suppose the current MTM of a portfolio is 20 and 15 of variation margin is held, and 5 of segregated initial margin is posted bilaterally. We have:

$$Exposure_{CCR} = \max(20-15-5,0) = 0$$

$$Exposure_{Funding} = 20-15 + 5 = 10$$

The current counterparty risk exposure is zero, since the initial margin makes up the gap between the MTM and variation margin (this could be because the MTM has increased rapidly). The amount that has to be funded is 10, which is the MTM not covered by variation margin (5) and the initial margin posted.

Example 3

Suppose the current MTM of a portfolio is –20 and 25 of variation margin has been posted, and 6 of initial margin is posted bilaterally. We have:

$$Exposure_{CCR} = \max(-20 + 25 - 6, 0) = 0$$

$$Exposure_{Funding} = -20 + 25 + 6 = 11$$

The current counterparty risk exposure is zero,[26] since the initial margin covers the excess variation margin that has been posted. However, there are significant funding costs of the excess variation margin (5) and the initial margin (6).

7.6 SUMMARY

In this chapter we have discussed exposure. Some key definitions of potential future exposure, expected exposure and expected positive exposure have been given. The factors impacting future exposures have been explained and we have discussed the impact of netting and collateral. The concept of funding exposure has been introduced, which will be important for defining FVA and MVA later (Chapters 15 and 16). Aspects such as segregation and rehypothecation and their impact on credit and funding exposure have been discussed.

---

[26] Note that the negative exposure is also zero.

8

Capital Requirements and Regulation

A camel is a horse designed by a committee.

Sir Alexander Arnold Constantine Issigonis (1906–1988)

This chapter discusses counterparty risk capital requirements, which have become increasingly important in recent years as they become more punitive and capital itself becomes more expensive. We also discuss other aspects such as the leverage ratio, liquidity coverage ratio and prudent valuation, which all have an impact on bank's capital and liquidity requirements.

A key form of regulation is determining the minimum amount of capital that a given bank must hold. Capital acts as a buffer to absorb losses during turbulent periods and, therefore, contributes significantly to defining creditworthiness. Ultimately, regulatory capital requirements partially determine the leverage under which a bank can operate. The danger of overly optimistic capital requirements has been often highlighted, with losses not just exceeding, but dwarfing, the capital set aside against them. Banks strive for profits and will therefore naturally wish to hold the minimum amount of capital possible in order to maximise the amount of business they can do and risk they are able to take. There is clearly a balance in defining the capital requirements for a bank; it must be high enough to contribute to a very low possibility of failure, and yet not so severe as to unfairly penalise the bank and have adverse consequences for their clients and the economy as a whole.

The definition of sound regulatory capital buffers is also plagued by the complexity of the underlying approach. A simple approach will be transparent and easier to implement but will not be able to capture any more than the key aspects of the risks arising from a complex web of positions often taken by a bank. As such, this may give rise to possible "arbitrages" of requirements arising from the ability to reduce capital, without a corresponding reduction in the associated risk. A more sophisticated model-based approach may more closely align capital and actual financial risk, but will be less transparent and harder to implement. Added to this is the fact that large banks may have the resources and expertise to implement complex regulatory capital approaches, whilst smaller banks may need to rely on a simpler approach, even if this is more conservative in ultimate capital requirements. Regulators generally define two or more alternative methodologies of varying sophistication.

Capital requirements are also split into various different and distinct areas such as market, credit, liquidity and operational risk. This leads to potential double-counting effects and failure to appreciate offsetting risks. Even in a seemingly individual risk type such as counterparty risk, capital requirements are defined by more than one set of requirements, with the overall capital being additive. A final problem is that regulation is not always consistent globally. Whilst Basel III, for example, constitutes a global set of capital rules, the precise implementation is decided by local regulators and may differ by region. The CVA capital charge exemption in Europe (Section 8.7.7) is one notable example of this.

Banks have been required to hold capital against counterparty risk since the 1988 Basel Capital Accord. However the Basel I rules lacked risk sensitivity, creating the wrong incentive and enabling banks to reduce regulatory capital without actually reducing the economic risks they were facing. To address this, a revised Capital Framework (Basel II) was imposed in 2006, allowing some banks to use their own models (once approved by supervisors) for measuring exposure and for assessing default probability and loss given default. However, Basel II did not include mark-to-market losses due to CVA. During the financial crisis, nearly two-thirds of counterparty risk losses were attributed to CVA losses and only one-third were due to actual defaults. The Basel III framework addressed this point and set out new capital rules for CVA that are significant.

8.1   BACKGROUND TO CREDIT RISK CAPITAL

Counterparty risk capital requirements are based on more general capital rules for credit risk and we first discuss this general approach taken to capitalise the default risk on typical credit risk instruments, such as loans. Since 1995, market risk capital requirements have been become model-based with the introduction of value-at-risk (VAR) (see Section 3.3.1), but this is not the case for credit risk. Such a limitation can be put down to the increased complexity of modelling credit risk, together with the limited data and longer time horizons involved. There are typically two methods used to define credit risk capital: the standardised approach and the internal ratings-based approach.

8.1.1   Standardised approach

In this simple approach, banks assess the risk of their exposures using external ratings. All non-retail exposures are assigned to risk buckets. BCBS (2006) provides tables that specify a capital charge for each risk bucket. This approach has its basis under Basel I but is more granular. Risk weights of 0%, 20%, 50%, 100% and 150% are assigned to the obligor depending on their rating to give the risk weighted asset (RWA) requirement. The RWA is then multiplied by 8% to convert it into a capital charge.

8.1.2   Internal ratings-based approach (IRB)

Here, banks rely on their own internal estimates of some (foundation IRB) or all (advanced IRB) risk components. These components are the probability of default, loss given default, exposure at default and effective maturity. The advanced IRB approach still uses a relatively simple formula, although the origins of this formula have a firm theoretical basis. The theory rests on the large homogeneous pool (LHP) approximation described in Appendix 8A. This is used to define a worst case ("unexpected") loss under the LHP assumptions of Vasicek (1997) and granularity adjustment formula of Gordy (2004) with a confidence level set at 99.9%. Under the advanced IRB approach, regulatory capital (RC) for a given instrument is defined by the following formula:

$$RC = EAD \times LGD \times PD_{99.9\%} \times MA(PD, M) \tag{8.1}$$

with the following definitions:

EAD   The exposure at default (e.g., the notional of a bond or loan).

LGD   The expected loss given default in relation to the *EAD* (estimated conditionally on an economic downturn).

$PD_{99.9\%}$ The obligor's probability of default (subject to a floor of 0.03%), with $PD_{99.9\%}$ representing an unexpected probability of default at the confidence level of 99.9%.[1] This incorporates an asset correlation parameter that may penalise more correlated or systemic exposures and is higher for financial institutions (Section 8.6.1).

MA   A maturity adjustment factor that partially accounts for the fact that an obligor's credit quality may deteriorate (credit migration via a rating downgrade, for example) and that this effect may be more significant for high quality obligors.

The above formula is intuitive: the capital should depend on the size of the position concerned (EAD) and on the probability of default, loss given default, effective maturity and correlation within the portfolio concerned. From the point of view of counterparty risk, the above formula makes up what will be referred to as the default risk capital charge (sometimes known as the CCR capital charge).

It is beyond the scope of this book to discuss the IRB methods in more detail and the reader is referred to BCBS (2006) for more information.

8.1.3   Double default

> **Spreadsheet 8.1**   Joint default probability calculation

Suppose the credit risk of an exposure is hedged with a product, such as a credit default swap, or otherwise guaranteed by a third party. Such hedging is quite common for xVA desks (Chapter 18). There should be capital relief due to this risk reduction, since there is now only risk in the case where both parties (the original counterparty and the party providing the guarantee) default. From Basel II onwards there are two possible ways in which to account for hedged or guaranteed exposures:

* *Substitution.* The default probability of the "guarantor" (provider of protection or guarantee) may be substituted for the default probability of the original "obligor" (original counterparty). Assuming the guarantor has a better credit quality, this will cause some reduction in risk.
* *Double default.* The "double default effect" is recognised via a formula to account for the fact that risk only arises from joint default. A key consideration in this formula is the correlation between the original counterparty and the guarantor.

The double default formula[2] (BCBS, 2005) is based on the treatment of the two-default case as described in Appendix 8B, where the joint default probability is expressed in

---

[1] Note that the default probability is subtracted from the worst case default probability, explained in Appendix 8A.

[2] This option is only available when using the IRB approach.

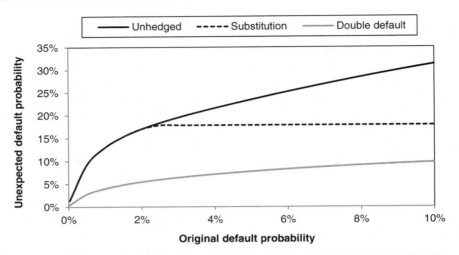

Figure 8.1   Default probability function in Basel II formula (the unexpected default probability term $PD_{99.9\%}$ in Equation 8.1) for unhedged and hedged exposures. In the latter case, both substitution assumptions and the double default formula are shown. All details are given in Appendix 8B. The guarantor default probability is assumed to be 2% for which the unexpected default probability is 17%.

terms of a bivariate normal distribution function. The main reduction in capital arises from the decrease in the default probability within the capital formula (together with less significant changes in effective maturity and loss given default). Figure 8.1 contrasts the difference between an unhedged exposure, the substitution and double default approaches. The substitution approach is beneficial only if the unexpected default probability of the guarantor is lower than that of the obligor. The double default formula is always beneficial, in recognition of the fact that the probability that both obligor and guarantor will default is usually significantly less than that of the obligor defaulting alone. The Basel Committee has also proposed a simple parametric formula. This approximation, described in Appendix 8B, works well for small obligor default probabilities but is less accurate for high probabilities. Indeed, it is possible for the adjustment factor to give a capital requirement higher than that for an unhedged exposure.

8.1.4   Exposure at default (EAD)

A primary emphasis of the Basel II framework was financial instruments with relatively fixed exposures, such as loans. In such cases, the definition of EAD for Equation 8.1 is trivial. However, the definition of EAD for derivative portfolios is challenging due to the inherent uncertainty of the underlying exposure. The credit exposure of a derivatives portfolio (netting set) is bilateral and driven by changes in risk factors (e.g. interest rates, FX rates), correlation and legal terms in relation to netting and collateral. This is complex and therefore difficult to represent in a simple regulatory formula.

The Basel II framework (BCBS, 2006) developed a choice of methods for banks to use when calculating EAD for each counterparty they faced. EAD is calculated at the netting set level: a netting set is a group of transactions with a single counterparty subject to a legally enforceable bilateral netting agreement that satisfies certain legal and operational criteria, described in Annex 4 of BCBS (2006). Each transaction that is not subject to a legally enforceable bilateral netting agreement is interpreted as its own netting set. The interpretation of a netting set according to Basel II is therefore consistent with the earlier definition of close-out netting (Section 5.2.6).[3]

The historical methods available for computing EAD under Basel rules are:[4]

- current exposure method (CEM);
- standardised method (SM); and
- internal model method (IMM) (including the so-called shortcut method).

The first two approaches above are normally referred to as the non-IMM methods. These methods are designed to provide a simple and workable supervisory methodology for those banks that do not have the sophistication to model credit exposure internally. The IMM involves sophisticated modelling of all the underlying risk factors; IMM approval is therefore costly to achieve (and maintain). For this reason, only the largest banks globally have IMM approval for counterparty risk.

As seen in Figure 8.2, banks generally use either the CEM or IMM. The SM is uncommon and some regulators (e.g. the US and Canada) do not allow it. For this reason, we do not discuss the SM below although details can be found in Appendix 8C. It can also be noted that a number of banks using the more basic CEM approach do aspire to gain IMM approval in the future which will be discussed later in Chapter 18. Finally, the CEM method is envisaged as being replaced in 2017 by the standardised approach for counterparty credit risk (SA-CCR) – see BCBS (2014d). It is therefore necessary to consider the following EAD approaches, which will be described in detail in the next sections:

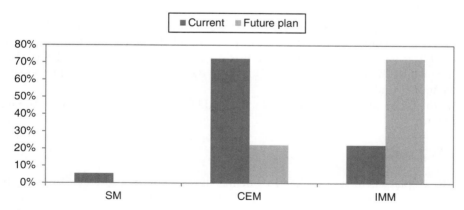

Figure 8.2 Illustration of market practice for exposure at default calculation. Note that the SA-CCR approach (Section 8.4) was not published at the time of this survey.
Source: Deloitte/Solum CVA survey, 2013.

---

[3] Although situations occasionally arise where a bank considers that they have sufficient legal opinion to assume that close-out netting is enforceable, but their regulator does not allow this for capital purposes.

[4] In addition, there are separate approaches to handle repo transactions (see Appendix 8D).

- *CEM*. The simplest method currently available and used by most banks but lacking risk-sensitivity across many aspects.
- *IMM*. The advanced model based method that the most sophisticated banks have gained approval to use. It is risk-sensitive but is very costly to implement.
- *SA-CCR*. A new, more risk-sensitive approach that aims to balance simplicity and risk sensitivity that will be introduced in 2017.

Note that the CEM and SA-CCR approaches are objective since they are based on prescribed formulas, whilst the IMM is subjective since it is based on a complex set of modelling assumptions.

8.1.5   Incurred CVA

It is possible to adjust the EAD for incurred CVA. Incurred CVA is defined as the CVA value on the balance sheet of a firm and should be recognised as being risk-reducing, since it is a loss that has already been accounted for. CVA can therefore be subtracted from the defined EAD. This could be best understood by considering a counterparty close to default: the CVA will be quite large but the capital charge is largely unnecessary since most of the anticipated default loss will be factored into the CVA. By removing the CVA from the EAD, the capital charge will therefore be correspondingly reduced. This reduction of EAD by incurred CVA losses does not apply to the determination of the CVA capital charge (Section 8.7), but only to the determination of the default-related (Basel II) risk capital charge. Pykhtin (2012) discusses this in more detail.

8.2   CURRENT EXPOSURE METHOD (CEM)

8.2.1   Add-ons

The CEM (originating from Basel I) is based on the fundamental idea that EAD arises from two components: the current exposure (CE) and the potential future exposure (PFE) as illustrated in Figure 8.3. The CE is obviously relatively easy to define (Section 7.1.1) whilst the PFE (Section 7.2.2) is more complex as it represents the possible exposure in the future.

Under the CEM rules (see BCBS, 2006), the EAD for a given transaction is computed according to:

$$EAD = RC + AddOn, \tag{8.2}$$

where RC (replacement cost) is used to define the current exposure (CE) and is the positive MTM of the portfolio, i.e. $\max(MTM, 0)$, and *AddOn* is the estimated amount of the PFE over the remaining life of the contract. The *AddOn* is calculated, for each single transaction, as the product of the transaction notional and the add-on factor, which is determined based on the remaining maturity and the underlying asset class (e.g. interest rates, foreign exchange, etc.) according to Table 8.1. For example, a six-year interest rate swap with a CE of 1% would have an add-on of 1.5% and therefore an EAD of 2.5%.

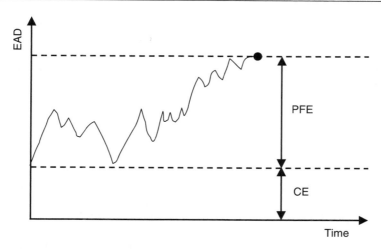

Figure 8.3 Illustration of the CEM approach at defining EAD via current exposure (CE) and potential future exposure (PFE).

Table 8.1 Add-on factors for the current exposure method (CEM) by the remaining maturity and type of underlying instrument

Remaining maturity	Interest rates	FX and gold	Equities	Precious metals (except gold)	Other commodities
< 1 year	0.0%	1.0%	6.0%	7.0%	10.0%
1–5 years	0.5%	5.0%	8.0%	7.0%	12.0%
> 5 years	1.5%	7.5%	10.0%	8.0%	15.0%

Whilst the CEM approach clearly captures in essence the differing exposure profiles for derivatives based on their asset class and maturity, it is not especially risk-sensitive (for example a two- and five-year interest rate swap have the same add-on). Another obvious issue is that a transaction with a negative MTM will have the same exposure as one with a zero MTM (in both cases the CE is zero and the add-on will be the same). In reality, a "negative exposure" should be expected to reduce the risk of a transaction.

8.2.2   Netting and collateral treatment

The CEM also provides recognition of close-out netting but does so in quite a simple way. In terms of the CE, it is possible to fully net transactions, covered by a legally enforceable bilateral netting agreement. This is trivial since it relates to current exposure and means that the RC for a netting set is defined by the net portfolio exposure, $RC_{NS} = \max(\Sigma_{i=1}^{n} MTM_i, 0)$. The add-on for a netting set of n transactions is then given by:

$$AddOn_{NS} = (0.4 + 0.6 \times NGR) \times \sum_{i=1}^{n} AddOn_i \tag{8.3}$$

where $AddOn_i$ is the add-on for transaction i and NGR (net gross ratio) is a quantity that determines the current impact of netting in percentage terms. (An NGR of zero implies perfect netting and an NGR of 100% implies no netting benefit.) The NGR is defined as the ratio of the current net exposure to the current gross exposure for all transactions within the netting set:[5]

$$NGR = \frac{RC_{NS}}{\sum_{i=1}^{n} \max(MTM_i, 0)} \tag{8.4}$$

This approach can be viewed as giving 60% of the current netting benefit to the future exposure. This is a compromise since the benefit of netting can change significantly over time as the MTM values of individual transactions change. Consider two transactions that net perfectly today since they have equal and opposite MTM values. Only if they are completely opposite transactions will the netting be perfect in the future. If the trades happened to net by chance, then some, or all, of this netting benefit will be lost over time. Essentially, giving only 60% of the current netting benefit recognises the fact that some netting benefit will be structural (such as hedges) but some will occur only transiently and by chance. This treatment seems conservative as it assumes that the current netting benefit will decay over time, whereas the reverse can also occur. In general, for directional portfolios (where netting is not particularly strong) banks find that the above treatment is not particularly punitive. However, it can appear so for more balanced portfolios with stronger netting.

Under the CEM, the impact of current collateral held against a netting set is incorporated into RC as follows:

$$RC = \max(RC_{NS} - C_A, 0) \tag{8.5}$$

where C_A is the volatility-adjusted collateral amount (i.e. the net value of collateral security after being adjusted for the haircut). This means that the current exposure for transactions within a netting set can be reduced by the current market value of the collateral, subject to a (potentially sizeable) haircut across the different collateral securities held.[6] Essentially, the benefit of collateral on current exposure is recognised via the reduction of CE, but the ability to call for collateral against future exposure is not. Furthermore, overcollateralisation (e.g. initial margin) will not reduce the PFE, since it is only applied to the CE as shown in Equation 8.5. This is especially problematic given the dramatic increase in the use of initial margin that is prescribed under the incoming bilateral margin rules (Section 6.7).

---

[5] NGR is used in bank capital requirements and the definition can be found in Annex IV of the Basel capital framework, paragraph 969(iv), Part 5, *Basel II: International Convergence of Capital Measurement and Capital Standards: A Revised Framework* (available at www.bis.org/publ/bcbs128d.pdf).

[6] This is referred to as "volatility adjusted collateral" – see www.bis.org/publ/bcbs116.pdf.

8.3   THE INTERNAL MODEL METHOD (IMM)

8.3.1   Background

The internal model method (IMM) is the most risk-sensitive approach for EAD calculation available under the Basel framework. Under the IMM, both EAD and maturity adjustment factor in Equation 8.1 are computed from the output of a bank's internal models for potential future exposure that must be approved by the bank's supervisors. Banks with IMM approval general make a moderate capital saving than under the more basic CEM approach. There are other IMM benefits that will be discussed later in Chapter 18.

Broadly speaking, an IMM implementation allows:

- accurate modelling of all underlying risk factors and the resulting future exposure of all transactions;
- full netting across asset classes as long as certain legal and operational requirements have been met; and
- collateral benefit, including aspects such as threshold and initial margin, and the modelling of future collateral received.

8.3.2   The alpha factor and EEPE

The IMM allows the calculation of an accurate exposure distribution at the counterparty level. However, since the regulatory capital calculation for counterparty risk requires a single EAD value per counterparty,[7] a key aspect of the IMM is being able to represent this distribution in a simple way.

The key basis for defining EAD was provided by Wilde (2001) who showed that it could be defined via the EPE under the following conditions:

- infinitely large portfolio (number of counterparties) of small exposures (i.e. infinite diversification);
- no correlation of exposures; and
- no wrong-way or right-way risk.

Whilst this is only relevant as a theoretical result, it implies that EPE is a good starting point. Picoult (2002) therefore suggests using a correction to account for the deviations from the idealistic situation above.[8] This correction has become known as the α multiplier and corrects for the finite size and concentration of the portfolio in question. Banks using the IMM have an option to compute their own estimate of α with a methodology that is approved by their regulator and subject to a floor of 1.2. However, this is relatively

---

[7] This is certainly the case for the default risk capital charge (CCR capital charge), but EAD is not used directly for the advanced CVA capital charge (see Section 8.7.3).

[8] According to Picoult (2002), alpha "expresses the difference between calculating economic capital with full simulation and with a simulation assuming the exposure profile of each counterparty can be represented by a fixed exposure profile".

uncommon[9] and most banks with IMM approval use a supervisory value, which is typically set to 1.4 or more.

Spreadsheet 8.2   Calculation of "alpha" factor

Table 8.2 shows some published estimates of α and Table 8.3 shows the value as a function of various portfolio inputs using Spreadsheet 8.1. We can see that the following aspects will all cause a decrease in the value of alpha:[10]

- larger portfolio;
- larger average default probabilities;
- larger correlations; and
- higher confidence levels.

Table 8.2   Regulatory results and published estimates of α. The study of Wilde (2005) includes wrong-way risk whilst the ISDA survey involved four banks making estimates based on their own portfolios and internal models.

	Alpha
Infinitely large ideal portfolio	1.0
Canabarro et al. (2003)	1.09
Wilde (2005)	1.21
ISDA (2003)	1.07–1.10
Regulatory prescribed value	1.4
Supervisory floor (if using own estimation)	1.2
Possible values for concentrated portfolios	2.5 or more

Table 8.3   Illustration of change in alpha values computed for different portfolio characteristics (size, default probability and correlation).

Portfolio size	Alpha	Default probability	Alpha	Correlation	Alpha	Confidence level	Alpha
50	1.45	0.5%	1.45	0%	1.80	90%	1.27
75	1.39	1.0%	1.35	10%	1.39	95%	1.26
100	1.25	1.5%	1.25	20%	1.25	99%	1.25
200	1.09	2.0%	1.16	30%	1.12	99.9%	1.22
400	1.04	2.5%	1.15	40%	1.05	99.97%	1.21

---

[9] For example, in the survey results shown in Figure 8.2, only one IMM bank reported using their own model to estimate α.

[10] We can also note that, as shown by Canabarro et al. (2003), the dispersion of exposures in a portfolio also causes the alpha value to increase. This is not surprising since it is a similar impact to decreasing the size of the portfolio.

Regulators made one other conservative modification under the IMM by requiring banks to use effective EPE (EEPE), which is, by definition, the same or higher than the EPE. EEPE was defined in Section 7.2.8 and is intended to capture[11] the roll-off impact for transactions that are close to maturity but may, in practice, be replaced. This is particularly true for portfolios such as, for example, short-dated FX positions. It could be argued that EEPE may sometimes be unnecessarily conservative. For example, a profile with a spike in exposure for a very short period (due, for example, to large cashflows) will create an EEPE that is much higher than the EPE.

Finally, the exposure at default under IMM is defined as:

$$EAD = \alpha \times EEPE \tag{8.6}$$

Since EAD is calculated at the netting set level, in contrast to the CEM, full cross-product netting and proper collateral modelling is allowable. Given the potential benefits of netting and collateral, this is clearly highly advantageous. Note that banks have also been allowed to use the so-called short-cut method for collateral modelling under the IMM but this is becoming less common and is also less relevant with the implementation of SA-CCR.

8.4 STANDARDISED APPROACH FOR COUNTERPARTY CREDIT RISK (SA-CCR)

8.4.1 Background

The CEM (and to some extent the SM mentioned in Section 8.1.4) has a number of shortcomings in its estimation of EAD:

- The add-ons were calibrated many years ago and do not reflect volatilities observed over recent stress periods, especially during the global financial crisis.
- The nature of the add-on methodology does not capture the fact that off-market transactions (negative MTM) should have a lower exposure than the equivalent par transactions.
- The recognition of netting benefits is simplistic and may produce estimates that are rather conservative for netting sets with strong netting benefit (offsetting and hedging transactions).
- The treatment of collateral is also simplistic and does not account for the benefit of receiving collateral in the future, and overcollateralisation (e.g. initial margin).

In order to address the above points, the SA-CCR (standardised approach for counterparty credit risk) has been developed to replace the CEM (and SM) methodologies from January 2017. In developing the SA-CCR, the aim was to introduce more risk sensitivity without introducing significantly greater complexity. The SA-CCR has also been conservatively calibrated to IMM results benchmarked from banks.

Note that the introduction of the SA-CCR has two general objectives: firstly to provide a simple but risk-sensitive capital methodology for bilateral OTC derivatives, and

---

[11] It could also be seen as assuming some worst-case default time within the one-year interval considered.

secondly to provide a similar more risk-sensitive foundation for the capital rules for central counterparties, which until 2017 are also based on the highly simplistic CEM (discussed in more detail in Gregory, 2014).

The benefits of the SA-CCR over the CEM are:

- a smoother representation of maturity;
- a better recognition of netting (although, as discussed below, netting is limited to products in the same asset class);
- more risk-sensitive treatment of collateral, in particular initial margin; and
- a recognition of negative MTM.

In general, the above points will tend to reduce capital but since there has been a reappraisal of the underlying calibration, the SA-CCR will potentially give higher capital requirements due to the use of more conservative parameters.[12]

Below is a basic overview of the key components of the SA-CCR. However, the methodology contains a reasonable amount of detail regarding aspects such as forward starting transactions, options and CDO tranches that are not explained. The reader is referred to BCBS (2014d) for more precise details. Some of the terminology below is shared with BCBS (2014d), but some additional terms are mentioned for explanation purposes.

8.4.2   Basic approach

The SA-CCR approach like the CEM treats the exposure at default as a combination of the RC and PFE.

$$EAD = \alpha \times (RC + PFE) \tag{8.7}$$

where the factor α is used to be consistent with the IMM methodology discussed in the last section and is therefore set to 1.4. It may seem surprisingly that the current MTM is essentially inflated by this factor but this is necessary to be consistent with the $\alpha \times EEPE$ treatment in the IMM (Equation 8.6). For non-collateralised transactions, the RC is defined by the netted MTM of the underlying contracts as in the CEM (Section 8.2.1). The PFE is essentially linked to $AddOn$ factors like in the CEM but also has direct sensitivity to the maturity of the contract. The $AddOn$ for a given transaction is:

$$AddOn_i = SF_i \times SD_i \tag{8.8}$$

where SF_i is a supervisory factor depending on the asset class and intended to capture a loss over a one-year (uncollateralised) or shorter (collateralised) period, and SD_i is an approximate measure of the duration.[13] An at market (zero MTM) seven-year interest rate swap (duration 5.91) would have a value of 2.95% (to be compared to the CEM equivalent of 1.5% in Table 8.1), since the supervisory factor for interest rates is 0.5%. This illustrates the generally more conservative underlying calibration of the SA-CCR.

---

[12] For example, see "Counterparty calamity: inside Basel's new standard charge", *Risk*, 26th June 2015.
[13] $SD_i = [1 - \exp(-0.05 \times M_i)]/0.05$ with M_i the maturity.

8.4.3   Netting

The treatment of netting in the SA-CCR is much more sophisticated than the basic NGR formula in the CEM (Equation 8.3). It is based on the concept of a hedging set, which is a representation of transactions with similar risk sensitivities. Within a hedging set, either full or partial netting is allowed depending on the underlying type or maturity. The hedging sets and offsets are defined within each of five asset classes as follows:

- *Interest rate*. Hedging sets are defined by currency and three maturity buckets: up to one year, one to five years and over five years. Full offset is given to transactions in the same maturity bucket whilst partial netting is achieved for transactions in different buckets. This partial netting is defined by correlations of 70% between the adjacent buckets and 30% otherwise.[14]
- *FX*. A hedging set is defined by all transactions referencing the same currency pair. Full netting is available within each hedging set and zero otherwise.
- *Credit and equity*. Each of these asset classes represents a hedging set. Full offset is allowed between transactions referencing the same name or index. Partial offset is allowed between other transactions with correlations of 64% (index, index), 40% (index, single name) and 25% (single-name, single-name).
- *Commodity*. There are four hedging sets (energy, metals, agriculture, other). Within a hedging set, full netting applies to transactions referencing the same commodity and partial netting applies otherwise (with a correlation of 16%).

Note that with respect to the correlations above, BCBS (2014d) essentially defines a systematic factor for each netting set that must be multiplied to get the correlation (for example, for single-name and index equity this gives $80\% \times 50\% = 40\%$). Supervisory factors for defining the PFE are defined for each of the hedging sets above with those for credit further divided by rating.

The above correlations specify the netting effect but must be combined with the direction of the underlying transactions, which is done via a delta adjustment. For linear transactions (not options or CDO tranches), delta is either $+1$ or -1 depending on whether or not the transaction is long[15] or short in the primary risk factor. Delta therefore serves two purposes:

- it specifies the direction of the trade with respect to the primary risk factor; and
- it serves as a scaling factor for trades that are non-linear in the primary risk factor (e.g. options).

For options and CDO tranches, the precise calculation of delta is covered in more detail in BCBS (2014d).

---

[14] Note that these correlations were calibrated to a continuous representation of correlation but this bucketing approach is used for tractability.

[15] Long (short) meaning that the MTM increases (decreases) as the primary risk factor increases.

8.4.4 Collateral

SA-CCR treatment of collateral accounts for the presence of both variation and initial margins in different ways. Haircuts are applied to convert non-cash collateral into cash equivalents: these haircuts reduce (increase) the value of collateral received (posted).

A key component is the net independent collateral amount (*NICA*), which defines a net amount of collateral that will available in default (it does not include variation margin). Referring to Equation 7.6 and the related discussion in last chapter:

$$NICA = CR - CP_{NS} \tag{8.9}$$

which is the collateral received (*CR*) less the non-segregated collateral posted (*CP*$_{NS}$). Any segregated collateral posted to the counterparty is ignored since it is assumed to be bankruptcy remote and returned in a default scenario. In our terminology, *NICA* refers to initial margin but BCBS (2014d) does not define it as such due to the different terminology used (such as "independent amount"). Note that *NICA* can be negative if a relatively large amount of initial margin is posted and not segregated. However, under bilateral rules (Section 6.7), posted initial margin must be segregated and therefore *NICA* would probably correspond only to the initial margin received.

In the presence of collateral, the first question is how to define the replacement cost. This is taken to be the higher value of:

- the current collateralised exposure (including variation margin and *NICA*); and
- the maximum possible uncollateralised exposure, which is the highest exposure that would not trigger a variation margin call (taking into account thresholds (*TH*), minimum transfer amounts (*MTA*) and initial margin).

Furthermore, the *RC* cannot be negative, and so:

$$RC = \max(V - C, TH + MTA - NICA, 0) \tag{8.10}$$

As an example, assume that $V = 7$, $C = 0$, $TH = 10$, $MTA = 1$ and $NICA = 0$. Although the current exposure is 7, the *RC* is 11 to represent the fact that the exposure could get to this level without collateral (variation margin) being received (note that threshold and minimum transfer amounts are treated as additive in a CSA – Section 6.2.5). The above representation can be quite conservative where relatively large threshold and/or minimum transfer is in place but bilateral rules (Section 6.7) specify these to be zero and €500,000 respectively.

The PFE for collateralised transactions can be multiplied by a factor of

$$\frac{3}{2}\sqrt{MPR/250} \tag{8.11}$$

where the margin period of risk (MPR) is typically ten business days for bilateral OTC derivatives (see discussion in Section 6.6.2). The above factor adjusts for the shorter risk horizon for collateralised transactions and will be discussed in more detail in Chapter 11. For the example of the interest rate swap mentioned in Section 8.4.2, the PFE would reduce[16] from 2.95% to 0.89% (the CEM equivalent would be 1.5% as in Table 8.1, since no benefit for collateral is recognised).

8.4.5   Overcollateralisation and negative MTM

A final component of the SA-CCR is the recognition of overcollateralisation (initial margin) and netting sets that are out-of-the-money (negative current MTM). Note that these two effects are similar because in both cases an increase in MTM will not cause an increase in exposure. SA-CCR allows this to be recognised via a multiplier of:

$$\min\left(1; Floor + (1 - Floor) \times \exp\left(\frac{V - C}{2 \times (1 - Floor) \times AddOn^{aggregate}}\right)\right) \qquad (8.12)$$

where *Floor* is 5% and $AddOn^{aggregate}$ is the total add-on for the netting set after application of the rules described in Section 8.4.3. The term $V - C$ can be negative due to a (uncollateralised) negative MTM netting set and/or the presence of initial margin in the total collateral determined by C. This will then cause a reduction in the add-on. Note that positive MTM benefits (Section 7.4.3) are not recognised and the presence of the floor means that the capital cannot go to zero, even in the case of a very large initial margin or extremely negative MTM.

8.5   COMPARISON OF EAD METHODS

Comparison of capital methodologies is difficult due to the different asset classes and number of different effects (e.g. MTM, netting and collateral) to consider. For this reason, we will base the results below on a simple interest rate swap example but will consider a number of important risk-mitigation effects. Note also that the IMM results are subject to a particular implementation that depends on the modelling and calibration choice made but is intended to be representative of a typical IMM approach (the currency chosen was US dollars). By contract, the CEM and SA-CCR approaches are prescriptive and currency-independent.

8.5.1   Impact of maturity

We consider the EAD of a par (zero MTM) interest rate swap with a notional of 1,000 as a function of maturity in Figure 8.4. The discrete behaviour of the CEM approach is due to the granularity of the add-ons calibrated to a continuous representation of correlation but this bucketing approach is used (Table 8.1). The SA-CCR shows a more realistic shape, which is comparable to the more sophisticated IMM method. Also noticeable is the more conservative nature of the SA-CCR calibration.

---

[16] Calculated from $1.5 \times \sqrt{(10/250)} = 0.3$.

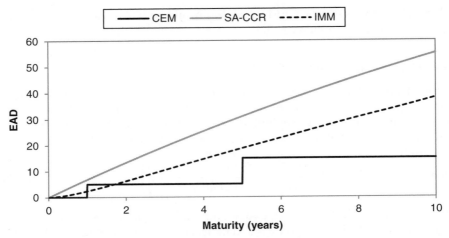

Figure 8.4   EAD for a ten-year USD par interest rate swap with a notional of 1,000 as a function of maturity for three possible regulatory capital approaches.

8.5.2 Collateral

Figure 8.5 shows the same result as the previous section but assumes a collateral agreement is in place. Specifically, we assume a two-way CSA with a zero threshold, zero minimum transfer amount and a MPR of ten (business) days. This reduces the IMM and SA-CCR results substantially, in the former case due to full collateral modelling whereas in the latter it arises due to the factor of 0.3 defined by Equation 8.11. The CEM approach gives no benefit for future collateral received and therefore the results are unchanged (since the MTM of the swap is zero then current collateral is not relevant).

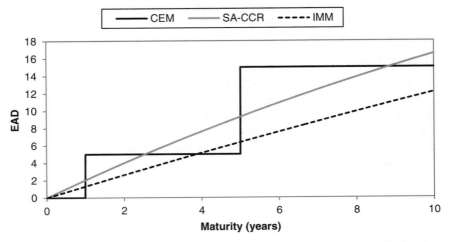

Figure 8.5   EAD for a ten-year USD collateralised par interest rate swap with a notional of 1,000 as a function of maturity for three possible regulatory capital approaches.

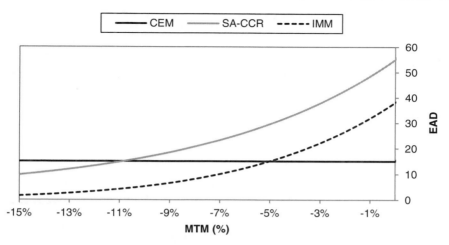

Figure 8.6   EAD for a ten-year USD off market interest rate swap with a notional of 1,000 as a function of maturity for three possible regulatory capital approaches.

8.5.3   Negative MTM

Another difficult aspect of a regulatory capital approach is to give benefit for the fact that off-market transactions generally have smaller PFEs (Section 7.4.3). This is particularly the case for transactions with negative MTM, which is considered in the example in Figure 8.6. Whilst the IMM captures the reduction in EAD, the CEM does not, as it makes no correction for negative replacement cost (see Equation 8.5). The SA-CCR does a reasonable job of reproducing the IMM behaviour although it is high in comparison: this is due to the relatively conservative add-on and floor included in Equation 8.12.

8.5.4   Initial margin and threshold

Initial margins and thresholds create over- and undercollaterlisation respectively. Figure 8.7 shows the impact of both, in each case assuming a two-way CSA with minimum transfer amount of zero (and zero threshold posting in the case of the initial margin).

The impact of initial margin is similar to the negative MTM considered above. This is captured quite well by the SA-CCR with the presence of the 5% floor again apparent. The CEM does not recognise overcollateralisation since the replacement cost cannot be negative, as discussed in Section 8.2.2. Since initial margins will become increasingly common (Section 6.7), this is clearly important.

The CEM does not treat the threshold case since no collateral benefit is given. The SA-CCR approach is quite conservative, since it assumes that the replacement cost will be exactly at the point where the threshold (plus any minimum transfer amount) is breached. Indeed, at a high enough threshold (30 and above) the SA-CCR collateralised EAD is bigger than the uncollateralised one, and the latter can therefore be used). Given material positive thresholds are becoming less important in collateral agreements, the relatively conservative behaviour of the SA-CCR in this regard is perhaps not of such great concern.

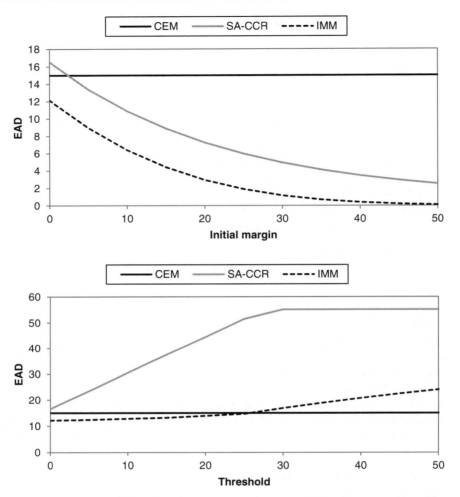

Figure 8.7   EAD for a ten-year USD interest rate swap with a notional of 1,000 as a function of a bilateral initial margin (top) and threshold (bottom) for three possible regulatory capital approaches.

8.5.5   Netting

Finally, we consider the impact of netting by using two interest rate swaps that are offsetting (i.e. one paying and the other receiving the fixed rate) in the same and different currencies. We hold the maturity of one swap fixed at ten years and vary the other between zero and 20 years to see the netting impact in each of the three methodologies (Figure 8.8).

In the case of the same currency, the CEM approach is very poor, since it gives a 60% netting regardless of the maturity mismatch and therefore shows the wrong behaviour entirely. The SA-CCR gives netting benefit since the swaps are in the same hedging set and matches the IMM results quite well. A noticeable aspect is the discontinuities at one and five years due to the three maturity buckets used by the SA-CCR. It could also be commented that the SA-CCR does not recognise the decorrelation of tenors when

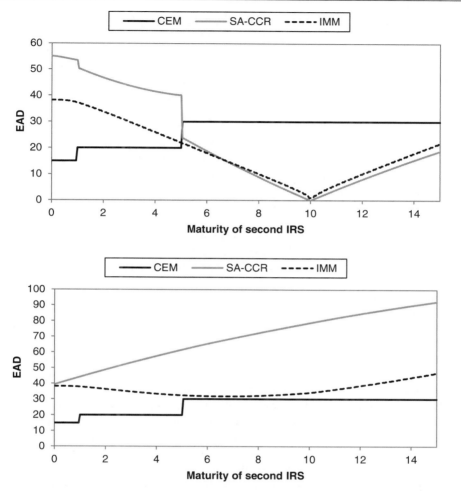

Figure 8.8   EAD for two offsetting interest rate swaps in the same currency (top) and different currencies (bottom) each with a notional of 1,000 as a function of the maturity of one swap (the other has a maturity of ten years) for three possible regulatory capital approaches.

the second swap has a maturity above ten years, which may be why the IMM results are higher in this region. For the swaps in different currencies, the SA-CCR appears too conservative compared to the IMM due to treating them in different hedging sets and giving no netting benefit.

8.6   BASEL III

8.6.1   Overview

As discussed in Chapter 1, the global financial crisis brought about regulatory changes, many of which aimed to reduce counterparty risk in OTC derivative markets. Two very significant initiatives in this respect are the clearing mandate (CCPs are discussed in the next chapter) and the bilateral collateral (margin) rules (Section 7.6). Additionally, under the Basel III (BCBS, 2009; BCBS 2011b) rules, the capital requirements for OTC derivatives will increase. A large portion of the Basel III changes relate to counterparty risk and credit value adjustment (CVA). In this section, we will explain the aspects of Basel III that concern counterparty risk that took effect from 1st January 2013 onwards (depending on the region). A brief summary of the changes (note that some affect over-all credit risk also) is given below:

- *Asset correlation multiplier.* Due to the view that financial firms are significantly interconnected, the correlation parameter in the Basel II IRB formula (Section 8.1.2) will be increased by a multiplier of 1.25 for regulated financial institutions whose total assets are greater than or equal to $100 billion, and also unregulated financial institutions. Note that this change is for credit risk capital in general and not specific to counterparty risk.
- *IMM methodologies.* This applies to banks with IMM approval for computing EAD.
  - ○ *Stressed EPE.* Expected positive exposure (EPE) must be calculated with parameters calibrated based on stressed data. This has arisen due to the procyclical issues of using historical data where non-volatile markets lead to smaller risk numbers, which in turn reduce capital requirements. This use of stressed data is also intended to capture general wrong-way risk.
  - ○ *Backtesting.* Validation of EPE models must involve backtesting up to a time horizon of at least one year.
  - ○ *Increased MPR.* In certain situations, the minimum MPR must be increased from ten days to 20 days or more. This has arisen due to the realisation that collateral management practices during the crisis were sometimes extremely suboptimal and issues such as collateral disputes severely influenced the timely receipt of collateral.
  - ○ *No recognition of triggers.* Under the IMM methodology, any reduction in exposure at default, due to the ability to change collateral requirements based on deterioration in counterparty credit quality, is not allowable. The basis of this preclusion is clearly due to situations such as AIG and monoline insurers (Section 6.2.2), where even an innocuous rating downgrade (e.g. triple- to double-A) caused a death spiral effect and, hence, was useless as a risk mitigant. A party may still potentially incorporate mitigants, such as rating triggers, into their documentation, pricing and valuation, but they cannot model any beneficial effects for capital purposes.
- *Stress-testing.* An increased focus on the stress-testing of counterparty risk exposures.
- *Specific wrong-way risk.* There must be procedures for identifying and dealing with specific wrong-way risk. Experiences with, for example, monoline insurers have shown the potentially devastating impact of ignoring such aspects.
- *CVA capital charge.* A capital charge must be included to account for CVA volatility, in *addition* to the current charges against counterparty risk.

The above will all increase counterparty risk capital requirements, via the additional CVA capital charge and also some more conservative assumptions in the EAD method-ologies. This, in turn, may incentivise active counterparty risk management (e.g. CVA hedging), and an increase in collateralisation and greater use of CCPs in order to benefit from the capital relief afforded in these situations. Note that introduction of the SA-CCR approach from 2017 (Section 8.4) as a more risk sensitive approach is also related to these changes. The SA-CCR is potentially more conservative for uncollateralised transactions but gives benefit to collateral (including initial margin).

The next sections discuss some of the above changes in more detail and Section 8.7 provides more detail on the CVA capital charge.

8.6.2 Stressed EPE

The requirements over stressed EPE parallel the rules introduced for market risk under Basel 2.5 (BCBS, 2011a). The danger in calibrating risk models with relatively recent historical data is that benign and quiet periods tend to precede major crises. This means that risk measures are particularly low at the worst possible time. The higher leverage levels that such low-risk measures ultimately allow may increase the likelihood and severity of any crisis. This problem is typically known as procyclicality.

In order to remedy for the above problem, it is necessary for IMM banks to use stressed inputs (e.g. volatility and correlation) when computing EPE. These stressed inputs must use three years of historical data that include a one-year period of stress (typically defined as increasing CDS spreads) or, alternatively, market-implied data from a stressed period. This stressed period must be used in addition to the "normal" period of at least three years of historical data, which itself should cover a full range of economic conditions (EBA, 2015b; note that most banks currently use a stress period around 2008–2009). The exposure at default must be on the set of parameters that result in the highest EPE at the portfolio (not by counterparty) level, i.e. the maximum[17] of the normal and stressed exposure calculations. It is not clear how often this comparison needs to be made, which is to be defined by the regulator. Daily comparisons could be computationally intensive and lead to unnecessary volatility in the EPE.

The use of the stressed period should reduce procyclicality problems by ensuring that EPE does not become artificially low during quiet periods in financial markets. In addition, it is viewed that the use of stressed EPE should improve the coverage of general wrong-way risk, as the dependencies that contribute to this may be more apparent in stressed periods. Otherwise the treatment of general wrong-way risk as EPE multiplied by the α factor is unchanged, except for some points related to the robust calculation of α.[18]

8.6.3   Increased margin period of risk

In certain situations, the MPR must be increased from a minimum of 10 days for OTC derivatives (discussed in Section 6.6.2). These situations are:

- For all netting sets[19] where the number of trades exceeds 5,000 at any point during a quarter, a longer 20-day period should apply for the following quarter.
- For netting sets containing one or more trades involving either illiquid collateral or an OTC derivative that cannot easily be replaced.

---

[17] Note that this is in contrast to the sum of stressed and non-stressed CVA capital charge discussed later.

[18] In particular, it seems banks cannot attain IMM approval without modelling wrong-way risk in some way.

[19] Note that the margin period of risk applies to netting sets and not at the counterparty level (unless there is only one netting set).

- If there have been more than two margin call disputes on a particular netting set over the previous two quarters that have lasted longer than the original margin period of risk (before consideration of this provision), then the period must be at least doubled.

This will obviously require more data to determine the appropriate margin period of risk for each netting set. Note that the margin period of risk must also include the contractual collateral posting frequency of N days. If this is not daily (N=1), then the period assumed must be increased by a further N – 1 days.

Whether or not the above rules are improving collateral management practices is not clear as there are potential problems and ambiguities with the above requirements. For example, if only a small fraction of the collateral is illiquid then the 20-day period assumed would be rather punitive. There could also be excess volatility from netting sets on the boundary (e.g. close to 5,000 trades) having unpleasant EAD variability from switching between ten and 20 days. Finally, market participants may behave sub-optimally, such as not disputing a collateral call to avoid triggering the move to a 20-day period, becoming less active in collateral management but reducing capital.

8.6.4   Backtesting

The Basel III required backtesting of EPE models follows the requirements over (market risk) VAR approaches. A backtesting procedure that could apply to quantile measures such as VAR or PFE is illustrated in Figure 8.9. VAR is typically defined as a 99% confidence level over a one-day time horizon.[20] Assuming that independence of daily forecasts would imply a simple binomial distribution for exceedances or violations, the expected number of violations over an annual period (250 business days) would be 2.5 and, to a

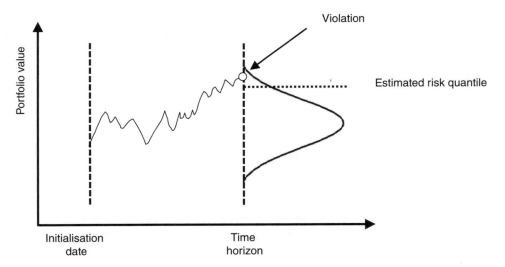

Figure 8.9   Illustration of backtesting via comparing a realised path, at some time horizon, to the estimated risk measure (assumed to be a quantile).

---

[20] This can then be scaled to the required ten-day interval, as mentioned previously.

95% confidence level, violations above six or below one are rejected.[21] The backtesting of VAR models is therefore relatively straightforward. Due to the nature of VAR, the severity of a violation does not need to be considered.

Backtesting of EPE is more challenging than that of market risk VAR for a variety of reasons:

- Multiple time horizons must be considered, which require more data to be stored and processed. The need to look at longer time horizons implies that a much larger historical dataset is used and creates problems with effects such as ageing. It is also necessary to keep track of the quarterly recalibration of EPE models.[22]
- Backtesting must be done for different portfolios of trades, as EPE is defined at the counterparty (or netting set) level. However, such portfolios cannot be assumed independent. For example, if one portfolio contains the hedges of another, then they will never be expected to have a high exposure at the same time.
- Measures such as EPE are based on expectations and not a quantile (which defines VAR). Non-quantile-based quantities are harder to backtest.

There are a number of considerations that are necessary to cope realistically with the above (see also the discussion in BCBS, 2010c). One is the use of overlapping windows (see Figure 8.10). However, it is then important to deal with the dependence of data (e.g. exceeding an exposure in one period leads to a greater likelihood of exceedance in an overlapping period). This leads to difficulties, as most simple statistical tests are based on the assumption of independent observations.

Backtesting should first be done at the risk factor level. The aim of this is to test the distributional assumptions for each risk factor individually and avoid the potential for these to be diluted or masked at the portfolio level. Secondly, backtesting must be done at the netting set or portfolio level. Assuming the risk factor backtesting shows acceptable results then the portfolio-level backtesting is relevant for testing the ability to capture important co-dependencies between different risk factors.

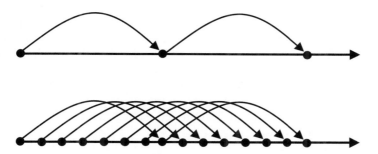

Figure 8.10   Use of non-overlapping (top) and overlapping (bottom) windows for backtesting.

---

[21] This can be shown via the relevant binomial probabilities or more robustly using the two-tailed approach of Kupiec (1995).

[22] For example, a three-month and six-month distribution generated today will be inconsistent with the three-month distribution generated three months from now, since a recalibration of the model will be performed.

Backtesting must involve multiple time horizons, up to at least one year, and multiple initialisation points. Furthermore, using different quantiles can effectively test across the whole exposure distribution. To simplify the workload, given the millions of transactions that may exist within a typical large OTC derivatives book, it is possible to backtest "representative portfolios". Such representative portfolios must be chosen based on their sensitivity to the significant risk factors and correlations to which a bank is exposed. This could be done via regression methods, principal components analysis or may be rather more ad hoc (e.g. based on the largest counterparties, exposures or overall capital contributions). Once representative portfolios have been chosen, a typical backtesting exercise may use, for example, tenors defined at (1W, 2W, 1M, 3M, 6M, 1Y, 2Y) and test 1%, 5%, 25%, 75%, 95% and 99% quantiles with weekly initialisation points. The data and systems implications of doing this are considerable. In addition, representative portfolios should presumably be reviewed on a periodic basis. Whilst a typical portfolio will not change materially over the short term, any large market move or significant trading in a particular asset class may create sensitivities in a bank's portfolio that need to be included in the representative portfolios.

8.6.5   Wrong-way risk

Wrong-way risk (WWR) is the term generally used to describe positive co-dependency between exposure and the credit quality of the counterparty, i.e. the exposure increases as the probability of default of the counterparty increases. Basel III characterises two broad forms of WWR:

- *General WWR.* This is driven by macroeconomic behaviour (for example, the fact that credit spreads and interest rate moves exhibit co-dependency).
- *Specific WWR.* This is related to the structural nature of individual trades or counterparty exposures (for example, a company writing put options on its own stock).

For IMM banks, general WWR is viewed as being partly captured by the stressed EPE calculation (Section 8.6.2). However, on top of this it may be necessary to incorporate a modelling of general WWR, driven by macroeconomic factors such as correlations between exposure drivers and credit spreads in the IMM exposure simulation (discussed later in Chapter 17). General WWR can also be included directly in the estimation of the α multiplier (Section 8.3.2). Clearly, a bank's regulator has the ability to impose a higher α if they are not comfortable with the coverage of general WWR elsewhere.

Whilst non-IMM banks are not required to implement any modelling of WWR, there is a greater burden in terms of identification and management, including the following with respect to general WWR:

- identification of exposures that give rise to a greater degree of general WWR;
- the design of stress tests and scenario analysis that specifically include WWR factor evolution (e.g. credit spreads strongly correlated with interest rates or FX moves);
- continuous monitoring of WWR by region, industry and other categories; and
- generation of reports for appropriate senior management and board members explaining WWR and mitigating action being taken.

Basel III seems to view specific WWR as being often due to badly designed transactions, which potentially should not even exist. It requires that there must be procedures in place to identify, monitor and control cases of specific wrong-way risk for each legal entity. Transactions with counterparties, where specific wrong-way risk has been identified, need to be treated differently when calculating the EAD for such exposures:

- each separate legal entity to which the bank is exposed must be separately rated and there must be policies regarding the treatment of a connected group of entities for the identification of specific WWR;
- transactions with counterparties where specific WWR has been identified need to be treated differently when calculating the EAD for such exposures; and
- instruments for which there exists a legal connection between the counterparty and the underlying issuer, and for which specific WWR has been identified, should not be considered to be in the same netting set as other transactions with the counterparty.

Furthermore, for single-name credit default swaps, where there exists a legal connection between the counterparty and the underlying issuer, and where specific wrong-way risk has been identified, the EAD should be 100%, less any current losses accounted for (e.g. via CVA). This is applied for other products also, such as equity derivatives, bond options and securities financing transactions that reference a single company, which has a legal connection to the counterparty. In such a case the EAD must be defined assuming a default of the underlying security.[23]

Whilst this treatment of specific wrong-way risk appears quite straightforward, it does create requirements in having the ability to have the correct legal information. Furthermore, it must be possible to define netting sets based on wrong-way risk rather than legal data alone.

8.6.6   Stress testing

Basel III makes more formalised requirements around stress tests, with the need to stress all principal market risk factors (interest rates, FX, equities, credit spreads and commodity prices) and assess material non-directional risks, such as curve and basis risks, at least quarterly. Other requirements noted by the BCBS include:

- proactively identify concentrations to specific directional sensitivities and concentrations of risk among industries and regions;
- identify general WWR by considering exposure and counterparty credit quality jointly in stress tests, which can give insights into WWR scenarios through a joint specification of market and credit events;
- concurrent stress testing of exposure and non-cash collateral for assessing wrong-way risk;
- stress-testing of CVA to assess performance under adverse scenarios, incorporating any hedging mismatches (severe historic or potential economic events may be considered); and
- integration of counterparty risk stress tests into firm-wide stress tests. Reverse stress testing (where scenarios are designed that create certain predefined losses) should also be used.

---

[23] The LGD must be set to 100% regardless of using a lower value elsewhere.

Some general principles for the design of a stress-testing framework are:

- *Multiple approaches.* Stress tests can be a combination of model-based scenarios, historical events and hypothetical scenarios.
- *Consistent definitions.* Scenarios should be consistent rather than being based on sets of independent and potentially misaligned moves.
- *Multiple specification methods.* There should be multiple methods for generating shocks to market variables.

A high-level framework for a counterparty risk stress testing programme may focus on:

- *Individual market risk stresses.* Separate stresses applied to individual market risk factors and their volatilities.
- *Multidimensional stress scenarios.* Joint movements of all market risk factors. Due to the exponentially increasing number of combinations, this is often best defined by a historical period such as around the Lehman Brothers bankruptcy.
- *Credit risk stresses.* Scenarios based upon defaults and credit migrations (generated, for example, via stressed default probabilities and default correlations) together with an assumed credit spread widening.
- *Market and credit stresses.* Joint co-movement of market and credit risk factors, such as interest rates and credit spreads.
- *Collateral stresses.* Scenarios based upon the movement in the value of collateral and choices of counterparties to post/substitute various collateral types.

The results of various stress tests can be shown in a number of different ways such as through MTM changes, capital changes and impact on collateral requirements.

8.7   CVA CAPITAL CHARGE

8.7.1   Rationale

The objective of the CVA capital charge is to supplement the Basel II requirements, which capitalise only potential losses due to default (and credit migration). In BCBS (2009) it is stated that, in the preceding crisis period, only one-third of counterparty risk-related losses were due to defaults, with the remaining two-thirds being MTM-based. This is clearly a very important statement, as it implies that capital for counterparty risk needs to be approximately trebled. Importantly, Basel III increases counterparty risk capital requirements primarily via a new and additional component related to CVA rather than, for example, simply imposing a higher multiplier or more conservative application of existing rules.

The precise empirical evidence for the value of two-thirds is not published, and it likely depends on aspects such as banks unwinding trades with monoline insurers (see Section 2.2). The highly distressed nature of monolines at the time could be used to argue that these were, in fact, more akin to default losses. Nevertheless, it seems hard to argue against the fact that CVA accounting volatility represents a substantial risk and, as such, must be capitalised. This risk is most obviously represented by the VAR, since CVA can be seen as a market risk for the trading book of a bank. Clearly calculating the

Table 8.4   Approaches used for the default risk and CVA capital charges.

	Default risk capital charge	CVA capital charge
IMM approval and specific risk approval	IMM	Advanced
IMM approval only No IMM approval	CEM or SA-CCR	Standardised

VAR of CVA is a challenging task and, as with EAD, there need to be different methodologies to suit the larger banks with sophisticated internal models and banks that do not have the resources and/or incentive to develop these.

Two factors are important in determining the approach that a bank will use for the CVA capital charge:

- *IMM approval.* Whether or not the bank has IMM approval for counterparty risk.
- *Specific risk approval.* Whether a bank has approval to use a specific risk VAR model. This model would basically allow a joint simulation of credit spreads of counterparties, which is clearly relevant in the case of quantifying CVA capital.

Table 8.4 describes the methodologies used for the default risk (sometimes referred to as CCR) and CVA capital charges. As discussed above, banks with approval may use their own IMM approach to define the default risk capital charge (via EAD). Otherwise they must use a simpler methodology that is probably the CEM and from 2017 will be the SA-CCR. Regarding CVA capital, if a bank has IMM approval for counterparty risk and specific risk approval (discussed more below), then they use the advanced CVA capital charge. If they do not have one or both of these approvals, then they use the standardised CVA capital charge. Note that the standardised CVA capital charge relies on the definition of EAD, which may make IMM approval even more desirable since a more simplistic EAD approach such as CEM will drive both the default risk and CVA capital charges.

The discussion below will show the formulas and requirements for CVA capital under Basel III but will include some interpretation and analysis that, although not particularly subjective, is not from BCBS (2009). The reader is also referred to Pykhtin (2012) for an analysis of the standardised formula. Finally, it should be noted that the BCBS have recently released a consultative document for an alternative specification of the CVA capital change (BCBS 2015). This may eventually resolve some of the criticisms discussed in Section 8.7.5.

8.7.2   Standardised formula

For more mathematical details showing derivation of the formulas below see Pykhtin (2012). For banks without the relevant IMM approvals a fairly simple formula is used to define the CVA capital charge. In order to explain more easily, we first show the formula for capital (K) assuming there are no CDS hedges involved (although this is not shown in BCBS 2009):

$$K = 2.33\sqrt{h} \sqrt{\left(\sum_i 0.5.X_i \right)^2 + \sum_i 0.75.X_i^2} \tag{8.13}$$

With the following definitions:

h relevant time interval which is set to 1 year.
n the total number of counterparties.
X_i the variability in the CVA.

The above formula can be interpreted as a simple representation of the worst case move in the CVA over a time horizon of one year and a confidence level of 99% (this is represented by 2.33 for a normal distribution). The movement in the CVA is represented by X_i, which is a product of three terms:

$$X_i = w_i . M_i . EAD_i^{total}$$

w_i a weight depending on the rating of the counterparty i. The weights are 0.7%, 0.7%, 0.8%, 1.0%, 2.0%, 3.0% and 10.0% for AAA, AA, A, BBB, BB, B and CCC ratings, respectively. This is most obviously interpreted as representing the (annual) credit spread volatility of the counterparty, with worse ratings having a higher volatility

M_i The effective maturity, which approximately represents the duration of the exposure to the counterparty (a longer duration will mean more volatility).

EAD_i^{total} The total exposure including netting and collateral for the netting set in question for the counterparty defined according to whatever method is used (CEM, SA-CCR, IMM).

The formula can be thought of as attempting to quantify in simple terms the increase in CVA from a widening in the credit spread of the counterparties. However, these credit spreads will not be perfectly correlated and there will be a diversification effect. This effect can be seen by assuming all counterparties are equivalent and looking at the capital per counterparty:

$$\frac{K}{n} = 2.33 . n^{-1} \sqrt{h} \sqrt{\left(\sum_i 0.5 . X_i \right)^2 + \sum_i 0.75 . X_i^2} \qquad (8.14)$$

$$= 2.33 . \sqrt{h} . X^2 \sqrt{0.25 + 0.75 / n}$$

This shows that the capital charge per counterparty would decrease with increasing numbers of counterparties, approaching a relative value of 0.5 (Figure 8.11). This is a result of an implicit correlation of 25% assumed between the different counterparty positions in the formula. This is most obviously interpreted as a credit spread correlation.

The standardised CVA capital charge formula allows for hedges in the form of single-name and index CDS. With these included the formula is:

$$K = 2.33 \sqrt{h} \sqrt{\left(\sum_i 0.5 . w_i . N_i - \sum_{ind} w_{ind} . M_{ind} . B_{ind} \right)^2 + \sum_i 0.75 . w_i^2 . N_i^2} \qquad (8.15)$$

$$N_i = M_i . EAD_i^{total} - M_i^{hedge} . B_i$$

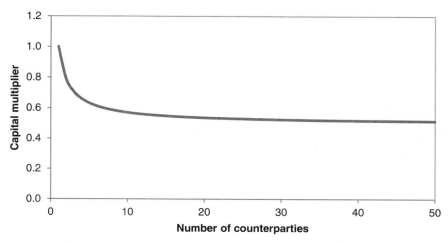

Figure 8.11   Impact of increasing number of counterparties on the standardised CVA capital change per counterparty for a homogenous portfolio. The capital multiplier is defined by $\sqrt{(0.25 + 0.75/n)}$.

with the following additional definitions:

B_i notional of single-name CDS.
B_{ind} notional of index CDS.
M_i^{hedge} maturity of single-name CDS hedge.
M_{ind} weighted maturity of index CDS hedge.

The first and second terms in the above formula can be interpreted as being systematic and idiosyncratic. The factors 0.5 and 0.75 above effectively assume that part of the credit spread component is systemic and, therefore, can be hedged with an index CDS (with adjustments for maturity effects).[24] Index hedges only reduce the systemic term in the formula and not the idiosyncratic one. Single-name CDS can reduce both terms and hence in theory can make the capital for a given counterparty zero if M_i^{hedge} is chosen to make the N_i term above equal zero. Note though that over-hedging, like under-hedging, will increase the capital charge. This penalises an open position (as seen from the formula at least) due to the hedge position being too large. Examples showing the capital relief achievable with single-name and index hedges are shown later in Section 8.7.4.

8.7.3   Advanced approach

As noted above, banks with IMM approval for both counterparty risk and specific risk must use the advanced approach for the CVA capital charge and cannot choose, instead, to adopt the standardised approach.[25]

---

[24] The correlation of 25% between spreads can be seen as being 50% × 50%, since each spread process is driven by a "global" index in a one-factor model.
[25] This is according to the Basel guidelines. Some regulators (e.g. the US) may allow advanced banks to use the standardised formula.

Developing a risk-sensitive methodology for CVA capital represents a significant challenge, since the aim is to quantify the uncertainty of the CVA itself. Computing CVA already requires a Monte Carlo simulation, as will be explained in Chapter 10. There is clearly a need to avoid a methodology requiring multiple Monte Carlo simulations and therefore certain simplifications will be required. The first proposal (BCBS, 2009) suggested a "bond-equivalent approach" as a reasonable simplification, but this received a critical response (e.g. see Rebonato et al., 2010) and the methodology was subsequently refined in the final Basel III rules (BCBS 2011b). Even these final rules have some potential drawbacks, most notably in the fact that they treat market risk hedges incorrectly. This is one reason for the alternative proposals published recently in BCBS (2015).

The advanced CVA capital charge defines CVA as follows:

$$CVA = LGD_{mkt} \sum_{i=1}^{T} PD\left(t_{i-1}, t_i\right)\left(\frac{EE_{i-1}D_{i-1} + EE_i D_i}{2}\right) \tag{8.16}$$

$$PD\left(t_{i-1}, t_i\right) = max\left(0; exp\left(-\frac{s_{i-1}t_{i-1}}{LGD_{mkt}}\right) - exp\left(-\frac{s_i t_i}{LGD_{mkt}}\right)\right)$$

with the following definitions:

LGD_{mkt} the loss given default of the counterparty.
$PD(t_{i-1}, t_i)$ the probability of default in the interval $[t_{i-1}, t_i]$.
s_i the counterparty spread for the tenor t_i.
EE_i the expected exposure at time t_i.
D_i the discount factor at time t_i.

The above can be seen as approximate representation of a one-dimensional integral defined by $[t_0, t_1, \ldots, t_n]$ and is similar to the market standard CVA formula discussed in Chapter 14. The default probability $PD(t_{i-1}, t_i)$ is an approximation based on the spreads at the beginning and end of the interval, and is floored at zero since it is a probability (see Chapter 12 for more discussion). CVA is very clearly defined as a market-implied quantity referencing credit spreads. The loss given default LGD_{mkt} is also supposed to be based on market expectations and not historical estimates that might be used for other capital charges. Note also that the same LGD must be used in both the numerator and denominator of the above formula although BCBS (2012) notes that when the underlying derivatives have a different seniority then this case be reflected. The sensitivity to LGD will be discussed in more detail in Chapter 12.

It is worth emphasising that the CDS spread defined by s_i in the Basel III CVA definition is clearly defined as a market-implied parameter. Indeed, the BCBS (2011b) states:

Whenever the CDS spread of the counterparty is available, this must be used. Whenever such a CDS spread is not available, the bank must use a proxy spread that is appropriate based on the rating, industry and region of the counterparty.

This is important because it implies that, even if a bank relied on historical default probabilities for calculating CVA for accounting purposes, then the CVA capital would need to use market-implied (risk-neutral) probabilities. Another point to note is that the

EE in the equation is the one calculated by an approved capital model (IMM) and not defined by accounting purposes when calculating CVA. This is likely to lead to efforts to align this exposure calculation with the one used by the CVA desk when pricing and hedging. This aspect will be discussed in more detail in Chapter 18.

A critical simplifying assumption is that the exposure (EE_i in Equation 8.16) should be held fixed and only the impact of credit spread changes is considered. This avoids a potentially extremely costly calculation but is a significant approximation because parameters such as interest rates, FX rates and volatilities are assumed to not change and therefore have no impact on CVA volatility. This may at first glance seem plausible, but means that any hedges that apply to the fixed terms (in practical terms, anything except credit hedges) will not be incorporated into the capital methodology. This has an important implication, which is discussed in Section 8.7.5.

With the above definition of CVA, the advanced approach requires a bank to use their VAR engine to calculate CVA VAR directly with the aforementioned simplification of fixed exposure. Formulas for delta and gamma of the CVA similar to the above are also provided for banks that calculate their VAR using these approximations. The approved specific risk model gives the ability to simulate the credit spreads that are required in order to calculate CVA, as in Equation 8.16. Such approaches tend to simulate spreads for generic or proxy curves, generally defined via ratings and potentially also regions and sectors. Hence, this is approximately aligned with the mapping procedures already required to estimate credit spreads for CVA valuation purposes. Regulators generally accept that, due to the illiquidity of the CDS and bond markets, proxying CDS spreads will be the norm and will be open to a reasonable amount of subjectivity. These aspects will be discussed in more detail in Chapter 12.

The advanced CVA capital charge methodology is illustrated in Figure 8.12. Generally, the methodology is analogous to market risk VAR, which requires a 99% confidence level, ten-day horizon and a multiplier of three to be used (although these may be changed under the Fundamental Review of the Trading Book, see Section 8.8.1). This multiplier can be increased by local regulators and may also depend on the performance of the model with respect to backtesting. In addition, the aforementioned changes that require an additional calculation with the simulation of stressed market data (similar to the EPE requirements discussed in Section 8.6.2) also apply. The stressed market

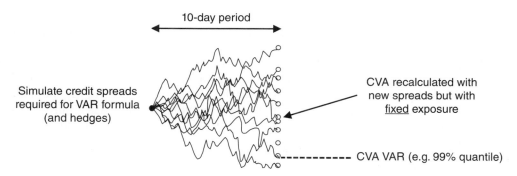

Figure 8.12   Illustration of advanced CVA capital methodology.

data corresponds to both the calculation of exposure with the CVA formula and the simulation of credit spread, and the final number is the sum of the normal and stressed calculations.[26] The choice of this stress period is subjective. EBA (2015b) report that most banks use a period around 2008–2009 giving a stressed CVA VAR between three and four times higher than the normal VAR, whilst some use a period around 2010–2012 and report a corresponding increase of between 1 and 2.5. Hence, the choice of stress period can clearly have a major impact on capital costs. Note finally that, despite the similarity to the general market risk VAR methodology of a bank, the advanced CVA capital calculation must be run separately.

As with the standardised formula, CDS hedges are incorporated in the above methodology. Since the volatility of exposure is not considered, it is clearly not possible to recognise hedges other than those in relation to the credit spread volatility. The eligible hedges are, therefore, single-name CDSs[27] (or single-name contingent CDSs), other equivalent hedges referencing the counterparty directly and index CDSs that may be treated within the CVA VAR methodology. Only hedges used for the purpose of mitigating CVA risk, and managed as such, are eligible (i.e. if a bank happens to have bought CDS protection on a counterparty for other purposes, then it is not eligible). Eligible hedges may be removed from the standard VAR calculation. Proxy hedges (where a bank has bought single-name protection on a different but highly correlated name) are not eligible for capital relief (although they are proposed to be eligible in the aforementioned BCBS (2015) consultative document).

With index CDSs, where an imperfect hedge clearly exists, the basis between the counterparty CDS and the index spread must be simulated in the calculation, as indicated in Figure 8.12. The extent to which this spread is correlated to the relevant index then defines the benefit through hedging. The index may be modelled as a linear combination of its components. However, "if the basis is not reflected to the satisfaction of the supervisor, then the bank must reflect only 50% of the notional amount of index hedges in the VaR" (BCBS, 2011b). This suggests that high correlations that lead to better hedging performance may be questioned by regulators.

8.7.4   Example

The CVA capital charge can easily be seen to be significant. Consider intuitively the multiplier that would be applied to the volatility of the CVA: the ten-day time horizon, 99% confidence level and multiplier of 3 lead to an overall multiplier of 1.4.[28] With the requirement to sum the capital from the normal and stressed calculations this should be more than doubled. Since credit spreads are relatively volatile, it is easy to imagine the CVA capital charge being far higher than the CVA itself.

We will show example CVA capital calculations for the standardised and advanced approaches described above and also illustrate the impact of hedges. We use the same collateralised ten-year swap shown previously in Section 8.5.2 which has a fairly similar EAD for all three regulatory capital approaches. Obviously, different transactions

---

[26] But the final number does not include the incremental risk charge (IRC), which measures the impact of effects such as default and credit migration risk over a one-year time horizon and is therefore similar to the Basel II IMM approach.

[27] Short bond positions are allowed if the basis risk is captured.

[28] $\sqrt{(10/250 \times 2.33 \times 3}=1.4.$

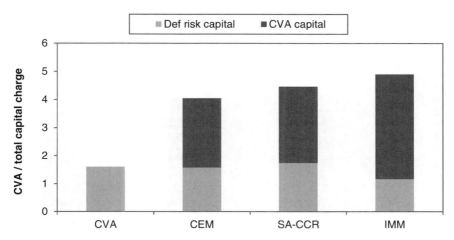

Figure 8.13   Example CVA capital calculations showing charge under the different regulatory approaches compared to the CVA itself. For the IMM calculation, the split arising from the standard and stressed calibrations is shown by the dotted line.

and portfolios can give rise to quite different results. Figure 8.13 shows the CVA capital charge for the example portfolio compared to the CVA itself. The latter is small in comparison but note that we are looking only at the capital charge and not the cost of holding regulatory capital, which will be discussed later (KVA, Chapter 16). Whilst the IMM method has a lower default risk capital charge, it has a larger CVA capital requirement and is therefore higher overall. This is most obviously arising from the need to sum normal and stressed CVA capital calculations.

Next, in Figure 8.14, we show the reduction of the CVA capital charge as a result of index hedges. In these calculations, we have assumed a perfect alignment between the CVA as seen by the CVA desk of the bank (which would drive the magnitude of the hedges) and advanced regulatory formula. As discussed later in Chapter 18, there is unlikely to be a perfect alignment here; therefore, in reality the capital relief from hedges may be weaker. Under such situations, single-name hedges could potentially reduce the capital to zero. The reduction arising from index hedges is moderate due to the nature of the index hedging: this is due to the imperfect correlation between index and counterparty credit spread, and the fact that index hedges do not reduce the default risk capital charge. In the IMM approach, the reduction is better, since we assume a higher correlation than the 50% required in the standardised formula (Equation 8.13). Note also that when we consider a portfolio rather than a single transaction, performance of index hedges improves. This is because there is diversification of idiosyncratic risk (for example, see Figure 8.11), leaving residual systematic risk, which can be hedged with the index. This will also be discussed in more detail in the examples in Chapter 18.

The above shows that significant benefit can be achieved when hedging with index and single-name CDS hedges. However, a question would obviously arise as to how well these hedges correspond to those for the reduction of CVA itself and what portfolio effects there may be. We will discuss this later in Chapter 18.

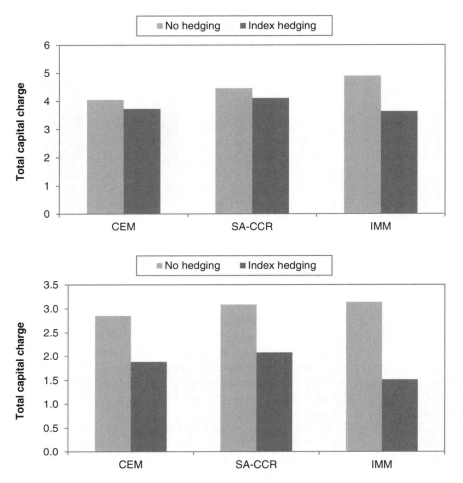

Figure 8.14   Potential reduction in total capital charge using index hedges for a single transaction (top) and assuming a portfolio effect (bottom). The portfolio effect considers 50 counterparties with the same transaction and shows the average capital charge per counterparty.

8.7.5   Criticisms

The CVA capital charge has been quite controversial and has attracted criticism. Some of the criticism concerns the significant increase in capital requirements, whilst some is more subtle and relates to the precise methodology. EBA (2015b) report that the CVA capital charge due to the potential increase in CVA is "very conservative" as it implies the CVA of most banks surveyed could increase between ten and 20 times over ten days.

Another important consideration is that the form of the CVA capital charge seems to incentivise hedging with CDS, since this is the only practical way to mitigate the charge for the significant (non-collateral posting) counterparties. Yet, in recent years, the liquidity of the CDS market has not improved. BIS (2013) report a general decline in CDS notional (especially single-name). ISDA (2013) report that the apparent decline in CDS liquidity is actually a reduction to notional driven by portfolio compression, but note a decline in single-name CDS trading. It is therefore questionable whether the form of the CVA capital charge in relation to index and single-name hedges was advisable given the poor development of the market liquidity in these hedging instruments.

The potential problems with the CVA capital charge are therefore:

- *Cost.* Banks have complained about the increased capital requirement for counterparty risk and the associated costs. (Under the advanced approach, capital is essentially three times the sum of the normal and stressed CVA VAR.) End-users have complained that such costs, when passed on to them, will mean that it will be inefficient for them to hedge their economic risk. Indeed, some end-users have experienced difficulty even transacting with banks in some products, regardless of the price.
- *De-recognition of DVA.* A second main criticism is that the benefit of DVA is not included,[29] even though it must be reported under accounting requirements (Section 4.3.4). This is not surprising given the controversial nature of DVA, as explained in Chapter 14, but more generally the focus of regulatory capital on CVA, with banks considering many more components to be important (xVA), is problematic. This will be discussed more in Chapter 18.
- *Recognition of hedges.* Both the standardised and advanced CVA capital charges represent credit hedging via CDS (single-name and index). The effectiveness of such hedges will be discussed in Chapter 18 – although, as noted above, the liquidity of the CDS market has not improved significantly. However, any other market risk hedges are not represented, and create a "split hedge" issue where these hedges increase, rather than reduce, the overall capital charge. Hence, a bank is given regulatory capital incentives not to hedge the market risk components of CVA. US and Canadian regulators have moved to exempt CVA-related market risk hedges and thus resolve this issue, and other regions may be expected to follow this lead (for example, see EBA, 2015b).[30] Note that some banks have tried to resolve this problem by including their CVA sensitivities in their market risk models.
- *Procyclicality.* The advanced capital charge for CVA is likely to be procyclical, since CDS spread volatility tends to increase with increasing spreads. In good economic climates, CDS volatility will be lower and will lead to an accordingly lower capital charge. However, the volatility and capital will tend to increase in more turbulent periods, although the use of stressed CDS spread data will partially alleviate this problem. This behaviour is equivalent to market risk VAR behaviour and at first glance may not appear any more problematic. However, CVA is defined primarily by credit spreads that are strongly cyclical (in terms of overall level and volatility) and cannot be as well hedged as traditional market risks. Hence, a bank has limited control over their CVA capital charge increasing during turbulent periods.

---

[29] "Application of own credit risk adjustments to derivatives", Basel Committee on Banking Supervision, www.bis.org/press/p111221.htm. "Additionally, DVA gains must be derecognised from the calculation of equity to ensure that an increase in the credit risk of a bank does not achieve an increase in its common equity due to a reduction in the value of its liabilities" – see www.bis.org/press/p120725b.htm.

[30] Although strangely, EBA (2015b) report that only three out of 18 banks reported a material benefit if such hedges were exempted, and several banks actually would see a negative impact from this exemption (i.e. the hedges offset other risks in their trading books).

- *Negative feedback loops.* Related to the above point, the potential for CDS hedging to create a doom loop has been highlighted (e.g. Murphy, 2012). This would occur when banks buy CDS protection and this drives CDS spreads wider, potentially creating higher CVA and CVA capital, creating the need for more hedging and so on (sometimes named the CDS "doom loop"). Obviously such an effect will be more significant given the relative illiquidity of the CDS market. Indeed, Kenyon and Green (2013) have showed that a significant component (up to 50%) of a single-name CDS spread could be related purely to the capital relief achievable (and not the default probability or related risk premium), thereby artificially inflating credit spreads. This aspect was considered particularly relevant during the sovereign debt problems in Europe around 2012 and is partially the source of exemptions to the CVA capital charge considered below.

The proposals in BCBS (2015) would improve on some of the above, notably given better recognition of hedges. However, they may also increase procyclicality.

8.7.6 US implementation

In addition to the exemption of market risk hedges mentioned above, there are some other deviations in the US implementation of the CVA capital charge compared to the Basel III text:

- US rules allow a bank to choose between the standardised and advanced approaches. This means that a bank with the relevant approvals to use the advanced method may be allowed to use the standardised method if there is a reasonable justification.
- Since the Dodd–Frank Act does not allow the use of credit ratings, credit quality in the standardised CVA capital charge formula is represented by weights related to default probabilities which are nevertheless similar in magnitude.
- The US rules do not allow the standardised method (Section 8.1.4) to be used. This is also the case for some other regions (e.g. Canada).

8.7.7 The European exemptions

It did not take long for some regulators to become worried about the unintended consequences of the CVA capital charge and the potential doom loop. For example, the Bank of England second quarter bulletin[31] in 2010 stated:

> ... given the relative illiquidity of sovereign CDS markets a sharp increase in demand from active investors can bid up the cost of sovereign CDS protection. CVA desks have come to account for a large proportion of trading in the sovereign CDS market and so their hedging activity has reportedly been a factor pushing prices away from levels solely reflecting the underlying probability of sovereign default.

The implication of this seems to be that the hedging of CVA was one factor in pushing credit spreads to excessively wide levels via a doom loop.

---

[31] See www.bankofengland.co.uk/publications/quarterlybulletin/index.htm.

Basel III defines global standards on capital requirements that are generally being implemented consistently, albeit with small differences and timescales depending on the region. However, one extremely significant divergence has occurred in Europe via the Capital Requirements Directive IV (CRD IV), which is the mechanism through which the European Union implements Basel III standards on capital. On the back of the sovereign debt crisis and related doom loop mentioned above, CRD IV exempted banks from holding CVA capital towards sovereign counterparties.[32] This was followed in 2013 by similar exemptions covering non-financial counterparties (below the clearing threshold) and pension funds (temporarily). CCP transactions between clearing members and clients are also exempt when the clearing member is essentially an intermediary between the client and the qualifying CCP (Section 9.3.7). These exemptions, which are relevant only for EU banks, do apply to counterparties outside of the EU. This is not driven by these counterparties being insignificant: indeed, quite the opposite is true as they do not post collateral and may trade relatively long-dated transactions. Rather, these exemptions were likely driven by a combination of a number of factors:

- *Structural differences in European markets.* Compared to the US market, the EU is more reliant on derivatives to hedge economic risks for end-users and has a less liquid underlying CDS market.
- *Cost.* Since banks pass on the cost of increased capital to their clients, then end-users of OTC derivatives would experience dramatically increasing costs. Concerns were particularly focused around the end-users who could not post collateral to mitigate the counterparty risks and therefore would otherwise experience much high prices.
- *Central clearing mandate.* One of the aims of high capital requirements for bilateral OTC derivatives is to incentivise the move to central clearing. Since these sovereign and non-financial counterparties are typically[33] exempt from the clearing mandate there is no need to create this incentive. The temporary exemption of pension funds from the CVA capital charge mirrors the same exemption with respect to the clearing mandate.
- *Doom loop.* These counterparties may create a significant doom loop since they typically do not post collateral, leading to large CVA capital charges that will attract large hedges. Sovereign entities are especially problematic since they typically trade large notional interest rate swaps to hedge bond issuance. This can mean that a bank's entire sovereign exposure could increase simultaneously due to a significant interest rate and/or credit spread move. The related hedging activity could create a doom loop, as discussed above. Since the liquidity of the (single-name) CDS market has not been improving, this may be considered a real problem.

The CVA capital charge exemption has had a significant impact, with European banks reporting a significant drop in capital requirements as a result.[34] A study by the EBA reported that without the exemptions then the total CVA capital of 18 banks surveyed would more than double from €12.4 to €31.1 billion, with sovereign exemptions being the most material and pension funds the least (EBA, 2015b). There have also been questions

---

[32] Including public bodies, multilateral development banks, public sector entities owned by central governments, central governments and central banks.

[33] Note that it is possible for a non-financial counterparty (NFC) with significant OTC derivative activity to be above the clearing threshold (NFC+) and then subject to clearing requirements.

[34] For example, see "UK banks face CVA exemption tension", *Risk*, 28th June 2013.

about the validity of the doom loop argument (e.g. IMF 2013) and some European regulators clearly did not agree with the form of the exemptions.[35] The exemptions have not been applied in any other region[36] and, at the time of writing, it seems they may be reversed in Europe at some point[37] – although this may only be achievable via imposing a similar capital requirement under some other legislation.

8.8   OTHER IMPORTANT REGULATORY REQUIREMENTS

This section reviews some other regulatory changes, that are not at the core of xVA assessment but have some related impacts.

8.8.1   Fundamental review of the trading book

The fundamental review of the trading book (FRTB) (BCBS, 2013b) can be seen as try-ing to define a more consistent set of market risk regulatory capital rules, balancing risk sensitivity and complexity, and promoting consistency. Key objectives are addressing the boundary between the banking and trading books, and enhancing the capitalisation of credit risk and liquidity risk in the trading book.

One aspect of the FRTB related to xVA is the use of expected shortfall (ES) as a re-placement for VAR as the risk measure for market risk capital based on internal models. This is due to the view that ES is better at capturing tail risk: VAR measures only a single quantile and does not consider the loss beyond this level whereas ES averages all losses above the confidence level. Since the ES is a naturally more conservative measure, it is proposed to replace 99% VAR with 97.5% ES (for a normal distribution the two are almost identical). The standard ten-day time horizon for VAR is also split into several categories based on the liquidity of the underlying. These aspects would likely have an impact on the advanced CVA capital charge (Section 8.7).

Another aspect considered in the FRTB was whether CVA risk could be captured in an integrated fashion with other forms of market risk rather than being a "standalone" capital charge. This would avoid the issue with some CVA-related hedges being charged capital rather than providing capital relief (Section 8.7.5). Under the proposed frame-work, such unification is not foreseen due to the potential complexity that would be required and model risk that would therefore be introduced,.

8.8.2   Leverage ratio

An often-cited cause of the global financial crisis was excessive on- and off-balance sheet leverage of banks, even when seemingly strong risk-based capital ratios were in place. The rapid deleveraging was seen as a key reason for the global financial crisis being so severe and long-lasting. This has led to the introduction of the leverage ratio (LR) described in BCBS (2014a).

Although increasing capital requirement should reduce leverage, they can be model-based (e.g. IMM) and vary significantly from bank to bank. The LR is seen as

---

[35] For example, see "Bafin weighing CVA charge despite European exemptions", *Risk*, 19th June, 2013.

[36] For example, see "No CVA exemptions in US Basel III rules", *Risk*, 3rd July 2013.

[37] For example, see "Corporate CVA exemption should be removed, says EBA", *Risk*, 5th December 2014.

complimenting regulatory capital requirements as a non-risk-based approach to the measurement of leverage with the aim of preventing it rising above a certain defined level across a bank. The LR can therefore be seen as a backstop to capital requirements, which mitigates the inherent uncertainties in these approaches. Implementation of the LR has already started via reporting to national supervisors and public disclosure. The final rules are yet to be finalised but implementation is planned from 2018.

The LR defines leverage via the ratio of a bank's exposure (non-risk-weighted assets) and its Tier 1 capital. Banks will be required to hold Tier 1 capital of at least 3% of their non-risk weighted assets, i.e.:

$$\text{Leverage ratio} = \frac{\text{Tier 1 capital}}{\text{Exposure}} \geq 3\%$$

Tier 1 capital comprises common share capital, retained earnings and other comprehensive income. The exposure in the above formula is made up of on-balance sheet assets, derivative exposures, securities finance transactions (e.g. repos) and other off-balance sheet exposures. For derivatives, the exposure is defined using the CEM (Section 8.2) and is therefore subject to some of the shortcomings of this approach. Generally, collateral and other credit risk mitigants cannot be used to offset exposures. This is fundamentally different to the fairly risk-sensitive treatment of capital in the SA-CCR and IMM approaches discussed above. An exemption (revised from the initial LR rules) is that cash variation margin can reduce the exposure subject to certain conditions.

The LR is particularly penalising with respect to repo transactions and centrally cleared transactions (another revision has removed a double-counting of client cleared exposures). Note also that in the US, separate from Basel III, an "enhanced supplementary leverage ratio" has been proposed for the largest banks with a more conservative 5% minimum.

A bank that is (or is close to) being LR-constrained may consider this to be more relevant than their actual capital charges. However, due to the LR being essentially a cap related to the total balance sheet of a bank, it is not completely clear how such capital would be priced in via a measure such as KVA.

8.8.3   Floors

Related to the leverage ratio is the use of capital floors for internal models based on the results of standardised approaches (BCBS, 2014f). This requirement has been driven by the observation that internal models can produce large variations in capital charges across banks for the same exposure and very small capital charges in certain situations. Such results suggest significant model risk and perhaps overly optimistic assumptions within the bank's internal models. By the use of a floor, excessively low capital charges would be prevented and there would be less variation between numbers.

From the counterparty risk perspective, the use of a floor would apply to an IMM bank and would require their capital to not fall below a certain percentage of that calculated using a standardised method (e.g. SA-CCR). Hence, IMM banks would need to implement such a standardised method alongside their more advanced framework.

Incorporating floors in internal model based capital approaches does not directly address the root cause of problems associated with model risk. Floors can also undermine the benefit of risk sensitive models and create adverse incentives.[38] It has also been suggested that such floors should be no higher than 75%, otherwise banks would no longer have the incentive to model their regulatory capital requirements.[39]

8.8.4   Liquidity coverage ratio and net stable funding ratio

The liquidity coverage ratio (LCR) aims to impose a more rigorous liquidity management regime on banks so that they can withstand a stress event. The stress event is envisaged as being associated with aspects such as increased market volatility, loss of secured and unsecured funding opportunities, and the additional outflows arising from a downgrading of the bank's external credit rating. In such a period, the LCR aims to ensure that a bank would maintain sufficient unencumbered high quality liquid assets (HQLAs) to meet all of their net outflows during a 30-day stress period, i.e.:

$$\frac{\text{Stock of HQLA}}{\text{Total net cash outflows over the next 30 calendar days}} \geq 100\%$$

One aspect that is particularly relevant for xVA is that the LCR requires the liquidity needs related to downgrade triggers embedded in derivative transactions to be assessed. A bank must include in the total net outflows 100% of any additional collateral that would have to be posted, or other contractual outflows in the event of a three-notch downgrade of the bank's external credit rating. This has an impact on pricing components such as margin valuation adjustment (MVA), where a bank, for example, may be required to post additional collateral (via initial margin) in connection with a downgrade. As discussed in Chapter 16, this may be priced in as having to hold HQLAs against a downgrade and is not materially different from actually posting the initial margin.

Whilst the LCR is relatively short-term and aims to ensure banks hold enough HQLAs that can be easily converted into cash to survive a 30-day stress scenario, the purpose of the net stable funding ratio (NSFR) is to ensure that banks hold a minimum amount of stable funding based on the liquidity characteristics of their assets and activities over a one-year time horizon (BCBS 2014b). The NSFR is calculated by dividing a bank's available stable funding by its required stable funding. As with the LCR, this ratio must always be greater than 100%.

8.8.5   Prudent value

In the EU, regulators (EBA, 2015a) have introduced the idea of prudent value (PruVal) via an additional value adjustment (AVA) to reflect the risks related to the valuation of financial instruments. The AVA can be thought of as the difference between a prudent (conservative) valuation and the value recorded in accounting. This value does not impact accounting numbers but must be deducted from Common Equity Tier 1 and therefore can be seen as an additional capital charge.

Amongst the components that must be assessed with AVA are:

---

[38] For example, see "Capital floors could spur risk-taking – Swedish FSA", *Risk*, 25th March 2015.
[39] See "Basel floors must be below 75% to preserve models, banks say", *Risk*, 26th January 2015.

- unearned credit spreads;
- model risk; and
- investing and funding costs.

The first component above clearly requires some credit value adjustment (CVA) consideration. The uncertainty in the CVA could be due to the credit spreads used for calculation and the model for calculating the counterparty exposure. Additionally, the second component above could be seen as requiring some consideration in relation to funding value adjustment (FVA). However, as discussed in Chapter 15, the reporting of FVA is not yet completely standard and many questions remain. Hence, FVA may not be seen as a realistic component of AVA in the short-term.

8.9   SUMMARY

In this chapter, we have described regulatory approaches to counterparty risk, in particular focusing on the regulatory capital requirements according to the Basel II and III guidelines. We have considered the different approaches available to compute counterparty risk capital charges, from the simple add-on rules to the more sophisticated internal model approach. We have also described the new SA-CCR methodology for capital that will be introduced from 2017. The more recent requirements of Basel III have also been addressed, including the CVA capital charge, stressed EEPE and backtesting requirements. Finally, we have described some other important impending regulation such as the leverage ratio, liquidity coverage ratio and prudent valuation.

9

Counterparty Risk Intermediation

If a financial institution is too big to fail, it is too big to exist.

Bernie Sanders (1941–)

9.1 INTRODUCTION

This chapter concerns counterparty risk mitigation via entities acting as intermediators and/or offering guarantees or insurance in relation to default events. This will cover the role played by derivative product companies (DPCs) and monoline insurers. Much of this discussion will be historical but is useful context and provides some lessons with respect to the underlying problems that such entities can create. We will also then cover the role of central counterparties (CCPs) in mitigation of OTC derivative counterparty risk, which is a key element due to the regulatory mandate regarding clearing of standardised OTC derivatives.

Exchange-traded derivatives have long used CCPs to control counterparty risk. Long before the global financial crisis of 2007 onwards, whilst no major derivatives dealer had failed, the bilaterally cleared dealer-dominated OTC market was perceived as being inherently more vulnerable to counterparty risk than the exchange-traded market. This larger and more complex OTC derivatives market has developed a number of methods to achieve counterparty risk mitigation, including through a CCP. Such methods are all based on some concept of counterparty risk intermediation (Figure 9.1), where a third party guarantor intermediates and guarantees the performance of one or both counterparties with the aim of reducing counterparty risk. Clearly the guarantor will need an enhanced credit quality for this to be beneficial.

There are a number of different forms of counterparty risk intermediation, which can be seen as a progression (although not necessarily a chronological one) towards central clearing, thus creating a number of other risks along the way (Figure 9.2):

Figure 9.1 Basic concept of counterparty risk intermediation between two bilateral counterparties, C1 and C2.

- *Special purpose vehicles.* An SPV is a wrapper aiming to create a bankruptcy-remote entity and give a counterparty preferential treatment as a creditor in the event of a default. It therefore introduces legal risk if this beneficial treatment is not upheld in the event of a default.
- *Guarantees.* A guarantee is where a third party guarantees the performance of a derivative counterparty. This introduces the concept of "double default" (Section 8.1.3) – both the original derivative counterparty and the guarantor must fail to lead to a loss. One common and simple sort of guarantee is intragroup, where a trading subsidiary is guaranteed by its parent company. Another example is a letter of credit from a bank, which will typically reference a specified amount. Clearly, to be effective, the party providing the guarantee should be of higher credit standing than the original counterparty, and there must be no clear relationship between them.
- *Derivative product companies.* A derivative product company (DPC) essentially takes the above idea further by having additional capital and operational rules, introducing operational and market risks. DPCs are a special form of intermediation where an originating bank sets up a bankruptcy-remote SPV and injects capital to gain a preferential and strong credit rating (typically triple-A). Monolines and credit DPCs can be seen as a specific application of this idea to credit derivative products where wrong-way risk is particularly problematic due to the obvious relationship between the counterparty and reference entities in the contracts.
- *Central counterparty (CCP).* A CCP extends the DPC concept by requiring collateral posting and default funds, and uses methods such as loss mutualisation to guarantee performance. This introduces liquidity risk since the CCP aims to replace contracts in the event of a default. The size of CCPs also creates systemic risk. A CCP clearing credit default swaps (CDSs) can be seen as a progression from a CDPC (see Section 9.2.4) and has arguably a more difficult role due to the underlying wrong-way risks.

Derivatives markets, like most markets, need some form of insurance or reinsurance in order to transfer risk or a method to mutualise losses. However, if this insurance or mutualisation fails, then it can be catastrophic. We will discuss how this was the case for monoline insurers and ask the question as to why this happened and whether there are lessons to be learned, especially in terms of the rapidly expanded role that CCPs will have in future OTC derivatives markets.

Figure 9.2   Illustration of the development of counterparty risk intermediation methods.

9.2   SPVS, DPCS, CDPCS AND MONOLINES[1]

9.2.1   Default remoteness and "too big to fail"

One concept at the heart of much of this discussion is that of the "default remote entity". The general idea of a default remote entity is that it provides a counterparty of such good credit quality that the default probability and thus the counterparty risk are essentially negligible. In the days when credit ratings were viewed as providing accurate and dynamic credit quality assessment, this generally applied to triple-A credit quality. Such entities have proved historically very useful for mitigating counterparty risk, as the default of the counterparty is argued to be a highly unlikely event. If this sounds too good to be true and implies a laziness in market practice, that is probably because it is, and it does.

Related to a default remote concept is the well-known "too big to fail" one. Such a counterparty may well fail, but it is simply too large and correlated to other risks to be *allowed* to fail. Hence, the same laziness in assessing counterparty risk may be applied. "Too big to fail" counterparties have been more formally known as systemically important financial institutions (SIFIs). Regulators are aiming to identify SIFIs (for example, via their size and linkage of assets and revenue from financial activities) and break them up or demand that they face higher capital requirements and tougher regulatory scrutiny. Such efforts are aimed at avoiding a repeat of the collapse of Lehman Brothers and the chaos in the OTC derivatives market that followed and the need to bail out institutions such as Bear Stearns and AIG to prevent worse chaos. Whilst these will be useful steps, a moral hazard problem will remain, since institutions may trade with SIFIs purely on the basis that they believe they have implicit support from governments and central banks.

The idea of default-remoteness or "too big to fail" has proved to be the Achilles heel of financial markets with respect to counterparty risk. Triple-A ratings have been assigned to counterparties or legal entities based on flawed logic in relation to aspects such as the underlying business model or legal structure. Triple-A ratings may have even been correct but were just potentially misunderstood. Furthermore, moral hazard causes a behaviour of market participants in relation to the "too big to fail" perception that further accentuates the illusion that there is little or no underlying counterparty risk. The failure of institutions such as monoline insurers and the rescue of AIG has had a massive impact on the way in which counterparty risk is perceived and managed.

We will review the role of derivatives product companies and monoline insurers within the OTC derivative markets and how ideas of their default-remoteness were so badly founded. Whilst this will be mainly a backward-looking reflection, the discussion will form the basis for some of the later discussion examining the concept of central counterparties.

9.2.2   Special purpose vehicles

A special purpose vehicle (SPV), sometimes called a special purpose entity (SPE), is a legal entity – for example, a company or limited partnership – typically created to

---

[1] Many of the aspects in this section could be described in the past tense. We use the present tense but note that many of the concepts around SPVs, DPCs and monolines are relevant only from a historical point of view.

isolate a party from counterparty risk. A company will transfer assets to the SPV for management, or use the SPV to finance a large project without putting the entire firm or a counterparty at risk. Jurisdictions may require that an SPV is not owned by the entity on whose behalf it is being set up. SPVs aim essentially to change bankruptcy rules so that, if a derivative counterparty is insolvent, a client can still receive their full investment prior to any other claims (e.g. bondholders and other creditors) being paid out. SPVs are most commonly used in structured notes where they use this mechanism to guarantee the counterparty risk on the principal of the note to a high level (triple-A, typically), better than that of the issuer. The creditworthiness of the SPV is assessed by rating agencies who look at the mechanics and legal specifics before granting a rating.

An SPV transforms counterparty risk into legal risk. The obvious legal risk is that a bankruptcy court consolidates the assets of the SPV with those of the originator. The basis of consolidation is that the SPV is substantially the same as the originator and would mean that the assets transferred to the SPV are treated like those of the originator and the isolation of the SPV becomes irrelevant. Consolidation may depend on many aspects such as jurisdiction: US courts have a history of consolidation rulings, whereas UK courts have been less keen to do so.

Unfortunately, legal documentation often evolves through experience and the enforceability of the legal structure of SPVs was not tested for many years. When it was tested in the case of Lehman Brothers, there were problems, although this depended on jurisdiction. Lehman essentially used SPVs to shield investors in complex transactions such as collateralised debt obligations (CDOs) from Lehman's own counterparty risk (in retrospect, a great idea). The key provision in the documents was referred to as the "flip" clause, which essentially meant that if Lehman were bankrupt, then the investors would be first in line for their investment. However, the US Bankruptcy Court ruled that the flip clauses were unenforceable – putting them at loggerheads with the UK courts, which ruled that flip clauses *were* enforceable.

Just to add to the jurisdiction-specific question of whether a flip clause (and therefore an SPV) was a sound legal structure, Lehman has settled cases out of court.[2] The only thing that can be stated with certainty is that mitigating counterparty risk with mechanisms that create legal risk is a dangerous process, as the SPV concept has illustrated.

9.2.3 Derivative product companies

The derivatives product company (or corporation) evolved as a means for OTC derivatives markets to mitigate counterparty risk (e.g. see Kroszner, 1999). A DPC is generally a triple-A rated entity set up by one or more banks that, unlike an SPV, is separately capitalised to obtain a triple-A credit rating.[3] The DPC structure provides external counterparties with a degree of protection against counterparty risk by protecting against the failure of the DPC parent. A DPC therefore provides some of the benefits of the exchange-based system while preserving the flexibility and decentralisation of the OTC market. Examples of some of the first DPCs include Merrill Lynch Derivative Products,

---

[2] For example, see "Lehman opts to settle over Dante flip-clause transactions", www.risk.net/risk-magazine/news/1899105/lehman-opts-settle-dante-flip-clause-transactions.

[3] Most DPCs derived their credit quality structurally via capital, but some simply did so more trivially from the sponsor's rating.

Salomon Swapco, Morgan Stanley Derivative Products and Lehman Brothers Financial Products.

DPCs maintain a triple-A rating by a combination of capital, collateral and activity restrictions. Each DPC has its own quantitative risk assessment model to quantify their current credit risk, benchmarked dynamically against that required for a triple-A rating. The rating of a DPC typically depends on:

- *Minimising market risk.* In terms of market risk, DPCs can attempt to be close to market-neutral via trading offsetting contracts. Ideally, they would be on both sides of every trade, as these "mirror trades" lead to an overall matched book. Usually the mirror trade exists with the DPC parent.
- *Support from a parent.* The DPC is supported by being bankruptcy-remote (like an SPV) from the parent to achieve a better rating. If the parent were to default, then the DPC is intended to either pass to another well-capitalised institution or be terminated in an orderly fashion with transactions settled at mid-market. As discussed below, this has not generally happened.
- *Credit risk management and operational guidelines (limits, collateral terms, etc.).* Restrictions are also imposed on (external) counterparty credit quality and activities (position limits, collateral, etc.). The management of counterparty risk is achieved by having daily MTM and collateral posting.

Whilst being of very good credit quality, DPCs also give further security by defining an orderly workout process. A DPC defines what events would trigger its own failure (rating downgrade of parent, for example) and how the resulting workout process would work. The resulting "pre-packaged bankruptcy" was therefore supposedly more simple (as well as less likely) than the standard bankruptcy of an OTC derivative counterparty.

The DPC idea apparently worked well since its creation in the early 1990s until the global financial crisis. One problem was the realisation that relying on credit ratings as a dynamic measure of credit quality is dangerous. For example, Lehman Brothers had a reasonably good single-A rating at the time of its bankruptcy[4] and Icelandic banks had the best quality triple-A ratings just weeks prior to their complete collapse. The voluntary filing for Chapter 11 by two Lehman Brothers DPCs, a strategic effort to protect the DPCs' assets, seemed to link a DPC's fate inextricably with that of its parent. After their parent's decline, the Bear Stearns DPCs were wound down by JP Morgan. Not surprisingly, the perceived lack of autonomy of DPCs led to a reaction from rating agencies, who withdrew ratings.[5]

As in the case of SPVs, it is clear that the DPC concept is a flawed one and the perceived triple-A ratings of DPCs had little credibility as the counterparty being faced was really the DPC parent, generally with a worse credit rating. Therefore, DPCs illustrate that a conversion of counterparty risk into other financial risks – in this case not only legal risk, as for SPVs, but also market and operational risks – may be ineffective.

---

[4] Standard & Poor's, one of the major credit rating agencies, have defended this since, claiming the Lehman Brothers' bankruptcy was a result of "a loss of confidence … that fundamental credit analysis could not have anticipated". See www2.standardandpoors.com/spf/pdf/fixedincome/Lehman_Brothers.pdf.

[5] For example, see "Fitch withdraws Citi Swapco's ratings", www.businesswire.com/news/home/20110610005841 /en/Fitch-Withdraws-Citi-Swapcos-Ratings.

However, such structures may again reappear from time to time depending on the market and regulatory environment.[6]

9.2.4 Monolines and CDPCs

As described above, the creation of DPCs was largely driven by the need for high-quality counterparties when trading OTC derivatives. However, this need was taken to another level with the birth and exponential growth of the credit derivatives market from around 1998 onwards. A CDS contract represents an unusual challenge since its value is driven by credit spread changes whilst its payoff is linked solely to one or more credit events. This so-called wrong-way risk (Chapter 17) means that the credit quality of the CDS counterparty is even more important than for other OTC derivatives, since CDS contracts reference relatively unlikely default events and will likely be triggered in quite difficult market conditions.

Monoline insurance companies (and similar companies such as AIG[7]) are financial guarantee companies with triple-A ratings that they utilise to provide financial guarantees. The monolines were established to provide financial guarantees for US municipal bond issues, effectively providing unrated borrowers with triple-A credit ratings and enabling them to sell their bonds to investors at attractive levels. These monolines then branched out into selling CDS protection via "credit wraps" across a wide range of the structured credit products with the aim of achieving diversification and better returns. In order to justify their ratings, monolines have capital requirements driven by the possible losses on the structures. These capital requirements are also dynamically related to the portfolio of assets that they wrap, which is similar to the workings of the DPC structure. Importantly, the monolines would typically not post collateral against their transactions.

A credit derivative product company (CDPC) is essentially a vehicle inspired by the DPC and monoline concepts described above and extending the DPC model to credit derivative products. A CDPC is a special purpose entity set up to invest in credit derivatives products on a leveraged basis, typically selling protection on corporate, sovereign and asset-backed securities in single-name or portfolio form as CDS contracts. Whereas a DPC is simply a bankruptcy-remote subsidiary of an institution, a CDPC is an entity set up with the aim of making profit from selling credit derivative protection. Unlike a traditional DPC, CDPCs have significant market risk due to not having offsetting positions. Like monolines, CDPCs act as high credit quality counterparties but do so largely on only one side of the market, as sellers of credit protection.

Prior to the global financial crisis, the market was, in general, comfortable that monolines and CDPCs were financially stable. For example:

---

[6] For example, see "RBS sets up first Moody's-rated DPC in 14 years", *Risk*, 7th May 2014.

[7] For the purposes of this analysis we will categorise monoline insurers and AIG as the same type of entity, which, based on their activities in the credit derivatives market, is fair.

Example

The credit quality of monolines (a quote[8] from 2001) "The major monoline bond insurers enjoy impeccably strong credit quality, offering investors excellent credit protection, which combined with the underlying issuer is tantamount to better than triple-A risk. In fact, the risk of capital loss for investors is practically zero and the risk of a downgrade slightly greater. Given the state of their risk profiles, the triple-A ratings of the monolines are well entrenched. Each of the four major monolines display adequate capital levels, ample claims paying resources against risk positions and limited if any single large exposures."

The triple-A ratings granted to monolines and CDPCs are interesting in that they were typically achieved due to the entity not being obliged to post collateral against transactions. This is significant since posting collateral crystallises MTM losses.

When the global financial crisis developed through 2007, monolines experienced major problems due to the MTM losses on the insurance they had sold. Concerns started to rise over their triple-A ratings and that they had insufficient capital to justify them. Critically, monolines had clauses whereby a rating downgrade (even below triple-A in some cases) could trigger the need to post collateral. For example, in November 2007 the ACA Financial Guarantee Corporation stated that a loss of its single-A credit rating would trigger a need to post collateral, which they would not be able to meet. Although rating agencies did not react immediately, once they began to downgrade monoline's credit ratings then their decline was swift as the need to post collateral essentially sent them into default. Figure 9.3 illustrates the extremely rapid decline of the monolines MBIA and AMBAC.

Many banks found themselves heavily exposed to monolines due to the massive increase in the value of the protection they had purchased. For example, as of June 2008, UBS was estimated to have $6.4bn at risk to monoline insurers whilst the equivalent figures for Citigroup and Merrill Lynch were $4.8bn and $3bn respectively (*Financial Times*, 2008). The situation with AIG was more or less the same, from the joint result of a ratings downgrade and AIG's positions moving against them rapidly, leading to the requirement to post large amounts of collateral. This essentially crystallised massive losses for AIG and led to potentially large losses for their counterparties if they were to fail. The latter did not happen, since AIG was bailed out by the US government to the tune of approximately $182bn. Why AIG was bailed out and the monoline insurers were not could be put down to the size of AIG[9] and the timing of their problems (close to the Lehman Brothers bankruptcy and Fannie Mae/Freddie Mac problems).

CDPCs, like monolines, are highly leveraged and typically do not post collateral. They fared somewhat better during the global financial crisis but only for timing reasons. Many CDPCs were not fully operational until after the beginning of the crisis

---

[8] See "Monolines deserve a good wrap", National Australia Bank Capital Markets, April 2001. It should be noted that this report was written a number of years before the global financial crisis and prior to the monolines undertaking the activities in structured credit that would lead to their downfall.

[9] Whilst the monolines together had approximately the same amount of exposure as AIG, their fortunes were not completely tied to one another.

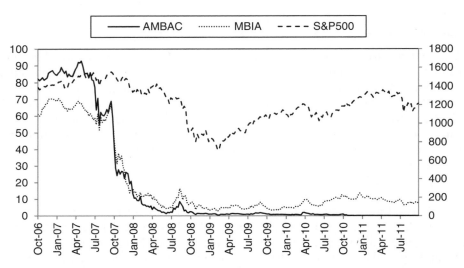

Figure 9.3 Share price (in dollars) of the monoline insurers AMBAC and MBIA (left axis) compared to the S&P500 index (right axis).

in July 2007. They therefore missed at least the first "wave" of losses suffered by any party selling credit protection (especially super senior[10]). Nevertheless, the fact that the CDPC business model is close to that of monolines has not been ignored. For example, in October 2008, Fitch withdrew ratings on the five CDPCs that it rated.[11]

There are strong arguments that the monoline/CDPC business model was fatally flawed. They acted as a central entity that was insuring large amounts of counterparty risk and therefore providing some sort of systemic risk shock absorber. But systemic risk insurance is a misnomer, since insurance relies on some level of diversification. The lessons from the failures of monolines and AIG are important, especially given the importance of CCPs in performing a similar role in the future. Whilst CCPs have many differences in the ways in which they operate, they do have similar positions as nodes for counterparty risk mitigation and may also concentrate systemic risk in a single place. They may become the biggest of all "too big to fail" entities.

9.3   CENTRAL COUNTERPARTIES

The lesson so far – after considering SPVs, DPCs, monolines and CDPCs – appears to be that relying on a default-remote entity as a major counterparty is a poor way to mitigate counterparty risk. It might seem strange then that CCPs have gained so much support from regulators in recent years. That said, there are many differences in the way that CCPs operate, although they do clearly have their own complexities and risks.

---

[10] The widening in super senior spreads was on a relative basis much greater than credit spreads in general during late 2007.

[11] See, for example, "Fitch withdraws CDPC ratings", Business Wire, 2008.

The rest of this chapter provides a summary of the operation of a CCP clearing OTC derivatives. A more in-depth description is given in Gregory (2014).

9.3.1 The clearing mandate

The global financial crisis from 2007 onwards triggered grave concerns regarding counterparty risk, catalysed by events such as the collapse of Lehman Brothers, the failure of monoline insurers and the bankruptcy of Icelandic banks. Counterparty risk in OTC derivatives, especially credit derivatives, was identified as a major risk to the financial system. There were also related operational and legal issues linked to aspects such as collateral management and close-out processes that result directly from counterparty risk mitigation. A CCP offers a potential solution to these problems as it guarantees counterparty risk and provides a centralised entity where aspects such as collateral management and default management are handled.

One of the largest perceived problems with bilateral OTC derivatives markets is the close-out process in the event of a major default, which can take many years and be subject to major legal proceedings (for example, see Figure 3.3). By contrast, CCPs can improve this process by establishing and enforcing the close-out rules, ensuring continuity and thereby reducing systemic risk. The default management of OTC derivatives by CCPs was viewed as being highly superior to bilateral markets in the aftermath of the Lehman bankruptcy. Although bilateral markets have made progress in certain aspects (see, for example, the adoption of the ISDA close-out protocol discussed in Section 5.2.6), they still cannot claim to be as coordinated as CCPs in this regard.

In 2010, both Europe (via the European Commission's formal legislative proposal for regulation on OTC derivatives, central counterparties and trade repositories) and the US (via the Dodd–Frank Wall Street Reform and Consumer Protection Act) put forward proposals that would commit all standardised OTC derivatives to be cleared through CCPs by the end of 2012. Part of the reason for this was that, when the financial markets were in meltdown after the collapse of Lehman Brothers in September 2008, CCPs were more or less alone in operating well. For example, LCH.Clearnet[12] and Chicago Mercantile Exchange (CME) were viewed as dealing well with the Lehman bankruptcy when virtually every other element of the financial system was creaking or failing. As a result, policymakers seemed to focus on CCPs as something close to a panacea for counterparty risk, especially with respect to the more dangerous products such as CDSs.

We will focus the discussion below on OTC derivatives clearing and not the broader role of CCPs in exchange-traded derivatives.

9.3.2 OTC clearing

Clearing is a process that occurs after the execution of a trade in which a CCP may step in between counterparties to guarantee performance. The main function of an OTC CCP is, therefore, to interpose itself directly or indirectly between counterparties to assume their rights and obligations by acting as buyer to every seller and vice versa. This means that the original counterparty to a trade no longer represents a direct risk, as the CCP to all intents and purposes becomes the new counterparty. CCPs essentially

---

[12] Formed via a merger between the London Clearing House (LCH) and Clearnet.

reallocate default losses via a variety of methods, including netting, collateralisation and loss mutualisation. Obviously, the intention is that the overall process will reduce counterparty and systemic risks.

CCPs provide a number of benefits. One is that they allow netting of all trades executed through them. In a bilateral market, a party with a position with counterparty A and the equal and opposite position with counterparty B has counterparty risk. However, if both contracts are centrally cleared then the netted position has no risk. CCPs also manage collateral (margin) requirements from their members to reduce the risk associated with the movement in the value of their underlying portfolios. All of these aspects can arguably be achieved in bilateral markets through mechanisms such as trade compression (Section 5.3) and increased collateral (Section 6.7).

However, CCPs do introduce features beyond those seen in bilateral markets. One is loss mutualisation; one counterparty's losses are dispersed across all clearing members rather than being transmitted directly to a smaller number of counterparties with potential adverse consequences. Moreover, CCPs can facilitate orderly close-outs by auctioning the defaulter's contractual obligations with multilateral netting reducing the total positions that need to be replaced which may minimise price impacts and market volatility. CCPs can also facilitate the orderly transfer of client positions from financially distressed members.

The general role of an OTC CCP is that it:

- sets certain standards and rules for its clearing members;
- takes responsibility for closing out all the positions of a defaulting clearing member;
- to support the above, it maintains financial resources to cover losses in the event of a clearing member default:
  - variation margin to closely track market movements;
  - initial margin to cover worst case liquidation or close-out costs above the variation margin; and
  - a default fund to mutualise losses in the event of a severe default.

The CCP also has a documented plan for the very extreme situation when all their financial resources (initial margin[13] and the default fund) are depleted. For example:

- additional calls to the default fund;
- variation margin haircutting;[14] and
- selective tear-up of positions.[15]

It is important to note that some banks and most end-users of OTC derivatives (e.g. pension funds) will access CCPs through a clearing member and will not become members themselves. This will be due to the membership, operational and liquidity requirements related to being a clearing member. In particular, participating in regular "fire drills" and bidding in a CCP auction are the main reasons why a party cannot be a clearing member at a given CCP.

---

[13] Note that only the defaulter's initial margin can be used.
[14] See Elliott (2013) or Gregory (2014) for more details.
[15] See previous footnote.

In a CCP world, the failure of a counterparty, even one as large and interconnected as Lehman Brothers, is supposedly less dramatic. This is because the CCP absorbs the "domino effect" by acting as a central shock absorber. In the event of default of one of its members, a CCP will aim to swiftly terminate all financial relations with that counterparty without suffering any losses. From the point of view of surviving members, the CCP guarantees the performance of their transactions. This will normally be achieved by replacement of the defaulted counterparty with one of the other clearing members for each transaction (generally done on a sub-portfolio basis). This is typically achieved via the CCP auctioning the defaulted members' positions amongst the other members, which allows continuity for surviving members.

9.3.3   The CCP landscape

A CCP represents a set of rules and operational arrangements that are designed to allocate, manage and reduce counterparty risk in a bilateral market. A CCP changes the topology of financial markets by inter-disposing itself between buyers and sellers, as illustrated in Figure 9.4. In this context, it is useful to consider the six entities denoted by D representing large global banks ("dealers"). Two obvious advantages appear to stem from this simplistic view. Firstly, a CCP can reduce the *interconnectedness* within financial markets, which may lessen the impact of an insolvency of a participant. Secondly, the CCP being at the heart of trading can provide more *transparency* on the positions of the members. An obvious problem here is that a CCP represents the centre of a "hub and spoke" system and consequently its own failure would be a catastrophic event.

The above analysis is clearly rather simplistic and although the general points made are correct, the true CCP landscape is much more complex than represented above because it ignores the following aspects:

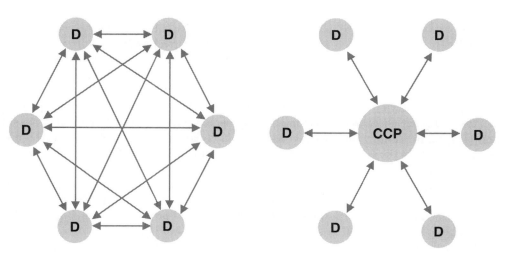

Figure 9.4   Illustration of bilateral markets (left) compared to centrally cleared markets (right).

- *Client clearing.* Parties that cannot be members of the CCP in question will have to clear through a clearing member. This creates additional complexity regarding operational aspects such as collateral transfer and what happens in a default scenario.
- *Bilateral trades.* Not all OTC derivatives are suitable for clearing and a reasonable population will always remain as bilateral transactions.
- *Multiple CCPs.* There are clearly a number of different CCPs globally that may be implicitly interconnected via sharing members.

9.3.4   CCP risk management

Given that CCPs sit at the heart of large financial markets, it is critical that they have effective risk control and adequate financial resources. The most obvious and important method for this is via the collateral that CCPs require to cover the market risk of the trades they clear. As mentioned above, CCPs require both variation and initial margins. Variation margin covers the net change in market value of the member's positions. Initial margin is an additional amount designed to cover the CCP's worst case close-out costs in the event that a clearing member defaults.

In the event of default of one of its members, a CCP will aim to swiftly terminate all financial relations with that counterparty without suffering any losses. This will normally be achieved by replacement of the defaulted counterparty with one of the other clearing members for each trade. This is typically achieved via the CCP auctioning the defaulted members' positions amongst the other members (although other methods are possible) by sub-portfolio (e.g. interest rate swaps in a given currency). Clearing members may have strong incentives to participate in an auction in order to collectively achieve a favourable workout of a default without adverse consequences, such as being exposed to losses through default funds or other mechanisms. This means that the CCP may achieve much better prices for essentially unwinding/novating trades than a party attempting to do this in an uncoordinated, bilaterally cleared market. However, if a CCP auction fails, the consequences are potentially severe, as other much more aggressive methods of loss allocation may follow.

The losses experienced during a clearing member default and the associated auction are absorbed primarily via the collateral the CCP holds. Collateral requirements by CCPs are in general much stricter than in bilateral derivative markets. In particular, variation margin has to be transferred on a daily or even intradaily basis, and must usually be in cash in the currency of the transaction. Initial margin requirements are conservative, will change with market conditions and must be provided in cash or liquid assets (e.g. treasury bonds). The combination of initial margins and increased liquidity of collateral, neither of which has historically been a part of bilateral markets, means that clearing potentially imposes higher costs via collateral requirements. However, bilateral markets in the future will experience similar higher collateral costs due to future regulatory rules (Section 6.7).

In case the initial margin and default fund contributions prove insufficient, and/or the auction fails, the CCP has other financial resources to cover the losses. In general, a "loss waterfall" defines the different ways in which resources will be used. Although they differ from CCP to CCP, a typical loss waterfall is represented in Figure 9.5.

The ideal way for CCP members to contribute financial resources is in a "defaulter pays" approach. This would mean that any clearing member would contribute all the

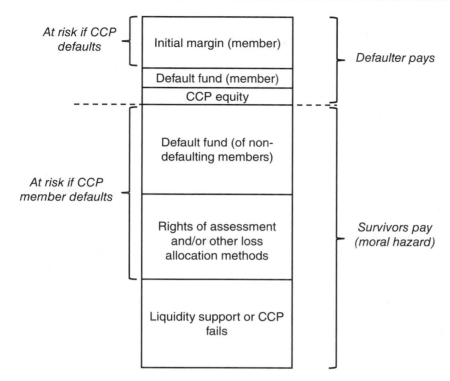

Figure 9.5   Illustration of a typical loss waterfall defining the way in which the default of one or more CCP members is absorbed.

necessary funds to pay for their own potential future default. This is impractical, though, because it would require very high financial contributions from each member, which would be too costly. For this reason, the purpose of financial contributions from a given member is to cover losses to a high level of confidence in a scenario where they would default. In extreme scenarios, where the initial margin and default fund contributions of the defaulted member(s) have been exhausted, further losses may be taken from some contribution ("skin in the game") of the CCP that would still allow it to function normally. As long as these aforementioned components are sufficient, then the "defaulter pays" approach will be fulfilled.

CCP initial margin calculations for OTC derivatives typically utilise the historical simulation approach. Historical simulation takes a period (usually several years) of historical data containing risk factor behaviour across the entire portfolio in question. It then resimulates over many periods how the current portfolio would behave when subjected to the same historical evolution. For example, if four years of data were used, then it would be possible to compute around 1,000 different scenarios of daily movements for the portfolio. CCPs general take the value-at-risk (VAR) or expected shortfall (ES) (Section 3.3.1) as a worst case measure of the performance over these scenarios, representing a statistical confidence level of at least 99%. This is done with the obvious intention that the initial margin in a default scenario is very likely to be sufficient to cover the associated losses. Initial margin approaches in bilateral markets will be broadly similar, as the SIMM (Section 6.7.7) can be seen as a more tractable version of CCP initial margin methodologies for OTC derivatives.

It is worth mentioning that CCPs reduce the margin period of risk (Section 6.6.2) by making daily and potentially also intradaily collateral calls in cash only (no settlement delays). They also have full authority over all calculations (no disputes allowed) and ensure that members can adhere to the operational requirement of posting collateral and that they guarantee to post on behalf of clients if necessary. They can also close-out positions more quickly than in bilateral markets, as they can declare a member in default without any external obstructions and aim to then invoke a swift and effective default management process. For these reasons, CCPs typically use a five-day assumption when calculating initial margins compared to a minimum of ten days under Basel III for bilateral transactions, as discussed in Section 8.6.3.[16]

Another basic principal of central clearing is that of loss mutualisation, where losses above the resources contributed by the defaulter are shared between CCP members. Generally, CCP members all contribute into a CCP "default fund", which is typically used after the defaulter's own resources to cover losses. The relative size of a default fund contribution will be broadly driven by a member's initial margin contribution, although it will be a less dynamic quantity. Since all members pay into this default fund, they all contribute to absorbing an extreme default loss. Losses wiping out a significant portion of the default fund of a CCP are clearly required to be exceptionally unlikely. However, if this does happen, the surviving members of the CCP are required to commit some additional default fund to support the CCP ("rights of assessment"). This contribution is not unlimited and is usually capped (often in relation to a member's initial default fund contribution) as a means to mitigate moral hazard. A CCP may have other methods besides an auction at their disposal such as selective tear-up of transactions or variation margin gains haircutting.[17] Compared to absorbing losses via a default fund, such methods may produce a more heterogeneous allocation of losses. The choice of loss allocation method is aimed to be fair and create the correct incentive for all clearing members.

Some loss allocation methods are theoretically infinite, i.e. the CCP would never fail but rather impose any level of losses on their clearing members to be able to continue to function themselves. Not surprisingly, these allocation methods (e.g. tear-up or forced allocation[18]) are fairly severe and may even cause surviving clearing members to fail.

Assuming loss allocation methods have a finite boundary, then a CCP could potentially fail unless they receive some external liquidity support (via a bailout from a central bank, for example). We should note that, in order to reach the bottom of the loss waterfall, many layers of financial support must be eroded. Hence, although unquantifiable to any relative precision, this should be an extremely low probability event. It is also important to note that a CCP can impose losses on its members via the default fund without being close to actually failing themselves. Hence a CCP's members can suffer

---

[16] This period generally applied to OTC CCPs. In exchange-traded derivatives, the greater underlying liquidity means that a one- or two-day assumption is more common.

[17] See footnote 14.

[18] See footnote 14.

from a "mini-default" of the CCP.[19] Note also that the default losses that a member incurs are not directly related to the transactions that they executed with the defaulting member. Indeed, a member can suffer default losses even if it never traded with the defaulted counterparty or has no net position with the CCP.

9.3.5   Comparing bilateral and central clearing

Table 9.1 compares bilateral and centrally cleared OTC markets. Only standardised, non-exotic and liquid products can be cleared. CCPs impose strong collateral requirements on their members (although regulation in bilateral markets is becoming stricter in this respect). CCP capital charges are relatively moderate and relate to trade level (e.g. initial margin) and default fund exposures. In bilateral markets, participants are exposed to the default risk and CVA capital charges discussed in the last chapter. As mentioned above, one important feature of central clearing is the centralised auction in a default scenario compared with the more uncoordinated bilateral equivalent. In bilateral markets, costs come from counterparty risk, funding and capital, whereas in CCP markets the costs are mainly funding (of initial margin and other financial contributions) related together with smaller capital charges (see Section 9.3.7).

Table 9.1   Comparing bilateral and centrally cleared OTC derivative markets.

	Bilateral	Centrally cleared
Counterparty	Original	CCP
Products	All	Must be standard, vanilla, liquid etc.
Participants	All	Clearing members are usually large banks Other collateral posting entities can clear through clearing members
Collateral	Bilateral, bespoke arrangements dependent on credit quality and open to disputes. New regulatory rules being introduced from September 2016 (Section 6.7)	Full collateralisation, including initial margin enforced by CCP
Capital charges	Default risk and CVA capital	Trade level and default fund related (see below)
Loss buffers	Regulatory capital and collateral (where provided)	Initial margins, default funds and CCP own capital
Close-out	Bilateral	Coordinated default management process (e.g. auctions)
Costs	Counterparty risk, funding and capital costs	Funding (initial margin) and (lower) capital costs

---

[19] For a recent example, see "Banks launch clearing review after Korean broker default", *Financial Times*, 7th March 2014.

9.3.6   Advantages and disadvantages of CCPs

Despite the obvious advantages, mandatory central clearing of OTC derivatives is not without criticism. CCPs have failed in the past (e.g. see Hills et al., 1999). Indeed, the difficulties faced by CCPs in a previous financial crisis, the stock market crash of 1987, posed a serious threat to the entire financial system.

CCPs offer many advantages and potentially offer a more transparent, safer market, where contracts are more fungible and liquidity is enhanced. The following is a summary of the advantages of a CCP:

- *Transparency.* A CCP may face a clearing member for a large proportion of their transactions in a given market and can therefore see concentration that would not be transparent in bilateral markets. If a member has a particularly extreme exposure, the CCP is in a position to act on this and limit trading. These aspects may, in turn, disperse panic that might otherwise be present in bilateral markets due to a lack of knowledge of the exposure faced by institutions.
- *Offsetting.* As mentioned above, contracts transacted between different counterparties but traded through a CCP can be offset. This increases the flexibility to enter new transactions and terminate existing ones, and reduces costs.
- *Loss mutualisation.* Even when a default creates losses that exceed the financial commitments from the defaulter, these losses are distributed throughout the CCP members, reducing their impact on any one member. Thus a counterparty's losses are dispersed partially throughout the market, making their impact less dramatic and reducing the possibility of systemic problems.
- *Legal and operational efficiency.* The collateral, netting and settlement functions undertaken by a CCP potentially increase operational efficiency and reduce costs. CCPs may also reduce legal risks in providing a centralisation of rules and mechanisms.
- *Liquidity.* A CCP may improve market liquidity through the ability of market participants to trade easily and benefit from multilateral netting. Barriers to market entry may be reduced. Daily collateral calls may lead to a more transparent valuation of products.
- *Default management.* A well-managed central auction may result in smaller price disruptions than the uncoordinated replacement of positions during a crisis period associated with default of a clearing member.

A CCP, by its very nature, represents a membership organisation, which therefore results in the pooling of member resources to some degree. This means that any losses due to the default of a CCP member may to some extent be shared amongst the surviving members and this lies at the heart of some potential problems. The following is a summary of the disadvantages of a CCP:

- *Moral hazard.* This is a well-known problem in the insurance industry that has the effect of disincentivising good counterparty risk management practice by CCP members (since all the risk is passed to the CCP). Parties have little incentive to monitor each other's credit quality and act appropriately because a third party is taking most of the risk.

- *Adverse selection.* CCPs are also vulnerable to adverse selection, which occurs if members trading OTC derivatives know more about the risks than the CCP themselves. In such a situation, parties may selectively pass these more risky products to CCPs that under-price the risks. Obviously, firms such as large banks specialise in OTC derivatives and may have superior information and knowledge on pricing and risk than a CCP. Anecdotal evidence on this point is already apparent with market participants aware that different CCPs are cheaper when clearing pay fixed and receive fixed interest rate swaps.
- *Bifurcations.* The requirement to clear standard products may create unfortunate bifurcations between cleared and non-cleared trades. This can result in highly volatile cashflows for customers, and mismatches for seemingly hedged positions.
- *Procyclicality.* Procyclicality refers to a positive dependence with the state of the economy. CCPs may create procyclicality effects by, for example, increasing collateral requirements (or haircuts) in volatile markets or crisis periods. The greater frequency and liquidity of collateral requirements under a CCP (compared with less uniform and more flexible collateral practices in bilateral OTC markets) could also aggravate procyclicality.

For the past century and longer, clearing has been limited to listed derivatives traded on exchanges. Bilateral OTC markets have been extremely successful and their growth has been greater than that of exchange-traded products over the last two decades. The trouble with clearing OTC derivatives is that they are more illiquid, long-dated and complex compared to their exchange-traded relatives.

9.3.7   CCP capital charges

An exposure to a CCP does not attract the capital charges associated with bilateral transactions discussed in the previous chapter.[20] However, there do exist CCP-specific capital charges that reflect the fact that CCPs are not risk-free and that default fund contributions can create losses without a CCP actually failing. The specific details are given in BCBS (2014c).

CCP capital requirements for qualifying CCPs (QCCPs[21]) come in two forms:

- *Trade exposures.* These exposures arise from the current mark-to-market exposure and variation margin, together with the potential future exposure (PFE) and also the initial margin posted to the CCP. Such an exposure is only at risk in the case of the CCP failure (not the failure of other CCP members). A relatively small risk weight of 2% is used for capitalising this component – to put this in context, the lowest risk weight possible under the IRB method discussed in Section 8.1.2 is about 34%[22]. So,

---

[20] This is true for a direct exposure to a CCP. For transactions cleared indirectly through a clearing member, the treatment varies depending on the set-up. For more details, see Gregory (2014).

[21] A QCCP complies with the global principles and is licensed to operate as a CCP (including via an exemption) in relation to the clearing services offered in the region in question.

[22] The risk weight would be the product of the three terms on the right of Equation 8.1 and multiplied by 12.5 to convert from a capital charge. In the number quoted, the minimal regulatory default probability of 0.03% was used together with an LGD of 40% and maturity of five years.

whilst the trade exposure can be very large (driven by the significant quantity of initial margin required by a CCP), the capital charge is relatively small.

- *Default fund exposures.* This covers the exposure via the contribution made to the CCPs default fund, that is at risk even if the CCP does not default. This exposure is problematic to quantify since it is possible for a CCP member to lose some or all of their default fund contribution, due to the default of one or more CCP members or other events such as operational or investment losses, even if the CCP itself does not fail. Furthermore, it may be necessary to contribute additionally to the default fund (rights of assessment) in the event of relatively large losses from the default of other members. The fact that each CCP sets default fund contributions itself further complicates this approach as this implies that each CCP will represent a specific risk. Finally, the potential application of other loss allocation methods, which may also be experienced by clients of clearing members, complicates this still further. The regulatory formulas consider a baseline one-to-one capital charge that, although default fund contributions are relatively small compared to initial margin requirements, is quite punitive. However, forthcoming rules from 2017 are likely to improve this as long as the CCP in question appears well-capitalised compared to the SA-CCR methodology (Section 8.4). More details can be found in Gregory (2014).

9.3.8   What central clearing means for xVA

Central clearing of OTC derivatives is aimed squarely at reducing counterparty risk through the risk management practices of the CCP, in particular with respect to the collateral they require. This would imply that CVA and associated capital charges (KVA) would no longer be a problem when clearing though a CCP. Given an increasing amount of OTC derivatives being centrally cleared (Figure 9.6), this would imply that CVA (and xVA) would become less of an issue in the light of the clearing mandate.

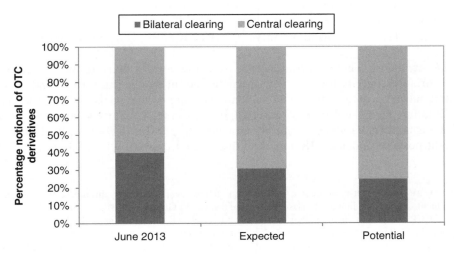

Figure 9.6   Bilaterally and centrally cleared OTC derivatives.
Source: Eurex (2014).

However, there are two problems with the above view. Firstly, it is important to realise that counterparty risk, funding and capital issues (CVA, FVA, KVA) predominantly arise from uncollateralised OTC derivatives with non-financial end-users (for example, see Section 3.1). Since such end-users will be exempt from the clearing mandate, they will not move to central clearing except on a voluntary basis. Since most such end-users find it difficult to post collateral, such voluntary clearing is unlikely. Hence, the uncollateralised bilateral transactions that are most important from an xVA perspective will persist as such.

Secondly, it is also important to note that central clearing and other changes such as the incoming bilateral collateral rules (Section 6.7) may reduce components such as CVA but will also increase other components (most obviously FVA and MVA which arise from funding variation and initial margins respectively, as discussed in Chapter 16). Hence, it will become even more important to consider xVA holistically to understand the balance of various effects.

9.4 SUMMARY

This chapter has described the historical development of various methods of counter-party risk mitigation via intermediation. Entities such as SPVs, DPCs and monoline insurers have been discussed mainly from a historical perspective to understand potential problems in terms of their operation and the financial risks they create. We have also described CCP operation in bilateral OTC derivatives markets in more detail. Due to the clearing mandate, OTC clearing will become increasingly important in the future and thus will be an important part of the xVA assessment. Central counterparties transform xVA: components such as CVA, FVA and KVA are reduced whilst MVA is increased and KVA changes form. This is why it is so important to consider all aspects of xVA holistically.

10
Quantifying Credit Exposure

> *The trouble with our times is that the future is not what it used to be.*
>
> Paul Valery (1871–1945)

10.1 INTRODUCTION

In this chapter, we present an overview of the various methods used to quantify exposure, focusing mainly on the most common and generic approach of Monte Carlo simulation. We will explain the methodology for exposure quantification, including a discussion of the approaches to modelling risk factors in different asset classes and their co-dependencies, and also the computational aspects. To illustrate many of the concepts, we will then show a number of examples, looking in particular at the impact of aspects such as model choice and calibration as well as the effect of netting. (Collateral is discussed in the next chapter.)

At the heart of the problem of quantifying exposure lies a balance between the following two effects:

- As we look into the future, we become increasingly uncertain about market variables. Hence, risk increases as we move through time.
- Many OTC derivatives have cashflows that are paid over their lifetime, and this tends to reduce the risk profiles as the portfolios in question "amortise" through time.

The practical calculation of exposure also inevitably involves a balance with respect to sophistication and resource considerations.

10.2 METHODS FOR QUANTIFYING CREDIT EXPOSURE

10.2.1 Parametric approaches

These approaches are not model-based but instead aim to parametrise exposure based on a number of simple parameters that have potentially been calibrated to more complex approaches. Their advantage is that they are simple, but they are not particularly risk-sensitive and often represent more complex features poorly.

The simplest such approach is the current exposure method (CEM) used in counterparty risk capital calculations, as discussed in Section 8.2. The new SA-CCR approach for capital (Section 8.4) is more sophisticated, although slightly more complicated. These approaches approximate the future exposure as the current positive exposure plus an "add-on" component that represents the uncertainty of the PFE in the future. At the transaction level, the "add-on" component should account for:

- the time horizon in question; and
- the volatility of the underlying asset class.

For example, longer time horizons will require larger add-ons and volatile asset classes, such as FX and commodities, should attract larger add-ons. Add-on approaches are fast and easy to implement but have a limited or non-existent treatment of more subtle effects, including:

- the specifics of the transaction in question (currency, nature of cashflows);
- if the transaction has a mark-to-market (MTM) very far from zero (other than the addition of this MTM when it is positive);
- netting; and
- collateral.

It is difficult to incorporate such effects except with rather crude rules (for example, the CEM method allows 60% of current netting benefit to apply to future exposure). More sophisticated add-on methodologies have been developed (e.g. Rowe, 1995; Rowe and Mulholland, 1999) and in the SA-CCR approach discussed already (see comparison results in Section 8.5). However, a simple parametric approach can never accurately represent exposure in all cases, especially the more complex ones.

10.2.2   Semi-analytical methods

Semi-analytical methods are generally more sophisticated than the simple parameter approaches as they are model-based. Their advantage lies in avoiding the time-consuming process of Monte Carlo simulation. A semi-analytical method will generally be based on:

- making some simple assumptions regarding the risk factor(s) driving the exposure;
- finding the distribution of the exposure as defined by the above risk factor(s); and
- calculating a semi-analytical approximation to a risk metric for that exposure distribution.

Some very simple and general semi-analytical expressions were described in Chapter 7 and formulas can be found in the appendices. One product-specific and well-known semi-analytical formula can be found in Sorensen and Bollier (1994) who show that the exposure of an interest rate swap can be defined in terms of a series of interest rate swaptions.[1] The intuition is that the counterparty might default at any time in the future and,

---

[1] We note that these semi-analytical formulas are generally concerned with calculating risk-neutral exposures using underlyings such as traded swaption prices. Such approaches can also be used for real-world calculations (as is usual for PFE) but this is not as straightforward.

hence, effectively cancel the non-recovered value of the swap, economically equivalent to exercising the reverse[2] swaption.

The swap exposure and swaption analogy is illustrated in Figure 10.1 with more mathematical details given in Appendix 10A. The expected exposure (EE) of the swap will be defined by the interaction between two factors: the swaption payoff and the underlying swap duration (these are the two components in the simple approach given in Equation 7.4 in Section 7.3.3). These quantities respectively increase and decrease monotonically over time. The overall swaption value therefore peaks at an intermediate point.

Spreadsheet 10.1 Semi-analytical calculation of the exposure for a swap	

This approach naturally captures effects such as the asymmetry between payer and receiver swap (Figure 10.2) and unequal payment frequencies such as in basis swap (Figure 10.3). In the former case, the underlying swaptions are in- or out-of-the-money for payer and receiver swaps respectively. In the latter case, the strike of the swaptions moves significantly out-of-the-money when an institution receives a quarterly cashflow whilst not needing (yet) to make a semi-annual one.

The Sorensen and Bollier formula gives a useful insight on exposure quantification: specifically that the exposure calculation will be more complex than pricing the underlying product itself. To quantify the exposure of a swap, one needs to know about swaption volatility (across time and strike), components far beyond those needed to price the swap itself. The value of the swap does not depend significantly on volatility and yet the EE for the swap does.

The above analogy can be extended to other products, since any non-path dependent transaction can be represented as a series of European options. A semi-analytical

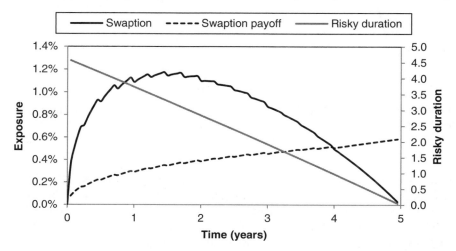

Figure 10.1 Illustration of swap EE as defined by swaption values which are given by the product of the swaption payoff and the risky duration value (shown on the secondary y-axis).

---

[2] From the counterparty's point of view.

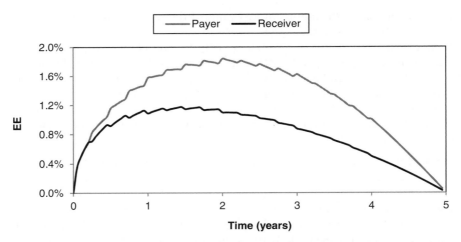

Figure 10.2   Illustration of swap EE for payer and receiver swaps as defined by swaption values.

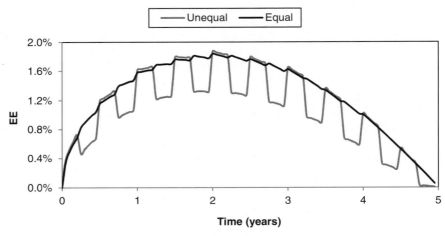

Figure 10.3   Illustration of swap EE for unequal (pay semi-annually, receive quarterly) swaps as defined by swaption values.

approach would clearly be the method of choice for evaluating the exposure of a single transaction, although in some cases, such as cross-currency swaps will still be problematic. In some circumstances semi-analytical approximations can also be extended beyond the single transaction level to, for example, a portfolio of interest rate swaps in a single currency as discussed by Brigo and Masetti (2005b). The ability to do this may often be useful, as some end-user counterparties may trade a rather narrow range of underlying products, the exposure of which may be modelled semi-analytically. However, multidimensional netting sets will typically need to be treated in a more generic approach.

Obvious drawbacks of such semi-analytical approaches are:

- Semi-analytical calculations depend on simplifying assumptions made with respect to the risk factors involved. Hence, complicated distributional assumptions cannot typically be incorporated.
- Path-dependent aspects (exercises, breaks) will be hard to capture, as will collateral, which is path-dependent, although approximations for collateralised exposures may be easier to formulate (as discussed in the next chapter).
- Such calculations typically ignore netting effects (Brigo and Masetti, 2005b is one exception), which are hard to incorporate in their most general fashion, although many netting sets (especially for non-collateralised counterparties) will actually be quite simple due to the rather narrow requirements of end-users of OTC derivatives.
- Such approaches may not be future-proof. In particular, the need to incorporate new products and changes in market practice (e.g. the increasing use of initial margins) may be hard to capture.

Whilst simple and/or collateralised netting sets may permit analytical calculations that will be much faster than Monte Carlo approaches, they may create difficulties from an operational point of view. A counterparty trading single currency swaps wanting to trade an FX forward may create a netting set that can no longer be handled within the analytical approximation used. Vanilla pricing may be straightforward, but more structured transactions may create problems. Hence, whilst Monte Carlo approaches may sometimes be unnecessarily complex, their generality is a significant advantage.

10.2.3 Monte Carlo simulation

Monte Carlo simulation, whilst the most complex and time-consuming method to assess exposure, is generic and copes with many of the complexities (such as transaction specifics, path dependency, netting and collateralisation) that simpler approaches may fail or struggle to capture. It is the only method that in the case of a high-dimensionality netting set can realistically be used with a relatively large number of risk factors and their correlations.

A generic approach also provides flexibility as market practice and regulation changes. For example, initial margins have in the past been rare but are becoming increasingly important with the central clearing mandate (Section 9.3) and bilateral collateral rules (Section 6.7). In more simple approaches, the incorporation of the impact of initial margin is unlikely to be easy and may require approximations, whereas in a Monte Carlo approach it will be more straightforward (although even dynamic initial margin will be a challenge, as discussed in Section 11.4.2).

So, whilst add-on and analytical approaches still sometimes exist, Monte Carlo simulation of exposure has been considered state-of-the-art for some time. Banks generally use Monte Carlo implementation across all products and counterparties, even when analytical approximations may be achievable in some cases. An obvious disadvantage of Monte Carlo simulation is computation time, which means that significant hardware is required to support its implementation.

10.3   MONTE CARLO METHODOLOGY

This section defines the general approach to Monte Carlo exposure computation without referencing more specific aspects such as model choice and calibration, which will be described in later sections.

Spreadsheet 10.2   Simple simulation of an interest rate swap exposure

---

10.3.1   Simulation model

The first task is to define the relevant risk factors and decide on the models to be used for their evolution. However, it is important to strike a balance between a realistic model and one that is parsimonious. For example, there are 50–60 or more risk factors defining an interest rate curve, whereas the simplest interest rate models involve only one factor. A model involving two or three factors may represent a compromise. Such an approach will capture more of the possible curve movements than a single-factor model would, but without producing the unrealistic curve shapes and arbitrageable prices that a model for each individual risk factor might generate. A more advanced model will also be able to calibrate more accurately and to a broader range of market prices (e.g. swaption volatilities).

Models must obviously not be too complex, as it must also be possible and practical to simulate discrete scenarios of the risk factors using the model. Typically, many thousands of scenarios will be required at many points in time and hence there must be an efficient way in which to generate these many scenarios. Another reason for simpler underlying models for risk factors is the need to incorporate co-dependencies (correlations)[3] in order to capture the multidimensional behaviour of the netting sets to be simulated. The correct description of the underlying risk factors and correlations leads to a significant number of model parameters. A balance is important when considering the modelling of a given set of risk factors (such as an interest rate curve) and the correlation between this and another set of risk factors (such as an interest rate curve in another currency). There is no point in having sophisticated univariate modelling and naïve multivariate modelling. Due to expertise in different product areas, an institution may have good univariate models for interest rates, FX, inflation, commodities, equities and credit. However, these may be linked via the naïve use of correlations. We will give examples of specific models in Section 10.4.5.

Whilst the choice of models for the underlying market variables is a key aspect, calibration of these models is just as important since future scenarios will depend on this. Models calibrated using historical data predict future scenarios based on statistical patterns observed in the past and assume that this previous behaviour is a good indicator of the future; such models are sometimes slow to react to changes in market conditions. Models calibrated to market prices tend to be more forward-looking but contain components such as risk premiums and storage costs that introduce bias. Furthermore, they

---

[3] Correlation is often the specific way in which to represent co-dependency and is very commonly used. We will use correlation from now on, but note that there are other ways to model co-dependency (as discussed further in Chapter 17).

may produce exposures that jump dramatically, for example during a period of high volatility. This will be discussed further in Section 10.4.

It is important to emphasise that the simulation model must be generic to support consistent simulation of the many risk factors that would be required to value a quite complex netting set. Calibrations also tend to be generic rather than netting set or transaction-specific. This is very different to classical modelling of OTC derivatives, where many models (and individual calibrations thereof) are typically used. This leads to unavoidable differences (hopefully small) between current valuation as seen from the xVA system and the relevant front-office systems. This will be discussed in Section 10.3.3.

10.3.2   Scenario generation

Having made a choice of risk factors and underlying model, it is necessary to generate scenarios via simulation of these risk factors. Each scenario is a joint realisation of risk factors at various points in time. Scenarios should be consistent since it must be possible to see the impact of various risks offsetting one another,[4] at least within a given netting set. Scenario consistency outside netting sets, where risks are additive, is not important for counterparty risk considerations but may be important for funding (Chapter 15).

One will first need to choose a grid for simulation, as illustrated in Figure 10.4. Note that the discussion on the choice of grid is important for aspects such as potential future exposure (PFE) assessment where the exposure needs to be visualised and not particularly relevant for quantification of metrics such as CVA.

The number of grid points must be reasonably large to capture the main details of the exposure, but not so large as to make the computations unfeasible. A typical value is in the region of 50–200. The final simulation date must obviously be greater than or equal to the longest maturity transaction under consideration. Note that the spacing of the above dates need not be uniform for reasons such as roll-off (discussed below) and identifying settlement risk. In addition, since intervals between simulation points are often greater than the length of the margin period of risk (Section 6.6.2), it may be necessary to include additional "look-back" points for the purposes of simulating the impact of collateral (Figure 10.5). This is discussed in more detail in the next chapter. Furthermore, the ability to change grids for different counterparties is beneficial due to different maximum maturity dates, collateral terms and underlying transaction type.

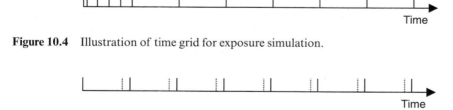

Figure 10.4   Illustration of time grid for exposure simulation.

Figure 10.5   Illustration of time grid for exposure simulation with additional points included for collateral calculations.

---

[4] So that a given scenario represents the same state of the world across trades.

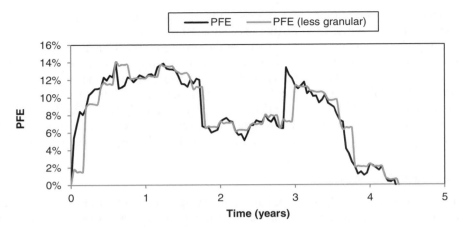

Figure 10.6   PFE for a counterparty calculated at different levels of granularity. In the normal case, the time intervals are spaced by ten business days, while in the less granular case, the interval is five times greater.

When exposure is calculated at only discrete points, it is possible to miss key areas of risk or "hotspots". Exposure profiles can be highly discontinuous over time due to maturity dates, option exercise, cashflow payments and break clauses. These aspects cause jumps, which may be small in duration but large in magnitude. Daily jumps correspond to settlement risk (Section 4.1.2). The impact of roll-off risk is shown in Figure 10.6.

The risk from the above jumps can be mitigated by using non time-homogeneous time grids (as in Figure 10.4), at least providing a better definition as discrepancies become closer. However, this can mean that the PFE may change significantly from day to day due to exposure jumps gradually becoming engulfed within the more granular short-term grid. A better approach is to incorporate the critical points where exposure changes significantly (for example, due to maturity dates, settlement dates and cashflow payment dates) into the time grid. This must be done separately for each netting set. The ability to use different grids is important; for example, to provide more granularity for certain instrument types or shorter maturities.

Another question to decide is whether the simulation should be done pathwise or via a direct simulation, as illustrated in Figure 10.7. As described by Pykhtin and Zhu (2007), a pathwise approach simulates an entire possible trajectory whereas a direct approach simulates each time point independently. Both methods should converge to the same underlying distributions and results; however, the pathwise method is more suitable for path-dependent derivatives, derivatives with Bermudan features and collateral modelling. Therefore, for simulating exposure for purposes such as PFE (although not necessarily for CVA calculations), the best approach is pathwise.

10.3.3   Revaluation

Once the scenarios have been generated, it is necessary to revalue the individual positions at each point in time in the future. For example, to revalue an interest rate swap in a

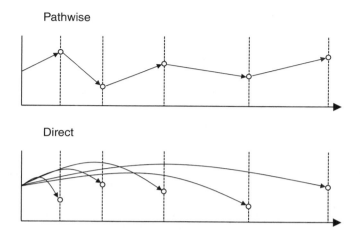

Figure 10.7   Illustration of the difference between pathwise and direct simulation. Note that the direct simulation may be more time-consuming and be problematic with respect to capturing path dependence because adjacent points are independent.

given scenario at a given point in time, one must calculate the corresponding risk factors (interest rates) and then use the standard pricing function for the swap as a function of these interest rates (for example, via a formula for reconstructing the yield curve at this particular point in time).

The revaluation step clearly requires the use of efficient valuation models and algorithms. Suppose the total population of transactions and exposure calculation involves:

- 250 counterparties;
- on average, 40 transactions with each counterparty;
- 100 simulation steps; and
- 10,000 scenarios.

Then the total number of instrument revaluations will be $250 \times 40 \times 100 \times 10,000 = 10,000,000,000$ (10 billion). This has very significant implications for the computation speed of pricing models, as this step usually represents the bottleneck of a PFE or xVA calculation.

Pricing functions for vanilla instruments must be highly optimised, with any common functionality (such as calculating fixings) stripped out to optimise the calculation as much as possible. Whilst such pricing functions are usually relatively fast, the sheer volume of vanilla products makes this optimisation important. Another important optimisation is to bucket cashflows in a single currency so as to reduce the number of pricing evaluations (Figure 10.8). Given the inherent approximation of using a relatively large discrete time-step, this should not represent a further significant approximation.

Exotic products may present more of a problem since, whilst there may be fewer of them, pricing often involves lattice-based or Monte Carlo methods that may be too slow. There are various ways to get around this problem, for example:

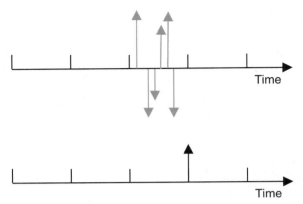

Figure 10.8 Illustration of cashflow bucketing in a single currency. The cashflows between the dates shown (top) can be realistically combined into a single payment (bottom) whilst preserving the MTM and potentially other aspects such as the sensitivity.

- *Approximations.* Sometimes crude ad hoc approximations may be deemed of sufficient accuracy; for example, approximating a Bermudan swaption as a European swaption (which allows a closed-form formula to be used).
- *Grids.* Grids giving the MTM of a transaction can be used as long as the dimensionality of the problem is not too large. Such grids may be populated by front-office systems and therefore be in line with trading desk valuation models. The exposure calculation will look up (and possibly interpolate) the relevant values on the grid rather than performing costly pricing.
- *American Monte Carlo methods.* This is a generic approach to utilising future Monte Carlo simulations to provide good approximations of the exposure[5] at a given point in time. Examples of this and related approaches can be found in Longstaff and Schwartz (2001), Glasserman and Yu (2002) and Cesari et al. (2009). This may be the best solution for xVA quantification but may be not as relevant for PFE and risk management (see Section 14.4.5).

Whilst there are many ways to improve the efficiency of the revaluation step, it is likely that this will have to be backed up by some quite significant hardware with hundreds or even thousands of CPUs. Given that a large institution may have to calculate each day the exposure of millions of trades in thousands of paths for hundreds of time steps, this is not surprising. Furthermore, the requirement to calculate exposure and price potential new transactions in sometimes no more than seconds also creates significant computational requirements.

Inevitably, even for simple products, there are MTM differences between the exposure calculation compared to official valuation. These differences are sometimes corrected for by applying shifts, as illustrated in Figure 10.9. Such shift can be proportional (as shown) or amortising. The latter case is relevant where MTMs differ because of model differences, since these may tend to converge as the transaction approaches maturity. The

---

[5] It can be used for both expected exposure (for xVA purposes) and PFE (for risk management purposes), although the accuracy in the latter case is typically worse. Furthermore, being a generic approach, this will not match front-office valuations exactly.

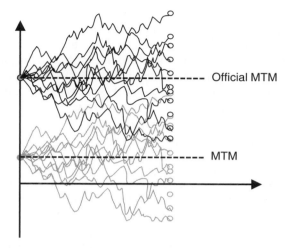

Figure 10.9 Illustration of the use of a proportion shift to correct an exposure simulation to the official MTM.

former is more appropriate when the valuation difference arises from contractual aspects (for example, a misspecification of a cashflow). Note that since different transactions vary significantly in terms of their contractual features and valuation methodologies, shifts should be applied at the transaction level.

10.3.4 Aggregation

Once the revaluation step has been done, there will be a large amount of data in three dimensions corresponding to the transaction (k), simulation (s) and time-step (t). We represent the future value as a function of each of these components as $V(k,s,t)$. This information may need to be aggregated at some level. Typically, it is needed at the netting set level but sometimes may need to be aggregated across counterparties or portfolios. Let us assume that transactions $k=1,K$ need to be aggregated. The future aggregate value is characterised by the matrix:

$$V_{Agg}(s,t) = \sum_{k=1}^{K} V(k,s,t)$$ (10.1)

Now $V_{agg}(s,t)$ defines the net future value of the aggregate set in simulation s and time step t. It may not be necessary to store all of the individual transaction information, $V(k,s,t)$, although this might be needed for calculating certain quantities (for example, see the discussion on marginal exposure in Section 10.7.3).

10.3.5 Post-processing

The previous step provides future values in all scenarios and time steps, aggregated to the appropriate level (e.g. netting set). The purpose of post-processing is to go through these values and apply the logic corresponding to a certain risk mitigant, the most obvious being collateral. Post-processing for a collateralised exposure means analysing each simulation path and applying the relevant logic to determine, at each point, how much collateral would be posted. Typically, this can be done independently of (but after) the previous steps under the assumption that the collateral parameters do not depend on any of the underlying market variables but only on the total exposure in one or more netting sets.

Post-processing can also apply to features such as termination events (Section 5.4.2) and resets (Section 5.4.3) although we note that these must be typically accounted for at the transaction level. These aspects will be discussed, together with collateral modelling, in more detail in the next chapter.

10.3.6   Extraction

Finally, once all the above steps have been completed, one can extract any metrics desired (for example, for risk management, pricing or regulatory purposes). Sometimes scenarios will be collapsed into metrics such as CVA. However, it is quite often desirable to store intermediate values in order to facilitate certain calculations. The classic example of this is storing values to facilitate the calculation of incremental CVA (or xVA), which is discussed later in Section 10.7.2.

10.4   REAL-WORLD OR RISK-NEUTRAL

10.4.1   Two fundamentally different approaches

Scenario generation for risk management purposes and arbitrage pricing theory tend to use different "measures". Arbitrage-based pricing uses the so-called risk-neutral measure, which is justified through hedging and arbitrage considerations. Parameters (and therefore probability distributions) such as drifts and volatilities are market-implied and need not correspond to the real distributions (or even comply with common sense). For a risk management application, one does not need to use the risk-neutral measure and may be focused rather on the real-world measure, estimated using, for example, historical data. Risk-neutral parameters are typically used in pricing applications (xVA), whilst real-world parameters generally form the basis of risk management models (PFE). There are therefore two fundamentally different ways in which to simulate exposure:

- *Real-world*. This refers to the attempt to simulate market variables based on the expected macroeconomic behaviour. Inevitably, this tends to use historical data for calibration.
- *Risk-neutral*. This refers to simulating market variables in a no-arbitrage framework, which requires calibration to market data.

For example, in a risk-neutral framework, interest rate volatilities (and associated parameters such as mean-reversions) would be derived from the prices of interest rate swaptions, caps and floors, rather than estimated via historical time series. In addition, the drift of the underlying variables (such as interest rates and FX rates) will need to be calibrated to forward rates, rather than coming from some historical or other real-world analysis.[6]

---

[6] As noted in Section 10.4.5 below, risk-neutral drift may often be used anyway for calculating exposure for risk management purposes.

As noted above, the choice of whether to use real-world or risk-neutral depends on the application. For risk management purposes, a model must provide a reasonable distribution of the possible risks of the transactions and thus account for a large fraction of the future plausible scenarios. The model will typically be calibrated to historical data in a real-world framework. Traditional VAR models are a classic example of this. For pricing, the most important aspect is matching current market data and explained MTM movements with respect to hedges and therefore a risk-neutral framework is preferable. In general, the application of the different approaches is as follows:

- *Real-world.* PFE simulation for credit limits purposes and capital calculations using the internal model method (IMM). This is often known as the P-measure. Real-world parameters are often used since the intention is to reflect the true economic reality and not be blurred by aspects such as the market price of risk or effects such as supply and demand.
- *Risk-neutral.* Pricing and valuation of CVA (and xVA) is generally under the Q-measure. In pricing and valuation of derivatives, market participants generally aim to calibrate to risk-neutral parameters where possible and resort only to real-world for the remaining non-observable parameters. This makes intuitive sense given that hedging can only perform in neutralising MTM changes with market instruments. It is also important to note that accounting rules (e.g. IFRS 13) suggest risk-neutral calibration since they require market observables to be used in valuation wherever possible.

The choice between real-world and risk-neutral approaches is a difficult one because each have various merits and weaknesses, as summarised in Table 10.1. In general, a historical approach reflects more appropriately the real-world nature of the problem but assumes that history is a good predictor of the future. On the other hand, market-implied approaches may be more indicative of current market conditions but, even if this is true, will be systematically biased upwards due to the existence of risk premiums and may be excessively erratic and procyclical as aspects such as the market price of risk change through time. This latter point would imply that limit breaches would be more common.

A more subtle problem with the separation between real-world and risk-neutral approaches is illustrated in Figure 10.10. Revaluation of transactions at future dates should always be done using risk-neutral valuation (Q-measure) as this is what happens in reality. If we simulate in the real-world (P-measure) then the resulting inconsistency can cause difficulties, for example, in using American Monte Carlo methods as discussed in Section 10.3.3. On the other hand, simulating in the Q-measure makes the set-up self-consistent.

A key high-level question is whether an exposure simulation should be real-world, risk-neutral or indeed if both approaches should be supported. This is a difficult question to answer and we will provide some additional theoretical discussion below before

Table 10.1   Comparison of real-world and risk-neutral approaches.

	Advantages	Disadvantages
Real-world	Unbiased	Not forward looking
Risk-neutral	May be more forward looking Retains consistency with underlying pricing approaches	Systematically biased Procyclical

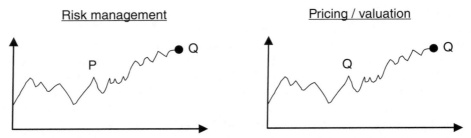

Figure 10.10   Illustration of the different requirements from scenario models for risk management and pricing/valuation. For risk management, simulations tend to be done under the real-world (P) measure whilst revaluations must be risk-neutral (Q measure). For pricing purposes, both scenarios and revaluations are risk-neutral.

returning to the question from a more practical point of view in Chapter 18. Some banks have separate implementations for counterparty risk and xVA across the front-office, and risk functions that will usually follow broadly risk-neutral and real-world approaches respectively.

As shown in Figure 10.11, there is certainly some debate between using real-world or risk-neutral approaches. However, it is important to understand the general differences between real-world and risk-neutral parameters. These can be generally be divided into three types:

- drift – the trend of market variables;
- volatility – the future uncertainty of market variables; and
- correlation – the co-movement between market variables.

These will be considered separately below.

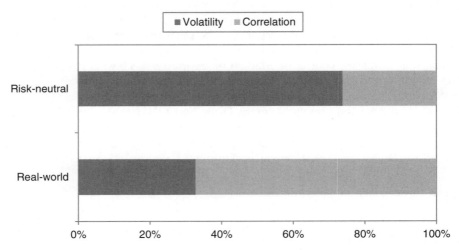

Figure 10.11   Exposure model calibration for volatilities and correlations using real-world and risk-neutral parameters.
Source: Deloitte/Solum CVA survey, 2013.

10.4.2   Drift

A key difference between value-at-risk (VAR) analysis for market risk (for example) and exposure quantification for xVA purposes is the time horizon concerned. In the relatively short market risk horizon (for example, ten days in VAR approaches), the drift of an underlying asset is of secondary importance vis-a-vis its volatility and is often ignored. However, in the longer time horizons required for assessing exposure and xVA, drift will be a key consideration alongside volatility. In other words, the trend (or drift) of an underlying variable can be just as important as its uncertainty.

The consideration of drifts is important since the impact of volatility approximately follows the square root of time scaling whereas the drift scales more linearly – so a strong drift will eventually dominate. Futures (or equivalently forward) prices have long been an important mechanism of price discovery in financial markets as they apparently represent the intersection of expected supply and demand at some future point in time. Forward rates can sometimes be very far from spot rates and it is important to understand whether or not this is truly the "view of the market". Some important technical factors are:

- *Interest rates.* Yield curves may be upwards-sloping or downwards-sloping (and a variety of other shapes) due to the risk appetite for short-, medium- and long-term interest rate risk and the view that rates may increase or decrease.
- *Foreign exchange (FX) rates.* Forward FX rates are determined from an arbitrage relationship between the interest rate curves for the relevant currency pair. Expectation of future FX rates may have an influence on the current interest rate curves in the corresponding currencies. However, there has long been doubt regarding the ability of long-term forward FX rates to predict future spot FX rates; see, for example, Meese and Rogoff (1983) and a review by Sarno and Taylor (2002).
- *Commodity prices.* In addition to market participants' view of the direction of commodity prices, storage costs (or lack of storage), inventory and seasonal effects can move commodities futures apart from spot rates. For high inventories the futures price is higher than the spot price (contango). When inventories are low, commodity spot prices can be higher than futures prices (backwardation).
- *Credit spreads.* Credit curves may be increasing or decreasing either due to demand for credit risk at certain maturities or the view that default probability will be increasing or decreasing over time. Historically, the shape of credit curves has not been a good predictor of future credit spread levels.

There has been much empirical testing of the relationship between spot and futures / forward prices across different markets. It is a generally held belief that the forward rate is a biased forecast of the future spot price. If we take the view that the forward rate is the best expectation of the future spot rate then this may lead to a strong drift assumption. If this view is wrong then it will significantly overstate or understate the risk, as the following example illustrates.

Example

Consider a transaction whose future value has a volatility of 10% and a drift of 5% over one year.

The expected exposure (EE) based on the usual formula (Appendix 7A) is

$$\left[5\% \times \Phi(5\%/10\%) + 10\% \times \varphi(5\%/10\%)\right] = 6.98\%.$$

On the other hand, consider the reverse transaction. The expected drift would be −5% and the expected exposure

$$\left[-5\% \times \Phi(-5\%/10\%) + 10\% \times \varphi(-5\%/10\%)\right] = 1.98\%.$$

In other words, different drift assumptions give EEs that differ by approximately three and half times.

10.4.3   Volatility

If one uses a historical estimate of volatility, then the implicit assumption is that the past will be a good indication of the future. It is also necessary to decide what history of data to use; a short history will give poor statistics, whereas a long history will give weight to "old", meaningless data. In quiet markets, the lack of variability in historical time series will give low volatility, which may give misleadingly risk numbers and lead to procyclicality. Using historical data from stress periods can alleviate this, but then yet more subjectivity is introduced in choosing the correct period of stress.

For most markets, there is likely to be implied volatility information, potentially as a function of strike and the maturity of the option. However, implied volatility will not be observed for out-of-the-money options and longer maturities. Since implied volatility will react quickly when the market becomes more uncertain, then its use can be justified via the "market knows best" view (or at least the market knows better than historical data). However, risk premiums embedded in market-implied volatilities will lead to a systematic overestimate of the overall risk. It has been argued that implied volatility is a superior estimator of future volatility (e.g. see Jorion, 2007, Chapter 9) compared with historical estimation via time series approaches. The stability of the volatility risk premium and the fact that an overestimate of volatility will always lead to a more conservative[7] risk number give greater credence to this idea.

Another difference between historical and implied volatility is the term structure impact (including aspects such as mean reversion in models). A volatility skew across time (e.g. long-dated volatility being higher than short-dated volatility) means that forward volatility is higher than spot volatility. However, empirical evidence does not always support forward volatility being predictive of actual future volatility.

---

[7] Using implied volatility might be expected to produce an upwards bias due to a risk premium, leading to higher (more conservative) risk numbers.

10.4.4   Correlation

Whilst it is at least conservative to assume volatilities are high, the same is not true of other quantities. When estimating correlation for modelling exposure, there may not be an obvious way of knowing whether a high or low (or positive or negative) value is more conservative. Indeed, in a complex portfolio it may even be that the behaviour of the exposure with respect to correlation is not monotonic.[8] Therefore, the use of some market-implied parameters cannot be justified on the basis that the resulting risk numbers will be conservatively high.

Implied correlations are sometimes available in the market. For example, a quanto option has a payoff in a different currency and thus gives information on the implied correlation between the relevant FX rate and the underlying asset. One key aspect of correlation is to determine wrong-way risk. For example, a quanto CDS (a CDS where the premium and default legs are in different currencies) potentially gives information on the correlation between the relevant FX rate and the credit quality of the reference entity in the CDS (Section 17.4.4).

Whilst implied correlation can sometimes be calculated, for most quantities no market prices will be available and so historical data will typically be used. This means that the sensitivity of xVA to correlations cannot generally be hedged. A sensitivity analysis of correlation will be useful to understand the importance of a particular correlation parameter.

10.4.5   Market practice

Table 10.2 summarises the general market practice for the use of real-world and risk-neutral parameters. Regarding drift, calibrations generally use risk-neutral parameters (e.g. forward rates) as this is more convenient from a modelling perspective (see Figure 10.10) and avoids the need for economic forecasting. Note that in risk and regulatory exposure calculations some banks may occasionally use a zero drift instead of calibrating to forward rates for certain risk factors. This is driven by the empirical experience that forward rates are often poor predictors of future spot rates, and avoids risk and capital quantities being biased due to the presence of aspects such as interest rate differentials, risk premiums and storage costs (e.g. backwardation) discussed in Section 10.4.2. It is

Table 10.2 Comparison of use of real-world and market implied parameters in exposure quantification.

	Real-world choice	Risk-neutral choice	General market practice
Drift	Economic forecasting	Forward rates	Risk-neutral
Volatility	Historical time-series	Implied volatility surface	Mixed
Correlation	Historical time-series	Spread options, quantos, baskets	Real-world

---

[8] Meaning, for example, that the worse correlation may not be equal to 100% or –100% but somewhere in between.

also worth mentioning that drift is less important for collateralised exposures. At the other extreme, correlations are usually real-world (historical data) based, since limited market prices are available for basket, quanto and spread option products that could define implied correlations. This leaves volatility assessment as the most subjective and important area to consider.

Risk-neutral approaches have become standard for quantification of components such as CVA and FVA. This has been catalysed by the more active management of such components and accounting standards. Where market practice differs is more in relation to PFE (credit limits) and capital calculations. Since KVA is typically not transfer priced (i.e. it is often seen only in hurdles and not charged), then it could be argued that a real-world approach to capital would be more relevant. However, some banks do use a risk-neutral approach for IMM capital calculations that should improve the capital relief from credit hedges executed by the xVA desk. However, this is not without problems: regulation capital requirements would still require the use of stressed calibrations (e.g. stressed implied volatility from a period in the past), which will be misaligned with the xVA desk view of current market implied volatility. Furthermore, the use of risk-neutral calibrations may make backtesting results (Section 8.6.4) harder to interpret. As mentioned in Section 8.7, BCBS (2015) may lead to a better capital framework with respect to these issues. These issues will be discussed further in Chapter 18.

10.5   MODEL CHOICE

In this section, we provide some broad details on models used for exposure simulation considering some basic points on the modelling in different asset classes (see also Appendix 10B for additional detail). We consider the calibration issues, the balance between complex and simple models, and make some comments for different asset classes We will provide only an overview and the reader is directed to Cesari et al. (2009) and Brigo et al. (2013) for a more mathematical treatment.

10.5.1   Risk-neutral or real-world?

Related to the discussion above, a first question is whether the model will be used in a real-world or risk-neutral context, or indeed will be required to support both. This is an important point since real-world and risk-neutral approaches would normally lead to different modelling choices. For example, when modelling interest rates using historical data, an approach such as principal component analysis (PCA) may be preferred as a means to capture historical yield curve evolution. However, a risk-neutral interest rate model would more naturally be an arbitrage-free term structure approach such as a Hull-White short-rate model or Libor Market Model (LMM). In order to support both real world and risk-neutral calibrations, it may be necessary to use an arbitrage-free model and calibrate this either historically or to market data. Whether to do this or have separate implementations will be discussed in Chapter 18.

In practical terms, comparing real world or risk-neutral calibrations can produce two different effects. These effects are illustrated for PFE only because EE (for example, for CVA and FVA quantification) is commonly computed only from a risk-neutral point of view.

- *Drift*. Risk-neutral drifts are derived from forwards rates whereas real-world drifts may incorporate historical data, an economic view to simply be set to zero. The difference in drift will "twist" the exposure distribution, as illustrated in Figure 10.12 for an interest rate swap. In this example, since the interest rate curve is upwards-sloping (long-term interest rates are higher than short-term rates), the risk-neutral drift is positive, leading to the 99% PFE being higher than the 1% PFE (this effect was explained in Section 7.3.3).
- *Volatility*. A larger volatility will increase both PFEs (in absolute terms). Figure 10.13 shows the expected exposure of a cross-currency swap under both real-world and risk-neutral volatility assumptions. Here the main impact is simply that risk-neutral volatilities tend to be higher than real-world ones and hence both the EE and NEE are bigger. Note that this may not be the case if stressed historical volatilities are used. When using risk-neutral volatility, the term structure is also important, as shown in Figure 10.14. An upwards-sloping volatility term structure leads to a higher exposure at longer maturities.

Note that even aside from the choice over calibration, there are a number of subjective choices to be made. For example, in real-world calibrations one must decide on the data set and use of any historical period of stress. In risk-neutral calibrations, it may be necessary to extrapolate implied volatility to estimate points not observed via market prices. Whilst in the past there has been much debate over the use of real-world or risk-neutral probability, current work (for example, Hull et al., 2014) is considering the possibility of utilising both.

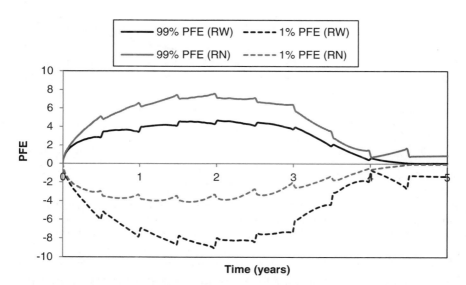

Figure 10.12   Illustration of the PFE for a five-year interest rate swap computed with both real-world (RW) and risk-neutral (RN) simulations for the drift. Note that, in order to isolate the drift impact, historical volatility has been used in both cases.

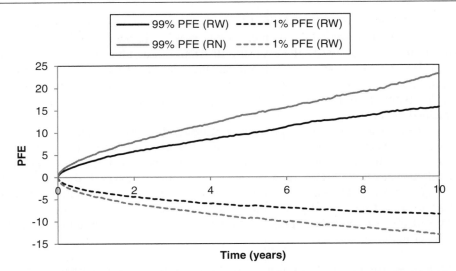

Figure 10.13   Illustration of the PFE for a ten-year cross-currency swap computed with both real-world (RW) and risk-neutral (RN) simulations for the volatility. Note that, in order to isolate this impact, risk-neutral drift (forward rates) has been used in both cases.

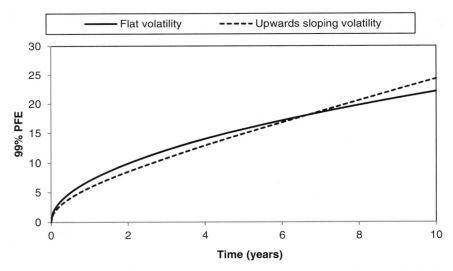

Figure 10.14   Illustration of the PFE for a ten-year cross-currency swap computed with flat and upwards sloping volatility term structures.

10.5.2   Level of complexity

Risk factor selection and modelling for exposure is a difficult problem, as it needs to balance the requirement for tractable and parsimonious models on the one hand with sophistication on the other. Market practice is somewhat divided on the subject, with some believing that the inherent uncertainties of xVA do not warrant advanced models, and others believing that more complex representation of aspects such as curve dynamics and volatility surfaces are important.

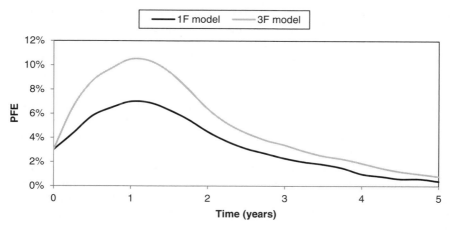

Figure 10.15   Exposure for an interest rate cap with both one-factor and three-factor models.

The following examples should be informative in understanding the problem. In Figure 10.15, we show the PFE of an interest rate cap with both one-factor and three-factor approaches calibrated against the same historical data. A one-factor model generally only captures parallel moves in the yield curve with some limited steepening and flattening movements. The more sophisticated three-factor approach, on the other hand, produces more complex changes in the shape of the yield curve, leading to a significantly greater exposure since the cap has a strong sensitivity to changes in yield curve shape.

A similar risk-neutral example is shown for an interest rate swap in Figure 10.16. Here the EE is materially different due to the different fits to the implied volatility surface (swaption prices) in each model. Note that this problem is magnified if we use a generic calibration approach, since the implied volatility calibration cannot be tailored to a particular transaction. For example, a calibration to swaption prices will be a compromise if the underlying portfolio contains swaps over a significant maturity range.

The problem with the above is that exposure quantification is mostly concerned with relatively simple products for which more basic models can be used. However, there will

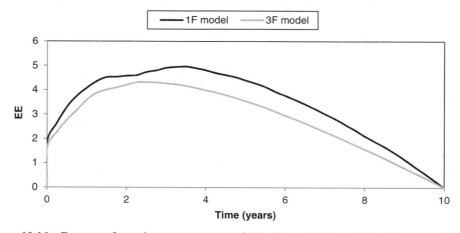

Figure 10.16   Exposure for an interest rate swap with both one-factor and three-factor models.

likely be a small amount of more complex products for which a more sophisticated approach is more relevant. Yet, it is not practical to mix approaches and using a more complex approach across the whole portfolio can be very resource-intensive.

It is important to note, therefore, that modelling choices depend very much on the nature of the problem at hand, important considerations being:

- *Complexity of portfolio.* As noted above, a simple portfolio with mainly vanilla transactions will not warrant a more sophisticated modeling approach, so it is more appropriate to focus on the correct treatment of vanilla products (for example, a reasonable swaption calibration).
- *Collateralisation.* Collateralised positions also suggest that more simple models can be used, since the nature of collateral is to shorten time horizons and make in- and out-of-the-money type optionality become at-the-money. Furthermore, the choice of margin period of risk (MPR) dominates in importance over the choice of exposure simulation model.
- *Dimensionality.* High dimensionality (e.g. several interest rate and/or FX risk factors for a given counterparty) may suggest simpler models due to the importance of considering the modelling of the underlying co-dependencies.
- *Wrong-way risk (WWR).* If WWR models are to be implemented then it is even more important to keep the basic set-up simple.
- *Computational workload.* Due to the likely need for rapid pricing, greeks and scenario analysis, then it is important that the modelling framework chosen does not lead to excessive hardware requirements.

10.5.3   General comments

Below are some general comments across various asset classes. It is worth noting in line with the above comments that many banks and other institutions modelling exposure have a portfolio mostly dominated by interest rate and FX products. Hence, it is likely that more attention will be paid to these asset classes than others.

- *Interest rates.* As noted above, multi-factor models can be important. In this context two fundamental types of model tend to be chosen: short-rate or LMM. Short-rate models have the advantage that they are typically numerically simpler in terms of calibration and simulation, and are usually easier to combine with models for other asset classes. LMM models tend to be more complex numerically, but are more flexible in terms of calibration to other instruments such as caplets and swaptions. Note that components such as the LIBOR-OIS basis (Chapter 13) may only be captured as a deterministic adjustment.
- *Foreign-exchange.* A simple geometric Brownian motion FX approach is still quite common here, calibrated by reference to either historical time series or options markets. The interrelated questions of how to deal with long-dated volatility and mean reversion do not have a clear solution and various ad-hoc methods are used in practice (for example, simple extrapolation of volatility). Jump-diffusion processes have often been used to characterise emerging markets or pegged currencies. The shorter the time horizon, the greater the importance of capturing such jumps (e.g. see Das and Sundaram, 1999).
- *Inflation.* Inflation products can be modelled in a similar way to FX since the underlying real and nominal rates can be treated as local and foreign currencies. The standard

yield curve essentially determines the local currency whilst inflation-linked bonds can be used to calibrate the foreign currency. Volatility may be calibrated to inflation-linked options.

- *Commodities*. Commodities tend to be highly mean-reverting around a level, which represents the marginal cost of production (e.g. see Pindyck, 2001; Geman and Nguyen, 2005). Furthermore, many commodities exhibit seasonality in prices due to harvesting cycles and changing consumption throughout the year. For commodities PFE, the use of risk-neutral drift may be particularly dangerous due to strong back-wardation and contango present for some underlyings (see Section 10.4.2). However, non-storable commodities (for example, electricity) do not have an arbitrage relation-ship between spot and forward prices, and therefore the forward rates might be argued to contain relevant information about future expected prices.
- *Equities*. The standard model for equities is a geometric Brownian motion, which as-sumes that the equity returns are normally distributed. The underlying volatility could also be either market-implied or determined from historical analysis. For practical purposes, it may not be advisable to attempt to simulate every single underlying stock. Not only is this highly time-consuming, but it also leads to a large correlation matrix that may not be of the appropriate form.[9] Rather, one may choose to simulate all major indices and then estimate the change in the individual stock price by using the beta[10] of that stock.

Model choice must also involve decisions over effects such as mean-reversion.[11] Failure to include mean-reversion can lead to unrealistically large exposures at long time horizons. However, calibration of these quantities may not be easy (mean-reversions, for example, are not trivial to calibrate from either historical or market data). Incorrect specifications of mean reversion together with other aspects (such as models allowing negative rates) can be particularly problematic for PFE, as a high quantile may be viewed as defining an economically unreasonable event. Sokol (2014) discusses this topic in more detail.

By necessity, exposure models cannot easily incorporate components such as stochas-tic volatility. More exotic aspects such as volatility smile are usually only incorporated approximately, and aspects such as volatility evolution typically ignored completely.

10.5.4 Correlations

A typical exposure simulation will model hundreds, perhaps even thousands, of risk factors. This then requires a large correlation matrix to specify the multidimensional dependency. Even for a single transaction, this dependency can be important: a cross-currency swap has risk to the FX rate and the two interest rates, and hence a minimum of three risk factors and the three correlations between them must be accounted for. However, individual correlations will have very different importance in defining future

---

[9] Such aspects can be solved; in particular, there are methods to regularise correlations, to obtain the closest possible valid (positive semi-definite) correlation matrix. However, this is time-consuming and may be viewed as being too complex with simpler methods preferred, especially if equity constitutes only a moderate portion of the overall exposure.

[10] As defined by the capital asset pricing model (CAPM), the beta represents the covariance of the stock and index returns divided by the variance of the index returns.

[11] Note that this comment is more relevant for PFE models. For CVA purposes, the question of mean ver-sion is linked to the calibration to the term structure of volatility.

exposure. For two interest rate swaps in different currencies, the correlation between the interest rates may be a very important parameter. However, the correlation between, for example, the price of oil and an FX rate may be unimportant or completely irrelevant. It will be informative to make a distinction between intra- and inter-asset class correlations.

The nature of a lot of client business for banks is asset class-specific by counterparty. For example, interest rate products may be traded with one counterparty and commodities with another. Intra-asset class dependencies (for example, the correlation between interest rates in different currencies) will be important components. Indeed, it may be a more important factor than the impact of subtle yield curve movements, which justifies the use of a relatively parsimonious (low-factor) interest rate model. Such correlations can be estimated from time series and may sometimes be observed via the traded prices of products such as spread options, baskets and quantos.

In some cases, the population of transactions with a given counterparty will cover two or more asset classes or contain cross-asset class transactions such as cross-currency swaps. The inter-asset class correlation between the risk factors must then be considered carefully. Inter-asset class correlations are harder to estimate from historical time series as the correlations are more likely to be unstable due to the more subtle relationship across asset classes. Furthermore, they are less likely to be able to be implied from the prices of market instruments. Inter-asset class correlations, especially for the non-collateral-posting counterparties, can often be less important due to single-asset class transactions. Having said that, even a relatively simple end-user of derivatives, such as an airline, could in theory trade across commodities, FX and interest rate products, creating a future exposure dependent on many inter- and intra-asset class correlation parameters.

The hundreds of risk factors required in a typical exposure simulation engine give rise to tens of thousands of correlations,[12] many of which will represent a minimal impact on future exposure. However, some will be very important and it is necessary to understand such effects and perform sensitivity analysis so as not rely solely on naïve correlation estimation from time-series data.

10.6   EXAMPLES

10.6.1   Data set

We now consider the netting benefit achieved in several examples.[13] The transactions considered are as follows:

- *Base case*. Seven-year pay fixed USD interest rate swap, "Payer IRS 7Y".
- *Transaction 1a*. Five-year pay fixed USD interest rate swap, "Payer IRS 5Y".
- *Transaction 1b*. The opposite (i.e. receiver) of the above. "Receiver IRS 5Y".
- *Transaction 2*. Five-year swaption on five-year pay fixed USD interest rate swap with physical delivery. "Payer swaption 5x5Y".
- *Transaction 3*. Five-year pay USD, rec JPY cross-currency swap "xCCY USDJPY".

---

[12] The number is $N(N-1)/2$ where N is the number of risk factors.

[13] I am grateful to Markit Analytics for using their xVA analytics tool, Integrated Resource Management (IRM) for providing the simulation data for these examples.

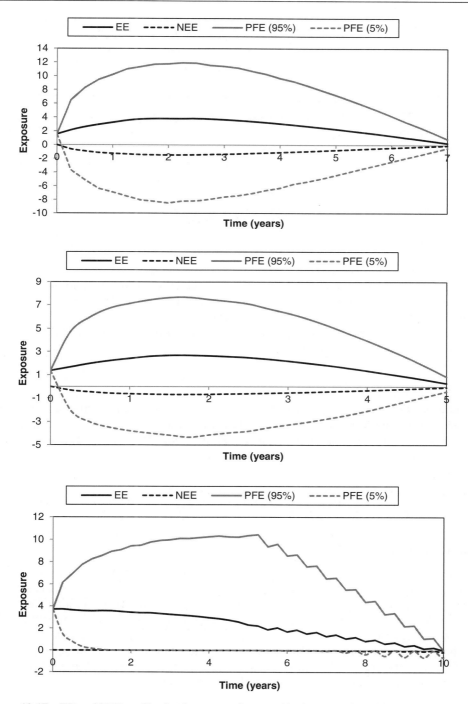

Figure 10.17   EE and PFE profiles for the transactions used in the examples. The exposure from the counterparty's point of view is represented by the NEE and 5% PFE. Note that the receiver swap (not shown) is simply the reverse of the equivalent payer. (*Continued*.)

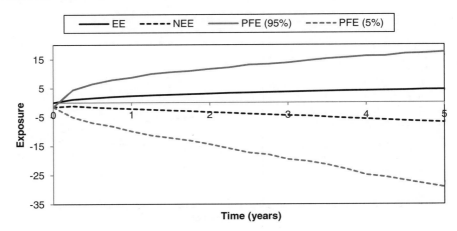

Figure 10.17 (*Continued.*)

All transactions have a notional of $100 except the cross-currency swap, which has a smaller relative notional of ¥10,000.[14] The exposures have been simulated at time intervals of three months with a total of 2,000 simulations. We show the transaction-level EE/NEE and PFE profiles (both positive and negative) in Figure 10.17. All the results below will be reported in US dollars.

10.6.2 Exposures profiles

We now consider exposure profiles that would arise in several different cases. In all examples, we start with the base case "Payer IRS 7Y" transaction and consider the impact of netting this with the other four transactions listed above. We will see different impacts depending on the relationship between the transactions in question.

Spreadsheet 10.3   Illustration of the impact of netting

Case 1: Payer IRS 5Y

This transaction is strongly positively correlated to the base case since they differ only in maturity date. An example scenario showing their simulated future values is given in Figure 10.18. The high structural correlation means that the values are highly dependent, similar to the example in Section 7.4.2. We note that the relationship between the two swaps depends subtly on the precise evolution in the shape of the yield curve that will be quite model-sensitive. In the path shown, there is a small amount of netting benefit from the two-year to the four-year point. However, even this small impact does not occur in most paths and the netting effect is minimal overall. We show the EE and NEE

---

[14] This is to prevent the inherently more risky cross-currency swap dominating the results. The USD notional was $43.5.

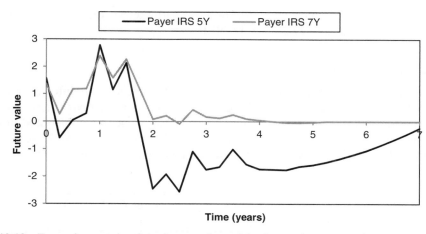

Figure 10.18   Example scenario of the future values of the five- and seven-year interest rate swaps.

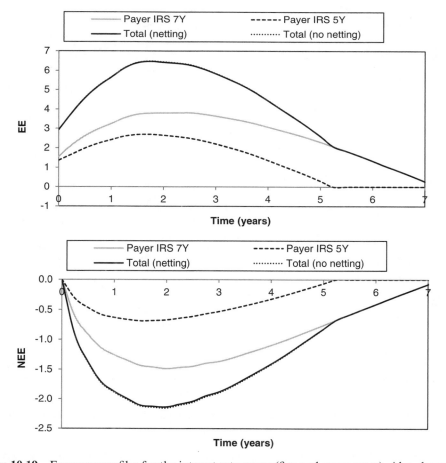

Figure 10.19   Exposure profiles for the interest rate swaps (five and seven years). Also shown are the total EE (top) and NEE (bottom) with and without netting. The EE and NEE components are almost additive due to the very high correlation.

values in Figure 10.19, which are almost additive with the average netting factor[15] being only 99.8% for the EE and 99.3% for the NEE.

Case 2: Payer swaption 5x5Y

In this case, although we are comparing a swap and swaption with different underlying maturities, the correlation is still high due to the first order sensitivity of each transaction being the same. There is a relatively small netting benefit, as illustrated in Figure 10.20, where the average netting factor is 98.1% (EE) and 88.7% (NEE). Note that the reduction of the NEE is larger since the swaption is a long position and therefore has a positive MTM.

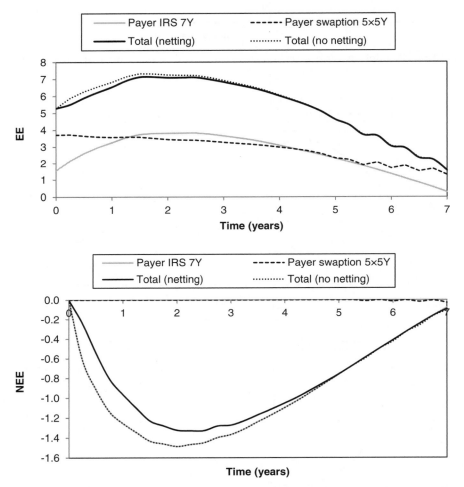

Figure 10.20   Exposure profiles for the interest rate swap and swaption. Also shown are the total EE (top) and NEE (bottom) with and without netting.

---

[15] As in Section 8.4.1, the netting factor is the ratio of net to gross exposure. We define the average netting factor as the ratio of the EPE with netting to the EPE without.

Case 3: xCCY USDJPY

We now consider the combination of the base case interest rate swap with the cross-currency swap. Since the cross-currency swap is dominated by the FX component, as described in Section 7.3.4, there is a small[16] correlation between the transactions and this should create a reasonable netting benefit. The EE profiles are shown in Figure 10.21 and the netting factor is 74.2% (EE) and 66.5% (NEE). This is quite close to the simple approximation of $1/\sqrt{2} = 70.7\%$ as discussed in Section 7.4.2.

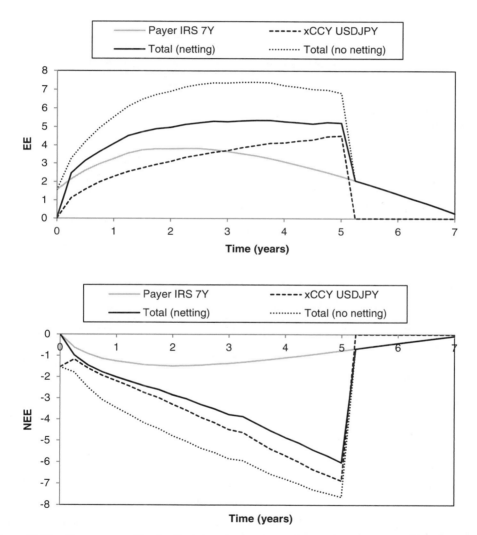

Figure 10.21   Exposure profiles for the interest rate swap and cross-currency swap. Also shown are the total EE (top) and NEE (bottom) with and without netting.

---

[16] The historical interest rate–FX correlation is small.

Case 4: Receiver IRS 5Y

Finally, we consider the combination of the base case interest rate swap with a reverse (receive fixed) interest rate swap of a different maturity. Although unlikely in practice, this represents a very strong netting benefit due to the structurally offsetting positions. The EE and NEE profiles are shown in Figure 10.22 and the netting factor is 44.3% (EE) and 26.5% (NEE). Note that the total EE with netting is less than that for the seven-year IRS alone.

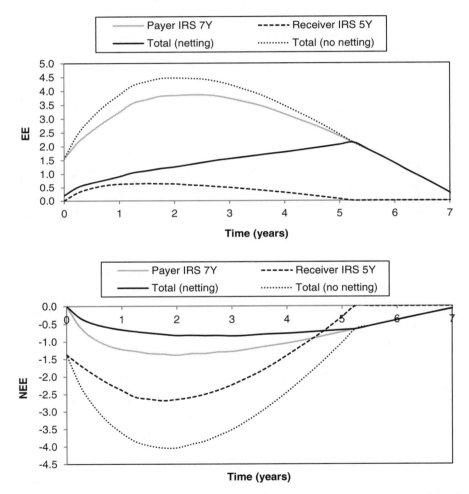

Figure 10.22   Exposure profiles for the interest rate swap and reverse interest rate swap. Also shown are the total EE (top) and NEE (bottom) with and without netting.

10.7   ALLOCATING EXPOSURE

It is clear from the above examples that netting benefits can be substantial. However, it is unclear how to allocate these benefits to the individual transactions. If the EE (and NEE) of the transactions is considered on a stand-alone basis then this will overstate the actual risk. However, there is no unique way to distribute the netted exposure amongst the transactions.

10.7.1   Simple two-transaction, single-period example

Suppose we have two exposures defined by normal distributions with different mean and standard deviation, as illustrated in Figure 10.23. The distributions are rather different, the first having a positive mean and a smaller standard deviation and the second a negative mean but a larger standard deviation. The result of this is that the EEs are similar at 7.69 and 7.63[17] for transaction 1 and transaction 2 respectively. Assuming zero correlation, the total expected exposure of both transactions would be 10.72.[18]

Now the question is how to allocate the exposure of 10.72 between the two transactions. The most obvious way to do this is to ask which order they arose in. If transaction 1 was first, then by definition it would contribute an EE of 7.69 at that time. By a simple subtraction, transaction 2 would then have to represent only 3.03. If the order were reversed, then the numbers would be almost the opposite. We will refer to this as *incremental exposure*, since it depends on the incremental effect, which in turn depends on the ordering. Incremental allocation is usually most relevant because the nature of trading is sequential, potentially with transactions being done years apart.

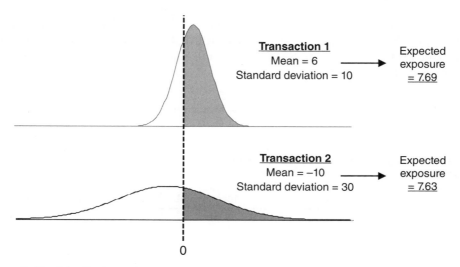

Figure 10.23   Distribution defining the exposures for the simple EE example.

---

[17] These EE numbers can be computed using the formula in Appendix 7A. This effect is similar to an in-the-money option having a similar value to an out-of-the-money option with a greater underlying volatility.

[18] Since the distributions are independent, we can calculate the combined mean and variance as $6 - 10 = -4$ and $10^2 + 30^2 = 1000$ respectively and then use the formula in Appendix 7A.

With incremental allocation the first transaction always gets charged more and the second transaction is given all the netting benefit. This may seem unfair, but life is unfair and, since we cannot (usually) predict future trading activity, incremental allocation is seemingly the only reasonable approach to use to form the basis of quoting prices. It is also consistent with a charging approach, where the charge must be defined at the time of initiation and must not subsequently change.[19]

Suppose that instead we did not wish to look at exposures sequentially but rather wanted to find a fair breakdown of exposure, irrespective of the order in which transactions were originated. This could be relevant if two transactions are initiated at the same time (e.g. two transactions with the same counterparty on the same day) or for analysing exposure to find the largest contribution. We could simply *pro rata* the values in line with the stand-alone EEs. Whilst this may seem reasonable, it is not theoretically rigorous. A more robust way to do this is via *marginal exposure*.

Marginal risk contributions are well-studied concepts due to the need to allocate risk measures back to individual constituents. For example, they have been described by Arvanitis and Gregory (2001) for credit portfolios and a discussion on marginal VAR can be found in Jorion (2007). In most situations, a marginal contribution can readily be calculated as the derivative of the risk measure with respect to its weight (Rosen and Pykhtin 2010). Hence, we need to calculate numerically the derivative of the total EE with respect to each constitution exposure in order to know the marginal EEs. This will be described more intuitively below. The marginal EEs will, under most circumstances,[20] sum to the total EE as required. More mathematical details are given in Appendix 10C.

We calculate the marginal EEs under the assumption of independence between the two exposure distributions and summarise the overall results[21] in Table 10.3 comparing also to incremental exposure and the crude pro rata approach. We can see that the marginal EE of transaction 2 is actually quite significantly higher than that of transaction 1, even though the standard EE is lower. The distribution with a smaller expected value and a larger standard deviation contributes more to the total exposure than the one with the opposite characteristics.

Spreadsheet 10.4   Example marginal exposure calculation

Table 10.3   Summary of different EE decompositions for the simple example in Figure 10.23, assuming independence between exposures.

	Incremental (1 first)	Incremental (2 first)	Pro rata	Marginal
Transaction 1	7.69	3.09	5.38	3.95
Transaction 2	3.03	7.63	5.34	6.77
Total	10.72	10.72	10.72	10.72

---

[19] This is leading to a transfer pricing concept for xVA at trade inception where a hard payment is made to the xVA desk.

[20] One obviously difficult case is where there is a collateral agreement with a threshold or an initial margin. This is discussed in more detail by Rosen and Pykhtin (2010).

[21] In the case of normal distributions, the analytical expression makes the calculation of marginal EE quite easy without the need for simulation, as shown in Spreadsheet 10.4.

Table 10.4   As Table 10.3, with a third transaction added.

	Incremental (1 first)	Incremental (2 first)	Pro-rata	Marginal
Transaction 1	7.69	3.09	4.86	4.45
Transaction 2	3.03	7.63	4.82	5.67
Transaction 3	3.76	3.76	4.79	4.36
Total	14.48	14.48	14.48	14.48

In summary, incremental exposure is relevant when exposure is built up sequentially, which is usually the case in practice. It is potentially unfair in that the incremental exposure depends on the timing as well as individual characteristics. Marginal allocation is fair but changes each time a new exposure is added, which is not appropriate for charging to the originator of the risk (directly via xVA or indirectly via PFE and credit limits). In order to illustrate this, consider adding a third exposure based on a normal distribution with mean 7 and standard deviation 7 (again with a similar stand-alone EE of 7.58). The change in numbers is shown in Table 10.4. Whilst the marginal EEs seem fairer, the impact of the third exposure is to change the magnitude of the first two (indeed, the first is increased while the second is reduced). By construction, the incremental exposures do not change.

We will now give some real examples of incremental and marginal exposure and discuss how they are both useful in practice.

10.7.2   Incremental exposure

The most common aggregation of exposure is done at the netting set level in order to asset the impact of a new transaction on the exposure with respect to that netting set. Exposures outside netting sets are usually additive, the only potential exception to this being FVA, as discussed in Chapter 15. The incremental exposure is defined via:

$$EE_i^{incremental}(u) = EE_{NS+i}(u) - EE_{NS}(u) \qquad (10.2)$$

In other words, it is the exposure of the netting set with the new transaction added ($NS+i$) minus that of the netting set alone (NS). A similar formula applies for other metrics such as NEE and PFE and for calculations requiring another type of aggregation.

Consider the examples shown in Section 10.6.2 showing the netting effect via the incremental exposure. Figure 10.24 shows the incremental exposure when the base case transaction (i) in Equation 10.2 is added to the four other example transactions. In other words, the netting set is originally assumed to contain one of the four transactions and we consider the impact of adding the Payer IRS 7Y to this. The stand-alone EE is always the same, whereas the incremental EE depends on the existing transaction.

Spreadsheet 10.5   Incremental exposure calculations

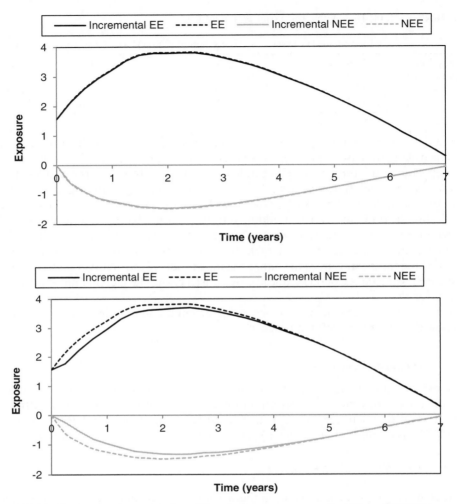

Figure 10.24   Incremental exposure for adding the base case transaction (Payer IRS 7Y) to each of the four different other example transactions. (*Continued.*)

We can explain the results as follows (note in all cases we are looking at the incremental effect for adding the base case transaction – Payer IRS 7Y):

- *Payer IRS 5Y*. This has virtually no impact, given the similarity with the transaction in question and with the incremental EE being very close to the stand-alone value.
- *Payer swaption 5x5Y*. Due to the directionality this has only a small but noticeable impact on both the EE and NEE.
- *xCCY USDJPY*. This has a much more significant impact due mainly to the low correlation between the interest rate and USD/JPY FX rate. Note that the impact on the NEE is more significant and it actually becomes positive (up to the five-year point when the cross-currency swap matures).

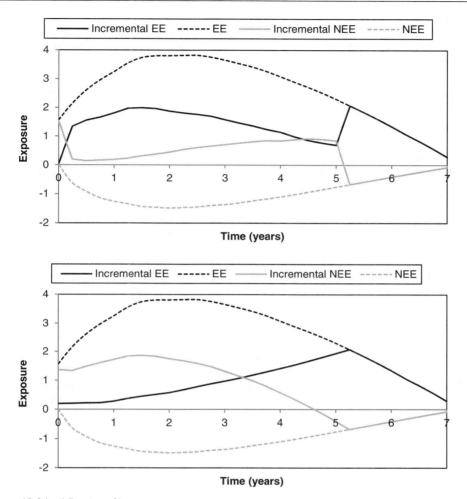

Figure 10.24   (*Continued.*)

- *Receiver IRS 5 Y.* This also shows a strong impact due to the structurally negative correlation between the transactions. Note that the NEE changes sign whereas the EE does not.

The above examples show that incremental exposure can vary dramatically depending on the existing netting set and can even change sign. It is clearly very important to be able to characterise the effect properly to understand the true magnitude of the risk being added or taken away. We also note that different parties will see different exposures for the same transaction with a given counterparty as they will have different existing netting sets. Indeed, a counterparty should find it easier to trade with a party with more favourable existing transactions. The extreme case of this is that it should be easiest to execute a reverse trade (unwind) with the same counterparty with which the existing transaction is done.[22]

---

[22] This may not necessarily be true as it depends also on the other trades in the netting set. Furthermore, a counterparty knowing this may not quote a competitive price.

10.7.3   Marginal exposure

In risk management, it is common and natural to ask where the underlying risk arises from. Risk managers and xVA desks may find it useful to be able to "drill down" from a number representing total exposure and understand which transactions are contributing most to the overall risk. This can be important information when considering whether to unwind transactions or enter into more business. Marginal exposure is useful in this context since, just because transaction level (stand-alone) exposures are similar, it does not mean that the contributions to the total netted exposure are also similar.

Let us first repeat the simple exercise in Section 10.7.1 for a range of correlation values as shown in Figure 10.25 (these calculations can be seen in the aforementioned Spreadsheet 10.4). The total EE is smallest at −100% correlation and increases with the correlation as the overall netting benefit is reduced. The breakdown of total EE into marginal components depends very much on the correlation. At zero correlation, as we have already seen, transaction 2 has a larger contribution to the overall EE. At negative correlation, the more "risky" transaction 2 has a positive marginal EE that is partly cancelled out by transaction 1 having a negative marginal EE. At high correlations, the marginal EEs are both positive and of almost equal magnitude (since there is little or no netting benefit).

The point being emphasised here is that for transactions with low or negative correlation, marginal EEs are particularly important to understand. The marginal EE of a transaction depends on the relationship of that transaction to others in the netting set. A transaction that is risk-reducing (negative marginal EE) in one netting set might not have the same characteristic in a different netting set.

There are two obvious reasons why marginal exposure might be a meaningful measure. Firstly, the situation where two or more transactions happen simultaneously (or

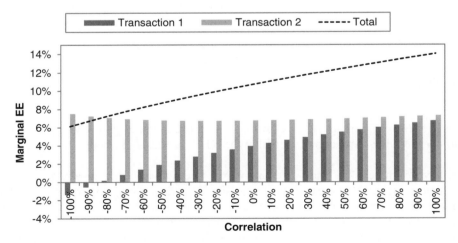

Figure 10.25   Marginal EEs for the simple two-transaction example shown in Figure 10.23 as a function of the correlation between the normal distributions.

within a short time interval) and incremental allocation would therefore be inappropriate (and arbitrary), and secondly, when it is important to allocate the exposure back to constituents in order to make some decision, such as which transactions to terminate or restructure. So, whilst incremental exposure is clearly useful for quantifying new individual transactions, marginal exposure can also be a useful measure in other situations.

Spreadsheet 10.6   Marginal exposure calculation

We now look at a general example of marginal EE calculation using the interest rate swap (Payer IRS 7Y) and cross-currency swap (xCCY USDJPY). Figure 10.26 shows the expected exposure allocated incrementally (in both ways) and marginally. We note that the top line is the same in all cases, as this represents the overall exposure. We can see that the second transaction allocated incrementally has a relatively small exposure, to the detriment of the first transaction. The marginal allocation is fairer and would be appropriate if the transactions occurred at the same time.[23] We will return to this example and show the respective CVA numbers in Section 14.4.3.

A reasonable question to ask is whether marginal exposure tells us anything significantly different than looking at the exposures of transactions in isolation. The answer is yes: let us look at the total expected exposure of the five aforementioned transactions (Section 10.6.1). The marginal allocation of expected exposure is shown in Figure 10.27 and compared to the stand-alone contributions (which are overall significantly larger due to the importance of netting) in Figure 10.28.[24]

Suppose it is desirable to reduce the overall exposure of the transactions in the above example. For example, this may be in order to comply with the credit limit[25] or because the xVA to a counterparty is deemed excessive (and cannot be readily hedged). All other things being equal, the transaction with the higher marginal EE (or PFE) is the most relevant to look at. There are two points of interest here:

- the marginal allocation is not homogeneous with time and so, depending on the horizon of interest, the highest contributor will be different; and
- it is not always easy to predict, a priori, which transaction will be the major contributor.

Figure 10.27 shows that the marginal allocation is relatively very different compared to the stand-alone contributions. Most obviously, the receiver interest rate swap has a negative contribution due to being risk reducing with respect to the payer interest rate swap (which has an equal and opposite marginal exposure) and the swaption. Aside from this, it can be seen that the relative contributions are generally different.

We will revisit incremental and marginal calculations in the discussion of CVA and DVA in Chapter 14.

---

[23] There is still some problem of allocation here, because we wish to allocate marginally for trades occurring at the same time whilst the total impact of the trades should be allocated incrementally with respect to existing trades in the netting set. An obvious way to get around this problem is to scale the marginal contributions of the trades so that they match the total incremental effect.

[24] These have been previously shown in Figure 10.23.

[25] In such a case, PFE rather than EE would be the appropriate metric to consider. Whilst the marginal PFE numbers are systemically higher than the EEs shown, there is no change in the qualitative behaviour.

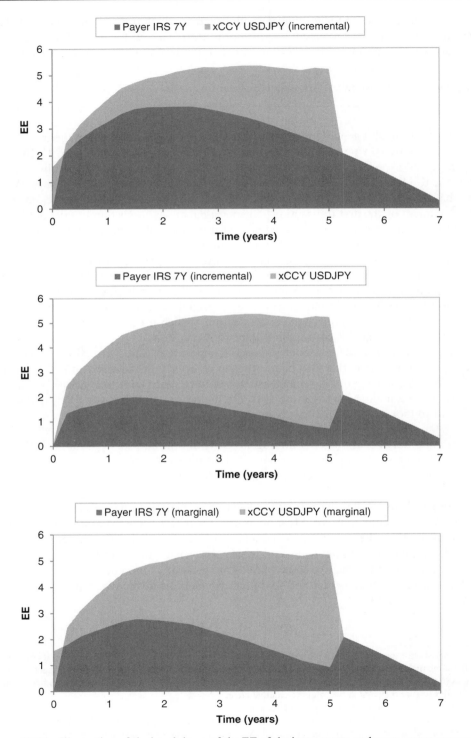

Figure 10.26   Illustration of the breakdown of the EE of the interest rate and cross-currency swaps via incremental (cross-currency swap first), incremental (interest rate swap first) and marginal.

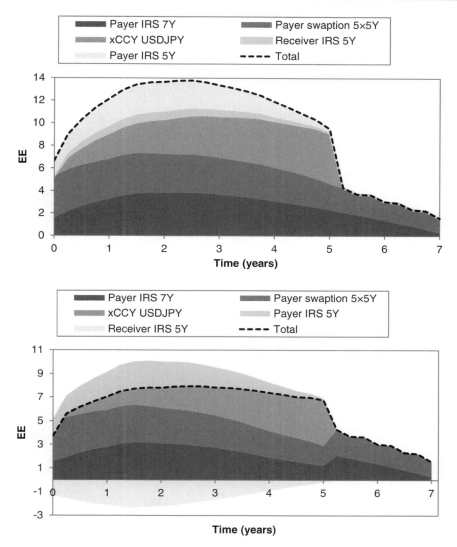

Figure 10.27 Illustration of the stand-alone (top) and marginal (bottom) expected exposure of the five transactions. Note that in the latter case the total reflects the subtraction of the negative contribution for the receiver interest rate swap.

10.8   SUMMARY

In this chapter, we have discussed the quantification of exposure and discussed the related modelling assumptions and numerical implementation of these models. The debate between using real-world and risk-neutral calibrations has been described. Some examples of exposures of actual transactions have been given and we have discussed the allocation of exposure using incremental and marginal measures. The next chapter will discuss the impact of collateral on exposure.

Exposure and the Impact of Collateral

11.1 OVERVIEW

The last chapter dealt with all aspects of quantifying uncollateralised exposure, including the treatment of netting terms. This chapter will now discuss how to overlay the treatment of collateral. Collateral can usually be treated separately and after the quantification of uncollateralised exposure, since it generally only depends on the mark-to-market (MTM) of the underlying portfolio. Furthermore, collateral terms usually (although not always) apply at the same or higher level as those of netting.

11.1.1 General impact of collateral

Uncollateralised exposure should be considered over the full time horizon of the transaction(s) in question. Long-term distributional assumptions such as drift, mean reversion and volatility term structure are important, and the specifics of the transactions, such as cashflow dates and exercise times, must be considered. Collateral changes this by transforming a risk that should be considered usually over many years into one that is primarily relevant over a much shorter period. As discussed previously, this period is commonly known as the margin period of risk (MPR). This is illustrated in Figure 11.1, which shows some future point where a position is well collateralised (e.g. no threshold in the collateral agreement) and hence the main concern is the relatively small amount of risk over the MPR. Note that due to the length of the MPR, aspects such as cashflows may not be important (as shown in Figure 11.1), although this will be discussed further below. Indeed, some of the intricacies of modelling exposure can often be ignored as long as the counterparty is well collateralised. The problem now becomes a short-term market risk issue and therefore shares many commonalities with market risk value-at-risk (VAR) methodologies (Section 3.3.1).

Whilst the above is generally true, we will see that the overall impact of collateral is not always straightforward and may not reduce the risk as much as might be hoped. Furthermore, certain contractual terms can be more difficult to assess and quantify. These will be covered later in this chapter. Note also that, whilst collateral may create residual market risk that is only a fraction of the uncollateralised risk, it will be more difficult and subjective to quantify (Section 11.3) and indeed hedge.

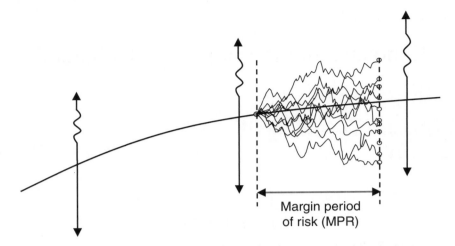

Figure 11.1   Schematic illustration of the impact of collateralisation on future exposure.

11.1.2   Modelling approach

As noted in Section 7.5.4 (but leaving aside aspects such as segregation for now), the impact of collateral on exposure can be written as:

$$Exposure_{CCR} = \max(value - C, 0), \tag{11.1}$$

where *value* represents the value of the portfolio of transactions under the relevant close-out assumptions (Section 7.1.3) and C represents the value of the collateral against the portfolio. In this general case, there are the following possibilities:

- $C = 0$, no collateral has been posted or received;
- $C > 0$, collateral has been received; and
- $C < 0$, collateral has been posted.

To quantify future exposure, one must understand the amount of collateral that would be held (or posted) in the future. Conventional models assume that the collateral available at a certain time t is determined by the portfolio value (MTM) at a previous time $t - MPR$.

$$Exposure_{CCR} = \max(value_t - C_{t-MPR}, 0) \tag{11.2}$$

The MPR is a ubiquitous parameter that captures the general uncertainty and delay inherent in the collateral process. However, it does express many uncertain aspects, such as collateral disputes and increased market volatility in a single variable. We will discuss the MPR in more detail in the next section so as to be completely clear as to what it should (and should not) represent.

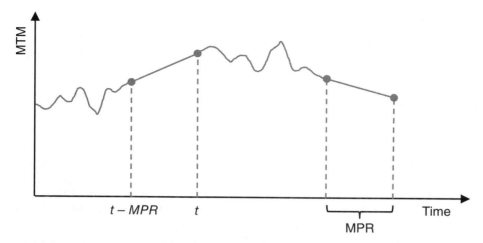

Figure 11.2   Schematic illustration of the use of MPR to model the impact of collateral.

11.2   MARGIN PERIOD OF RISK

11.2.1   Setup

Figure 11.2 illustrates the general setup for quantifying the impact of collateral using the MPR. We assume that the uncollateralised MTM as discussed in the last chapter has already been generated. In order to quantify the collateralised exposure at a given time t, we need to know (at a minimum) what amount of collateral would have been requested previously at a time $t-MPR$. This amount of collateral will in turn be defined by the MTM at this time (MTM_{t-MPR}), which must be known (as described in Section 6.2.8).

Note that the literal interpretation of the mechanics of default in relation to this MPR definition are:

1 the counterparty ceases to perform on contractual payments, including posting collateral;
2 the counterparty is determined to be in default; and
3 the party initiates the close-out process at a time exactly MPR later than (1) and this occurs instantaneously. Prior to this point, all contractual obligations other than the posting of collateral (e.g. cashflow payments) continue to happen.

The above is stylised: in reality between (1) and (2) above, where the counterparty is not yet deemed to be in default (the pre-default period as discussed in Section 6.6.2), it will be unlikely to perform on any contractual payments (such as cashflows). The party themselves may cease their own contractual obligations at time (2). The close-out process is not instantaneous and it may take a few days for illiquid products and/or large portfolios. The following sections will discuss a number of complexities that may all need to be considered in the MPR estimation.

11.2.2   Amortisation

As noted above, in reality the close-out process in the aftermath of a default will not occur instantaneously but rather will be a gradual process involving a combination of:

- delay before the counterparty is deemed in default;
- hedging and replacement of transactions; and
- liquidation of collateral.

In reality, the situation is represented by Figure 11.3. During the pre-default period, there is no reduction of risk, as the close-out process has not been initiated. During the post-default period, the risk is reduced gradually as a result of the three points above. This shows that the MPR should not be interpreted literally as the sum of the pre- and post-default periods. For example, suppose that during the post-default period of n days, the risk reduces linearly, equivalent to closing-out a relative amount of $1/n$ on each day (so over five days we would close-out 20% on each day). The effective post-default period (with the equivalent variance) would be:[1]

$$1 + \frac{n}{3} \times \left(1 - \frac{1}{n}\right) \times \left(1 - \frac{1}{2n}\right) \text{days} \qquad (11.3)$$

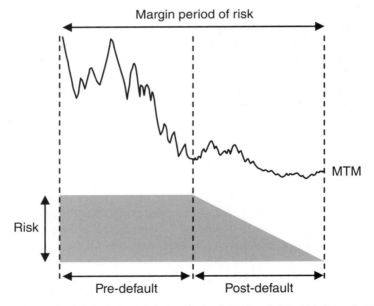

Figure 11.3   Illustration of the pre- and post-default periods and the reduction of risk during the close-out process. In the post-default period, MTM volatility reduces in line with the underlying risk.

---

[1] This result can be found in Jorion (2007).

This would mean that if one believed that the actual post-default period would be ten days but that the close-out would occur linearly as above then the actual MPR to be used in modelling should be 3.85 days plus the assumed pre-default period.

11.2.3   Conditionality

Another component of the MPR is the conditionality (or lack thereof) in the modelling of the MTM after a default event. Traditional exposure quantification generally assumes implicitly that after a counterparty default, the MTM of the underlying portfolio will simply continue with the same underlying properties (distributional assumptions). In reality, as shown in Figure 11.4, market conditions in the aftermath of a default may be different – most obviously, there may be increased volatility. This will be particularly significant for a large financial counterparty. Indeed, in the aftermath of the Lehman Brothers bankruptcy, the volatility in the credit default swap market was five times greater than in the preceding period (Pykhtin and Sokol 2013). Counterparties that post collateral generally tend to be more significant and have larger OTC derivatives exposures. The impact of their default, notwithstanding any collateral considerations, may be considered to be more significant than a typical uncollateralised counterparty.

If an exposure simulation does not quantify the above effect, then a longer MPR may be an obvious and easy method to incorporate it. Following the "square root of time" rule (Section 7.3.2), the standard deviation of a position over a time t (in years) will follow $\sigma\sqrt{t}$ where σ is the annual volatility. In order to mimic the impact of volatility doubling in the aftermath of a default then it would be necessary to *quadruple* the MPR.

11.2.4   Disputes

Yet another component embedded within the MPR is the possibility of a collateral dispute: indeed, this is one of the aspects under Basel III that can lead to an increase in the regulatory MPR (Section 8.6.3). In the case of a dispute, the protocol that should be followed is that the undisputed amount is transferred and then the parties involved enter

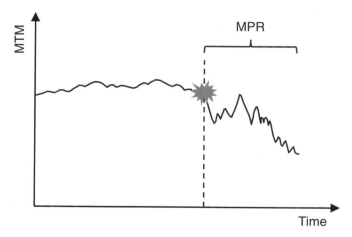

Figure 11.4   Illustration of the likely increase in MTM volatility in the aftermath of a default event.

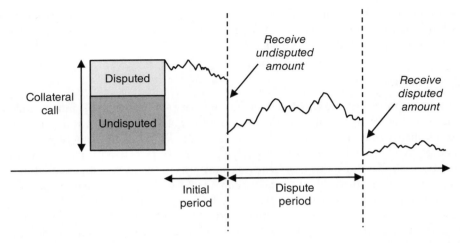

Figure 11.5 Illustration of the impact of a dispute on the MPR assuming that the full amount of collateral is eventually received.

into negotiations to agree on the disputed amount. The latter procedure may take some significant time, as experienced by many parties during the global financial crisis. This process is illustrated in Figure 11.5. In theory, receiving collateral should be divided into two parts: the undisputed and disputed amounts with associated periods. In practice this is probably extraneous, but the MPR should not ignore this aspect.

11.2.5   MPR discretisation and cashflows

Given the choice of MPR, there is a necessary discussion around the discretisation of the exposure simulation. Fundamentally, there are two choices, as illustrated in Figure 11.6. The lookback approach includes a single point at time $t-MPR$ prior to each required exposure quantification so as to determine the amount of collateral that would be asked for at this point. The continuous[2] approach simulates at all points with a time step equal to the MPR, which is clearly more costly.

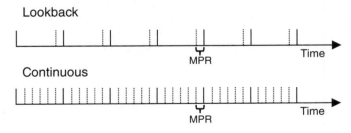

Figure 11.6 Illustration of different discretisation schemes for collateral modelling.

---

[2] Continuous with respect to the MPR unit.

Although the lookback method depicted in Figure 11.6 is clearly less costly, it requires further simplification. The amount of collateral called at a given time will obvious depend on the amount currently held (see Equation 6.1 in Chapter 6). With the lookback discretisation scheme it would not be known how much collateral would be held at this point. It could be that the exposure happens to be overcollateralised and therefore less collateral (if any) need be called for. For this reason, a quantity such as the minimum transfer amount (MTA) cannot be treated in the lookback approach, because the proper treatment of the MTA requires knowledge of the current collateral balance. In the continuous approach there will be a completely pathwise representation of collateral balances and hence aspects such as MTAs can be treated precisely.

Related to the above point is the assumption of the return of collateral. The MPR is representative of the fact that the counterparty is defaulting and prior to this will at some point stop posting collateral. But would a surviving party return excess collateral held during the MPR? They likely would in the pre-default period, although possibly not in the post-default one. There is also a point regarding the treatment of cashflows during the MPR. Would the defaulting counterparty and surviving party pay cashflows during the pre- and post-default periods? One obvious choice might be to resort to conservative assumptions:

- the surviving party posts or returns collateral and pays cashflows; and
- the defaulting party does not pay collateral or cashflows.

However, these assumptions might be further changed depending on the pre- or post-default period. Note that Basel III regulation does not specify any requirements in this regard, only defining the minimal MPR to be used (as discussed in Section 8.6.3). This means that for regulatory capital considerations the MPR must be at least ten business days, but for CVA itself, other periods may be used.[3]

11.2.6   MPR modelling

The discussion in the sections above should illustrate that the MPR is a parameter that may incorporate many effects and it should not be interpreted as being precisely related to the actual time to close-out a portfolio in a counterparty default scenario. A typical exposure simulation model effectively assumes that the whole portfolio will be closed-out and replaced at the end of the MPR, and ignores effects such as higher volatility and the possibility of collateral disputes. The MPR is clearly a difficult and subjective parameter to quantify, but all of the above considerations should be included in its estimation.

Very little attention has been given to the precise modelling of the events during the MPR. One recent exemption looking at the impact of cashflow payments is Andersen et al. (2015). It is important to balance the incremental benefit of more advanced collateral modelling against the fact that the MPR is by nature very hard to quantify. In Section 11.3 we will present an example showing the potential differences from different assumptions during the MPR. However, it may be viewed that the MPR itself is so uncertain that more advanced modelling is meaningless or of limited value.

---

[3] Although there are instances of auditors requiring banks to follow the regulatory capital definitions of MPR.

11.3 NUMERICAL EXAMPLES

11.3.1 Collateral assumptions

We will now give some numerical results from modelling collateral. As discussed above, collateral can be accounted for after the simulation of exposure, under the assumption that the collateral agreement depends only on the net MTM and not other market variables.[4] We have described in Section 6.2.8 the specifics of the calculation of the amount of collateral that may be called, considering the impact of parameters such as thresholds and MTAs. We have also discussed the choice of MPR, with around ten business days being a reasonably standard choice (although this may differ between CVA and regulatory capital considerations). Note also, as mentioned previously, that the MPR for funding purposes could be assumed to be negligible since this requires the exposure in a non-default scenario where collateral may be received relatively quickly.

Spreadsheet 11.1   Quantifying the impact of collateral on exposure

---

In the collateral simulations that will be shown below, the following assumptions apply:

- The underlying portfolio consists of three interest rate swaps and one cross-currency swap with a total notional of £325. More details can be found in Spreadsheet 11.1.[5]
- The exposure simulation uses a "continuous" grid (Figure 11.6) with a time-step of ten calendar days. This means that the MPR can be assumed to be ten calendar days or any multiple thereof.
- The collateral amounts to be called by either party will be calculated as described in Section 6.2.8.
- Collateral called for will take 20 calendar days[6] to arrive (this is between the ten and 20 business days that may be required under Basel III). Collateral posting to the counterparty will be immediate.
- There are no other assumptions on collateral disputes other than those captured by the 20-day MPR assumption.
- Collateral posted is not retrievable in the event of a counterparty default unless it is initial margin (which will be stated explicitly). This assumes that it is not held in a segregated account (and can be rehypothecated).
- All collateral will be in cash (non-cash collateral will be discussed later) in a liquid currency so that any mismatch can be hedged in the FX market.

---

[4] There are situations where this assumption may not be entirely appropriate; for example, collateral parameters may be defined in different currencies to the deals to which they apply. In practice, this means that some FX translations may be required when the collateral parameters are applied within the simulation. However, in the majority of situations the assumptions made will be valid and will greatly simplify the analysis of collateralised exposures.

[5] I am grateful to IBM for providing the underlying portfolio MTM simulations that were first used in the second edition of this book.

[6] This is because the simulations used are discretised in calendar and not business days with a step size of ten days.

Table 11.1   Base case parameters used for the collateral examples (two-way CSA).

	Party A (institution)	Party B (counterparty)
Initial margin	–	–
Threshold	–	–
Minimum transfer amount (MTA)	1	1
Rounding	0.05	0.05

For the purposes of general discussion, we will use the following general definitions:

- *Under-collateralised.* This refers to a collateral agreement (e.g. CSA) with a threshold amount.
- *Collateralised.* This refers to a zero threshold CSA.
- *Over-collateralised.* This refers to a zero threshold CSA with additional initial margin (sometimes called independent amount – see Section 6.2.4).

The base case parameters, representing a collateralised scenario, are shown in Table 11.1 and will be varied in the examples below where stated.

11.3.2   Margin period of risk impact

We start by assessing the risk of a collateralised position with the parameters as defined above. To understand the impact of collateral, first consider a single simulation path, as illustrated in Figure 11.7. We can see that the impact of collateral on exposure is not perhaps as strong as one might first have thought. Firstly, whilst the collateral amount approximately tracks the exposure, this is imperfect due to the MPR and the MTA, which create a delay effect. Secondly, collateral can also increase exposure, such as during the

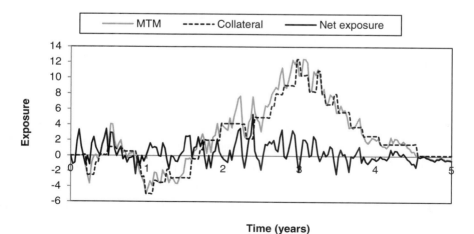

Figure 11.7   Illustration of an individual simulation path and the impact of collateral on that path.

first period when the MTM is negative. This leads to a posting of collateral, which is not retrievable,[7] when the future value increases and the counterparty defaults.

The overall impact of collateral on EE and PFE (the latter at the 95% confidence level) is shown in Figure 11.8. Whilst there is a benefit, a significant exposure remains: the prominent spikes due to the payment of cashflows (for which collateral is not received immediately), which creates a peak in the exposure for a length of time corresponding to the MPR. The overall reduction in exposure (measured via the EPE) is 2.66 times, which is surprisingly low since a five-year uncollateralised exposure has been collater-alised with a zero threshold and only a 20-day (91 times shorter than the maturity!) risk horizon. Note also that that reduction in the PFE is relatively better, since not all

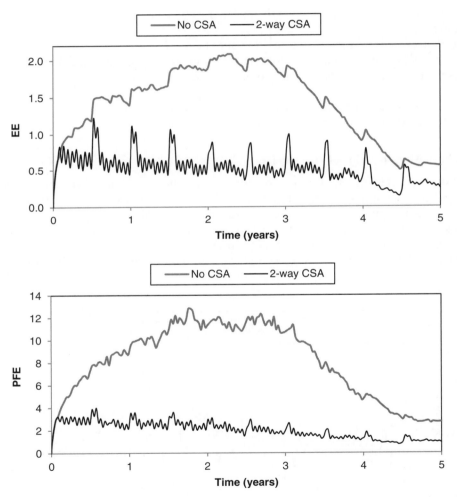

Figure 11.8   Illustration of EE (top) and 95% PFE (bottom) calculated with and without collateral assumptions.

---

[7] This is the assumption of non-segregated or rehypothecated collateral, as discussed in Section 6.4.5.

simulations contribute equally to the PFE and those with the largest contribution (when the exposure is high) are precisely the ones where the most collateral is taken (the average improvement in PFE is 3.99 times).

11.3.3   Simple approximations

It is possible to have relatively simple representations for the impact of collateral in some circumstances. In Appendix 11A we give simple formulas for the PFE and EE for a collateralised exposure based on normal distribution assumptions. For example, the EE in our case is given by:

$$EE(u) \sim 0.4 \times \sigma_p \times \sqrt{MPR} \times (T-u), \qquad (11.4)$$

where σ_p represents the (annual) volatility for the underlying portfolio of maturity T. The factor $(T-u)$ is an amortisation component, which assumes linear decay.[8] The volatility of the positions can be estimated from a variance/covariance-type analysis, which is well known from market risk VAR calculations. This approximation implicitly assumes that the position is collateralised with zero threshold, MTA and rounding (but no initial margin). Figure 11.9 shows this approximation, which is reasonable, but underestimates the exposure due to the MTA and spikes caused by cashflows.

Another simple approximation (Appendix 11B) relates the uncollateralised and collateralised EPE as a ratio. This approximation can be written as:

$$\frac{EPE\,(no\ CSA)}{EPE\,(collateralised)} \approx 0.5 \sqrt{\frac{T}{MPR}} \qquad (11.5)$$

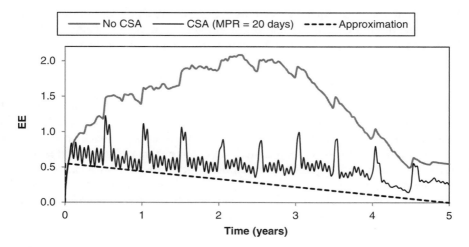

Figure 11.9   Illustration of EE compared with the simple approximation described.

---

[8] This is a rather crude approximation in this case, because it is a reasonable assumption for interest rate swaps but not for the cross-currency swap due to the exchange of notional. In the latter case no amortisation should be assumed. This also assumes constant volatility across time.

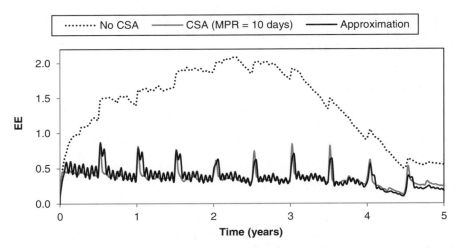

Figure 11.10   Illustration of EE calculated with a smaller MPR of ten calendar days and comparing to the previous result scaled by $1/\sqrt{2}$.

This is similar to the collateral multiplier for the SA-CCR capital methodology shown in Equation 8.11 (Section 8.4.4). This is a useful ballpark for the reduction in an uncollateralised EPE in the case of collateralisation. This in turn suggests, not surprisingly, that we can also estimate the impact of changing the MPR by multiplying by the square root of the ratio of the relevant MPRs. Figure 11.10 shows the EE with a shorter MPR of ten calendar days compared to the approximation by scaling the 20-day result by $\sqrt{(10/20)} = 1/\sqrt{2}$.

We note that analytical formulas such as the one above can be useful for characterising the impact of collateral, although such approximations become increasingly difficult when aspects such as thresholds and initial margins are present, as discussed below.

11.3.4   Discretisation and cashflows

In Section 11.2.5 we discussed the discretisation of the exposure simulation in relation to collateral modelling and the related aspect of cashflow payments. Figure 11.11 shows the collateralised EE computed with both the continuous and lookback approaches. The latter approach clearly misses the potential risk arising from cashflow payments during the MPR. It also generally gives lower numbers due to the MTA (in the lookback approach, the MTA cannot be included since this requires a continuous sampling of the exposure and collateral values). This illustrates that the continuous approach is clearly preferable, although this does require significantly more calculation effort: 183 simulation steps compared to 40.[9]

---

[9] In the continuous approach, there is a simulation point every ten days for five years, whereas in the lookback approach there are 20 original points (quarterly discretisation) plus another 20 lookback points for collateral evaluation.

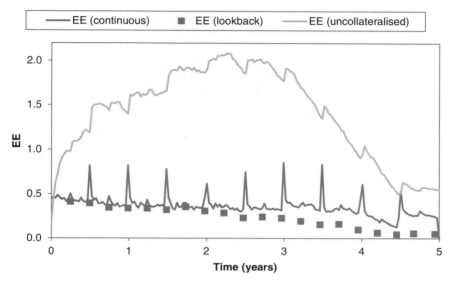

Figure 11.11   Illustration of collateralised EE using the continuous and lookback approaches illustrated in Figure 11.6.

11.3.5   Impact of threshold

One important use of thresholds is to minimise the operational and liquidity costs associated with exchanging collateral at the expense of increasing future exposure.[10] This balance between risk reduction and operational workload is sometimes important in collateral management. A low threshold will significantly reduce the exposure with a higher liquidity cost. On the other hand, decreasing the number of collateral calls can only be achieved by accepting a larger exposure. We consider the impact of a bilateral threshold in Figure 11.12. As expected, it makes the reduction in exposure worse (the EPE is improved by only a factor of 1.50 with a threshold of 5 compared to the aforementioned 2.66 reduction in the zero-threshold case).

Analytical approximations are harder to define in the presence of thresholds. However, Gibson (2005) derives a simple semi-analytical formula for a collateralised exposure incorporating collateral thresholds, and the SA-CCR approach discussed in Section 8.4.4 also incorporates the approximate effect of a threshold, albeit in a conservative fashion.

Whilst the reduction and comments above are reasonable for credit limits purposes (and indeed the PFE is improved by a slightly more significant amount for the zero-threshold case discussed above and shown in Figure 11.8), they are not so relevant or useful for mitigating CVA, as discussed in more detail in Chapter 14. From the perspective of central counterparties, for example, there is a need to mitigate exposure more strongly. This can only be achieved by using initial margin.

---

[10] We note that this might come from an institution or their counterparty's point of view; if the CSA is likely to give rise to operational effort, the counterparty may be unable to commit to collateral posting.

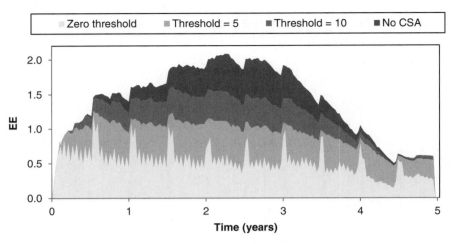

Figure 11.12   Illustration of EE calculated with different threshold assumptions.

11.3.6   Do two-way CSAs always reduce exposure?

Two-way collateral agreements may in some specific cases increase exposure. Take the example of CDS protection. Such products create a very skewed exposure distribution: when selling CDS protection, exposure is moderate compared with the negative exposure, due to the possibility of an extreme credit spread widening and/or credit event(s). The overall result of this is that in a short CDS protection position, collateral is much more likely to be posted than received, as illustrated for one simulation in Figure 11.13. The net result is to increase the overall EE, as shown in Figure 11.14. The increased risk

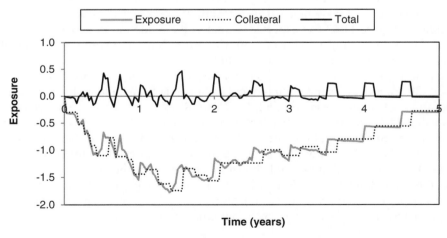

Figure 11.13   Illustration of an individual simulation path and the impact of collateral on that path for a single-name CDS protection position (short protection) calculated with and without a two-way collateral agreement (as defined in Table 11.1).

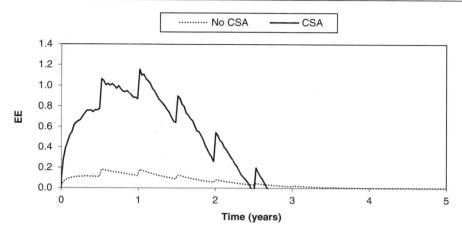

Figure 11.14   EE for a single-name CDS protection position (short protection) calculated with and without a two-way collateral agreement (as defined in Table 11.1).

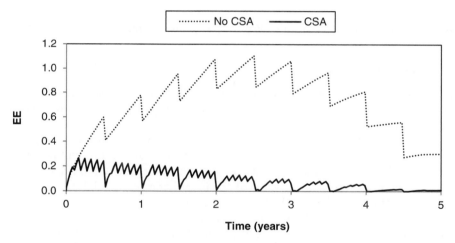

Figure 11.15   EE for a single-name CDS protection position (long protection) calculated with and without a two-way collateral agreement (as defined in Table 11.1).

from posting collateral has dominated the reduced risk from receiving it. For a long protection single-name CDS position (Figure 11.15), the situation is reversed and the CSA is seen to be beneficial.

There are other cases where the skew of the exposure distribution is important to consider when looking at the benefit of collateral. Examples would be long option positions, strongly off-market netting sets and wrong-way risk exposures (Chapter 17).

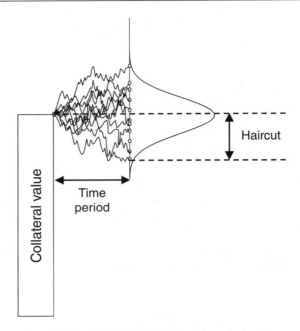

Figure 11.16   Illustration of the methodology for estimating a haircut.

11.3.7   Non-cash collateral

Non-cash collateral will have a price volatility that should be considered, since a decline in collateral value will potentially lead to an uncollateralised exposure. For this reason, haircuts are used to essentially discount the value of securities posted. The levels of haircuts are usually estimated according to price and FX (where relevant) volatility. Furthermore, typical haircuts take into account the type of security, its credit rating and its maturity. An obvious way in which to derive a haircut would be to require that it covers a potential worst-case move in the value of the underlying collateral during a given time period, as illustrated in Figure 11.16. The time would depend on the liquidity of the underlying collateral but would typically be in the region of a few days.

Under normal distribution assumptions, such a formula is easy to derive:

$$haircut = \Phi^{-1}(\alpha) \times \sigma_C \times \sqrt{\tau}, \tag{11.6}$$

where $\Phi^{-1}(\alpha)$ defines the number of standard deviations the haircut needs to cover involving the cumulative inverse normal distribution function and the confidence level α (e.g. 99%). Also required is the volatility of the collateral, σ_C, and the liquidation time (similar to the MPR concept but typically shorter) denoted τ. For example, in Table 6.7 (Chapter 6), the regulatory collateral rules require a haircut of 2% to be used for a ten-year high quality government bond. Assuming a 99% confidence level and two-day time horizon, this would equate to an interest rate volatility of around 1%,[11] which is reasonable.[12]

---

[11] $2\%/\Phi^{-1}(99\%)/\sqrt{(2/250)} = 9.6\%$ and then dividing by an approximate duration of 8.5 years.

[12] This should not be taken to imply that these assumptions were used to derive the results in Table 6.7.

Haircuts applied in this way should not only compensate for collateral volatility but also reduce exposure overall, since they will create an overcollateralisation in 99% of cases and only 1% of the time will they be insufficient. Indeed, for a short MPR the use of even quite volatile non-cash collateral does not increase the exposure materially, and a reasonably conservative haircut will at least neutralise the additional volatility. The major issue that can arise with respect to collateral type is where there is a significant a relationship between the value of the collateral and the exposure or credit quality of the counterparty. We will describe this as wrong-way collateral and discuss further in Chapter 17.

11.3.8   Collateral and funding liquidity risk

Many end-users have not traditionally posted collateral due to the liquidity implications. For example, EBA (2015b) note:

It is however more difficult to convince counterparties without collateral agreements to operate on a collateralised basis because most of them do not have the treasury function to exchange collateral on a frequent basis.

Nevertheless, in recent years, a number of parties have been under pressure to move to transact under two-way CSAs, driven by the large costs experienced by banks for uncollateralised transactions. Before entering into a collateral arrangement, it would be naturally important to make an analysis of the funding implications that may arise and put in place a "liquidity buffer" to mitigate the risk of having to post a substantial amount of liquid collateral in a relatively short space of time. In sizing this liquidity buffer, there are subjective questions such as what time horizon should be considered and what form of cash and/or securities should make up the buffer. As an example of the type of analysis that might be used, Figure 11.17 shows the worst case quarterly collateral outflow for

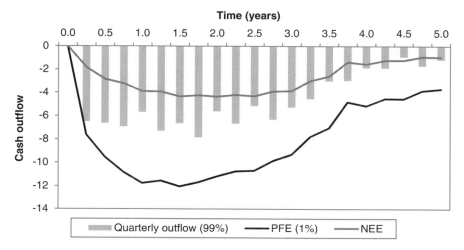

Figure 11.17   Worst case quarterly outflow for a two-way CSA with zero threshold compared to the NEE and PFE.

the portfolio in the examples above, compared to the NEE and PFE. Note that, with a zero threshold assumed, the NEE and PFE represent approximately the expected and worst case cumulative amount of collateral posted.

11.4   INITIAL MARGIN

11.4.1   Impact of initial margin on exposure

Although historically rare, as noted previously, initial margins (IMs) will be increasingly common due to the central clearing mandate (Section 9.3.1) and bilateral collateral rules (Section 6.7). An obvious question is then to look at the impact of IM on exposure as described in Section 7.5.4. Taking the base case above (zero threshold variation margin posting), and including bilateral IM posting, leads to the results in Figure 11.18. Clearly IM can potentially reduce exposure to negligible levels if it is substantial enough. Note that the IM posted by the party in question does not appear, since it is assumed that this is segregated (Equation 7.8). Also notice that since these results use a fixed IM, the residual exposure falls over time as the shorter maturity portfolio becomes less sensitive to market movements.

One way of looking at an IM is that it converts counterparty risk into gap risk. The gap risk is defined in this case by the chance of the exposure "gapping" through the IM during the MPR. Quantifying the residual exposure now becomes more difficult, since it is driven by more extreme events and will be very sensitive to modelling assumptions. When assessing gap risk one should be more concerned about distributional assumptions such as fat tails, jumps and extreme co-dependency. None of these is considered in the modelling of the exposure, but for cases without IM this is less of a concern. Note that IMs are essentially the first line of defence through which central counterparties mitigate their risk. The difficulty in setting the correct IM should be clear, since this depends so subtly on the assessment of the gap risk that remains.

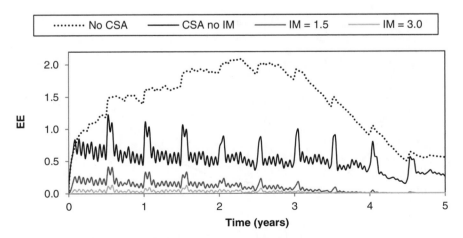

Figure 11.18   EE computed under different bilateral IM assumptions.

11.4.2   Dynamic initial margins

Whilst IMs are sometimes static, as in the above example (for example, they may be a percentage of notional), they can also be dynamic. Indeed, central counterparties typically base their IM requirements on a VAR-like model (Section 9.3.4). The incoming bilateral rules on collateral also allow a similar dynamic approach such as the SIMM to be used (although simpler formulas can also be applied – Section 6.7.6). It will therefore become increasingly important in the future to be able to model stochastic IM. Assuming the IM is static at the current level will be unacceptable since IM requirements on a portfolio will reduce through time. This is therefore a very challenging computational task, since it would require a calculation of the future IM that would be held at every single scenario in the exposure calculation. Green and Kenyon (2015) give one potential framework for how this might be achieved.

One could question whether the computational intensive calculation of the impact of IM on exposure is really necessary, since high confidence levels are generally used for IM calculations (regulation requires both central counterparties and bilateral markets to use a minimum of 99% and use stressed data in the calculation). Take a simple example of the EE of a normal distribution with IM taken at a confidence level of α. The reduction compared with having no IM (i.e. the uncollateralised EE divided by the EE collateralised with IM) can be shown (Appendix 11C) to be:

$$R_{\alpha} = \left[\phi\left(\sqrt{\lambda} K\right) - \sqrt{\lambda} K \Phi\left(-\sqrt{\lambda} K\right) \right]^{-1} (2\pi)^{-0.5}, \tag{11.7}$$

where $\lambda = \tau_{IM}/\tau_{MPR}$ is the ratio of the time horizon used (τ_{IM}) for the IM calculation divided by the MPR for the exposure quantification (τ_{MPR}) and $K = \Phi^{-1}(\alpha)$ where $\phi(.)$ is a standard normal density function and $\Phi(.)$ is the cumulative standard normal density function.

Table 11.2 shows the reduction in EE calculated at various confidence levels and values of λ. For example, under normal distribution assumptions, taking IM at the 99% confidence level will reduce the EE by over two orders of magnitude (117.7 times) if the time horizons for IM and exposure are identical. Of course, it is possible that the horizon for MPR could be greater than the time horizon for the IM calculation: for example, 20 days' MPR as required in some cases under Basel III (Section 8.6.3) combined with a bilateral initial margin calculation using only ten days (Section 6.7.3). Even this case gives a reduction of 19.1 times with a 99% confidence level IM.

There are clearly drawbacks to the above example, such as the fact that the distributions used for IM estimation and exposure quantification are identical. In reality these will be different, although both will include aspects such as stressed data. Whilst the above is a simple illustration, it does suggest that if IM is indeed taken to a high

Table 11.2   EE for a normal distribution with IM at different confidence levels. The ratio is defined as the EE with no IM divided by the ratio with IM.

Confidence level	$\lambda = 1$	$\lambda = 0.5$	$\lambda = 0.25$
90%	8.4	4.0	2.5
95%	19.1	6.6	3.5
99%	117.7	19.1	6.6
99.5%	252.4	29.5	8.5

confidence level then any residual exposure should be small. Even if this is not the case, the exposure quantification model is unlikely to show significant residual risk when a broadly similarly calibrated IM model operates at a confidence level of 99% or more and the horizon for IM computation is broadly similar to the MPR. Perhaps it is better to focus attention on IM quantification standards rather than on modelling dynamic IM within exposure models that will inevitably produce very favourable reductions.

The above analysis does, however, assume that a full IM to a high confidence will be taken against the entire exposure in question. In reality, in bilateral markets this is not completely true for the following reasons (Section 6.7.3):

- the requirement to post initial margin where it applies only impacts new transactions and so legacy trades will not have IM held against them (although this effect will fade over time until all such legacy trades have matured);
- there is a threshold of up to €50m that can be applied to the IM amount; and
- there are exempt transactions (e.g. some FX).

This means that a portfolio of transactions may collectively appear to have only a relatively moderate IM associated with it and will therefore have a material residual exposure, although this effect will lessen as more transactions become subject to the bilateral rules through time. We will therefore look at dynamic IM again in the KVA discussion in Chapter 16.

11.4.3   Segregation and funding exposure

Segregated collateral aims to reduce counterparty risk for the receiving party without increasing it for the collateral giver. This is why the IM posted does not show up in the previous result in Figure 11.18, even though the IM posting is assumed to be bilateral. However, as described in Section 7.5, posted IM does increase funding costs. Figure 11.19

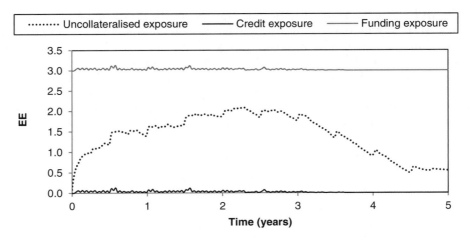

Figure 11.19   Credit exposure compared to funding exposure for the example in Figure 11.18 with bilateral initial margin of 3. Note that the uncollateralised exposure applies for both credit and funding.

shows the credit exposure (as previously discussed in this chapter) compared to the funding exposure for the previous example. As discussed in Section 7.5.4, the segregated IM that is posted does not increase the credit exposure but does create funding exposure. The credit exposure is close to zero due to the IM held, whilst the funding exposure is broadly characterised by the posted IM. The funding exposure in this example is the source of MVA discussed in Chapter 16.

11.5   SUMMARY

This chapter has discussed the impact of collateral on exposure. We have described the general methodology for accounting for collateral in exposure simulations. A number of examples have been used to show the impact of aspects such as thresholds, initial margins and non-cash collateral. Some simple formulas to approximate the impact of collateral in certain situations have also been shown. We have also shown the impact of segregated collateral (initial margin) on both credit and funding exposure.

12

Default Probabilities, Credit Spreads and Funding Costs

12.1 OVERVIEW

This chapter discusses default probabilities, funding spreads and return on capital, which represent the cost components of the xVA terms. Default probability, and associated recovery rates, are required in order to define CVA and DVA in counterparty risk quantification. There is significant subjectivity in obtaining default probabilities for illiquid credits, since they must usually be derived via a credit spread mapping procedure. Terms such as FVA and MVA require an assessment of the relevant funding costs that are required when funding a position or posting initial margin. Funding costs are also difficult to define, since they depend on the overall funding strategy as well as the nature of the funding requirements and any remuneration of collateral. KVA requires an assessment of the required return on capital. Capital costs are also subjective to define, as they are based on the perceived return that shareholders require together with effects such as tax. All of these costs terms may also have important term structure effects and may therefore impact different tenors differently.

12.2 DEFAULT PROBABILITY

12.2.1 Real-world and risk-neutral

In Section 10.4, we discussed the difference between real-world and risk-neutral parameters for exposure quantification. There is a even more significant difference between real world and risk-neutral default probabilities that has been at the heart of the increased importance of CVA in recent years.

A real-world default probability is typically estimated from historical default data via some associated credit rating. A risk-neutral default probability is derived from market data using instruments such as bonds or credit default swaps (CDSs). It would be expected that risk-neutral default probabilities would be higher than their real-world equivalents, since investors are risk-averse and demand a premium for accepting default risk. This is indeed observed empirically: Altman (1989), for example, tracks the performance of portfolios of corporate bonds for a given rating and finds that the returns outperform a risk-free benchmark (which is a portfolio of Treasury bonds). This

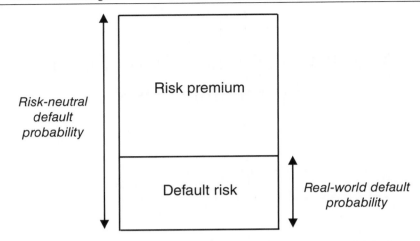

Figure 12.1 Illustration of the difference between real-world and risk-neutral default probabilities.

outperformance shows that the return on the corporate bonds is more than adequate to cover the default losses experienced and that bond investors are being compensated for material components above expected default rates and the resulting losses.

We depict the difference between a real-world and a risk-neutral default probability in Figure 12.1. The risk-neutral default probability is larger due to an embedded premium that investors require when taking credit risk. There has been research based on understanding the nature and behaviour of the risk premium depicted in Figure 12.1 (see, for example, Collin-Dufresne et al., 2001, Downing et al., 2005 and Longstaff et al., 2005). For our purposes, we do not need to know more about the nature of this premium, although it is interesting to understand its magnitude.

The difference between real-world and risk-neutral default probabilities have been characterised in a number of empirical studies. For example, Giesecke et al. (2010) used a dataset of bond yields that spans a period of almost 150 years from 1866 to 2008 and found that average credit spreads (across all available bond data) have been about twice as large as realised losses due to default. Studies that are more specific include Fons (1987), the aforementioned work by Altman (1989) and Hull et al. (2004). For example, Fons found that one-year risk-neutral default probabilities exceed actual realised default

Table 12.1 Comparison between real-world and risk-neutral default probabilities in basis points.

Credit rating	Real-world	Risk-neutral	Ratio
Aaa	4	67	16.8
Aa	6	78	13.0
A	13	128	9.8
Baa	47	238	5.1
Ba	240	507	2.1
B	749	902	1.2
Caa	1690	2130	1.3

Source: Hull et al. (2005a).

rates by approximately 5%. The difference between real and risk-neutral default probabilities from Hull et al. (2004) is shown in Table 12.1 as a function of credit rating. We see that the difference is large, especially for better quality credits.

12.2.2   The move to risk-neutral

In the early days of counterparty risk assessment it was common for banks to use real-world default probability (based on historical estimates) in order to quantify CVA, which was not universally considered a component of the fair value of a derivative. With this as a background, the Basel III capital requirements for CVA (Section 8.7) were outlined with a risk-neutral based CVA concept irrespective of whether or not the bank in question actually accounted for their CVA in this fashion.

As discussed in Section 4.3.4, it has been increasingly common in recent years for risk-neutral default probabilities to be used when calculating CVA. For example, in an Ernst and Young Survey in 2012,[1] 13 out of 19 participating banks used risk-neutral ("market data") for default probability estimation. The move to risk-neutral has been catalysed by accounting requirements and Basel III capital rules. IFRS 13 requires entities to make use of market-observable inputs wherever possible, and Basel III makes explicit reference to the credit spread in the underlying CVA formula (Section 8.7.3). Some small regional banks still use real-world default probabilities, but this is becoming increasingly rare and harder to defend to auditors and regulators. For example, Ernst and Young (2014) state that "the use of historical default rates would seem to be inconsistent with the exit price notion in IRFS 13".

As discussed in Section 4.3.4, the use of risk-neutral default probabilities changes the interpretation of CVA to be a market price of counterparty risk rather than some actuarial reserve. In some sense this is not surprising, given the development of the CDS market and the fact that CVA hedging has become more commonplace. On the other hand, it is important to emphasise that many counterparties are "illiquid credits" in the sense that there is no direct market observable from which to directly define a risk-neutral default probability. This is particularly true for banks who may have thousands of counterparties, many of whom are relatively small and do not have bonds or CDSs referencing their own credit. It is also more significant in regions outside Europe and the US, where CDS and secondary bond markets are more illiquid and sometimes non-existent.

The requirement to use risk-neutral default probabilities for illiquid credits creates a further problem with hedging: risk-neutral probabilities suggest the existence of a hedge, but without a liquid CDS on the counterparty in question, such a hedge does not exist. This is problematic, since CVA will be generally much larger and more volatile (compared to using historical default probabilities) but without the availability of the natural hedging instruments to manage this volatility. For these reasons, banks have sometimes attempted to follow an intermediate approach such as using a blend of historical and risk-neutral default probabilities (including two banks from the aforementioned Ernst and Young survey in 2012). Another approach has been to use risk-neutral default probabilities for "liquid credits" (i.e. those with an active CDS market or equivalent) and historical or blended probabilities for illiquid credits.

---

[1] Ernst and Young CVA Survey 2012, www.ey.com.

However, regulators and auditors generally do not support the deviation from risk-neutral default probabilities, even in cases of illiquid credits. For example, the CVA challenger model imposed by the ECB states:[2]

> The CVA challenger model then calculates an estimate of the CVA based on Benchmark PD [probability of default] parameters estimated from current index CDS curves and a market standard LGD parameter. The source of any significant deviations should then be understood.

Basel III capital rules impose similar requirements for capital allocation against CVA, requiring CDS spreads to be used where available and for non-liquid counterparties stating (BCBS, 2011b):

> Whenever such a CDS spread is not available, the bank must use a proxy spread that is appropriate based on the rating, industry and region of the counterparty.

Using the current credit environment (via CDS spreads) as a reference would seem to be preferable to a backward-looking and static approach using historical data. However, the large non-default component in credit spreads (Section 12.2.1), the inability to define CDS spreads for most counterparties and underlying illiquidity of the CDS market do create problems with such an approach. Furthermore, the unintended consequences of the use of CDS implied default probabilities has potentially adverse effects such as the "doom loop" discussed in Section 8.7.5. Some authors (e.g. Gregory, 2010) have argued against this requirement and noted that banks do not attempt to mark-to-market (MTM) much of their illiquid credit risk (for example, their loan books). However, whilst using subjective mapping methods to determine a credit spread may seem rather non-scientific, it is generally a necessary process for banks to value illiquid assets, such as bonds and loans, held on their trading books. Accordingly, regulators clearly see risk-neutral default probabilities as a fundamental building block for CVA calculations and they are clearly the basis for defining exit prices for fair value accounting purposes.

In line with the above, market practice (especially in the larger banks) has converged on the use of risk-neutral default probabilities. For example, EBA (2015b) states:

> The CVA data collection exercise has highlighted increased convergence in banks' practices in relation to CVA. Banks seem to have progressively converged in reflecting the cost of the credit risk of their counterparties in the fair value of derivatives using market implied data based on CDS spreads and proxy spreads in the vast majority of cases. This convergence is the result of industry practice, as well as a consequence of the implementation in the EU of IFRS 13 and the Basel CVA framework.

---

[2] European Central Bank, Asset Quality Review, March 2014.

12.2.3   Defining risk-neutral default probabilities

Risk-neutral default probabilities are those derived from credit spreads observed in the market. There is no unique definition of a credit spread and it may be defined in slightly different ways and with respect to different market observables such as:

- single-name CDSs;
- asset swaps[3] spreads;
- from bond or loan prices; and
- using some proxy or mapping method.

All of the above are (broadly speaking) defining the same quantity, but the CDS market is the most obvious clean and directly available quote, since the CDS premium defines the credit spread directly. In contrast, to calculate a credit spread from a bond price requires various assumptions such as comparing with some benchmark such as a treasury curve. Where observable, the difference between CDS and bond-derived credit spreads (the "CDS-bond basis") can be significant. For now, we will not be concerned with the precise definition of the credit spread, but simply how to extract the risk-neutral default probability.

Spreadsheet 12.1   Calculating risk-neutral default probabilities

---

Appendix 12A gives more detail on the mathematics of deriving risk-neutral default probabilities. For quantifying a term such as CVA, we require the default probability between any two sequential dates. A commonly used approximation for this is:

$$PD(t_{i-1}, t_i) \approx \exp\left(-\frac{s_{t_{i-1}} t_{i-1}}{LGD}\right) - \exp\left(-\frac{s_{t_i} t_i}{LGD}\right), \tag{12.1}$$

where $PD(t_{i-1}, t_i)$ is the default probability between t_{i-1} and t_i, s_t is the credit spread at time t and LGD is the assumed loss given default (discussed below). Note that this probability is unconditional (i.e. it is not conditional upon the counterparty surviving to t_{i-1}). Table 12.2 illustrates this for a simple example using annual default probabilities. To obtain a more granular representation then the most obvious solution would be to interpolate the credit spreads.

Table 12.2   Annual default probabilities for an example credit curve using Equation 12.1. An LGD of 60% is used.

Time	Credit spread	PD
1Y	300 bps	4.88%
2Y	350 bps	6.13%
3Y	400 bps	7.12%
4Y	450 bps	7.79%
5Y	500 bps	8.16%

---

[3] An asset swap is essentially a synthetic bond, typically with a floating coupon.

Equation 12.1 is only an approximation because it does not account for the shape of the credit spread curve prior to the time t_{i-1}, and the more sloped the curve is, the worse the approximation. In Spreadsheet 12.1, it is possible to compare the simple formula with the more accurate calculation.

12.2.4   Term structure

Spreadsheet 12.2   Impact of credit curve shape on risk-neutral default probabilities

Suppose we take three different credit curves: flat, upwards-sloping and inverted, as shown in Figure 12.2. The cumulative default probability curves are shown in Figure 12.3. Note

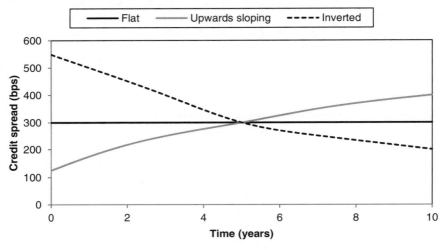

Figure 12.2   Three different shapes of credit curve all with a five-year spread of 300 bps.

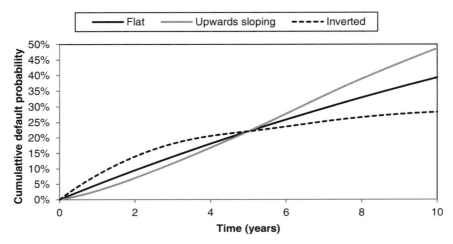

Figure 12.3   Cumulative default probabilities for flat, upwards-sloping and inverted credit curves. In all cases, the five-year spread is 300 bps and the LGD is assumed to be 60%.

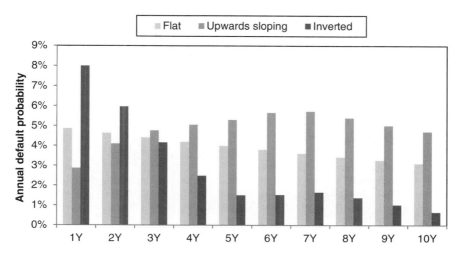

Figure 12.4   Annual default probabilities for flat, upwards-sloping and inverted curves as described in the text. In all cases, the five-year spread is 300 bps and the LGD is assumed to be 60%.

that all have a five-year credit spread of 300 bps and assumed LGD of 60%. The only thing that differs is the shape of the curve. Whilst all curves agree on the five-year cumulative default probability of 22.12%, the precise shape of the curve up to and beyond this point gives very different results. This is seen in Figure 12.4, which shows annual default probabilities for each case. For an upwards-sloping curve, default is less likely in the early years and more likely in the later years, whilst the reverse is seen for an inverted curve. In order to calculate risk-neutral default probabilities properly, in addition to defining the level of the credit curve, it is also important to know the precise curve shape. Extrapolation to the ten-year point, if that information is not available, is very sensitive.

12.2.5   Loss given default

In order to estimate risk-neutral default probabilities, we must know the associated loss given default (LGD), which refers to the percentage amount that would be lost in the event of a counterparty defaulting (all creditors having a legal right to receive a proportion of what they are owed). Equivalently, this is sometimes defined as one minus the recovery rate. LGD depends on the seniority of the OTC derivative claim – normally this ranks *pari passu* (of the same seniority) with senior unsecured debt, which, in turn, is referenced by most CDS contracts. However, sometimes derivatives may rank more senior (typically in securitisations) or may be subordinated, in which case further adjustments may be necessary.

Historical analysis on recovery rates show that they vary significantly depending on sector, seniority of claim and economic conditions. As an example, Table 12.3 shows some recovery values of for financial institutions, which spans the whole range from virtually zero to full recovery. For CVA computation, the recovery rate (or equivalently LGD) estimate is not of primary importance due to a cancellation effect, which will be

Table 12.3 Recovery rates for CDS auctions for some credit events in 2008. The Fannie Mae and Freddie Mac subordinated debt traded at higher levels than the senior debt because of a "delivery squeeze" due to a limited amount bonds in the market to deliver against CDS protection.

Reference entity	Seniority	Recovery rate
Fannie Mae	Senior	91.5%
	Subordinated	99.9%
Freddie Mac	Senior	94.0%
	Subordinated	98.0%
Washington Mutual		57.0%
Lehman		8.6%
Kaupthing Bank	Senior	6.6%
	Subordinated	2.4%
Landsbanki	Senior	1.3%
	Subordinated	0.1%
Glitnir	Senior	3.0%
	Subordinated	0.1%
Average		38.5%

discussed in Chapter 14. Hence, the assessment of recovery is not as important as that of the credit spread curve.

A final point on recovery is related to the timing. CDSs are settled quickly following a default and bondholders can settle their bonds in the same process (the CDS auction) or simply sell them in the market. However, bilateral OTC derivatives cannot be settled in a timely manner. This is partly due to their bespoke nature and partly due to netting (and collateral), which means that many transactions are essentially aggregated into a single claim and cannot be traded individually. The net claim (less any collateral) is then often quite difficult to define for the portfolio of trades (see Figure 3.3 in Chapter 3). This creates two different recovery values:

- *Settled recovery.* This is the recovery that could be achieved following the credit event by trading out of a claim; for example, by selling a defaulted bond.
- *Actual recovery.* This is the actual recovery received on a derivative following a bankruptcy or similar process.

In theory, settled and actual recoveries should be very similar, but in reality – since bankruptcy processes can take many years – they may differ materially. This is illustrated in Figure 12.5. It should be possible to agree on the claim with the bankruptcy administrators prior to the actual recovery, although this process may take many months. This would allow an institution to sell the claim and monetise the recovery value as early as possible. In the case of the Lehman Brothers bankruptcy, the settled recovery was around 9%, whereas some actual recoveries received since have been substantially higher (in the region of 30–40%).

It should also be noted that recoveries on derivatives may be improved due to offsetting against other claims or other assets held (e.g. see the discussion on set-off in Section 5.2.5). These components may not be priced into transactions (they are not consistent with the exit price concept applied to accounting CVA), but may give some additional benefit in a default workout process.

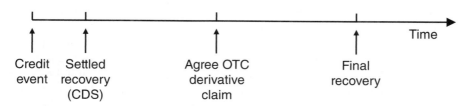

Figure 12.5 Schematic illustration of recovery settlement after a credit event. The settled recovery rate is achieved very close to the credit event time (for example, by participating in the CDS auction). The final recovery occurs when the company has been completely wound up. The actual recovery for a derivative claim may be realised sometime between the settled and final recoveries.

12.3 CREDIT CURVE MAPPING

12.3.1 Overview

Credit curve estimation is a key but subjective input into the CVA calculations. Banks will have many hundreds and (for the larger ones) thousands of derivatives counterparties, which will be entities such as sovereigns, supranationals, corporates, SMEs and financial institutions. The vast majority of these counterparties may not have liquid CDS quotes, bond prices or even external ratings associated with them. This is in contrast to end-users, who will generally only trade with a relatively small number of (bank) counterparties for which the required information (CDS market) may well be readily available. For banks with many illiquid names, credit curve mapping is a significant challenge.

No standard method exists for defining a credit curve for a given counterparty. This is not surprising given the subjectivity of the problem, and although some basic principles apply, there are many different ways in which to do this. Much of the regulatory guidance is generally quite broad and only makes reference to general aspects such as the rating, region and sector being considered when determining the appropriate credit spread. The European Banking Authority (EBA 2013) have expanded on the suggested methodology behind this. Some of the general issues to be faced with credit curve mapping are:

- *Reference instrument.* As noted above (Section 12.2.3), there are a number of potential source of credit spread information such as CDSs or bonds.
- *Tenor.* As discussed in Section 12.2.4, it is important to define fully the term structure of credit spreads up to the maturity of the counterparty portfolio in question. Available market data may mean that some tenors may be more easy to map that others. Defining tenors above ten years will be particularly challenging.
- *Seniority.* It may be that the instrument used to define the credit spread has a different seniority to that of the potential derivative claim with the counterparty.
- *Liquidity.* Some instruments, such as CDS indices, will be more liquid but less appropriate from a fundamental point of view for mapping a given credit. Other more relevant sources may be rather illiquid.
- *Region.* Whilst European and US debt markets may provide a reasonable amount of liquidity (for traded credit), other regions (e.g. Asia) are generally much more limited. Regional banks may therefore face an even greater challenge for determining credit spreads.
- *Hedging.* Related to the above liquidity comments, some reference instruments may provide reasonable mapping information but may not facilitate the hedging of

counterparty risk. This could be due to a lack of liquidity or for practical reasons (for example, not being able to short a corporate bond).

- *Capital relief.* Related to hedging will be the potential capital relief that will be available from various hedges, which can sometimes create problems. For example, proxy single-name CDS[4] may be considered good hedges but attract no capital relief (Section 8.7.3).[5] Index hedges do allow capital relief, but the magnitude of this may not align with the view of the bank. Note that for banks using the advanced CVA capital charge, the mapping methodology must be consistent with the specific risk model used for simulating credit spreads.

The above will lead to some rather difficult and subjective decisions over the choice of mapping methodology. For example, is it appropriate to map to an illiquid bond price observed in the secondary market for the counterparty in question or to use a CDS index that is much more liquid and can provide a hedge? Should one use a single-name CDS on a similar credit, which is believed to represent an excellent reference point but under (current) Basel III rules does not attract any capital relief? The next sections will define the general approach and choices to be made.

12.3.2   The CDS market

There are many hundreds of names with liquid CDS quotes: mainly large corporates, banks and sovereigns, although the liquidity of this market has not been improving in recent years. There are also credit indices, which are generally more liquid. Figure 12.6 gives an overview of the main CDS instruments available for mapping purposes in Europe. Reading from the bottom, the first choice could obviously be to map to a single-name CDS or a relevant proxy such as a parent company. If such information were not available then the counterparty would be mapped to the relevant index depending on whether it is a corporation, financial or sovereign entity. Corporations may be further sub-divided according to credit quality (for example, iTraxx Non-financials, Crossover and High volatility – see Table 12.4).

Table 12.4 lists some of the most liquid credit indices globally. Generally indices reference liquid credits that trade in the single-name CDS market or secondary bond market. Note that more detailed classifications exist that are not shown. For example, iTraxx financials is divided into senior and sub, iTraxx SovX is sub-divided into various regions (Western Europe, CEEMEA, Asia Pacific, Latin America, G7, BRIC*)*. The main non-financials index is sub-divided into sectorial indices (TMT, industrials, energy, consumers and autos). Whilst these sub-divisions give a more granular representation, they have to be balanced against the available liquidity in the CDS market. The liquid indices trade at maturities of three, five, seven and ten years, whilst for the less liquid ones then the five- and ten-year tenors are the most traded.

There are some additional technical issues with using CDS to derive credit spreads for calculating CVA. First, the credit events under an ISDA standard CDS are failure to pay, restructuring or bankruptcy. Failure to make a derivative payment may not constitute a trigger under a CDS contract. Ideally, there would be a cross-default of

---

[4] A single-name proxy is one that is viewed as giving a good representation of the credit spread in question. This may be a similar company or sovereign entity.

[5] Although BCBS (2015) proposes to give capital relief for proxy single-name CDS.

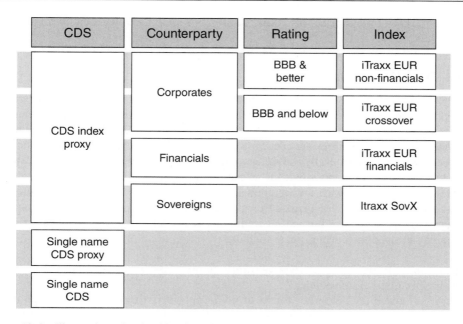

Figure 12.6   Illustration of a classification of counterparties according to European credit indices.

Table 12.4   Universe of key credit indices globally.

	Index	Size	Comment
iTraxx	Main	125	Most actively traded investment grade names
Europe	Non-financials	100	Non-financial credits
	Crossover	40	Sub-investment grade credits
	High volatility	30	Widest spread credits from main index
	LevX	30	First lien loan CDS
CDX	Main	125	Most actively traded investment grade credits
	High yield	100	High yield credits
	Emerging markets	14	Emerging markets CDS
	LCDX	100	First lien leverage loans CDSs
iTraxx	Asia	50	Investment grade Asian (ex-Japan) credits
Asia	Asia HY	20	High yield Asian (ex-Japan) credits
	Japan	50	Investment grade rated Japanese entities
	Australia	25	Liquid investment grade Australian entities

these obligations in documentation. Indeed, sometimes CDS do include such a trigger explicitly, although they are inevitably more expensive. Note also that the deliverable in a CDS contract is typically a bond or loan, and not a derivative receivable. This leaves a potential basis risk between the LGD on the derivative and the payout on the CDS, as discussed in Section 12.2.5.

Liquidity in the CDS market (especially single-name) has not significantly improved the global financial crisis. There is a general issue with the depth and liquidity of single-name CDS markets and the calculation and management of CVA. Despite this, the CDS market is still believed (by regulators and auditors, at least, if not all banks) to provide the best market-implied price for credit risk and is widely used in credit curve mapping approaches.

12.3.3   Loss given default

Ideally, LGDs would be derived from market prices, but this is not generally possible since current market levels for implied recovery do not really exist. A recovery lock or recovery swap is an agreement between two parties to swap a realised recovery rate (when or if the relevant recovery event occurs) with a defined recovery rate (fixed at the start of the contract and is generally the same as the standard recovery rates outlined above). Recovery swaps do not generally trade, except occasionally for distressed credits.

CDS contracts trade with an assumed LGD depending on the underlying reference entity (for example, 60% for iTraxx Europe and CDX NA). Generally, these standard recoveries are used to mark individual credit curves. Sometimes, more favourable (lower) LGDs may be used to reflect aspects such as:

- Structural seniority of the derivative transaction(s). For example, trades with securitisation special purpose vehicles.
- Credit enhancements or other forms of credit support, although aspects such as derivatives collateral should generally be modelled within the exposure simulation, as discussed in the last chapter.
- The assumption of a favourable work-out process based potentially on experience. Often banks may have experienced recovery rates on their derivative portfolios that are higher than the standard recovery rates, even though in terms of seniority they should be the same. One reason for this is the Lehman case mentioned in Section 12.2.5. Auditors and regulators may not accept such assumptions without stronger evidence.

The choice of LGD is therefore driven by market convention but is not implied directly from market prices.

12.3.4   General approach

In general, there are three different sources of credit spread information for a given counterparty:

- *Direct observables.* In this situation, the credit spread of the actual counterparty in question is directly observable in the market. Note that even when this data exists, there may only be one liquid tenor (for example, typically five-year for single name CDS), which is a clear problem, especially for long-dated trades. If it is possible to short the credit (e.g. buy CDS protection) then it may be possible to hedge and gain capital relief.
- *Single-name proxies.* This is a situation where another single reference entity trades in the market, which is viewed as a good proxy for the counterparty in question. This may be a parent company or the sovereign of the region in question, and may be used directly or have an additional component added to the credit spread to reflect a greater riskiness. Hedging with such a name may provide a spread hedge but not

Table 12.5 Comparison of different mapping approaches.

	Liquidity	Hedging	Capital relief
Direct observables	Poor	Spread and default hedge	Full
Single-name proxies	Medium	Partial spread hedge only	None
Generic proxies	Good		Partial

a default hedge, and capital relief will not be achieved (under the current regulatory rules although as noted previously, BCBS 2015 proposes to change this).

• *Generic proxies.* This is the case where there is no defined credit spread that can be readily mapped directly and some sort of generic mapping via rating, region and sector is required. Such a mapping may use CDS indices, which do not provide default protection but allow spread hedging and will provide partial capital relief.

A summary of the above approaches is given in Table 12.5.

The above rules need to be implemented via some sort of decision tree, as illustrated in Figure 12.7. The typical benchmark choice is CDS, where available and other instruments such as bonds will normally only be considered where the single-name CDS is not

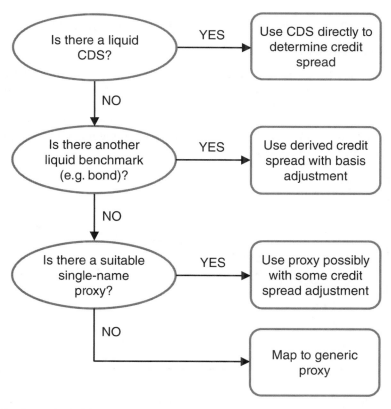

Figure 12.7 Example decision tree in order to map a given counterparty credit spread.

liquid. Other quotes, such as bond spreads, will have to be derived using some methodology and then potentially basis-adjusted to attempt to estimate the equivalent CDS value. Single-name proxies may attract a small spread adjustment to account for a perceived higher (or lower) credit risk. This spread adjustment could be because a parent company is being used as a proxy but does not offer an explicit guarantee and the child company is viewed as more risky. Sovereign CDS are also quite common proxies, especially in markets where single-name CDSs are limited, and a spread will be added to reflect the additional idiosyncratic risk with respect to the sovereign credit quality. Clearly, if a significant spread adjustment needs to be made, then this suggests that the proxy is not a particularly good choice.

Is it also important to note that single-name proxies may increase volatility, since any idiosyncratic behaviour of the proxy will be incorrectly reflected in the mapped credit spread.

With respect to the decision tree in Figure 12.7, it is important to note that a typical bank will end up with many names mapped to generic proxies. This is due to the likelihood of having many clients who have relatively small balance sheets (e.g. corporates, SMEs) and therefore do not have liquid instruments traded in the credit markets. Although the exposure to these clients may be relatively small, the total exposure is likely to collectively be very significant, and therefore the construction of general curves as proxies is important.

12.4   GENERIC CURVE CONSTRUCTION

12.4.1   General approach

The fundamental aim of generic credit curve mapping is to use some relevant classified points to achieve a general curve based on observable market data, as illustrated in Figure 12.8. This represents the case seen in the CDS market where only a few maturity points will be available. In the case of the secondary bond market, more maturity points may be available. Some methodology will be required to combine points at a given tenor

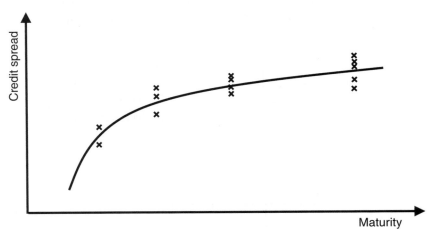

Figure 12.8   Illustration of a generic curve construction procedure. The crosses represent observable credit spreads as a function of maturity.

(perhaps with some underlying weighting scheme also used to bias towards the more liquid quotes) and interpolate between tenors.

The above classification may be rather broad (e.g. a single-A curve), in which case there will be a large number of data points to fit, but less distinguishing between different counterparties. By contrast, a more granular classification (e.g. rating, region and sector such as a single-A US utility company) distinguishes better between different counterparties but provides less data for each curve calibration. Mapping has to consider granularity carefully: a more granular mapping is preferable only if there are sufficient data points for each categorisation. With few data points, there is a danger of the idiosyncratic risk of a particular credit creating unrealistic and undesirable volatility.

Whilst regulators generally propose a mapping based upon rating, country and sector, they seemingly accept more sparse representation when data does not clearly allow this. Even within these categories, the classification is generally kept fairly narrow, for example:

- *Regions*. Western Europe, Eastern Europe, North America, South America, Middle East, Oceania and Asia.
- *Rating*. AAA, AA, A, BBB, BB, B and CCC. For non-externally rated names, banks will typically use their internal rating mapped to external ratings.
- *Sectors*. Financials, corporates and sovereigns.

The approach to classification may differ between banks. For example, a large global bank may believe that they have an exposure that is not concentrated from a regional or sectorial point of view. On the other hand, a local bank will necessarily have a more geographically concentrated exposure and may be more exposed to certain sectors that are more active in their own region.

Note that even the above broad classification gives a total of $7 \times 7 \times 3 = 147$ possible combinations. Given the number of liquid CDS, it is clear that even this categorisation will have the problem of limited or no CDS quotes in some rating, region or section buckets. Expanding the representation is clearly impractical without either many extrapolation and interpolation assumptions or a more liquid underlying CDS market.

12.4.2 Third party curves

Some generic curves are available from third party providers. These offer a potentially cheaper solution and are independent (which may be desirable from an auditor's perspective). On the other hand, they have the drawback of being rigid in their classification and will produce behaviour beyond the control of the user (such as MTM volatility).

One example of such generic curves is the Markit sector curves.[6] These are based on senior unsecured CDS spreads for publicly rated entities with liquid single-name CDS at the one-, five- and ten-year points. Between tenors, credit spreads are interpolated and, depending on the number of points available, various top and tailing and averaging are done to produce the final curve. Curves are constructed across ratings (AAA, AA, A, BBB, BB, B and CCC) and sectors (basic materials, consumer goods, consumer services, financials, government, healthcare, industrials, energy, technology, telecommunications

---

[6] See www.markit.com.

services and utilities). With seven ratings classes and 11 sectors, a total of 77 possible curves exist. Region is not currently considered as a component of the generic curve construction, but this is planned.

Another provider of generic curves is S&P through its group curves.[7] This uses a broadly similar methodology with the same seven rating categories and eight sectors (basic materials, consumer cyclical, consumer non-cyclical, financials, healthcare, industrials, oil and gas, and SSAs), giving a total of 56 potential buckets. Like Markit, regions are not currently defined.

12.4.3   Mapping approach

Figure 12.9 illustrates market practice for the construction of generic curves for non-tradable credits. In addition to the obvious use of indices, it can be seen that bespoke curves are generated as a function of rating, region and industry. Not surprisingly, whilst classification via rating is common, the use of region and industry grouping is less prevalent. In other words, banks will classify by all three if possible, and drop the industry and possibly also regional categorisation if necessary. Clearly, in regions such as the US and Europe, the most granular definition may be possible; but in smaller regions, sector classification will almost certainly need to be excluded. Internal spread corresponds to using some internal estimation of spread, potentially from the pricing of loans to the same or similar counterparties. This is clearly less in line with the concept of defining spreads with respect to external pricing and market observables.

A typical approach to generic curve construction is to produce bespoke curves by some rating, regional and sector classification based upon a chosen universe of liquid single-name CDS. This will be broadly achieved as follows:

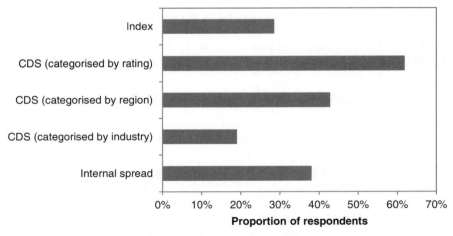

Figure 12.9   Market practice for marking non-tradable credit curves.
Source: Deloitte/Solum CVA survey, 2013.

---

[7] See www.capitaliq.com.

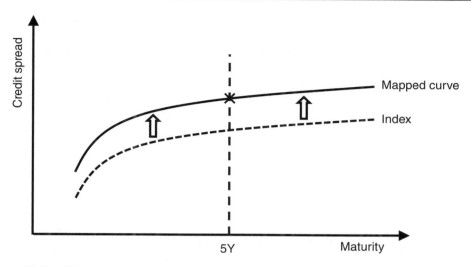

Figure 12.10   Illustration of defining a curve shape based on the shape of the relevant index. The cross shows the five-year point that is assumed to be known for the curve in question.

- define the universe of available CDS via a minimum liquidity threshold (for example, more than three quotes);
- bucket this universe by the agreed upon classification (rating, region and sector where appropriate), and depending on the data available;
- exclude outliers in each bucket according to some given metric such as more than a certain number of standard deviations from the median (this can clearly only be done with a reasonably large data set);
- fill in missing data points via various interpolation and extrapolation methods; and
- define the resulting curve via an average of the relevant points or a weighted average depending on the relative liquidity of different points.

Indices are an alternative for mapping purposes and banks sometimes map to some beta-adjusted index directly. Indices can also be used to fill in missing points. For example, in circumstances where a curve has one liquid point that is well characterised (e.g. a five-year) but the curve shape is not, it may be appropriate to use the curve shape inferred from the index (Figure 12.10). Due to the importance of term structure noted in Section 12.2.4, it is important to make a reasonable assumption on curve shape. Indices can also be used to fill in missing ratings points. For example, one may look at the ratio of single-A to triple-B spreads in iTraxx or CDX, and use this ratio to infer one rating curve from another in the more granular generic curve representation.

12.4.4   Cross-sectional approach

The above mapping approach has drawbacks driven by the limited liquid CDS data available in the market. A very broad definition of generic curves is less descriptive, whereas a detailed categorisation is limited by the illiquidity of the CDS market, meaning that buckets would have limited or no data points. As a result, there would be potentially large jumps in credit spreads due to idiosyncratic behaviour of names in a given bucket. This behaviour will be particularly adverse for buckets with fewer CDS quotes to calibrate to.

An alternative approach to credit spread mapping is proposed by Chourdakis et al. (2013) and is based on a cross-section methodology involving a multi-dimensional regression.[8] This approach still uses a categorisation based across rating, region and sector, but generates the spread via a factor approach rather than a direct mapping to the names in a given bucket. A given spread is generated as the product of five factors:

- global;
- rating;
- region;
- industry sector; and
- seniority.

The advantage of a cross-sectional is that there will be much more data available to calibrate each of the factors. For example, the single-A factor will be calibrated to all such credits, irrespective of region and section. This should give rise to smoother behaviour. This approach has recently been adopted by Markit within their aforementioned CDS sector curve product.

12.4.5   Hedging

An important consideration in the choice of mapping methodology is the potential hedging of CVA. Here, the appropriate strategy depends on the liquidity of the counterparty. For liquid counterparties, the single-name CDS is the most obvious hedging instrument. For illiquid counterparties, proxy single-name hedges may be less liquid and do not allow capital relief (at the current time). Credit indices are therefore the most efficient macro-hedges. Whilst a more granular mapping methodology may reflect the underlying economic behaviour more accurately, it may make such hedging less effective. Ultimately, mapping and hedging can be a self-fulfilling prophecy, since the mapping mechanism ultimately defines the effectiveness of the hedge.

In order to macro-hedge credit risk under a generic curve approach, it is necessary to construct a "beta mapping" to a given index or set of indices. This involves performing a regression of the generic curve against the index to obtain the optimum hedge ratio. There is no definitive consensus as to over what time period such regression should be performed: longer time periods will be less noisy, but shorter periods may be more accurate. Another important consideration is the recalibration frequency: daily recalibration minimises the potential for large, discrete changes, but may be operationally cumbersome. From a practical perspective, a periodic (e.g. monthly) recalibration may be more appropriate, but will lead to potentially significant changes that cause MTM impacts and required adjustment of hedges. Some banks actually map to the beta-adjusted indices directly, which produces more stability in between recalibration dates but may be harder to defend to regulators and auditors. We will discuss hedging in more detail in Chapter 18.

---

[8] Note that this approach is proposed in relation to the specific risk model required as part of the advanced CVA capital charge (Section 8.7.1) and not for the quantification of CVA for accounting purposes, although there is no obvious reason why it might be used for the latter.

12.5   FUNDING CURVES AND CAPITAL COSTS

12.5.1   Background

Historically, banks and other financial institutions did not consider funding costs in the valuation of derivatives. This was for a number of interrelated reasons:

- banks could fund rather easily via deposits or raising money in the wholesale market;
- through the above, banks could fund at LIBOR or better and LIBOR was viewed as being a close proxy for the risk-free rate; and
- banks generally treated derivatives (from a funding point of view) as short-term assets and therefore considered only short-term funding costs where relevant.

Funding costs and associated funding risk was rarely considered in relation to derivatives, even those which were very long-dated.

The above changed very dramatically in the global financial crisis and, in particular, after the Lehman Brothers bankruptcy in 2008, where wholesale markets dried up – creating a huge funding problem for banks and forcing them to ultimately rely on central bank liquidity. Whilst funding costs have eased in the years since, they are still high compared to pre-crisis, and the market has experienced a regime shift: funding costs are now important. Additionally, some of the regulatory response to the crisis will make funding of derivatives positions increasingly costly. For example:

- *The clearing mandate.* The requirement to centrally clear standardised OTC derivatives will create significant funding costs due to the requirement to post initial margins and default funds to CCPs (Section 9.3).
- *Bilateral collateral rules.* The requirements to post collateral against non-clearable OTC derivatives (Section 6.7) will increase funding requirements, again predominantly through initial margin.
- *Liquidity coverage ratio.* This requires banks to have sufficient high-quality liquid assets to withstand a 30-day stressed funding scenario and will restrict the use of short-term funding, again creating additional cost (Section 8.8.4).
- *Net stable funding ratio.* This requires banks to use more stable sources of funding, which again will be more expensive (Section 8.8.4).
- *Increased capital requirements.* The increased capital for OTC derivatives under some of the Basel III requirements will constrain banks and make funding more expensive.
- *Leverage ratio.* Similar to the above, OTC derivatives will impact the leverage ratio (Section 8.8.2) and have an associated knock-on effect for funding costs.

All of the above has led banks to become much more aware of the need to quantify and manage funding costs alongside more traditional areas such as counterparty risk. This has created the concept of funding value adjustment (FVA) and margin value adjustment (MVA), which will be discussed in more detail in Chapter 16. FVA is generally associated with funding derivatives assets whilst MVA arises from the need to post initial margin. Both FVA and MVA create a clear need to define funding curves, just as credit curves are required for CVA.

12.5.2 Funding costs

An important concept is that funding costs are asset-specific. For example, a high-quality treasury bond can be repoed fairly easily and it is therefore the financing cost via the repo market (haircut and spread) that is relevant. The existence of the repo market means that it is not necessary to consider the cost of borrowing money on an unsecured basis to buy the bond (which would be considerably higher).

Derivatives assets can be effectively used for collateral for other derivatives liabilities (through netting) but they cannot be repoed. This suggests that an unsecured term funding rate would be more applicable for assessing the underlying funding costs of derivatives. However, a bank will fund itself through a variety of different sources. The bank's treasury department will typically generate a blended cost of funds curve in all major currencies to be used internally for pricing purposes. This is often called a funds transfer pricing (FTP) curve. Ultimately, the assessment of a funding curve will be, like the credit curve mapping in Section 12.3, subjective and open to debate.

Funding costs may arise from a variety of different sources and may be different in each case. The obvious difference may arise from variation and initial margin. Variation margin is posted against a MTM loss and therefore may not be considered as an actual funding cost. (This is the Hull and White debate on FVA, which will be discussed in more detail in Chapter 15.) Initial margin is not posted against MTM losses and so is a direct funding cost. This is another reason for splitting funding costs into FVA and MVA terms. The type of collateral is also relevant, because posting non-cash collateral may be considered cheaper depending on the relevant haircuts. The return paid on collateral is also important, though: variation margin in a CSA is generally remunerated at the overnight indexed swap (OIS) in the relevant currency, which is often viewed as a reasonable proxy for the risk-free rate. In such a case, the cost of funding is the cost above the risk-free rate. However, if remuneration of collateral is less than OIS (for example, in the case of initial margin posted to a CCP), then the overall funding cost should be higher: even funding at OIS may be seen as costly. Indeed, segregation may be seen to create additional funding costs: initial margin received may be costly to segregate and cannot earn a return.

12.5.3 Defining a funding curve

In terms of defining funding costs for FVA and MVA purposes, a number of questions arise. Firstly, as noted above, banks have a number of sources of funding through the debt markets, including:

- customer deposits;
- wholesale money markets;
- private or public unsecured borrowing (e.g. normal or structured bonds); and
- private or public secured borrowing (e.g. covered bonds).

A bank funding themselves predominantly in short-term money markets should probably not evaluate funding costs based on unsecured bond issuance at much longer maturities. There are also other sources that may be considered to be representative references for the current funding costs on an entity, such as secondary bond or CDS markets.

Another issue is that the funding of an asset should possibly depend on the credit quality of the asset itself, as lenders will charge funding rates that inevitably depend on the quality of the balance sheet of the borrower. For example, a bank trading with a triple-A counterparty should have lower *incremental* funding costs than doing the same business with a lower-rated counterparty. This suggests that a single "funding curve" should not be applied to all types of derivatives clients.

A final competing point is that from an accounting view, an entity should actually be attempting to incorporate the cost of funding of other market participants in order to adhere to the exit price concept. There is also the question of whether the full contractual maturity of a transaction should be used or some shorter period, based on the fact that the transaction could be exited early if required. However, this could become difficult, since an entity might argue that they would tactically exit certain transactions with parties with different funding costs depending on the characteristics of the transaction at the time (for example, whether it is in-the-money and the tenor).

All the above points have left market participants, accountants and regulators having much debate over defining the cost of funding. As can be seen from Figure 12.11, banks are divided on how to do this, with further differences seen between accounting and pricing practices (some banks do not account for funding costs but do price them into transactions). Some of the questions that arise when incorporating funding into pricing are as follows:

- What instruments should a funding cost be calibrated to (e.g. primary issuance, secondary bond trading or internal assessment of cost of funding)?
- Should a party use their own cost of funding, a counterparty's cost of funding (with whom they might exit the transaction if required) or a curve that is blended based on cost of funding of market participants in general?
- Should term funding using the final contractual maturity of a transaction be used, or rather a shorter tenor assumed, based on the fact that term funding is not required and/or that the transaction may be terminated early?

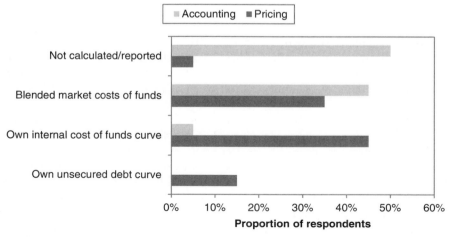

Figure 12.11   Market practice for defining funding costs for accounting and pricing purposes.
Source: Solum CVA survey, 2015.

It is also useful to characterise the funding cost as the sum of two distinct components:

- *Credit funding cost.* This is the cost of the credit risk of a party that would be charged as part of a cost of unsecured funding. Obviously, more risky parties would be expected to have higher funding costs.
- *Funding liquidity risk premium.* This is a cost in addition to the pure credit risk that should not be entity-specific and may be relevant in secured funding (e.g. covered bonds).

The full unsecured funding cost is the sum of the above components. However, as discussed in Chapter 15, it may be relevant to include only the funding liquidity risk premium in pricing FVA, since the first component should already been priced via CVA.

We will discuss the definition of funding costs in more detail in relation to FVA and MVA calculations in Chapter 15.

12.5.4   Cost of capital

The regulatory changes over the past few years have generally made banks focus less on actual profits from their OTC derivative activities and more on the return on capital. Cost of capital is usually quantified via a benchmark percentage return on capital (ROC) that should ideally be achieved in order to pay a return to the investors who have provided the capital.

Since a company typically finances itself via both debt and equity, the cost of each should be calculated on a forward-looking basis to reflect future expectations. The cost of debt is relatively straightforward, since it is just the rate for borrowing money, adjusted for tax deductions available on the interest paid. The cost of equity is more subjective, since it is the return paid to shareholders that is a policy decision by the bank but must deliver a satisfactory return from the shareholders' point of view (or they will sell their shares). Cost of equity can be assessed via either the historical dividend policy of a company or a more forward-looking approach such as with the capital asset pricing model (CAPM).

The costs of debt and equity are often blended to give the weighted average cost of capital (WACC). This WACC is often used as a discount rate for the projected cash flows of a project. However, since regulation has become stricter in both the definition and quantity of Tier 1 capital (which is mainly made up of equity capital), banks will generally more look to the cost of equity capital when assessing ROC for OTC derivatives transactions.

Banks' OTC derivative businesses, like any other, are typically subject to capital hurdles due to the associated costs. The given ROC applied is an internal and somewhat subjective parameter; around 8–10% is a commonly used base assumption. However, since profits generating a ROC will be taxed, an effective tax rate (for the region in question) will also be incorporated, leading to a higher effective rate. Kenyon and Green (2015) define this term, namely TVA (tax valuation adjustment), more rigorously. The number may be grossed up further by other costs and so the gross ROC that banks aim for on their OTC derivative activities is probably more in the region of 15–20%. Traditionally capital hurdles have represented guidelines but are now becoming more rigorously priced in via KVA (Chapter 16).

Given the amount of regulation-affected OTC derivatives, it is not surprising that banks are generally struggling to meet traditional hurdles for ROC. This has arisen for a number of reasons such as the costs that must be netted from profits (e.g. CVA and FVA), the higher capital requirements for OTC derivatives, and the cost of raising new capital. Yet most banks will not consider exiting the derivatives business to be a viable strategy. Ideally, the ROC would be evaluated at the client level and not consider only one business area. Banks may ultimately have to accept that ROC for OTC derivatives will be low but partially subsidised by revenues from other business, sometimes even with the same clients.

12.6   SUMMARY

This chapter has been concerned with an overview of methods used to determine default probabilities, funding costs and return on capital, which are the major cost components of xVA. We have described the differences between real and risk-neutral default probabilities, and the methods used in practice to estimate credit spreads and LGDs of counterparties. The generation of generic curves in order to map illiquid credits has been covered, emphasising important points such as term structure. The nature of funding costs and obtained associated funding curves has also been discussed. Finally, we have discussed the cost of capital concept as applied to OTC derivative transactions.

13

Discounting and Collateral

If you put the federal government in charge of the Sahara Desert, in five years there'd be a shortage of sand.

Milton Friedman (1912–2006)

13.1 OVERVIEW

Recent years have seen a paradigm shift in the pricing of derivatives, with even the very basic principles changing. This chapter will discuss OIS discounting, a benchmark and common starting point for valuation. We will then consider related aspects concerned with the valuation of certain collateral terms, generally known as ColVA (collateral valuation adjustment). Generally, both OIS discounting and ColVA adjustments relate primarily to the basic discounting assumptions used when valuing derivatives, although there are some special cases, such as one-way CSAs (Section 6.2.2), which will also be discussed.

In Figure 4.12 of Chapter 4 we showed the hierarchy of xVA components with reference to what was defined as the "basic valuation". The first question will be how to define the basic valuation. There is no unique choice for this, but an obvious choice is a collateralised transaction. Indeed, by gross notional, the majority of derivatives are collateralised, either bilaterally or via exchanges or central counterparties (see Figure 3.2 in Chapter 3).

In order to provide a starting point, we will define the concept of "perfect collateralisation", which will be the case where a derivative can be valued easily and without any further xVA adjustments. Such a concept is largely theoretical (except perhaps from the point of view of a central counterparty) but is a convenient base case.

13.2 DISCOUNTING

13.2.1 Introduction

Pricing derivatives has always been relatively complex. However, prior to the global financial crisis, pricing of vanilla products was understood and most attention was on exotics. Credit and liquidity were ignored, since their effects were viewed as negligible. The old-style framework for pricing financial instruments is now undergoing a revolution in order to address the shortcomings highlighted by the crisis and properly incorporate aspects such as funding and collateral agreements in the analysis.

One relatively recent change in pricing assumptions has been the move away from the use of LIBOR (London inter-bank offered rate) to discount future cashflows. LIBOR has been one of the most crucial interest rates in finance, referenced in trillions of dollars of derivatives and other contracts such as loans. LIBOR rates represent indicative unsecured lending between banks and it is the rate charged (determined daily) for banks to borrow from other banks, usually for terms of three months on an uncollateralised basis. LIBOR is risky in the sense that the lending bank loans cash to the borrowing bank on an unsecured basis, albeit for a relatively short period. LIBOR is supposed to represent an average interest rate that a bank would be charged if borrowing from other such banks. For many years, LIBOR was seen as a good proxy for the risk-free rate that was used to discount cashflows and therefore define the "time value of money".

It is important to note that both the time value of money and concept of a risk-free rate are essentially theoretical constructs. Furthermore, traditional LIBOR discounting of risk-free cashflows, so standard for many years, was generally used with two key assumptions in mind:

- LIBOR is (or at least is a very good proxy for) the risk-free interest rate; and
- there are no material funding considerations that need to be considered, i.e. an institution can easily borrow and lend funds (including for collateral purposes) at LIBOR.

13.2.2   OIS rates

OIS (overnight indexed swap) is generally the (unsecured) interest rate that large banks use to borrow and lend from one another in the overnight market. Some example of OIS rates are:

- Fed Funds (US Federal Reserve overnight rate);
- EONIA (euro overnight index average);
- SONIA (sterling overnight index average); and
- MUTAN (Japanese uncollateralised overnight call rate).

Collateral arrangements involve parties posting cash or securities to mitigate counterparty risk, usually governed under the terms of an ISDA Credit Support Annex (Section 6.2.1). The standard frequency of posting is daily and the holder of collateral typically pays an overnight interest rate such as EONIA or Fed Funds. As discussed in Chapter 6, the use of collateral has increased steadily as the OTC derivatives market has developed.

There are conceptual similarities between OIS and LIBOR rates. Both are unsecured and whilst the former reflects a single-day time horizon, the latter is longer (e.g. three months). Furthermore, OIS rates are averages from actual transactions whereas LIBOR is just the average (with the highest and lowest submissions removed) of banks' stated opinions. Indeed, there have been problems over the manipulation of LIBOR rates.[1]

---

[1] For example, see "Timeline: Libor-fixing scandal", BBC News, 6th February 2013, www.bbc.co.uk.

13.2.3   The risk-free rate

Traditionally, there have been two different measures of a risk-free interest rate. Historically, LIBOR rates were thought to be largely free of credit risk[2] due to the extremely small default probabilities of banks and short tenor (three or six months). An alternative risk-free proxy has been the yields of triple-A treasury bonds, again considered being largely free of credit risk due to the extremely high quality rating of the sovereign issuer. LIBOR rates were generally thought to be preferable to treasury bonds due to better liquidity, the lack of problems with technical factors (such as repo specialness and tax issues), and the close links between LIBOR rates and funding costs. Hence, pre-2008 the market standard discount (or funding) curve was the three- or six-month LIBOR curve.[3]

Before the global financial crisis, the basis between OIS and LIBOR was tight (less than 10 bps). However, the crisis caused the LIBOR-OIS basis to widen dramatically, as can be seen in Figure 13.1. The difference between US three-month LIBOR and Fed Funds (OIS) was only a few basis points prior to the crisis but spiked to hundreds of basis points in the aftermath of the Lehman Brothers bankruptcy of September 2008 and has remained material ever since. This could also be seen in other ways such as via basis swap spreads, which represent the exchange of rates in the same currency. For example, the EURIBOR (LIBOR rate in Euros) three-month versus EURIBOR six-month basis swap spread went from less than 1 bp to more than 40 bps in October 2008 after the Lehman Brothers bankruptcy. This represents the additional unsecured credit

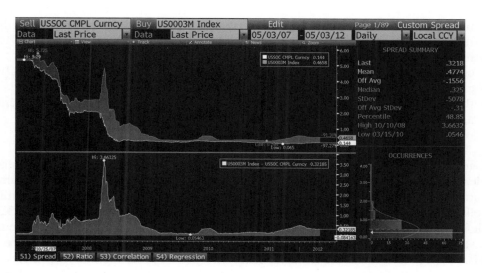

Figure 13.1   Illustration of the historical relationship in US dollars between OIS (Fed Funds) and three-month US LIBOR. The top graph shows the respective levels while the bottom line shows the difference between the two.
Source : Bloomberg (www.bloomberg.com), reproduced with permission.

---

[2] For example, a typical quote from a paper discussing derivative pricing prior to the crisis states that "LIBOR is not a risk-free rate, but it is close to it as the participating banks have very strong credit ratings".

[3] Depending on the currency, the most liquid point may have been either maturity. However, the differences between LIBOR at different tenors was extremely small.

risk in the six-month tenor versus the three-month tenor. When banks were perceived as risk-free, such differences did not exist; but as soon as this myth dissolved, basis swap spreads blew up dramatically.

Due to the short tenor and unbiased submission process, OIS would seem to be a more logical "risk-free rate". The daily tenor of transactions such as EONIA means that they should carry a minimal amount of credit risk. OIS can be observed across a term structure in major currencies via products such as OIS–LIBOR swaps. The difference or "spread" between the LIBOR and OIS rates is an important measure of risk and liquidity. A higher spread is typically interpreted as an indication of decreased willingness to lend by major banks. Whilst this basis has tightened in recent years, the use of LIBOR as a ubiquitous risk-free rate is considered wrong.

13.2.4   Perfect collateralisation and discounting

Whilst it useful to have the idea of a risk-free rate, as already mentioned, it is nothing more than a theoretical concept used when defining the time value of money. However, under certain conditions, it can be shown that the correct discounting rate for a derivative is the rate of return of collateral. We will define these conditions as "perfect collateralisation" and they are:

- the transaction is covered by a symmetric (two-way) collateral agreement based on the mark-to-market (MTM) of the underlying transaction with zero threshold, minimum transfer amount and rounding (i.e. the exact amount of required collateral can be received);
- there is no overcollateralisation (initial margin);
- collateral is settled continuously (i.e. there is no delay in paying or receiving collateral);[4]
- collateral can be reused and is not segregated;
- there are no close-out costs (or equivalently, the MTM referenced by the collateral agreement includes such costs already); and
- collateral is paid in cash in the currency of the transaction.

Under the above assumptions, the amount of collateral held (posted) will be at all times identical to the MTM (negative MTM) of the transaction and denominated in the same currency. In such a situation the correct discounting rate is that of the return paid on the collateral, as shown by Piterbarg (2010). This is illustrated qualitatively in Figure 13.2, showing symmetry between the collateral balance and the discounted value of a given cashflow. The aim is to find the MTM of a cashflow by deciding on the discounting rate. The MTM in turn equals the collateral held today (perfect collateralisation). This collateral must be returned at maturity plus the collateral interest rate, which needs to balance the cashflow. The collateral rate is therefore the appropriate discount rate for the cashflow. If the collateral for a transaction is remunerated in one rate and the rate for discounting the cashflow is in another, then there is a conflict leading to arbitrage opportunities.[5]

---

[4] It also needs to be assumed that the underlying exposure changes continuously and that, in the event of default, transactions can be closed-out instantaneously.

[5] For example see "Goldman and the OIS gold rush: How fortunes were made from a discounting change", *Risk*, 29th May 2013.

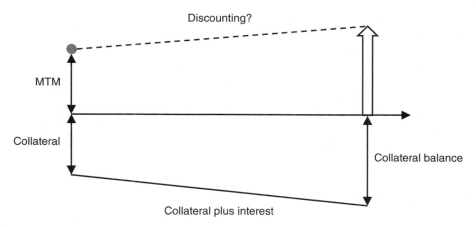

Figure 13.2 Illustration of the concept of collateral discounting. The current MTM of a single cashflow will give rise to a collateral balance, which will grow according to the contractual return paid by the collateral receiver and can then offset the final payment of the cashflow. By symmetry, the MTM must be equal to the collateral balance and therefore the correct discount rate is the collateral rate.

13.2.5 OIS discounting

The standard collateral rate specified in a collateral agreement is the OIS rate (Section 6.3.4). This is not because OIS is the risk-free rate, but rather because (with daily calls) collateral is only guaranteed to be held for one day (although in practice it can be held for much longer, which is an important consideration). Hence, in this situation, "OIS discounting" is the correct valuation. Whilst the above assumptions defining perfect collateralisation are somewhat stylised in reality (especially the continuous settlement of collateral), they are a reasonable starting point, and some transactions are considered by the industry to be close to this theoretical ideal, notably:

- centrally cleared trades – from the central counterparty (CCP) point of view, due to initial margins, default funds and daily or intradaily collateral posting; and
- interbank trades, due to CSAs with zero thresholds, low MTAs and daily collateral posting. Note that the Standard CSA (Section 6.4.6) and the incoming bilateral collateral rules (Section 6.7) can be seen as requiring collateral terms that are closer to "perfect collateralisation".

It is therefore not surprising that such transactions have experienced a move to OIS discounting in recent years. One could also argue below that this is a reasonable starting point for all transactions, and additional xVA components can then be added on to this base case as required. However, the OIS rate is not relevant in uncollateralised transactions unless it is viewed as the risk-free rate.

As noted in Section 13.2.3, the OIS rate is also an obvious proxy for the risk-free rate. However, this is not why it is the appropriate discount rate. In cases where another rate is referenced in the collateral agreement, then this is the appropriate discount rate. If this rate were zero, then no discounting should be applied. OIS is simply an obvious benchmark of overnight lending and so is used as a convenient return on cash collateral deposited overnight. However, OIS is not the "fair" return for long maturity transactions, since collateral may be posted for long periods whilst only receiving an overnight return.

Even without the intervention of the global financial crisis, OIS discounting should always have been the more correct way to approach valuation. However, prior to the crisis, the difference between this and traditional LIBOR discounting was not particularly material, as shown in Figure 13.1. There has been a gradual shift from LIBOR to OIS discounting for valuing collateralised transactions in recent years, although the extent of this move depends on the underlying product and region (for example, see ISDA, 2014).

13.2.6   OIS methodology

OIS discounting complicates matters for a number of reasons. Pricing a single interest rate swap once used the same rate (LIBOR) for both projecting the future cashflows and discounting them; now, it is necessary to account for the difference between projected rates for cashflows (e.g. LIBOR) and the rates used for discounting (e.g. OIS). This is often known as "dual curve"[6] pricing. Pricing and risk management of a single currency interest rate swap is now an exotic problem involving multiple curves and basis risks.

Traditional interest rate curve building typically follows the following steps:

- select a set of liquid securities (cash deposits, futures and swaps);
- make decisions on overlapping, interpolation, etc.; and
- fit a single curve via a "bootstrap" procedure, which solves sequentially to fit market prices or a more complex algorithm.

OIS discounting complicates this process. LIBOR–OIS swaps are generally more liquid than OIS swaps, so OIS and basis curves[7] have to be built simultaneously from these market prices together with standard LIBOR-based swaps. In this calibration, discounting is assumed based on OIS whilst cash-flows are projected in the relevant rate (OIS or LIBOR). This dual curve problem means that standard simpler bootstrap methods are not applicable. More details on these issues can be found in, for example, Mercurio (2010) and Morini and Prampolini (2010) and Kenyon and Stamm (2012).

Whilst OIS discounting is emerging as a standard, it has not yet been fully implemented across all banks and other financial institutions. Where trading desks use LIBOR discounting, there is a LIBOR-OIS basis that should be managed, possibly via an xVA desk. This will be discussed in more detail in Chapters 15 and 18.

---

[6] Noting that dual curve pricing is relevant for a single interest rate transaction, but different currencies and cross-currency products will require many curves that incorporate the various tenor basis and cross-currency basis effects. Optionality from collateral agreements will, in theory, introduce even more curves into the pricing problem.

[7] This defines the basis between LIBOR and OIS.

13.3   BEYOND PERFECT COLLATERALISATION

13.3.1   The push towards perfect collateralisation

Many transactions are close to the theoretical ideal of OIS discounting, especially through interbank and centrally cleared trades as mentioned above. There is also clearly a push towards this standard of OIS discounting through the following aspects:

- *CSA renegotiation.* Market practice over recent years has been to renegotiate CSAs bilaterally, often aiming to bring them closer to some of the ideal characteristics listed in Section 13.2.4. This may involve more frequent exchange of collateral (e.g. daily), reducing thresholds and minimum transfer amounts, and restricting the cash and securities that can be delivered. This also includes the introduction of the standard CSA (SCSA) discussed in Section 6.4.6.
- *Bilateral collateral rules.* The incoming bilateral rules discussed in Section 6.7 require frequent collateral exchange, a zero threshold and minimum transfer amount of no more than €500,000. They also penalise certain types of collateral through haircuts, in particular when cash is posted in a currency different from that of the transaction (see Table 6.7 although as discussed in Section 6.7.4 the European Union implementation may not include haircuts on cash collateral). The US rules may restrict variation margin to cash only.
- *Clearing mandate.* The mandate to clear standardised OTC derivatives (Section 9.3.1) is important, since CCP rules on collateral can be seen to broadly follow the perfect collateralisation ideal. Notably, CCPs have zero thresholds and minimum transfer amounts, and usually require collateral (variation margin) in cash in the currency of the transaction. They also make daily, and sometimes intradaily, collateral calls. However, the requirement for initial margin (and default fund contributions) goes clearly against perfect collateralisation. This is not a problem for the CCP itself: indeed, it goes further to ensuring that the CCP is perfectly collateralised. However, for clearing members or clients, the initial margin takes them away from perfect collateralisation, as will be discussed below.

The above comments generally apply to banks and other financial institutions that have already engaged in two-way collateral agreements and are not exempt from the bilateral collateral rules or clearing mandate. They are less relevant for end-users who transact without a collateral agreement or with a one-way agreement in their favour. However, through the pricing they receive from banks, such end-users are also under pressure to move closer to the perfect collateral ideal.

13.3.2   The xVA terms

It is useful to recap on the xVA terms first discussed in Section 4.4.3, but from the perfect collateralisation point of view. In theory, it is possible to use OIS discounting for all transactions, even those far away from the theoretical ideal – although when no collateral exists, this seems to require viewing OIS as a risk-free rate. With respect to perfect collateralisation, the xVA components are:

- *ColVA.* Collateral adjustments due to deviations from a perfect collateral agreement, in terms of collateral type and remuneration. This will be discussed in Section 13.4.

- *Credit value adjustment (CVA).* The negative adjustment for the counterparty risk due to the non-collateralised exposure in the event of the default of the counterparty. This will be discussed in Chapter 14.
- *Debt value adjustment (DVA).* The positive adjustment for the counterparty risk due to the non-collateralised negative exposure in the event of own default. This will be also discussed in Chapter 14.
- *Funding value adjustment (FVA).* The adjustment for the costs and benefits arising from funding the MTM of a transaction due to imperfect collateralisation. This will be discussed in Chapter 15.
- *Margin valuation adjustment (MVA).* The negative adjustment as a result of the need to post initial margin against bilateral or centrally cleared transactions. This may also include the need to post default funds to a central counterparty (Section 9.3.2), which could be termed "default fund VA" (although we will consider default fund costs as part of MVA). This is sometimes referred to as IMVA and will be discussed in Chapter 16.
- *Capital value adjustment (KVA).* The negative adjustment as a result of the need (for banks) to hold regulatory capital against transactions to the extent that they are imperfectly collateralised (according to the capital methodology used). This will be discussed in Chapter 16.

Note that different authors may use different terminology, although the above terms are now reasonably market-standard. Note that we distinguish between FVA (the funding costs associated with uncollateralised MTM and/or posting variation margin on hedges) and MVA (the funding costs for initial margin) – these funding costs are very different in nature and it will be relevant to separate them.

Not surprisingly, under different contractual terms across bilateral and centrally cleared trades, different xVA terms will be more or less important. When changing contractual terms, it may be that value is moved between different xVAs. For example, increased collateralisation tends to reduce CVA, FVA and KVA, but increase MVA. Table 13.1 illustrates the importance of each of the xVA terms in a number of classic situations discussed below:

- *Uncollateralised.* An uncollateralised transaction has all xVA components except ColVA and those relating to initial margins and default funds.
- *One-way collateralised.* A one-way collateral agreement against the institution in question would be as above but without material benefit from their own default (DVA), since they post collateral against this eventuality. There may be ColVA depending on the terms of the underlying agreement.
- *Traditional two-way collateralised.* In this case, the CVA and DVA terms will be less significant due to the collateral posting. The FVA will likely be insignificant unless the collateral terms are weak (see Chapter 16). There will likely be ColVA due to the relative flexibility of the CSA (e.g. the choice of the type of collateral to post). The KVA may be reduced but will still be material, and the extent of the reduction will depend on the methodology used for capital calculations (Section 8.1.4).
- *Single-currency two-way collateralised.* Compared to the above, this case will likely remove the ColVA due to the need to post in the currency of the transaction (although there may be other effects, as discussed in Section 13.4). The FVA will likely be

immaterial due to the likelihood of daily posting and the ability to intrinsically reuse cash collateral.

- *Collateralised with bilateral initial margin.* Due to the high confidence level used for initial margin calculations (99% or more, as discussed in Section 6.7.3), CVA and DVA will likely become insignificant.[8] KVA will also become small under the SA-CCR and IMM methodologies (but not CEM, as seen in Section 8.5.4). There will be MVA from the posted initial margin (and also potentially the received initial margin that must be segregated).

- *Centrally cleared (direct).* A centrally cleared trade cleared directly (as a clearing member) attracts MVA from the initial margin and default fund requirements respectively. There are also associated capital charges with respect to these components that may be relatively small compared to bilateral capital requirements (Section 9.3.7). There is no ColVA due to the use of cash collateral in the transaction currency for variation margin. In theory there should be a CVA via the default fund and initial margin exposures, although this is often not generally considered relevant.

- *Centrally cleared (indirect).* For a client-cleared trade, this is as above but with no default fund exposure. The MVA may be higher due to the need to post additional initial margin to the clearing member. Depending on the account setup, the CVA component and capital charges may be more significant since the client will have some risk to their clearing member (and potentially the other clients of their clearing member) defaulting.

- *Centrally cleared (CCP).* From a central counterparty's (CCP's) point of view there are no material xVAs, since a CCP benefits from intraday margining, cash variation margin, substantial initial margins and default funds, and the ability to close-out clearing members in a timely manner. This is obviously not supposed to mean that CCPs are risk-free; just that they do not have any material valuation adjustments.

The above is a general characterisation of the importance of xVA in different situations that is useful as a reference. More details on the specifics will be given below and in the forthcoming chapters.

Table 13.1 Illustration of the importance of xVA terms in different relationships. A tick indicates a significant xVA consideration and a tick in brackets a less significant one.

	ColVA	CVA	DVA	FVA	KVA	MVA
Uncollateralised		✓	✓	✓	✓	
One-way collateralised	(✓)	✓	(✓)	✓	✓	
Traditional two-way collateralised	✓	(✓)	(✓)		✓	
Single-currency two-way collateralised	(✓)	(✓)	(✓)		✓	
Collateralised with bilateral initial margin	(✓)				(✓)	✓
Centrally cleared (direct)		(✓)			(✓)	✓
Centrally cleared (indirect)		(✓)			(✓)	✓
Centrally cleared (CCP view)						

[8] Noting the previous comments that initial margin need not be posted on legacy transactions and the presence of thresholds (Section 6.7.3).

13.4   COLLATERAL VALUATION ADJUSTMENTS

13.4.1   Overview

"ColVA" is a generic term used for adjustments to collateralised transactions, related to contractual terms that differ from those of a perfect collateral agreement. Broadly speaking, there are two components to consider:

- differences in the remuneration of collateral paid and/or received compared to the discount rate (e.g. collateral remunerated at OIS plus or minus a spread); and
- optionality over collateral that can be posted and received (cash in other currencies and non-cash collateral).

The first component above is quite easy to account for, at least in symmetric cases, since it simply requires a rate other than OIS to be used to discount cashflows. It is just a question of whether this is done directly (i.e. changing the discount rate) or indirectly (i.e. by adjusting via ColVA to effect the discounting change). The second component is more complex, as it reflects the optionality, future changes in OIS rates and contractual terms. We will consider these components separately below.

13.4.2   Collateral rate adjustments

The appropriate rate at which cashflows should be discounted when valuing a perfectly collateralised transaction is the rate at which collateral earns interest. In a general setting, we can define the ColVA as:

$$ColVA = -\sum_{i=1}^{m} ECB(t_i) \times CS_X \times (t_i - t_{i-1}) \times S(t_i), \tag{13.1}$$

where $ECB(.)$ is the expected collateral balance, CS_X is the spread paid on the collateral with respect to the discount rate used in valuation (e.g., the OIS rate) and $S(.)$ is the joint survival probability (i.e. the probability that neither the party or their counterparty defaults). Note that the joint survival probability suggests that the party making the calculation should adjust by their own probability of default. This is slightly problematic and may sometimes therefore be ignored in general for xVA, but is discussed more in the next chapter with respect to CVA and DVA. Some technical aspects related to the computation of the above type of expression are also discussed in the next chapter.

Equation 13.1 essentially requires an integral over the ECB for the lifetime of the transaction. We implicitly assume that the collateral spread is symmetric with respect to posting and receiving collateral. This is generally the case, but if it were not – for example, if parties in a CSA remunerated collateral at different rates – then we would need to split the above into two terms, similar to the way that FVA is split up (see Section 15.2.1).

Obviously, if the collateral spread (CS_X) is zero, then the ColVA is zero. Beyond this, there are a number of distinct cases that can be considered:

- *Uncollateralised.* The ECB will be zero and therefore there will be no ColVA.
- *Strongly two-way collateralised.* With zero thresholds and small minimum transfer amounts, the ECB will closely track the future MTM of the transaction (note that

since this scenario is not default-related, there is no need to consider a MPR concept) although strictly speaking there will be a delay in receiving collateral – in practice this might be ignored. This term, defined as expected future value (EFV), is quite easy to calculate (Section 7.2.1). The ColVA adjustment will change the discounting rate by the collateral spread CS_x and it may be more relevant to use this rate directly in valuation. For example, in a portfolio or transaction with a positive ECB and a positive spread, the ColVA will be negative, which reflects having to pay a higher return on received collateral.

- *Weak two-way collateralised.* In this case of undercollateralisation, the ECB will depend on the size of contractual terms such as thresholds, which tend to lessen the adjustment. As the thresholds increase, the ColVA will reduce towards zero, as in the uncollateralised case.
- *One-way collateralised.* In a one-way collateral agreement, collateral will be posted in only one direction. If the threshold is zero then the ECB will be very close to the expected exposure (EE) or negative expected exposure (NEE) defined in Sections 7.2.6 and 7.2.7 respectively. EE and NEE will be relevant when the one-way CSA is in favour and against the party making the calculation respectively. For example, a one-way CSA against a party will have an ECB approximately equal to the NEE and with a positive spread would give a positive ColVA, which reflects receiving a higher return on collateral posted.

Note that in the first two cases above, ColVA is not really necessary as it is either zero or simply a facet of using a different rate (than the collateral rate) for discounting. The second two cases are more complicated and require an explicit adjustment to be calculated.

The following example aims to illustrate the above. We consider the EFV and ECBs corresponding to Equation 13.1 for a five-year interest rate swap with a negative MTM in Figure 13.3. The resulting ColVA adjustments are given in Table 13.2, assuming a constant spread CS_x of –25 bps.[9] This negative adjustment could be relevant for different reasons such as:

- due to the valuation being done with LIBOR rates and needing to be adjusted according to OIS rates; or
- since the CSA contractually specifies that collateral is remunerated with a return of OIS minus 25 bps (this is uncommon but does sometimes occur, for example for sovereign and supranational counterparties).

Note that there may, of course, be a term structure on the spread in the former case above (and also in the latter case where the OIS rate is contractually floored at zero as is sometimes the case).

The EFV for the portfolio is mostly positive and so in a two-way CSA, collateral is generally expected to be received rather than posted. In most cases, the ColVA is positive and the overall valuation higher due to the benefit of paying a lower return on the collateral received. Note that a negative MTM would normally be expected to produce a negative ColVA for a negative spread, since collateral may be currently posted at a sub-OIS

---

[9] The discount factors and survival probabilities are ignored since they would only act as multipliers and not change the qualitative behaviour.

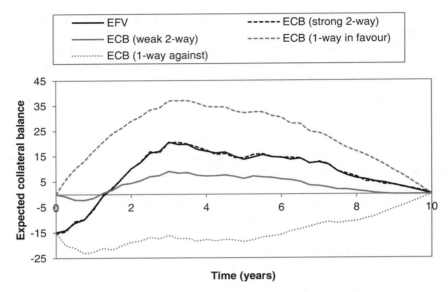

Figure 13.3   Illustration of the expected future value (EFV) and expected collateral balance (ECB) for a five-year interest rate swap under different collateral relationships.

Table 13.2   Collateral valuation adjustment corresponding to the cases shown in Figure 13.3.

	ColVA	Adjusted MTM
One-way (in favour)	0.582	−14.318
Strong two-way	0.211	−14.689
Weak two-way	0.090	−14.810
Base case	n/a	−14.900
One-way (against)	−0.373	−15.274

rate. However, since the EFV becomes positive and is on average positive overall, this is not the case. More specifically, the three different cases are explained as follows:

- *Strong two-way.* The ECB is approximately equal to the EFV of the transaction. The ColVA adjustment is then positive due to paying a lower rate on the received collateral and the adjusted MTM higher than the base case. Note that since the ECB is almost equal to the EFV, this is very close to simply discounting the portfolio with a rate 25 bps lower. Indeed, it is likely that this would be the valuation method used in practice.
- *Weak two-way.* In a two-way CSA with bilateral threshold (at a value of 50), the above effect is reduced due to the fact that less collateral is received. The ColVA adjustment is still positive, but smaller. There is not a simpler way to reflect this component since the transaction is partial collateralised.

- *One-way (in favour)*. Since collateral is only received, the ECB is higher and approximately equal to the EE. The ColVA adjustment is correspondingly positive due to paying a lower return on received collateral.
- *One-way (against)*. Collateral is only posted. The ECB is approximately equal to the NEE and the adjustment is negative (due to receiving a lower return on the collateral posted).

13.4.3   Collateral optionality

Collateral arrangements are historically quite flexible. A typical collateral agreement will allow a range of cash and other assets that may be posted as collateral. This range of eligible collateral will comprise some or all of the following (in approximate decreasing order of likelihood):

- cash in different currencies;
- government bonds;
- covered and corporate bonds;
- equities;
- MBS (mortgage-backed securities); and
- commodities (e.g. gold).

There will also be contractual haircuts specified for all of the above (cash in major currencies may be zero). This creates a choice for the giver of collateral who should pick the most optimal collateral to post. This optimal choice will depend on:

- the return paid on the collateral (as usually specified by the OIS rate in the currency in question);
- the haircut required (generally only for non-cash securities); and
- the availability of the collateral in question (although if repo or reverse repo markets exist then this is less of a concern as the assets in question can be readily acquired or lent).

This creates a valuation problem linked to the ability to optimise the collateral that a party posts, noting that their counterparty holds, analogously, a similar option for the collateral that is received. The market volatility experienced as a result of the global financial crisis exposed, in dramatic fashion, the potential collateral optionality value embedded within the contractual collateral definitions. As a result, parties (especially the more sophisticated ones) began to value and monetise this embedded optionality. Collateral management, which used to be mainly a reactive back-office function, has moved on to become a proactive front-office process. Some banks and large financial institutions have become fairly optimal in managing current collateral. However, it is a great challenge to price and monetise the future value of collateral optionality and "lock in" the value that is effectively embedded in contractual terms. Furthermore, this optionality clearly represents a zero-sum game, and in many situations the bilateral nature of most collateral agreements reduces the overall benefit unless a portfolio is very in- or out-of-the-money.

Let us deal with optionality around different currencies of cash first. Cash collateral returns are tied to the OIS in the corresponding currency (EONIA, SONIA, Fed Funds). This means that the choice of which currency to post collateral in materially affects the return received. A party should optimally post the collateral in the highest yielding currency and maximise their "cheapest-to-deliver option". This refers to posting the highest yielding collateral at a given time, which is calculated by comparing yields earned in other currencies after exchanging them back into the base currency at the relevant forward FX rates. This adjustment is typically done by adjusting with cross-currency basis spreads, which have widened in recent years.[10] The counterparty should be expected to follow the same optimal strategy in terms of collateral posting. Clearly this is a dynamic process, since the cheapest-to-deliver collateral may change through time.

A key question is whether collateral can be substituted. This will give greater value to the party with a negative MTM since they can replace the posted collateral with a more optimal choice (for example, if the OIS in one currency widens with respect to another). Collateral agreements not allowing substitution (or requiring consent[11]) should have less optionality but a party can still optimise by posting the highest yielding collateral as a MTM becomes more negative. However, there are two points to consider:

- *Positive MTM reduces.* In such a case, collateral may be held that needs to be returned and the collateral giver may request specific assets back.
- *Negative MTM reduces (becomes more negative).* In this case, collateral must be posted outright and optionality is clearly present.

The most common method used to reflect the above optionality in valuation is to form a cheapest-to-deliver curve, as illustrated schematically in Figure 13.4. The projected collateral return in each currency is converted into some base reference and then the maximum is chosen as the reference. The cheapest-to-deliver curve is then a composite of all of the admissible curves, with FX adjustments derived from cross-currency basis spreads. This curve can either be used to discount the collateralised transactions in question directly or to define a spread in order to calculate the appropriate ColVA adjustment from Equation 13.1. Assuming that currency 1 is used as the base currency, this basis is shown in Figure 13.5.

For portfolios where the ECB is expected to be generally positive (as in the example shown in Figure 13.3 in the previous section), the value would be expected to be lower (negative ColVA) due to the counterparty posting collateral requiring a higher return. Higher valuations would generally arise when the ECB is negative, although the overall effect clearly depends on the term structure of the cheapest-to-deliver spread. As discussed in Section 13.4.2, asymmetric terms (such as in a one-way CSA), thresholds and rating triggers can all be important.

The above treatment, whilst relatively simple, makes two very important implicit assumptions:

---

[10] Ideally, the OIS FX basis is required, but this can be implied from the LIBOR FX basis (which is often more liquid) if required.

[11] Since the counterparty's optimal strategy would be to not give consent.

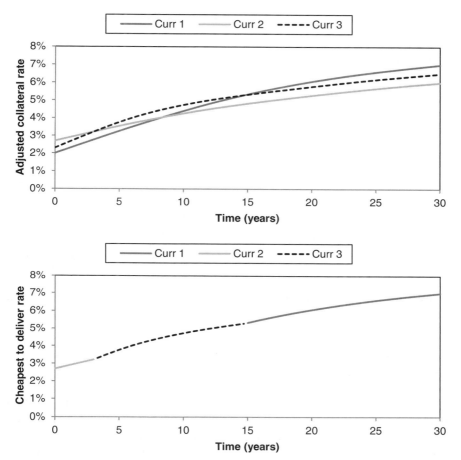

Figure 13.4 Schematic illustration of the pricing of intrinsic collateral posting optionality. The top graph represents three currencies in which collateral can be posted or received converted into a base currency, and the bottom graph the resulting "cheapest-to-deliver" curve used for valuation purposes.

- It assumes that collateral is always held in full in the currency that earns the highest rate for the poster of collateral. This requires a collateral balance to be freely and immediately substituted to the cheapest-to-deliver asset – in practice, consent must often be given for such a substitution (Section 6.4.2). Given the party wishing to switch collateral finds it optimal, then the counterparty's optimal action may be to refuse such consent. The assumptions here may also be jurisdiction-specific: for example, substitution rights are generally viewed as enforceable under New York but not UK law. However, anecdotal evidence suggests that there is a "gentleman's agreement" not to refuse such requests. Even then, switching collateral gives rise to settlement risk and may cause associated trading and hedging costs.
- It captures only the intrinsic value of the collateral optionality and does not price the time value of the optionality due to potential curve co-movements over time. Indeed,

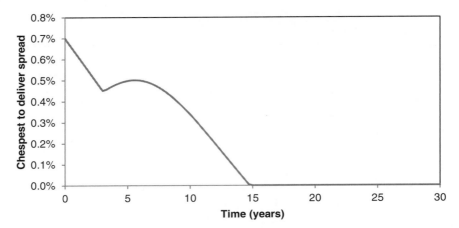

Figure 13.5 Cheapest to deliver spread implied from Figure 13.4 using currency 1 as the base currency.

in many situations the intrinsic value of the optionality is zero (i.e. the adjusted curves do not cross as in Figure 13.4, although if they do cross then there will be a MTM jump).

Note that since the above components have value for both parties, it is not clear whether the above approximations lead to a value that is too high or too low. It should also be noted that pricing via a cheapest-to-deliver curve may result in complex risk management considerations, since even relatively small movements can result in dramatically different risk profiles (for example EUR exposure shifting to USD exposure on any given day). As shown in Figure 13.6, this intrinsic cheapest-to-deliver valuation method is most common, although some banks do use a more sophisticated option-based valuation. This

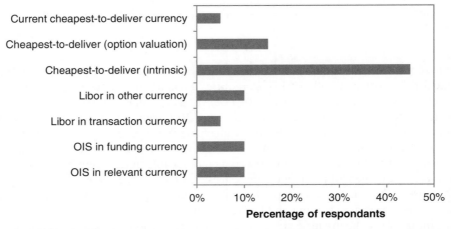

Figure 13.6 Market practice around the discounting curve used for collateralised transactions.
Source: Solum FVA survey, 2015.

component is challenging to deal with fully as it requires a model for the joint evolution of all eligible currencies for the lifetime of the transactions in question. Note also that a more sophisticated representation of the substitution of collateral is a path-dependent problem for a given collateral balance; it must be known how much of the collateral has already been posted (and would therefore need to be substituted) and how much needs to be posted (for which the optimal currency can be chosen). More sophisticated pricing of collateral optionality has been discussed, for example, by Fuji and Takahashi (2011) and Piterbarg (2012 and 2013). However, market practice often relies on the more simple methods outlined above.

13.4.4   Non-cash collateral

Applying the above analysis to non-cash collateral requires the consideration of the relevant haircuts. Consider a party posts collateral in either cash or securities with the following economic situations:

- post one unit of cash directly at a return defined by the collateral agreement (usually OIS); or
- reverse repo cash to give securities that can be posted in the collateral agreement with H_{repo} and H_{CSA} denoting the haircuts in the repo market and collateral agreement respectively.

We can therefore see that the relevant repo rate for a security should be multiplied by the factor $(1 + H_{CSA})/(1 + H_{repo})$ and compared with the cash rates discussed above in order to decide whether the relevant securities are cheapest-to-deliver. A given security will become more advantageous to post as its repo haircut increases and its CSA haircut decreases. This ratio will change as haircuts in the repo market change compared to the relatively static contractual haircuts in collateral agreements. Note also that technical factors and balance sheet considerations may also be important: there may be benefit in posting non-cash collateral that cannot easily be repoed and aspects such as the leverage ratio (Section 8.8.2) may also be relevant. Additionally, not all parties may have the same access to the repo market.

13.4.5   The end of ColVA

As discussed in Section 13.3.1, market practice has evolved over recent years to restrict some of the embedded value and optionality inherent in collateral agreements. Over the coming years, it is likely that CSAs will become simpler, partly to minimise ColVA components wherever possible. Regulation such as the bilateral collateral rules may also have the same ColVA reducing impact: for example, by penalising non-cash collateral or even variation margin posted in the "wrong currency" by requiring haircuts (Section 6.7.6).

Not surprisingly, CCPs have been switching to OIS discounting for valuations. In order to mitigate some of the problems with substitutions and cheapest-to-deliver collateral, CCP collateral terms are much simpler than in a CSA. A common approach is to require collateral (variation margin) to be posted in the currency of the underlying transaction. Cross-currency products are currently not cleared, partly due to the obvious problems this would create. This currency-mixing problem is also one of the reasons why cross-product netting of CCP variation margins is not recognised. Even then, some practical issues exist, such as if there is no liquid reference for OIS in a currency.

However, this reduction of ColVA will not be absolute. Single-currency collateral agreements create additional challenges such as settlement risk (the main obstacle to the development of the standard CSA, as discussed in Section 6.4.6). Many end-users (for example, pension funds) will struggle to move to posting cash collateral since they prefer to post directly the assets they hold. Problems will also remain with multi-currency products (e.g. cross-currency swaps).

Note also that ColVA adjustments may be present in other situations, such as those involving posting initial margin. Both bilateral markets and CCPs permit initial margin to be posted in a variety of different assets and there is similar optionality to that described above for variation margin. However, in these situations, any optionality may be incorporated in the determination of the underlying funding costs rather than being adjusted directly.

13.5 SUMMARY

This chapter has defined the starting point for OTC derivatives valuation and a reference point for xVA computation. We have introduced the concept of perfect collateralisation and explained that it leads to discounting at the collateral rate. This defines OIS discounting, which is commonly applied for valuation of many collateralised derivatives. We have then discussed all xVA adjustments with reference to the notion of perfect collateralisation. Finally, we have introduced the first xVA component, ColVA, which adjusts for certain features of the collateral agreement such as the remuneration rate and cheapest-to-deliver option.

14

Credit and Debt Value Adjustments

> *Do not worry about your difficulties in Mathematics. I can assure you mine are still greater.*
> Albert Einstein (1879–1955)

14.1 OVERVIEW

This chapter will introduce the next members of the xVA family, namely CVA (credit or counterparty value adjustment) and DVA (debt or debit value adjustment). We will show that under fairly standard assumptions, CVA and DVA can be defined in a straightforward way via credit exposure and default probability. We will then discuss computational aspects and show example calculations.

CVA has become a key topic for banks in recent years due to the volatility of credit spreads and the associated accounting (e.g. IFRS 13) and capital requirements (Basel III). However, note that whilst CVA calculations are a major concern for banks, they are also relevant for other financial institutions and corporations that have significant amounts of OTC derivatives to hedge their economic risks. Indeed, CVA and DVA should only be ignored for financial reporting if they are immaterial which is not the case for any significant OTC derivative user.

A key and common assumption made in this chapter will be that credit exposure and default probability[1] are independent. This involves neglecting wrong-way risk, which will be discussed in Chapter 17. We will also discuss CVA and DVA in isolation of other xVA terms, which will then be dealt with in more detail in later chapters. This is an important consideration since xVA terms cannot, in reality, be dealt with separately, and possible overlaps should be considered (Chapter 18). Standard reference papers on the subject of CVA include Jarrow and Turnbull (1992, 1995, 1997), Sorensen and Bollier (1994), Duffie and Huang (1996) and Brigo and Masetti (2005a).

14.2 CREDIT VALUE ADJUSTMENT

14.2.1 Why CVA is not straightforward

Pricing the credit risk for an instrument with one-way payments, such as a bond, is relatively straightforward – one simply needs to account for default when discounting the cashflows and add the value of any payments made in the event of a default. However, many derivatives instruments have fixed, floating or contingent cashflows or payments that are made in both directions. This bilateral nature characterises credit exposure and makes the quantification of counterparty risk significantly more difficult. Whilst this will become

---

[1] As well as the recovery value.

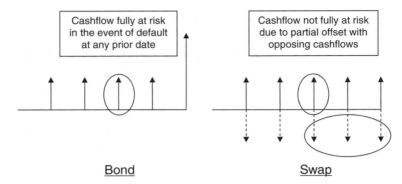

Figure 14.1 Illustration of the complexity when pricing the counterparty risk on a derivative instrument such as a swap, compared with pricing credit risk on a debt instrument such as a bond. In the bond the cashflow circled is fully at risk (less recovery) in the event of default of the issuer, but in the swap the equivalent cashflow is not due to the ability to partially offset it with current and future cashflows in the opposite direction (the three dotted cashflows shown circled).

clear in the more technical pricing calculations, a simple explanation is provided in Figure 14.1, which compares a bond to a similar swap transaction. In the bond case a given cashflow is fully at risk (a portion of its value will be lost entirely) in the event of a default, whereas in the swap case, only part of the cashflow will be at risk due to partial cancellation with opposing cashflows. The risk on the swap is clearly smaller due to this effect.[2] However, the fraction of the swap cashflows that are indeed at risk is hard to determine as this depends on many factors such as yield curve shape, forward rates and volatilities.

14.2.2   History of CVA

CVA was originally introduced as an adjustment to the risk-free value of a derivative to account for potential default via the relationship:

Risky value = Risk-free value – CVA   (14.1)

The above separation is theoretically rigorous, with the full derivation given in Appendix 14A. This separation is clearly useful because the problem of valuing a transaction and computing its counterparty risk can be completely separated. The obvious proxy for the risk-free value is OIS discounting (Section 13.2.5). Historically, the CVA in Equation 14.1 this was seen as a "credit charge" for pricing and a "reserve" or "provision" for financial reporting purposes.

A clear implication of the above is that it is possible to deal with all CVA components centrally and "transfer price" away from the originating trader or business. This is critical, since it allows separation of responsibilities within a financial institution: one desk is responsible for risk-free valuation and one for the counterparty risk component. Transactions and their associated counterparty risk may then be priced and risk-managed separately. This idea generalises to all xVA components. (although such a set-up may not always be the most optimal solution).

---

[2] It is also smaller due to the lack of a principal payment, but this is a different point.

There is a hidden complexity in the seemingly simple Equation 14.1, which is that it is not naturally additive across transactions. Due to risk mitigants such as netting and collateral, CVA must be calculated for all transactions covered by these risk mitigants. We will therefore have to consider the allocation of CVA just as we considered allocation of exposure in Chapter 10. The impact of collateral will also be non-additive.

14.2.3   CVA formula

The standard formula for computation of CVA (see Appendix 14B for more detail) is:

$$CVA = -LGD\sum_{i=1}^{m}EE\left(t_{i}\right)\times PD(t_{i-1},t_{i}) \tag{14.2}$$

The CVA depends on the following components:

- *Loss given default (LGD)*. This is the percentage amount of the exposure expected to be lost if the counterparty defaults. Note that sometimes the recovery rate is used with $LGD = 100\% - Rec$.
- *Expected exposure (EE)*. This term is the discounted expected exposure (EE) for the relevant dates in the future given by t_i for $i = 1, m$. Calculating EE was the subject of Chapter 10. Although discount factors could be represented separately, it is usually most convenient to apply (risk-free) discounting during the computation of the EE.
- *Default probability (PD)*. This expression requires the marginal default probability in the interval between date t_{i-1} and t_i. Default probability estimation was covered in Chapter 12.

CVA is hence proportional to the likelihood of default (PD), the exposure (EE) and the percentage amount lost in default (LGD). The formula has a time dimension, since EE and PD have been previously shown to be rather time-inhomogeneous (see Sections 7.3.3 and 12.2.4 respectively). Therefore, the formula must integrate over time to take into account the precise distribution of EE and PD, and not just their average values. Note that there is a minus sign to signify CVA is a loss – this convention was not always followed in the past, but is relevant since xVAs in general can have both positive and negative impacts. An illustration of the CVA formula is given in Figure 14.2.

A further important advantage of computing CVA via Equation 14.2 is that default enters the expression via default probability only. This means that, whilst one may require a simulation framework in order to compute CVA, it is not necessary to simulate default events, only the exposure (EE). This saves on computation time by avoiding the need to simulate relatively rare defaults.

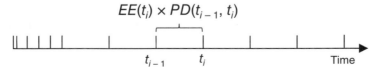

Figure 14.2   Illustration of CVA formula. The component shown is the CVA contribution for a given interval. The formula simply sums up across all intervals and multiplies by the loss given default.

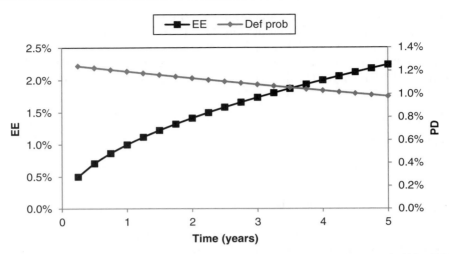

Figure 14.3   Illustration of the discounted expected exposure (EE) and default probability (PD) for the example CVA calculation.

14.2.4   CVA example

We illustrate the above CVA formula with a simple example of a forward contract-type exposure[3] using the simple expression from Equation 7.3 in Section 7.3.2, and a risk-neutral default probability defined by Equation 12.1 in Section 12.2.3. We use a constant credit spread of 300 bps and an LGD of 60%. We assume an interval of 0.25 years between the dates in Equation 14.2, which involves evaluation at a total of 20 points. With these assumptions, the expected exposure and marginal default probability are as shown in Figure 14.3. The CVA is calculated to be –0.200%, which is expressed in terms of percentage of notional value (the EE was expressed in percentage terms).

Spreadsheet 14.1   Simple CVA calculation

In terms of the accuracy of the integration, the exact result is –0.193%. One can obviously improve the accuracy by choosing more than 20 points. However, it is also best to approximate the exposure by the average of those at the beginning and end of each period, i.e.:

$$EE(t_i) \rightarrow [EE(t_i) + EE(t_{i-1})]/2 \tag{14.3}$$

This gives the more accurate result of –0.192% with the 20 points used above.

---

[3] The expected exposure is given by $EE(t) = 0.01 \times \sqrt{t}$ as a percentage of notional.

14.2.5   CVA as a spread

Suppose that instead of computing the CVA as a stand-alone value, one wanted it to be expressed as a spread (per annum charge). A simple calculation would involve dividing the CVA by the risky annuity[4] value for the maturity in question. For the previous calculation, a risky annuity of 4.42 would be obtained using the simple formula described in Appendix 14B. From the result above, we would therefore obtain the CVA as a spread, being $-0.200\%/4.42 \times 10,000 = -4.52$ bps (per annum).

There is also a quicker way to estimate the above result (Appendix 14C) that is useful for simple calculations and intuition (and similar approximations will be used also for other xVA terms). The formula assumes that the EE is constant over time and equal to its average value (EPE). This yields the following approximation based on EPE:

$$CVA \approx -EPE \times Spread, \tag{14.4}$$

where the CVA is expressed in the same units as the credit spread, which should be for the (maximum) maturity of the transaction (portfolio) in question, and EPE is as defined as in Section 7.2.6.[5] For the example above, the EPE is 1.54%[6] and therefore the CVA approximation is $-1.54\% \times 300 = -4.62$ bps.

The approximate calculation can therefore be seen to work reasonably well in this case. This approximate formula tends to be more accurate for swap-like profiles, where the symmetry of the profile helps, but is less accurate for monotonically increasing profiles such as the one used in the example above. It is also more accurate where the default probabilities are relatively constant (as in the example above). Whilst not used for actual calculations, the approximate formula in Equation 14.4 is useful for intuitive understanding of the drivers of CVA, because it separates the credit component (the credit spread of the counterparty) and the market risk component (the exposure, or EPE).

14.2.6   Exposure and discounting

In the CVA formula above, we assume that the EE is discounted, which is generally a better solution than expressing discount factors separately. Care must be taken if explicit discount factors are required; for example, in an interest rate product where high rates will imply a smaller discount factor and vice versa. To account for this convexity effect technically means quantifying the underlying exposure using the "T-forward measure" (Jamshidian and Zhu, 1997). By doing this, discount factors depend on expected future interest rate values, not on their distribution. Hence, moving the discount factor out of the expectation term (for exposure) can be achieved.

Working with separate discount factors may sometimes be convenient. For example, the approximation in Equation 14.4 requires the EPE to be undiscounted,[7] as described

---

[4] The risky annuity represents the value of receiving a unit amount in each period as long as the counterparty does not default. In this case we are assuming zero interest rates.

[5] This is the simple average of the EE values in our example, although for non-equal time intervals it would be the weighted average. In the approximate formula, the undiscounted EPE is required, although in a low interest rate environment the discounting differences may be small, especially for short-dated transactions.

[6] This is using the previous discretisation of 0.25. The analytical result is 1.49%.

[7] In other words, the EPE in Equation 14.4 does not contain any discounting effects.

in the derivation in Appendix 14C. However, often EE for CVA purposes is discounted during the simulation process. This is generally the more practical solution.

14.2.7   Risk-neutrality

In Chapter 10, we discussed in detail how to quantify exposure, which covers the EE term in Equation 14.4. Section 10.4 discussed the difference between real-world and risk-neutral exposure quantification. In general, CVA is computed with risk-neutral (market-implied) parameters where practical. Such an approach is relevant for pricing, since it defines the price with respect to hedging instruments and supports the exit price concept required by accounting standards (Section 2.1 in Chapter 2). Of course, certain parameters cannot be risk-neutral, since they are not observed in the market (e.g. correlations), or may require interpolation or extrapolation assumptions (e.g. volatilities). Risk-neutral parameters such as volatilities may generally be higher than their real-world equivalents (e.g. historical estimates).

A more controversial issue is the reference to default probability in Equation 14.4. Risk-neutral default probabilities were discussed and defined in Chapter 12. As for exposure, the use of risk-neutral parameters is relevant for pricing purposes. However, the use of risk-neutral default probabilities may be questioned for a number of reasons:

- risk-neutral default probabilities are significantly higher than their real-world equivalents (Section 12.2.1);
- default can, in general, not be hedged, since most counterparties do not have liquid single-name credit default swaps referencing them; and
- the business model of banks is generally to "warehouse" credit risk, and they are therefore only exposed to real-world default risk.

The above arguments are somewhat academic, as most banks (and many other institutions) are required to use credit spreads when reporting CVA. There are, however, cases where historical default probabilities may be used in CVA calculations today:

- smaller regional banks with less significant derivatives businesses who may argue that their exit price would be with a local competitor who would also price the CVA with historical default probabilities; and
- regions such as Japan where banks are not subject to IFS 13 accounting standards.

In situations such as the above, which are increasingly rare, banks may see CVA as an actuarial reserve and not a risk-neutral exit price. We will discuss this problem more in Chapter 18 in relation to the mandate of an xVA desk.

14.2.8   CVA semi-analytical methods

In the case of some specific product types, it is possible to derive relatively simple formulas for CVA. Whilst such formulas are of limited use, since they do not account for aspects such as netting or collateral, they are valuable for quick calculations and an intuitive understanding of CVA.

The first simple example is the CVA of a position that can only have a positive value, such as a long option position with an upfront premium. In this situation, it is possible to show (Appendix 14D) that the CVA is simply:

$$CVA \approx -LGD \times PD(0, T) \times V, \tag{14.5}$$

where T is the maturity of the transaction in question and V is its current (standard) value. The term $PD(0, T)$ represents the probability that the counterparty will default at any point during the lifetime of the transaction in question. It is intuitive that one simply multiplies the standard risk-free price by this default probability and corrects for the loss given default.

Another more sophisticated approach is the Sorensen-Bollier semi-analytical formula mentioned in Section 10.2.2, in which the EE in Equation 14.4 can be replaced by the value of European swaptions. This can be extended to a portfolio in a single currency (e.g. see Brigo and Masetti, 2005b) but cannot be used for more multidimensional problems.

Note that the above approaches are risk-neutral by their nature and therefore would not naturally support the use of real-world calibrations (although this may not be a major concern).

14.3   IMPACT OF CREDIT ASSUMPTIONS

We now consider the impact of default probability and LGD on CVA. There are several aspects to consider, such as the level of credit spreads, the overall shape of the credit curve, the impact of LGD and the basis risk arising from LGD assumptions. In all the examples below, we will consider the CVA of the same simple example as in Section 14.2.4. The base case assumptions will be a flat credit curve of 300 bps and an LGD of 60%. Assuming a notional of 1m then the base case CVA is −1,999 (the percentage result of −0.200% above).

14.3.1   Credit spread impact

Let us first review the impact of increasing the credit spread of the counterparty in Table 14.1. The increase in credit spread clearly increases the CVA, but this effect is not linear

Table 14.1   CVA as a function of the credit spread of the counterparty.

Spread (bps)	CVA
150	−1,074
300	−1,999
600	−3,471
1,200	−5,308
2,400	−6,506
4,800	−6,108
9,600	−4,873
Default	0

Table 14.2   CVA of five- and ten-year forward-type transactions for different shapes of credit curve. The five-year credit spread is assumed to be 300 bps and the LGD 60% in all cases.

	Five-year	Ten-year
Upwards-sloping	−2,179	−6,526
Flat	−1,999	−4,820
Downwards-sloping	−1,690	−2,691

since default probabilities are bounded by 100%. Another way to understand this is that the "jump to default" risk[8] of this swap is zero, since it has a current value of zero and so an immediate default of the counterparty will (theoretically) not cause any loss. As the credit quality of the counterparty deteriorates, the CVA will obviously decrease (become more negative) but at some point, when the counterparty is close to default, the CVA will increase again. This point will be discussed again in Chapter 18, as it has hedging implications.

Next we look at the impact of changes in *shape* of the credit curve. In Chapter 12 (Section 12.2.4), we considered upwards-sloping, flat and inverted credit curves, all of which assumed a five-year credit spread of 300 bps. We discussed how, whilst they gave cumulative default probabilities that were the same at the five-year point, the marginal default probabilities differed substantially. For a flat curve, default probability is approximately equally spaced, whilst for an upwards (downwards)-sloping curve, defaults are back (front) loaded. We show the impact of curve shape on the CVA in Table 14.2. For the five-year swap, even though the spread at the maturity is fixed, there are quite different results for the different curve shapes. Indeed, going from an upwards-sloping to a flat curve changes the CVA by around 10%. For the ten-year swap, we are extrapolating the known five-year spread and the differences are even more extreme: the upwards-sloping curve gives a CVA more than double the downwards-sloping curve. This illustrates why we emphasised the shape of the credit curve as being an important part of the mapping process (Section 12.4.3).

14.3.2   Recovery impact

In Chapter 12 (see Figure 12.5), we discussed that the settled recovery defines the (expected) LGD at the time of default (for example, settled in the CDS auction) whilst the actual recovery defines the (expected) LGD that will actually be experienced (i.e. used in Equation 14.2). Substituting the default probability formula (Equation 12.1) into the CVA formula (Equation 14.2) gives:

$$CVA = -LGD_{actual} \sum_{i=1}^{m} EE\left(t_i\right) \times \left[\exp\left(-\frac{s_{t_{i-1}}t_{i-1}}{LGD_{settled}}\right) - \exp\left(-\frac{s_{t_i}t_i}{LGD_{settled}}\right) \right], \tag{14.6}$$

where we explicitly reference the actual and settled LGDs. Whilst they are different conceptually, if a derivatives claim is of the same seniority as that referenced in the CDS (as

---

[8] This term is generally used to mean a sudden and immediate default of the counterparty, with no other factors changing.

Table 14.3 CVA of the base case IRS for different recovery assumptions. Simultaneous changes in the settled and final recovery ("both") and a 10% settled recovery and 40% final recovery are shown.

LGD (settled/final)	CVA
80% both	−2,072
60% both	−1,999
40% both	−1,862
90%/60%	−1,398

is typically the case), then we should assume that $LGD_{actual} = LGD_{settled}$ (i.e. the expected LGDs are equal). In this case the LGD terms in Equation 14.6 will cancel to first order and we will expect an only moderate sensitivity to changing this parameter.[9] The simple approximation in Equation 14.4 has no LGD input reflecting this cancellation.

Table 14.3 shows the impact of changing settled and actual LGDs. As expected, changing both LGDs has a reasonably small impact on the CVA, since there is a cancellation effect: increasing LGD reduces the risk-neutral default probability but increases the loss in the event of default. The net impact is only a second-order effect, which is negative with reducing LGD: halving the LGD only changes the CVA by around 10%. Using different assumptions for settled and actual LGDs will obviously change the CVA more significantly. For example, assuming a 90% settled LGD and a lower 60% actual LGD (similar to the values experienced in the Lehman Brothers bankruptcy, as discussed in Section 12.2.5) gives a much higher (less negative) CVA.

14.4   CVA ALLOCATION AND PRICING

Risk mitigants, such as netting and collateral, reduce CVA, but this can only be quantified by a calculation at the netting set level. It is therefore important to consider the allocation of CVA to the transaction level for pricing and valuation purposes. This in turn leads to the consideration of the numerical issues involving the running of large-scale calculations rapidly.

14.4.1   Netting and incremental CVA

When there is a netting agreement then the impact will reduce the CVA and cannot increase it (this arises from the properties of netting described in Section 7.4). We therefore know that for a netting set (a group of transactions with a given counterparty under the same netting agreement):

$$CVA_{NS} \geq \sum_{i=1}^{n} CVA_i,$$ (14.7)

---

[9] This is because $\exp(-x) \approx 1-x$ for small values of x. This is therefore more accurate for smaller spread values.

where CVA_{NS} is the total CVA of all transactions under the netting agreement and CVA_i is the stand-alone CVA for transaction i. The above effect (CVA becoming less negative) can be significant and the question then becomes how to allocate the netting benefits to each individual transaction. The most obvious way to do this is to use the concept of *incremental CVA*, analogously to incremental EE discussed in Section 10.7.2.[10] Here the CVA of a transaction i is calculated based on the incremental effect this transaction has on the netting set:

$$CVA_i^{incremental} = CVA_{NS+i} - CVA_{NS} \qquad (14.8)$$

The above formula ensures that the CVA of a specified transaction is given by its contribution to the overall CVA at the time it is executed. Hence, it makes sense when the CVA needs to be charged to individual salespeople, traders or businesses. The CVA depends on the order in which transactions are executed but does not change due to subsequent transactions. An xVA desk (Chapter 18) charging this amount will directly offset the instantaneous impact on their total MTM from the change in CVA from the new transaction.

As shown in Appendix 14E, we can derive the following fairly obvious formula for incremental CVA:

$$CVA_i^{incremental} = -LGD \sum_{i=1}^{m} EE_i^{incremental}\left(t_i\right) \times PD(t_{i-1}, t_i) \qquad (14.9)$$

This is the same as Equation 14.2 but with the incremental EE replacing the previous stand-alone EE. This should not be surprising since CVA is a linear combination of EE, and netting changes only the exposure and has no impact on the credit components (LGDs or default probabilities). The quantification of incremental EE was covered in detail in Section 10.7. Incremental EE can be negative, due to beneficial netting effects, which will lead to a CVA being positive and, in such a case, it would be a benefit and not a cost.

It is worth emphasising that, due to the properties of EE and netting, the incremental CVA in the presence of netting will never be lower (more negative) than the stand-alone CVA without netting. The practical result of this is that a party with existing transactions under a netting agreement will be likely to offer conditions that are more favourable with respect to a new transaction. Cooper and Mello (1991) quantified such an impact many years ago, showing specifically that a bank that already has a transaction with a counterparty can offer a more competitive rate on a forward contract.

The treatment of netting makes the treatment of CVA a complex and often multidimensional problem. Whilst some attempts have been made at handling netting analytically (e.g. Brigo and Masetti, 2005b, as noted in Section 14.2.8), CVA calculations incorporating netting accurately typically require a general Monte Carlo simulation for exposure (EE) quantification. For pricing new transactions, such a calculation must be run more or less in real-time.

---

[10] The reader may wish to refer back to the discussion around incremental exposure in Chapter 10, as many of the points made there will apply to incremental CVA also.

Table 14.4 Incremental CVA calculations for a seven-year USD swap paying fixed with respect to four different existing transactions and compared to the stand-alone value. The credit curve is assumed flat at 300 bps with a 60% LGD.

Existing transaction	Incremental CVA
None (stand-alone)	−0.4838
Payer IRS USD 5Y	−0.4821
Payer swaption USD 5x5Y	−0.4628
xCCY USDJPY 5Y	−0.2532
Receiver IRS USD 5Y	−0.1683

14.4.2   Incremental CVA example

We now look at an example of incremental CVA following the previous results for incremental exposure in Section 10.7.2 As before, we consider a seven-year EUR payer interest rate swap and in Table 14.4 consider the CVA under the assumption of five different existing transactions with the counterparty.

We can make the following observations:

• The incremental CVA is never lower (more negative) than the stand-alone CVA, since netting cannot increase exposure.
• The incremental CVA is only slightly less negative for a very similar existing transaction (five-year payer EUR swap). This follows from the high positive correlation between the two transactions. The swaption also leads to only a small reduction due to the directionality.
• The incremental CVA is increased (less negative) significantly for the cross-currency swap and the receiver swap. In the latter case, we may have expected a positive CVA, which is not the case (but this reversal effect is seen for DVA later).

14.4.3   Marginal CVA

Following the discussion in Section 10.7.3, we can define marginal CVA in a similar way by simply including the marginal EE in the CVA formula (Equation 14.2). Marginal CVA may be useful to break down a CVA for any number of netted transactions into transaction-level contributions that sum to the total CVA. Whilst it might not be used for pricing new transactions (due to the problem that marginal CVA changes when new transactions are executed, implying MTM adjustment to trading books), it may be required for pricing transactions executed at the same time[11] (perhaps due to being part of the same deal) with a given counterparty. Alternatively, marginal CVA is the appropriate way to allocate a CVA to transaction level contributions at a given time. This may be useful for reporting purposes or to give an idea of transactions that could be usefully restructured, novated or unwound.

---

[11] This could also cover a policy where CVA adjustments are only calculated periodically and several trades have occurred with a given counterparty within that period.

Table 14.5 Illustration of the breakdown of the CVA of an interest rate (IRS) and cross-currency (CCS) swaps via incremental and marginal. The credit curve is assumed flat at 300 bps and the LGD is 60%.

	Incremental (IRS first)	Incremental (CCS first)	Marginal
IRS	−0.4838	−0.2587	−0.3318
CCS	−0.1990	−0.4241	−0.3510
Total	−0.6828	−0.6828	−0.6828

Table 14.5 shows the incremental and marginal CVA corresponding to the interest rate swap (Payer IRS 7Y) and the cross-currency swap (xCCY USDJPY) with exposures previously shown in Figure 10.26 assuming a credit curve at 300 bps flat. We see the effect that the first transaction is charged for the majority of the CVA, as seen before, whilst the marginal CVA charges are more balanced.

Different CVA decompositions can obviously lead to rather different results. Table 14.6 shows contrasting decompositions for the five transactions described in Section 10.6.1. Incremental CVA depends very much on the ordering of the transactions. For example, the incremental CVA of the cross-currency swap is significantly less negative in the first compared to the second incremental scenario. Clearly, the amount of CVA charged can be very dependent on the timing of the transaction. This may be problematic and could possibly lead to "gaming" behaviour. However, this is not generally problematic for two reasons:

- a given client will typically be "owned" by a single trading desk or salesperson, and will therefore be exposed only to the total charge on a portfolio of transactions (although certain transactions may appear beneficial at a given time); and
- most clients will execute relatively directional transactions (due, for example, to their hedging requirements) and netting effects will therefore not be large.

Whilst the marginal contributions are fair, it is hard to imagine how to get around the problem of charging traders and businesses based on marginal contributions that change as new transactions are executed with the counterparty.

Table 14.6 Illustration of the breakdown of the CVA for five transactions via incremental (the ordering of transactions given in brackets) and marginal contributions. The credit curve is assumed flat at 300 bps and the LGD is 60%.

	Stand-alone	Incremental (1-2-3-4-5)	Incremental (5-4-3-2-1)	Marginal
Payer IRS 7Y	−0.4838	−0.4838	−0.3287	−0.3776
Payer swaption 5x5Y	−0.5135	−0.4925	−0.3437	−0.4447
xCCY USDJPY	−0.4296	−0.1258	−0.4296	−0.2798
Receiver IRS 5Y	−0.0631	0.1964	0.2587	0.2093
Payer IRS 5Y	−0.2587	−0.1964	−0.2587	−0.2093
Total	−1.7487	−1.1021	−1.1021	−1.1021

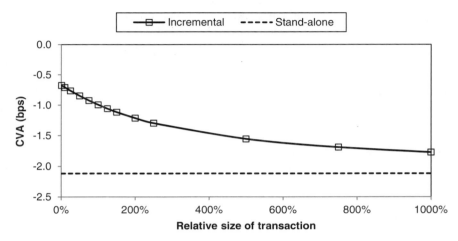

Figure 14.4   Incremental CVA (as a spread in basis points per annum) for a five-year swap within a portfolio with significant netting benefit.

14.4.4   CVA as a spread

Another point to consider when pricing CVA into transactions is how to convert an upfront CVA to a running spread CVA. This would facilitate charging a CVA to a client via, for example, adjusting the rate paid on a swap. One simple way to do such a transformation would be to divide the CVA by the risky duration for the maturity in question, as shown in Section 14.2.5.

However, when adding a spread to a contract such as a swap, the problem is non-linear, since the spread itself will have an impact on the CVA. The correct value should be calculated recursively, which would ensure that the CVA charge precisely offsets the CVA bedded in the contract. Using this accurate calculation for the example in Section 14.2.5 gives a spread of –4.83 (compared to –4.79 bps previously). For relatively small CVA charges, this effect is small, although Vrins and Gregory (2011) show that it is significant in certain cases (typically more risky counterparties and/or long-dated transactions).

Another point to emphasise is that the benefit of netting seen in the incremental CVA of a new transaction also depends on the relative size of the new transaction. As the transaction size increases, the netting benefit is lost and the CVA will approach the stand-alone value. This is illustrated in Figure 14.4, which shows the incremental CVA of a five-year swap as a function of the relative size of this new transaction. For a smaller transaction, the CVA decreases to a lower limit of –0.67 bps, whereas for a large transaction size it approaches the stand-alone value (–2.12 bps). Clearly, a CVA quote in basis points is only valid for a particular transaction size.

14.4.5   Numerical issues

The CVA calculation as represented by Equation 14.2 is costly due to the large number of calculations of the future value of the underlying transaction(s). For example, for

10,000 simulations and 100 time points, each individual transaction must be valued one million times. This is likely to be the bottleneck of the CVA calculation, and standard pricing functions may be inadequate for CVA purposes since they are not optimised to this level of performance. Furthermore, complex products may be even more problematic, since they often use Monte Carlo or lattice-based modelling for valuation.

The first and most obvious method for improving the efficiency of the CVA calculation will be to speed up the underlying pricing functionality. There are many methods that may achieve this, such as (see also discussion below on exotics):

- stripping out common functionality (such as cashflow generation and fixings), which does not depend on the underlying market variables at a given point in time;
- numerical optimisation of pricing functions;
- use of approximations or grids; and
- parallelisation.

Another aspect to consider when computing CVA is whether to use pathwise or direct simulation, as discussed in Section 10.3.2. Whilst evaluation of pathwise simulations would seem to be best for PFE purposes, this is not the case for CVA, which is an integral over the exposure distribution. We compare the evaluation of the CVA of a five-year interest rate swap based on a direct and pathwise simulation approach. The former case uses 10,000 paths for the exposure at a total of 183 time steps. In the latter approach, there is no time grid and, instead, default times are drawn randomly in the interval up to five years.[12] The exposure is then calculated at each of these points directly and a total of 1.83m default times are generated, so that the number of swap evaluations is the same as in the pathwise case. The comparison of the CVA estimates is given in Figure 14.5,

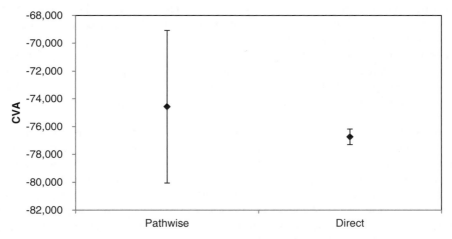

Figure 14.5 Estimate of the CVA for a five-year swap with pathwise and direct simulation approaches. In each case, the same numbers of evaluations of the swap are used. The pathwise approach uses 183 time-steps.

---

[12] The approach of Li (2000) allows this to be done in a way that is consistent with the underlying cumulative default probability.

with error bars representing one standard deviation of uncertainty. We can see that the direct simulation approach is much more accurate for CVA than the pathwise approach for the same number of underlying pricing calls. The pathwise simulation approach is less efficient, since the points along a given path will be correlated, leading to a slower convergence of the CVA integral approximation.

The improvement above is quite dramatic, with the standard deviation 9.7 times smaller in the direct approach. Since Monte Carlo error is approximately proportional to the square root of the number of simulations, this actually represents a speed improvement of $9.7 \times 9.7 = 94$ times. In other words, we can do 94 times fewer simulations to achieve the same accuracy. Whilst the above may sound appealing, we must consider the overall improvement. Amdahl's law (Amdahl, 1967) gives a simple formula for the overall speedup from improving one component of a calculation. This formula is $((1-P)+P/S)^{-1}$, where P is the percentage of the calculation that can be improved and S is the relative speed improvement. For example, if 90% ($P = 0.9$) of the time is spent on pricing function calls and these can be speeded up by 94 times, then the overall improvement is 9.1 times. A direct simulation approach for CVA may be faster but this will depend on the precise time spent on different components in the Monte Carlo model and other overheads such as data retrieval. This approach is less obviously applied to portfolios with path dependency, such as collateralised transactions and some exotics.

The calculation of CVA with reference to EE calculated at discrete points in time can cause issues for certain path-dependent derivatives based on a continuous sampling of quantities (for example, barrier options). Such cases will also require approximations like those introduced by Lomibao and Zhu (2005), who use a mathematical technique known as a Brownian bridge to calculate probabilities of path-dependent events that are intermediate to actual exposure simulation points.

Regarding exotic products and those with American-style features, as discussed in Section 10.3.3, there are typically three approaches followed. The first is to use approximations and a second, more accurate approach involves using pre-calculated grids to provide the future value of instruments as a function of the underlying variables. This second approach works well as long as the dimensionality is not high. Thirdly, American Monte approaches can be used to approximate exposures, handling any exotic feature as well as path dependencies. This is described in detail by Cesari et al. (2009) and is becoming increasingly commonly used for xVA computation to provide a generic framework in which any product can be handled – even those with complex features.

14.5   CVA WITH COLLATERAL

The impact of collateral on CVA follows directly from the assessment of the impact of collateral on exposure in Chapter 11. As with netting before, the influence of collateral on the standard CVA formula given in Equation 14.2 is straightforward: collateral only changes the EE and hence the same formula may be used with the EE based on assumptions of collateralisation. The results below will use the example portfolio presented in Section 11.3. The base case exposure, with and without collateral, can be seen in Figure 11.8. This assumes a zero-threshold, two-way CSA with a minimum transfer amount of 0.5 and a rounding of 0.1. For the CVA calculation, a flat credit curve of 500 bps and LGD of 40% is assumed. The base case CVA without any collateral considered is –0.2932.

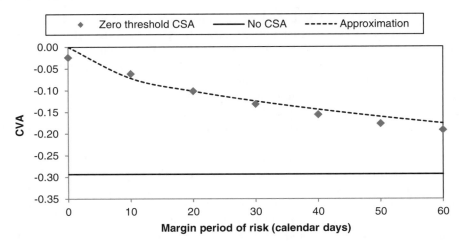

Figure 14.6   Impact of the margin period of risk on CVA. The uncollateralised CVA is shown by the solid line. Also shown is the approximation from scaling the 20-day MPR according to the square root of time rule.

14.5.1   Impact of margin period of risk

We can also use the simple approximation in Equation 11.5 to estimate the CVA reduction directly. For example, for a margin period of risk (MPR) of 30 calendar days, this would give –0.075.[13] The actual result in this case is considerably lower at –0.131. The smaller absolute value given by the approximation can be attributed to the fact that it implicitly assumes a zero minimum transfer amount and does not consider the risk from posting collateral (which is assumed to be not segregated as is usual). Nevertheless, this can produce a ballpark figure for the reduction in CVA.

We now consider the impact of changing the MPR on the zero-threshold CVA calculation, as considered previously in Figure 14.6. At zero MPR, the CVA is obviously small (but not zero due to the minimum transfer amount and rounding) and then decreases towards the uncollateralised value. At a margin period of risk of 30 calendar days (similar to the Basel III requirement of 20 business days discussed in Section 8.6.3), the CVA is almost half the uncollateralised CVA. We can also see that an approximation based on the square root of time scaling via the 20-day result is reasonably accurate (for example, we approximate the 30-day result as $\sqrt{(30/20)}$ times the 20-day result).

14.5.2   Thresholds and initial margins

Figure 14.7 shows the impact of initial margins or thresholds on the CVA. Note that an initial margin can be considered as a negative threshold. We can see a reduction from zero, where the initial margin is large, to the uncollateralised CVA (dotted line) where the threshold is large.

Whilst increased initial margin reduces CVA, the determination of the correct initial margin is extremely subjective. We can see this in Figure 14.8, which shows the impact

---

[13] $0.5 \times \sqrt{(365 \times 5/30)} = 3.9$ times smaller.

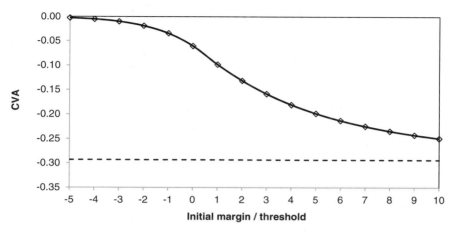

Figure 14.7 Impact of the initial margin (negative values) and threshold (positive values) on CVA. A one-way CSA in the party's favour is assumed, with an MPR of 30 calendar days. The dotted line is the uncollateralised CVA.

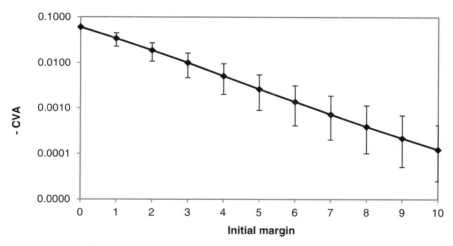

Figure 14.8 Impact of initial margin on CVA with a logarithmic y-axis (note that the negative CVA is shown, i.e. a positive number). Also shown are error bars corresponding to changing the assumed margin period of risk by +/–10 calendar days.

of the initial margin on the CVA with error bars arising from an assumed uncertainty in the margin period of risk of +/–10 days (i.e., 20 days or 40 days). Whilst an increase in the initial margin reduces the CVA substantially, the uncertainty is relatively greater.

Note that any initial margin posted would not show up in any of the above calculations as long as it is segregated (Section 7.5.4). However, it will represent a cost from the point of view of MVA (Chapter 16).

14.6   DEBT VALUE ADJUSTMENT

14.6.1   Overview

A key assumption above in the definition of CVA was that the party making the calculation could not default. This may have seemed like a fairly innocuous and straightforward assumption. Indeed, it is consistent with the "going concern" accountancy concept, which requires financial statements to be based on the assumption that a business will remain in existence for an indefinite period. However, as discussed below, international accountancy standards allow (and potentially *require*) a party to consider their own default in the valuation of their liabilities. Since credit exposure has a liability component (the negative exposure as defined in Section 7.2.7), this can be included in the pricing of counterparty risk, as the debt value adjustment (DVA) component.

DVA is a double-edged sword. On the one hand, it will resolve some theoretical problems with CVA and create a world where price symmetry can be achieved. On the other hand, the nature of DVA and its implications and potential unintended consequences are troubling. Indeed, as will be discussed in the next chapter, market practice can be seen to generally disregard DVA in aspects such as pricing and replace it with funding considerations (FVA). However, it is still important to understand DVA from an accounting standpoint and its subsequent relationship to FVA.

14.6.2   Accounting standards and DVA

Consideration of a party's own default, together with that of its counterparty, leads to bilateral CVA (BCVA), which is made up of CVA and DVA. The use of BCVA has been largely driven by accounting practices and formally began in 2006, when the FAS 157[14] determined that banks should record a DVA entry. FAS 157 states:

> Because non-performance risk includes the reporting entity's credit risk, the reporting entity should consider the effect of its credit risk (credit standing) on the fair value of the liability in all periods in which the liability is measured at fair value.

This led to a number of large US (and some Canadian) banks reporting DVA in financial statements, a practice that was followed by some large European banks. The use of DVA was combined with the use of credit spreads and not historical default probabilities, as discussed in Section 2.1. However, the treatment of DVA from an accounting standpoint was not consistent, and many banks ignored it. These participants would also generally use historical (or blended) default probabilities (see discussion in Section 12.2.2).

The accounting position was made clearer with the introduction of IFRS 13 from January 2013 where derivatives must be reported at "fair value", the definition of which includes the following comment:

> The fair value of a liability reflects the effect of non-performance risk. Non-performance risk includes, but may not be limited to, an entity's own credit risk.

---

[14] The Statements of Financial Accounting Standard, No. 157.

The interpretation of auditors has generally been that IFRS 13 accounting standards require the use of risk-neutral default probabilities (via credit spreads) and both CVA and DVA components to be reported. This has led to a convergence over recent years, although there are still some exceptions : Japan, for example, where banks do not report under IFRS 13 accounting standards. Furthermore, whilst banks have converged in their DVA reporting practices, this is somewhat undermined by their introduction of FVA, as discussed in the next chapter.

14.6.3   DVA and pricing

CVA has traditionally been a charge for counterparty risk that is levied on the end-user (e.g. a corporate) by their counterparty (e.g. a bank). Historically, banks charged CVAs linked to the credit quality of the end-user and the exposure in question. An end-user would not have been able to credibly question such a charge, especially since the probability that a bank would default was considered remote (and indeed the credit spreads of banks were traditionally very tight and their credit ratings were very strong). The idea that a large bank such as Lehman Brothers would default was, until 2008, an almost laughable suggestion.

Obviously this changed during the global financial crisis, and the credit spreads of the "strong" financial institutions widened dramatically. Banks struggled for creditability for charging even more to end-users when their own credit quality was clearly worsening dramatically. Furthermore, there was a question of two banks trading in the interbank market. Would both banks not need to report a loss for the CVA they faced to each other, even though the transactions would be collateralised? (As shown in Section 14.5.1, even a zero-threshold CSA does not eradicate CVA entirely.) Hence, in a world where all parties use CVA, how can two counterparties ever agree a price, even under a collateral arrangement?

One important feature of DVA is that it solves the above issues and creates "price symmetry" where, in theory, parties can agree on prices. However, it is important to note that price symmetry is not generally a requirement for markets anyway: banks determine prices and end-users decide whether or not to transact at these quoted prices. Furthermore, the use of DVA causes other issues that will be discussed below.

14.6.4   Bilateral CVA formula

BCVA means that a party would consider a CVA calculated under the assumption that they, as well as their counterparty, may default. In Appendix 14F we derive the formula for BCVA under these conditions. Ignoring the relationship between the two default events and related close-out assumptions (discussed in Section 14.6.5), gives BCVA as a simple sum of CVA and DVA components:

$$BCVA = CVA + DVA \tag{14.10a}$$

$$CVA = -LGD_C \sum_{i=1}^{m} EE(t_i) \times PD_C(t_{i-1}, t_i) \tag{14.10b}$$

$$DVA = -LGD_P \sum_{i=1}^{m} NEE(t_i) \times PD_P(t_{i-1}, t_i) \tag{14.10c}$$

The suffixes P and C indicate the party making the calculation and their counterparty respectively. The CVA term is unchanged from Equation 14.2 and the DVA term is the mirror image based on the negative expected exposure (NEE), the party's own default probability and LGD. DVA is positive due to the sign of the NEE and it will therefore oppose the CVA as a benefit. The DVA term corresponds to the fact that in cases where the party themselves default, they will make a "gain" if they have a negative exposure. A gain in this context might seem unusual but it is, strictly speaking, correct, since the party, in the event of their own default, pays the counterparty only a fraction of what they owe, and therefore gains by the LGD portion of the NEE. The negative expected exposure, defined in Section 7.2.7, is the opposite of the EE.

Note that NEE is also the negative EE from the counterparty's point of view. This shows an important feature of Equation 14.10a, which is that a party's CVA loss is exactly their counterparties DVA gain and vice versa. This is the price symmetry property of BCVA. To understand this price symmetry more easily, let us return to the simple formula in Equation 14.4. An obvious extension including DVA is:

$$BCVA = -EPE \times Spread_C - ENE \times Spread_P, \tag{14.11}$$

where the expected negative exposure (ENE) is the opposite of the EPE, as defined in Section 7.2.7. The ENE is the negative of the counterparty's EPE. If we assume that $EPE = -ENE$,[15] then we obtain $BCVA \approx -EPE \times (Spread_C - Spread_P)$. A party could therefore charge their counterparty for the *difference* in their credit spreads (and if this difference is negative then they should pay a charge themselves). Weaker counterparties pay stronger counterparties in order to trade with them based on the differential in credit quality. Theoretically, this leads to a pricing agreement (assuming parties can agree on the calculations and parameters), even when one or both counterparties has poor credit quality.

14.6.5   Close-out and default correlation

The above formula for BCVA ignored three important and interconnected concepts:

- *Survival.* The survival probability of the non-defaulting party is not included in the CVA and DVA representation. For example, when calculating CVA, a party may wish to condition on their own survival, since if they default before their counterparty then they will suffer no loss. Indeed, Equations 14.10a–c include the potential default of both parties where there is a clear "first-to-default" effect: the underlying contracts will cease when the first party defaults and therefore there should be no consideration of the second default.
- *Default correlation.* Related to the above, the correlation of defaults between the party and their counterparty is not included. If such a correlation is positive then they would be more likely to default closer together, which would be expected to have an impact on CVA and DVA.
- *Close-out.* Finally, as discussed in Section 7.1.3, the definition of the EE and NEE as referenced in Equations 14.10b and 14.10c is typically based on standard valuation

---

[15] This is sometimes a reasonable approximation in practice, especially for a collateralised relationship, but we will discuss the impact of asymmetry below.

assumptions and does not reflect the actual close-out assumptions that may be relevant in a default scenario. In other words, in the event of a default it is assumed that the underlying transactions will be settled at their MTM value at the default time, which is inconsistent with the reality of close-out. Close-out assumptions are now relevant since we are considering that the surviving party is no longer "risk-free".

The above points have been studied by various authors. Gregory (2009a) shows the impact of survival probabilities and default correlation on BCVA but in isolation of any close-out considerations. Brigo and Morini (2010) have considered the impact of close-out assumptions in the unilateral (i.e. one-sided exposure) case. The importance of close-out assumptions can be understood as follows. When a counterparty defaults, the value of the underlying transactions will still contain a DVA benefit to the surviving party. Mechanisms for close-out (Section 5.2.6) seem to support realising such a DVA, since they may allow a party's own creditworthiness to be a consideration.

Given the above, either party can potentially gain their DVA in the default of their counterparty and this is not accounted for in the standard BCVA calculation that likely relies on "risk-free" valuation (Section 7.1.3). However, monetising such a gain depends on the specifics of the close-out specification, for example (refer to Section 5.2.6):

- *Market quotation.* Here, DVA would be naturally seen as the CVA that another counterparty would charge in a replacement transaction. However, such a quotation would generally be on a collateralised basis and therefore the DVA benefit would be difficult to claim unless it were possible to get a firm market quotation on an uncollateralised transaction.
- *Close-out amount.* Defined in the 2002 ISDA documentation, this would seem to be more conducive to the inclusion of DVA in the close-out price since it does not require an actual market quotation and specifies that the claim "may take into account the creditworthiness of the Determining Party".

Not only are close-out assumptions very difficult to define but quantification becomes difficult because it involves including the future BCVA at each possible default event in order to eventually determine the current BCVA. This creates a difficult recursive problem. Brigo and Morini (2010) show that for a loan, the assumption that the DVA can be included in the close-out assumptions ("risky close-out") leads to a cancellation, with the survival probability of the party making the calculation. This means that the formula in Equation 14.10 is correct in a one-sided situation with risky close-out. Gregory and German (2012) consider the two-sided case and find that a simple result does not apply but that the formulas used in Equations 14.10a–c are probably the best approximation in the absence of a much more sophisticated approach.

Generally, market participants do not follow a more advanced approach and simply include survival probabilities (or not) directly. For example, in an Ernst and Young Survey in 2012,[16] six out of 19 respondents report making CVA and DVA "contingent" (survival probability adjusted), seven non-contingent (Equations 14.10a–c) with the remainder not reporting DVA at the time. Equations 14.10a–c do have the nice feature that

---

[16] Ernst and Young CVA Survey 2012, www.ey.com.

CVA and DVA are specific to the counterparty's and party's own credit spreads respectively and will show generally monotonic behaviour with respect to spread movements.

14.6.6   Example

> **Spreadsheet 14.2**   Simple BCVA calculation

We will consider an example of BCVA computation based on the CVA calculations shown in Section 14.2.4, for which the associated EE and NEE are shown in Figure 14.9 (the EE has been previously shown in Figure 11.8). This portfolio, although currently at market, has a skewed EE/NEE distribution with the latter being higher. Figure 14.9 also shows the impact of a two-way, zero-threshold CSA as defined at the start of Section 14.5, assuming an MPR of 20 calendar days. Note that the CSA makes the exposure distribution more symmetric.

Assume that the counterparty's and party's own credit spread (CDS) curves are flat at 200 bps and 100 bps respectively, and both LGDs are 60%. CVA and DVA values are shown in Table 14.7 for both the uncollateralised and collateralised cases. In the uncollateralised case, the DVA is slightly dominant over the CVA, since the NEE is significantly bigger (even though the party's own spread is lower). This represents a net benefit overall via BCVA. Note that this risky derivatives portfolio is therefore worth more than the equivalent default-free portfolio where the BCVA would be zero.

The collateralised results change the sign of the BCVA, which becomes a cost and not a benefit. This means that the party would make a loss in the event of moving to a two-way CSA and their counterparty would make the equivalent gain. Whilst this shows that in the symmetric world of BCVA the CSA has a price, it is perhaps troubling that the significant reduction in counterparty risk seen in Figure 14.9 is not supported by BCVA valuation.

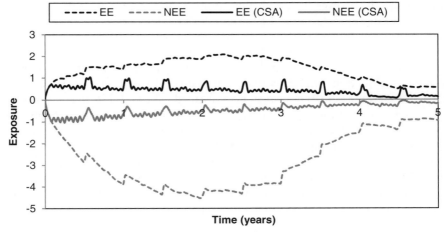

Figure 14.9   EE and NEE for a swap portfolio both uncollateralised and with a (zero-threshold, two-way) CSA.

Table 14.7 CVA and DVA values for a swap portfolio with counterparty and own credit spread assumptions of 200 and 100 bps respectively. LGDs are assumed to be 60%. Results with and without a two-way CSA are shown.

	No CSA	Two-way CSA
CVA	−0.1309	−0.0408
DVA	0.1357	0.0222
BCVA	0.0048	−0.0185

A CVA-only world would suggest that both parties in the above example would make valuation gains from moving to a two-way CSA: this is clearly incorrect. On the other hand, a CVA and DVA treatment suggests that the party making the calculation would not move to a two-way CSA due to the loss of their DVA benefit, even though this may have other beneficial effects such as reducing PFE or capital requirements. This is not correct either and shows how important it is to consider other components such as FVA and KVA.

14.6.7   DVA and own-debt

The issue of DVA in counterparty risk is a small part of a broader issue, which is the general incorporation of credit risk in liability measurement. Accountancy standards have generally evolved to a point where "own credit risk" can (and should) be incorporated in the valuation of liabilities. For example (relevant for the US), in 2006 the FASB[17] issued SFAS 157, relating to fair value measurements, which became effective in 2007. This permits a party's own credit quality to be included in the valuation of their liabilities, stating that "the most relevant measure of a liability always reflects the credit standing of the entity obliged to pay". Amendments to IAS 39 by the International Accounting Standards Board (IASB) in 2005 (relevant for the EU) also concluded that the fair value of a liability should include the credit risk associated with that liability. This position is reinforced with the introduction of IFRS 13 from the beginning of 2013.

DVA was a very significant question for banks in the years following the global financial crisis since their "own credit risk" (via credit spreads) experienced unprecedented volatility. Banks reported massive swings in accounting results as their credit spreads widened and tightened. Articles reporting such swings did not seem to take them seriously, making statements such as:

> The profits of British banks could be inflated by as much as £4bn due to a bizarre accounting rule that allows them to book a gain on the fall in the value of their debt.[18]
>
> [DVA is] a counter-intuitive but powerful accounting effect that means banks book a paper profit when their own credit quality declines.[19]

---

[17] Financial Accounting Standards Board of the United States.
[18] "Banks' profits boosted by DVA rule", *The Daily Telegraph*, 31st October 2011.
[19] "Papering over the great Wall St Massacre", efinancialnews, 26th October 2011.

There is logic to the use of DVA on own debt, since the fair value of a party's own bonds is considered to be the price that other entities are willing to pay for them. However, it is questionable whether a party would be able to buy back their own bonds without incurring significant funding costs. It therefore became typical for equity analysts to remove DVA from their assessment of a company's ongoing performance with the view that DVA is no more than a strange accounting effect.

14.6.8 DVA in derivatives

DVA in derivatives has probably received more scrutiny than in own debt since derivatives valuation has received much attention and is based on rigorous hedging arguments. The criticism of DVA stems mainly from the fact that it is not easily realisable (Gregory, 2009a). Other criticisms include the idea that the gains coming from DVA are distorted because other components are ignored. For example, Kenyon (2010) makes the point that if DVA is used, then the value of goodwill (which is zero at default) should also depend on a party's own credit quality. Losses in goodwill would oppose gains on DVA when a party's credit spread widened.

This debate really hinges around to what extent a party can ever *realise* a DVA benefit. Some of the arguments made in support of DVA have proposed that it can be monetised in the following ways:

- *Defaulting.* A party can obviously realise DVA by going bankrupt but, like an individual trying to monetise their own life insurance, this is a clearly not a very good strategy.
- *Unwinds and novations.* A party unwinding, novating or restructuring a transaction might claim to recognise some of the DVA benefit since this is paid out via a CVA gain for their counterparty. For example, monolines derived substantial benefits from unwinding transactions with banks,[20] representing large CVA-related losses for the banks and associated DVA gains for the monolines. The monoline MBIA monetised a multi-billion dollar derivatives DVA in an unwind of transactions with Morgan Stanley.[21] However, these examples occurred because the monolines were so close to default that the banks preferred to exit transactions prior to an actual credit event. Banks would have been much less inclined to unwind in a situation where monolines credit quality had not been so dramatically impaired. Furthermore, if a transaction is unwound, then it would generally need to be replaced. All things being equal, the CVA charged on the replacement transactions should wipe out the DVA benefit from the unwind.
- *Close-out process.* As discussed above (Section 14.6.5), another way to realise DVA might be in the close-out process in the event of the default of the counterparty. In the bankruptcy of Lehman Brothers, these practices have been common, although courts have not always favoured some of the large DVA (and other) claims.
- *Hedging.* An obvious way to attempt to monetise DVA is via hedging. The obvious hedging for CVA is to *short the credit of their counterparty*. This can be accomplished

---

[20] Due to different accountancy standards for insurance companies, the monolines did not see this gain as a DVA benefit.

[21] See "MBIA and Morgan Stanley settle bond fight", *Wall Street Journal*, 14th December 2011. Although MBIA paid Morgan Stanley $1.1 billion, the actual amount owed (as defined by Morgan Stanley's exposure) was several billion dollars. The difference can be seen as a DVA benefit gained by MBIA in the unwind.

by shorting bonds or buying CDS protection. It is possible that neither of these may be achievable in practice, but they are theoretically reasonable ways to hedge CVA. The CVA (loss) is monetised via paying the carry in the repo transaction or the premiums in the CDS protection position. However, in order to hedge DVA, a party would need to go *long their own credit*. This would be achieved by selling CDS protection on themselves (which is not possible[22]). An alternative is therefore to sell protection on similar correlated credits. This clearly creates a major problem, as banks would attempt to sell CDS protection on each other, and is also inefficient to the extent that the correlation is less than 100%. An extreme example of the latter problem was that some banks had sold protection on Lehman Brothers prior to their default as an attempted "hedge" against their DVA.

Most of the above arguments for monetising DVA are fairly weak. It is therefore not surprising that (although not mentioned in the original text), the Basel committee determined (BCBS, 2011c) that DVA should be de-recognised from the CVA capital charge (Section 8.7). This would prevent a more risky bank having a lower capital charge by virtue of DVA benefits opposing CVA losses. This is part of a more general point with respect to the Basel III capital charges focusing on a regulatory definition of CVA and not the CVA (and DVA) defined from an accounting standpoint. Even accounting standards have recognised problems with DVA with the FASB, for example, determining that DVA gains and losses be represented in a separate form of earnings known as "other comprehensive income".

Market practice has been somewhat divided over the inclusion of DVA in pricing, as shown in Figure 14.10, with many banks giving some, but not all, of the DVA benefit in pricing new transactions. Even those quoting that they "fully" include DVA would not

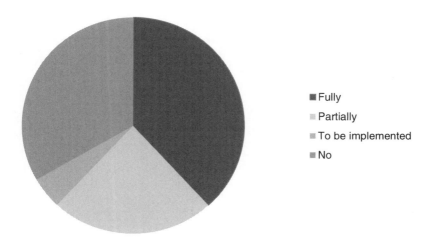

■ Fully

■ Partially

■ To be implemented

■ No

Figure 14.10   Market practice around including DVA in pricing.
Source: Deloitte/Solum CVA survey, 2013.

---

[22] Either because it is illegal or because of the extreme wrong-way risk it would create (Section 17.4.5), meaning that no party should be willing to enter such a trade except at a very low premium.

do this on all transactions (an obvious exception being where the DVA is bigger than the CVA and they would not "pay through mid").

Market practice has generally resolved the debate over DVA by considering it a funding benefit. Indeed, in the hedging argument above, buying back one's own debt could be seen as a practical alternative to the obviously flawed idea of selling CDS protection on one's own credit. However, buying back debt clearly creates a link to funding that must therefore be considered.

Most banks therefore see DVA as a funding benefit from a negative exposure (NEE) and believe there should be an associated funding cost from a positive exposure (EE). This funding benefit is seen as a more economically realistic version of DVA. We will therefore discuss FVA in the next chapter.

14.7 SUMMARY

This chapter has described the calculation and computation of CVA under the commonly made simplification of no wrong-way risk, which assumes that the credit exposure, default of the counterparty and recovery rate are not related. We have shown the relevant formulas for computing CVA and given simple examples. Incremental and marginal CVA have been introduced and illustrated for pricing new or existing transactions. We have discussed the specifics of calculating CVA, including collateral and netting, and covered some more complex aspects and numerical implementation. We have also discussed DVA, which is a controversial component of counterparty credit risk arising from a party's ability to value the potential benefits they make from defaulting. The theoretical background to DVA has been discussed and its inherent problems highlighted. We have described how most market participants view DVA as a funding benefit. In the next chapter, we will tackle the issue of funding and the calculation of FVA.

15
Funding Value Adjustment

> *Price is what you pay. Value is what you get.*
>
> Warren Buffett (1930–)

This chapter will describe the consideration of funding with respect to derivatives valuation through funding value adjustment (FVA). We will describe the nature of funding costs and benefits, and the underlying formulas and examples. We will also discuss the view of debt value adjustment (DVA) as a funding benefit, as mentioned in the last chapter.

FVA, like CVA, is predominantly considered for uncollateralised transactions. However, since no collateralisation is perfect, it will also be a component for collateralised ones (although in some cases this may be neglected). FVA was not considered prior to 2007 because unsecured funding for institutions, such as banks, was trivial, and could be achieved at more or less risk-free rates. (Bank credit spreads were typically only a few basis points prior to 2007. but since then have been more in the region of hundreds of basis points.) This means that transactions, especially those that are uncollateralised, are now typically treated including the party's own funding as a component of their price. This is the role of FVA, although its use in accounting statements has been more controversial. From a quantification point of view, FVA is similar in many ways to CVA, and many of the components to calculate the two are the same.

15.1 FUNDING AND DERIVATIVES

15.1.1 Why there are funding costs and benefits

Despite the increased use of collateral, a significant portion of OTC derivatives remain uncollateralised (for example, see Figure 3.2). This arises mainly due to the nature of the counterparties involved, such as corporates and sovereigns, without the liquidity and/or operational capacity to adhere to frequent collateral calls. In general, funding costs (and benefits) in derivatives portfolios can be seen as arising from the following situations:

- *Undercollateralisation.* Transactions that are undercollateralised give rise to funding costs and benefits. This includes completely undercollateralised (no CSA) but also cases of partial collateralisation (e.g. a two-way CSA with a material threshold). One-way CSAs are also a special case, since one party is collateralised whilst the other is not.
- *Non rehypothecation and segregation.* Even if a party can receive collateral, there is a question of whether or not this collateral can be used. If the collateral cannot be rehypothecated and/or must be segregated, this will deem it useless from a funding point of view.

Note that we will not include initial margin in the FVA discussion, as it will be considered separately as margin value adjustment (MVA). This chapter will therefore focus solely on variation margin considerations. This will often mean that the rehypothecation and segregation points above will not be important, since variation margin is generally reused. However, if variation margin is received in securities that cannot easily be rehypothecated into cash in the repo market or posted in another collateral agreement, then FVA will still apply.

Derivatives can be both assets and liabilities. When they are assets they create funding costs, but as liabilities they provide funding benefits. Transactions with large CVA (and DVA) components are also likely to have significant funding components.

In some sense, FVA is not a particularly new concept. Prior to the global financial crisis, LIBOR was used to discount cashflows: not because it was the risk-free rate (which in any case is a theoretical construct), but because it was a good approximation of a bank's unsecured funding costs that were considered short-term. Post-crisis, banks have realised that they cannot be as reliant on short-term funding or fund at LIBOR, and have therefore sought to incorporate these higher costs through FVA.

15.1.2   The nature of funding costs and benefits

The most common (but potentially misleading) way to explain funding costs and benefits is as follows. A party such as a bank trading an uncollateralised derivative will hedge it with transaction(s) that will typically be collateralised due to being transacted with other banks bilaterally or in an exchange/CCP environment. This is because banks aim to run mainly flat (hedged) derivatives books. The situation is shown in Figure 15.1. Consider what happens when the bank has a positive MTM on the client transaction(s): the hedge(s) will have an offsetting negative value and the bank will need to post collateral to cover this amount. The return paid on the collateral will typically be the OIS rate (Section 6.3.4). Hence, unless the bank can fund the collateral they post at the OIS rate, then there will be an associated cost. In recent years, funding costs have become significant and borrowing cash at the OIS rate is not practical for most parties (including investment banks). The cost above OIS of borrowing the collateral to post should therefore be considered. On the other hand, when the bank has a negative MTM on the client transaction(s), they will receive collateral from the hedge(s), which creates a funding benefit – they have effectively borrowed money at the OIS rate. Note that this funding benefit requires the reuse of the collateral (e.g. rehypothecation must be allowed).

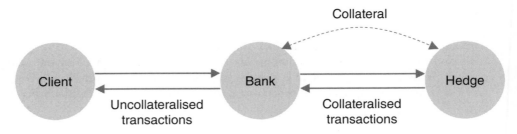

Figure 15.1   Illustration of the origin of funding costs and benefits. A bank trades with a client with no collateral arrangement and hedges with a collateralised transaction(s).

The above analogy is commonly used to justify FVA. For example:[1]

> When a dealer is in-the-money on the client trade, it would have to post collateral to its hedge counterparty, and would therefore need to borrow money from its internal treasury, which is a funding cost. ... If the dealer is out-of-the-money on the client trade, it receives collateral from its hedge counterparty, and if the collateral is assumed to be rehypothecable, the dealer should be able to lend that collateral to its treasury, which is a funding benefit.

Although useful for explanation purposes, the above analogy must not be taken too literally, as it may suggest the wrong FVA in certain situations. For example:

- *The bank does not hedge the transactions in question*. Here, there should still be a FVA adjustment, even though there is no movement of collateral.
- *Profit margin*. The profit that a bank makes on a transaction will not be a component of the MTM of the hedges and therefore will not be posted as collateral, and yet a FVA is likely to still be charged on this amount.
- *Intermediation/novation*. Here a bank might effectively step-in to a portfolio with an up-front payment but any hedges executed would likely be at par (zero MTM) and therefore not require collateral posting. This certainly does not mean that there would be no FVA incorporated in the price.
- *Restriking a portfolio*. If a bank restrikes the MTM of a client portfolio involving paying or receiving an up-front amount in cash but again without impacting the hedges, then there are still FVA considerations (indeed, FVA may be one reason for doing this, and is discussed in Chapter 19).
- *Change of CSA terms*. If the bank and client change their CSA terms (e.g. move from a one-way to two-way CSA), there will be FVA considerations even though the hedges are again not impacted.

The above points illustrate that the hedging argument is potentially misleading. In reality, funding costs arise from the uncollateralised positive MTM of a portfolio. This is a value that has not been realised and therefore has to be funded. By contrast, the uncollateralised negative MTM creates a funding benefit. From the definition of funding exposure (Section 7.5.1) and assuming reuse of collateral, then:

$$Exposure_{Funding} = MTM - Collateral \tag{15.1}$$

Funding costs (benefits) arise when the above term is positive (negative). Equation 7.7 shows this for the case where collateral may be segregated. The analogy in Figure 15.1 can still be used, but the hedge should be assumed to be an idealistic hedge (i.e. exactly the opposite of the transaction at all times) performed under a perfect collateral agreement (according to the terms at the start of Section 13.2.4). The actual hedge transactions are not relevant.

A simpler way to think of this funding cost (benefit) is that a party would receive (pay) the exposure (negative exposure) in cash if a transaction was terminated, and

---

[1] *Risk*, February 2011, pages 18–22.

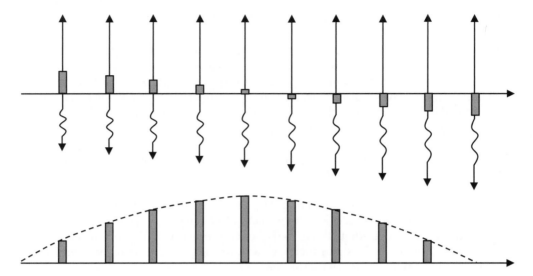

Figure 15.2   (Top) Illustration of the funding needs on a payer interest rate swap which arise due to the future cashflow differential. The grey bars show the net projected funding cost (based on risk-neutral valuation). (Bottom) The cumulative effect over time of the cashflow differential and resulting funding profile.

hence there is a funding position in order to maintain the transaction. Another way to think of funding costs is that they relate to cash paid or received in transactions (e.g. via upfront premiums or differentials in swap cashflows). Consider Figure 15.2, which shows the cashflows and associated funding considerations for a payer interest rate swap assuming an upwards-sloping yield curve (this is similar to the discussion on exposure in Section 7.3.3). In the early stages of the swap, the fixed cashflows being paid are expected (risk-neutrally) to be greater than the floating ones received. This creates a positive exposure that needs to be funded and is real, since cash is being paid out. The exposure increases cumulatively for the first five[2] payment dates and then reduces as the projected floating payments start to exceed the fixed ones. This creates an overall funding cost based on the discounted expected future value (EFV) of the swap. The corresponding receiver swap would have precisely the opposite profile, creating a funding benefit overall.

The key point is that, however it is defined, exposure drives a funding cost, just as it drives CVA. By symmetry, negative exposure drives a funding benefit analogous (or perhaps identical) to DVA.

15.1.3   Relationship to CVA and DVA

Although this will be discussed in more detail in Section 15.3.2, it is useful to characterise the approximate relationship between CVA, DVA and FVA (Figure 15.3). FVA is generally made up of funding cost adjustment (FCA) and funding benefit adjustment

---

[2] Note that the reduction in this case occurs exactly halfway through the profile. This is for illustration purposes only and the true profile depends on the precise shape of the yield curve.

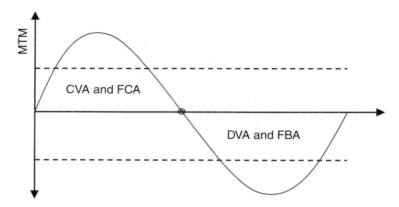

Figure 15.3   Illustration of the relationship between BCVA (CVA and DVA) and FVA (FCA and FBA). The dotted lines represent thresholds in the collateral agreement for each party.

(FBA). This is analogous to bilateral CVA, or BCVA (Section 14.6.4), which consists of CVA and DVA. CVA and FCA are related to the positive exposure, whilst DVA and FBA arise from negative exposure. A threshold in a collateral agreement should have the effect of reducing FCA and FBA (just as it does for CVA and DVA). Note that this may be asymmetric: for example, we would expect a one-way CSA acting against a party to remove their FBA, since they must post collateral against any negative MTM value, but leave the FCA unaffected.

Whilst the above is useful intuition, we will need to discuss more on the overlap between the above terms in more detail. In particular, as already noted in the previous chapter, there is general agreement that the DVA and FBA terms overlap.

15.1.4   FVA in financial statements

FVA has generally been reported in financial statements alongside CVA and DVA components. The inclusion by banks of FVA in pricing and accounting statements has been somewhat controversial as academics (notably Hull and White, 2012a) have argued that FVA should not be reflected in the valuation of derivatives. Furthermore, FVA is generally seen by banks as an internal cost of financing their uncollateralised derivatives portfolios, which involves their own cost of funding – this does not sit well with the accounting concept of exit price, which would involve another party's funding costs. Nevertheless, the adoption of FVA has become common in the last few years. FVA reporting is becoming the norm (Figure 15.4) and at the time of writing there are well over 20 banks (mainly the largest) that have reported an FVA number.[3] The total FVA reported by these banks amounts to many billions of US dollars.

---

[3] For example: ANZ, Bank of America, Barclays, BNP Paribas, Crédit Agricole, CIBC, Citigroup, Credit Suisse, Deutsche Bank, Goldman Sachs, HSBC, JP Morgan, Lloyds, Morgan Stanley, NAB, Nomura, RBC, RBS, SocGen, UBS and Wespac.

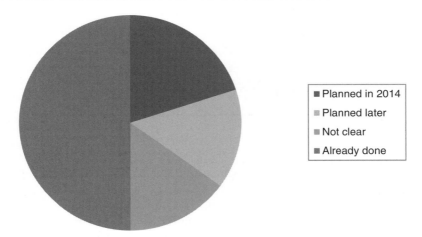

Figure 15.4   Market practice around including FVA in accounting.
Source: Solum FVA survey, 2015.

It is interesting to look at some of the statements made in this regard:

A fair-value adjustment was applied to account for the impact of incorporating the cost of funding into the valuation of uncollateralised derivatives. [Barclays, 2012 annual report]

The group has recognised a funding valuation adjustment to adjust for the net cost of funding certain uncollateralised derivative positions where the group considers that this cost is included in market pricing. [Lloyds Banking Group, 2012 annual report]

In general, FVA reflects a market funding risk premium inherent in the uncollateralised portion of derivative portfolios, and in collateralised derivatives where the terms of the agreement do not permit the reuse of the collateral received. [Citigroup, third quarter 2014]

The Firm implemented a funding valuation adjustments ("FVA") framework this quarter for its OTC derivatives and structured notes, reflecting an industry migration towards incorporating the cost or benefit of unsecured funding into valuations. For the first time this quarter, we were able to clearly observe the existence of funding costs in market clearing levels. As a result, the Firm recorded a $1.5b loss this quarter. [JP Morgan, fourth quarter 2014]

Note that whilst it is clear that banks consider FVA to arise from their own internal costs of funding uncollateralised derivatives, there is some reference to market pricing. Whilst the exit price concept is not completely compatible with the view of FVA as an internal cost, it is obviously acceptable to report FVA if market practice is to incorporate this into pricing. Hence, the inclusion of FVA (and indeed any other xVA component) in financial statements can be supported via a self-fulfilling prophecy.

Let us also use the case of JP Morgan to illustrate an important aspect of banks reporting FVA.[4] JP Morgan reported an FVA charge (as discussed below, this charge is likely to be more akin to what is defined here as FCA) of $1.5 billion in its fourth quarter earnings in 2013, and noted that future FVA/DVA volatility was expected to be significantly lower as a result. In order to understand this statement, assume that JP Morgan used an effective funding spread of 60 bps in the calculation. This would therefore imply a sensitivity of $25 million per basis point. In the same period, JP Morgan's DVA had changed by $536 million (a loss) since their credit default swap (CDS) spread had tightened from 93 bps to 70 bps. This suggests an opposite $23 million per basis point sensitivity for DVA.[5] Hence, if JP Morgan's credit spread widens by 1 bp, then they expect to lose approximately $25 million due to increased funding cost but gain $23 million in DVA benefit.[6] It therefore appears as if FVA is being used to partially cancel the impact of DVA. This overlap will be discussed in more detail below, together with the criticisms and definition problems associated with FVA (Section 15.3).

15.2 FUNDING VALUE ADJUSTMENT

15.2.1   Intuitive definition

Since the important paper of Piterbarg (2010), there has been a significant theoretical effort put into characterising FVA. The mathematical derivation for FVA has been made by a number of authors, notably Burgard and Kjaer (2011a, 2011b and 2012b). They also show that the precise formula achieved depends on the assumptions made, and therefore there is no unique definition of FVA. For example, an assumption that leads to the setup discussed below is that excess collateral can be used to buy back one's own debt and therefore gives a funding benefit. We give an intuitive derivation of the FVA formula that is consistent with this more formal approach. We will initially assume a completely uncollateralised situation but will then discuss how situations such as partial collateralisation can be treated quite naturally.

According to the discussion in Section 15.1.2, FVA exists due to the funding associated with the MTM of a given portfolio. To calculate FVA we first need to know the expected MTM over the lifetime of the portfolio. In Section 7.2.1, this was introduced and defined as the expected future value (EFV). The EFV therefore will define the amount that has to be funded (if positive) or that will create a funding benefit (if negative). As with xVA in general, we will need to integrate over the EFV profile through time and take into account the cost of funding at each point in time defined as a funding spread (FS) with respect to the rate used for valuation (e.g. OIS). Hence, the intuitive FVA formula is:

$$FVA = -\sum_{i=1}^{m} EFV\left(t_i\right) \times FS(t_i) \times (t_i - t_{i-1}) \times S\left(t_i\right) \tag{15.2}$$

---

[4] Note that this analysis is based on market information and the statements of JP Morgan, and is not their own analysis.

[5] The loss of $536 million divided by the change in CDS of 23 bps.

[6] Ignoring any basis between their own CDS and funding costs.

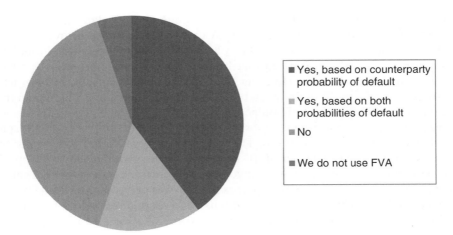

Figure 15.5   Market practice around including survival probabilities in FVA computation. *Source*: Solum CVA Survey 2015.

Note that $FS(t_j)$ is the forward funding spread for the time t_i and that the *EFV* should be discounted. The term $S(.)$ represents a survival probability for either or both of the two parties concerned (the probability of no default). This formula would be expected to produce a negative (funding cost) for the example in Figure 15.2 whilst the schematic profile in Figure 15.3 would be expected to produce a small or zero FVA due to a cancellation of funding costs and benefits across time. The implementation of the above formula is often done via a CVA-like representation (Equation 14.6) using an LGD of 100% with (spot) funding spreads in place of the credit spread.

Regarding the adjustment for survival probability in Equation 15.2, this is similar to the discussion on close-out assumptions for CVA and DVA in the last chapter (Section 14.6.5) and depends on whether or not funding costs would be part of the close-out amount in a default scenario. As shown in Figure 15.5, market practice is divided on which survival probabilities to adjust for in the FVA calculation. Using the counterparty survival probability would be most consistent with a likely discounting approach, where the counterparty's default probability would be included. Furthermore, some banks adjust FCA and FBA terms differently; for example, to reflect a view that they would claim funding costs but not pay funding benefits in a default scenario.

Equation 15.2 represents the overall economic value adjustment associated with respect to funding without showing costs and benefits explicitly. This is not problematic in the completely uncollateralised and symmetric[7] case, but does not give any insight into other cases such as partial collateralisation. However, a very simple transformation can produce a more intuitive formula: recall the definitions of EE and NEE from Sections 7.2.3 and 7.2.7 respectively. EE is the expected positive value whilst NEE is the expected negative value; rather trivially, we therefore have $EE + NEE = EFV$ and so can decompose the above formula into:

---

[7] Meaning we consider funding costs and benefits to be associated with the same funding spread.

$$FVA = -\sum_{i=1}^{m} EE\left(t_i\right) \times FS_B\left(t_i\right) \times \left(t_i - t_{i-1}\right) - \sum_{i=1}^{m} NEE\left(t_i\right) \times FS_L\left(t_i\right) \times \left(t_i - t_{i-1}\right)$$

$$= FCA + FBA \tag{15.3}$$

In certain situations this might complicate things unnecessarily, since EFV is relatively easy to compute, depending mainly on forward rates, whilst EE/NEE are more complex to quantify and depend on factors such as volatilities. However, the advantage of Equation 15.3 is that it decomposes FVA into the cost (FCA) and benefit (FBA) components, and uses quantities that would already be calculated for CVA and DVA purposes.[8] This will allow the treatment of aspects such as one-way CSAs and any other asymmetries. Indeed, we could include different funding spreads to express a view that funding costs and benefits should not be treated symmetrically. In Equation 15.3, this is expressed via $FS_B(.)$ and $FS_L(.)$ representing the funding spreads for borrowing and lending respectively. However, in this case the FVA calculation would need to be done at the entire portfolio level (as opposed to the netting set level for CVA/DVA), since MTM and collateral values can be offset at this level (discussed later in Section 15.2.5).

Similarly to equation (14.12) and assuming a flat funding spread curve, we can also have the following simple approximation for FVA, expressed as a spread:

$$FVA \approx -FS_B \times EPE - FS_L \times ENE \tag{15.4}$$

Spreadsheet 15.1   Example FVA calculation

15.2.2   Discounting approach

In the completely uncollateralised case where borrowing and lending rates are the same, the application of the FVA formula is equivalent to discounting at a rate including the funding spread, as illustrated in Figure 15.6 (to be compared with Figure 4.12). This method is a simple way to incorporate funding for uncollateralised transactions that is commonly used.

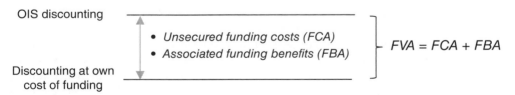

Figure 15.6   Illustration of equivalence between discounting at own cost of funding versus applying a standard FVA adjustment.

---

[8] When collateral is involved there is a potential difference relating to the margin period of risk that will be discussed in Section 15.2.3.

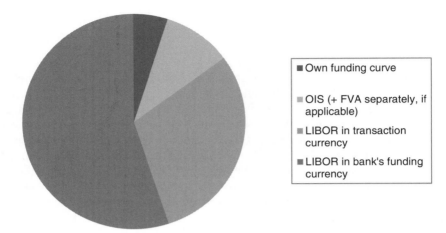

Figure 15.7   Market practice for valuing uncollateralised transactions.
Source: Solum CVA survey, 2015.

Figure 15.7 shows market practice for valuing uncollateralised transactions. Banks generally do not apply the same discounting assumption used for collateralised transactions (e.g. OIS discounting). Without a collateral agreement then a rate such as OIS only has relevance if viewed as a good proxy for the risk-free rate. Although a small proportion of banks do value uncollateralised transactions with OIS discounting (and make an FVA adjustment), the majority report using LIBOR discounting. This is consistent with the historical view stated in Section 15.1.1 that the discounting rate should be primarily related to the cost of funding unsecured transactions rather than some risk-free proxy.

To give an example of the simple FVA adjustment for an uncollateralised portfolio, we return to the example in Section 14.6.6 in the last chapter.[9] The EE and NEE profiles are shown in Figure 15.8 together with the EFV (which is the sum of the two). The FVA values are shown in Table 15.1, assuming a flat and symmetric funding spread of 100 bps. The FVA is positive overall since the portfolio has a net funding benefit (EFV negative and FBA therefore bigger than FCA). If the cashflows are discounted at the funding cost (the original discounting rate plus the 100 bps funding spread) then the same result is achieved: the discounted valuation would be higher by the FVA benefit of 0.0640).

There are two more points to notice from the results in Table 15.1. Firstly, adjustment by survival probabilities can have a material impact on the resulting FVA. As shown in Figure 15.5, there is no market consensus on this point. Secondly, the FBA value is close to the DVA number shown in the last chapter in Table 14.7. This is related to the double-counting associated with DVA and FBA that will be discussed in Section 15.3.1.

---

[9] As in the last chapter, we also assume that the counterparty's and party's own credit spread (CDS) curves are flat at 200 bps and 100 bps respectively, and both LGDs are 60%.

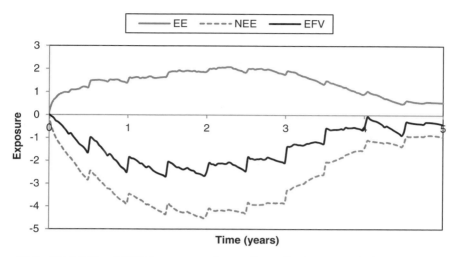

Figure 15.8 EE, NEE and EFV for an example uncollateralised swap portfolio.

Table 15.1 FVA values for the portfolio of four swap transactions with a funding spread assumption of 100 bps. Results with different adjustments for survival probabilities are shown.

	No survival adjustment	Counterparty survival adjustment	Joint survival adjustment
FCA	−0.0690	−0.0640	−0.0617
FBA	0.1377	0.1281	−0.1237
FVA	0.0687	0.0641	0.0620

15.2.3   More complex cases

The discount curve method is clearly a simple way to take funding into account, but there are two obvious drawbacks with this approach. Firstly, it implicitly assumes a symmetry between funding costs and funding benefits. Secondly, it does not allow the treatment of situations such as thresholds, or one-way CSAs. These aspects will be considered in more detail below. Equation 15.3 can be used directly to deal with more complicated FVA cases where symmetry does not permit simple calculations such as discounting with the cost of funding. The most obvious cases to be considered are those of imperfect collateralisation such as:

- two-way CSAs with material threshold and/or minimum transfer amounts;
- one-way CSAs; and
- collateral that cannot be rehypothecated.

To properly account for the above, all that is required is to model the EE/NEE consistently with the collateral terms in question and using the definition of funding exposure instead of credit exposure (Section 7.5.2). This has been discussed already for CVA computation in Section 14.5. There is just one caveat regarding the margin period of

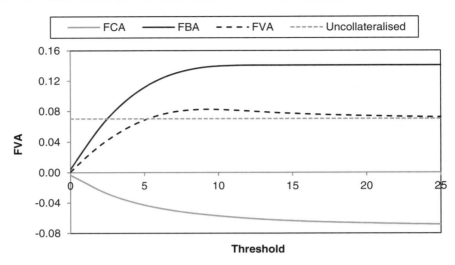

Figure 15.9   FVA for a two-way CSA as a function of the threshold.

risk (MPR). In CVA/DVA calculations, the MPR reflects the relevant time horizon to consider over the default and close-out period (Section 6.6.2) and is typically taken to be ten business days or more. For FVA purposes, the equivalent time horizon should only be the time taken to receive collateral in a normal (not default) scenario and would therefore assumed to be much shorter. This may create a practical problem, since a CVA calculation may use a step-size of the MPR to represent collateral (Section 11.2.5) and an FVA calculation will ideally use a different step-size.

Let us first consider the impact of thresholds. A positive exposure creates a funding cost only up to the threshold amount, after which collateral would be taken and the exposure above the threshold would essentially be capped, reducing the FCA term (Figure 15.3). Correspondingly, the negative exposure defining the funding benefit would also be capped (at a potentially different threshold), reducing the FBA term. Figure 15.9 shows the impact of an increasing bilateral threshold for the swap portfolio shown previously, assuming no delay in receiving collateral. At a zero threshold, the FVA is very close to zero and driven by the minimum transfer amount of 0.5. As the threshold increases, so do both the FCA and FBA terms tending towards the uncollateralised (no CSA) value of 0.0641 shown in Table 15.1. Due to the asymmetry of the portfolio, the increase in the FCA and FBA is not the same, and the overall FVA term does not approach the uncollateralised value monotonically.

Note that small funding costs theoretically occur in the zero-threshold, two-way CSA case since OIS discounting alone requires continuous collateral posting and zero minimum transfer amounts. However, market practice is generally to ignore such impacts.

The case of a one-way CSA also fits naturally into the framework from Equation 15.3, since it simply requires the correct EE and NEE quantification with an infinite threshold on one side. This is shown in Figure 15.10, assuming the one-way CSA is in the favour of the counterparty and the threshold for the party posting is zero.[10] The EE is virtually

---

[10] This type of CSA is relatively common for high-quality entities such as sovereigns and supranationals.

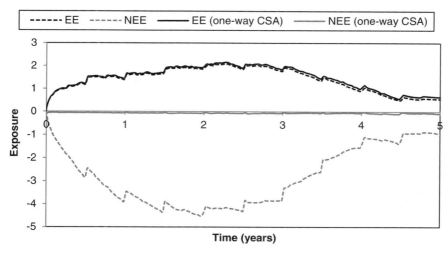

Figure 15.10   EE and NEE for a one-way CSA in favour of the counterparty compared to the uncollateralised values.

Table 15.2   FVA values for a swap portfolio with a funding spread assumption of 100 bps comparing a one-way CSA with the uncollateralised case.

	No CSA	One-way CSA
FCA	–0.0690	–0.0760
FBA	0.1377	0.0072
FVA	0.0687	–0.0688

unchanged except for the small impact of the MTA (the need to post collateral actually makes the funding exposure slightly higher than in the uncollateralised case), whilst the NEE is virtually zero since the party must post collateral against any beneficial negative exposure. This means that the FCA is similar to the uncollateralised case whilst the FBA almost disappears. The results are shown in Table 15.2, with FVA now being an overall cost.

15.2.4   Contingent FVA

Note also that FVA may sometimes be contingent. Consider the rating-linked CSA parameters shown in Table 6.2. Parties with ratings of A+/A1 or below would be posting collateral at a zero threshold and there would therefore be virtually no FVA. However, if either party were upgraded, this would create an FBA benefit and an associated FCA loss for their counterparty due to the need to post less collateral (higher threshold). We illustrate the change in FVA for different thresholds in Table 15.3 for the example in the last section. This shows the gain in FVA when a party's own threshold increases and a loss when their counterparty moves to a higher threshold. Note that, since the example is for an at-market portfolio, these impact do not arise from the necessity of one party to post collateral immediately but the change in future expected collateral payments.

Table 15.3 FVA values as a function of thresholds for a swap portfolio with a funding spread assumption of 100 bps.

	Own threshold			Counterparty threshold	
	0	5	10	5	10
FCA	−0.0034	−0.0009	−0.0009	−0.0459	−0.0607
FBA	0.0042	0.1133	0.1422	0.0030	0.0030
FVA	0.0008	0.1124	0.1413	−0.0429	−0.0577

Note that the above effect is difficult to price because it would require ratings transaction probabilities to be defined. It is therefore commonly ignored or priced only approximately. This is in contrast to the initial margin posting that may be contingent to ratings discussed later in Section 16.2.1, where the requirement to hold a liquidity buffer means that the full effect (for a certain number of rating changes) is generally priced in fully. Since the development of FVA, contractual features such as ratings triggers have been seen as a difficult legacy problem from a valuation perspective.

15.2.5   Allocation of FVA

Like CVA, it is important to be able to allocate FVA to transaction level for pricing and valuation purposes. One advantage of the framework presented above is that the FVA is additive across transactions in the symmetric case (funding costs and benefits are equal). To understand this, suppose we are quantifying a new transaction with a net funding cost at some tenor. This funding cost will either increase existing funding costs at this tenor or reduce benefits, and the impact will be the same. However, if we assess costs and benefits differently, it will be important to know if the existing portfolio (total transactions) has a net cost or benefit at a given tenor and the resulting impact that a new transaction has on this with asymmetric funding assumptions..

Symmetric funding assumptions are useful, since otherwise there would be a portfolio effect similar to the effect of netting characterised in Section 7.4. However, whereas CVA must be calculated at the netting set level, funding would need to be considered at the overall portfolio level and incremental exposure calculations (Section 10.6) would be needed in order to allocate funding at transaction level at the total portfolio level. This would lead to very significant computational requirements for pricing new transactions and allocating FVA to existing ones. Albanese and Iabichino (2013) discuss computational aspects in such a situation.

In symmetric cases, the above methodology will correctly represent overall funding costs across transactions. For example, consider the total funding cost of a non-collateralised transaction hedged via a partially collateralised transaction represented via the sum of the relevant FVAs. Suppose an uncollateralised receiver swap has an overall funding benefit. By symmetry, the payer hedge will have an equal and opposite funding cost. However, this cost will be smaller due to the ability to receive collateral above the threshold. Hence, the combination of the two transactions has an overall funding benefit. This can be seen as the benefit from receiving collateral above the threshold on the hedge but not posting collateral on the uncollateralised transaction minus the cost from posting on the hedge and not receiving.

15.3   THE PRACTICAL USE OF FVA

15.3.1   Link to DVA

In the discussion on monetising DVA (Section 14.6.8), it was mentioned that DVA is generally now seen as a funding benefit. Indeed, there is a generally agreed double-counting (e.g. Tang and Williams, 2010) of DVA and FBA illustrated in Figure 15.11, meaning that only one should be considered. Comparison of the DVA and FBA formulas in Equations 14.10c and 15.3 respectively does indeed suggest that they are equivalent, since the NEE term appears in both and LGD and default probabilities terms in the former are similar to the forward funding spreads in the latter. Hence, we can see both DVA and FBA as the benefit of a negative MTM: the former because in default some of this is not paid whilst the latter as a funding benefit. Morini and Prampolini (2010) first looked theoretically at this effect and showed that explicit inclusion of DVA leads to a duplication of the funding benefit in a transaction and therefore would be equivalent to discounting cashflows twice.

Although they are similar both conceptually and mathematically, there are differences between DVA and FBA, notably:

- *Spread.* The calculation of DVA requires the risk-neutral default probability of the party, which is most obviously derived from their credit spread, probably defined via the CDS market. FBA, on the other hand, requires a party's own cost of funding, which would be more closely linked to their bond spread.
- *Portfolio effect.* DVA, like CVA, should be applied at the netting set level with respect to the close-out process in a default. As discussed above, FBA would be relevant for an entire portfolio across counterparties or at the transaction level, depending on the assumptions made.

The choice of DVA or FBA will therefore have implications on pricing and valuation, and will define the extent of the coherence with regulatory capital and accounting frameworks.

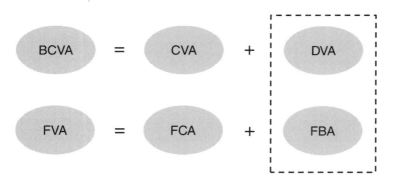

Figure 15.11   Illustration of the link between FBA and DVA.

15.3.2   CVA/DVA/FVA framework

To avoid double-counting of a funding benefit, there are two obvious potential frameworks for treating counterparty risk and funding consistently. These are:

- *CVA and symmetric funding* (CVA + FCA + FBA). This would ignore the DVA benefit on the basis that monetisation of DVA (purely as a self-default component) is problematic (Section 14.6.8).
- *Bilateral CVA and asymmetric funding* (CVA + DVA + FCA). This includes DVA alongside a funding cost only.

The symmetric funding case would be more consistent with Basel III capital rules where DVA cannot be recognised (Section 14.6.8) but inconsistent with accounting requirements (e.g. IFRS 13) where DVA must be included (Section 14.6.2). Symmetric funding may also be more closely aligned to the treatment of funding in a bank where a "funding desk" (typically, the treasury department) considers both funding costs and benefits, and views that two hedged transactions with the same collateral terms (but potentially different counterparties) have a net zero funding cost as their benefits and costs cancel perfectly.[11] It also allows a CVA desk to consider CVA but ignore DVA, which may be considered to be a benefit that is hard to monetise.

The asymmetric funding is obviously more consistent with accounting standards but at odds with Basel III capital requirements. It may lead to the CVA desk attempting to hedge DVA, which creates a problem since only funding costs and not associated benefits would be considered by the funding unit. Furthermore, incorporating DVA into credit hedges will likely worsen any capital relief achievable under Basel III.

Market practice over the last few years has generally evolved to consider the symmetric funding case most relevant in terms of pricing (Figure 15.12). This is consistent with

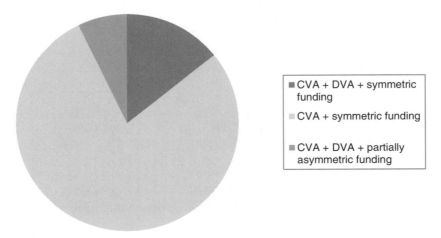

Figure 15.12   Market practice around including DVA and funding benefits in pricing.
Source: Deloitte/Solum CVA Survey 2013.

---

[11] Aside from the time delay in receiving collateral, discussed in Section 15.3.5.

the Basel III capital requirements, the view that DVA is a "bizarre accounting rule" and hard to monetise, and that funding of derivatives should consider both costs and benefits. It is obviously incompatible with accounting requirements, but we will see below that banks are circumventing this problem in their FVA reporting.

15.3.3   Is FVA really symmetric?

One of the interesting aspects of FVA is that different frameworks can be derived depending on the assumptions made regarding the funding instruments that a party has at their disposal. For example, Burgard and Kjaer (2011b) assume that cash generated can be used to buy back bonds, whilst Albanese and Iabichino (2013) propose a view where excess cash for derivatives books is an unstable source of funding and should be assumed to only earn the risk-free lending rate.[12] Burgard and Kjaer (2012b) also assume asymmetry regarding unsecured borrowing and lending where unsecured lending may be assumed to yield only the risk-free rate,[13] whilst borrowing will require the unsecured term funding rate. Choosing between the extremes where a negative MTM on a derivatives portfolio is either a full funding benefit or of no practical use (i.e. there are no activities in the bank that can benefit from this liability) is clearly difficult. A cash-rich bank may find it difficult to justify pricing in net funding benefits into a transaction such as in Table 15.1. It may also be that market participants do not view funding as completely symmetric but require the tractability in this framework where funding costs can be additive over transactions. Note that even in the standard symmetric funding framework, FVA may not be treated completely symmetrically; for example, banks may use slightly skewed funding spreads for costs and benefits, and may include survival probabilities differently for FCA and FBA.

At the time of writing, most banks use the framework outlined above, although there are criticisms in the market that some banks are overly aggressive in their approach (or lack thereof) to FVA.[14] There is also the debate of the reality of FVA and where it should be reflected on the balance sheet, as discussed in Section 15.3.5. The Totem consensus pricing service (Section 15.3.6) also broadly supports symmetric funding assumptions for most contributors.

15.3.4   Defining the funding rate

Section 12.5.1 discussed the definition of funding curves in relation to quantifying funding. We now look a little closer into the cost of funding and the relationship to credit spreads and risk-free rates, with Figure 15.13 depicting the various components. Note that the terms on the left-hand side are all theoretical constructs, while those on the right are market observables.

As discussed in Section 13.2.2, OIS is the obvious proxy for the risk-free rate, and LIBOR rates could be seen as representing a small amount of short-term funding potentially related to generic bank credit risk on top of this – indeed, OIS and LIBOR rates diverged

---

[12] Furthermore, in Burgard and Kjaer (2012b), symmetric funding arises when a zero-coupon bond is a sole funding instrument, whilst the asymmetric funding is a consequence of assuming a single bond with recovery is freely tradable.

[13] Of course, unsecured lending can yield more than the risk-free (or OIS) rate, but this then involves taking additional credit risk.

[14] "Small banks underpricing FVA, dealers claim", *Risk*, 9th April 2015.

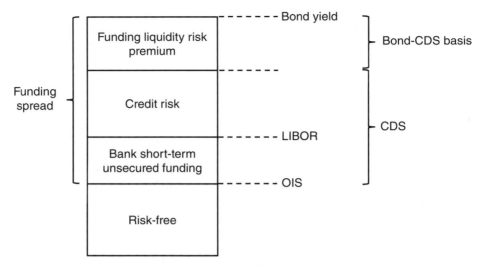

Figure 15.13 Illustration of the differing funding rates together with the CDS–bond basis (note that a negative basis is illustrated, although this does not have to be the case in practice). The unsecured funding spread is defined with respect to the OIS rate.

mainly due the perceived worsening of bank's credit quality). There is then the cost of the longer-term credit risk of banks and their funding risk premium on top of that. In terms of defining these components, the CDS market could be seen as providing the most natural price for traded credit risk. Finally, the bond yield may be assumed to represent additional liquidity risk on top of the credit risk (e.g. Longstaff et al., 2005) which compensates a bondholder for a potential illiquidity when selling a bond. This represents (by convention) a negative CDS–bond basis (bond spreads higher than CDS spreads) – although this does not necessarily have to be the case, and nor has it always been the case historically.

Defining the funding spread to use in the FVA formula is difficult. Derivatives, due to their dynamic nature and the funding approach of banks, are not *term-funded*.[15] Traditionally, the funding has been generally considered to be short-term, but regulation (e.g. the liquidity coverage ratio and net stable funding ratio – Section 8.8.4) is pushing banks to rely less on short-term funding. Overall, this means that a party defining their appropriate funding curve represents a difficult and subjective problem.

15.3.5   The Hull and White and accounting arguments

FVA is problematic, since including a party's individual funding cost in the price of a derivative breaks the price symmetry of CVA/DVA and goes against basic foundations of valuation, notably those used in risk-neutral pricing and the accounting notion of exit price. FVA also suggests that parties may be unable to agree a price due to their unique funding costs and that arbitrage opportunities will therefore be present in the market.

There has been a significant amount of discussion around the validity of FVA in pricing and valuation. This was largely catalysed by Hull and White (2012a), who argued

---

[15] Meaning, for example, that a five-year swap is not funded via a five-year bond issue.

that it was not appropriate to use FVA in pricing decisions, nor report FVA in financial statements. The Hull and White argument can be broadly explained as follows:

- standard valuation arguments dictate that derivative cashflows should be valued in a risk-neutral world using a risk-free discount rate to calculate the expected cashflows;
- a transaction should be assessed based on its expected return and not the average funding costs of the entity making the calculation; and
- if funding costs are applied, then arbitrage opportunities will exist via transacting with parties that have different funding costs and who will therefore price FVA differently.

There have been opponents of the Hull and White view (for example, see Carver, 2012, Castagna, 2012 and Laughton and Vaisbrot, 2012, with a response in Hull and White, 2012b). An alternative general view is that funding costs prove that standard risk-neutral pricing assumptions do not hold (not vice versa). It should also be noted that funding costs are generally not considered when buying assets (e.g. US treasury bonds), since the assets can be readily repoed to generate cash. Derivatives, on the other hand, cannot be repoed, and FVA may therefore be considered relevant – indeed, Burgard and Kjaer (2011b) note that FVA disappears if the derivative can be used as collateral. There are other practical problems with the Hull and White view. For example, they propose (Hull and White 2014) that a bank's treasury should not charge the derivatives desk a funding cost, which, even if correct, is a long way from reality in most banks.

Even if one were to reject the Hull and White view, there are some clear problems with FVA. The first is that funding costs represent credit risk and yet credit risk has already been priced in via CVA. The second is that the funding cost applied to a derivative transaction should be the incremental one and not the average funding cost of the party in question. Indeed, this is why many assets have no funding costs, since they can be effectively self-funded via repo. These examples are illustrated in Figure 15.14. On the left-hand side, a bank charges a counterparty CVA based on the counterparty credit spread of 100 bps. However, the bank's funding cost is also 100 bps, which they charge via FVA. But surely the bank's funding cost is related to the credit risk of their counterparty and so they are in danger of effectively charging CVA twice?

Hull and White (2012a) argue that the apparent excess funding cost that the derivatives desk faces should not be considered when a trading decision is made. On the right-hand side of Figure 15.14, suppose the bank now transactions with a less risky counterparty with a credit spread of 50 bps. Should they charge an FVA based on their higher funding

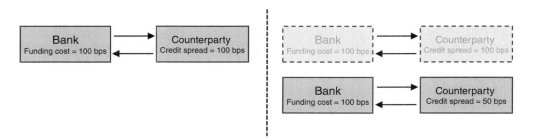

Figure 15.14   Illustration of the difficulty with applying FVA.

cost when this transaction should actually bring their overall cost of funding down? When buying poor-quality assets, lenders should be charged a higher funding rate than for high-quality assets: the quality of the derivative should drive the asset's funding cost. But the quality of a derivative portfolio is already priced in with the CVA.

Furthermore, FVA creates a problem for accountants, since a party's own cost of funding does not represent the correct component to be included in an exit price. Indeed, FVA as an exit price component could be extremely problematic: in exiting a derivative with a larger FCA (FBA), it is optimal to find a counterparty with a lower (higher) cost of funding. This would imply that funding spreads would be transaction-specific and change with market factors.

15.3.6   Resolving the FVA debate

Some of the above issues have generally been resolved via a compromise approach to FVA without the need to prove any of the aforementioned points as definitely correct or incorrect. One important idea is that only the funding liquidity risk premium (Figure 15.13) should be priced into FVA. This is the result of Morini and Prampolini (2010), who state that this liquidity spread (or equivalently the CDS–bond basis) contributes as a net funding cost to the value of a transaction. Hull and White (2014) seem to accept this viewpoint by stating that "FVA is justifiable only for the part of a company's credit spread that does not reflect default risk". The liquidity risk premium component of the credit spread is sometimes estimated from the CDS–bond basis, which is defined as the CDS spread minus the bond yield spread. If the CDS spread is assumed to be a "pure credit spread" reflecting only default risk, then the liquidity component of the credit spread equals the negative of the CDS–bond basis. This is often known as liquidity value adjustment (LVA), which might be defined to account for "liquidity related costs not already accounted for by the CVA".

Although the use of the funding liquidity risk premium in pricing and accounting is not always obvious, it can be generally identified either explicitly or implicitly. For example, a "market funding risk premium" is mentioned in the Citigroup statement quoted in Section 15.1.4. Barclays state in their 2012 annual report using a scaling factor when calculating FVA to estimate "the extent to which the cost of funding is incorporated into observed traded levels". Banks may use an "own internal cost of funds curve" (Figure 12.11) for FVA purposes that will likely be lower than their actual unsecured funding rate as implied via bond spreads.

Referring to the different funding rates explained previously (Figure 15.13), we explain the above view in Figure 15.15. Banks generally discount uncollateralised transactions at LIBOR, which already incorporates some short-term funding costs. To get to the banks' full cost of funding would involve adding both the full funding cost related to their own credit risk and the funding liquidity risk premium. However, the former component should have already been priced in via the CVA and so only the latter component is included.

Risk-neutral pricing should depend on the cost of replicating a position and should therefore refer to internal funding costs. However, as noted above from the accounting point of view of exit price, it is the funding cost of the counterparty with whom you exit the transaction that is relevant. The problem of course is that you do not know who this counterparty is, and any assumptions over choosing the "best counterparty" (e.g. the

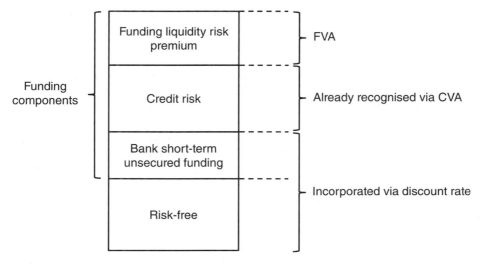

Figure 15.15   Illustration of the role of FVA.

one with the lowest funding costs) are subjective and hard to defend. Another pragmatic solution to the FVA debate which is supported by the above representation is a move to using a "market cost of funding" curve (Figure 12.11) derived from observable funding costs of other banks rather than an internal assessment.

Note that whether or not there is agreement on the above is a somewhat academic argument. Markit's Totem[16] service provides consensus market prices (each firm submits prices for specific transactions and is returned information on the distribution of prices) from which FVA levels can be extracted (see Section 19.2.2). This and anecdotal evidence from the industry suggests that at the current time, most banks have converged to pricing funding using a spread in the region of 50 bps. The qualitative view of what this spread should represent may differ significantly between market participants, but the resulting FVA shows less variation. Note that the spread used for pricing FVA will likely change when there are significant changes in funding levels in the market.

15.3.7   Remaining issues

There are also opposing views on the correct FVA setup, such as those of Albanese et al. (2015), who argue that FVA losses should not hit earnings and instead should give rise to a capital adjustment. Some banks are reported to be reassessing their calculation framework with this in mind.[17] The Albanese et al. argument is that FVA cancels across the entire balance sheet of a firm, with the shareholders seeing a cost of funding with an equal and opposite benefit to bondholders. Indeed, Burgard and Kjaer (2012b) note that derivatives funding strategies can result in windfalls or shortfalls to bondholders in a firm's default. From an accounting point of view, the FVA cancellation argument

---

[16] See www.markit.com/product/totem.
[17] For example, see "The black art of FVA, part III: a \$4 billion mistake?", *Risk*, 2nd April 2015.

requires fair value to be represented as a combined value to the shareholders and bond-holder of a firm (which is not the case).

In summary, there are currently at least two key questions around the use of FVA:

- What funding strategy should be assumed in defining FVA? Should it be assumed that excess cash can always be recycled as in the framework described above?
- What is the correct definition of fair value? Should it focus only on shareholders or rather look at the combined view of shareholders and bondholders? In the former case, an FVA accounting adjustment is relevant (as is currently market practice), but in the latter there need be no adjustment since FVA represents an internal transfer from shareholders to bondholders.

Another potential issue is that FVA charges are generally not counterparty-specific. Economically, this does not make sense, since trading with poor-quality counterparties will likely drive up funding costs and vice versa. Such effects might only be applied in an ad hoc manner; for example, high-quality counterparties may not be charged a full FVA. Another point to mention is that the set-up of a bank may lead to an incorrect FVA being charged. Treasury will likely dictate a funding rate to derivatives desks or an xVA desk. To the extent that the treasurer defines such a funding cost, it will likely be passed on – even if this is not viewed as the correct economic cost of funding.

Market participants have generally aligned pricing and valuation, i.e. the components that are priced into a transaction are also reflected in accounting statements. This is not surprising, but some authors argue that the entry price of a transaction can be entity-specific and subjective, but that the exit price for fair value accounting purposes must respect concepts such as the law of one price and should not therefore contain compo-nents such as FVA. That said, as seen from Figure 12.11, there are still differences in FVA from pricing and valuation perspectives, and so transactions may generate profits or losses based on their prices compared with the accounting valuations.

Although some sort of broad market standard exists with respect to the use of FVA, there will still clearly be much debate about its precise use in pricing and financial state-ments. Not surprisingly, given the number of banks reporting FVA in their accounts, the Basel Committee have launched an FVA project to determine their position with respect to this adjustment.[18]

15.3.8   Example

We show the same example as shown in Section 14.6.6 of the last chapter, but have in-cluded FVA in the pricing according the "CVA + symmetric funding" pricing approach (Section 15.3.2). Table 15.4 shows that the move to a two-way CSA (not favoured in the CVA/DVA world, as shown previously in Table 14.7) is now beneficial due to a reduction in both CVA and FCA, which dominate the loss from a lower FBA (or DVA).[19]

In Table 15.5 we show the same situation but from the counterparty's viewpoint. Note that price symmetry is broken and the parties (in theory) would not agree on a price. However, another consequence of the price symmetry is that they both gain from the

---

[18] See "Basel Committee launches FVA project", *Risk*, 24th April 2015.
[19] In this case we consider FBA and not DVA, which results in some small differences.

Table 15.4   CVA and FVA values for a swap portfolio with counterparty and own credit spread assumptions of 200 and 100 bps respectively. Funding costs are assumed to be 100 bps for both counterparties[20] and LGDs are assumed to be 60%. Results with and without a two-way CSA are shown.

	No CSA	Two-way CSA
CVA	−0.1309	−0.0408
FCA	−0.0706	−0.0034
FBA (DVA)	0.1407	0.0042
Total	−0.0608	−0.0400

Table 15.5   As Table 15.4 but from the counterparty's point of view.

	No CSA	Two-way CSA
CVA	−0.1357	−0.0222
FCA	−0.1407	−0.0042
FBA (DVA)	0.0706	0.0034
Total	−0.2058	−0.0230

move to the two-way CSA. This suggests that terms such as FVA will lead to more renegotiation of contractual terms like CSAs under the belief that both parties can benefit. We will discuss this in more detail in Section 19.4.

15.4   SUMMARY

In this chapter we have described the issues relating to funding, which are, in many ways, entwined with the problems of counterparty credit risk and BCVA. We have described the definition of FVA and the source of funding costs and benefits from derivatives transactions. We have also considered the linkages between CVA, DVA and FVA. Some of the implications of FVA are difficult, such as its relevance in pricing and financial statements, and the fact that it breaks price symmetry and the law of one price. FVA is therefore controversial; we have analysed the FVA debate and suggested that the market is currently operating under some form of compromise solution. In the next chapter we discuss KVA and MVA, which are related to funding costs but reflect the cost of holding regulatory capital and posting initial margin respectively.

---

[20] Note that the funding costs are assumed to be the same for each counterparty whilst their credit spreads differ. This may seem unusual but is consistent with the idea that funding costs not not include the credit risk of the party in question.

16
Margin and Capital Value Adjustments

I don't want to tell you how much insurance I carry with Prudential. All I can say is: When I go, they go!

Jack Benny (1894–1974)

16.1 OVERVIEW

This chapter follows on from the discussion about funding in the last chapter and focuses on the cost of initial margin and regulatory capital. These components are of growing importance, because two very significant aspects of regulatory reform since the global financial crisis are:

- *Initial margin.* Both the clearing mandate (Section 9.3.1) and the bilateral collateral rules for non-cleared transactions (Section 6.7) require significant initial margin (IM) posting. FVA, discussed in the last chapter, generally deals with cases of undercollateralisation, where the unsecured MTM of a derivative can be viewed as leading to funding costs or benefits. As discussed in Section 15.1.2, FVA is not really driven by collateral posting *per se*, although it is sometimes explained in this context. Nevertheless, FVA is largely a result of imperfect variation margin posting. It is appropriate to deal with margin valuation adjustment (MVA) separately from FVA. MVA will quantify the cost of posting IM and any other overcollateralisation such as the requirement for liquidity buffers.
- *Regulatory capital.* As discussed in Chapter 8, capital requirements for counterparty risk have become significantly more punitive with the advent of Basel III. Aspects such as the CVA capital charge (Section 8.7) and leverage ratio (Section 8.8.2) are having significant implications on the capital structures of banks. Historically, capital (often economic and not regulatory) has been priced implicitly into derivatives transactions via hurdle rates. However, given the importance of capital requirements, regulatory capital is now being considered more precisely via capital value adjustment (KVA), which aims to price the cost of holding regulatory capital over the lifetime of transactions. Since capital comes in several forms (market risk capital, default risk capital and CVA capital), and a bank's capital requirements may be impacted by the leverage ratio, KVA is complex.

Another important feature is the increased complexity of IM and capital methodologies. Historically, IM amounts have been defined using relatively simple metrics, such as percentage of notional, whereas the significant IM requirements in the future are likely to rely predominantly on more risk-sensitive methodologies such as the SIMM (Section 6.7.7). More banks are aiming for model method (IMM) approval (Section 8.3) in order to quantify their capital requirements in a more risk-sensitive manner. When IM and capital requirements are driven by relatively sophisticated methodologies, MVA and KVA quantification is a significant computational challenge. This is because it is necessary to project the output of these methodologies at any future date to be able to price the lifetime cost. There is also the problem that receiving IM should lead to a reduction in capital charges. However, to work out the reduced KVA under this assumption is yet more challenging.

16.2   MARGIN VALUE ADJUSTMENT

16.2.1   Rationale

MVA will cover the cost of the following components.

- *IM and other financial resources required by a central counterparty (CCP).* As discussed in Section 9.3.4, CCPs require IM to cover a worst-case scenario in the event of a default of a clearing participant. They also require other financial commitments, notably via the default fund contributions and rights of assessment (future default fund contributions). Such requirements are definitely costly, since IMs and default funds are held by the CCP or third party and are not remunerated at anything more than a "risk-free" rate (and typically less). It would seem logical to include the cost of default fund contribution alongside IM in MVA. Rights of assessment and other contingent loss allocation methods are unfunded and potentially heavily capitalised (Section 9.3.7), and so would more likely appear via KVA.
- *Bilateral IM.* As discussed in Section 6.7, bilateral derivatives are subject to incoming rules (from September 2016) that require posting of IM by both parties. This IM must be segregated and cannot typically be rehypothecated (except in one situation mentioned in Section 6.7.5), and so will be costly due to the need for segregation.
- *Contingent IM posting.* Some collateral agreements require contingent IM posting in certain situations, most commonly upon a ratings downgrade (see the example in Table 6.1). Regulatory rules in the liquidity coverage ratio (LCR) require banks to hold a liquidity buffer to cover such outflows in the event of a three-notch ratings downgrade, and such an outflow therefore needs to be prefunded (Section 8.8.4). Note that it may be beneficial for a bank to actually post a smaller IM[1] in order to have such rating-based triggers removed, since the IM needs to be held in high-quality assets in their liquidity buffer anyway. Sometimes, there may be alternatives to the IM posting, such as transactions being terminated: this is even more of a challenge to quantify, since it would require the estimation of the price charged by a replacement counterparty. Note that a bank does not generally derive any benefit from contingent triggers in their favour, because the prudent LCR rules would require the assumption that these triggers were not breached. As seen in Figure 16.1, market practice is divided on the treatment of such contingent liquidity requirements but many banks do price them in, especially in relation to their own potential rating downgrade.

---

[1] Ideally this IM should then be segregated to avoid creating additional CVA.

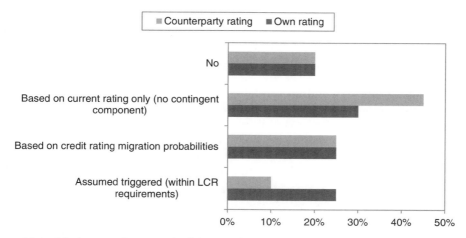

Figure 16.1   Market practice around pricing contingent funding requirements.
Source: Solum CVA survey, 2015.

Note that all of the above requirements are costly, since they involve posting high-quality IM that is usually not rehypothecated and is segregated, so is therefore remunerated at a low return. If the IM was allowed to be rehypothecated, a higher return may be achievable but it would then create additional counterparty risk via CVA.

16.2.2   IM profiles

The valuation of MVA is illustrated in Figure 16.2 and involves pricing the cost of holding IM for the lifetime of the transaction(s) in question. As noted above, there may be non-contingent (e.g. currently posted IM) and contingent (e.g. liquidity buffer)

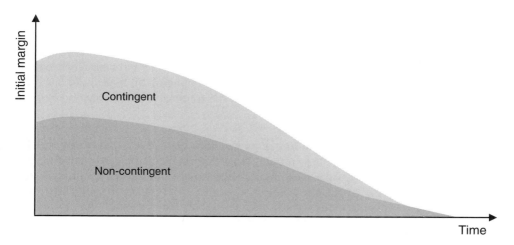

Figure 16.2   Illustration of MVA with both contingent and non-contingent components.

components. The amount may be deterministic, such as a percentage of notional (e.g. see Table 6.1), but is more commonly an uncertain amount based on a quantitative model (e.g. the SIMM discussed in Section 6.7.7).

IM requirements for OTC derivatives are increasingly being calculated using measures such as value-at-risk (VAR) or expected shortfall (ES): this is the case for both CCP and bilateral transactions. A typical methodology uses historical simulation and a VAR or ES metric at the 99% confidence level or more over a time horizon of five (CCP) or ten (bilateral) business days (see discussions in Sections 6.7.3 and 9.3.4). It is now common for a stressed period of data to be included in the calculation to dilute any procyclical problems where consistent periods of low volatility may lead to excessively low IMs. Examples of centrally cleared and bilateral markets in this regard are:

- *Bilateral.* The BCBS-IOSCO (2015) recommends IM to be based on a 99% confidence level with a ten-day time horizon and calibrated to a period including financial stress.
- *CCP.* SwapClear[2] uses historical simulation with a five-day time horizon calibrated to a period of ten years (so including the last crisis) with the IM defined by the average of the worst six moves in this period. This equates to an expected shortfall at the 99.76% confidence level.

Figure 16.3 illustrates the potential evolution of IM through time for a five-year swap using historical simulation and ten-day VAR[3] at the 99% confidence level. Two different examples are used: the first has a fixed data history ("lookback period") of three years, while the second additionally includes a fixed annual period of stress. Calculation of current IM may be relatively trivial; even CCPs typically make their methodologies available. It is therefore possible to calculate the projected IM through time using forward rates via a number of discrete IMs as the underlying portfolio approaches maturity. For a single transaction with periodic cashflows, this profile, not surprisingly, decays to zero monotonically: for a portfolio there can be discrete changes in future projected IM due to transactions maturing (and IM may therefore increase over the lifetime). However, when calculating the actual IM we also see discrete changes due to the changing historical data set through time. With the three-year data window these changes are quite significant, which is not surprising given the associated procyclicality of such a period – indeed, this is not acceptable for either bilateral or CCP IM calculation standards. Using a period of stress actually makes the IM more predictable (although significantly higher and therefore more costly), since the 99% confidence level is more likely to be consistently defined by the fixed stress period and not by the continuously changing three-year history.

In reality, IM requirements can evolve in many different ways depending on a number of factors:

- Changes in the portfolio composition as transactions mature (excluding new transactions, which can be priced as they occur). Note that the profile may actually increase when transactions that are offsetting longer-dated transactions in the portfolio mature and therefore drop out of the portfolio.

---

[2] See www.lchclearnet.com/risk_management/ltd/margining/swapclear.asp.
[3] As is often done in practice, the one-day VAR has been calculated and scaled by $\sqrt{10}$.

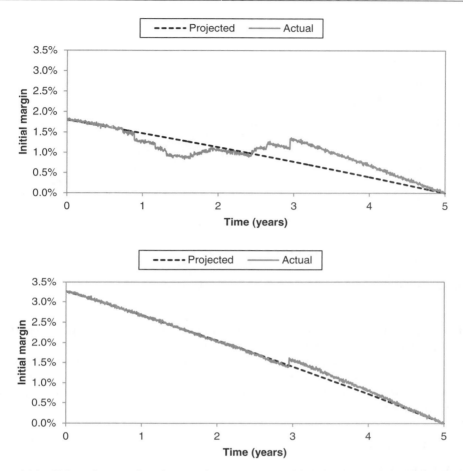

Figure 16.3 IM requirement for a five-year interest rate swap showing an actual realisation and the projected result as seen from today. Historical simulation is used and a metric of VAR at the 99% confidence level and ten-day time horizon is assumed. The top graph uses three years of data and the bottom additionally uses a one-year stress period.

- Continuous changes in the lookback period (in particular when important days drop in and out of the dataset).
- Changes in methodology such as change in underlying assumptions, recalibration of parameters and change in stress periods used. For example, most CCPs have recently switched from the assumption of "relative returns" to "absolute returns"[4] for interest rates movements, which in a falling interest rate environment is usually more conservative.

The first two components above are possible to calculate up-front, whilst the third is unpredictable and may lead to IM requirements changing in the future in a non-predictable

_____

[4] To understand this effect, suppose rates are currently at 2% but a move in the historical data involved an increase from 3% to 3.3%. Relative returns would interpret this as a 10% increase and shift rates to 2.2%, whereas absolute returns would interpret the increase as 0.3% and shift rates higher to 2.3%.

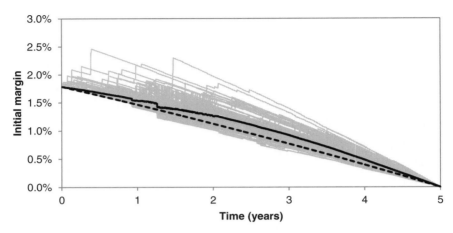

Figure 16.4   Initial actual IM requirement for a five-year swap based on a Monte Carlo simulation of interest rates and a VAR model using a three-year lookback period, 99% confidence level and ten-day time horizon. The dotted line shows the projected IM as seen from today and the solid line is the average of the scenarios defined as the expected IM (EIM).

fashion. Figure 16.4 shows a number of different possible IM profiles based on a Monte Carlo simulation of interest rates. Clearly there is a reasonable variation in IM requirements through time, even ignoring the possibility of methodology changes. The behaviour is also asymmetric: IM can increase substantially but substantial reductions are not seen. For this reason, the expected IM (EIM) requirements are significantly higher than the projected value seen from today.

16.2.3   MVA formula

The MVA formula can be written as:

$$MVA = -\sum_{i=1}^{m} EIM\left(t_i\right) \times \left(FC\left(t_i\right) - s_{IM}\right) \times \left(t_i - t_{i-1}\right) \times S\left(t_i\right), \tag{16.1}$$

where $EIM(.)$ is the discounted expected IM, $FC(.)$ is the funding cost of posting the IM with s_{IM} being the remuneration of this amount and $S(.)$ is the (joint) survival probability (i.e. the probability that the party and/or their counterparty do not default). Note that IM may be remunerated at rates below OIS, especially on CCPs, in which case the term $(FC(t_i) - s_{IM})$ will be higher to account for this.

There will be cheapest-to-deliver optionality (Section 13.4.3) with respect to the posting of IM, since both bilateral and CCP requirements will typically permit IM to be posted in different currencies and types of securities – this is in contrast to variation margin, which is generally cash in the currency of the transaction. This optionality would be most obviously accounted for in the estimation of the funding cost term. Note that received IM may also constitute a cost, since it will typically have to be segregated, and this segregation cost may be viewed as contributing to the MVA. This would involve computation of the EIM on the reverse portfolio.

The form of MVA as an integral over the EIM profile leads to computation problems, since a traditional approach would require a Monte Carlo simulation similar to the exposure methodology but with IM calculations at each point. Noting that an IM calculation itself may require another simulation, this leads to a classic computational bottleneck similar to the one discussed in Section 10.3.3 for exposure simulation involving transactions with relatively complex valuation models. One obvious way to get around this would be to rely on traditional VAR simplifications involving local approximations to the valuation such as delta and gamma. As in the previous case, another way to get around this problem is with American Monte Carlo methods as described by Green and Kenyon (2015).[5] However, it should be noted that even with accurate numerical methods to calculate the EIM profile, there are still future aspects that remain uncertain, such as the changing IM dataset and potential methodology changes.

Note that the IM in Equation 16.1 will also be typically defined for a portfolio of transactions with a bilateral counterparty or CCP. In particular:

- *Bilateral.* The bilateral rules (Section 6.7.6) require IM to be calculated across four asset classes (currency/rates, equity, credit, commodities). If a model-based approach is being used, there will be a portfolio IM for all transactions within a given asset class.
- *Centrally cleared.* CCPs generally net IMs across transactions in the same asset class (e.g. rates in different currencies) although they may not net across asset classes. This means that there will be a total IM requirement for all CCP netted transactions.

This means that there will be a need for an "incremental MVA", similar to the incremental CVA defined in Section 14.4.1. This increases the computational requirements further, since it will be necessary to calculate a portfolio MVA with and without the impact of a new transaction. Such incremental MVA effects have already become apparent in the market such as in the case of the CME-LCH basis.[6]

For centrally cleared transactions, it may be convenient to include the default fund contribution with the IM requirement in Equation 16.1. Furthermore, the relatively small capital charges arising from IM and default fund contributions may be incorporated qualitatively at this stage or assessed more accurately via capital value adjustment (KVA) discussed in Section 16.3.

16.2.4   Example

It is interesting to compare MVA with funding cost adjustment (FCA). The former can be seen as a funding cost based on the worst-case move of a portfolio during a short period (e.g. ten days), whilst the latter is an expected cost of funding over the portfolio lifetime. The effect of the shorter time horizon has been previously approximated for collateralised portfolios (Section 11.3.2) as $0.5\sqrt{(T/\tau_{IM})}$, with T being the maturity of the portfolio and τ_{IM} being the assumed time horizon. This would reduce the MVA compared to the FCA. However, since IM is taken at a high confidence level, whereas FCA is

---

[5] Green and Kenyon argue that VAR approximations such as delta-gamma may be too approximate due to the fairly extreme moves involved over the time horizon in question.

[6] For example, see "Bank swap books suffer as CME-LCH basis explodes", *Risk*, 15th May 2015. This is due to the directionality of positions at CME and LCH leading to a large differential in incremental IM charges.

Table 16.1   MVA values for the swap portfolio with a funding spread assumption of 100 bps.

	xVA
FCA	−0.0706
MVA (five-day, 99%)	−0.0467
MVA (ten-day, 99%)	−0.0688

based on the expected cost, this will increase the IM in relation to FCA by a factor that we approximate as $\Phi^{-1}(\alpha)/\varphi(0)$.[7] We therefore would expect the FCA to be related to the MVA by the following approximate factor:

$$2 \times \sqrt{\frac{\tau_{IM}}{T}} \times \frac{\Phi^{-1}(\alpha)}{\phi(0)} \tag{16.2}$$

We show an example MVA calculation for the same five-year portfolio of swaps used previously (see Section 11.3) and with the same funding cost assumption and compared to the FCA (funding cost adjustment) previously calculated in Section 15.3.8. For a ten-day horizon and 99% confidence level, the MVA is approximately the same as the FCA. The above formula would give a value of 1.04,[8] which is broadly consistent with this. This example suggests that in funding terms, it is slightly beneficial to be in an IM environment rather than an FCA one at this particular maturity (five-years). The further reduction in CVA and capital costs would be likely to further support an IM framework, although the loss of funding benefit (FBA) and liquidity considerations may make the IM environment less attractive. If the posting of IM is seen as beneficial from an xVA point of view, then it would be due to dramatically shortening the time horizon for funding from many years to just a few days (albeit with the consideration of a worst-case scenario in the latter case). This implies that IM posting will be more favourable against longer-dated transactions and vice versa. We will consider this aspect in Chapter 19.

16.3   CAPITAL VALUE ADJUSTMENT

16.3.1   Rationale

As discussed in Chapter 8, banks need to hold considerable counterparty risk-related regulatory capital against OTC derivative transactions. Capital is a cost because investors require a return on their investment. Capital costs can be seen as another type of funding and therefore there will be an analogy with FVA and the aforementioned MVA. Regulatory capital requirements will drive the split between debt and equity in funding a bank's balance sheet.

Banks have historically implicitly charged capital to transactions by setting limits on capital usage or requiring a certain capital hurdle to be achieved in transactions. Whilst these actions discourage capital intensive transactions to a degree, they do not properly price in the lifetime costs associated with holding regulatory capital. In recent years,

---

[7] This is the α quantile of the distribution divided by the average positive value.

[8] $2 \times \sqrt{(10/1250)} \times 2.33/0.40$ using normal distribution assumptions.

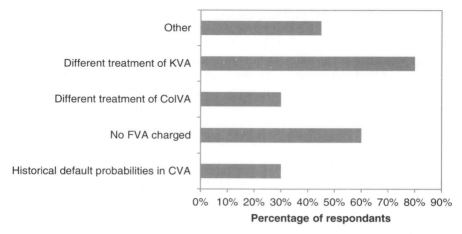

Figure 16.5 Market view on the most significant cause of divergence in market prices.
Source: Solum CVA survey, 2015.

increased capital requirements via Basel III with the CVA capital charge (Section 8.7), other capital constraints such as the leverage ratio (Section 8.8.2), together with the increased cost of raising new capital, have meant that pricing capital properly via capital value adjustment (KVA) has become key. Indeed, at the time of writing, the pricing of capital seems to represent one of the biggest divergences of pricing within OTC derivatives (Figure 16.5). The move from capital hurdles to KVA can be seen as being similar to the move from PFE and credit limit monitoring to CVA pricing and reporting.

Capital requirements linked to OTC derivatives and counterparty risk come in three forms:

- *Default risk capital charge.* This aims to capitalise the potential default of the counterparty. This is sometimes known as the CCR capital charge.
- *CVA capital charge.* This aims to capitalise for the mark-to-market (MTM) volatility from changes in CVA driven by credit spread movements in the absence of an actual default event.
- *Market risk capital charge.* Banks will normally aim to hedge the market risk in a transaction and it will therefore not be expected to attract a market risk capital charge. However, as discussed in Section 8.7.5, CVA related hedges may attract additional capital charges via appearing "naked" in a market risk capital framework.

The third component above has been shown by Kenyon and Green (2014) to be potentially significant, where back-to-back hedges will create spurious capital charges due to being ineligible hedges (irrespective of the counterparty risk capital methodology used). However, as noted in Section 8.7.5, US and Canadian regulators have exempted such hedges from capital charges and Europe, and other regions may be expected to follow this lead. BCBS (2015) also proposes capital framework where such market risk hedges would be capital efficient. We will therefore only consider the first two capital charges above. We will also not consider KVA on the capital requirements for exposures to central counterparties, which, as explained in Section 9.3.7, are (usually) relatively small. As noted in Section 16.2.2, these might be more easily incorporated as small adjustments in the MVA calculation.

With respect to the above calculations, Sections 8.1 and 8.7 explain the default risk and CVA capital charges in detail. The three relevant methodologies for calculating these charges, namely CEM (current exposure method), IMM (internal model method) and SA-CCR (standardised approach for counterparty credit risk) are discussed in Sections 8.2, 8.3 and 8.4 respectively, with comparisons examples given in Section 8.5. The results below will focus on the total capital charge as a sum of the default risk and CVA capital as is required.

16.3.2   Capital profiles

In order to calculate KVA, we need to be able to generate capital profiles over time for the different methodologies in question. This is similar to the generation of IM profiles discussed in Section 16.2.2. We use an example of an uncollateralised at-market seven-year maturity interest rate swap. We assume a single-A counterparty with a credit spread of 200 bps and default probability of 0.2%. The rating is relevant to determine the weight in the standardised CVA capital charge (Section 8.7.2) and the default probabilities in the default risk capital charge (Equation 8.1). The spread and its volatility drive the advanced CVA capital charge (Section 8.7.3). The projected capital profiles for the different methodologies are shown in Figure 16.6. Note that these are the result of running the capital calculation through time using forward rates. Such profiles are relatively easy to calculate but do not take into account the variability in future capital requirements. All profiles decay to zero as the swap approaches maturity, with the CEM approach being rather inelegant due to the simple add-ons used (Table 8.1).

Obviously capital requirements can be quite volatile over time as market factors move. Whether or not this volatility is not being hedged, it is important to have an idea of the potential variability of the capital through time. In order to do this, we would run the standard exposure simulation (Section 10.3) and calculate the new capital requirement at each point in the future. For the CEM and SA-CCR approaches, this is relatively straightforward, since methodologies are based on simple formulas. Due to the

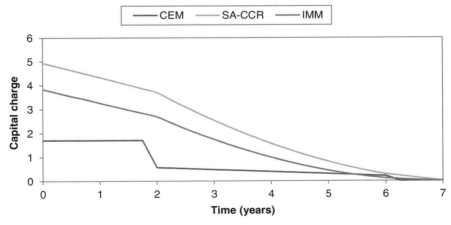

Figure 16.6   Total projected counterparty risk capital charge for a seven-year interest rate swap of notional 1,000 using the CEM, SA-CCR and IMM methodologies described in Chapter 8.

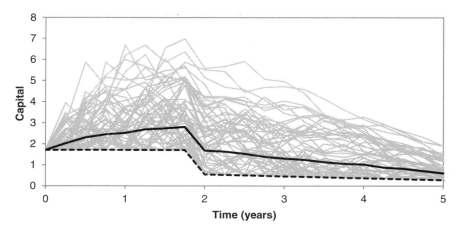

Figure 16.7 Simulations showing the evolution of counterparty risk capital for a seven-year interest rate swap with notional 1,000 using the CEM (top), SA-CCR (middle) and IMM (bottom) methodologies. The dotted line shows the projected value and the solid line shows the expected capital.

complexity of the method, simulating future capital requirements for the IMM would be extremely time-consuming, since this method itself is Monte Carlo-based.

Figure 16.7 shows the evolution of the counterparty risk capital charge over time for the three methodologies, showing the projected[9] and expected values. The capital requirements under the CEM approach cannot get any smaller for an at-market transaction (except where it moves into a shorter maturity bucket), since the current exposure is based on the positive MTM and therefore negative MTM values do not create any offset (see Section 8.2.1). This means that the expected capital is significantly higher than the projected value. For the SA-CCR and IMM approaches, the paths are more symmetric around the projected value due to the fact that both approaches recognise the risk-reducing benefit of negative MTMs (albeit with a 5% floor in the SA-CCR case, as discussed in Section 8.4.5). In these approaches, the expected capital is only slightly higher than the projected capital. This is especially useful in the IMM case, where a proper calculation of the expected capital value would be computationally expensive. However, the large variability of the future capital requirements illustrates the potential need to hedge counterparty risk capital requirements.

16.3.3   Formula

The KVA formula (e.g. Green et al., 2014) can be written as:

$$KVA = -\sum_{i=1}^{m} EC(t_i) \times CC(t_i) \times (t_i - t_{i-1}) \times S(t_i),$$ (16.3)

where $EC(.)$ is the (discounted) expected capital profile as illustrated in the examples in Section 16.3.2. The results in the last section suggest that it may be reasonable to use the

---

[9] As noted above, this takes a single deterministic capital requirement projected in the future via current forward rates.

projected capital to approximate the true EC. This may only be a relatively small underestimate in some cases and is much easier to quantify. There is also a certain cost of capital (*CC*) assumption (as discussed in Section 12.5.4) with *S*(.) the (joint) survival probability, as with previous xVA terms. The EC is traditionally discounted by the cost of capital; for example, based on the bank's own dividend policy or CAPM. However, others argue that it should be discounted by the risk-free rate or even not discounted at all. Some banks may also increase the capital cost over time, which will penalise longer-dated transactions (for example, to price in the perceived cost of future regulatory change).

Note that the above formula must be calculated for a bank's entire portfolio simultaneously. Whilst the default risk capital charge is additive across netting sets, the CVA capital charge is a portfolio level calculation in both the standardised and advanced versions. As usual, this will potentially create a computational challenge for pricing KVA on new transactions, especially in an IMM approach. Note also that the impact of any capital reducing hedges should be included in the EC profile. As stated above in the last section, this requires certain subjective assumptions about how much capital relief can actually be achieved.

As discussed above, the EC profile will be defined by the future capital methodology that applies to the bank, the three most common methods being CEM, SA-CCR and IMM. The bank may attempt to incorporate a likely change in methodology within the integral: for example the SA-CCR is only relevant from 2017 and some banks currently using CEM will expect to move to SA-CCR or gain IMM approval at some point in the future. Finally, banks may also attempt to incorporate the impact of the leverage ratio (Section 8.8.2) in this calculation, especially if this becomes a major constraint to business.

16.3.4   Term structure behaviour

Projected and expected capital costs do not always amortise as in the above examples. For the case of a forward transaction, since there are no periodic cashflows the capital will project approximately flat, as shown in Figure 16.8 for an FX forward. Similar behaviour will also be seen for cross-currency swap (although they will likely amortise slightly due to the interest rate cashflows).

Another important term structure effect can be seen when using an IMM approach where different projections will occur depending on whether real-world (e.g. historical volatility) or risk-neutral (e.g. implied volatility) parameters are used. Figure 16.8 shows the expected exposure (EE) and projected capital for the FX forward under these different assumptions. In the historical calibration, the volatility is flat and the EE will follow a familiar "square root of time" shape and the projected capital projection is therefore flat. Using implied volatility will change the shape of the EE, making it lower in the short term and higher in the longer term. This means that the expected capital also increases over time.

The above differences between real-world and risk-neutral parameterisations are important. Because terms such as CVA and FVA are generally hedged and reflected in financial statements, risk-neutral calibrations are relevant (as discussed in Section 10.4). However, KVA is typically not charged directly to desks, hedged or reflected in accounting statements. Hence, there is a question as to whether pricing KVA with risk-neutral parameters is relevant. Of course, a bank may have a view that KVA will be hedged at some point in the future, in which case a risk-neutral approach for capital calculations may be preferable.

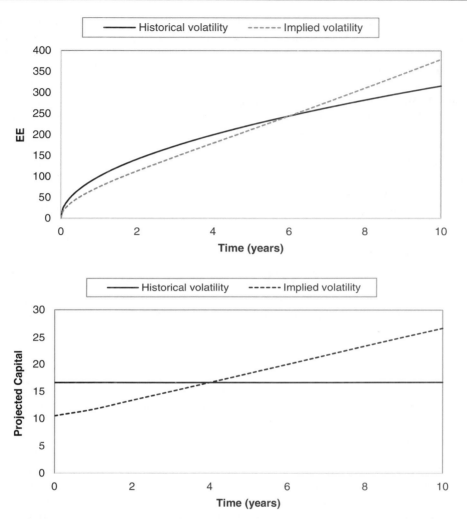

Figure 16.8 Expected exposure (EE) (top) and projected capital charge (bottom) for a ten-FX forward transaction using historical and implied volatility. The implied volatility is assumed to be upwards sloping.

16.3.5   Behavioural aspects and regulatory change

KVA is the most subjective xVA component.[10] This is due to the difficulty in predicting future regulatory regimes and behaviour of counterparties. For example, when assessing the capital costs of a transaction (especially a long-dated one), banks currently need to consider issues such as:

[10] See "KVA: banks wrestle with the cost of capital", *Risk*, 2nd March 2015.

- *Regulatory capital methodology.* Some banks may currently be using the CEM but will anticipate at some point in the future using the SA-CCR or IMM methodologies. There is also a new proposed approach for CVA capital described in BCBS (2015).
- *Regulatory changes.* Whilst there are complete unknowns in the regulatory landscape, there are also uncertainties. For example, the leverage ratio is currently set to 3% in Europe, with the US considering a scale of 4–6%. However, the final number will not be calibrated until 2017. Also proposed are floors set for banks using IMM approaches (Section 8.8.3), although at the time of writing these have not been determined.
- *Exemptions.* In Europe, banks currently enjoy exemptions with respect to the CVA capital charge for many counterparties (Section 8.7.7), but these are likely to be reversed at some point. A complete reversal is unlikely in the short term, although local regulators may require some sort of overlay. Hence, the actual amount of capital required is unknown and the presence or not of exemptions has a significant impact on prices.[11]
- *Capital relief through hedges.* Hedging with index hedges gives partial capital relief but the extent of this depends to some degree on future behaviour of market variables such as credit spreads. Whilst capital for a given counterparty may not currently be directly hedgeable (for example, due to illiquidity of the relevant single-name credit default swap), then it may be assumed to be hedged at some point in the future. The reverse may also be true: a counterparty may currently trade in the single-name CDS market but this may not be the case in the future.

Furthermore, banks may also incorporate certain behavioural factors into their assessment of future capital requirements. For example, a client may be expected to unwind a transaction early, and this may lead to a reduced KVA charge. This will, of course, be related to the motive and past behaviour of the client: a hedge fund is likely to unwind transactions whilst a corporate hedging debt issuance is not.

The above assumptions are relevant at the current time since KVA, unlike CVA and FVA, is generally not hedged, and therefore it is the actual real-world capital requirements that are relevant. This also implies that KVA should be calculated with real-world and not risk-neutral parameters, as mentioned in Section 16.3.4. From the point of view of a sales or trading desk, KVA is generally not transfer-priced to an internal xVA desk and so not meeting a target return on capital, and will not show up as loss for their book. Whether this will change in the future is discussed in Section 16.3.9.

16.3.6   Example

Table 16.2 shows the KVA values for the interest rate swap illustrated in Section 16.3.2. The collateralised results are shown in addition to the previous uncollateralised example. As expected from the profiles in Figure 16.6, the CEM method is the cheapest in the uncollateralised case – but note that, as discussed in Section 8.2.2, this method performs badly in representing netting and collateral, and is less favourable at the portfolio level. The approximate (projected) value for the SA-CCR and IMM approaches are quite close to the actual calculation (requiring Monte Carlo simulation), as expected from Figure 16.7. For the CEM, the actual capital is almost double the projected value. Regarding the collateralised results, the actual and projected results are much closer. They are the

---

[11] For example, see "Sovereigns facing price hike if CVA exemption is axed", *Risk*, 6th January 2015.

Table 16.2 KVA values for a seven-year interest rate swap of notional 1,000 with the three different capital methodologies assuming a cost of capital of 10%. In the collateralised case, a MPR of ten days is assumed.

	Uncollateralised		Collateralised	
	Projected	Actual	Projected	Actual
CEM	−0.457	−0.881	−0.457	−0.457
SA-CCR	−1.502	−1.758	−0.451	−0.451
IMM	−0.991	−1.249	−0.343	−0.367

same for the CEM and SA-CCR approaches, since we always assume the correct amount of collateral is held. In the collateralised case, the SA-CCR and IMM, not surprisingly, give lower values than the CEM. Note that in the collateralised case, the KVA is reduced (due to the assumption of taking collateral against positive MTM), even though the spot capital is not.

16.3.7 KVA and MVA

KVA and MVA are not mutually exclusive, but since IM should reduce capital, we would generally expect one of them to be significant and one of them to not be significant in a given situation (indeed, IM can be seen as capital provided by a counterparty). For example, in an uncollateralised transaction, KVA is clearly significant, whereas for a central cleared transaction, MVA is most important and KVA would be expected to be small. It is therefore interesting to consider the impact on increasing IM amounts, which should reduce KVA whilst increasing MVA.

Figure 16.9 shows the KVA and MVA for the three capital methodologies as a function of a bilateral IM for the same example as in the last section assuming an IM funding cost of 50 bps. Obviously the cost of posting IM will increase linearly with the amount, but the received IM will correspondingly produce a reduction in KVA (except in the CEM case, which does not capture IM in the methodology). The gain in KVA is not as

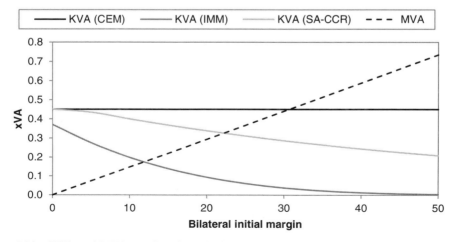

Figure 16.9 KVA and MVA as a function of a bilateral IM for the seven-year interest rate swap.

good in the SA-CCR case compared to the IMM: this can be seen as related to the floor of 5% used (see Equation 8.12) and the relatively conservative add-on in this approach (Section 8.4.2). Under IMM, there is actually an overall benefit to a moderate bilateral IM posting. This is perhaps not surprising as debt should be less expensive than equity. However, since there is a law of diminishing returns, every unit of IM received has a smaller overall reduction on the KVA.

The above suggests that incoming bilateral IM requirements (which require a conservatively high amount to be exchanged) as discussed in Section 6.7 should not be favoured purely via a reduction in KVA. This is not surprising, as this would imply a form of regulatory arbitrage where it is cheaper for banks to give each other capital than holding it themselves. However, when considering the benefit of IM on reducing CVA and FVA as well as KVA, it may be that higher levels of IM posting can be seen as beneficial. We will consider this in Chapter 19.

16.3.8   Overlaps and hedging

We have mentioned previously the potential problem of overlaps with xVA terms, most significantly those involving CVA, DVA and FVA (Section 15.3.2). KVA also presents some problems with respect to overlap, the main issue being with respect to CVA.

CVA using risk-neutral default probabilities as implied by regulatory and accounting standards (Section 12.2.2) is the theoretical cost of hedging counterparty risk. However, KVA represents the capital that must be held, because CVA cannot be perfectly hedged. Indeed, it is possible to achieve full capital relief using a single-name CDS (Section 8.7.2). Some banks sometimes make ad hoc adjustments to correct for this potential double-counting, for example by charging the maximum of the two possible extremes (in addition to other components):

$$\max(CVA, EL + KVA), \tag{16.4}$$

where the first term reflects the perfect hedging of counterparty risk with no additional capital requirements and the second term represents the warehousing of counterparty risk leading to a KVA charge together with the expected loss (EL). The EL is essentially a CVA but quantified with real-world parameters. This may seen like an obvious approach but is in fact flawed since an xVA desk will generally operate under a limits framework and will therefore not be able to warehouse credit risk. If the CVA (first term above) is charged then the return on capital will be expected to be zero as the CVA will be lost by the xVA desk in hedging. Alternatively if the EL and KVA (second term above) is changed then there will seemingly be no cash to use for CVA hedging.

A preferable approach to the above is to charge the standard CVA and a proportion of the capital charge depending on the capital relief expected through CVA hedging. This approach is shown more mathematically in Kenyon and Green (2014). To the extent the CVA is being hedged (with eligible instruments such as CDS), then the capital relief achieved should be reflected in the KVA formula as discussed above.

One of the reasons that banks may sometime still use ad hoc representations such as Equation 16.4 is due to the problems with CVA hedging. In Section 8.7.5, we discussed some criticisms of the CVA capital charge. Some potential problems with this form of capital charge have already been seen. A large bank reported significant CVA losses associated with their RWA reduction programme (Carver, 2013). In other words, by reducing counterparty risk capital, they were actually increasing the accounting volatility in their CVA (DVA and FVA) numbers. This is obviously an unpleasant side-effect of capital rules not being perfectly risk-sensitive and being inconsistent with accounting standards and market practice with respect to CVA, DVA and FVA (note that the regulatory capital proposals in BCBS (2015) are potentially more beneficial in this regard).

Another consideration is that capital might be assumed to reduce funding requirements. This may be represented by a reduction in the FCA term discussed in the last chapter (discussed by Green et al., 2014).

16.3.9   KVA reporting

In general, individual xVA components have initially developed as non-standard and lenient adjustments to prices but have then developed into standard and rigorous charges with accounting implications. Given the increasing prominence of KVA, it is natural to ask whether or not it be eventually seen as an accounting adjustment, like CVA and FVA before it. On the one hand, this may seem natural, since capital costs measured by KVA have similarities to the funding costs represented by FVA. There are potential benefits of this:

- *Return on capital.* When KVA is only a hurdle, this implies that return on capital in the first year will be very strong, since it will be based on the total profit of a transaction but will then drop to zero for the remaining lifetime. Taking KVA as an accounting item would allow profits to be released over the lifetime of the transaction, thereby generating the required return on capital.
- *Incentives.* With capital hurdles, sales and trading in a bank will still gain from the entire profit of a transaction at inception. Taking KVA into accounting numbers would allow profits to be deferred and released over the lifetime of a transaction, arguably creating the right incentive for front-office staff.
- *Management.* Like other xVAs, KVA could be transfer priced to a central xVA desk and managed accordingly. Without this a bank may suffer from extremely volatile capital numbers, especially using methodologies such as the IMM. Some banks have experienced significant changes in regulatory capital driven by aspects such as large FX moves.

However, given that most banks have relatively long-dated derivatives books, the one-off adjustment that would be required to achieve the above would be large compared to the fairly significant FVA reported values discussed in the last chapter. It is therefore difficult to see how a bank would satisfy its staff and shareholders by making such a fundamental change, especially if competitors were not doing so also. Furthermore, there are still arguments that FVA should not be an accounting adjustment (Section 15.3.7), which would need to be resolved before considering representing KVA in financial statements.

16.4   SUMMARY

In this chapter, we have discussed the final two components of xVA: MVA and KVA. MVA will become increasing important in the future in determining the cost of posting initial margin both bilaterally and to central counterparties. KVA is important given the increased capital requirements that have been imposed on banks since the global financial crisis and aims to calculate the cost of holding regulatory capital over the lifetime of a transaction. We also illustrated the balance between MVA and KVA, where increasing initial margin can generate capital relief.

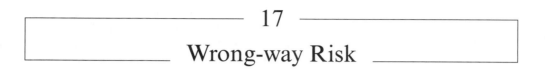

17

Wrong-way Risk

I never had a slice of bread, particularly large and wide, that did not fall upon the floor, and always on the buttered side.

Newspaper in Norwalk, Ohio, 1841

17.1 OVERVIEW

In the quantification of xVA presented in the previous chapters, wrong-way risk (WWR) was ignored. WWR is the phrase generally used to indicate an unfavourable dependence between exposure and counterparty credit quality: the exposure is high when the counterparty is more likely to default and vice versa. Such an effect would have a clear impact on CVA and DVA. Moreover, certain WWR features can also apply to other situations and impact other xVA terms through dependencies related to collateral, funding and other factors. Most of this chapter will be dedicated to the assessment of WWR in CVA, but mention will be made of other important considerations. WWR is difficult to identify, model and hedge due to the often subtle macro-economic and structural effects that cause it.

Whilst it may often be a reasonable assumption to ignore WWR, its manifestation can be potentially dramatic. In contrast, "right-way" risk can also exist in cases where the dependence between exposure and credit quality is a favourable one. Right-way situations will reduce counterparty risk and CVA. We will identify causes of WWR and discuss the associated implications on exposure estimation and quantification of CVA. We will then outline the quantitative approaches used and examine some important specific examples. The impact of collateral on WWR will be analysed and the central clearing implications will be discussed.

17.2 OVERVIEW OF WRONG-WAY RISK

17.2.1 Simple example

In Chapter 14, we saw that CVA could be generally represented as credit spread multiplied by exposure (Equation 14.2). However, this multiplication relies on a key assumption, which is that the different quantities are *independent*. If this is not the case, then one must consider how to integrate the quantification of credit risk (default probability) and market risk (exposure), which is a complex task.

A simple analogy to WWR is dropping (the default) a piece of buttered bread. Many people believe that in such a case, the bread is most likely to land on the wrong, buttered side (exposure). This is due to "Murphy's Law", which states that "anything that can go wrong, will go wrong". This particular aspect of Murphy's Law has even been empirically tested[1] and, of course, the probability of bread landing butter side down is only 50%.[2] People have a tendency to overweight the times when the bread lands the wrong way against the times they were more fortunate. Since it is in human nature to believe in WWR, it is rather surprising that it has been significantly underestimated in the derivatives market! The market events of 2007 onwards have illustrated clearly that WWR can be extremely serious. In financial markets, the bread always falls on the buttered side, has butter on both sides or explodes before hitting the ground.

17.2.2   Classic example and empirical evidence

WWR is often a natural and unavoidable consequence of financial markets. One of the simplest examples is mortgage providers who, in an economic regression, face both falling property prices and higher default rates by homeowners. In derivatives, classic examples of trades that obviously contain WWR across different asset classes are as follows:

- *Put option.* Buying a put option on a stock (or stock index) where the underlying in question has fortunes that are highly correlated to those of the counterparty is an obvious case of WWR (for example, buying a put on one bank's stock from another bank). The put option will only be valuable if the stock goes down, in which case the counterparty's credit quality will be likely to be deteriorating. Correspondingly, equity call options should be right-way products.
- *FX forward or cross-currency products.* Any FX contract should be considered in terms of a potential weakening of the currency and simultaneous deterioration in the credit quality of the counterparty. This would obviously be the case in trading with a sovereign and paying their local currency in an FX forward or cross-currency swap (or, more likely in practice, hedging this trade with a bank in that same region). Another way to look at a cross-currency swap is that it represents a loan collateralised by the opposite currency in the swap. If this currency weakens dramatically, the value of the collateral is strongly diminished. This linkage could be either way: a weakening of the currency could indicate a slow economy and hence a less profitable time for the counterparty, but alternatively, the default of a sovereign, financial institution or large corporate counterparty may itself precipitate a currency weakening.
- *Interest rate products.* Here, it is important to consider a relationship between the relevant interest rates and the credit spread of the counterparty. A corporate paying the fixed rate in a swap when the economy is strong may represent WWR, since interest rates would be likely to be cut in a recession. However, interest rates may rise during an economic recovery suggesting that a receiver swap may have right-way risk.
- *Commodity swaps.* A commodity producer (e.g. a mining company) may hedge the price fluctuation they are exposed to with derivatives. Such a contract *should* represent right-way risk, since the commodity producer will only owe money when the commodity price is high and when their business should be more profitable. The right-way risk arises due to hedging (as opposed to speculation).

---

[1] On the UK BBC TV science programme *Q.E.D.* in 1993.

[2] Matthews (1995) has shown that a butter-down landing is indeed more likely, because of gravitational torque and the height of tables rather than Murphy's Law.

- *Credit default swaps.* When buying protection in a CDS contract, an exposure will be the result of the reference entity's credit spread widening. However, one would prefer that the counterparty's credit spread is not widening also! In the case of a strong relationship between the credit quality of the reference entity and counterparty, clearly there is extreme WWR. A bank selling protection on its own sovereign would be an obvious problem. On the other hand, with such a strong relationship, selling CDS protection should be a right-way trade with little or no counterparty risk.

There is also empirical evidence supporting the presence of WWR. Duffee (1998) describes a clustering of corporate defaults during periods of falling interest rates, which is most obviously interpreted as a recession leading to both low interest rates (due to central bank intervention) and a high default rate environment. This has also been experienced in the last few years by banks on uncollateralised receiver interest swap positions, which have moved in-the-money together with a potential decline in the financial health of the counterparty (e.g. a sovereign or corporate). This effect can been seen as WWR creating a "cross-gamma" (Chapter 18) effect via the strong linkage of credit spreads and interest rates, even in the absence of actual defaults.

Regarding the FX example above, results from Levy and Levin (1999) look at residual currency values upon default of the sovereign and find average values ranging from 17% (triple-A) to 62% (triple-C). This implies the amount by which the FX rate involved could jump at the default time of the counterparty. Losses due to WWR have also been clearly illustrated. For example, many dealers suffered heavy losses because of WWR during the Asian crisis of 1997/1998. This was due to a strong link between the default of sovereigns and corporates, and a significant weakening of their local currencies. A decade later, the credit crisis that started in 2007 caused heavy WWR losses for banks buying insurance from so-called monoline insurance companies (Section 9.2.4).

17.2.3   General and specific WWR

Regulators have identified both general (driven by macro-economic relationships) and specific (driven by causal linkages between the exposure/collateral and default of the counterparty) WWRs as critical to measure and control (Section 8.6.5). Not surprisingly, Basel III has made strong recommendations over quantifying and managing WWR. There is clearly a need to address WWR for correctly pricing and hedging xVA. General and specific WWR are compared in Table 17.1.

Table 17.1   Characteristics of general and specific WWR.

General WWR	Specific WWR
Based on macro-economic behaviour	Based on structural relationships that are often not captured via real-world experience
Relationships may be detectable using historical data	Hard to detect except by a knowledge of the relevant market, counterparty and the economic rationale behind their transaction
Can potentially be incorporated into pricing models	Difficult to model and dangerous to use naïve correlation assumptions; should be addressed qualitatively via methods such as stress-testing
Should be priced and managed correctly	Should in general be avoided, as it may be extreme

17.2.4   WWR challenges

Quantifying WWR will involve somehow modelling the relationship between credit, collateral, funding and exposure. At a high level, there are a number of problems in doing this, which are:

- *Uninformative historical data.* Unfortunately, WWR may be subtle and not revealed via any empirical data such as a historical time series analysis of correlations.
- *Misspecification of relationship.* The way in which the dependency is specified may be inappropriate. For example, rather than being the result of a correlation, it may be the result of a causality – a cause-and-effect type relationship between two events. If the correlation between two random variables is measured as zero, this does not prove that they are independent.[3]
- *Direction.* It may not be clear on the direction of WWR. For example, low interest rates may be typically seen in a recession when credit spreads may be wider and default rates higher. However, an adverse credit environment when interest rates are high is not impossible.

WWR by its very nature is extreme and often rather specific. For example, in 2010, the European sovereign debt crisis involved deterioration in the credit quality of many European sovereigns and a weakening of the euro currency. However, historical data did not bear out this relationship, largely since most of the sovereigns concerned nor the currency had ever previously been subject to such adverse credit effects.

17.3   QUANTIFICATION OF WRONG-WAY RISK

17.3.1   Wrong-way risk and CVA

Incorporation of WWR in the CVA formula is probably most obviously achieved simply by representing the exposure *conditional* upon default of the counterparty. Returning to Equation 14.2, we simply rewrite the expression as:

$$CVA = LGD \sum_{i=1}^{m} EE\left(t_i \mid t_i = \tau_C\right) \times PD(t_{i-1}, t_i), \tag{17.1}$$

where $E(t_i \mid t_i = \tau_C)$ represents the expected exposure (EE) at time t_i conditional on this being the counterparty default time (τ_C). This replaces the previous exposure, which was unconditional. As long as we use the conditional exposure[4] in this fashion, everything is correct.

Equation 17.1 supports approaching WWR quantification heuristically by qualitatively assessing the likely increase in the conditional EE compared to the unconditional one. An example of a qualitative approach to WWR is in regulatory capital requirements and the alpha factor (Section 8.3.2). A more conservative value for alpha, together with

---

[3] A classic example of this is as follows. Suppose a variable X follows a normal distribution. Now choose Y = X^2. X and Y have zero correlation but are far from independent.

[4] We note that there are other ways to represent this effect. For example, we could instead look at the conditional default probability, as will be done in Section 17.4.2.

the requirement to use stressed data in the estimation of the exposure (Section 8.6.1), represents a regulatory effort to partially capitalise general WWR.

Alternatively, one can attempt to model correctly the relationship between default probability and EE, which is much harder to achieve and may introduce computational challenges. Some of the potential modelling approaches will be discussed below.

17.3.2   Simple example

In Appendix 17A, we derive a simple formula for the conditional expected exposure for a forward contract-type exposure (an extension of the previous unconditional case given in Appendix 7B). The relationship between exposure and counterparty default is expressed using a single correlation parameter. This correlation parameter is rather abstract, with no straightforward economic intuition, but it does facilitate a simple way of quantifying and understanding WWR.

Spreadsheet 17.1   Simple wrong-way risk example

Figure 17.1 shows the impact of wrong-way (and right-way) risk on the EE. We can see that with 50% correlation, WWR approximately doubles the EE, whilst with −50% correlation, the impact of right-way risk reduces it by at least half. This is the type of behaviour expected: positive correlation between the default probability and exposure increases the conditional expected exposure (default probability is high when exposure is high), which is WWR. Negative correlation causes right-way risk.

Let us look into this simple model in a bit more detail. Consider the impact of the counterparty default probability on the EE with WWR. Figure 17.2 shows the EE for differing counterparty credit quality, showing that the exposure increases as the credit

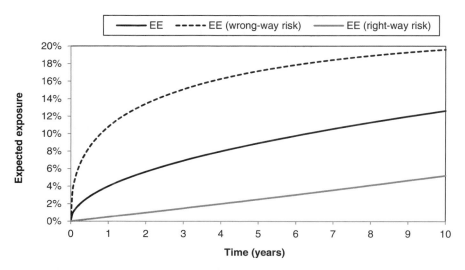

Figure 17.1   Illustration of wrong-way and right-way risk expected exposure profiles using a simple model with correlations of 50% and −50% respectively.

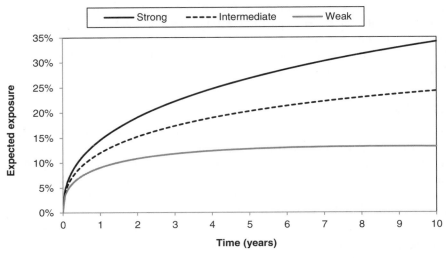

Figure 17.2   Illustration of expected exposure under the assumption of WWR for different credit quality counterparties.

quality of the counterparty also increases. This result might seem counterintuitive at first, but it makes sense when one considers that for a better credit quality counterparty, default is a less probable event and therefore represents a bigger surprise when it comes. We note an important general conclusion, which is that WWR therefore *increases* as the credit quality of the counterparty *improves*.

17.3.3   Wrong-way collateral

Consider a payer interest rate swap collateralised by a high-quality government bond. This would represent a situation of general WWR, since an interest rate rise would cause the value of the swap to increase whilst the collateral value would decline. In the case of a receiver interest rate swap, the situation is reversed, and there would be a beneficial right-way collateral position. However, given the relatively low volatility of interest rates then this is not generally a major problem.

A more significant example of general wrong-way (or right-way) collateral could be a cross-currency swap collateralised by cash in one of the two underlying currencies. If collateral is held in the currency being paid, then an FX move may simultaneously increase the exposure and reduce the value of the collateral. An example of this is shown in Figure 17.3. As the potential amount of collateral held increases over the lifetime of the transaction, the potential impact of an adverse FX move becomes more significant. Overall, the wrong-way collateralised exposure is around 50% higher than the normal uncollateralised exposure (assuming cash in another independent currency). Note that, due to the margin period of risk, it is not possible to completely hedge the FX risk.

There can also be cases of specific wrong-way collateral where there is a more specific relationship between the collateral value and the counterparty credit quality. An entity posting their own bonds is an example of this: this is obviously a very weak mitigant

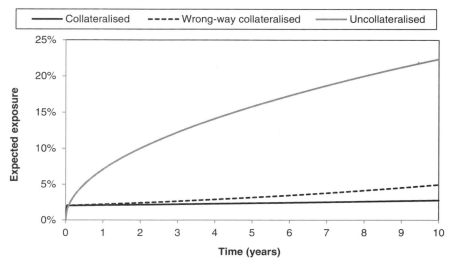

Figure 17.3   Illustration of the impact of collateral on the expected exposure of a cross-currency swap assuming normal and wrong-way collateral. In the latter case, it is assumed that cash in the pay currency will be posted.

against credit exposure and CVA although it may mitigate FVA, as discussed in Section 7.5.3. A bank posting bonds of their own sovereign can also be a problem here, and may not be prevented within the collateral agreement.

17.4   WRONG-WAY RISK MODELLING APPROACHES

This section explains some of the commonly used approaches to WWR, highlighting the relative strengths and weaknesses of each method.

17.4.1   Hazard rate approaches

An obvious modelling technique for WWR is to introduce a stochastic process for the credit spread (or "hazard rate", which is a mathematical concept directly related to the credit spread) and correlate this with the other underlying processes required for modelling exposure. Default will be generated via the credit spread process and the resulting conditional EE will be calculated in the usual way, but only for paths where there has been a default. This approach can be implemented relatively tractably, as credit spread paths can be generated first and exposure paths need only be simulated in cases where some default is observed. The required correlation parameters can be observed directly via historical time series of credit spreads[5] and other relevant market variables.

---

[5] Noting that the credit spread may be determined by some proxy or generic curve, in which case this historical time series should be used.

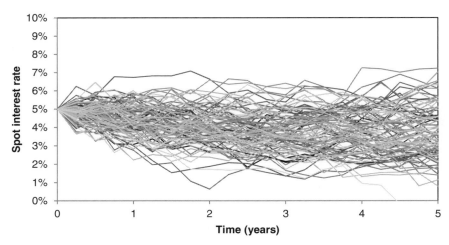

Figure 17.4   Interest rate simulations conditional on counterparty default (at some point in the five-year period) for the hazard rate model.

Let us illustrate this approach for an interest rate swap. We assume a Vasicek (1977) interest rate model[6] with a flat interest rate term structure (spot rate equal to long-term mean) leading to a symmetric exposure profile that will make the wrong- and right-way risk effects easier to identify. We assume a lognormal hazard rate approach so that credit spreads cannot become negative and use a volatility of 80%.[7] The counterparty CDS spread and LGD are 500 bps and 60% respectively.

The relationship between changes in interest rates and default rates has been shown empirically to be generally negative.[8] Figure 17.4 shows the interest rates paths generated conditional on default in a case where the correlation is negative. This is because defaults typically happen where credit spreads are wider when interest rates will generally be lower due to the negative correlation.

Figure 17.5 shows the swap values resulting from the paths in Figure 17.4. Not surprisingly the swap tends to be more in-the-money in default scenarios. This is a WWR effect and we would therefore expect a higher CVA for negative correlation and a lower CVA for positive correlation.

However, simple hazard rate approaches generate only very weak dependency between exposure and default. The correlation used in this example is –90% and the WWR effect is not particularly strong, even though the correlation is close to the maximum negative value. Hence, whilst this type of approach is the most obvious to implement and tractable, it will probably only ever generate relatively small WWR effects.

---

[6] The mean reversion parameter and volatility are set at 0.1 and 1% respectively.

[7] The volatility used is 50%.

[8] See, for example, Longstaff and Schwartz (1995), Duffee (1998), and Collin-Dufresne et al. (2001).

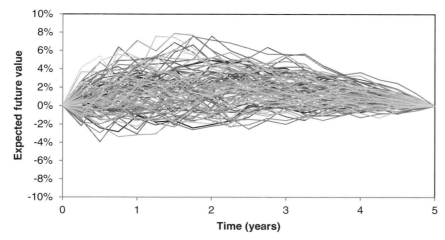

Figure 17.5   Future values for a receiver interest rate swap conditional on counterparty default for a hazard rate approach with negative correlation.

17.4.2   Structural approaches

An even more simple and tractable approach to general WWR is to specify a dependency directly between the counterparty default time and exposure distribution as illustrated in Figure 17.6 (for example, see Garcia-Cespedes et al., 2010). In this approach, the exposure and default distributions are mapped separately onto a bivariate distribution. Positive (negative) dependency will lead to an early default time being coupled with a higher (lower) exposure, as is the case with wrong-way (right-way) risk. Note that there is no need to recalculate the exposures, as the original unconditional values are sampled directly. The advantage of this method is that pre-computed exposure distributions are

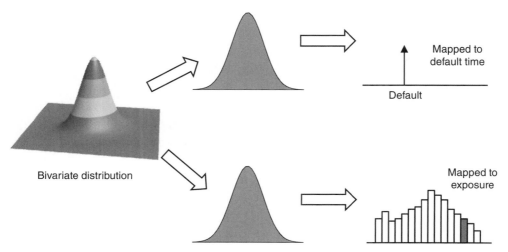

Figure 17.6   Illustration of the structural approach to modelling general WWR, assuming some underlying bivariate distribution.

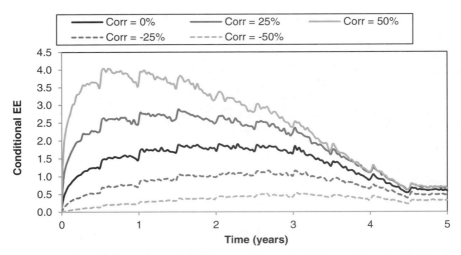

Figure 17.7 Conditional expected exposure (EE) calculated with various levels of correlation using the structural approach.

used and WWR is essentially added on top of the existing methodology. However, this is also a disadvantage, since it may not be appropriate to assume that all the relevant information to define WWR is contained within the unconditional exposure distribution.

We show an example of this approach using the same portfolio as before (see Section 14.6.6), assuming the counterparty CDS curve is flat at 500 bps and the LGD is 60%. If a bivariate Gaussian distribution is assumed, then conditional expected exposure is as shown in Figure 17.7 for various correlation values. We see that positive (negative) correlation leads to a higher (lower) conditional exposure, reflecting wrong-way (right-way) risk. This effect is stronger for shorter maturities, since an early default is more unexpected.

Figure 17.8 shows the CVA as a function of correlation. Negative correlation reduces the CVA due to right-way risk and WWR, created by positive correlation,

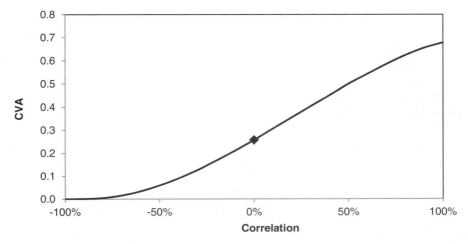

Figure 17.8 CVA as a function of the correlation between counterparty default time and exposure. The point marked shows the standard CVA (0% correlation).

increases it. The effect is reasonably strong, with the CVA approximately doubled at 50% correlation.

The big drawback with the structural model is that the correlation parameter described above is opaque and therefore difficult to calibrate. Discussion and correlation estimates are given by Fleck and Schmidt (2005) and Rosen and Saunders (2010). More complex representations of this model are suggested by Iscoe et al. (1999) and De Prisco and Rosen (2005), where the default process is correlated more directly with variables defining the exposure. Estimation of the underlying correlations is then more achievable.

17.4.3   Parametric approach

Hull and White (2011) have proposed a more direct approach by linking the default probability parametrically to the exposure using a simple functional relationship. They suggest using either an intuitive calibration based on a what-if scenario or calibrating the relationship via historical data. This latter calibration would involve calculating the portfolio value for dates in the past and examining the relationship between this and the counterparty's credit spread. If the portfolio has historically shown high values together with larger-than-average credit spread, then this will indicate WWR. This approach obviously requires that the current portfolio of trades with the counterparty is similar in nature to that used in the historical calibration, in addition to the historical data showing a meaningful relationship.

In the Hull and White WWR model, the single parameter (b) drives the relationship, which has an impact similar to the correlation in the structural model. As shown in Figure 17.9, a positive gives a WWR effect and a higher CVA, whilst a negative value gives the reverse right-way risk effect. The overall profile is similar (although more dramatic) than that seen in the correlation model above. Whether or not this is economically reasonable, it illustrates that 100% correlation in the structural model should not be taken to imply a limiting case.

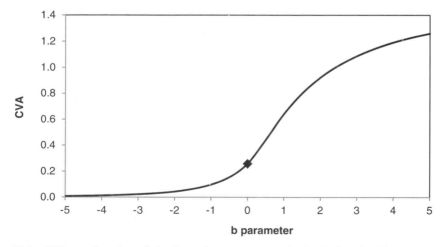

Figure 17.9   CVA as a function of the dependency parameter in the Hull and White approach.

17.4.4   Jump approaches

Jump approaches may be more relevant in cases of specific WWR, an obvious example being the aforementioned FX case. Ehlers and Schönbucher (2006) have considered the impact of a default on FX rates and illustrated cases where a hazard rate approach such as described in Section 17.4.1 is not able to explain empirical data, which implies a significant additional jump in the FX rate at default. A simple approach proposed by Levy and Levin (1999) to model FX exposures with WWR is to assume that the relevant FX rate jumps at the counterparty default time, as illustrated in Figure 17.10. The jump factor is often called a residual value (RV) factor of the currency and the assumption is that the currency devalues by an amount (1 – RV) at the counterparty default time and the relevant FX rate jumps accordingly.

As mentioned previously, an empirical estimate of the magnitude of the jump via the residual value (RV) of the currency for sovereign defaults is made by Levy and Levin (1999) based on 92 historical default events, and is shown in Table 17.2. The RV is larger for better-rated sovereigns, presumably because their default requires a more severe financial shock and the conditional FX rate therefore should move by a greater amount. Such an approach can also be applied to other counterparties, as described by Finger (2000). For example, a default of a large corporate should be expected to have quite a significant impact on their local currency (albeit smaller than that due to sovereign default).

The conditional expected exposure implied by the devaluation approach is shown in Figure 17.11 (and the calculations are described in Appendix 17B). The impact is fairly time-homogeneous, which may be criticised based on the previous observation that WWR may have a different impact for different future horizons.[9] For example, we may think that an immediate default of a sovereign may produce a large currency jump (small RV in the short term), whereas a later default may be less sudden and therefore lead to a smaller effect (larger RV in the medium to longer term).

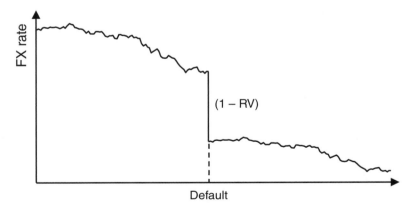

Figure 17.10   Illustration of the currency jump approach to WWR for FX products.

---

[9] Although the market data shown below approximately supports this homogeneous assumption.

Table 17.2 Residual currency values
(RV) upon sovereign default as a function
of the sovereign rating prior to default.

Rating	Residual value
AAA	17%
AA	17%
A	22%
BBB	27%
BB	41%
B	62%
CCC	62%

Source: Levy and Levin (1999).

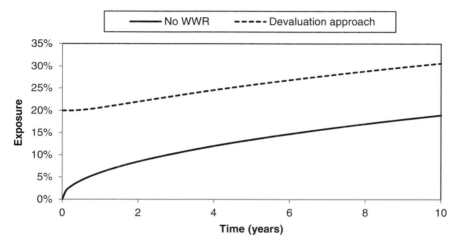

Figure 17.11   Illustration of the conditional expected exposure for the devaluation WWR approach
for an FX forward assuming a residual value factor RV = 80%. The FX volatility is assumed to be
15%.

The devaluation approach is also supported by observations in the CDS market. Most
CDSs are quoted in US dollars, but sometimes simultaneous quotes can be seen in other
currencies. For example, Table 17.3 shows the CDS quotes on Italian sovereign protection in both US dollars and euros. These CDS contracts should trigger on the same
credit event definitions, and thus the only difference between them is the currency of
cash payment on default. There is a large "quanto" effect, with euro-denominated CDS
cheaper by around 30% for all maturities. This shows an implied RV of approximately[10]
69% in the event of the default of Italy using five-year quotes (91/131). Not only is the
RV time-homogeneous, supporting the approach above, but it is also apparent several
months before the euro sovereign crisis developed strongly in mid-2011 and Italian credit
spreads widened significantly from the levels shown.

---

[10] This calculation would require adjustment for forward FX and cross-currency basis spreads.

Table 17.3   CDS quotes (mid market) on Italy in both US dollars and euros from April 2011.

Maturity	USD	EUR
1Y	50	35
2Y	73	57
3Y	96	63
4Y	118	78
5Y	131	91
7Y	137	97
10Y	146	103

Similar effects during the European sovereign crisis were seen later in 2011. For example, implied RVs of the euro were 91%, 83%, 80% and 75% for Greece, Italy, Spain and Germany respectively.[11] This is again consistent with a higher credit quality sovereign creating a stronger impact. The CDS market therefore allows WWR effect in currencies to be observed and potentially also hedged.

17.4.5   Credit derivatives

Credit derivatives are a special case as the WWR is unavoidable (buying credit protection on one party from another party) and may be specific WWR (e.g. buying protection from a bank on their sovereign). A number of approaches have been proposed to tackle counterparty risk in credit derivatives such as Duffie and Singleton (1999), Jarrow and Yu (2001), and Lipton and Sepp (2009).

In Appendix 17C, we describe the pricing for a CDS with counterparty risk using a simple model. We will ignore the impact of any collateral in the following analysis. Due to the highly contagious and systemic nature of CDS risks, the impact of collateral may be hard to assess and indeed may be quite limited (for example, see Section 11.3.6). We note also that many protection sellers in the CDS market such as monolines and CDPCs did not traditionally enter into collateral arrangements anyway (although this point is probably only of historical note).

We calculate the fair price for buying or selling CDS protection as a function of correlation between the reference entity and counterparty (the counterparty is selling protection). We assume that the reference entity CDS spread is 250 bps whereas the counterparty CDS spread is 500 bps.[12] Both LGDs are assumed to be 60%. Figure 15.22 shows the fair premium – i.e., reduced to account for CVA – that an institution should pay in order to buy CDS protection. Selling protection will require an increased premium. We can observe the very strong impact of correlation: one should be willing to pay only around 200 bps at 60% correlation to buy protection compared with paying 250 bps with a "risk-free" counterparty. The CVA in this case is 50 bps (per annum) or one-fifth of the risk-free CDS premium. At extremely high correlations, the impact is even more severe and the CVA is huge. At a maximum correlation of 100%, the CDS premium is

---

[11] For example, see "Quanto swaps signal 9 percent Euro drop on Greek default", Bloomberg, June 2010.

[12] These are assumed to be free of counterparty risk.

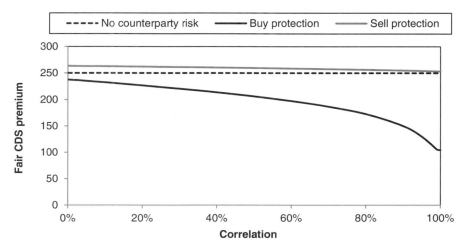

Figure 17.12   Fair CDS premium when buying protection subject to counterparty risk compared with the standard (risk-free) premium. The counterparty CDS spread is assumed to be 500 bps.

just above 100 bps, which relates entirely to the recovery value.[13] When selling protection the impact of CVA is much smaller and reduces with increasing correlation due to right-way risk.[14]

17.4.6   Wrong-way risk and collateral

Collateral is typically assessed in terms of its ability to mitigate exposure. Since WWR potentially causes exposure to increase significantly, the impact of collateral on WWR is very important to consider. However, this is very hard to characterise, because it is very timing-dependent. If the exposure increases gradually prior to a default then collateral can be received, whereas a jump in exposure deems collateral useless.

To understand the difficulty in characterising the impact of collateral, consider first the approach taken for general WWR in Section 17.4.2. Recalculating the CVA under the assumptions of a zero-threshold, two-way collateral agreement gives the results shown in Figure 17.13. The collateralised CVA is rather insensitive to WWR, with the slope of the line being quite shallow. This is because (according to the model) the greater the WWR, the more collateral is generally taken. The relative benefit of collateral is greatest when there is the most WWR (at +100% correlation) and has a negative impact when there is extreme right-way risk (less than –40% correlation) due to the need to post collateral.

---

[13] The premium based only on recovery value (i.e. where there is no chance of receiving any default payment) is $250 \times 40\% = 100$ bps.

[14] For zero or low correlation values, the protection seller may possibly suffer losses due to the counterparty defaulting when the CDS has a positive MTM (requiring a somewhat unlikely tightening of the reference entity credit spread). However, for high correlation values, the MTM of the CDS is very likely to be negative at the counterparty default time, and – since this amount must still be paid – there is virtually no counterparty risk.

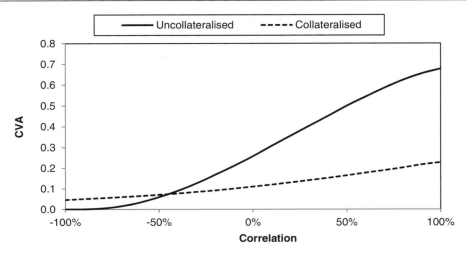

Figure 17.13 Combined impact of collateral (via a two-way collateral agreement) and WWR on the CVA of the swap portfolio considered previously in Figure 17.8.

In the above example, collateral seems to mitigate most of the impact of WWR as more collateral can be taken in WWR scenarios. However, let us instead consider the impact of collateral in the FX example from Section 17.4.4. The effect here is fairly obvious, but nevertheless is shown in Figure 17.14. Clearly, the jump effect cannot be collateralised and the exposure cannot be below the assumed devaluation of 20%. In this case, the ability of collateral to reduce WWR is very limited. If the weakening currency is gradual then the exposure can be well collateralised prior to the default. However, if devaluation of a currency is linked very closely to a sovereign default, it may be likely to result in a jump in the FX rate that cannot be collateralised in a timely manner.

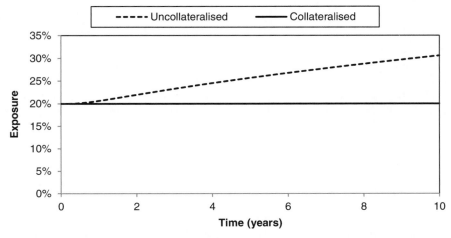

Figure 17.14 Impact of collateral on the conditional expected exposure of the FX forward shown previously in Figure 17.11.

Not surprisingly, approaches such as the devaluation approach for FX tend to quantify collateral as being near useless, whereas more continuous approaches such as the hazard rate and structural approaches suggest that collateral is an effective mitigant against WWR. The truth is probably somewhere in between and depends on the type of counterparty. Pykhtin and Sokol (2013) consider that the quantification of the benefit of collateral in a WWR situation must account for jumps and a period of higher volatility during the margin period of risk. They also note that WWR should be higher for the default of more systemic parties such as banks. Overall, their approach shows that WWR has a negative impact on the benefit of collateralisation. Interestingly, counterparties that actively use collateral (e.g. banks) tend to be highly systemic and will be subject to these extreme WWR problems, whilst counterparties that are non-systemic (e.g. corporates) often do not post collateral anyway.

17.4.7 Central clearing and wrong-way risk

Given their reliance on collateral as protection, central counterparties (CCPs) may be particularly prone to WWR, especially those that clear products such as CDS. A key aim of a CCP is that losses due to the default of a clearing member are contained within resources committed by that clearing member (the so-called "defaulter pays" approach described in Section 9.3.4). A CCP faces the risk that the "defaulter pays" resources of the defaulting member(s) may be insufficient to cover the associated losses. In such a case, the CCP would impose losses on their members and may be in danger of becoming insolvent themselves.

CCPs tend to disassociate credit quality and exposure. Parties must have a certain *credit* quality – typically, as defined by the CCP and not external credit ratings – to be clearing members. However, they will then be charged initial margins and default fund contributions driven primarily[15] by the *market* risk of their portfolio (that drives the exposure faced by the CCP). In doing this, CCPs are in danger of implicitly ignoring WWR.

For significant WWR transactions such as CDSs, CCPs have a problem of quantifying the WWR component in defining initial margins and default funds. As with the quantification of WWR in general, this is far from an easy task. Furthermore, WWR increases with increasing credit quality, as shown quantitatively and empirically in Figure 17.2 and Table 17.2 respectively. Similar arguments are made by Pykhtin and Sokol (2013), in that a large dealer represents more WWR than a smaller and/or weaker credit quality counterparty. Perversely, these aspects suggest that CCPs should require greater initial margin and default fund contributions from *better* credit quality members.[16]

Related to the above is the concept that a CCP waterfall may behave rather like a collateralised debt obligation (CDO), which has been noted by a number of authors including Murphy (2013), Pirrong (2013) and Gregory (2014). The comparison, illustrated in Figure 14.1, is that the "first loss" of the CDO is covered by "defaulter pays" initial margins and default funds, together with CCP equity. Clearing members, through their

---

[15] Some CCPs do base margins partially on credit quality but this tends to be a secondary impact.

[16] Of course, better credit quality members are less likely to default, but the impact in the event that they do is likely to be more severe.

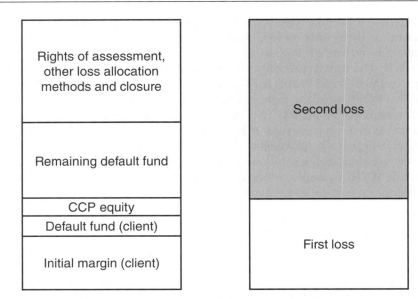

Figure 17.15   Comparison between a CCP loss waterfall and a CDO structure.

default fund contributions and other loss-allocation exposures, have a second loss position on the hypothetical CDO. Of course, the precise terms of the CDO are unknown and ever-changing, as they are based on aspects such as the CCP membership, portfolio of each member and initial margins held. However, what is clear is that the second loss exposure should correspond to a relatively unlikely event, since otherwise it would imply that initial margin coverage was too thin.

The second loss position that a CCP member is implicitly exposed to is therefore rather senior in CDO terms. Such senior tranches are well-known to be heavily concentrated in terms of their systemic risk exposure (see, for example, Gibson, 2004, Brennan et al., 2009, and Coval et al., 2009). This is a worrying aspect for the risk from default funds and other loss allocations methods of CCPs.

CCPs also face WWR on the collateral they receive. They will likely be under pressure to accept a wide range of eligible securities for initial margin purposes. Accepting more risky and illiquid assets creates additional risks and puts more emphasis on the calculation of haircuts that can also increase risk if underestimated. CCPs admitting a wide range of securities can become exposed to greater adverse selection as clearing members (and clients) will naturally choose to post collateral that has the greatest risk (relative to its haircut) and may also present the greatest WWR to a CCP (e.g. a European bank may choose to post European sovereign debt where possible). However, unlike bilateral counterparties, CCPs can change their rules to prevent this, such as imposing significant haircuts of various assets, although this in turn may create liquidity problems their members.

17.5 SUMMARY

In this chapter we have discussed the impact of WWR on counterparty risk. WWR is a subtle but potentially strong effect that can increase counterparty risk and CVA substantially. We have contrasted general and specific WWR and have described some common approaches to modelling WWR, highlighting some inherent weaknesses. We have considered the impact of WWR on collateral and the impact of WWR for central counterparties.

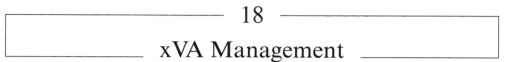

18

xVA Management

18.1 INTRODUCTION

In this chapter we look at the ways in which banks and other significant derivative users manage counterparty risk, funding, collateral and capital. Large banks have generally had "CVA desks" for many years to facilitate the pricing and hedging of counterparty risk. These units have evolved into "xVA desks" with a broader mandate that includes aspects such as funding, collateral optimisation and capital reduction. Smaller banks have in recent years embarked on the same process, driven by aspects such as IFRS 13 and Basel III. Even other financial institutions (e.g. supranationals) and non-financials (e.g. large corporates) have had the need to build some sort of xVA function driven by accounting needs and pricing optimisation.

18.2 THE ROLE OF AN xVA DESK

18.2.1 Motivation

xVA is derivatives pricing. Historically, derivatives trading and risk management would be siloed according to asset class (e.g. rates, FX, commodities, equities and credit) with the associated expertise. As CVA and other xVA terms have become increasingly important, there has been a clear need to manage these components. However, xVA is not asset class-specific and requires broad knowledge, not only of all asset classes, but also of underlying credit, collateral, funding and capital implications. Therefore, it has been common to have central functions to address two primary needs:

- *Pricing.* xVA arises heterogeneously. Long-dated trades, lower quality and uncollateralised counterparties will be the most significant contributors. It is important to charge the correct xVA to each transaction, taking into account the underlying incremental impact on counterparty risk, collateral, funding and capital. Failure to incorporate xVA correctly represents a failure to price properly.
- *xVA management.* New transactions have impacts on credit limits, collateral, funding and capital requirements. These aspects are unpredictable and can also give rise to significant mark-to-market volatility. It is therefore necessary for the xVA desk to take ownership and manage these components where possible. The general aim should be

that the xVA priced at trade inception is "locked in" over the lifetime without any additional costs (or benefits).

An xVA desk is generally set up as a central unit within an institution. There is a benefit in centralising all the required expertise and systems in one place. This does introduce clear challenges, such as when an xVA desk is perceived to be charging excessive premiums leading to reduced client revenue and lost business opportunities.

18.2.2   Role

An xVA desk is responsible for some or all of the components below, which collectively represent the cost of holding an OTC derivative transaction to maturity:

- *Counterparty risk.* The most common and fundamental role of the xVA desk is to own the counterparty risk in the event of a counterparty default, but also to manage the mark-to-market (MTM) volatility of the CVA.
- *Collateral optimisation.* The xVA desk may be involved in collateral optimisation by choosing the most efficient collateral to post in line with pricing the "cheapest-to-deliver" collateral (Section 13.4.3). Collateral also mitigates various xVA components such as CVA, FVA and KVA, and therefore the negotiation and renegotiation of collateral terms is a critical component to managing xVA.
- *Funding and margin.* The xVA desk may be responsible for managing funding and initial margin posting requirements and costs, for example via hedging internally with a treasury department. The overlap between CVA, DVA and FVA (Section 15.3.2) is also important in this respect.
- *Capital.* Under Basel III (Chapter 8), capital requirements for counterparty risk can be large and there are associated aspects such as the leverage ratio (Section 8.8.2). There may be responsibility to manage the potential increase in capital requirements and reduce capital usage, for example by hedging CVA with credit default swaps (CDSs).

Note that some of the above roles are complimentary. For example, hedging counterparty risk with CDS with respect to either default events (single-name CDS) or generic credit spread movements (index CDS) would be expected to also provide capital relief. However, these aspects are not always complimentary, as discussed later.

From a pricing perspective, broadly speaking there are two roles that an xVA desk performs:

- *Transfer pricing.* Here, xVA pricing is similar to buying insurance. The xVA desk requires a hard transfer of cash, at inception, to a trading or sales desk, with respect to a given new transaction. The trading or sales desk in turn will charge this to the client and any margin they can make on top of this is generally realised. It is hard for the originator (e.g. trading desk) to avoid passing on the charge in full, since this would be likely to lead to them generating a loss (although in limited situations they may do this in order to build or maintain the client relationship).
- *Hurdles.* In this case, the xVA desk only sets a hurdle for the trading or sales desk to achieve and there is no actual transfer of profit or risk. The originating desk is guided but not forced to charge this full amount to the client, although if they do not then

there is an indication that the transaction will not maintain the desired profitability for its lifetime (for example, in terms of return on capital metrics).

Historically, xVA has tended to migrate from the latter to the former category as xVA desks have been built out. Smaller banks tend to follow more of a hurdle approach, whilst larger and more sophisticated ones transfer price. The increasing impact of accounting standards (e.g. IFRS 13), regulatory rules (Basel III capital requirements, leverage ratio) and market practice (FVA, MVA) has increased the need for active management of xVA which has led in turn to the need for transfer pricing. However, not all xVA components are routinely transfer priced: the obvious current exception is capital where hurdles to achieve the correct return on capital are defined but most banks have not yet moved to up-front transfer pricing of KVA.

Note that xVA charges are typically not returned to the point of origination, even in the event of favourable outcomes (e.g. counterparties not defaulting). In reality, xVA premiums charged may be used indirectly or to offset other costs. For example, an xVA desk may use CVA premiums to buy options: this is not offsetting the CVA *per se*, but is one component in managing CVA volatility. However, any other economic decision in relation to the transaction (for example, unwind, option exercise, cancellation, termination, change in risk mitigants) should trigger an xVA adjustment. Indeed, in recent years optimisation via various restructurings (unwinds, change in collateral terms, etc.) have been proactively used by banks to minimise costs and maximise returns. An xVA desk should price such restructurings to give trading and sales desks the right incentive in such situations.

Note also that, when pricing a new transaction, aspects such as hedging activities have become increasingly important. For example, suppose a client executes a swap that is in turn hedged with the reverse swap. Since this hedge is likely with a financial counterparty then it will give rise to initial margins costs either bilaterally or due to the requirement for central clearing. The cost of this initial margin (MVA) may be charged to the original client, even though they themselves may be exempt from posting initial margin.

18.2.3   Profit centre or utility?

Another question is whether or not an xVA desk is a "profit centre" or a "utility", although these terms are not particularly distinct. It is generally agreed that an xVA desk should be a utility function with a zero P&L target. A zero P&L target should incentivise good behaviour for an xVA desk compared to a traditional trading desk. There should be no incentive to overcharge (or undercharge) xVA and active management via hedging, and paying out for risk-reducing transactions is encouraged. In an ideal world, the xVA would represent the total cost of a transaction and there would be no chance of experiencing future losses in excess of this amount.

Obviously, the above ideal is extremely impractical, as hedging xVA is imperfect. It is therefore important for a given institution to define their risk appetite to xVA. In general, the more one seeks to reduce the volatility of xVA, then the greater will be the long-term cost. This is particularly true for counterparty risk: warehousing credit risk will lead to massive CVA volatility, but expected long-term gains as actual credit losses are smaller than those priced in via risk-neutral default probabilities (Section 12.2.1). Banks traditionally warehouse credit risk arising from lending activities and have often looked at counterparty risk from derivatives in a similar fashion. This is particularly true for smaller and regional banks, and is especially relevant since the relative illiquidity of the CDS market makes hedging of counterparty risk on a single-name basis impossible in most cases.

The warehousing approach has become increasingly impractical over the years with developments such as IFRS 13 and Basel III. An xVA desk will need to have a carefully defined limits structure so that they cannot run significant open risks. That said, they should also have leeway to make tactical decisions where hedges might be expensive and inefficient, and subject to their limits, they may prefer to warehouse the risk. Some components will be relatively easy to hedge, some less easy and some will be unhedgeable, as discussed in Section 18.3.

It is therefore clear that, whilst an xVA desk may have a zero P&L target, it is important to consider the allocation of potential excess gains or losses periodically in some way. Some of these gains or losses may be accounting-driven (e.g. from a credit spread widening) whilst some will be actually realised (e.g. default losses). In the former case, a homogenous allocation back to the point of origination would be most obvious, potentially weighted by the xVA charge (i.e. those paying the most xVA will experience most of the excess gains or losses). In some scenarios, such as defaults, it may be appropriate to consider a more heterogeneous allocation to the point of origination. In the event of default, the workout process (the process of negotiating claims with a defaulted counterparty) is also important and the xVA desk should be an active participant, managing their claims optimally.

It may be helpful to maintain some "constructive ambiguity" in the possible future allocation of xVA losses. There is otherwise an adverse selection problem that the originating salesperson or trader may choose to transact with the wrong type of clients (e.g. lower credit quality) based on the fact that all risks are perceived to be passed through fully to the xVA desk. If there is a chance that some losses could one day make their way back to the point of origination, then this may incentivise better behaviour. In some client relationships, the originating trader or business may be the best placed to understand the nature of the underlying risk, especially in relation to complex aspects such as wrong-way risk. Of course, this type of allocation may also be seen as unfair in some situations.

18.2.4   Operation and rollout

A challenge for an xVA desk, especially in the early stages of development, is the coverage of transactions. It is important to address the biggest xVA users, which tend to be uncollateralised, long-dated transactions. For CVA assessment, it is possible to ignore many transactions such as those that are well collateralised or with high-quality counterparties. However, the biggest xVA-related losses for banks in the last crisis arose from transactions with monoline insurers, which were generally ignored for these reasons. Furthermore, xVA generally applies to every transaction in some way (e.g. see Table 13.1) and it is important to correctly assess all components. This also applies to being able to price the costs of hedges (e.g. initial margin requirements) and charge the client with whom the originating transaction is being made.

The xVA charge is often the key determinant in the price of an OTC derivative. A key aspect of the transfer pricing of xVA is therefore that there must be a robust and industrialised process in place for calculation of xVA charges in real time. To do this properly is complex from a systems point of view and simple methods are often used by necessity. The ways in which real-time pricing is implemented vary in sophistication, as below:

- *Lookup tables.* A lookup table will provide a rapid estimation of an xVA charge based on grids, which may be produced separately for each product type, maturity and credit quality. Such calculations cannot, of course, account for trade specifics or risk mitigants, but they do make for a very simple, rapid and transparent approach.
- *Stand-alone calculations.* Stand-alone xVA pricing for given products can be implemented relatively simply (for example, in spreadsheets) and does capture more transaction-specific aspects, but ignores potential risk mitigants and portfolio effects. For directional transactions, this is sometimes not as problematic, because components such as netting may be only weak.
- *Full simulation-based pricing.* Incorporation of all aspects (especially netting, collateral and portfolio effects) can only be done accurately with simulation-based approaches that can run an entire group of transactions (usually at the counterparty level but potentially at the portfolio level). Practically, this requires a simulation engine that can generate all relevant market variables and compute values of the current transactions and the new transaction in all required scenarios through time. This requires very rapid processing power and/or use of significant data storage (for example, see the discussion in Section 10.3.3).

Full simulation-based quantification is a requirement for accurate incremental pricing at the counterparty or portfolio level. This is likely to be a requirement for some or all of the xVA components. In particular:

- *CVA and DVA.* CVA and DVA are typically required at the netting or collateral set level (Section 14.4). This will be the same, or a sub-set, of the counterparty portfolio.
- *FVA.* Depending on the nature of the collateral agreement and the underlying assumptions, FVA may need to be calculated at the stand-alone (transaction) level or potentially the entire portfolio level (Section 15.2.5).
- *MVA.* The computation of initial margin for bilateral transactions will be at the portfolio level, unless a simple methodology such as the standardised schedule shown in Table 6.8 is used. For centrally cleared transactions, the initial margin will be calculated depending on the extent of the cross-margining at the CCP. Typically, this may mean that all transactions within an asset class at the same CCP will constitute the portfolio for the calculation.
- *KVA.* The default risk capital charge (Section 8.1.2) is additive across netting sets and therefore follows a similar calculation to CVA. However, due to the portfolio-level assumptions underlying the standardised and advanced CVA capital charges (Section 8.7) and even the leverage ratio (Section 8.8.2), pricing KVA will likely constitute a calculation for the whole portfolio, although simple approximations may be reasonable in many cases.

The requirement for counterparty and portfolio-level calculations in real time clearly requires relatively sophisticated systems implementations that will be discussed below

(Section 18.4). Even if a bank has a relatively advanced set-up that allows accurate, real-time, incremental xVA, there may be certain non-trivial manual aspects to pricing a new transaction. It is therefore likely that trading, sales and marketing may have only relatively simple pricing tools and must rely on the xVA desk to calculate the official price. In some markets, such as short-dated FX transactions, a price must be quoted in minutes and the operational aspects to achieving this are clearly a challenge.

Note that it is not only new transactions that need to be priced. It is also necessary to price unwinds, restructuring of transactions, changes in risk mitigants (e.g. CSA renegotiation), novations, moving a bilateral portfolio to a CCP (often known as "backloading") and even moving a portfolio from one CCP to another. All of these will have an impact of one or more xVA terms, and may need to be quantified on a dynamic basis. Some examples of the different xVA terms in these situations are given in the next chapter.

Decisions where there is a choice, such as the exercise or cancellation of an option or the utilisation of an ATE (Section 5.5.2) also depend on xVA. For example, the exercise of a physically settled swaption should be done optimally with respect to the xVA components of the underlying swap. Failure to do so may lead to sub-optimal exercise where the risk-free value of the swap is positive but the xVA adjusted value is not. There is a potential transfer pricing problem here if the xVA is charged upfront: this removes the incentive for an originating trader to exercise or break a transaction optimally, since the P&L impact resides on the xVA desk (who may experience losses due to sub-optimal behaviour). Ideally, an xVA desk would impose a cost or refund on any economic decision to avoid this. This would usually translate into a conditional charge for exercising an option or a rebate for cancelling a transaction.

Note finally that there will be cases where banks may adjust the theoretical xVA in a charge to a client. This could arise due to a number of reasons, such as:

- *Credit risk warehousing.* Due to the belief that warehousing credit risk will generate profits and therefore a lower CVA can be charged (see also the comments in Section 16.3.8).
- *Work-out process.* The assumption of a lower LGD from the view that the claim is more senior or will have a favourable work-out process.
- *Client relationships.* Behaviour driven by the client relationship could include charging less for a transaction in anticipation of future, more profitable, transactions, or the assumption that it will be unwound early and the lifetime xVA costs will not therefore be realised.
- *Capital relief.* Reduction in KVA due to the capital relief achieved from hedging (for example, with CDS indices). See also the discussion in Section 16.3.8.
- *Change in regulation and policy.* The assumption of changes in internal policy (e.g. cost of capital or funding), or relaxation or tightening of regulation (e.g. the removal of the CVA capital charge exemption – see Section 8.7.7).

Any of the above must be clearly rationalised and balanced against accounting policy, especially with respect to CVA, where accounting requirements are relatively prescriptive. For example, charging a lower CVA due to the view that credit risk would be warehoused would likely lead to accounting losses due to the need to use credit spreads for CVA quantification under IFRS 13 (Section 12.2.2). On the other hand, in the current environment, transactions may be executed even though their KVA is not sufficient to meet the relevant return on capital hurdle. This situation will not lead to immediate losses, but will lead to poor returns compared to the required regulatory capital actually deployed over the lifetime of the transaction.

18.3   HEDGING xVA

18.3.1   Motivation

A key aspect of xVA, as mentioned first in Section 4.4.3, is the ability to separate the basic valuation of a derivative with the xVA adjustments. The same applies to hedging (Figure 18.1): whilst the market risks on a derivative may be hedged by a trading desk in isolation, the xVA desk will seek to hedge their own market risk. This separation of the xVA is relevant due to the asset-specific nature of different classes of derivatives, combined with the fact that xVA depends generally on counterparty risk, collateral, funding and capital. Additionally, whilst the basic valuation of any derivative portfolio is additive, the xVAs generally are not. This requires a special treatment of xVA hedging at the portfolio level. Furthermore, xVA tends to be more complex than basic valuation, often involving components such as volatility and cross-gamma, which may not be as complex, especially for linear products.

18.3.2   xVA as an exotic option

It is possible to see xVA terms as driven by a series of option payoffs. For example, see the definition of exposure (Section 7.1.4) or the Sorensen–Bollier analogy that represents swap exposure as a series of European swaptions (Section 10.2.2). This implies that the problem of hedging should be approached in a similar way to that of hedging options (potentially quite complex ones). However, there are some important considerations to keep in mind:

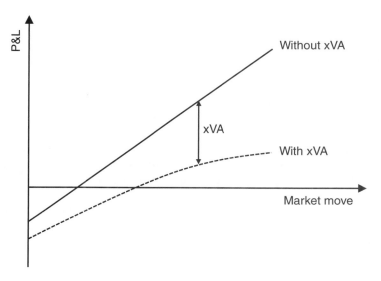

Figure 18.1   Illustration of xVA hedging.

- *Documentation aspects.* The option payoff in exposure is not precisely defined, as it depends on the documentation of legal aspects such as the close-out value in the event of a default (Section 5.2).
- *Complexity.* Even if xVA is defined by the prices of various options, these options may be complex such as being in- or out-of-the-money and long-dated. Hence, the pricing and hedging will be difficult.
- *Credit, collateral, funding and capital costs.* xVA is generally an option payoff integrated against some credit, collateral, funding or capital cost. These underlying costs are quite opaque, subjective to estimate and difficult or impossible to hedge.
- *Cross-dependency.* The dependency or relationship between different variables (for example, interest rates and credit spreads) may be impossible to hedge and lead to difficult cross-gamma effects.
- *Lack of arbitrage.* When pricing derivative products, arbitrage is a key aspect. Mispricing leads to arbitrage as other market participants can transact at these incorrect prices and hedge in order to lock in a profit. However, a mispricing of xVA is not directly arbitrageable since it usually represents a private transaction between two parties.

For the above reasons, it is important to be pragmatic and bear in mind that some xVA components can be hedged, some can be hedged with difficulty leading to residual basis risks, and some cannot be hedged at all. In order to understand this, take a simple example of hedging the CVA on an interest rate swap. The CVA is sensitive to interest rates, interest rate volatility and credit spreads, and so to hedge will require an interest rate future/swap, single-name CDS and interest rate swaption. In theory, these hedges would not be single transactions (e.g. one would hedge with a series of swaptions to match the vega profile). The single-name CDS that would ideally be used is likely to be illiquid and so some index or other proxy must be used. The hedges will also require frequent rebalancing as market movements occur. Finally, even if the xVA is hedged on rates and credit, then a simultaneous move where interest rates go down and credit spreads widen can cause significant P&L movements (cross-gamma). The function of an xVA desk is therefore part trading desk and part portfolio management group.

18.3.3   Misalignment

An xVA portfolio will experience sensitivity to every single market parameter for the underlying transactions in every currency, asset class and product type. Furthermore, there will be sensitivities specific to xVA such as where volatility risk arises from non-volatility-sensitive products.

The increasing volatility of xVA has led more banks to consider some sort of hedging strategy. Such a strategy will ultimately be a compromise. Firstly, there is the question of what is the purpose of the hedging. There could be at least three different aspects here:

- *Actual economic risk.* The actual underlying economic financial risk (e.g. defaults).
- *Accounting xVA.* The changes in xVA driven by the accounting practices (e.g. credit spread widening).
- *Regulatory capital.* The regulatory capital requirements.

In an ideal world, the above would be perfectly aligned, but in reality the misalignment can be significant. For example, DVA is a component of accounting xVA that is not generally recognised as being economically realistic (Section 14.6.8). On the other hand, banks generally view FVA as being an important consideration (Section 15.1), but it is not yet mentioned in accounting standards or regulatory capital rules. Different banks will have a different focus on the above: a bank that is capital-constrained may have the primary aim to reduce capital, whereas another may focus on reducing accounting volatility. Recall also the potential issues with market risk hedges increasing capital according to Basel III rules (Section 8.7.5), although some local regulators have implemented exemptions. EBA (2015b) report that banks are sensitive to these capital-consuming hedges, with interest rate swaps, FX forwards, interest rate options and cross-currency swaps mentioned in particular.

Finally, any change in funding and capital costs will potentially impact the P&L of the xVA desk. However, this generally reflects internal parameters such as a funds transfer pricing (FTP) curve or a return on equity (ROE) target. These parameters are likely to be semi-stationary although indirectly driven by continuously evolving market rates (e.g. see Figure 12.11). Any changes here will cause a P&L move that is very difficult to hedge and it is probably not relevant to continuously remark such parameters, since this will merely cause spurious MTM volatility.

In general, xVA can be represented as a combination of market risk with some underlying credit, collateral, funding or capital cost. We will consider these terms below.

18.3.4   Market risk

The market risk sensitivity of xVA can be broadly broken down into:

- *Spot/forward rates.* The sensitivity to spot and forward rates, such as interest rates and FX. This is generally hedgeable with the underlying hedging instruments being liquid, potentially exchange-traded or centrally cleared.
- *Volatility.* The sensitivity to implied volatility, such as FX options or interest rate swaptions. This is also hedgeable, although the underlying instruments will generally be bilateral OTC products and may be illiquid and unavailable in some cases. For example, hedging long-dated volatility may not be possible.
- *Correlation.* The sensitivity to correlation between different exposure variables (such as two different interest rates). This is generally unhedgeable except via exotic product such as quantos, basket options and spread options, which are not usually liquid.

Note that we can combine market risk hedges across some or all xVA terms. For example, an interest rate hedge may apply because an increase in rates could cause both CVA and FVA to increase. If an xVA desk does not have a mandate to hedge the change in a particular component (e.g. capital costs via KVA), then this would obviously not be included in their P&L.

The number of sensitivities that the above categories can constitute is large, even in some rather simple cases, let alone for large portfolios of trades. For example, a single cross-currency swap gives rise to interest rate risk (in two currencies and potentially also OIS-LIBOR basis risk), interest rate volatility risk (two currencies), FX risk, FX volatility risk and correlation risk (between both interest rates and between interest rates and the FX rate). All hedges should also ideally be considered across the term structure, which is often impractical as it leads to increasing numbers of hedging transactions.

18.3.5   Credit, funding and capital hedging

Whilst market risk hedging is reasonably practical, the hedging of credit and funding aspects less straightforward. Credit hedging is clearly more difficult due to the illiquidity of the underlying CDS market. Potential hedging instruments are:

- *Single-name CDS.* If liquid, then this is the ideal hedge against counterparty credit quality. However, there is a difference between hedging the credit spread and the "jump-to-default" risk. In the former case, the focus is on a small credit spread change and the latter an actual default event. It is important to be aware also of the counterparty risk of the protection seller. Ideally, one should buy protection from a high-quality counterparty with minimal correlation to the original counterparty (if the CDS is centrally cleared then this may be viewed as resolving this problem).
- *Single-name proxy CDS.* Hedging using a similar credit may be viewed as efficient, although this obviously depends on the underlying credit spread correlation. Also important is whether the proxy credit would default in the same situations. In some situations, this may be the case (e.g. the proxy is a sovereign that would always support the counterparty in question) and in some cases not (e.g. a name in a similar region and sector).
- *Index CDS.* Credit indices are more liquid and can be used to provide a macro hedge of a general credit spread widening, but do not provide any protection against actual counterparty defaults.[1] The benefit of index hedging (and associated capital relief) also depends heavily on there being a significant correlation between index and single-name CDS, which may not always be observed in practice.[2]

Due to the above, most banks would consider some credit hedging to be relevant in order to avoid excessive fluctuation in their accounting CVA. They may also use, where possible, credit options to manage convexity and single-name CDS to hedge large exposures.

Hedging of funding costs is generally not possible, but in case the xVA desk is responsible for these costs then credit indices would be one potential proxy. This obviously depends on the policy for setting the funding cost for FVA purposes. Capital costs would most obviously be hedged via equity (e.g. stock buyback), although this again depends also on the actual policy in setting return on capital hurdles.

18.3.6   Cross-gamma

"Cross-gamma" is the term used to describe a dependency between two underlying variables due to non-zero correlation. The most problematic cross-gamma is between credit spreads and other market variables, which may be linked to wrong-way risk components. The definition of cross-gamma is that even if the two variables are hedged independently, their *joint* move will have a material impact. In practical terms, cross-gamma might be

---

[1] Except implicitly, because the name happened to be referenced in the index.
[2] For example, see "CDS de-correlation a threat to CVA hedging, traders warn", *Risk*, 3rd September 2015.

experienced due a major market movement such as interest rates falling together with a credit spread widening. In such a situation, the larger uncollateralised exposures on receiver swap positions will then require more credit hedges, but the cost of these hedges will not be funded by gains on existing interest rate hedges, unless these accounted for the underlying cross-gamma effect.

18.3.7   P&L explain

It is important to be able to predict and explain P&L changes in relation to xVA. This is a common requirement for trading desks to understand the performance of their hedging and the source of any material unhedged moves. "P&L explain" aims to decompose the P&L changes into simple drivers that may be related to market movements that can be hedged or changes to contractual terms or data that cannot. The following components need to be included in a P&L explain for xVA:

- Market risk:
  - time decay (theta);
  - deltas (interest rates, FX, etc);
  - volatility (vega);
  - credit spreads;
  - cross-gamma correlation;
  - default events; and
  - funding and capital costs.
- Trading decisions:
  - new transactions;
  - unwinds;
  - novations;
  - terminations; and
  - exercise decisions.
- Contractual terms and other changes:
  - changes to netting terms;
  - changes in collateral terms (CSA renegotiation);
  - rating changes (leading to a change in credit spread mapping, for example); and
  - model changes or recalibration of semi-static parameters (e.g. mean reversion).

18.3.8   Capital relief from hedges

Capital charges are expensive, so potential capital relief achievable from hedges would be welcome. This could be seen as a joint reduction of CVA and KVA. However, achieving capital relief is problematic due to the relatively simplistic and conservative methodologies used for defining capital charges.

Under Basel III, market risk hedges cannot create any capital relief since they are not included in either the standardised or advanced methodologies. These methodologies actually implicitly assume the market risk is already being hedged by an xVA desk. Market risk hedges will actually cause an increase in capital charges, as illustrated in Figure 18.2. Here, suppose an uncollateralised transaction is hedged back-to-back with a collateralised transaction. Note that the market risk capital framework would see no net market risk.

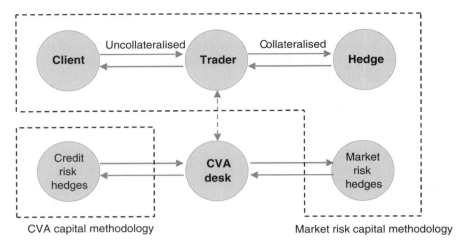

Figure 18.2   Illustration of xVA market risk hedges increasing capital requirements.

However, there is of course xVA associated with this situation, but any xVA market risk hedges are not recognised in the CVA capital charge and must therefore be recognised under the standard market risk rules where they will increase capital. As mentioned in Section 8.7.6, some regulators have exempted CVA-related market risk hedges, preventing them from adding to capital. A better solution would be to integrate the CVA capital charge methodology into the market risk methodology, but this is currently viewed by some regulators as being too complicated (e.g. see the discussion on the fundamental review of the trading book in Section 8.8.1). A potential solution is proposed in BCBS (2015).

The only hedges that can currently reduce counterparty risk capital are credit-related. This includes single-name and index CDS, and also even some more complex hedges such as swaptions.[3] Single-name CDS hedges are obviously most effective. They can reduce default risk capital charges subject to the double default formula (Section 8.1.3) and can reduce CVA capital charges for a given counterparty, as shown in Figure 18.3 for a single transaction example. The main problem here is that the delta-neutral hedge (which would minimise the accounting CVA) will not necessarily give the optimal capital relief. This misalignment is particularly acute for the standardised CVA capital charge, since its definition of exposure is rather crude. For an IMM bank using the more sophisticated advanced methodology, then the agreement is better. However, even under IMM there is a likely misalignment between the regulatory and front-office calculations that may be driven by:

- the use of risk-neutral (front-office) or real world (regulatory) parameters;
- the requirement to use stressed data in determining EEPE for capital calculations (Section 8.6.2);
- the requirement to use stressed market data and add this to the standard calculation for CVA capital (Section 8.7.2);[4]

---

[3] For example, see "CVA hedge losses prompt focus on swaptions and guarantees", *Risk*, 28th October 2014.

[4] This may be a limited impact but is relevant since the delta hedge is likely to perform worse with stressed parameters.

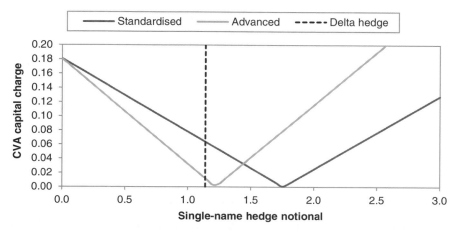

Figure 18.3 Impact of a single-name CDS hedge on the standardised and advanced CVA capital charges for a single six-year interest rate swap. The delta-neutral CDS hedge is also shown (dotted line).

- the requirement to include an alpha multiplier in the EEPE from the point of view of capital calculations (Section 8.3.2)[5] – indeed, as noted by Pykhtin (2012), the use of the alpha factor incentivises systematic overhedging of CVA;[6] and
- the requirement to use EEPE instead of EPE in capital calculations (Section 8.3.2).[7]

The above misalignment leaves an xVA desk in a difficult situation, since they have to choose between hedging the CVA as defined by their own calculations and accounting rules or maximising capital relief via counterparty risk-related capital charges.

In practice, the majority of credit hedging will be performed using indices; Figure 18.4 illustrates the impact of index hedging on the capital charge for the same example as above. Under the standardised CVA capital charge the benefit is poor for the same reason as in the single-name case, and also because of the 50% correlation between index and counterparty spread that is assumed in the standardised formula (Section 8.7.2). Under the advanced approach, a higher correlation is usually modelled and the capital relief is therefore better, although the delta hedge is still not optimal from a capital relief point of view.

Finally, it should be noted that the above examples are for a single counterparty (and transaction), and there will also be a portfolio effect that will potentially make the index hedging more efficient, as shown in Figure 18.5. For a larger portfolio, index hedging becomes beneficial due to a diversification of the idiosyncratic risk, leaving more systemic risk that can be hedged with the index. This effect is actually more beneficial in the standardised case due to the relatively low 25% correlation implicitly assumed between counterparty spreads (Section 8.7.2).

---

[5] This would apply to a bank with IMM but not specific risk approval (Table 8.4).

[6] Note that this point and the last three of the five bullet points only apply to an IMM bank using the standardised CVA capital charge. An advanced bank will model CVA according to the formula in Section 8.7.3 and will not be exposed to the calculation of EEPE or use the alpha factor.

[7] As previous footnote.

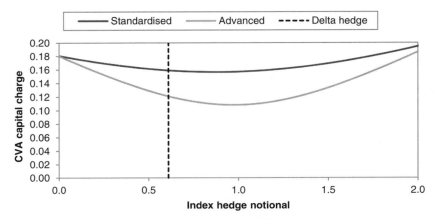

Figure 18.4 Impact of an index CDS hedge on the standardised and advanced CVA capital charges for a single six-year interest rate swap. The dotted line represents the hedge that minimises the P&L variance.

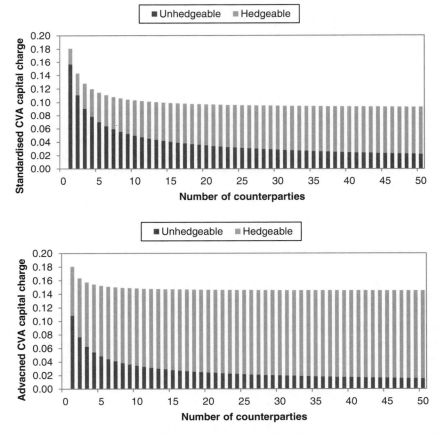

Figure 18.5 Impact of an index CDS hedging as the size of the portfolio increases for the standardised (top) and advanced (bottom) CVA capital charges.

18.3.9   Market practice and hedging

Many banks have been hedging CVA for a number of years and are incorporating other xVA components (e.g. FVA) as appropriate. Hedging is generally discretionary in nature to a degree (Figure 18.6) due to the complexity of the xVA risk and the underlying illiquidity or lack of availability of hedges. Market risk hedges are most common, which is not surprising due to the underlying instruments being the most liquid and not subject to significant additional counterparty risks. Credit spread risk is the next most common but is less liquid and, as noted above, banks would prefer in general to warehouse some counterparty risk. The hedging of credit spreads is generally driven by the need to reduce accounting P&L volatility and/or capital rather than reducing the actual economic risk. Not surprisingly, vegas, gammas and other terms are less commonly hedged.

It is important to have limits in place to define the appetite for P&L volatility for the various different Greeks (Figure 18.7). Credit spread delta limits are probably the most

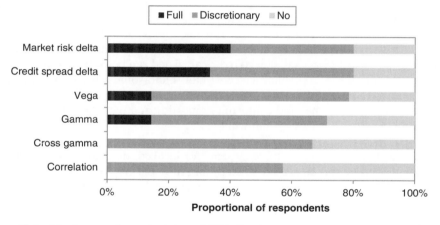

Figure 18.6   Market practice on hedging of CVA Greeks.
Source: Deloitte/Solum CVA survey, 2013.

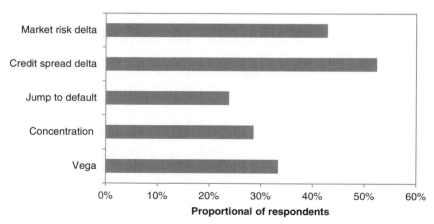

Figure 18.7   Market practice on CVA limits.
Source: Deloitte/Solum CVA survey, 2013.

important to define since, whilst it may be profitable to warehouse credit risk, this is usually the biggest driver of accounting volatility. Credit spread hedging is therefore a balance between reducing the volatility of xVA but without paying away the full credit risk premium. (As noted above, credit options may be preferable for this reason.) Other important limits are market risk delta and vega, which can both be significant. Finally, it is important to have jump-to-default limits (to avoid a single counterparty exposure being too high although this is more the purpose of credit limits as discussed in Section 4.3.1) and concentration limits (for example with respect to a given region).

18.4   XVA SYSTEMS

18.4.1   Overview

The underlying complexity of xVA, the need for accurate real-time calculations and related regulatory requirements lead to significant systems demands. The calculation of Greeks for xVA is potentially very time-consuming due to the high dimensionality (e.g. multiple currencies and FX pairs) involved and the significant inherent nonlinearities (which imply that term structure and cross-gamma components can be significant). This means that the number of Greeks that need to be calculated can be extremely large, which in turn requires optimisation. This has led most banks and some other significant users of OTC derivatives to invest heavily in xVA systems to be able to support pricing and risk management in a timely manner and conform to reporting and regulatory requirements.

The building blocks of an xVA system will be:

- *Data.* Most institutions have multiple systems for legal, trade, market and historical data. Data collection and storage is substantial and must be obtained from various front-office trading and back-office systems and external sources. Data requirements cover the following aspects:
  - o trade population (including hedges);
  - o legal entities;
  - o netting agreements;
  - o collateral agreements;
  - o market data;
  - o historical data (including stress periods);
  - o credit ratings, default probabilities and loss given defaults (internal and external);
  - o credit spreads; and
  - o simulation data storage (for intraday pricing).
- Rapid data retrieval is also important so that incremental calculations can be made at the netting set or portfolio level.
- *Simulation engines.* The heart of the xVA calculation is a simulation that must be able to efficiently generate the evolution of all relevant risk factors with an underlying correlation structure. It must also be possible to generate additional scenarios maintaining "scenario consistency", for example in order to run an intraday calculation without re-running an entire netting set or portfolio.
- *Revaluation functionality.* After generating a large number of scenarios, it is necessary to revalue every single transaction in each scenario. Whilst most common products are fast to value, the scale is huge, with potentially trillions of valuation calls required.

Valuations can be speeded up significantly via applying both financial and computational optimisations. The key point is not to refine valuations far beyond the error margins of the underlying variables being simulated, especially in the case of long time horizons where there is significant uncertainty. In such a context, multidimensional interpolation of prices and the use of approximate pricing functions should not necessarily be a major issue, although regulators and users may be concerned about such approximations.

- *Collateral.* It must be possible to track existing collateral (whether this be in cash or other securities), calculate the projected future collateral in each simulation, and calculate the impact of this (together with current collateral) on exposure. This must include impacts such as segregation and also be able to simulate future initial margin.
- *Reporting.* Reporting functionality such as xVA for financial statements, limit breaches, P&L explain, and scenario analysis should be available.
- *Greeks.* Hedging and P&L explain requires Greeks for all relevant risk factors covering both market and credit risk. Due to the number of Greeks, calculation by finite difference ("bump and run") methods may be extremely time-consuming.
- *Backtesting and stress testing tools.* Basel III is introducing significant requirements over the backtesting of EPE, which will involve the storage and tracking of hypothetical portfolios and the checking of PFE at multiple confidence levels and time horizons (Section 8.6.4). Basel III also requires stress-testing of counterparty risk, as discussed in Section 8.6.6.

18.4.2   Optimisations

It is inevitable that some optimisation will be required in order to manage the volume of calculations and likely requirements for near-real-time xVA. Such optimisations can be in relation to hardware, software or numerical methods. Typical methods used are:

- *Pre-calculations.* It has been common to rely on pre-calculations and intermediate storage to circumvent the xVA real-time workload (for example, see Section 10.7.2). This involves simulating only new transactions and relying on pre-computed values for an existing netting set or portfolio. This does, however, require significant data storage, and will probably become less common as processing power and other optimisations become more common.
- *Numerical optimisations.* Relatively straightforward numerical approximations such as random number generation (low discrepancy sequences and using the same random numbers each day to avoid unnecessary noise), cashflow bucketing (Section 10.3.3), or optimisation of revaluation functionality (Section 14.4.5) are often used with good speed-up at minimum loss of accuracy. When calculating sensitivities, it is important to avoid the need to revalue certain positions that have no sensitivity to a given variable. This can be implemented algorithmically (e.g. if a valuation does not change in a given simulation then other instances in other simulations are not revalued) or via a mapping of each trade to the dependent market data.
- *American Monte Carlo.* As mentioned in Section 14.4.5, American Monte Carlo (AMC) is an approach to optimisation quite commonly used in the industry (Cesari et al., 2009). This produces speed improvement since the pricing overhead is absorbed within the simulation via regressing with respect to the relevant market variables.

There is significant implementation work involved in AMC and the specification of the regressions is not trivial. AMC can be particularly advantageous for portfolios with significant numbers of exotics (especially those with embedded Bermudan-style optionality).

- *Processors.* The use of parallel processing involves splitting xVA computations across different processors. However, it is important to balance splitting calculations evenly, but also avoid repeating calculations (such as calibrations). Additionally, some implementations have relied on more specialised hardware solutions such as graphics processing units (GPUs) that offer potential speed-up of traditional CPUs but with implementation effort and additional expense.
- *Adjoint algorithmic differentiation.* One of the more recent but increasingly popular applications to xVA is adjoint algorithmic differentiation (AAD). AAD is specific to the generation of sensitivities (Greeks) and requires significant implementation and architecture design. However, AAD allows the calculation of an arbitrary number of Greeks at a cost that is a small fixed multiple often claimed to be in the region of 4 (for example, see Capriotti and Lee, 2014). For large portfolios where the number of required sensitivities is large (potentially in the hundreds), the additional overhead in implementing AAD is probably worthwhile.

18.4.3   Shared or separate implementations

There may be a number of different areas with xVA-related requirements in an institution, notably:

- *Front-office.* The calculation of xVA for pricing purposes.
- *Finance.* Daily valuation of transactions and the representation of this both internally for management purposes and externally for financial reporting (accounting) purposes.
- *Risk and regulatory.* The generation of PFE for limits monitoring. This may also apply to regulatory capital calculations if the bank has, or intends to achieve, IMM approval.

In an ideal world, all xVA pricing, valuation, risk management and regulatory requirements would be addressed via a single holistic solution. However, in practice, it is not uncommon to see separate risk and front-office implementations. Whilst systems separation may occur due to organisational or historical reasons, there are more relevant explanations as to why they may be divided. Risk management and regulatory models have to support a very large trade coverage (upwards of 95% of the trade population), but tend not to have the same level of model sophistication or computational intensity as the front office models and systems for pricing and valuation. On the other hand, front-office xVA implementations tend to have a reduced product coverage (in the short- to medium-term, at least) but require much more precision and high calculation speed (for example, due to the requirement for Greeks). Table 18.1 below compares different xVA implementations.

Nevertheless, there are institutions that are aligned with respect to xVA infrastructure. In such a situation, it may still be necessary to support different calculations such as the need for stressed data in regulatory calculations and some other minor aspects (e.g. the treatment of certain netting terms or break clauses). The advantages and disadvantages of such consistency are outlined in Table 18.2. When combining approaches, there is

Table 18.1   Comparison of risk & regulatory and front-office requirements for xVA implementations.

	Risk and regulatory	Front-office
Focus	Limits monitoring and counterparty risk regulatory capital requirements (IMM)	xVA pricing and valuation
Trade coverage	High and may only exclude some exotic trades or those referencing usual underlyings. Capital charges for trades not modelled under IMM can be very punitive	Likely to be quite low, at least in the first stages of development, with a small population of trades potentially capturing a large fraction of the total xVA
Counterparty coverage	High, with few exceptions (e.g. central counterparties)	May ignore well-collateralised transactions and high credit quality counterparties
Optimal simulation approach	Pathwise (to support the calculation of quantities such as EEPE and PFE)	Direct (to optimise convergence of xVA integrals – Section 14.4.5)
Calibration	Generally real-world-based, although risk-neutral is becoming more common	Generally risk-neutral
Speed	Less important as long as entire batch can be run overnight and intraday limits checking can be done using stored simulations	More critical as intraday CVA calculations must be very fast, even for large netting sets. Significant Greeks requirement also
Architecture	Batch-driven process with limited intraday functionality (e.g. for limits checking)	More real-time calculations and Greeks required (may use AMC and/or AAD)
Release cycle	Infrequent, due to less frequent changes and regulatory requirements	Frequent, due to rapidly evolving front-office needs (e.g. new Greeks and new measures such as FVA)

Table 18.2   Strengths and weaknesses of consistent and separate xVA frameworks.

	Advantages	Disadvantages
Single xVA solution	• Consistent calculations for risk management, accounting and internal pricing. This can be particularly advantageous when hedging CVA for accounting and/or capital reduction purposes • More alignment between KVA and actual return on capital	• Excessive limits breaches due to the use of risk-neutral calibrations and potentially less stable backtesting results • Still need to incorporate stressed parameters (e.g. implied volatility from the past) in exposure calculation (Basel III)
Separate solutions	• Separate ownership of methodologies • Changes can be made in one system without impacting the other • Optimisations can be specific to each implementation	• Extra workload due to having two sets of calculations and calibrations • Lack of consistency between accounting, capital and internal pricing numbers

likely to be a need for very robust controls across risk and front-office. It should be noted that consistency can also be inefficient with respect to calculations; for example, there are optimisations that can speed up xVA calculations but are detrimental to PFE quantification.

Note that irrespective of the choice over systems, there are always aspects that can be readily shared: one example being data, where having a "Golden Source" of market data, counterparty data, trade data, netting information and collateral terms can be used across multiple environments.

18.4.4   Internal and vendor systems

Over the past decade, a number of software vendors have invested significantly in the development of counterparty risk and xVA solutions. Some of the significant vendors in this respect are CompatibL, Fincad, IBM (previously known as Algorithmics), Markit Analytics (previously known as QuIC), Murex, Numerix, Pricing Partners, Quantifi Solutions, RiskMetrics, SunGard and TriOptima. Not surprisingly, vendor solutions differ significantly, with two clear axes of differentiation being:

- *Sophistication.* Some vendors offer cheaper and less sophisticated solutions, whereas others offer greater sophistication at a higher cost.
- *Application.* Vendors are more focused on a particular implementation (e.g. front-office or risk).

Most vendors provide reasonable product coverage across rates, FX, credit, inflation, equity and commodity products. Some have implemented a deal structuring framework (generic language) to capture non-standard products, in theory, to allow a broad range of payoffs and optionality to be represented. Some also offer AMC to handle exotic products. Sensitivity calculations may also be provided, although the use of AAD for efficient computation of sensitivities is not yet common.

Large banks have tended to build xVA systems internally, driven by economies of scale and the desire to maintain full control over the framework and its development. Smaller institutions have tended to use external vendor solutions that may offer time savings. In general, in-house builds are preferred for front-office xVA implementations, with vendor implementations being more common for risk and regulatory functionality.

Both internally developed and external vendor solutions have their respective advantages and disadvantages (Table 18.3). An internally developed solution can offer greater control over the development process and future flexibility. On the other hand, internal development from a limited starting point can be a substantial undertaking and may require significant time and resources, especially with respect to aspects such as achieving a satisfactory coverage of the many underlying products.

The following is a list of the broad considerations when choosing a vendor-based xVA solution:

- Modelling:
  - ○ availability of different models across each asset class;
  - ○ calibration choices (e.g. real-world and risk-neutral);

Table 18.3 Comparison of an internal approach versus an external vendor solution for xVA.

	Internal approach	External vendor solution
Implementation time	Full development can be time-consuming and resource-intensive, and may result in a significant delay before functionality can be delivered	Implementation time should be reduced, although integration with internal systems can still be a lengthy process
Coverage	Depends upon the underlying portfolio, but can be slow to achieve close to full product coverage	Better coverage due to the significant vendor investment in development risk factor modelling and payoff descriptions
Flexibility	Offers flexibility for future development and allows greater control over functionality and implementation timeframes	Typically a less flexible approach and development may be slow. An institution will still need its own resources to customise various aspects
Support	Internal support is easier to control	Outsourcing of support may result in issues and delays
Regulatory considerations	Regulatory guidelines must be factored into modelling assumptions, and high product coverage is required before the system can be compliant. Regulators may impose punitive capital requirements on products not covered	Allows the bank to leverage off previous experiences gained during regulatory processes (e.g. IMM approval)

- o how collateral is modelled (margin period of risk, non-cash collateral, rehypothecation, etc.); and
- o treatment of specific and general wrong-way risk.
- Calculation:
  - o methodology for calculating xVA in real-time;
  - o approach for exotic payoffs and/or path dependency where the computation time for valuation is prohibitive (e.g. AMC);
  - o what sensitivities can be calculated and how the calculation is implemented (e.g. finite difference, AAD);
  - o if a P&L explain is implemented; and
  - o speed and recommended hardware requirements for the portfolio in question.
- Data and implementation:
  - o approaches for data capture (market, legal) and data maintained by vendor (e.g. market conventions and calendars);
  - o product coverage and how non-standard payoffs can be represented (e.g. generic scripting language);
  - o if it is possible to match day zero pricing (for example, by offering parallel or amortising shifts – Section 10.3.3); and
  - o if it is possible to implement a user's own pricing library or pricing grids (for exotics) in the revaluation stage.

- Regulatory and risk functionalities:
  - PFE and credit limits functionality;
  - regulatory capital approaches (CEM, SA-CCR, standardised and advanced CVA capital charge);
  - approach for scenario analysis and stress-testing;
  - whether the system has been through an IMM approval process with one or more banks; and
  - reporting functionality and feeding of downstream systems (e.g. accounting, general ledger).
- General:
  - other institutions that use the system and for what purposes;
  - cost structure (upfront, costs per licence, computing services, consultants cost per day); and
  - likely implementation time.

18.4.5   IMM approval

In recent years, more banks have pursued IMM approval (for example, see BCBS, 2014e) for counterparty risk to reduce (current) capital requirements. Figure 8.2 illustrates these intentions. Most banks report material savings in capital under an IMM approach and anecdotally other benefits such as improved risk culture and alignment of incentives. However, it should be emphasised that the potential capital reduction (if any) in achieving IMM approval can vary substantially based on a number of factors, including:

- the nature of the underlying portfolio, specifically the type of transactions, their directionality (which impacts netting) and tenor;
- the overall exposure to the various different types of counterparties (corporate, sovereign, supranational, financial institution);
- the nature of collateralised transactions (thresholds, type of collateral, dispute history, etc.);
- the IMM modelling and calibration assumptions made, including the specific risk model (relevant for credit spread evolution) and the choice of stress periods under Basel III; and
- the current market conditions (level of credit spreads and interest rates).

The IMM approval process takes a significant time and it may also be necessary to provide a history of backtesting for the approval process. It is also important to note that capital requirements, whilst lower overall, may be more volatile. With the more risk-sensitive SA-CCR approach due to be implemented in 2017, some regulators may be more reluctant to allow banks to use their own models via an IMM approval. Regulators may also be unwilling to allow dramatic capital savings (over CEM or SA-CCR) to be recognised, and may impose floors (see Section 8.8.3) in this regard. As noted above, transactions not captured under IMM (Figure 18.8) must generally be treated separately and conservatively, and can therefore be very capital-intensive. Note also that the implementation of the proposals in BCBS (2015) would likely mean that IMM approval may be less relevant in the future since the IMM methodology may only be required for the default risk (and not CVA) capital charge.

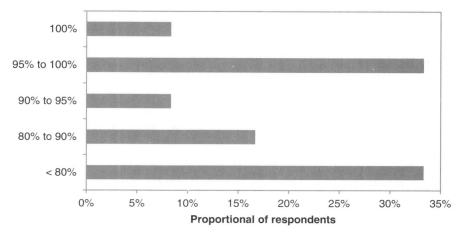

Figure 18.8   Percentage of exposures measured under IMM by trade count.
Source: Deloitte/Solum CVA survey, 2013.

There is of course another IMM benefit beyond capital reduction, which is the alignment of xVA within the front office and regulatory formulas (particularly relevant with respect to hedging[8]). This also allows a link between market KVA charges and a running accrual of actual capital charges. Banks without IMM approval may feel that there is a disconnect between appraising and managing the business (i.e. the capital charges against trades do not reasonably reflect their true risks). IMM approval may also promote portfolio optimisation exercises such as unwinds, restructuring, novations and backloading to CCPs, since it will align the reduction in economic risk with the actual capital relief achieved.

18.5   SUMMARY

This chapter has considered the management of counterparty risk within an institution and the role of the so-called xVA desk. We have outlined the role and responsibilities of an xVA desk and the various styles of approach from passive to more active management. The hedging of xVA has been discussed, as have the complexities related to the large number of variables, relative illiquidity of the CDS market and aspects such as cross-gamma and jump-to-default risk. The capital implications of hedging have been analysed and we have also outlined the systems requirements to support active xVA management, looking at aspects such as optimisations and whether to implement internal builds or vendor systems. Finally, we have discussed the relative merits of achieving IMM approval for regulatory capital purposes.

---

[8] For example, see "Deutsche Bank loses €94 million on CVA mismatch", *Risk*, 13th August 2013.

19

xVA Optimisation

> *A banker is a fellow who lends you his umbrella when the sun is shining, but wants it back the minute it begins to rain.*
>
> Mark Twain (1835–1910)

19.1 OVERVIEW

Previous chapters in this book have analysed xVA components to a large extent in isolation. This chapter will give some examples of complete xVA calculations, incorporating all relevant terms. In doing this, we will aim to give insight into the relative importance of xVA terms in different trading situations and consider potential optimisations that may arise from this.

In Section 19.2, we will discuss market practice around xVA computation and outline some of the likely differences in approach and their impact on pricing. Examples in Section 19.3 will then look at the pricing of xVA in a variety of situations. Clearly, there can be many different results depending on the transaction type, counterparty and collateral terms in place. Other more technical points, such as regulatory approvals for a bank, can also play a part here. We will use some classic examples, based on the typical transacting behaviour of end-users such as pension funds, corporates and supranationals to illustrate the different breakdown of xVA that can be seen. We will also look at situations that will be more common in the future with bilateral initial margins and centrally cleared transactions.

Section 19.4 will then consider the balance of xVA components and ask where the optimal terms for transacting would be. For example, taking bilateral initial margins increases costs through MVA but will reduce other components such as CVA and KVA. There is an obvious question regarding how much initial margin (if any) might be optimal in a given situation.

Finally, one feature of the xVA world is that parties will see economic costs differently due to their own views and the internal and external policies and regulation that they have to follow. For example, a large bank is likely to consider all xVA terms to be relevant, driven by a combination of their own assessment of the economics of a transaction together with their accounting and regulatory (e.g. capital) requirements. An end-user may have a more limited view of xVA, driven potentially by the accounting requirements involving CVA and DVA but not components such as KVA, since regulatory capital is specific to banks. The result of this is that the "law of one price" will not apply and end-users will not agree with the prices charged by banks (although end-users in general probably believe that the prices they must pay for goods are too high). A related point will be that certain xVA optimisations, such as changing collateral terms, may be seen as optimal from both parties perspective. We will give some examples of this in Section 19.5.

The examples in this chapter are single transactions only and are based on approximate xVA calculations. Although such calculations are not sophisticated enough for actual xVA implementation, they are likely to be reasonable enough to show the qualitative features, as is the intention. Whilst all the calculation details are not given, I will be happy to provide any details on precise assumptions to anyone on request.

19.2   MARKET PRACTICE

19.2.1   General approach to xVA

The number of xVA components and their relative magnitude has grown over the last few years driven by regulation and market practice. This in turn has led to clients regarding xVA charges as higher and also more divergent between different banks. Banks in turn have sometimes been surprised at the magnitude by which they have lost transactions. Table 19.1 outlines market standards and best practice with respect to pricing xVA into transactions and shows which deviations may be experienced.

Even many years ago, when CVA was potentially the only significant component that was priced into transactions, there were deviations. Many banks would base their CVA calculations on historical default probabilities and were viewed as underpricing the

Table 19.1   General market standards and best practice for pricing xVA components and areas where some market participants may deviate.

	General market standard/best practice	Other assumptions
Counterparty risk (CVA/DVA)	Risk-neutral approach Credit spread mapping IFRS 13 reporting Some or all DVA included as a funding benefit	Historical PDs CVA not reported in financial statements No DVA
Collateral (ColVA)	OIS discounting for collateralised transactions ColVA adjustments Intrinsic cheapest-to-deliver valuation (at least)	LIBOR discounting without ColVA adjustments No cheapest-to-deliver valuation
Funding (FVA and MVA)	Funding liquidity costs No double-counting with DVA Initial margin priced where relevant	FVA not included in price DVA double-counted Cost of initial margin ignored
Capital (KVA)	Projected cost of capital to term Based on sum of default risk and CVA capital	Deviation from capital hurdles Capital not calculated to Basel III (e.g. legacy economic capital methodology) Behavioural assumptions (exemptions, early termination, etc.)
Overall (xVA)	Correct economic combination of terms based on business model	Compromise based on charging the maximum of different combinations of terms

credit risk compared to banks using risk-neutral default probabilities via credit spreads. The advent of IFRS 13 has largely produced alignment in this regard (Section 12.2.2), although some banks (notably some Japanese megabanks and some smaller regional banks) may still deviate from "best market practice".

Whilst CVA has become more standard and best market practice can be defined, increased divergence has been seen in the treatment of collateral, funding and capital.[1] With respect to collateralised transactions, some smaller banks still use LIBOR discounting and do not adjust for ColVA. They may also ignore any cheapest-to-deliver optionality (Section 13.4.3). With respect to FVA, some banks will not price this into transactions; where it is included, there may be differences over the interpretation of the underlying funding costs. Some participants may also ignore initial margin costs (MVA) in pricing, since this usually requires assessing the cost of hedging transactions that may need to be centrally cleared.

Probably the biggest divergence in market practice comes in pricing capital. Some banks are more capital-constrained than others and may naturally price capital more carefully. Whilst virtually all banks will have some implicit capital hurdle embedded into a price, there are significant deviations in the way this may be applied:

- *Cost of capital.* This is generally in the region of 8–10% (net), but this level can vary and may differ across maturities. Furthermore, adjustments for aspects such as tax rates will increase this cost but will again differ between banks (Section 12.5.4). Finally, the discount rate (if any) applied to future capital requirements is also relevant, especially for longer-dated transactions.
- *Capital metric.* Rather than being based on the real future regulatory capital required, another simpler metric (such as some approximate economic capital) may be used.
- *Transacting within hurdle.* Capital is generally not transfer priced to an xVA desk (Section 18.2.2); capital hurdles may therefore be soft targets and certain transactions may be allowed to be executed within these hurdles.
- *Projection.* Capital may not be priced rigorously via KVA with the correct projection of costs over time (for example, see the discussion on term structure in Section 16.3.4).
- *Behavioural assumptions.* Banks may price in various subjective behavioural assumptions. Examples are the view that a transaction may be unwound early and therefore not be subject to capital requirements for its entire lifetime. Current or future exemptions may also be looked upon favourably.
- *Hedging.* Hedging may lead to a reduction of capital requirements, but this is hard to predict a priori. The reduction of capital in this regard will differ depending on whether a bank is actively hedging their counterparty risk and their view on the availability of the underlying hedges. A bank with a view that a single-name CDS will remain liquid through the lifetime of the transaction in question may not charge any capital.

There are also differences in the precise quantification of the above terms and their combination. An example is whether survival probabilities should be included in xVA terms (e.g. see the discussion in Section 14.6.5 and 15.2.1). Finally, the combination of the xVA

---

[1] For example, see "Small banks underpricing FVA, dealers claim", *Risk*, 9th April 2015.

terms may differ, with some banks pricing "either/or" scenarios; one example is pricing the maximum of the CVA or the counterparty risk capital, as discussed in Section 16.3.8.

With the above in mind, the later examples in Section 19.3 will give an idea of the potential impact of different pricing assumptions. Due to the significant debate around aspects such as FVA and the complexities in quantifying terms such as MVA and KVA, it is likely that significant price divergence will be seen in the market for some time to come. The impact of incoming regulation such as the leverage ratio and bilateral collateral rules (which are likely not yet priced in by most participants) will only increase future divergence.

19.2.2   Totem

Markit's Totem service provides consensus market prices across OTC derivatives.[2] Banks submit prices for hypothetical transactions and receive information on other submissions that allow benchmarking and indicate if they are an outlier in each particular pricing example. The Totem service has recently been expanded to include xVA quotations. This is done by defining a variety of counterparties (credit spreads), contractual situations (collateral terms) and transactions (interest rate swaps of different maturities and moneyness). Although only the total xVA is transparent, the range of different situations allows quite a lot of information to be implied from the submissions. The results are not made publically available and so the discussion below is anecdotal.

Totem provides all important market data (yield curves, volatility surfaces and counterparty credit spreads), and so certain aspects such as credit curve mapping are not being benchmarked. Moreover, capital is currently not included in the prices – the bank is asked to assume that they have sufficient capital to support the transactions – and no cases with initial margin are specified. Hence, Totem allows information on CVA, FVA and ColVA, but not KVA and MVA, to be assessed. More precisely, information on the following components can be realistically extracted:

- *Breakdown of xVA.* Given that a number of different collateral agreements are specified, it is possible to breakdown quotes into their respective components. For example, the use of a two-way CSA, but where the bank segregates the counterparty's collateral, seems designed to isolate funding costs (FCA) – although such a situation is unlikely to occur in practice.[3] From this, uncollateralised and one-way CSA submissions can be used to extract CVA, FBA and/or DVA. Note that this may not be completely straightforward, as it depends on more subtle aspects such as participants' approaches to pricing the margin period of risk (MPR) in a collateralised transaction. (Some can be clearly seen to ignore this whilst others seemingly do not.)
- *Exposure quantification.* Although exposure profiles are not observed directly, it should be possible to broadly benchmark the exposure quantification through observed submissions for different maturities and in- and out-of-the-money transactions. It may be possible, for example, to extract information on calibration to swaption prices, which

---

[2] See www.markit.com/product/totem.

[3] As discussed in Section 7.5.4, variation margin is generally not segregated; nor is this required by future regulation.

in turn may provide information on the model being used and/or whether a calibration is generic or transaction specific.

- *Approach to funding.* Since CVA can be extracted, it is possible to observe the overall funding cost and benefits via specified one-way CSAs both against (funding cost only) and in favour (funding benefit only), again with some potential MPR consideration. Since both pay and receive positions are included, it would be apparent if symmetric funding assumptions are being used since in this case the FCA on a pay transaction would equal the FBA on a receive transaction and vice versa.
- *Other assumptions.* It may be possible to extract information on more subtle aspects such as the use of survival probabilities (the longest maturity is 30 years, for which this is a particularly important assumption, since the risk-neutral default probability of a bank for this period could easily be 30% or higher[4]).

The above initiative will inevitably help some convergence in market practice, especially as more smaller and regional banks join the submission process. However, submissions may not be totally aligned with the pricing policies of the participants, which may lead to a false sense of security. Furthermore, at the time of writing, the most subjective component of pricing (capital costs via KVA) is not included in the Totem analysis.

19.3 EXAMPLES

Spreadsheet 19.1   Simple xVA calculator

19.3.1   xVA assumptions

This section shows various examples of xVA calculations for different counterparty types and contractual agreements. The aim is to present cases that would be relevant to the way in which derivatives would be priced in the current market environment. Following the exposition in Section 4.4.3 and subsequent discussion regarding the various xVA terms (in particular the overlap between CVA, DVA and FVA discussed in Chapter 15), we will consider the bank making the calculation uses the following pricing terms:

- *CVA and DVA.* The bilateral price of counterparty risk based on the counterparty credit spread. Due to looking at a single transaction, the potential netting benefit is not considered.
- *FCA.* The funding cost under the assumption that the funding benefit is already priced via DVA (we will assume zero basis between own credit spread and funding below, and therefore DVA and FBA can be considered equivalent except for a small MPR component which will be mentioned). The funding spread is considered symmetric and so there would be no portfolio effect.
- *ColVA.* The adjustment due to any non-standard collateral terms or optionality where a collateral agreement is in place.

---

[4] For example, assuming a bank's credit spread is 75 bps and the LGD is 60%, then the 30-year default probability is 31.1% (Equation 12.1).

- *KVA*. The cost of holding regulatory capital for the lifetime of the transaction (no exemptions are assumed). Due to looking at a single transaction, the potential portfolio effect is not considered. We do not consider any reduction in capital from potential CVA hedges.
- *MVA*. The cost of posting initial margin over the lifetime of the transaction, where relevant.

We will not consider any other overlap between the above terms such as the representation discussed in Section 16.3.8. Unless stated otherwise, the examples below will assume the following:

- a par (zero MTM) ten-year interest rate swap;
- a triple-B rated counterparty with credit spread of 175 bps;
- own credit spread and funding cost of 75 bps (the funding cost applies also to initial margin posting where relevant);
- the bank in question uses the current exposure method (Section 8.2) and standardised CVA capital formula (Section 8.7.2) for regulatory capital calculations and prices KVA with a required return on capital of 10%;
- the collateral agreement is cash in the currency of the transaction and collateral (including initial margin) is remunerated at the OIS rate; and
- where relevant, the margin period of risk (MPR) is assumed to be ten days for computation of CVA, DVA and KVA.[5] From the point of view of FCA, no delay is assumed when receiving collateral and so for a transaction collateralised with a zero threshold and minimum transfer amount the FCA component will be zero.

The xVA terms that represent costs will be shown as negative, whilst benefits will be positive. Note that the figures are normalised to the overall xVA magnitude and therefore not all shown with the equivalent scales. We will refer to the price maker as the bank and the price taker as the end-user. We choose examples where the end-user could be classified as a typically medium credit quality counterparty such as a corporate, or high credit quality counterparty such as a sovereign or supranational entity.

19.3.2   Uncollateralised

In the first example, we look at an uncollateralised transaction for which the xVA terms are shown in Figure 19.1 showing both the payer and receiver swaps. Due to the relative riskiness of the counterparty, CVA is the most significant term, followed by KVA. The FCA and DVA partially offset one another. The difference between payer and receiver transactions arises due to the assumed positive slope on the yield curve: in this case the expected future value of the payer swap is positive (Section 7.3.3), which increases the CVA and FCA components and reduces the DVA benefit. In the case of the receiver, the opposite occurs, leading to a significantly lower overall price. Note that under the IMM method, the same asymmetric effect would be seen on KVA (i.e. a larger KVA for the payer swap) but the CEM approach used (and also the SA-CCR methodology) gives a capital charge that is symmetric in this respect.

---

[5] In the case of KVA, this is relevant when we consider IMM capital calculations later.

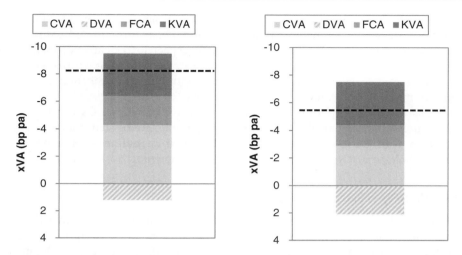

Figure 19.1   xVA components for an uncollateralised swap paying (left) and receiving (right) the fixed rate. Asssumptions and parameters as defined in Section 19.3.1. The dotted line represents the overall price.

19.3.3   Off-market

This example shows an off-market transaction where the current mark-to-market (MTM) is negative (Figure 19.2). The pricing of such a transaction shows a large DVA that would be monetised via a funding benefit due to receiving an up-front payment if entering into the transaction (most likely as a novation or intermediation). For the same reason, the CVA and FCA components are small, since the transaction is unlikely to be in-the-money. The KVA component is not reduced accordingly, since the current

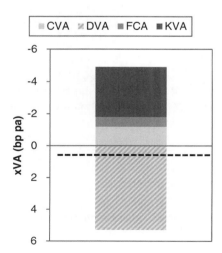

Figure 19.2   xVA components for an off-market uncollateralised swap transaction with assumptions and parameters as defined in Section 19.3.1. The dotted line represents the overall price.

exposure method does not recognise the risk-reducing benefit of a negative MTM.[6] The overall price is negative, implying that the bank should "pay through mid". It is unlikely they would do this but such a transaction may be expected to clear at a price close to mid-market levels with no or minimum xVA charge applied. It is also worth commenting that a party aiming to novate this transaction may optimally choose a counterparty with a high funding cost, since they may be willing to pay for a larger DVA (funding) benefit.

Note that this effect is not only seen for off-market transactions. Cases where the expected future value is particularly negative (for example, a cross-currency swap paying the currency with the lower interest rate, as illustrated in Section 7.3.3) can also have dominant DVA (or equivalently funding benefit) components.

19.3.4   Partially collateralised

This example (Figure 19.3) assumes partial collateralisation via a two-way CSA with a relatively high threshold but where parties must post cash collateral in the currency of the transaction (this means that there is no ColVA term). In this case, CVA and FCA are reduced due to the ability to receive collateral, whilst DVA is reduced due to the requirement to post. The dominant component is KVA due to the lack of recognition of future collateral within the current exposure method, as described in Section 8.2.2. (Note that, as discussed in Section 16.3.6, the KVA is reduced moderately in this example even though the spot capital is not.) The overall price is reduced compared to the uncollateralised case, although, due to the only partial collateralisation and lack of KVA benefit, this is only moderate. This situation is often seen by banks with institutional investors where capital charges/hurdles drive pricing.

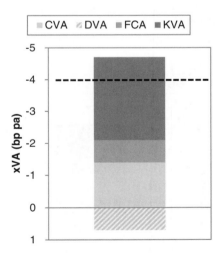

Figure 19.3   xVA components for a partially collateralised swap transaction (two-way collateral agreement with material thresholds) with other assumptions and parameters as defined in Section 19.3.1. The dotted line represents the overall price.

---

[6] Note that even under the CEM, the negative MTM may be beneficial if netting were considered since it would potentially reduce the exposure and NGR (Section 8.2.2) of existing transactions.

19.3.5 One-way collateralised

This example assumes a one-way CSA against the bank in question (Figure 19.4). Such a situation has been historically common with highly rated counterparties, and so we now assume that the counterparty credit quality is triple-A and their credit spread is 50 bps (flat). Furthermore, we assume that the bank must post cash in the currency of the transaction but that this collateral will be remunerated at OIS minus 25 bps (all other assumptions are as before).

The first observation is that DVA is close to zero due to the need to post collateral. There is a small DVA due to the assumed MPR, although in reality it is likely that this component would be ignored. The CVA is relatively small due to the high credit quality and lower credit spread. However, the FCA is larger, since the bank's funding cost is assumed to be worse than the credit spread of the counterparty – this assumption could be challenged, as discussed previously in Section 15.3.4.[7] Finally, the largest term is the KVA due to the relatively high weight in the CVA capital charge assumed for a triple-A counterparty, which is only 30% smaller than the previous triple-B case (Section 8.7.2).

Due to the assumption that collateral is remunerated at OIS minus 25 bps, there is an additional ColVA component. This can be seen as the bank charging for the collateral they have posted being remunerated below the rate used in their basic valuation. Note that if we consider OIS to be the risk-free rate, then we can see the FCA as a charge for the bank's cost of funding above this rate and ColVA as the fact that, even if they can fund at the risk-free rate, they have a negative carry on posting collateral due to the sub-OIS remuneration.

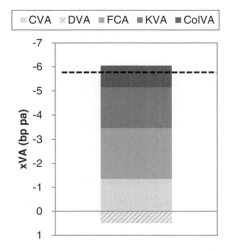

Figure 19.4 xVA components for a one-way collateralised swap transaction against the bank (i.e. they post but do not receive and collateral is remunerated at OIS minus 25 bps) with a triple-A counterparty with credit spread of 50 bps but otherwise with assumptions and parameters as defined in Section 19.3.1. The dotted line represents the overall price.

---

[7] In particular, refer to Figure 15.15.

We can comment that from a purely CVA point of view, this example is substantially better than the uncollateralised case in Section 19.3.2 due to the significantly better counterparty credit quality. However, when FCA and KVA are considered, the situation is only slightly improved. This is one of the reasons why in recent years high quality end-users have considered posting collateral (Section 7.5.3). We can also see why posting own bonds may be particularly optimal in such situations: these will reduce the larger FCA (as long as the bonds can be rehypothecated) although not the CVA or KVA components (Section 7.5.4). This will be demonstrated in the next example. Since the CVA is the smallest of the components in this example, posting other forms of collateral in order to reduce this might be considered suboptimal.[8]

19.3.6   Collateralised

We now consider a collateralised example, assuming a two-way CSA with zero threshold and small minimum transfer amount (but no initial margin) for a triple-A counterparty. In this case, the CVA and DVA are small and driven largely by the MPR assumption. We assume two situations: firstly, where the entity posts their own bonds as collateral, and secondly, where they post cash (or generally collateral with no wrong-way risk). These are shown together with the one-way collateralised situation in Figure 19.5. In both collateralised situations there is no FCA adjustment, since collateral is assumed to be received immediately in non-default situations. (Note that if DVA were instead viewed as FBA, then this term too would be zero.) In the case of the end-user posting their own bonds, we assume these can be rehypothecated.

We can see that the posting of own bonds has some benefits, since it reduces the quite significant FCA component. This can be seen as the counterparty utilising their likely cheap funding costs to mitigate those of the bank. In this scenario there is CVA and KVA, which are both material despite the strong credit rating, but the potential benefit of the end-user reducing the price without detrimental liquidity costs (Section 7.5.3) can be seen. If the counterparty posts collateral that is not wrong-way, then the CVA can be further reduced. The major component driving the price is then KVA, which is especially large due to the lack of recognition of future collateral in the current exposure method mentioned above. This illustrates clearly the importance of better treatment of collateralised transactions, as can be achieved under the IMM or SA-CCR methodologies (Section 8.5.2).

19.3.7   Overcollateralised (initial margin) and backloading

Future rules for bilateral transactions will potentially require significant amounts of initial margin to be posted. Figure 19.6 shows the result of such an arrangement assuming a two-way collateral agreement with zero threshold and bilateral initial margin posted on a segregated basis. The initial margin amount is broadly consistent with a ten-day worst-case move and as a result the CVA and DVA terms are practically zero since the overcollateralisation removes any residual counterparty risk over the MPR (Section 11.4.2). Since the FCA is also zero, the only remaining components are the cost

---

[8] Although under other capital methodologies such as SA-CCR and IMM, KVA would be reduced also (Section 8.1.4).

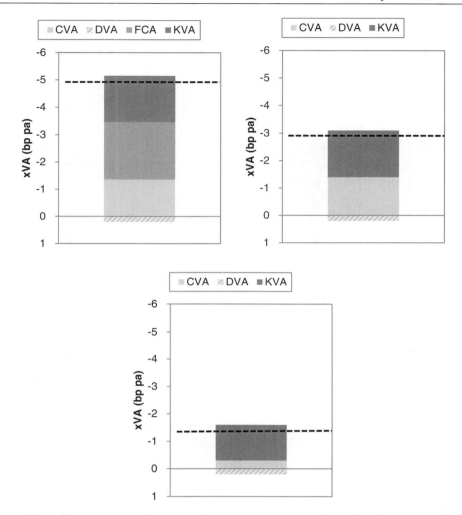

Figure 19.5 xVA components for transactions that are one-way collateralised (top left), collateralised where the end-user posts their own bonds (top right) and collateralised with cash (bottom). In the collateralised cases a two-way agreement with zero threshold is assumed, and other assumptions and parameters as defined in Section 19.3.1. The dotted line represents the overall price.

of posting initial margin (MVA) as well as the KVA. Since KVA is important, we will consider the different capital methodologies in this example.

Comparing methodologies, we see that the CEM gives a large KVA due to not recognising the impact of overcollateralisation (although it is assumed to provide benefit in offsetting future positive MTM in the KVA formula). The SA-CCR method is smaller but not as small as the IMM (due to the relatively conservative add-ons and floor of 5% used in the former). The significance of KVA illustrates the importance of the SA-CCR methodology for capital currently aiming to be introduced in 2017. Aside from this, we see that MVA is the main driver of the economics and the size and cost of the initial

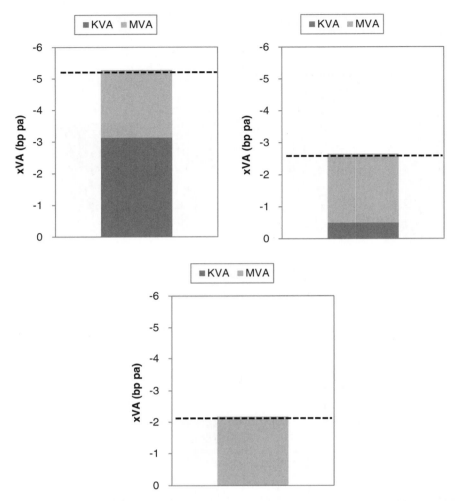

Figure 19.6   xVA components for an overcollateralised transaction (two-way collateral agreement with zero threshold and bilateral initial margin posting) for CEM, SA-CCR and IMM approaches respectively, and with other assumptions and parameters as defined in Section 19.3.1. The dotted line represents the overall price.

margin are crucial components. Note that we have ignored the cost of segregation in this example but in reality, there would be a cost of segregating initial margin received and for the same reason posted initial margin may be remunerated at a sub-OIS rate.

Also note that this example is broadly consistent with the assessment of a centrally cleared transaction. In this case, the relevant considerations would be:

- *CVA.* This is likely to be considered small and may be neglected due to the strong credit quality of central counterparties (CCPs). As in the above case, DVA and FCA will be negligible.

- *MVA.* The cost of initial margin and other contributions required by the CCP. A number of aspects could make this larger than the bilateral case; for example, the use of default funds and more conservative initial margin methodologies by a CCP. However, portfolio diversification and a shorter time horizon in the CCP initial margin calculation (typically five days compared to ten days for bilateral transactions) can make this smaller.
- *KVA.* This would now reference the capital charges against central counterparties (discussed in more detail in Gregory, 2014). There are separate charges for CCP initial margin and default fund exposures, which are not immaterial but are likely to be smaller than the MVA component.

19.4   COSTS AND THE BALANCE OF xVA TERMS

19.4.1   Spectrum of transaction

The examples in the previous section illustrate the extent to which the overall xVA components can change depending on the situation in question, most obviously in relation to collateral posting (since such contractual terms can potentially be changed). It is therefore interesting to ask the question as to what contractual situation is optimal. Generally, there are three situations of interest:

- *Uncollateralised.* In this case, the main costs arise from counterparty risk (CVA), associated capital charges (KVA) and funding (FCA). There are potential funding benefits via DVA although subjectivity exists over the precise use of CVA, DVA and FCA.
- *Collateralised.* A collateral agreement has the impact of reducing the above components although the extent of this reduction is subjective and depends on the treatment of collateral in the regulatory capital methodology. Moreover, there is a loss of any DVA or funding benefit. However, the potential reduction of counterparty risk and funding would be expected to give a lower price in most situations.
- *Overcollateralised.* By receiving initial margin or facing a CCP, CVA and KVA should be reduced even further (subject again to the regulatory capital treatment). However, at the same time, MVA will appear due to the need to post initial margin.

Although there is often not free choice over the above due to the constraints of end-users (e.g. inability to post collateral) or regulation (clearing mandate or bilateral collateral rules), it is interesting to consider the above cases from a cost point of view. Moreover, there are some cases where choices exist. For example, a small financial institution will typically transact on a collateralised basis but may consider voluntarily clearing trades (they may remain exempt from initial margin posting due to their size). A supranational may currently be uncollateralised (from a bank's point of view) but may consider transacting on a collateralised basis (or even clearing). Some large corporates may also consider moving to two-way collateral agreements.

Table 19.2 contrasts the costs (and benefits) of the three situations in terms of xVA components. Overcollateralised transactions have mainly initial margin (MVA) and some capital costs. At the other extreme, uncollateralised transactions have high counterparty risk, funding and capital costs, but also high funding benefits. Collateralised transactions have medium counterparty risk and capital costs.

Table 19.2 Qualitative assessment of the contribution of each xVA component under different collateral assumptions.

	Overcollateralised	Collateralised	Uncollateralised
CVA	Low cost	Medium cost	High cost
DVA	Low benefit	Medium benefit	High benefit
FCA	Low cost	Low cost	High cost
KVA	Low / Medium cost*	Medium / High cost*	High cost
MVA	High cost	n/a	n/a

*Dependent on the regulatory capital methodology used.

19.4.2   Optimising xVA

We now consider looking at xVA costs as an optimisation problem in order to understand preferences with respect to aspects such as collateral posting. We note that a quantitative analysis based on xVA components is not a comprehensive analysis of the total costs. For example, aspects such as the leverage ratio (Section 8.8.2) and liquidity coverage ratio (Section 8.8.4) are not assessed; nor are the liquidity costs for end-users posting collateral (Section 11.3.8) considered. Nevertheless, the assessment of total xVA should give a good guide to the total economic costs of transacting an OTC derivative in various situations.

One simple way to look at the move from uncollateralised to collateralised and overcollateralised is to plot the xVA terms against the threshold and initial margin as previously shown in Figure 14.7. Symmetric collateral assumptions are made, otherwise one-way CSAs in favour of the party in question would clearly be favoured. This varies the terms of the collateralisation although it does not change other quantities that may be relevant such as credit quality (for example, generally uncollateralised counterparties may have lower credit quality). We will use the same example as defined in Section 19.3.1 but use a seven-year transaction (the impact of maturity together with credit quality will be shown afterwards). We also assume that the bank has IMM approval for regulatory capital purposes. Because an IMM is risk-sensitive, this will be expected to give smoother behaviour and not lead to a solution that is favoured simply due to the inadequacy of the regulatory capital approach.

Figure 19.7 shows the xVA arising from a bilateral collateral arrangement as a function of threshold and initial margin (note that an initial margin can be represented as a negative threshold). The behaviour is as expected with the counterparty risk, funding and capital components reducing as the collateralisation level increases (lower threshold), and then the initial margin cost (MVA) increasing as the transaction becomes overcollateralised. Note that received initial margin is not a benefit as it is assumed to require segregation, but it does reduce CVA and KVA.

The sum of the components from Figure 19.7 is shown in Figure 19.8. The cases of uncollateralised and overcollateralised are not favoured, with a minimum price seen at a moderate bilateral initial margin that amounts to about 1% of the transaction notional. This is a small initial margin by the standards of the bilateral collateral rules that, based on a 99% confidence level and ten-day time horizon, would imply something in the region

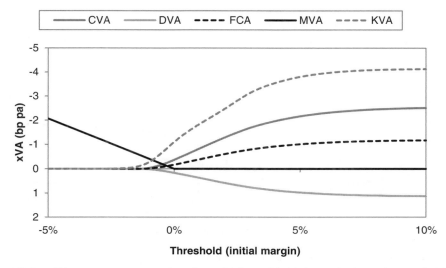

Figure 19.7   xVA components as a function of bilateral initial margin (negative x-values) and bilateral threshold (positive x-values) for a seven-year interest rate swap.

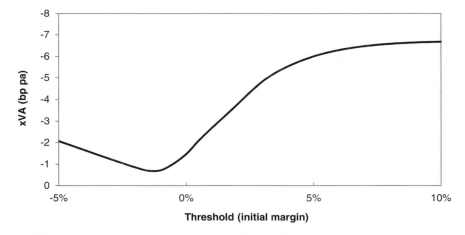

Figure 19.8   Total xVA from the components in Figure 19.7.

of three or more times greater.[9] In price terms, a small initial margin can be beneficial thanks to the reduction in counterparty risk and capital that it provides. However, initial margins at a high confidence level are expensive and may not be favoured due to a law of diminishing returns with respect to CVA and KVA reduction as previously illustrated in Section 16.3.7.

---

[9] For example, assuming a 1% interest rate volatility, duration of six years, ten-day time horizon and 99% confidence level, the initial margin would be $1\% \times 6 \times \sqrt{(10/250)} \times 2.33 = 2.8\%$.

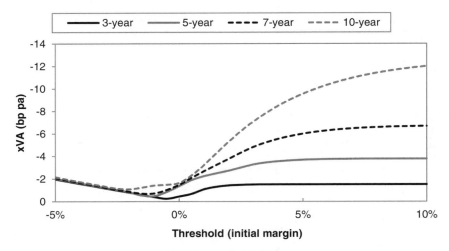

Figure 19.9   Total xVA as a function of maturity for a seven-year interest rate swap.

19.4.3   Impact of credit quality and maturity

Figure 19.9 shows the same example as in the previous section for different maturities. We can see that the uncollateralised case becomes significantly more expensive at an exponential rate, which is due to a longer maturity increasing both the exposure (e.g. see Figure 7.9) and default probability. The cost of required initial margin will also increase with maturity but this will be at a lower rate (approximately proportional to maturity). This suggests that initial margins will be favoured for longer-dated products due to the benefit of reducing the time horizon from the maturity in question (considered when calculating terms such as CVA and KVA) to a short-term horizon of typically five to ten days.

Figure 19.10 shows the example for different credit quality counterparties. The uncollateralised case is more costly as credit quality declines due to an increase in CVA and

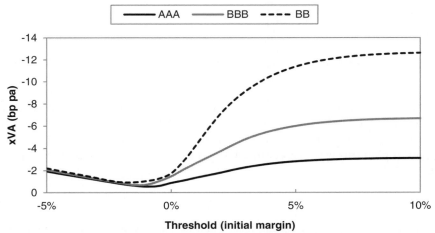

Figure 19.10   Total xVA as a function of counterparty credit quality.

KVA terms, and initial margins become increasing beneficial by comparison. Note that initial margin methodologies are typically not strongly linked (if at all) to credit quality. This implies that initial margins will be more favoured for poorer credit quality parties (although such parties will have higher funding costs and liquidity risks when posting initial margin).

19.4.4 Summary

The results above highlight a number of important aspects for bilateral (and centrally cleared) OTC derivatives. In terms of the three broad choices in relation to collateralisation as represented in Table 19.2, the optimum is the collateralised case which has broadly medium costs associated with all components but avoids the potential high costs of counterparty risk and funding at one extreme or initial margin at the other. Small bilateral initial margins may be favoured in many situations due to the counterparty risk and capital relief they represent (assuming the capital methodology is sensitive to initial margin), but due to a law of diminishing returns, initial margins at a high confidence level as required by regulation do not seem to be favoured.

We have also shown some important features of initial margin requirements in relation to maturity and credit quality, which can be seen to be relevant for cases in bilateral and centrally cleared markets. Initial margins (or central clearing) should be more favoured for longer maturity products. This is because in an initial margin world, risk is assessed via a rolling window of a few days and not the full term of the transaction. Credit quality is also (to a large extent) ignored and so lower credit quality parties may experience preferable costs due to an implicit homogenisation of default probability.

19.5 xVA OPTIMISATION

The presence of components related to funding and capital may lead to potential xVA optimisations between parties. Some of these optimisations may relate to parties considering terms differently (for example, a bank pricing and accounting for funding costs). Some may arise from different regulatory treatments (for example, a bank having to hold regulatory capital and pricing this into transactions). We will analyse some of these potential optimisations below. They generally fall into two categories:

- an intermediation (or novation), whereby one party replaces another in a transaction; or
- a renegotiation of collateral terms between parties (e.g. a bank and an end-user).

19.5.1 Intermediation

A novation is the transfer of a transaction from one party to another with consent. The advent of funding and capital costs suggests opportunities for more highly rated banks to step into transactions. As an example, Table 19.3 shows the xVA charges from the uncollateralised example in Section 19.3.5 (one-way CSA against the bank) and computes the same charges from the point of view of a more highly rated bank with lower funding costs and internal model method approval for capital calculations. The CVA component

Table 19.3 xVA example shown in Section 19.3.5 calculated with the original and a (stronger credit quality) replacement counterparty.

	Original counterparty	Replacement counterparty
CVA	1.4	1.4
DVA	−0.5	−0.3
FCA	2.1	1.2
KVA	1.7	1.1
Total	4.7	3.5

is unchanged, as it is driven only by the counterparty credit quality. The DVA reduces due to the party's stronger credit quality but, due to the one-way CSA in this case, this term is negligible. The FCA reduces due to the lower funding costs of the replacement bank and the KVA reduces due to the more favourable capital calculation.[10]

This example suggests that there are optimisations available such as from a lower-rated bank with higher funding costs novating client transactions to a more highly rated bank with lower funding costs. Table 19.3 suggests that both banks can gain from such a transaction. The end-user in the example will be relatively indifferent quantitatively, with the only difference being a slightly improved CVA[11] and potentially facing a bank of better credit quality. There may be other qualitative reasons why the original bank may wish to do this (for example, freeing up balance sheet capacity).

With respect to funding, this example is related to the Hull and White arguments discussed in Section 15.3.5 and represents an arbitrage due to funding costs. It supports a bank pricing at a "market cost of funds" (Section 15.3.6) rather than their own internal funding cost. This would still leave potential "arbitrages" due to different capital rules unless all banks were forced to use the same objective regulatory capital methodology. Even with the implementation of the SA-CCR mentioned above in 2017, this is unlikely to occur unless IMM banks are forced to move away from their more complex and risk-sensitive IMM implementations and use the same cost of capital in their calculations.

19.5.2 Restrikes

Some uncollateralised end-users have experienced problems when hedging transactions have moved heavily against them. Not only do banks' xVAs increase, but they may also breach credit limits and be unable to transact and provide hedges anymore. One potential solution in this situation is to "restrike" transactions so they are less in-the-money for the bank. This is similar at the outset to the effect of entering into a collateral agreement but without the uncertainty of future collateral requirements and related liquidity costs. Table 19.4 shows the impact of moving from an in- to at-the-money transaction showing a very significant xVA reduction from the bank's point of view (13.9 bps), which dominates the end-users loss of net CVA/DVA benefit (3.6 bps).

---

[10] Note that this depends on the precise IMM implementation, but IMM banks do generally achieve lower capital charges (as discussed in Chapter 8).

[11] Note that the end-user's CVA will be the opposite of the bank's DVA, which is very small due to the collateral posting.

Table 19.4 xVA example (in bp pa) for an in-the-money to at-the-money transaction (the latter case is shown in Section 19.3.2).

Bank point of view			End-user point of view		
	In-the-money	At-the-money		In-the-money	At-the-money
CVA	−7.0	−4.3	CVA	−0.7	−1.2
DVA	0.7	1.2	DVA	7.0	4.3
FCA	−3.4	−2.1			
KVA	−12.5	−3.1			
Total	−22.2	−8.3		6.7	3.1

Of course, the above does not consider the ability and cost of the end-user funding the cash that would be required to be paid to the bank in order to restrike the transaction. Nevertheless, unlike entering into a collateral agreement, this represents a one-off cost and there are no uncertain liquidity aspects. There are also potential regulatory arbitrages that arise from the above, where a bank may lend money to an end-user in order for them to undertake this. This practice is incentivised by regulation since a bank does not experience anything analogous to the CVA capital charge for a loan and so essentially can reduce KVA without changing the real economic risk they face. EBA (2015b) comment on this as follows:[12]

From the point of view of the bank, there is a transformation of counterparty risk (coming from the derivatives) into credit risk (coming from the loan). But assuming the loan will roll over until the maturity of the derivative contracts, the overall level of risk has not changed. However, the net level of capital has.

19.5.3   Uncollateralised to collateralised

Table 19.5 shows the impact of moving from no CSA (the uncollateralised case in Section 19.3.2) to a two-way zero threshold cash CSA (the collateralised case in Section 19.3.6). Purely from a pricing point of view, the bank gains by 6.9 bp pa from being collateralized by the removal of FCA and the reduction of CVA and KVA, which dominate the smaller DVA loss. The end-user in this example would potentially experience an

Table 19.5 xVA example (in bp pa) from Sections 19.3.2 (uncollateralised) and 19.3.6 (collateralised).

Bank point of view			End-user point of view		
	Uncollateralised (no CSA)	Collateralised (two-way CSA)		Uncollateralised (no CSA)	Collateralised (two-way CSA)
CVA	−4.3	−0.3	CVA	−1.2	−0.2
DVA	1.2	0.2	DVA	4.3	0.3
FCA	−2.1	n/a			
KVA	−3.1	−1.3			
Total	−8.3	−1.4		3.1	0.1

---

[12] Note that the comment on the loan rolling is relevant if the end-user is entering into a collateral agreement rather than just restriking the derivative.

equal and opposite loss from their net CVA/DVA, which would go from a benefit of 3.1 bp pa to a negligible amount. However, this clearly suggests both parties can gain from the change in collateral terms.

Some end-users have increased their level of collateralisation in recent years, as implied from the above example. However, the question of how to price the liquidity impact of such a move is not easy to answer. On the one hand, the "benefit" of not having to post collateral can be seen in the end-user's DVA of 4.3 bps which they give up when moving to a two-way CSA. On the other hand, the more qualitative consideration of the cost of holding a liquidity buffer against potential contractual collateral requirements may seem much more expensive than this, due to being based on a worst-case scenario (see the example in Section 11.3.8). It is perhaps not surprising that, based on their assessment of such liquidity costs, some end-users have moved to an increased level of collateralisation whilst others have not. This also depends on a bank's willingness to pay out their xVA gains on existing transactions.

19.5.4   Backloading to a CCP

One feature of the clearing mandate and bilateral collateral rules are that they only impact future and not existing transactions. However, the question arises as to whether or not it may be optimal to "backload" legacy transactions to a CCP or voluntarily post initial margin against bilateral transactions that were transacted before the bilateral rules or which are within the specified €50m threshold. To show an example of this, we take the case from Section 19.3.2, which represents an intermediate credit quality counterparty (triple-B rating, credit spread 175 bps) and look at the effect of collateralisation and overcollateralisation, in the latter case either bilaterally or via a CCP (Table 19.6). In the bilateral case, it is assumed that the bank is using the IMM method for capital calculations so as to show full risk sensitivity.

This example suggests that bilateral initial margin would be favoured due to the reduction in CVA and KVA being greater than the additional cost of MVA. Central clearing is not favoured since the MVA is higher due to the (assumed) more conservative initial margin methodology used by the CCP for initial margin and default fund costs (even though the time horizon is shorter).[13]

Table 19.6   xVA example shown in Section 19.3.2 calculated under assumptions of bilateral collateralisation (zero threshold), bilateral with initial margin and centrally cleared.

	Bilateral collateralised	Bilateral with initial margin	Centrally cleared
CVA	0.5	–	–
DVA	−0.2	–	–
KVA	3.4	0.5	0.4
MVA	–	2.5	3.4
Total	3.7	3.0	3.9

---

[13] As discussed in Section 9.3.4.

However, it is also important to take into account portfolio effects; of particular relevance here would be the reduction in MVA from the transactions already cleared with the CCP in question. If there is any material offset between the cleared and legacy portfolio, then backloading would appear to be efficient. However, as can be seen from Figure 19.9 and Figure 19.10, the balance between collateralised and overcollateralised is subtle and depends, amongst other things, on the credit quality and tenor of the transaction in question. Portfolio effects may therefore be important in determining the overall benefit.

19.6 SUMMARY

This chapter has illustrated some real-life pricing examples, including all relevant xVA terms according to market practice at the current time. We have shown how xVA can change significantly in different situations, driven by aspects such as the collateral terms in place. It is also clear that xVA is always material (except perhaps for a CCP), it is just a question of which components are large, medium and small. We have also illustrated the optimal xVA scenario (assuming symmetry in collateral terms) in terms of price minimisation that appears to be collateralisation with potentially a small bilateral initial margin. Finally, we have illustrated how, given that the market approach to xVA violates the "law of one price", there are optimisations whereby both parties in a transaction can gain. This can partly explain some of the market behaviour such as the movement to two-way collateral agreements or entities posting their own bonds in collateral arrangements.

20
The Future

The subject area covered in this book has changed dramatically over recent years and continues to evolve at pace. This final chapter aims to briefly consider some of the likely future trends as a result of xVA and related topics discussed in this book.

xVA concepts are currently still developing and no clear market standard can be defined precisely. A potential exception to this is CVA, where a best market practice does, more or less, exist. It seems likely that eventually the same thing will occur to all xVA components, although this undoubtedly will require much intellectual thought and debate first. A likely consequence of the standardised treatment of terms such as FVA, MVA and KVA may well be that the ideal of the "law of one price" will be forever gone, although it will be interesting to see how aspects such as accounting standards react to this.

Banks have struggled greatly with regulatory requirements in the last few years and will continue to do so. It is unlikely that they will be able to generate a strong return on capital for OTC derivative activities and will require a combination of exiting businesses and cross-subsidising OTC derivatives via other revenue streams with the same clients. Banks will also continue to optimise their xVA across bilateral and centrally cleared transactions via a combination of methods such as changing collateral terms, backloading and hedging. More responsibility and workload will likely be channelled through centralised xVA desks, potentially even charging for regulatory capital utilisation (KVA) and then releasing this profit to businesses more appropriately over the life of a transaction. The control of xVA will become increasingly important: in doing this there will be balances such as whether to hedge for optimum CVA reduction of capital (KVA) relief.

End-users will continue to find it difficult and costly to transact with banks due to the high xVA charges. As a result they will likely spend much more time than historically was the case in understanding and optimising their relationships and xVA charges. This may involve broadening the range of counterparties they transact with, posting (more) collateral or changing the terms of their hedging transactions (for example, using futures rather than OTC products).

Not surprisingly, given the above, there is likely to be a continued focus on xVA model, analytics and systems. Here, there will be emphasis not only on flexibility but also on speed. Being able to rapidly calculate the price of new transactions, change in contractual terms or value of moving to or between CCPs will be crucial. Banks will likely require many greeks and scenarios to support their increasing active management of xVA.

Another interesting dynamic will be the increased use of initial margins in both centrally cleared and bilateral markets. Whilst this reduces CVA and KVA, it creates MVA and leads to an interesting optimisation problem with many dimensions such as credit quality and maturity. In turn, the increasing use of bilateral initial margins will push banks to seek to use more advanced and risk-sensitive regulatory capital approaches such as the IMM. This will also direct more attention towards CCPs and understanding if they really are "too big to fail" and how the risk to a CCP should be assessed and quantified.

Another key feature will be the development of the CDS market. A more liquid market may make xVA hedging (CVA and KVA mainly) more realistic, but if this liquidity does not develop then the whole ethos of aspect such as IFRS 13 accounting standards and the Basel III CVA capital charge may be challenged. Irrespective of this, it may be that at some point regulation begins a journey to simplicity. The proliferation of different requirements and standards together with jurisdictional differences may catalyse this. The recent regulatory capital proposals in BCBS (2015) may already reflect this.

Glossary

AAD	adjoint algorithmic differentiation
AIG	American International Group
AMC	American Monte Carlo
AVA	additional valuation adjustment
ATE	additional termination events
Basel III	Basel III International Banking Regulatory Framework
BCBS	Basel Committee on Banking Supervision
BRIC	Brazil, Russia, India and China
CAPM	capital asset pricing model
CCP	central counterparty
CCR	counterparty credit risk
CDS	credit default swap
CEEMEA	Central & Eastern Europe, Middle East & Africa
CEM	current exposure method
ColVA	collateral value adjustment
CRD IV	Capital Requirements Directive IV
CSA	credit support annex
CVA	credit value adjustment
Dodd-Frank	Dodd–Frank Wall Street Reform and Consumer Protection Act
DVA	debt value adjustment
EAD	exposure at default
EBA	European Banking Authority
ECB	European Central Bank/expected collateral balance
EE	expected exposure
EMIR	European Market Infrastructure Regulation
EPE	expected positive exposure
ES	expected shortfall
EU	European Union
FAS	Financial Accounting Standards
FASB	Financial Accounting Standards Board
FBA	funding benefit adjustment
FCA	funding cost adjustment
FTP	funds transfer pricing
FVA	funding value adjustment
FX	foreign exchange
G7	"Group of Seven" countries (Canada, France, Germany, Italy, Japan, the UK and the USA)
G20	"Group of Twenty" countries (Argentina, Australia, Brazil, Canada, China, France, Germany, India, Indonesia, Italy, Japan, Mexico, Russia, Saudi Arabia, South Africa, South Korea, Turkey, the UK and the USA)

GFC	global financial crisis
GPU	graphical processing unit
HQLA	high quality liquid asset
IAS	International Accountancy Standards
IFRS	International Financial Reporting Standards
IM	initial margin
IMM	internal model method
IRS	interest rate swap
ISDA	International Swaps and Derivatives Association, Inc.
KVA	capital value adjustment
LCR	liquidity coverage ratio
LGD	loss given default
LHP	large homogeneous pool
LIBOR	London Interbank Offered Rate
LVA	liquidity value adjustment
LR	leverage ratio
MTA	minimum transfer amount
MVA	margin value adjustment
MTM	mark-to-market
MPR	margin period of risk
NEE	negative expected exposure
NSFR	net stable funding ratio
OIS	overnight indexed spread
OTC	over-the-counter
P&L	profit and loss
PD	probability of default
PFE	potential future exposure
ROC	return on capital
ROE	return on equity
QIS	quantitative impact study
SA-CCR	standardised approach for counterparty credit risk (regulatory capital)
SIFI	systemically important financial institution
SIMM	standard initial margin method
SPV	special purpose vehicle
TMT	technology, media & telecommunications
US	United States
VAR	value-at-risk
WACC	weight average capital cost
WWR	wrong-way risk
xVA	CVA, DVA, FVA, ColVA, MVA, KVA, LVA, etc.

References

Albanese, C., Andersen, L. and Iabichino, S. (2015) "FVA accounting, risk management and collateral trading", *Risk*, January.

Albanese, C. and Iabichino, S. (2013) "The FVA–DVA puzzle: risk management and collateral trading strategies", working paper.

Albanese, C., D'Ippoliti, F. and Pietroniero, G. (2011) "Margin lending and securitization: regulators, modelling and technology", working paper.

Altman, E. (1968) "Financial ratios, discriminant analysis and the prediction of corporate bankruptcy", *Journal of Finance*, 23, 589–609.

Altman, E. (1989) "Measuring corporate bond mortality and performance", *Journal of Finance*, 44(4 September), 909–22.

Altman, E. and Kishore, V. (1996) "Almost everything you wanted to know about recoveries on defaulted bonds", *Financial Analysts Journal*, Nov/Dec.

Amdahl, G. (1967) "Validity of the single processor approach to achieving large-scale computing capabilities", AFIPS Conference Proceedings (30), 483–5.

Andersen, L. and Piterbarg, V. (2010a) *Interest Rate Modelling Volume 1: Foundations and Vanilla Models*, Atlantic Financial Press.

Andersen, L. and Piterbarg, V. (2010b) *Interest Rate Modelling Volume 2: Term Structure Models*, Atlantic Financial Press.

Andersen, L. and Piterbarg, V. (2010c) *Interest Rate Modelling Volume 3: Products and Risk Management*, Atlantic Financial Press.

Andersen, L., Pykhtin, M. and Sokol, A. (2015) "Modeling credit exposure for margined" counterparties, working paper.

Artzner, P., Delbaen, F., Eber, J.-M., Heath, D. (1999) "Coherent measures of risk", *Mathematical Finance* 9 (July), 203–28.

Arvanitis, A. and Gregory J. (2001) *Credit: The Complete Guide to Pricing, Hedging and Risk Management*, Risk Books.

Arvanitis, A, Gregory, J. and Laurent, J.-P. (1999) "Building models for credit spreads", *Journal of Derivatives*, 6(3 Spring), 27–43.

Baird, D.G. (2001) *Elements of Bankruptcy*, 3rd edn, Foundation Press, New York, NY.

Bank for International Settlements (BIS) (2013) "OTC derivatives statistics at end-December 2013", May, www.bis.org.

Basurto, M.S. and Singh, M. (2008) "Counterparty risk in the over-the-counter derivatives market", November, IMF Working Papers, pp. 1–19, available at SSRN: http://ssrn.com/abstract=1316726.

Basel Committee on Banking Supervision (2004) "An explanatory note on the Basel II IRB risk weight functions", October, www.bis.org.

Basel Committee on Banking Supervision (BCBS) (2005) "The application of Basel II to trading activities and the treatment of double default", www.bis.org.

Basel Committee on Banking Supervision (BCBS) (2006) "International convergence of capital measurement and capital standards, a revised framework – comprehensive version", June, www.bis.org.

Basel Committee on Banking Supervision (BCBS) (2009) "Strengthening the resilience of the banking sector, consultative document", December, www.bis.org.

Basel Committee on Banking Supervision (BCBS) (2010a) "Basel III: a global regulatory framework for more resilient banks and banking systems", December (Revised June 2011), www.bis.org.

Basel Committee on Banking Supervision (BCBS) (2010b) "Basel III counterparty credit risk – frequently asked questions", November, www.bis.org.

Basel Committee on Banking Supervision (BCBS) (2010c) "Sound practices for backtesting counterparty credit risk models", December, www.bis.org.

Basel Committee on Banking Supervision (BCBS) (2011a) "Revisions to the Basel II market risk framework", February, www.bis.org.

Basel Committee on Banking Supervision (BCBS) (2011b) "Basel III: a global regulatory framework for more resilient banks and banking systems", June, www.bis.org.

Basel Committee on Banking Supervision (BCBS) (2012) "Basel III counterparty credit risk and exposures to central counterparties – frequently asked questions", December, www.bis.org.

Basel Committee on Banking Supervision (BCBS) (2013a) "Basel III: the liquidity coverage ratio and liquidity monitoring tools", January, www.bis.org.

Basel Committee on Banking Supervision (BCBS) (2013b) "Fundamental review of the trading book: a revised market risk framework, Consultative document", October, www.bis.org.

Basel Committee on Banking Supervision (BCBS) (2014a) "Basel III leverage ratio framework and disclosure requirements", January, www.bis.org.

Basel Committee on Banking Supervision (BCBS) (2014b) "Basel III: the net stable funding ratio", January, www.bis.org.

Basel Committee on Banking Supervision (BCBS) (2014c) "Capitalisation of bank exposures to central counterparties", April, www.bis.org.

Basel Committee on Banking Supervision (BCBS) (2014d) "The standardised approach for measuring counterparty credit risk exposures", March (rev. April), www.bis.org.

Basel Committee on Banking Supervision (BCBS) (2014e) "Regulatory Consistency Assessment Programme (RCAP) assessment of Basel III regulations – Canada", June, www.bis.org.

Basel Committee on Banking Supervision (BCBS) (2014f) "Capital floors: the design of a framework based on standardised approaches", December, www.bis.org.

Basel Committee on Banking Supervision, Board of the International Organization of Securities Commissions (BCBS-IOSCO) (2015) "Margin requirements for non-centrally cleared derivatives", March, www.bis.org.

Basel Committee on Banking Supervision (BCBS) (2015) "Review of the Credit Valuation Adjustment (CVA) risk framework", consultative document, July, www.bis.org.

Black, F. and Cox, J. (1976) "Valuing corporate securities: some effects of bond indenture provisions", *Journal of Finance*, 31, 351–67.

Black, F. and Scholes, M. (1973) "The pricing of options and corporate liabilities", *Journal of Political Economy*, 81(3), 637–54.

Bliss, R.R. and Kaufman, G.G. (2005) "Derivatives and systemic risk: netting, collateral, and closeout (May 10)", FRB of Chicago Working Paper No. 2005-03, available at SSRN: http://ssrn.com/abstract=730648.

Bluhm, C., Overbeck, L. and Wagner, C. (2003) *An Introduction to Credit Risk Modeling*, Chapman and Hall.

Brace, A., Gatarek, D. and Musiela, M. (1997) "The market model of interest rate dynamics", *Mathematical Finance*, 7(2), 127–54.

Brennan, M.J., Hein, J. and Poon, S.-H. (2009) "Tranching and rating", *European Financial Management*, 15(5), 891–922.

Brigo, D., Chourdakis K. and Bakkar, I. (2008) "Counterparty risk valuation for energy-commodities swaps: impact of volatilities and correlation", available at SSRN: http://ssrn.com/abstract=1150818.

Brigo, D. and Masetti, M. (2005a) "Risk neutral pricing of counterparty risk" in *Counterparty Credit Risk Modelling*, M. Pykhtin (ed.), Risk Books.

Brigo, D. and Masetti, M. (2005b) "A formula for interest rate swaps valuation under counterparty risk in presence of netting agreements", www.damianobrigo.it.

Brigo, D. and Morini, M. (2010) "Dangers of bilateral counterparty risk: the fundamental impact of closeout conventions", working paper.

Brigo, D. and Morini, M. (2011) "Closeout convention tensions", *Risk*, December, 86–90.

Brigo, D., Morini, M. and Pallavicini, A. (2013) *Counterparty Credit Risk, Collateral and Funding: With Pricing Cases for All Asset Classes*, John Wiley and Sons.

Brouwer, D.P. (2012) "System and method of implementing massive early terminations of long term financial contracts", 6th November, US Patent 8,306,905 B2.

Burgard, C. and Kjaer, M. (2011a) "Partial differential equation representations of derivatives with counterparty risk and funding costs", *The Journal of Credit Risk*, 7(3), 1–19.

Burgard, C. and Kjaer, M. (2011b) "In the balance", *Risk*, November, 72–5.

Burgard, C. and Kjaer, M. (2012a) "A generalised CVA with funding and collateral", working paper.

Burgard, C. and Kjaer, M. (2012b) "Funding costs, funding strategies", working paper.

Canabarro, E. and Duffie, D. (2003) "Measuring and marking counterparty risk" in *Asset/Liability Management for Financial Institutions*, L. Tilman (ed.), Institutional Investor Books.

Canabarro, E., Picoult, E. and Wilde, T. (2003) "Analyzing counterparty risk", *Risk*, 16(9), 117–22.

Capriotti, L. and Lee, J. (2014) "Adjoint credit risk management", *Risk*, August.

Carver, L. (2012) "Traders close ranks against FVA critics", *Risk*, September.

Carver, L. (2013) "Capital or P&L? Deutsche Bank losses highlight CVA trade-off", *Risk*, October.

Castagna, A. (2012) "Yes, FVA is a cost for derivatives desks", working paper.

Cesari, G., Aquilina, J., Charpillon, N., Filipovic, Z., Lee, G. and Manda, I. (2009) *Modelling, Pricing, and Hedging Counterparty Credit Exposure*, Springer Finance.

Chourdakis, K., Epperlein, E., Jeannin, M. and McEwen, J. (2013) "A cross-section across CVA", *Nomura*, February.

Collin-Dufresne, P., Goldstein, R.S. and Martin, J.S. (2001) "The determinants of credit spread changes", *Journal of Finance*, 56, 2177–207.

Cooper, I.A. and Mello, A.S. (1991) "The default risk of swaps", *Journal of Finance*, 46, 597–620.

Coval, J., Jurek, J. and Stafford, E. (2009) "Economic catastrophe bonds", *American Economic Review*, 99(3), 628–66.

Das, S. (2008) "The credit default swap (CDS) market – will it unravel?", 2nd February.

Das, S. and Sundaram, R. (1999) "Of smiles and smirks, a term structure perspective", *Journal of Financial and Quantitative Analysis*, 34, 211–39.

De Prisco, B. and Rosen, D. (2005) "Modelling stochastic counterparty credit exposures for derivatives portfolios" in *Counterparty Credit Risk Modelling*, M. Pykhtin (ed.), Risk Books.

Downing, C., Underwood, S. and Xing, Y. (2005) "Is liquidity risk priced in the corporate bond market?", working paper, Rice University.

Duffee, G. (1998) "The relation between treasury yields and corporate bond yield spreads", *The Journal of Finance*, LIII (6 December).

Duffee, G.R. (1996a) "Idiosyncratic variation of treasury bill yields", *Journal of Finance*, 51, 527–51.

Duffee, G.R. (1996b) "On measuring credit risks of derivative instruments", *Journal of Banking and Finance*, 20(5), 805–33.

Duffie, D. (1999) "Credit swap valuation", *Financial Analysts Journal*, January–February, 73–87.

Duffie, D. (2011) "On the clearing of foreign exchange derivatives", working paper.

Duffie, D. and Huang, M. (1996) "Swap rates and credit quality", *Journal of Finance*, 51, 921–50.

Duffie, D. and Singleton, K.J. (1999) "Modeling term structures of defaultable bonds", *The Review of Financial Studies*, 12(4), 687–720.

Duffie, D. and Singleton, K.J. (2003) *Credit Risk: Pricing, Measurement, and Management*, Princeton University Press.

Duffie, D. and Zhu, H. (2009) "Does a central clearing counterparty reduce counterparty risk?", Stanford University Working Paper No. 46: Stanford University Graduate School of Business Research Paper No. 2022, April.

Edwards F.R. and Morrison, E.R. (2005) "Derivatives and the bankruptcy code: why the special treatment?", *Yale Journal on Regulation*, 22, 91–122.

Ehlers, P. and Schönbucher, P. (2006) "The influence of FX risk on credit spreads", working paper.

Elliott, D. (2013) "Central counterparty loss-allocation rules", Financial Stability Paper No. 20 – April, Bank of England, www.bankofengland.co.uk.

Engelmann, B. and Rauhmeier R. (2006) *The Basel II Risk Parameters: Estimation, Validation, and Stress Testing*, Springer.

Ernst and Young (2014) "Credit valuation adjustments for derivative contracts", April, www.ey.com.

Eurex (2014) "How central counterparties strengthen the safety and integrity of financial markets", www.eurexchange.com.

European Banking Authority (EBA) (2013) "Consultation paper on draft regulatory technical standards (RTS) on credit valuation adjustment risk for the determination of a proxy spread and the specification of a limited number of smaller portfolios under Article 383 of Regulation (EU) 575/2013 (capital requirements regulation – CRR)", July, www.eba.europe.eu.

European Banking Authority (EBA) (2015a) "EBA final draft regulatory technical standards on prudent valuation under Article 105(14) of Regulation (EU) No 575/2013 (capital requirements regulation – CRR)", January, www.eba.europe.eu.

European Banking Authority (EBA) (2015b) "On credit valuation adjustment (CVA) under Article 456(2) of Regulation (EU) No 575/2013 (capital requirements regulation – CRR)", February, www.eba.europe.eu.

Financial Times (2008) "Banks face $10bn monolines charges", June 10.

Finanzmarktaufsicht (FMA) (2012) "Rundschreiben: zu Rechnungslegungsfragen bei Zinssteuerungsderivaten und zu Bewertungsanpassungen bei Derivaten gemäß §57 BWG", www.fma.gv.at.

Finger, C. (2000) "Towards a better understanding of wrong-way credit exposure", RiskMetrics working paper number 99-05, February.

Fitzpatrick, K. (2002) "Spotlight on counterparty risk", *International Financial Review*, 99, 30th November.

Fleck, M. and Schmidt, A. (2005) "Analysis of Basel II treatment of counterparty risk" in *Counterparty Credit Risk Modelling*, M. Pykhtin (ed.), Risk Books.

Fleming, M.J. and Sarkar, A. (2014) "The failure resolution of Lehman Brothers", Federal Reserve Bank of New York Economic Policy Review, December, www.ny.frb.org.

Fons, J.S. (1987) "The default premium and corporate bond experience", *Journal of Finance*, 42(1 March), 81–97.

Fuji, M. and Takahashi, A. (2011) "Choice of collateral currency", *Risk*, 24, 120–25.

Garcia-Cespedes, J.C., de Juan Herrero, J.A., Rosen, D. and Saunders, D. (2010) "Effective modelling of wrong-way risk, CCR capital and alpha in Basel II", *Journal of Risk Model Validation*, 4(1), 71–98.

Gemen, H. (2005) *Commodities and Commodity Derivatives*, John Wiley & Sons Ltd.

German, H. and Nguyen, V.N. (2005) "Soy bean inventory and forward curve dynamics", *Management Science*, 51(7 July), 1076–91.

Ghosh, A., Rennison, G., Soulier, A., Sharma P. and Malinowska, M. (2008) "Counterparty risk in credit markets", Barclays Capital Research Report.

Gibson, M., (2004) "Understanding the risk of synthetic CDOs", Finance and Economics Discussion Paper, 2004–36, Federal Reserve Board, Washington DC.

Gibson, M.S. (2005) "Measuring counterparty credit risk exposure to a margined counterparty" in *Counterparty Credit Risk Modelling*, M. Pykhtin (ed.), Risk Books.

Giesecke, K., Longstaff, F.A., Schaefer, S. and Strebulaev, I. (2010) "Corporate bond default risk: a 150-year perspective", NBER Working Paper No. 15848, March.

Glasserman, P. and Li, J. (2005) "Importance sampling for portfolio credit risk", *Management Science*, 51(11 November), 1643–56.

Glasserman, P. and Yu, B. (2002) "Pricing American options by simulation: regression now or regression later?" in *Monte Carlo and Quasi-Monte Carlo Methods*, H. Niederreiter (ed.), Berlin, Springer.

Gordy, M. (2004) "Granularity adjustment in portfolio credit risk management" in *Risk Measures for the 21st Century*, G.P. Szegö (ed.), John Wiley & Sons Ltd.

Gordy, M. and Howells, B. (2006) "Procyclicality in Basel II: can we treat the disease without killing the patient?", *Journal of Financial Intermediation*, 15, 395–417.

Gordy, M. and Juneja, S. (2008) "Nested simulation in portfolio risk measurement", working paper.

Green, A.D. and Kenyon, C. (2015) "MVA: initial margin valuation adjustment by replication and regression", working paper.

Green, A.D., Kenyon, C. and Dennis, C. (2014) "KVA: capital valuation adjustment", *Risk*, December 2014.

Gregory, J. (2009a) "Being two faced over counterparty credit risk", *Risk*, 22(2), 86–90.

Gregory, J. (2009b) *Counterparty Credit Risk: The New Challenge for Global Financial Markets*, 1st edn, John Wiley and Sons Ltd.

Gregory, J. (2010) "Counterparty casino: the need to address a systemic risk", European Policy Forum working paper, www.epfltf.org.

Gregory, J. (2011) "Counterparty risk in credit derivative contracts" in *The Oxford Handbook of Credit Derivatives*, A. Lipton and A. Rennie (eds), Oxford University Press.

Gregory, J. (2012a) *Counterparty Credit Risk and Credit Value Adjustment: A Continuing Challenge for Global Financial Markets*, 2nd edn, John Wiley and Sons Ltd.

Gregory, J. (2014) *Central Counterparties: Mandatory Central Clearing and Initial Margin Requirements for OTC Derivatives*, John Wiley and Sons Ltd.

Gregory, J. and German, I. (2012b) "Closing out DVA", working paper.

Hamilton, D.T., Gupton, G.M. and Berthault, A. (2001) "Default and recovery rates of corporate bond issuers: 2000", *Moody's Investors Service*, February.

Hille, C.T., Ring J. and Shimanmoto, H. (2005) "Modelling counterparty credit exposure for credit default swaps" in *Counterparty Credit Risk Modelling*, M. Pykhtin (ed.), Risk Books.

Hills, B., Rule, D. and Parkinson, S. (1999) "Central counterparty clearing houses and financial stability", *Bank of England Financial Stability Review*, June, 122–34.

Hughston, L.P. and Turnbull, S.M. (2001) "Credit risk: constructing the basic building block", *Economic Notes*, 30(2), 257–79.

Hull, J. (2010) "OTC derivatives and central clearing: can all transactions be cleared?", working paper, April.

Hull, J., Predescu, M. and White, A. (2004) "The relationship between credit default swap spreads, bond yields, and credit rating announcements", *Journal of Banking & Finance*, 28(11 November), 2789–811.

Hull, J., Predescu, M. and White, A. (2005) "Bond prices, default probabilities and risk premiums", *Journal of Credit Risk*, 1(2 Spring), 53–60.

Hull, J. and White, A. (1990) "Pricing interest-rate derivative securities", *The Review of Financial Studies*, 3(4), 573–92.

Hull, J. and White, A. (2011) "CVA and wrong way risk", working paper, University of Toronto.

Hull, J. and White, A. (2012a) "The FVA debate", *Risk* (25th Anniversary Edition), August.

Hull, J. and White, A. (2012b) "The FVA debate continues: Hull and White respond to their critics", *Risk*, October.

Hull, J. and White, A. (2014) "Valuing derivatives: funding value adjustments and fair value", *Financial Analysts Journal*.

Hull, J.C., Sokol, A. and White, A. (2014) "Modeling the short rate: the real and risk-neutral worlds", Rotman School of Management Working Paper No. 2403067 (June).

International Monetary Fund (IMF) (2013) "A new look at the role of sovereign credit default swaps" in *Global Financial Stability Report*, Chapter 2, www.imf.org.

International Swaps and Derivatives Association (ISDA) (2003) "Counterparty risk treatment of OTC derivatives and securities financing transactions", June, www.isda.org.

International Swaps and Derivatives Association (ISDA) (2009) "ISDA close-out protocol", www.isda.org.

International Swaps and Derivatives Association (ISDA) (2010) "Market review of OTC derivative bilateral collateralization practices", March, www.isda.org.

International Swaps and Derivatives Association (ISDA) (2012) "Initial margin for non-centrally cleared swaps: understanding the systemic implications", November, www2.isda.org.

International Swaps and Derivatives Association (ISDA) (2013) "CDS Market summary: market risk transaction activity", October, www.isda.org.

International Swaps and Derivatives Association (ISDA) (2014) "ISDA margin study 2014", April, www.isda.org.

Iscoe, I., Kreinin, A. and Rosen, D. (1999) "An integrated market and credit risk portfolio model", *Algo Research Quarterly*, 2(3), 21–38.

Jamshidian, F. and Zhu, Y. (1997) "Scenario simulation: theory and methodology", *Finance and Stochastics*, 1, 43–67.

Jarrow, R.A. and Turnbull, S.M. (1992) "Drawing the analogy", *Risk*, 5(10), 63–70.

Jarrow, R.A. and Turnbull, S.M. (1995) "Pricing options on financial securities subject to default risk", *Journal of Finance*, 50, 53–86.

Jarrow, R.A. and Turnbull, S.M. (1997) "When swaps are dropped", *Risk*, 10(5), 70–75.

Jarrow, R.A. and Yu, F. (2001) "Counterparty risk and the pricing of defaultable securities", *Journal of Finance*, 56, 1765–99.

Johnson, H. and Stulz, R. (1987) "The pricing of options with default risk", *Journal of Finance*, 42, 267–80.

Jorion, P. (2007) *Value-at-Risk: The New Benchmark for Managing Financial Risk*, 3rd edn, McGraw-Hill.

Kenyon, C. (2010) "Completing CVA and liquidity: firm-level positions and collateralized trades", working paper, www.defaultrisk.com.

Kenyon. C. and Green, A. (2013) "CDS pricing under Basel III: capital relief and default protection", *Risk*, 26(10).

Kenyon, C. and Green, A.D. (2014) "CVA under partial risk warehousing and tax implications", working paper.

Kenyon, C. and Green, A.D. (2015) "Warehousing credit (CVA) risk, capital (KVA) and tax (TVA) consequences", working paper.

Kenyon, C., and R. Stamm, 2012, "Discounting, LIBOR, CVA and Funding", Palgrave Macmillan.

Kroszner, R. (1999), "Can the financial markets privately regulate risk? The development of derivatives clearing houses and recent over-the-counter innovations", *Journal of Money, Credit, and Banking*, August, 569–618.

Kupiec, P. (1995) "Techniques for verifying the accuracy of risk management models," *Journal of Derivatives*, 3, 73–84.

Laughton, S. and Vaisbrot, A. (2012) "In defence of FVA: a response to Hull and White", *Risk*, September.

Laurent, J.-P. and Gregory, J. (2005) "Basket default swaps, CDOs and factor copulas", *Journal of Risk*, 7(4), 103–22.

Levy, A. and Levin, R. (1999) Wrong-way exposure, *Risk*, July.

Li, D.X. (2000) "On default correlation: a copula function approach", *Journal of Fixed Income*, 9(4 March), 43–54.

Lipton, A. and Sepp, A. (2009) "Credit value adjustment for credit default swaps via the structural default model", *The Journal of Credit Risk*, 5, 123–46.

Lomibao, D. and Zhu, S. (2005) "A conditional valuation approach for path-dependent instruments" in *Counterparty Credit Risk Modelling*, M. Pykhtin (ed.), Risk Books.

Longstaff, F.A., Mithal, S. and Neis, E. (2005) "Corporate yield spreads: default risk or liquidity? New evidence from the credit default swap market", *The Journal of Finance*, LX (5 October).

Longstaff, F.A. and Schwartz, S.E. (1995) "A simple approach to valuing risky fixed and floating rate debt", *The Journal of Finance*, L (3 July).

Longstaff., F.A. and Schwartz, S.E. (2001) "Valuing American options by simulation: A simple least squares approach", *The Review of Financial Studies*, 14(1), 113–47.

Matthews, R.A.J. (1995) "Tumbling toast, Murphy's Law and the fundamental constants", *European Journal of Physics*, 16, 172–6.

Meese, R. and Rogoff, K. (1983) "Empirical exchange rate models of the Seventies", *Journal of International Economics*, 14, 3–24.

MacKenzie, D. (2006) *An Engine, Not a Camera: How Financial Models Shape Markets*, MIT Press.

Mercurio, F. (2010) "A LIBOR market model with stochastic basis", available at SSRN: http://ssrn.com/abstract=1583081.

Merton, R.C. (1974) "On the pricing of corporate debt: the risk structure of interest rates", *Journal of Finance*, 29, 449–70.

Moody's Investors Service (2007) "Corporate default and recovery rates: 1920–2006", Moody's Special Report, New York, February.

Morini, M. and Prampolini, A. (2010) "Risky funding: a unified framework for counterparty and liquidity charges", working paper, http://ssrn.com/abstract=1669930.

Murphy, D. (2012) "The doom loop in sovereign exposures", *FT Alphaville Blog*, April.

Murphy, D. (2013) *OTC Derivatives: Bilateral Trading and Central Clearing: An Introduction to Regulatory Policy, Market Impact and Systemic Risk*, Palgrave Macmillan.

O'Kane, D. (2013) "Optimizing the compression cycle: algorithms for multilateral netting in OTC derivatives markets", working paper.

Ong, M.K. (2006) *The Basel Handbook: A Guide for Financial Practitioners*, 2nd edn, Risk Books.

Picoult, E. (2002) "Quantifying the risks of trading" in *Risk Management: Value at Risk and Beyond*, M.A.H. Dempster (ed.), Cambridge University Press.

Picoult, E. (2005) "Calculating and hedging exposure, credit value adjustment and economic capital for counterparty credit risk" in *Counterparty Credit Risk Modelling*, M. Pykhtin (ed.), Risk Books.

Pindyck, R. (2001) "The dynamics of commodity spot and futures markets: a primer", *Energy Journal*, 22(3), 1–29.

Pirrong, C. (2009) "The economics of clearing in derivatives markets: netting, asymmetric information, and the sharing of default risks through a central counterparty", available at SSRN: http://ssrn.com/abstract=1340660.

Pirrong, C. (2011) "The economics of central clearing: theory and practice", ISDA Discussion Papers Series Number One (May).

Pirrong, C. (2013) "A bill of goods: CCPs and systemic risk", working paper, Bauer College of Business, University of Houston.

Piterbarg, V. (2010) "Funding beyond discounting: collateral agreements and derivatives pricing", *Risk*, 2, 97–102.

Piterbarg, V. (2012) "Cooking with collateral", *Risk*, July, 58–63.

Piterbarg, V. (2013) "Stuck with collateral", *Risk*, October, 60–65.

Pykhtin, M. (2012) "Model foundations of the Basel III standardised CVA charge", *Risk*, July, 60–66.

Pykhtin, M. and Sokol, A. (2013) "Exposure under systemic impact?", *Risk*, September, 100–105.

Pykhtin, M. and Zhu, S. (2007) "A guide to modelling counterparty credit risk", *GARP Risk Review*, July/August, 16–22.

Rebonato, R. (1998) *Interest Rate Options Models*, 2nd edn, John Wiley and Sons Ltd.

Rebonato, R., Sherring, M. and Barnes, R. (2010) "Credit risk, CVA, and the equivalent bond", *Risk*, 23(9) 118–21.

Reimers, M. and Zerbs, M. (1999) "A multi-factor statistical model for interest rates", *Algo Research Quarterly*, 2(3), 53–64.

Rosen, D. and Pykhtin, M. (2010) "Pricing counterparty risk at the trade level and CVA allocations", *Journal of Credit Risk*, 6(Winter), 3–38.

Rosen, D. and Saunders, D. (2010) "Measuring capital contributions of systemic factors in credit portfolios", *Journal of Banking and Finance*, 34, 336–349.

Rowe, D. (1995) "Aggregating credit exposures: the primary risk source approach" in *Derivative Credit Risk*, R. Jameson (ed.), Risk Publications, 13–21.

Rowe, D. and Mulholland, M. (1999) "Aggregating market-driven credit exposures: a multiple risk source approach" in *Derivative Credit Risk*, 2nd edn, R. Jameson (ed.), Risk Publications, 141–7.

Sarno, L. (2005) "Viewpoint: Towards a solution to the puzzles in exchange rate economics: where do we stand?" *Canadian Journal of Economics*, 38, 673–708.

Sarno, L. and Taylor, M.P. (2002) *The Economics of Exchange Rates*, Cambridge University Press.

Segoviano M.A. and Singh, M. (2008) "Counterparty risk in the over-the-counter derivatives market", November, IMF Working Papers.

Shadab, H.B. (2009) "Guilty by association? Regulating credit default swaps", (19th August), *Entrepreneurial Business Law Journal*, forthcoming, available at SSRN: http://ssrn.com/abstract=1368026.

Singh, M. (2010) "Collateral, netting and systemic risk in the OTC derivatives market", (November), IMF Working Papers.

Singh, M. and Aitken, J. (2009) "Deleveraging after Lehman – evidence from reduced rehypothecation", March, IMF Working Papers, 1–11, available at SSRN: http://ssrn.com/abstract=1366171.

Sokol, A. (2010) "A practical guide to Monte Carlo CVA" in *Lessons From the Crisis*, A. Berd (ed.), Risk Books.

Sokol, A. (2014) *Long-Term Portfolio Simulation – For XVA, Limits, Liquidity and Regulatory Capital*, Risk Books.

Sorensen, E.H. and Bollier, T.F. (1994) "Pricing swap default risk", *Financial Analysts Journal*, 50(3 May/June), 23–33.

Soros, G. (2009) "My three steps to financial reform", *Financial Times*, 17th June.

Standard & Poor's (2007) "Ratings performance 2006: stability and transition", New York, S&P, 16th February.

Standard & Poor's (2008) "Default, transition, and recovery: 2008 annual global corporate default study and rating transitions", 2nd April.

Tang, Y. and Williams, A. (2010) "Funding benefit and funding cost" in *Counterparty Credit Risk*, E. Canabarro (ed.), Risk Books.

Tennant, J., Emery, K. and Cantor, R. (2008) "Corporate one-to-five-year rating transition rates", Moody's Investor Services Special Comment.

Thompson, J.R. (2009) "Counterparty risk in financial contracts: should the insured worry about the insurer?", available at SSRN: http://ssrn.com/abstract=1278084.

Vasicek, O. (1977) "An equilibrium characterisation of the term structure", *Journal of Financial Economics*, 5, 177–188.

Vasicek, O. (1997) *The Loan Loss Distribution*, KMV Corporation.

Vrins, F. and Gregory, J. (2011) "Getting CVA up and running", *Risk*, October.

Wilde, T. (2001) "In ISDA's response to the Basel Committee on Banking Supervision's Consultation on the New Capital Accord", May 2001, Annex 1.

Wilde, T. (2005) "Analytic methods for portfolio counterparty risk" in *Counterparty Credit Risk Modelling*, M. Pykhtin (ed.), Risk Books.

Index